MW01630583

Real Estate

Valuation in

Litigation

Real Estate

Valuation in

Litigation

J.D. Eaton, M.A.I.

American Institute of Real Estate Appraisers

430 N. Michigan Ave., Chicago, Illinois 60611

ACKNOWLEDGMENTS

A project of this scope cannot be accomplished without the support and assistance of a great many people. I would like to thank James H. Pritchett, MAI, Atlanta, GA, and David W. Craig, MAI, Topeka, KS, who encouraged me to undertake this project as long ago as 1977. Their input throughout the project is appreciated.

The American Institute of Real Estate Appraisers' publication staff has been a pleasure to work with. Karla Heuer, Director of Publications, has made my job easier by her cooperation and ability. I would particularly like to thank my primary editor, Stephanie Shea-Joyce, who took a manuscript that read like an appraisal report and turned it into a manuscript that reads like a book.

The contribution by the reviewers of my manuscript is also hereby acknowledged. The recommendations made by Stanley D. Moe, MAI, Boise, ID, and David W. Craig, MAI, were particularly helpful.

Without my wife Carol's encouragement and assistance in proofreading and her help in researching case references and preparing the index, this work might not have seen the light of day. Also, the contribution of my secretary, Nancy Brett, is acknowledged and appreciated. With the number of drafts she has typed and the number of times she has proofed the manuscript, she is the only one who has the entire book memorized.

James D. Eaton, MAI
Longview, Washington
August, 1982

ABOUT THE AUTHOR

James D. Eaton, MAI, is president/owner of Eaton & Associates, Inc., a real estate appraisal and consulting firm in Longview, Washington. Mr. Eaton has been active in the appraisal of all types of property since 1961, and has held his present position since 1971. He specializes in litigation appraising and consulting, and has testified as an expert witness in a number of state and federal courts in the Northwest.

As an active Realtor®, Mr. Eaton has been president of the Cowlitz County Board of Realtors, Realtor of the Year 1975, and has served on the Board of Directors and Executive Committee of the Washington Association of Realtors. He also holds the CRA designation awarded by the National Association of Review Appraisers.

Mr. Eaton has been active in real estate education, serving as a trustee of the Washington Real Estate Educational Foundation for six years and as the Foundation's president for two years. He has taught real estate courses at the community college level and for the state Realtors'® GRI program. He has also taught the American Institute of Real Estate Appraisers' litigation valuation course.

EPIGRAPH

"Nothing that I [will hereafter say] should be construed to place the appraiser in the role of an advocate. However, much as the expert appraiser trains his lawyer, it is the lawyer who must lead in the courtroom; it is the lawyer who has the ultimate responsibility to his client. Therefore, the determinations as to the variant and proper legal approaches are his alone to make. They are never the responsibility of the appraiser. The worst thing an appraiser can do is to become an advocate except for his opinion, for, if he does, his bias and his prejudice will show through. He must stick to the fundamental facts."

Sidney Z. Searles

Examination and Cross-Examination
of Appraiser in Eminent Domain

FOREWORD

Although *Real Estate Valuation in Litigation* is designed as a textbook, it is also a reference guide for both experienced real estate appraisers and attorneys who deal in valuation litigation cases.

The author has presented appraisal theory as well as the legal precedents that affect the appraiser's approach, preparing the appraisal report for litigation purposes, dealing with review appraisers, and court testimony. With appraisers playing an increasing role in estate valuation, IRS disputes, condemnation proceedings, boundary line disputes, divorce actions, and other legal procedures, much of the text's information, which is not usually readily available to the appraiser, makes this book even more useful for solving the complex problems faced by appraisers today.

Because condemnation assignments have traditionally comprised a significant portion of the professional appraiser's litigation work, the author has placed a great deal of emphasis on condemnation valuation methods, thus providing a valuable tool for appraisers with limited experience in condemnation appraising.

The Institute is pleased to offer a publication of this quality and depth, and extends its thanks and appreciation to James D. Eaton for sharing his more than two decades of appraisal expertise.

John D. Dorchester, Jr., MAI
1982 President
American Institute of Real Estate Appraisers

TABLE OF CONTENTS

PREFACE

The format of this publication has been dictated somewhat by the fact that it is a textbook. The material is presented in the order that a student might receive it in a typically structured course in litigation appraising. The book is not intended to be an appraisal principles textbook; rather, it is directed to the real estate appraiser who has a basic understanding of real estate valuation principles and techniques and to the attorney who is interested in the various valuation techniques applied by appraisers in litigation appraising.

Although it is not a law book, this book has been written under the premise that, in many cases, applicable law and valuation procedures are so interrelated that a thorough study and understanding of valuation procedures cannot be made without a general understanding of the law. The attorney practicing in the field of real estate litigation must have a basic understanding of real estate valuation principles to properly fulfill his professional obligations. For these reasons, applicable law and court rulings have been cited throughout this text. Because laws and court rulings vary from state to state, the author has made no attempt to cover all applicable laws in each jurisdiction. The cases cited were selected to illustrate a general rule. Readers are encouraged to research the applicable law in their jurisdictions.

There is no doubt that condemnation, or eminent domain, assignments have historically been the largest segment of the professional appraiser's litigation work. In recognition of this fact, and because many other litigation valuation problems follow the ground rules established for eminent domain valuations, the primary emphasis of this text is on condemnation appraising. Other types of litigation appraising are covered in chapter 20 of this text. Appraising for various types of litigation is compared with condemnation, or eminent domain, valuation procedures; where the methodologies differ, or when a specific type of litigation requires special treatment, a detailed discussion is provided.

Much has been written for and by the legal profession on eminent domain law and valuation. The material directed toward appraisers has generally consisted of articles in professional journals or compilations of articles published in book form.

The number of condemnation cases has dropped substantially in the past few years, because the Federal Interstate Highway system is nearing completion. However, current trends indicate that our society is *litigation happy*. Even professional real estate appraisers who say, "I don't do court work," will inevitably find themselves testifying about property value before one tribunal or another. They may fight a valiant battle, kicking and screaming all the way, but they will, nevertheless, be there. For this reason, professional appraisers, whether they consider themselves *litigation specialists* or not, must have a working knowledge of applicable valuation law to serve clients properly and to fulfill professional obligations.

This text includes an explanation of valuation procedures and observations and comments on presenting valuation evidence as a witness. The well-written, well-documented appraisal report is of little value if the appraiser is unable to present the findings to the court persuasively. Similarly, the well-prepared appraisal witness is little help to his client or the trier of fact unless the attorney understands the valuation methods and techniques employed by the appraiser and knows what questions to ask.

There is no publication now in general circulation that has the proper content and format to be used as a condemnation appraisal textbook, nor is there any authoritative text which covers real estate valuation for other forms of litigation. It is the purpose of this publication to fill both of these voids.

CHAPTER 1
ORIGIN OF EMINENT DOMAIN
AND JUST COMPENSATION

Eminent domain is the right of the sovereign government to take private property for public use upon payment of *just compensation*. This right can be, and has been, conveyed to other public and quasi-public bodies such as public utility districts, development commissions, and railroad companies.[1] Condemnation is the act of the government, or other authorized public or quasi-public agencies, taking private property for public use upon payment of just compensation to the owner of the property.[2]

The distinction between the two terms is quite simple. Eminent domain is the *right* of the government to take private property for public use upon payment of just compensation, while condemnation is the *act* of doing so.

It is not absolutely necessary for the real estate appraiser to have any more understanding of the sovereign's right of eminent domain and its act of condemnation than that written above. However, greater understanding of these terms will lead to better comprehension of the reasoning behind many court decisions relative to eminent domain valuation and to more effective communication with members of the law profession and others involved in eminent domain and condemnation. Some appraisers feel that it is almost impossible to have meaningful communication between appraisers and attorneys under the best of circumstances. It therefore behooves the appraiser to acquire a thorough understanding of legal terms so that he does not compound the confusion in the already complex field of eminent domain litigation.

Eminent Domain

The origin of the concept of eminent domain seems lost in history, but it is acknowledged that the sovereign's right of eminent domain is well established. The first recorded condemnation action occurred in the year 871 B.C.[3] The condemnor, King Ahab, attempted to acquire Naboth's vineyard. Naboth refused to voluntarily sell the vineyard, and King Ahab exercised the right of eminent domain. Jezebel became, in effect, the trier of fact. The decision at the end of trial was that King Ahab did, in fact, have the right of eminent domain and title to the vineyard was transferred to him. By way of just compensation for the taking, Naboth was stoned to death for his refusal to sell the land voluntarily. There was no appeal! It appears that no appraiser was involved in the case.

The previous definition of eminent domain could be termed the *modern definition* inasmuch as it includes the provision for payment of just compensation. Many early definitions of eminent domain, including those applied in the United States, did not include the provision of just compensation. Until after the Civil War, several states exercised the power of eminent domain without paying compensation. It is now well settled, however, that the right of eminent domain cannot be exercised in this country without payment of just compensation.

Many believe that the government's right of eminent domain comes from its constitution. This belief is false.[4] The sovereign has always had the right of eminent domain. Some theorize that this right originates from the principle that the sovereign owns all of the property within its boundaries, and that private ownership and possession of property is always subject to reversion or repossession by the sovereign. In fact, some jurisdictions use the term *expropriation* interchangeably with, or in place of, eminent domain.

Expropriation is defined as a "Canadian and British term representing the act of a sovereign in reclaiming its inherent ownership in real estate which in law was never given up. It is similar to the taking of private property under the law of eminent domain in the United States."[5] Some disagree with this theory of sovereign ownership because two sovereignties cannot hold ultimate title to the land at the same time and both the state and the U.S. Government have the right of eminent domain. It was not until 1875 that it was clearly established that the federal government does, in fact, have the power of eminent domain.[6]

It is now generally acknowledged that the power of eminent domain is not a property right, but an inherent right of the sovereign.[7] The powers of the sovereign are broad enough to include the power of eminent domain, so the right does not specifically have to be granted to the sovereign by its constitution, and the states are not prohibited from exercising their powers of eminent domain by the federal constitution.

The power of eminent domain, by its very definition, is limited in that it cannot be exercised unless the proposed taking is for a public use. For example, a public agency could not invoke its power of eminent domain to take a property from one individual for the sole benefit of another individual. The determination that the exercise of eminent domain is for a *public use* is generally made by the appropriate court in a *public use and necessity* hearing. This determination is made well before any condemnation trial, so the issue of public use is not considered in a condemnation trial. Recent trends indicate that the courts interpret *public use* quite liberally. Thus, takings for scenic easements, golf courses, and open space have been held to be for *public use*. But, when the City of Oakland attempted to purchase the Oakland Athletics from Charlie Finley under its power of eminent domain, the court ruled that the acquisition of a baseball club, under the right of eminent domain, did not constitute a public use.

Insofar as eminent domain is an inherent right of the sovereign, the right cannot be limited by the legislature. The power of eminent domain will exist, in unlimited form, as long as the sovereign itself exists.[8] The only way the power can be limited is by the sovereign's constitution. The U.S. Constitution states "[n]o person shall be deprived of life, liberty, or property without due process of law, nor shall private property be taken for public use without just compensation."[9] This provision of the Constitution does not grant the U.S. Government the right of eminent domain, but it does limit the sovereign's inherent power by providing that it cannot be exercised without payment of just compensation to the owner of the property taken.

This provision has no effect on the powers of the states. However, Section 1 of the Fourteenth Amendment of the U.S. Constitution reads in part, "nor shall any state deprive any person of life, liberty, or property without due process of law." The *due process of law* provision of the amendment has been interpreted as requiring payment of just compensation for the taking of property. In fact, every state in the Union, except North Carolina, makes provision in its constitution for the payment of compensation to an owner when his or her property is acquired by the sovereign through eminent domain.[10]

Just Compensation

As stated above, it has been held that an individual has a fundamental right to compensation when his land is taken for the public use and that the legislature is bound by unwritten restrictions to respect this right. Disregard of this right has been held to be a violation of the "unwritten law," of the "spirit of the Constitution," and of "common law principles," against "natural equity," and a travesty on "natural justice."[11]

Not all state constitutions refer to *just compensation*. Terms such as *adequate, reasonable,* and *due* are used in some constitutions in conjunction with *compensation*. The adjectives used to describe compensation do not alter its meaning, but rather emphasize it. It has been said that it is difficult to imagine *unjust compensation*. About half of the state constitutions provide for compensation to be paid for the taking of, or *damage* to, private property by the sovereign.[12]

Even in jurisdictions that do not have such a constitutional provision, it universally has been held that damages to a remainder parcel in a partial taking case are part and parcel of *just compensation* in a constitutional sense. The basic premise is that the owner must be compensated for the *taking of the land,* as opposed to being compensated for the *land taken.*[13] It is also generally recognized that *property* encompasses the entire bundle of rights inherent in the ownership of the real estate and that the taking or infringement on these rights often constitutes a *taking,* even if no part of the physical real estate is taken. The taking of all access rights is an example of such a taking. "Clearly an owner of land abutting on a street or highway cannot constitutionally be deprived of all access to his premises without compensation . . . total deprivation of access is equivalent to a taking requiring compensation . . ."[14]

It is imperative that the appraiser be aware of the *damage* provisions in the constitution, or adopted by statute, in the jurisdiction where the property under appraisal is located. In many jurisdictions that have no *damage* provision, there must be an actual *taking* before damages can be recovered; thus, in these jurisdictions, damages are only recoverable in partial taking cases. The importance of this provision is further discussed and demonstrated later in this work.[15]

Just compensation is defined as ". . . the amount of the loss for which a property owner has established a claim to compensation. It is the payment of the market value of the real estate which was taken."[16] Another definition says, "just compensation means value of land taken and damage, if any, to land not taken."[17]

The term *just compensation* is not defined in the U.S. Constitution or in any state constitution. It has been up to the courts to interpret and define the term, and they have generally held that just compensation is measured by market value.[18] On occasion, the courts have deviated from this concept, most notably when the property has no ascertainable market value.

Citing a multitude of federal and state cases, *Nichols* defines market value as follows:

> By "fair market value" is meant the amount of money which a purchaser willing but not obliged to buy the property would pay to an owner willing but not obliged to sell it, taking into consideration all uses for which the land was suited and might in reason be applied.[19]

The *Uniform Eminent Domain Code* defines market value as:

> . . . the price which would be agreed to by an informed seller who is willing but not obligated to sell, and an informed buyer who is willing but not obligated to buy . . .[20]

A generally accepted definition of market value in the appraisal profession is:

Market Value—The most probable price in terms of money which a property should bring in competitive and open market under all conditions requisite to a fair sale, the buyer and seller, each acting prudently, knowledgeably and assuming the price is not affected by undue stimulus.

Implicit in this definition is the consummation of a sale as of a specified date and the passing of title from seller to buyer under conditions whereby:

1. buyer and seller are typically motivated.
2. both parties are well informed or well advised, and each acting in what they consider their own best interest.
3. a reasonable time is allowed for exposure in the open market.
4. payment is made in cash or its equivalent.
5. financing, if any, is on terms generally available in the community at the specified date and typical for the property type in its locale.
6. the price represents a normal consideration for the property sold unaffected by special financing amounts and/or terms, services, fees, costs, or credits incurred in the transaction.

Numerous definitions of Market Value have been devised over the years by professional organizations, government bodies, courts, et cetera.

The Supreme Courts of most states have handed down definitions of Market Value for use in the state courts. These definitions are subject to frequent change.

Persons performing appraisal services which may be subject to litigation are cautioned to seek the exact definition of Market Value in the jurisdiction in which the services are being performed.[21] [emphasis added]

Various jurisdictions have different definitions of market value. The definition in most jurisdictions assumes a cash sale or its equivalent, but there are exceptions.[22] If an appraisal is to be valid for condemnation purposes, the appraiser must utilize a definition of market value acceptable to the courts where the condemnation trial on the property will be held. Thus, it is imperative that the real estate appraiser be aware of the applicable definition of market value and include it in his appraisal report; otherwise, the entire appraisal report and/or the appraisal testimony may be rejected. The safest procedure for the appraiser, if in doubt as to the proper definition of market value within the jurisdiction, is to request the applicable market value definition from legal counsel, with supporting authority therefor.

Market value is not an end in itself, but merely a measure to an end; the objective being the ascertainment of just compensation, *but not by the appraiser.* The appraiser's function in eminent domain valuation is to estimate market value—no more, no less. It is the responsibility of the trier of fact, be it a judge, jury, or another tribunal, to determine just compensation. " 'Market value' is not necessarily the equivalent of just compensation but rather a useful and generally sufficient tool for arriving at this."[23] Market value is not the only value which the trier of fact may consider in arriving at a determination of just compensation.

The appraiser who attempts to determine just compensation, instead of estimating market value, is usurping the right and responsibility of the trier of fact. While, from a practical standpoint, it is difficult for the appraiser to avoid arriving at some opinion of just compensation in the process of the appraisal assignment, he or she must suppress this opinion in arriving at an estimate of market value and in testifying. He should make it as clear as possible that his estimate is of market value only. To avoid misunderstanding, he should inform his attorney that if he is asked the question, "Have you arrived at a conclusion as to the just compensation for this acquisition?" the response will be an emphatic "no," or he will say, "estimating just compensation was beyond the scope of my assignment."

Considerable case law supports this position. For instance, in an Illinois case an expert witness was asked, "Would you say that this is just compensation for the owner of a piece of property located at 1762-64 North Larrabee, the sum of twenty-six thousand dollars?" The trial court refused to allow the expert to answer the question and the case was appealed. On appeal the court said, "We find that no error occurred when the trial court refused to permit the expert witness to give his conclusions as to the ultimate issue of just compensation."[24]

The courts have intentionally avoided rulings that would infer that just compensation is always equal to market value. The U.S. Supreme Court ruled:

> The court in its construction of the constitutional provision has been careful not to reduce the concept of "just compensation" to a formula. The political ethics reflected in the Fifth Amendment reject confiscation as a measure of justice. But the Amendment does not contain any definite standards of fairness by which the measure of "just compensation" is to be determined. The Court in an endeavor to find working rules that will do substantial justice has adopted practical standards, including that of market value. But it has refused to make a fetish even of market value, since it may not be the best measure of value in some cases.[25] [citations omitted]

The term just compensation has been determined to mean compensation that is just not only to the person whose property is being taken, but also to the condemnor, who is, in fact, the general public, or society as a whole. Thus, just compensation is "[r]easonable compensation" and "compensation which is just, not merely to the individual whose property is taken, but to the public which is to pay for it."[26]

Also, while the price paid for the property may have a bearing on its market value, "[i]t is not the investment, but the 'value of the interest' in land taken by eminent domain that is guaranteed to the owner; the government may neither confiscate the owner's bargain, nor be required to assume his loss."[27]

Generally, market value is the measure of just compensation, but it is often difficult for the appraiser to estimate market value without considering the influence of the pending public improvement for which the property is being acquired. In eminent domain valuation, the appraiser must appraise the property assuming the owner is a willing seller, which is seldom the case. He must also assume that there is no pending condemnation action against the property being appraised and that there is, in fact, no public improvement project in progress which would require the taking of the property. This can be difficult when a public improvement such as a new interstate highway has been in the planning and construction stages for years. The proposed right-of-way may have been on the local municipality's planning maps for some time, and zoning changes may have actually occurred with the proximate cause of the change being the anticipated highway.[28]

The appraiser must also disregard *project enhancement* and *condemnation blight* in appraising the property.[29] If the property is being appraised in conjunction with a partial acquisition, the appraiser's problems are often compounded. In many cases, it must be assumed that the public improvement is complete, viewing the property in its after situation even though the public improvement will not be completed for several years. In estimating the market value of a property in the after situation, the appraiser must also consider the possible existence of *compensable damages, noncompensable damages,*[30] *special benefits,* and *general benefits.*[31]

Summary

Eminent domain is the right of the sovereign to take private property for a public use upon payment of just compensation. The sovereign's act of taking property under its right of eminent domain is called *condemnation.* The appraiser should have a complete understanding of these two terms to communicate effectively with others active in the field of eminent domain litigation.

The sovereign's right of eminent domain is well established as an inherent right, which need not be specifically granted. This right is limited in two ways: 1) the use for which the land is being taken must be a *public use,* a term which the courts interpret liberally; and 2) the property owner must be justly compensated by the sovereign for its acquisition. The requirement for the payment of just compensation by the federal government is specified in the Fifth Amendment to the U.S. Constitution. The requirement that states must pay just compensation when invoking their right of eminent domain is provided in Section 1 of the Fourteenth Amendment to the U.S. Constitution. Also, every state constitution, except one, requires payment of just compensation for the taking of private property for public use.

Just compensation is not defined by any constitution, but has generally been held to be market value. The property owner is to be compensated for the *taking of his property,* as opposed to being compensated for *the property taken.* This provides that an owner is to be compensated for damages to his remainder property occasioned by the taking as well as for the property actually taken. The courts have refused to rule that just compensation is always measured by market value. Other means of measuring value, or just compensation, have upon occasion won court approval.

The appraiser's function is to assist the court in its determination of just compensation by furnishing an opinion of market value, which is one element the court will consider in making its determination. The appraiser does not estimate just compensation directly; this is the function of the court.

In estimating market value in the before situation for eminent domain proceedings, the appraiser must exclude from consideration the influences of the proposed public improvement. He must also analyze the remainder property in a partial taking for potential damages and/or benefits arising from the taking and proposed public improvement.

Notes

1. American Institute of Real Estate Appraisers and the Society of Real Estate Appraisers, *Real Estate Appraisal Terminology,* rev. ed., Byrl N. Boyce, ed. (Cambridge, Mass.: Ballinger Publishing Co., 1981), p. 89.
2. Ibid., p. 55.
3. 1 Kings XXI.
4. Joiner v. City of Dallas, 380 F.Supp. 754.
5. *Real Estate Appraisal Terminology,* p. 96.
6. Kohl v. United States, 91 U.S. 367, 23 L.Ed. 449.
7. Joiner v. City of Dallas, 380 F.Supp. 754.; Jockheck v. Shawnee County Comrs., 53 Kan. 780, 37 P. 621.
8. Town of Durham, N.H. v. United States, 167 F.Supp. 436.
9. 5th Amendment, U.S. Constitution.
10. Julius L. Sackman, *Nichols' The Law of Eminent Domain,* rev. 3rd ed. (New York: Matthew Bender, 1979), Vol. 1, § 1.3.
11. Ibid., Vol. 3, § 8.1[1].
12. Ibid., Vol. 2, § 6.1[3], f.n.29.
13. Bauman v. Ross, 167 U.S. 548, 17 S.Ct. 966.
14. 26 *AM. Jur. 2d, Eminent Domain,* § 200, p. 882.
15. See Chapter 11, "Damages in Partial Takings."
16. *Real Estate Appraisal Terminology,* p. 143.
17. Los Angeles v. Oliver, 102 Cal. App. 299, 283 P. 298.

18. Harwell v. United States, 316 F.2d 791.

19. *Nichols'*, Vol. 4, § 12.2[1].

20. "Uniform Eminent Domain Code," 1974, § 1004, p. 10.7.

21. *Real Estate Appraisal Terminology*, pp. 160-161.

22. Baucum v. Arkansas Power & Light Co., 179 Ark. 154, 15 S.W.2d 399.

23. United States v. Certain Property, 306 F.2d 439.

24. City of Chicago v. Budd 12 Ill. App.2d 51, 257 N.E.2d 161.

25. United States v. Cors, 337 U.S. 325, 69 S.Ct. 1086.

26. James A. Ballentine, *Ballentine's Law Dictionary*, 3rd ed., William S. Anderson, ed. (Rochester, N.Y.: The Lawyers Co-operative Publishing Co.; San Francisco: Bancroft-Whitney Co., 1969), pp. 695-696.

27. Ibid.; Kinter v. United States, 156 F.2d 5.

28. See Chapter 6, "Land Use Regulations."

29. See Chapter 5, "Highest and Best Use."

30. See Chapter 11, "Damages in Partial Takings."

31. See Chapter 13, "Benefits—Special and General."

CHAPTER 2
LEGAL MEASUREMENTS OF JUST COMPENSATION

Due to conflicting case law and differing constitutional provisions in the various jurisdictions, several different methods for computing just compensation have been promulgated. Although appraisers do not estimate just compensation, it is necessary that they report findings of market value and the difference in value before and after a partial taking in a manner usable to those charged with the responsibility of computing just compensation.

The various condemning agencies have adopted computational rules, often in modified form, to be used by their appraisers in eminent domain valuation. The law recognizes that there are exceptions to the general rule that just compensation is equal to market value, but the acquisition policies of condemning agencies seldom provide for such exceptions. Therefore, many condemning agencies use appraisal forms and guidelines which require modification to ensure that all parties understand that the estimate being made is an estimate of market value, which may or may not represent just compensation within the legal meaning of the term. Policy statements such as "[u]nder established law the criterion for just compensation is the fair market value of the property at the time of the taking"[1] and "[t]he mathematical difference between the two values ('market value before minus market value after') is the just compensation . . ."[2] typify condemning agencies' reluctance to acknowledge any measure of just compensation other than market value.

The specific rules for computing just compensation are almost as numerous as the states in the Union. Two general rules predominate; and others are merely modifications to ensure compliance with applicable constitutional and statutory provisions. The two general rules are the *before-and-after rule* (often referred to as the *federal rule*) and the *value of the take plus damages rule* (or the *state rule*).

Federal Rule

The federal (before-and-after) rule is somewhat of a misnomer. This rule is applicable in federal condemnation cases, but it is also applicable in a number of state jurisdictions. In its simplest form, the federal rule is: *value before taking minus value after taking equals just compensation.* Graphically, this would be shown as:

Value of property before take	+ $________
Value of property after take	− ________
Difference (just compensation)	= $________

Under the federal rule, no further breakdown is necessary for trial purposes. However, the Federal Uniform Relocation Assistance and Real Property Acquisitions Policy Act of 1970[3] requires the condemnor to furnish the property owner with a written statement summarizing how the figure offered as just compensation was reached. "Where appropriate, damages for the land acquired and consequential damages to the remaining land not taken should be shown separately."[4] The provisions of this act relate not only to federal land acquisitions, but also to acquisitions made by the states and their various subdivisions if federal matching funds are involved in either the land acquisition or construction of the public improvement. For this reason, it is often necessary for the appraiser to give a detailed breakdown of the value estimates within the appraisal report.

For purposes of illustration, consider the following sample property valued under two different premises. Figure 2.1 shows a single-family property on a site 100 feet × 300 feet, or 30,000 sq. ft. The site is improved with a 980-sq. ft., single-family dwelling with an attached 280-sq. ft. garage and miscellaneous on-site improvements such as trees, landscaping, and a driveway. The site has very poor surface drainage and is zoned for a single-family dwelling with a minimum lot size of 25,000 sq. ft. and a minimum front-yard setback of 25′. The estimated market value of the property before any acquisition is $47,500, which can be broken down for analytic purposes only, as follows:

Site (30,000 sq. ft. @ 50¢)	$15,000
Dwelling	28,800
Garage	1,200
On-site improvements	2,500
Total	$47,500

Premise 1

Assume the local municipality will acquire the easterly (front) 10 feet of the site for a road-widening project. Within the take area are two trees and a portion of the driveway. The acquisition will create a zoning nonconformance because the dwelling and garage will not meet the minimum required front-yard setback.

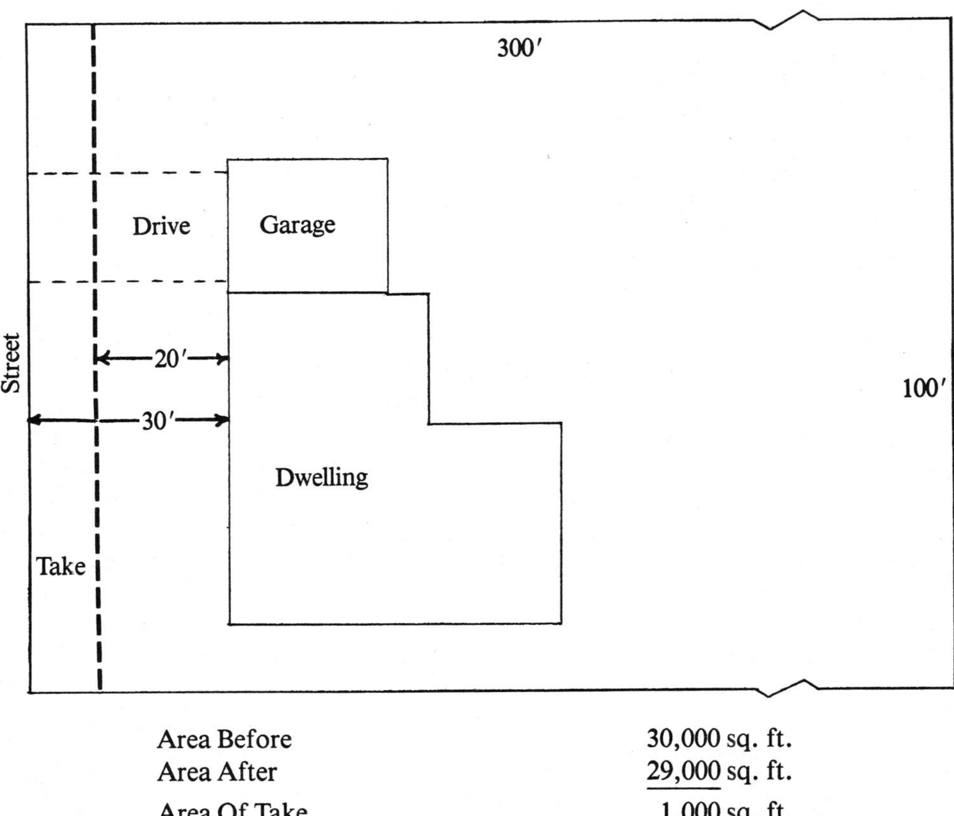

Area Before	30,000 sq. ft.
Area After	29,000 sq. ft.
Area Of Take	1,000 sq. ft.

Figure 2.1. Plot Plan—Partial Taking

Market analysis indicates that dwellings and garages that are nonconforming in front-yard setback sell for 20% less than comparable, conforming dwellings. The contributory value of the on-site improvements remaining after the taking is estimated at $2,000. Table 2.1 tabulates the property's value before and after the taking under Premise 1.

Utilizing the information in Table 2.1, the appraiser's conclusion would be shown as follows:

Value of property before take	$47,500
Value of property after take	40,500
Difference (just compensation)	$7,000

Table 2.1

Summary of Conclusions
(Accounting tabulation—NOT Indicative of appraisal method employed)

Indicated Value Before Acquisition:
  Highest and Best Use: Residential

Land Area		Unit Value			
30,000 sq. ft.		.50	$15,000		
Total Area 30,000 sq. ft.		Total Land		$15,000	

Improvements

Type	Size	Unit Value			
Dwelling	980 sq. ft.	29.39	$28,800		
Garage	280 sq. ft.	4.29	1,200		
On-site		Lump Sum	2,500		
		Total Improvements		32,500	
		Total Indicated Value			$47,500

Indicated Value of Remainder:
  Highest and Best Use: Residential

Land Area		Unit Value			
29,000 sq. ft.		.50	$14,500		
Total Area 29,000 sq. ft.		Total Land		$14,500	

Improvements

Type	Size	Unit Value			
Dwelling	980 sq. ft.	23.51	$23,040		
Garage	280 sq. ft.	3.43	960		
On-site		Lump Sum	2,000		
		Total Improvements		26,000	
		Total Indicated Value			40,500

Breakdown of Acquisition:

Land Area		Unit Value			
1,000 sq. ft.		.50	$ 500		
Total Area 1,000 sq. ft.		Total Land		$ 500	

Improvements

Type	Size	Unit Value			
On-site		Lump Sum	$ 500		
		Total Improvements		500	

Damages

Item					
Non-conforming House & Garage			$ 6,000		
		Total Damages		6,000	
		Sub-total		$ 7,000	

Benefits (Subtract)

Item					
None			$ 0		
		Total Benefits		0	
		Difference Between Before and After Values			$ 7,000

Table 2.2

Summary of Conclusions
(Accounting tabulation—NOT Indicative of appraisal method employed)

Indicated Value Before Acquisition:
  Highest and Best Use: Residential

Land Area		Unit Value			
30,000 sq. ft.		.50	$15,000		
Total Area 30,000 sq. ft.		Total Land		$15,000	

Improvements

Type	Size	Unit Value			
Dwelling	980 sq. ft.	29.39	$28,800		
Garage	280 sq. ft.	4.29	1,200		
On-site		Lump Sum	2,500		
		Total Improvements		32,500	
		Total Indicated Value			$47,500

Indicated Value of Remainder:
  Highest and Best Use: Residential

Land Area		Unit Value			
29,000 sq. ft.		.75	$21,750		
Total Area 29,000 sq. ft.		Total Land		$21,750	

Improvements

Type	Size	Unit Value			
Dwelling	980 sq. ft.	23.51	$23,040		
Garage	280 sq. ft.	3.43	960		
On-site		Lump Sum	2,000		
		Total Improvements		$26,000	
		Total Indicated Value			47,750

Breakdown of Acquisition:

Land Area		Unit Value			
1,000 sq. ft.		.50	$ 500		
Total Area 1,000 sq. ft.		Total Land		$ 500	

Improvements

Type	Size	Unit Value			
On-site		Lump Sum	$ 500		
		Total Improvements		500	

Damages

Item					
Non-conforming Garage & House			$ 6,000		
		Total Damages		6,000	
		Sub-total		$ 7,000	

Benefits (Subtract)

Item					
Improved Drainage (29,000 sq. ft. @ .25)			$ 7,250		
		Total Benefits		7,250	
	Difference Between Before and After Values				$ 0

Premise 2

Consider the same property described above. Assume that, as a part of the road-widening project, the municipality will install storm sewers which will eliminate the surface drainage problems on the property being appraised. Market investigation and analysis indicates that sites with no drainage problems will sell for 75¢ per square foot, as compared to 50¢ per square foot for sites which have drainage problems. The property's value before and after the taking under these conditions is mathematically computed in Table 2.2.

Utilizing the information in Table 2.2, the appraiser's conclusion would be shown as follows:

Value of property before take	$47,500
Value of property after take	47,750
Difference (just compensation)	$ 0

The difference between the before value and the after value (or just compensation) cannot, of course, be less than zero. The *summary of conclusions* form shown in Tables 2.1 and 2.2 is typical of the type required by a condemnor using the before-and-after rule.[5] This format satisfies condemnors' reporting requirements and helps them comply with the Federal Uniform Relocation Assistance and Real Property Acquisition Policies Act of 1970. It should be noted that the phrase, "Accounting tabulation—NOT indicative of appraisal method employed," is printed on the form. This is imperative to ensure that the purpose of the summary is not misconstrued; the appraiser must not be put on the witness stand to defend why he estimated the contributory value of a tree at $250 instead of $300.

It is also advisable that the appraiser include in the limiting conditions section of the appraisal report a statement such as the following:

> Where the value of the various components of the property are shown separately, the value of each is segregated only as an aid to better estimating the value of the whole; the independent value of the various components may, or may not, be the market value of the component.

Even in jurisdictions that strongly adhere to the before-and-after rule, there are generally provisions allowing deviation from the rule under certain circumstances. Such deviation may be necessary when a minimal taking is involved or when a total before-and-after appraisal would not be economically practical. The formula applied in these instances is generally: *the value of the part taken (as a part of the whole), plus damages to the remainder, less special benefits, equals difference in value* (just compensation). Graphically, this can be shown as:

<pre>
Value of taking   + $________
Plus damages   + ________
Less special benefits   − ________
Difference (just compensation) $_________
</pre>

As stated in the *Uniform Appraisal Standards for Federal Land Acquisitions,*

[a]nother approach [besides the before-and-after approach] is to find the value of the part taken on the date of taking; and add to or subtract from that figure an allowance for diminution or enhancement in value of the remainder. This method may or may not be more complicated. It usually is more subject to error, however, and is more apt to result in duplication.

It should be borne in mind that there are situations in which insistence upon strict adherence to the "before and after" rule would impose costly and sometimes nearly impossible burdens upon the appraisers and the courts. Examples of such situations, in which the second method discussed above would generally be applicable, are minor easement takings (for flowage, roads, pipe lines, transmission lines, etc.) from large ranches, industrial complexes, etc., where the cost of valuing the whole unit before and after the taking is simply unwarranted in view of the minor easement being acquired.

In short, where its application would be logical, practical, and capable of understanding, the "before and after" method of determining compensation in partial taking cases is preferred. Fortunately, this method is generally applicable and it is the exceptional case where the cost of valuing the whole is unreasonable.[6]

This type of appraisal, sometimes called a *strip appraisal,* is seldom used to appraise a property that may be subject to damages and/or benefits by reason of the proposed acquisition. Such a report is not generally detailed enough for trial purposes, so it is often necessary for the appraiser to convert a strip appraisal into a complete before-and-after appraisal prior to trial.

Regardless of the reporting requirements, it is generally advisable for the appraiser to break down the value estimates in a manner similar to that shown in Tables 2.1 and 2.2. Such a breakdown provides for easier and more accurate comparative analysis between the property under appraisal and comparable properties and will often reveal any flaw in the logic the appraiser applied in reaching his value estimates. If such a flaw in logic does exist, it is much more comfortable for the appraiser to find it in the privacy of his office than on the witness stand while under cross-examination.

State Rule

The state rule requires greater in-depth analysis than the before-and-after rule.
The procedural steps in applying the state rule are:

1. Value before take $_______
2. Value of part taken   –_______
3. Remainder value before take   = $_______
4. Remainder value after take   –_______
5. Damages   = $_______
6. Special benefits   –_______
7. Net damage   = $_______
8. Value of part taken   +_______
9. Total difference (just compensation) $_______

The results of the computations made in Step 5 (damages) and Step 7 (net damage) cannot be less than zero. This formula can be applied to the circumstances described in Premise 1 as follows:

1. Value before take $47,500
2. Value of part taken   – 1,000
3. Remainder value before take $46,500
4. Remainder value after take   – 40,500
5. Damages $ 6,000
6. Special benefits   –   0
7. Net damages $ 6,000
8. Value of part taken   + 1,000
9. Total difference (just compensation) $ 7,000

Premise 2 computations would be:

1. Value before take $47,500
2. Value of part taken   – 1,000
3. Remainder value before take $46,500
4. Remainder value after take   – 47,750
5. Damages $ 0*
6. Special benefits   – 7,250
7. Net damages $ 0*
8. Value of part taken   + 1,000
9. Total difference (just compensation) $ 1,000

*As mentioned earlier, Steps 5 and 7 cannot be less than zero

There are a number of variations on this formula. In a few jurisdictions, the basic state rule must be modified because the jurisdiction does not allow benefits to be offset against either the value of the taking or the damages to the remainder. This formula eliminates Steps 6 and 7 from the basic state formula. This revised formula can be shown as:

1. Value before take	+ $_______
2. Value of part taken	− _______
3. Remainder value before take	= $_______
4. Remainder value after take	− _______
5. Damages	= $_______
6. Value of part taken	+ _______
7. Total difference (just compensation)	$_______

Applying this formula to Premise 1, described earlier in this chapter, would result in the following:

1. Value before take	$47,500
2. Value of part taken	− 1,000
3. Remainder value before take	$46,500
4. Remainder value after take	− 40,500
5. Damages	$ 6,000
6. Value of part taken	+ 1,000
7. Total difference (just compensation)	$ 7,000

Premise 2 would be computed as:

1. Value before take	$47,500
2. Value of part taken	− 1,000
3. Remainder value before take	$46,500
4. Remainder value after take	− 40,500
5. Damages	$ 6,000
6. Value of part taken	+ 1,000
7. Total difference (just compensation)	$ 7,000

By comparing the computations it can be seen that the results of Premise 1 and Premise 2 are identical. In the standard state formula, Item 5 (damages) can never be less than zero; also, under this modified rule, Item 4 (remainder value after take) can never be greater than Item 3 (remainder value before take) because the appraiser is prohibited from considering any benefits whatsoever in estimating the value of the remainder after the take. It is therefore impossible for the value of the remainder after the take to be greater than the remainder value before the take.

Many of these rules have been developed to avoid a chronic and dangerous problem—*double damage,* or duplication of just compensation. To illustrate how easy it is to double damage using the *taking plus damages* rule, consider the situation depicted in Figure 2.2. Assume that the property's annual economic rent prior to the take is $5,000 net to the lessor, and the applicable overall capitalization rate is 10.5%, indicating a before value of $47,600 ($5,000 ÷ .105), rounded.

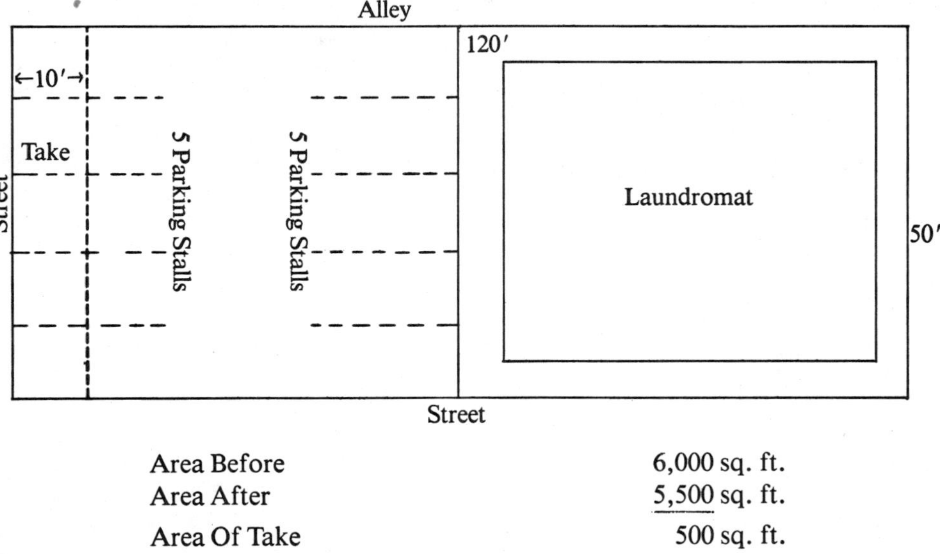

Area Before	6,000 sq. ft.
Area After	5,500 sq. ft.
Area Of Take	500 sq. ft.

Figure 2.2. Plot Plan—Partial Taking

Market evidence indicates that the land has a value of $2.00 per square foot, or $12,000; thus, the before value can be segregated for analytical purposes as follows:

Land	$12,000
Improvements	35,600
Total	$47,600

Now, assume that the municipality takes a 10 ft. strip from the southerly side of the property, which eliminates five parking stalls. Analysis indicates that the economic rent after the take is $3,500 per year. Under the state, or take plus damages, rule, the computations made by the uninitiated appraiser might be:

Value of take (500 sq. ft @ $2.00)	$ 1,000
Damages ($1,500 rent loss ÷ .105)	14,286
Total difference (just compensation)	$15,286
Rounded	$15,500

This procedure results in compensating the landowner twice for the taking. Use of the correct state rule formula would result in the following:

1.	Value before take	$47,600
2.	Value of part taken (500 sq. ft. @ $2.00)	− 1,000
3.	Remainder value before take	$46,600
4.	Remainder value after take ($3,500 income ÷ .105)	− 33,333
5.	Damages	$13,267
6.	Special benefits	0
7.	Net damages	$13,267
8.	Value of part taken	+ 1,000
9.	Total difference (just compensation)	$14,267
9.	Rounded	$14,500

This illustrates the importance of following a set forumla when using the state rule. The courts are plagued with appraisals which double damage the property when the state rule is used.

When applying the state rule, the part taken generally is valued as a part of the whole property prior to the taking.[7] There have been, however, court rulings that conflict with this position. If the part taken has an independent economic use and a market value as a separate entity greater than its value as a part of the whole, it has been held proper to value the part taken as a separate tract, not as a part of the whole.[8] A considerable amount of case law exists on this point. Analysis of this case law clearly illustrates that these conflicting rulings are not due to differing constitutional and/or statutory provisions in the various jurisdictions, but are caused by insufficient or improper analysis on the part of the appraiser in arriving at a conclusion of *highest and best use*[9] and/or a determination of the *larger parcel.*[10]

If, as the court rulings assert, the part taken has an independent economic use and its market value as a separate entity is greater than as a part of the whole, the appraiser has erred in determining the larger parcel and/or highest and best use because the area taken and the remainder parcel had no unity of use prior to the taking. Therefore, the *larger parcel* to be appraised in the before situation is the taken area itself, and there is no after situation because the taking was, in effect, a *total take* of the larger parcel.

This situation is illustrated in a Louisiana decision wherein the court said:

> A landowner is always entitled to the fair market value of the land actually taken.
>
> The fair market value of the front land in certain situations is higher than the average unit price of the tract. The fact that adjacent areas of land which have different highest and best uses are all under the same ownership, and together compose a large ownership tract, does not presuppose that they would be developed or marketed as a single tract. In fact, market realities dictate otherwise. An owner ordinarily will sell a portion of his property for the highest price the market will deliver so long as that use does not damage the value of the remainder. This jurisdiction has long recognized that different portions of an ownership tract may have different highest and best uses and, thus, different per unit values.[11]

When evaluating the part taken as a part of the whole, the appraiser must carefully determine whether the area taken contributes an equal pro rata value, a greater than pro rata value, or a less than pro rata value to the whole. The courts have ruled that it is improper to use an average unit value, e.g., per square foot or per acre, as developed for the whole tract in evaluating the part taken unless each unit in the tract has the same value.[12] As one court put it:

> The landowner is thus to be awarded the actual market value of the particular portion of the property taken, valued according to its highest and best use. He is not limited to its average per acre value as a pro rata portion of the parent tract where the front portion has a different highest and best value.
>
> . . . [W]here the evidence shows that the front portion of the tract taken has a higher value than the rear portion not taken, the landowner must be awarded the higher value for the land actually taken rather than an average value based on its proportionate portion of the land-area of the parent tract.[13] [citations omitted]

Considerable case law has developed over the use of a valuation procedure variously referred to as the *backland theory,* the *slide back theory,* or the *front land—rear land concept.* Figure 2.3 illustrates a situation where this theory might be applicable.

Assume that market evidence shows that the highest and best use of the property depicted in Figure 2.3 is for commercial development. Analysis indicates that tracts 200 feet wide and 200 feet deep will bring a price of $4.00 per square foot,

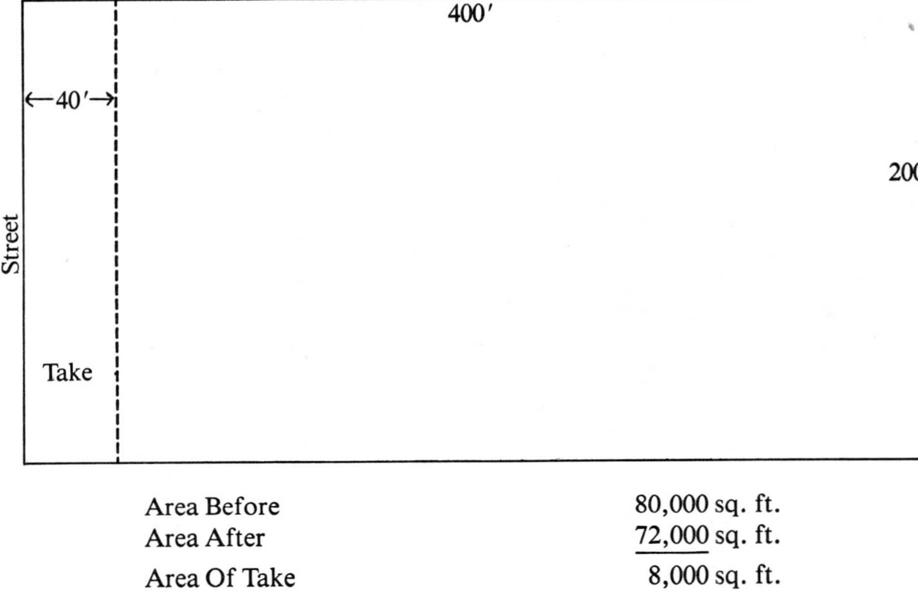

Area Before	80,000 sq. ft.
Area After	72,000 sq. ft.
Area Of Take	8,000 sq. ft.

Figure 2.3. Plot Plan—Partial Taking

or $160,000, on the open market; tracts 200 feet wide and 400 feet deep will bring a price of $200,000. It can be assumed then that the front 200 feet of the tract has a value of $4.00 per square foot, and the rear 200 feet of the tract has a value of $1.00 per square foot. The front 40 feet of the tract will be acquired for road widening. Two diametrically opposed approaches to this situation have been developed by courts in jurisdictions using the state (taking plus damages) rule. The two views are exemplified by two cases from different jurisdictions.

A California court, citing *City of Los Angeles* v. *Allen,*[14] stated:

> On appeal, the condemnee contended that the strip taken was frontage and that he should have been allowed the commerical value. The Supreme Court disagreed. It reasoned that if to widen the public highway, a strip of land is taken from a larger parcel under one ownership and if it is clear that the main parcel has more than one theoretical zone of value, not because of any unique characteristic in the land itself, but rather because of the proximity of the theoretical zones to the public highway or similar factors affecting property values, and if it is also clear that the same zones may be immediately reestablished after

the "take," the owner is unjustly enriched if he is compensated on the basis of the highest zone of value; under these circumstances, the strip must be treated as an integral part of the whole and not as a separate piece of property having an independent value.[15]

On the other hand, a Louisiana case stated:

> We consider the Louisiana jurisprudence to be settled, therefore, that generally the market value of the particular part of a tract expropriated is determined by the actual market value of the portion taken, and not by its average per acre or per square foot value as a pro rata portion of the parent tract. Also, a landowner is entitled to receive the full and actual market value of highway frontage expropriated for further highway purposes, without deduction therefrom because of the fact that by reason of the taking a new highway frontage will be provided for the formerly rear portions of the parent tract.[16]

In the *Allen* case[17] the trial judge used a weighted average in determining just compensation. Applying this procedure to the above circumstances would result in the following computations:

1. Value before take (40,000 sq. ft. @ $4.00 + 40,000 sq. ft. @ $1.00) — $200,000
2. Value of take ($200,000 ÷ 80,000 sq. ft. × 8,000 sq. ft.) — – 20,000
3. Remainder value before take — $180,000
4. Remainder value after take (40,000 sq. ft. @ $4.00 + 32,000 sq. ft. @ $1.00) — – 192,000
5. Damages — $ 0
6. Special benefits — 0
7. Net damages — $ 0
8. Value of part taken — + 20,000
9. Total difference (just compensation) — $ 20,000

Under the Louisiana rule, just compensation would be:

1. Value before take (40,000 sq. ft. @ $4.00 + 40,000 sq. ft. @ $1.00) — $200,000
2. Value of take (8,000 sq. ft. @ $4.00) — – 32,000
3. Remainder value before take — $168,000
4. Remainder value after take (40,000 sq. ft @ $4.00 + 32,000 sq. ft. @ $1.00) — – 192,000
5. Damages — $ 0

6. Special benefits	0
7. Net damages	$ 0
8. Value of part taken	+ 32,000
9. Total difference (just compensation)	$ 32,000

Applying the before-and-after rule, compensation would be:

1. Value before take (40,000 sq. ft. @ $4.00 + 40,000 sq. ft. @ $1.00)	$200,000
2. Value after take (40,000 sq. ft. @ $4.00 + 32,000 sq. ft. @ $1.00)	− 192,000
3. Total difference (just compensation)	$ 8,000

Comparing the results of these computations clearly illustrates the need for the appraiser to be fully familiar with eminent domain laws in the applicable jurisdiction.

Comparison of Rules

The two different rules in computing just compensation have been brought about by various judicial attitudes regarding the practice of offsetting the benefits created by a project against the value of the taking and/or the damages caused by the taking. The rules relating to benefits are covered at length later in this work.[18] Generally, jurisdictions that use the state rules do not allow the offsetting of benefits against the value of the part taken. Some, in fact, will not allow a project benefit to be set off against either the part taken or the damages caused by the taking. The before-and-after rule is generally utilized in jurisdictions that allow benefits to offset both the value of the taking and the damages.

The two primary weaknesses of the before-and-after rule are: 1) it does not provide a mechanism to exclude benefits from the after value, and 2) it does not provide a mechanism to exclude *noncompensable damages*[19] from the after value.

Some authorities assert that the state rule's complexity and its potential for double damages are so great that the before-and-after rule should be adopted despite its weaknesses. *Orgel* advocates

> . . . the abandonment of the attempt to find the separate value of the part taken, in favor of the rule that recovery should be based on the difference between the value of the whole before and after the taking. The adoption by all courts of this rule should be far less confusing to a jury and would probably avoid a very practical objection that may be urged against the more popular rule of "value of part taken plus damages to the remainder"—the objection that a jury may include in

"damages to the remainder" a part of the very injury which it incorporates in "value of the part taken."[20]

Nichols states

> [i]t is quite apparent, of course, that some of the practical difficulties and complexities involved in the application of the first rule [the value of the part taken plus damages rule] are obviated by use of the latter method [before-and-after rule] of valuation. The relationship of the part taken to the whole tract need not be considered under the latter method, nor need consideration be given to the relationship of the remainder area to the original tract. Duplicate consideration of the same elements of damage are thereby avoided. Although theoretically both methods should lead to the same result, as a matter of practical application this is not always the case. Despite such fact, however, the simplicity of application of the before and after rule commends itself to the courts as a method most likely to attain a result that is fair both to the condemnor and the condemnee.[21]

The *Uniform Eminent Domain Code*[22] recommends the adoption of a modified before-and-after rule. This modified rule would simply ensure that just compensation could not be less than the market value of the part taken.

Summary

Two basic rules have been developed in measuring just compensation in eminent domain litigation. These rules are the *before-and-after rule,* often referred to as the *federal rule,* and the *value of the part taken plus damages rule,* often referred to as the *state rule.* The federal rule is generally used in jurisdictions that allow benefits caused by the public improvement to be set off against the value of the property taken and damages to the remainder land due to the taking and the construction of the public improvement. The federal rule has two weaknesses: there are no procedures inherent in the application of the rule to exclude benefits (for those jurisdictions which do not allow a setting off of benefits) in the after valuation or to exclude noncompensable damages in the after value of the property. Applying the federal rule can result in no difference between the before and after values (or zero just compensation), if benefits are equal to or greater than the aggregate amount of the value of the part taken plus damages.

The state rule is generally used in jurisdictions that do not allow benefits to be set off against the value of the part taken and/or damages. The state rule is more complex than the federal rule, and there is considerable danger that the unwary appraiser, or jury, could double the damages to a property by compensating the owner twice for the taking—once for the value of the take and again for damages to the remainder. Because of this potential for double damaging, it is essential that the appraiser utilize a standard formula in making value computations. Applying the state rule will never result in a difference in value (or just compensation) less than the value of the part taken.

There is considerable amount of conflicting case law in regard to whether the value of the part taken should be valued as a part of the whole property or as a separate entity. If the appraiser properly analyzes the highest and best use of the property and the question of what constitutes the larger parcel, this inconsistency can be largely alleviated.

The two rules will generally result in the same conclusion, if they are properly applied and if benefits do not exceed damages. The appraiser must know which rule is applicable in the jurisdiction where a trial on the property being condemned may be held. Using the wrong rule will often result in rejection of the appraiser's report and/or appraisal testimony. It is also essential that the appraiser investigate the applicable rule in the jurisdiction to determine whether the rule has been modified from the standard rule applicable in other jurisdictions.

Notes

1. *Uniform Appraisal Standards for Federal Land Acquisitions* (Washington, D.C.: U.S. Government Printing Office, 1973), § A-2, p. 3.
2. Washington State Dept. of Transportation, *Right of Way Manual,* Chapter 4, Appendix 4-2, Appraisal Report Guide, Part 1, § A, ¶3, (Revised 11/10/76).
3. Public Law 91-646.
4. Ibid., Title III, § 301 (3).
5. Washington State Dept. of Transportation Form 261-016 (Revised 3/78).
6. *Uniform Appraisal Standards for Federal Land Acquisitions,* § A-11, p. 25.
7. Department of Public Works and Bldngs. v. Oberlaender, 235 N.E.2d 3 (Ill.).
8. Southwestern Bell Telephone Co. v. Ramsey, 542 S.W.2d 466 (Tex.).
9. See Chapter 5, "Highest & Best Use."
10. See Chapter 4, "The Larger Parcel."
11. State, Dept. of H'wys. v. Stegemann, La., 269 So.2d 480.
12. Los Angeles County Flood Control Dist. v. McNulty, 59 Cal.2d 347, 29 Cal. Rptr. 13, 379 P.2d 493.
13. State, through Department of Highways v. Hoyt, La., 284 So.2d 763.
14. City of Los Angeles v. Allen, 1 Cal.2d 572, 36 P.2d 611.
15. City of Fresno v. Cloud, 26 CA.3d 113, 102 Cal. Rptr. 874.
16. State, Dept. of H'ways v. LeDoux, La., 184 So.2d 604.
17. City of Los Angeles v. Allen, 1 Cal.2d 572, 36 P.2d 611.
18. See Chapter 13, "Benefits—General and Special."
19. See Chapter 11, "Damages in Partial Takings."
20. Lewis Orgel, *Valuation Under Eminent Domain,* Vol. 1, § 52, p. 238.
21. Julius L. Sackman, *Nichols' The Law of Eminent Domain,* rev. 3rd. ed. (New York: Matthew Bender, 1979), Vol. 4A, § 14.232[1].
22. "Uniform Eminent Domain Code," (1974) § 1002, p. 10.2.

CHAPTER 3
PROPERTY RIGHTS

In appraisal terminology the term *real estate* refers to "[t]he physical land and appurtenances, including structures affixed thereto"[1]; the term *real property* refers to "[t]he interests, benefits, and rights inherent in the ownership of the physical real estates."[2] The appraiser must be careful using these terms because many states consider them synonymous by statute.

Property is defined "[a]s the term appears in constitutional provisions respecting taking of property: a word of most general import, extending to every species of right and interest, capable of being enjoyed as such, upon which it is practical to place a money value."[3] Property rights are "[e]conomic interests supported by the law."[4] In real estate, these property rights are referred to as the *bundle of rights* because "[o]wnership of a parcel of real estate may embrace a great many rights, such as the right to its occupancy and use; the right to sell it in whole or in part; the right to bequeath; the right to transfer, by contract, for specific periods of time, the benefits to be derived by occupancy and use of the real estate. These rights of occupancy and use are called beneficial interests."[5]

Bundle of Rights

The bundle of rights inherent in the ownership of real estate has often been likened to a bundle of sticks because, like a bundle of sticks, the various rights may be separated and held by a number of individuals or entities. When an individual is in full possession of all property rights, he is said to have fee (meaning title) simple (meaning unencumbered) ownership, which, of course, represents maximum value. Orignially, this term meant absolute ownership, from the center of the earth, through the earth's surface, and upward to infinity. Thus, from a theoretical standpoint, it can be said that real estate owned absolutely is in the form of an inverted pyramid.

This absolute ownership has been limited, however, by the sovereign's inherent rights, constitutional provisions, and legislative actions. For example, the Air Commerce Act of 1926[6] and the Civil Aeronautics Act of 1938[7] limit air rights to the height necessary for the full enjoyment of the property. Later legislation and court rulings further defined the real estate owner's rights to air space above the ground. The treatment of avigation easements, as well as other forms of easements, are covered later in this work.[8]

As stated earlier,[9] the sovereign has the inherent power of eminent domain, which is a further limitation on property rights. In addition, the sovereign has the power of taxation, police power, and the power of escheat, all of which limit property rights. The appraiser must be aware of the existence of escheat[10] as it restricts property rights, but a detailed treatment of this subject is beyond the scope of this work. Appraising in conjunction with the sovereign's power of taxation will be discussed elsewhere in this text.[11]

Police Power

The government's police power is "[t]he right of the government to limit the exercise of property rights in real estate, without compensation, provided the limitation is not specific to one parcel. The limitation is to serve the interest of public health, public safety, public morals and the general welfare."[12] The government's police power generally takes the form of zoning codes, building codes, subdivision ordinances, shorelines management ordinances, rent controls, and the like.

The government's police power is constantly being broadened by legal interpretation and by new legislation. Actions which formerly would have been considered *takings* under the government's right of eminent domain, for which compensation would be required, are now often viewed as matters of the government's police power, for which no compensation is required.[13] The distinction between a *taking* in the constitutional sense and the government's proper use of police power is often unclear. As one court put it:

> Plaintiffs have presented this court with an issue that commonly arises when governmental activity benefits the public generally at the expense of private interests: when does a publicly inflicted private injury rise to the level of a "taking," for which the Constitution requires payment of compensation? The general question admits of no easy answer, for the courts in grappling with this issue have produced decisions as diverse as the factual situations that called for judicial decision-making.[14]

The other side of the question is well illustrated by the decision in a New

Hampshire case involving the denial of a landowner's request for a permit to fill the salt marsh on his property. The court stated:

> We hold that the denial of the permit to fill the salt marsh of the plaintiffs was a valid exercise of the police power prescribing future activities that would be harmful to the public and that, therefore, there was no taking under the eminent domain clause.[15] [citations omitted]

However, in dissenting, one judge expressed the opposing view very well. He said:

> I am in complete sympathy with those who wish to preserve the marshes. However, I continue to agree with Judge Smith when over one hundred years ago he said that great public benefit "may afford an excellent reason for taking the plaintiff's land in a constitutional manner but not for taking it without compensation."
>
> Because I fear the decision destroys private ownership in all undeveloped property in this state, I can concur in the result only as to that part of the marsh which lies below the mean high water mark of the Atlantic Ocean. I can concur to this extent because the state has an interest in the public waters which would be reduced by the fill.
>
> The master [original trier of fact] has found that the unfilled marsh is of practically no pecuniary value to the plaintiffs. As to the marsh above mean high water, the effect of the State's action is to compel the plaintiff to devote his land to a public purpose without compensation by denying him the right to put it to any other reasonably profitable use.
>
> This constitutes a taking. The effect of the principle adopted in today's decision is to undermine a great constitutional safeguard.[16] [citations omitted]

Zoning and other land-use regulations have been the subject of considerable litigation. Case law is extensive and the questions of zoning and other land-use regulations have such bearing on the appraiser's determination of highest and best use and the estimate of market value that these subjects are treated separately in this work.[17]

Access Rights

Access, or abutter's, rights have also been the subject of considerable litigation, much of which occurred during right-of-way acquisitions in conjunction with the interstate highway system. Access, or abutter's, rights are a part of the real estate owner's bundle of rights. These rights include the right of reasonable ingress and egress, the right to reasonable light and air, and the reasonable right to see and be seen. These rights are often referred to as the rights of access, light, view, and air.

Access rights are subject to governmental alteration by two means—police power and eminent domain. The government's use of its police power must, of course, be reasonable, and, when this power is reasonably applied, the abutting property owner is not entitled to any compensation, even though the government's action may decrease the value of the property. Examples of such police power would be the conversion of a two-way street into a one-way street, the elimination of left turns into or out of a property, or the diversion of street traffic to an alternate route. Under the second form of governmental alteration of access rights, the sovereign's invocation of its right of eminent domain, the property owner is entitled to compensation. *Unreasonable* access restrictions would fall into this category.

In all jurisdictions, the damaging alteration of a street grade would be compensable if the alteration involves a partial taking of the property affected. However, many jurisdictions have neither constitutional nor statutory provisions for payment of *damages* in addition to payment for a *taking,* so a damaging change of street grade which does not involve a physical taking is noncompensable.[18] On the other hand, if the property were in a jurisdiction that provided compensation for damages, by its constitution or by statute, the grade change would be a compensable damage.[19]

There is a gray area between police power and the sovereign's power of eminent domain when it comes to the right of access. This is why access and abutter's rights have been called the *elastic right.*[20] Although private, adjacent property owners have the right to ingress, egress, and a view from their land onto the public way, these rights are not unlimited. They are subordinate to the public's enjoyment and safe use of the route.[21] Expansion of the road surface within the existing right-of-way has therefore been ruled a police power action for which no compensation is required.[22]

In defining the limits of a property owner's access rights, the courts have referenced "reasonable access,"[23] "suitable access,"[24] and "free and convenient access"[25] and have stressed the need to obtain a "balance of public and private interests"[26] in regard to utilization of the traveled way. It is well settled that abutting owners "are not entitled to access to their properties at any and all points along"[27] the public way. In other words, case law indicates that an abutting owner is entitled to reasonable, convenient, and adequate access for proper use and enjoyment of his property for its present use and for its reasonable uses in the foreseeable future. For instance, consider the property shown in Figure 3.1. If this property's highest and best use is for a single-family dwelling as improved, and

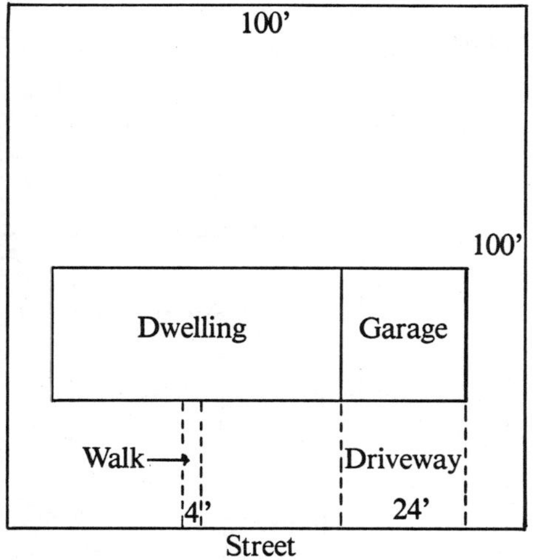

Figure 3.1. Plot Plan

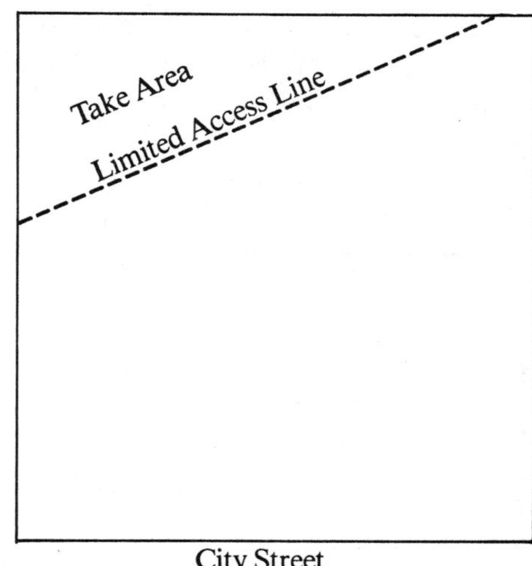

Figure 3.2. Plot Plan—Partial Taking

there is no likelihood that the highest and best use of the property will change in the foreseeable future, the legal access afforded to the subject could be limited to 28 feet (the width of the driveway plus the width of the walk) of the property's 100 feet of frontage without payment of compensation.

When a partial acquisition occurs for the construction of a limited-access highway, the remainder parcel cannot be damaged for lack of access to the new highway.[28] Figure 3.2 demonstrates this situation. The owner cannot receive compensation for lack of access to the new facility because the owner had no prior rights of access to the road.

The courts have ruled that an abutting property owner has special rights to the abutting roadway, beyond the rights of the public at large, and that these special rights take the form of an easement in the roadway;[29] however, alteration of a formerly unlimited access road into a partially limited, or even fully limited, access facility does not necessarily mean that damages are due the abutting owner.

Figure 3.3 illustrates a property in a before-and-after situation, where the easterly 450 feet of the property's frontage become limited access in the after situation, leaving only the westerly 50 feet as accessible frontage. Figure 3.4 depicts a similar situation, but here the property is a corner location and access to and from the frontage road is totally restricted in the after situation.

If the highest and best use of the illustrated property is for a restaurant, and the property continues to have reasonable access and can continue to operate as a restaurant in these after situations, it is probable that no compensable damage has accrued to the property by reason of the access limitation. If, however, the property becomes a second-rate highway retail location due to unreasonably restricted, remote, and congested access, substantial compensable damage may result.

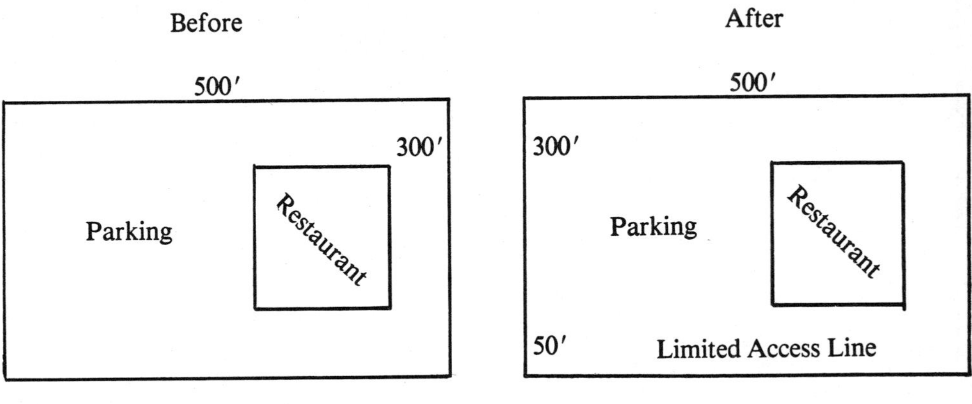

Figure 3.3. Access Taking

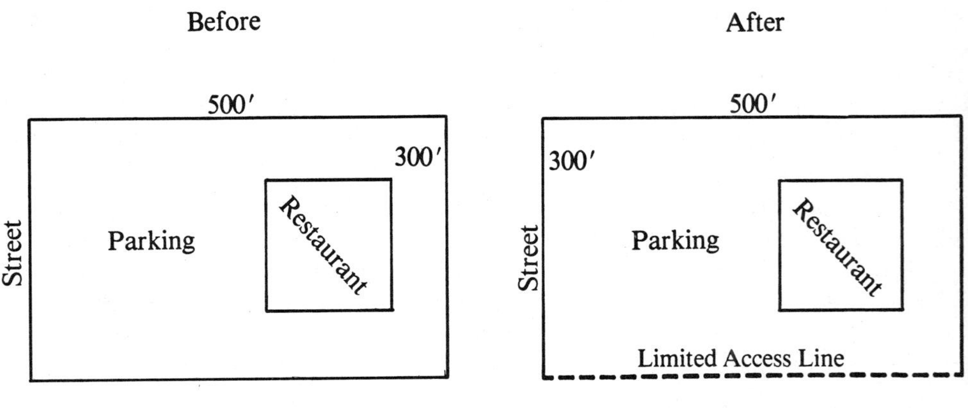

Figure 3.4. Access Taking

There is some inconsistency in case law in regard to replacing access with substitute access to a frontage or service road. Consider Figure 3.5. In this type of situation, some courts have ruled that the access to the new frontage road may partially mitigate the damages for the loss of access to the main highway.[30] How-

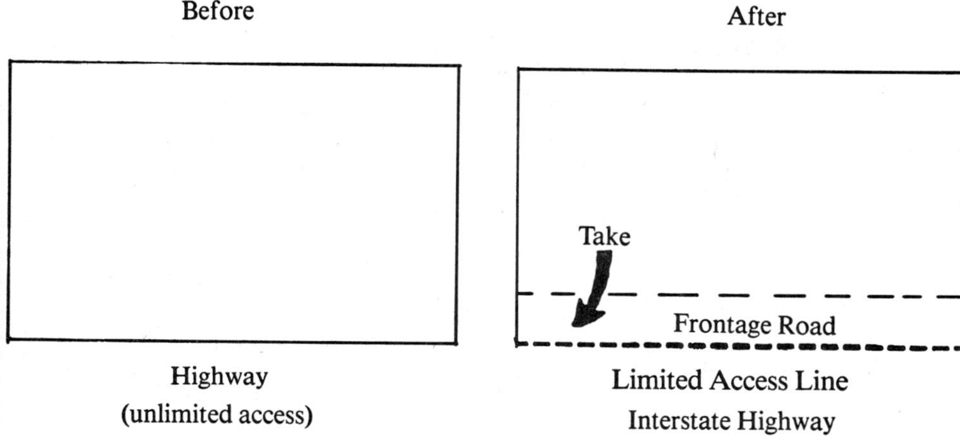

Figure 3.5. Access Taking

ever, other courts have ruled that the access along the new frontage road totally replaces the access lost, so there can be no compensable damages.[31]

Some elements of damage, in relation to access and abutter's rights, have universally been held noncompensable.
These elements include:

1. Increases,[32] decreases,[33] or diversions of[34] traffic on the roadway. The abutting owner retains access and rights of access to and from the highway, but no right to the traffic that uses the highway.

2. Circuity of travel[35] caused by government exercise of police power. It must be kept in mind, however, that the property owner is entitled to *suitable* access. " 'Circuitous,' in its commonly accepted understanding, indicates that which is round-about and indirect but which nevertheless leads to the same destination. 'Suitable,' in its commonly accepted understanding, describes that which is adequate to the requirements of or answers the needs of a particular object. The concepts are not mutually exclusive and, therefore, a finding that a means of access is indeed circuitous does not necessarily eliminate the possibility that that same means of access might also be unsuitable in that it is inadequate to the access needs inherent in the highest and best use of the property involved."[36]

At least one court has ruled that although an abutting property owner has an inherent right of access to the abutting street, the right extends only to those lanes of travel that actually abut the property. This situation is depicted in Figure 3.6. The jury that heard this case was instructed:

> [Y]ou may allow such compensation to respondents as you find is established by the evidence because the owners or others must take a more circuitous route in going to or leaving their remaining property as a result of the loss of direct access for northbound traffic only.[37]

On appeal, this instruction was upheld as proper.

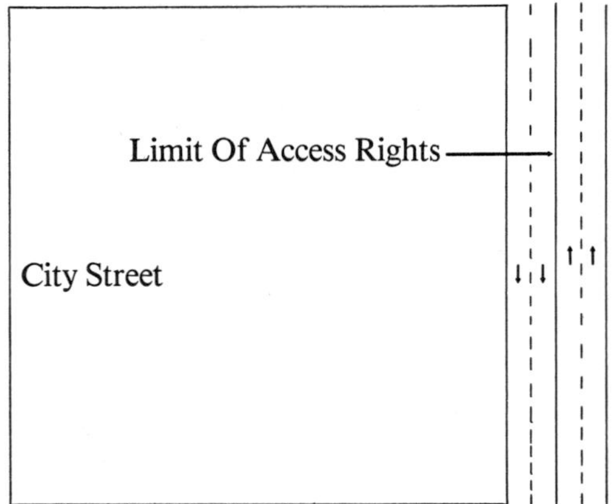

Figure 3.6. Limits of Access Rights

3. Relocation of highways. The government has no obligation to maintain the location of a street right-of-way, nor does it have any obligation to continue to lead customers past a retail location. The desires, convenience, and safety of the general public has greater weight than the desires of retail street merchants. However, if a through street is dead-ended, the resultant traffic diversion has been held to be compensable as an unreasonable limitation of access rights.[38] The discontinuance, abandonment, or obstruction of a highway has also been held to be compensable,[39] but the loss in value must be specific to the property in question because losses common to the general public are noncompensable.[40] The temporary closure of a highway is generally noncompensable,[41] but there is case law in some jurisdictions to the contrary.[42]

4. Changes in highway width. As previously noted, the widening of a highway within the existing right-of-way has universally been held to be noncompensable. However, the narrowing of a highway has been considered a *partial street closing* and, therefore, compensable.[43] The damage resulting from the narrowing of a highway is usually not as great as that which results from the dead-ending or total abandonment of a highway.

Multiple Estates

Real estate may be divided into more than one estate, and these various estates are often owned by different individuals or entities. Nevertheless, a condemnor generally instructs its appraiser to evaluate the property as if the title were held by a single entity. This procedure has won court approval[44] and is often referred to as the *unit rule*[45] or the *undivided fee rule.*[46]

The philosophy of the unit rule is described in the *Uniform Appraisal Standards For Federal Land Acquisition:*

> The unit rule: The fair market value concept which has been adopted by the courts to determine the just compensation required by the Constitution generally requires application of the so-called "unit rule," which is another principle designed to reflect the true situation in the market. This rule has two aspects:
>
> First, the unit rule requires valuing property initially as a whole rather than by the sum of the values of the various interests into which it may have been carved, such as lessor and lessee, life tenant and remainderman, etc. This is an application of the principle that it is the property, not the various titles, which is being taken. Under this rule, the award for the whole is later apportioned among the claimants (lessor and lessee, life tenant and remainderman, etc.) as a second phase in the procedings. . . .
>
> The second aspect of the unit rule is that different elements of a tract of land are not to be separately valued and added together. For example, the value of timber is not added to a value for the house and those, in turn, added to a value for the remainder of the property. The property is to be valued as a whole and its constituent parts considered only in light of how they enhance or diminish the value of the whole, with care being exercised to avoid so-called "cumulative" appraisals.[47] [citations omitted]

The *Washington State Department of Transportation Appraisal Report Guide* states: "[G]enerally, in the appraisal of real estate for the purpose of acquiring rights of way, the considerations are confined to estimating the market value of the fee interest, i.e. all the property rights inherent in ownership."[48]

Therefore, when engaged by a condemnor, the appraiser must often ignore the fact that the property is held by various estates and appraise only the fee simple estate. This is the case even though the knowledgeable appraiser is aware that the value of the various estates, when added together, may or may not equal the value of the fee simple estate. When appraising for the condemnor, the appraiser's assignment is often complete upon estimating the market value of the fee simple estate. However, the condemnor may ask the appraiser to allocate the value of the fee simple estate to the various lesser estates in the property to help him arrive at a negotiated settlement with all of the parties who hold interests in the property.

When the appraiser's client is not the condemnor, but an individual who holds an estate less than the fee simple estate in the affected property, the appraiser's assignment often is not the simple estimation of the market value of the fee simple estate. In most instances, after estimating the market value of the fee simple estate, the appraiser allocates proportionate shares of the total estate to the various lesser estates. The separation of the fee simple estate most often encountered is its division into the leased fee estate and leasehold estate. The valuation of leased fee and leasehold estates is covered later in this work.[49]

The *life estate* is also considered on occasion, and the question of its value has been addressed by the courts. The creation of a life estate divides the fee simple estate into two lesser estates held by the *life tenant* and the *remainderman.* The life tenant holds the beneficial interest in the property for his life, or the life of a third party; the remainderman holds all other rights to the fee simple estate, plus the right to the beneficial interest in the property upon death of the life tenant or third party. A life estate has been defined as "[a]n ownership interest with the right of use or enjoyment limited to the owner's own life or the lifetime of another."[50] It has been well established that a life tenant is an *owner* in the constitutional sense and is entitled to compensation in an eminent domain proceeding.[51]

Early English law required that one-third of the fee simple value (or the total condemnation award or settlement) go to the life tenant, with the balance going to the remainderman. Since the advent of statistically accurate mortality tables, the courts have generally held that proper apportionment is accomplished by evaluating the present worth of the life estate, through discounting the income stream from the property (or the worth of the beneficial interest therein) to a present worth at an appropriate discount rate.[52] The remainderman is then entitled to the difference between the market value of the fee simple estate and the present value of the life estate.[53]

For example, assume a life tenant with a remaining life expectancy of 20 years, based on accepted mortality tables. Further assume the property in question is under a 25-year absolute net lease with an annual rental of $5,200 per year. The current market value of the undivided fee (fee simple estate) has been estimated at $85,000, and an interest, or discount, rate of 8% is considered appropriate. The market value of the property would be apportioned as follows:

Market value of unencumbered fee	$85,000
Present value of life estate ($5,200 × 9.818147)[54]	− 51,054
Present value to remainderman	$33,946

It is extremely important that the appraiser fully understand two factors in this process. First, the interest, or discount, rate selected should reflect the risks of the future earnings of the real estate (i.e., quality and durability of the income stream) as opposed to the risk of the life tenant living for a shorter or longer period than indicated by the mortality tables.

Secondly, while financial tables and the financial calculator are excellent appraisal tools, the appraiser must avoid using them without a complete understanding of the formula utilized to arrive at the results shown in the table or on the calculator display. If the appraiser is going to use the present worth of one per annum factor noted above (9.818147), he must be prepared to demonstrate, in the presence of a judge and jury, how this factor is manually constructed.

In some jurisdictions, the entire condemnation award is placed in trust and the income from the trust is used by the life tenant until his death, at which time the trust is terminated and the original principal of the award is transferred to the remainderman.[55] This procedure eliminates the necessity of allocating the award between the life tenant and the remainderman.

Natural Assets

Property's natural assets may include mineral deposits, such as gas, oil, gravel, and sand, and growing crops, including timber stands. The unit rule has been strictly adhered to in the valuation of mineral deposits and crops. The rules of evidence and valuation testimony were clearly set forth in *U.S. v. Land in Drybed of Rosamond Lake* as follows:

> (1) that a landowner in dealing with a parcel of land on which there is a mineral, timber or like substance may not introduce expert testimony by which the expert multiplies the gross material present by the market value per unit thereof and thereby arrives at a figure which purports to be fair market value for the parcel;

> (2) that a landowner may not by expert testimony capitalize the present or future value of a business enterprise and thereby arrive at fair market value; that rental value may, however, be capitalized;

> (3) that the landowner is entitled to have an expert or lay witness describe the commodity or substance on the land, the quantity thereof, the going price thereof as *factors* only, upon which the expert may in part base his value as to the *fair market value* of the parcel in question; that a landowner is not entitled to present testimony as to the fair market value of the mineral or timber or other substance apart from the value of the land. . . . In other words, a clear distinction must be

drawn between what is presented and considered as a *factor* underlying the expert's opinion as contrasted with opinion as to the fair market value of the substance, timber or mineral itself, apart from the land.

(4) that a landowner must make a showing of some sort of market, poor or good, great or small, for the commodity in question before the quantity and price of the commodity or substance may be presented to the jury to be used as a factor in the expert's opinion testimony;

(5) that since the inquiry is essentially one as to what would have been the negotiations between the willing buyer and the willing seller, there may be taken into consideration by the expert only those *factors* which would have been reasonably so considered;

(6) that except in cases where the matter is so clear that it becomes a question of law it is generally a question for the jury to determine whether the proposed *factor* underlying in part the opinion of the expert as to the fair market value, is one which would have reasonably been considered by the willing buyer and the willing seller;

(7) that where the commodity in place on the land has a defect, or is deficient in quality, testimony may be introduced showing that the defect or lack of quality may be remedied or cured by scientific or business methods if the willing buyer and willing seller in the marketplace would have reasonably considered such a *factor;*

(8) that in such instance, unless that matter is so clear that it becomes a question of law, the question is one of fact for the jury to determine whether the commodity could be so remedied or cured and such a factor may only be considered by the jury as supporting the expert's opinion if the commodity could reasonably be corrected or remedied.[56]

These rules are not universal, but they are generally followed in most jurisdictions. They provide excellent guidelines for making an appraisal, writing a report, and testifying in regard to mineral deposits and crop lands.

In appraising property that may possibly contain mineral deposits, the appraiser's first step is to determine whether there is a market for the mineral deposits if they do, in fact, exist. If there is no market for the minerals, their presence or absence will have little, if any, effect on the market value of the property. Without a potential market, the quantity and price of the minerals present lends little, if anything, to the estimate of the market value of the property and, in accordance with Rule 4, this information is inadmissible.

In determining whether or not a market exists for mineral deposits, it is improper for the appraiser to consider the government project for which the property is being condemned as a possible market for the minerals.[57] For instance, if a property is being condemned for construction of a new highway, and the property has a gravel deposit on it, the quantity, quality, or price of the gravel cannot be considered by the appraiser in his estimate of market value if the only present, or reasonably foreseeable, future market for such gravel deposit would be for construction of the same new highway.

If a market does exist for mineral deposits thought to be on a property, the appraiser should attempt to determine the quantity and quality of the minerals. This is usually accomplished by retaining specialists such as geologists or mining engineers. If the appraiser can determine whether or not there is a market for the mineral deposits before retaining a specialist, he can often save his client a substantial sum of money; if there is no market for the minerals, the specialist is not needed.

It is improper to simply multiply the quantity of mineral deposits or crops present by a price per unit and add the results of this computation to the value of the land to arrive at a market value for the whole property. Again, the unit rule must be adhered to, thus it is the enhancement of the land value by the mineral deposits or crops which must be considered, not the results of some mathematical computation. It is not improper, however, for the appraiser to consider the results of such a mathematical computation as a factor affecting the market value of the property as a whole. It is apparent that the appraiser cannot simply adopt a specialist's value estimate of mineral deposits or crops and add it to his own estimate of the land value. Such a procedure even goes beyond the forbidden *summation* or *cumulative* appraisal because the resultant value is not even the opinion of one individual, but of two or more.

For the above reasons, it is extremely important that the appraiser be very careful in writing his appraisal report and in testifying in court. In both instances he must make it clearly understood that his final value estimate is not derived by simply multiplying the number of units (mineral deposits or crops) by a price per unit; rather, the appraiser has considered such a computation as only one factor in arriving at the final value estimate.

When a property being condemned has immature crops on it, a specific procedure for valuing such crops has been developed and accorded court approval in some jurisdictions.[58] The procedure involves three steps:

1. Estimate the quantity of the crops if they were allowed to mature.
2. Estimate the value of the crops if they were mature on the date of taking (or date of destruction).

3. Deduct from (2) all cost of producing, cultivating, harvesting, and marketing the crops.

Again, the result of this process is a factor for the appraiser to consider in arriving at an estimate of the market value of the property as a whole: it is not an independent value of the immature crops to be added to the compensation due for the taking and/or damage to the land.

In the appraisal of land with mineral deposits or timber, the appraiser must always adhere to the *consistent use theory,* which maintains "that a property in transition to another use cannot be valued on the basis of one use for the land and another for improvements."[59] Applying this theory to mineral deposits, it would not be proper to value land for agricultural purposes and then add a substantial value increment for gravel deposits under the surface of the land. If the gravel is mined, the land, in all probabilty, will have no value for agricultural purposes at the conclusion of the mining operation.

The above example is, of course, somewhat oversimplified. To demonstrate the necessity of adhering to the consistent use theory, and the complexity sometimes involved, assume that a 100-acre tract of land is being acquired for park purposes. The tract includes a lake of 10 acres, and the balance of the land is covered with merchantable timber. Market analysis indicates that the property, as is, would sell for $2,000 per acre, including the area of the lake, for recreational development. A timber cruise is made on the property and the cruiser's report shows 810 MBF (thousand board feet) of merchantable timber on the site. The cruiser estimates a value for the timber of $290 per MBF delivered at the mill, and a logging cost of $60 per MBF based upon clear-cutting (removal of all) of the timber. This indicates a value for the standing timber (stumpage value) of $290-$60, or $230 per MBF. Based on the timber appraisal, the uninitiated appraiser might violate the consistent use theory and evaluate the property as follows:

Land (100 acres @ $2,000)	$200,000
Timber (810 MBF @ $230/M)	+ 186,300
Total indicated value	$386,300
Rounded	$386,000

The two uses, recreational development and clear-cut timber harvesting, are incompatible with one another. The land will lose its aesthetic appeal for recreational development if all of the timber is removed. However, it would not necessarily be correct for the appraiser to assume that the highest and best use of the property is limited to only one of the two uses. If market evidence had indicated that clear-cut timberland was selling for $300 per acre of usable land area, a value estimate for timber purposes for the property might be developed as follows:

Land (90 acres @ $300)	$ 27,000
Timber (810 MBF @ $230)	+ 186,300
Total indicated value	$213,300
Rounded	$213,000

It may be erroneous for the appraiser to conclude at this point that the highest and best use of the property is exclusively for timber harvesting, simply because the value of the property for this use is $13,000 greater than its value exclusively for recreational development ($200,000). Further investigation and analysis may show that a portion of the timber could be harvested through selective cutting without affecting the land's value for recreational development. Analysis may indicate that 30% of the timber could be removed without affecting the value of the property for recreational purposes or exposing the balance of the timber to blow down. Selective cutting typically increases logging costs; in this case, assume it will cost $10 more per MBF. Under these circumstances, the value of the property could be computed as follows:

Land (100 acres @ $2,000)	$200,000
Contributory value of timber	53,460*
Total indicated value	$253,460
Rounded	$253,000

*Timber available for harvesting (810 MBF × .30 = 243 MBF). Stumpage value of timber ($290/M − $70/M = $220). Timber value (243 MBF @ $220/M = $53,460).

This analysis clearly indicates that the two users are not necessarily exclusive of each other. In fact, it would be prudent for the appraiser to make further analysis. If it is found that land that was clear-cut 10 years ago has regained all of its recreational value due to the new growth of the timber, and the appropriate discount, or interest, rate in valuing the present worth of a land reversion is 10%, the following analysis might be applicable:

Timber value (810 MBF @ $230/M)	$186,300
Land value (100 acres @ $770*)	77,000*
Total indicated value	$263,300
Rounded	$263,000

*Present worth of $1 discounted for 10 years at 10% = .385543.[60] $2,000/ acre value × .385543 = $771.09 present value per acre. Rounded to $770/acre current value.

To make this type of analysis more easily understood, particularly by a jury, the appraiser could explain that the acreage value, above that price the property would bring for timber reproduction purposes, is a value increment that reflects the property's potential for future recreational development.

The preceding examples demonstrate the various types of analysis which may arise when valuing land with mineral deposits or crops. The best analysis is the one that most closely duplicates the actions of buyers and sellers in the market and results in a final value estimate which represents the price at which the property, as a single unit, would sell on the open market.

Personal Property and Fixtures

Personal property is defined as:

> Generally, movable items; that is, those not permanently affixed to and a part of real estate. In deciding whether or not a thing is personal property or real estate, usually there must be considered (1) the manner in which it is annexed; (2) the intention of the party who made the annexation (that is, to leave permanently or to remove at some time); (3) the purpose for which the premises are used. Generally, and with exceptions, items remain personal property if they can be removed without serious injury either to the real estate or to the item itself.[61]

Fixture is defined as:

> A tangible thing, which previously was personal property, and which has been attached to or installed in land or a structure thereon in such a way as to become a part of the real property. The legal interpretation of what constitutes a fixture varies among states.[62]

The determination of whether an item is a fixture or personal property is of utmost importance to the appraiser, because the condemnation of a parcel of real estate does not include the condemnation of personal property on the premises. Thus personal property used on the real estate taken cannot be considered in the determination of just compensation.[63] However, if the item in question is determined to be a fixture, it is part of the real estate taken and compensation must be paid.[64]

A real problem arises in determining whether an item is personal property or a fixture, because the determination is based, in part, on ". . . the intention of the parties who made the annexation." In other words, when the annexation was made, did the person making the annexation intend for the item to remain in place as a part of the real estate, or did the individual anticipate the removal of the item, as personalty, at some later date?

Often, the final determination of the item's status is a legal question rather than an appraisal determination. It is therefore advisable for the appraiser to obtain legal instruction as to the inclusion or exclusion of questionable items in his value estimate. It is imperative that the appraiser specify in his report which items have been considered as fixtures, and are therefore included in the value estimate, and which items have been excluded from the value estimate as personal property. The appraiser should be prepared to extract the contributory value of any questionable fixture included in his value estimate, so he can testify as to the market value of the property excluding this fixture if the court rules it to be personal property.

If fixtures are of a specialty nature, such as lumber mill machinery or other manufacturing equipment with which the appraiser is not totally familiar, it is often advisable for the appraiser or his client to retain the services of one or more specialists in the field to evaluate the fixtures. Such fixtures are generally valued on the basis of their depreciated reproduction cost.

It is not proper for the appraiser to merely accept the value estimate of a fixture specialist and add this figure to the estimate of the market value of the balance of the real estate. It is not the value of the fixture alone that is compensable, but rather the enhancement in value of a whole property by reason of the fixture's existence. As one court put it:

> To the extent that the value of the real property as a whole is enhanced by the fixtures annexed thereto, the value of the fixtures must be included, in what the city pays, and the tenant is entitled to part of the award, not because the fixtures added to the value of the leasehold, but because they belonged to him and their value enters into the value of what the city has taken.[65]

The court in this decision is applying the *unit rule,* which has already been discussed.

It is a univeral rule that fixtures are a part of the real estate and compensation must be paid for them, but the general rule that compensation need not be paid for personal property on the realty being taken does have some exceptions. For instance, a California court[66] refused to rule, as a matter of law, that personal property on a property being condemned is noncompensable. Michigan also allows compensation awards to include personal property.[67] By statute, Iowa courts allow compensation for personal property.[68] Because of these exceptions to the general rules of compensability, it is always advisable for the appraiser to consult with legal counsel.

Other Estates

Other estates can also be segregated from the bundle of rights inherent in real estate ownership. Some of the more common divisions are: between an underlying fee owner and a *reverter;* between the various owners within a condominium project; between an underlying fee owner and the balance of the real estate owners within a platted neighborhood (e.g., plat restrictions); and between underlying fee owners and lien holders.

In some instances, owners of these estates are said to be *owners* from a constitutional sense,[69] while in other instances, these interests in property are not considered estates and, therefore, are not compensable upon a public taking.[70] The latter is generally the ruling in a case involving a *reverter,* one to whom a property will revert if it ceases to be used for a specific purpose. The courts generally hold such an estate to be so speculative as to hold no material monetary value.[71] However, the appraiser should obtain legal instructions in all such cases. As one court put it:

> We decline to follow the majority rule which denies compensation to owners of all future interest taken by the state. There is no rational basis for such a general doctrine. It is not equitable, and is not consistent with other legal principles related to such existing estates in land. In each case it should be determined whether the particular interest is of a sufficiently substantial character to warrant protection, or whether it is too tenuous for that purpose.[72]

Summary

The absolute ownership of real estate is limited by the sovereign's rights of taxation, eminent domain, escheat, and police power. The sovereign has further limited absolute ownership of real estate by constitutional and statutory provisions. The line between the government's police power and its power of eminent domain is often fuzzy and has been the subject of considerable litigation. For example, fee simple interest in real estate includes an easement in the abutting roadway for the purposes of ingress and egress, light, view, and air. This easement, however, is subordinate to the public's rights to the roadway, and the abutter's rights are subservient to those of the public. The abutter's rights of access, light, view, and air can be limited by the sovereign's police power, without compensation to the abutter, so long as the limitation of these rights is reasonable and the abutter retains *adequate* access, light, view, and air to his property.

The bundle of rights also includes crops that grow on the land and mineral deposits under the land as parts of the real estate. Therefore, when such property is condemned, these items are included in the valuation of the real estate, inasmuch as they contribute to the value of the whole property as a single unit. Fixtures are also included as part of the real estate and must be considered in arriving at a final value estimate. Personal property, however, is not generally included in the valuation of the real estate, and personal property located on a property being condemned is not considered *taken* or *damaged* from a constitutional sense, and, therefore, no compensation is due.

The bundle of rights may also be divided by private action, such as in the creation of a leasehold estate, a life estate, or a private easement. However, the appraiser must keep in mind that it is generally the rule that the value of the various estates cannot, for the purposes of condemnation, exceed the market value of the unencumbered fee of the real estate. When more than one state exists, the compensation paid for the fee taken is generally "apportioned in accordance with the respected interests of such owners. The matter of such apportionment is of no concern to the condemnor and is a problem in which only the claimants are involved. The compensation that must be paid is for the land, and not for the different interests therein."[73]

As stated in *Lewis on Eminent Domain,* "[w]hen there are different interests or estates in the property the proper course is to ascertain the entire compensation as if the property belonged to one person and then apportion this sum among the different parties according to their respective rights. The value of the property cannot be enhanced by any distribution of the title or estate among different persons or any contract arrangements among the owners of different interests. Whatever advantage is secured by one interest must be taken from another, and the sum of all the parts cannot exceed the whole."[74]

Due to the potential complexity of the various estates which may, together, constitute the fee simple estate of a parcel of real estate, and because the courts are inconsistent in their treatment of estates of various natures, it behooves the real estate appraiser to insist on reviewing a title report on any property being appraised for the purpose of litigation. This is the only way he can be sure that he is aware of all interest of record in the property being appraised. In addition, the appraiser is advised to obtain legal instruction, with documenting citations, as to the proper treatment of the various estates, if multiple estates do, indeed, exist.

Notes

1. American Institute of Real Estate Appraisers and the Society of Real Estate Appraisers, *Real Estate Appraisal Terminology,* rev. ed., Byrl N. Boyce, ed. (Cambridge, Mass.: Ballinger Publishing Company, 1981), p. 200.

2. Ibid., pp. 200-201.

3. James A. Ballentine, *Ballentine's Law Dictionary,* 3rd ed., William S. Anderson, ed. (Rochester, N.Y.: The Lawyers Co-operative Publishing Co.; San Francisco: Bancroft-Whitney Co., 1969), pp. 1009-1010.

4. Ibid., p. 1010.
5. *Real Estate Appraisal Terminology*, pp. 35-36.
6. *The Appraisal of Real Estate,* 7th ed., (Chicago: American Institute of Real Estate Appraisers, 1978) p. 12.
7. Ibid.
8. See Chapter 14, "Easement Acquisitions."
9. See Chapter 1, "Origin of Eminent Domain and Just Compensation."
10. *Real Estate Appraisal Terminology*, p. 94.
11. See Chapter 20, "Appraisals for Tax Hearings and Other Litigation."
12. *Real Estate Appraisal Terminology*, p. 188.
13. Michael M. Berger, "To Regulate, or Not to Regulate—Is That the Question? Reflections on the Supposed Dilemma Between Environmental Protection and Private Property Rights," *Loyola of Los Angeles Law Review,* Vol. 8, June 1975, No. 2.
14. Shrader v. Horton, 471 F.Supp. 1236.
15. Sibson v. State, N.H., 336 A.2d 239.
16. Ibid.
17. See Chapter 6, "Land Use Regulations."
18. McGarrity v. Commonwealth, 311 Pa. 436, 166 A. 895, App. Dism. 292 U.S. 19, 54 S.Ct. 565.
19. Chicago v. Taylor, 125 U.S. 161, 8 S.Ct. 820.
20. Henry J. Kaltenbach, "The Elastic Right—Access," *The Appraisal Journal,* Vol. 35, January 1967, pp. 9-16.
21. State v. Lavasek, N.M., 385 P.2d 361.
22. Julius L. Sackman, *Nichols' The Law of Eminent Domain,* rev. 3rd ed. (New York: Matthew Bender, 1979), Vol. 3, § 9.21.
23. City of Houston v. Fox, Tex., 429 S.W. 2d 201.
24. Priestly v. State, 23 N.Y.S.2d 152, 295 N Y.S.2d 659, 242 N.E.2d 827.
25. Iowa State Highway Comm. v. Smith, 248 Iowa 869, 82 N.W.2d 755.
26. Wilson v. Iowa State Highway Comm., 249 Iowa 994, 90 N.W.2d 161.
27. Iowa State Highway Comm. v. Smith, 248 Iowa 869, 82 N.W.2d 755.
28. State v. Fonburg, 80 Idaho 269, 328 P.2d 60.
29. State v. Wilson, 4 Ariz. App. 420, 420 P.2d 992.
30. Balog v. State, Dep't of Roads, 131 N.W.2d 402 (Neb.).
31. State, Commissioner of Transportation v. Charles Investment Corp., 143 N.J. Super 541, 363 A.2d 944.
32. State Highway Comm, v. Chatham, 173 Miss. 427, 161 So. 674.
33. Mabe v. State, 83 Idaho 222, 360 P.2d 799.
34. People v. Sayig, 101 Cal. App.2d 890, 226 P.2d 702.
35. State, ex rel. Merritt v. Linzell, 163 Ohio St. 97, 126 N.E.2d 53.
36. Priestly v. State, 23 N.Y.2d 152, 295 N.Y.S.2d 659, 242 N.E.2d 827.
37. State v. Wineberg, 74 Wn.2d 372, 444 P.2d 787.
38. O'Brien v. Central Iron & Steel Co., 158 Ind. 218, 63 N.E. 302.
39. Wolfe v. City of Providence, 77 R.I. 192, 74 A.2d 843.
40. Department of Public Works & Buildings v. Hubbard, 363 Ill. 99, 1 N.E.2d 383.
41. Commonwealth Dept. of H'ways v. Sherrod, 367 S.W.2d 844 (Ky.).
42. State v. Widen, 268 Minn. 209, 128 N.W.2d 755.
43. City of Beaumont v. Marks, 443 S.W.2d 253 (Tex.).
44. United States v. 70.39 Acres of Land, 164 F.Supp. 451.
45. *Uniform Appraisal Standards for Federal Land Acquisitions* (Washington, D.C.: U.S. Government Printing Office, 1973) § A-12, pp. 25-28.
46. George L. Schmutz, *Condemnation Appraisal Handbook,* revised by Edwin M. Rams (Englewood Cliffs,

N.J.: Prentice-Hall, Inc., 1963), pp. 75-76; Nichols, Vol. 4, § 12.36[1].

47. *Uniform Appraisal Standards for Federal Land Acquisitions,* § A-12, pp. 25-28.

48. Washington State Dept. of Transportation, *Right of Way Manual,* Chapter 4, Appendix 4-2, Appraisal Report Guide, Part II, § A, ¶2, (Revised 11/10/76).

49. See Chapter 16, "Leasehold Valuations."

50. *Real Estate Appraisal Terminology,* p. 151.

51. Stubbs v. United States, 21 F.Supp. 1007.

52. *Nichols',* Vol. 4, § 12.46[1].

53. Ibid., § 12.46[2].

54. L.W. Ellwood, *Ellwood Tables for Real Estate Appraising and Financing,* Part II, 3rd ed. (Chicago: American Institute of Real Estate Appraisers, 1970), p. 84.

55. Redevelopment Comm. of Greenville v. Capehart, 268 N.C. 114, 150 S.E.2d 62.

56. United States v. Land in Dry Bed of Rosamond Lake, 143 F.Supp. 314.

57. Volbrecht v. State Highway Comm., 31 Wis.2d 640, 143 N.W.2d 429.

58. State v. Dillon, 175 Neb. 350, 121 N.W.2d 798.

59. *Real Estate Appraisal Terminology,* p. 57.

60. *Ellwood Tables,* p. 116.

61. *Real Estate Appraisal Terminology,* p. 184.

62. Ibid., p. 106.

63. United States v. Certain Lands, 69 F.Supp. 815.

64. Carmichall v. United States, 273 F.2d 392.

65. In re Allen St. & 1st Ave., Borough of Manhattan, City of New York, 256 N.Y. 236, 176 N.E. 377.

66. Community Redevelopment Agency of Los Angeles v. Abrams, 116 Cal. Rptr. 308.

67. City of Fenton v. Lutz, 250 N.W. 2d 579 (Mich.).

68. Iowa Code § 472.14 (1971).

69. Lancaster School Dist. v. Lancaster County, 295 Pa. 112, 144 A. 901.

70. People v. City of Fresno, 210 Cal. App.2d 500, 26 Cal. Rptr. 853.

71. State v. Independent School Dist. No. 31, 266 Minn. 85, 123 N.W. 2d 121.

72. Patrick v. Mississippi State H'way Comm., 184 So.2d 850.

73. *Nichols',* Vol. 4, § 12.42[2].

74. *Lewis on Eminent Domain,* Vol. 2, 3rd ed., § 716, p. 1253.

CHAPTER 4
THE LARGER PARCEL

The appraiser seldom encounters a valuation or analytical premise in condemnation appraising that is not also found in general appraisal assignments. However, the concept of the *larger parcel* is an exception; it is an analytical premise unique to the field of eminent domain valuation. Generally, the appraiser is retained to estimate the value of a parcel of land which has specific boundaries and he knows the parameters of the property before any in-depth analysis is made. This is not, or should not be, the case in condemnation appraisals.

Real Estate Appraisal Terminology defines the *larger parcel* as:

> In condemnation, that portion of a property which has unity of ownership, contiguity, and unity of use. These are the three conditions which must be present to establish the larger parcel for the purpose of considering the extent of severance damage in most states.[1]

Understanding the concept of the *larger parcel* is paramount to the condemnation appraiser. The appraiser cannot determine the highest and best use of a property before a conclusion as to the larger parcel is reached. The larger parcel may be all of one parcel, part of a parcel, or several parcels, depending to varying degrees on unity of ownership, unity of use, and contiguity.

It is helpful to understand how parcel, or right-of-way, maps are developed by a condemnor. If, for instance, a roadway is to be constructed or widened, the condemnor's engineers prepare a survey of the proposed right-of-way limits. This survey is then given to the title section within the condemning agency, or to a title company, with instructions to determine all ownerships within the proposed right-of-way and the property boundaries of each parcel. These boundaries include all land that is contiguous and under identical ownership to that within the proposed right-of-way. A right-of-way map like the one shown in Figure 4.1 is then prepared. Figure 4.2 illustrates the typical ownership information included

48

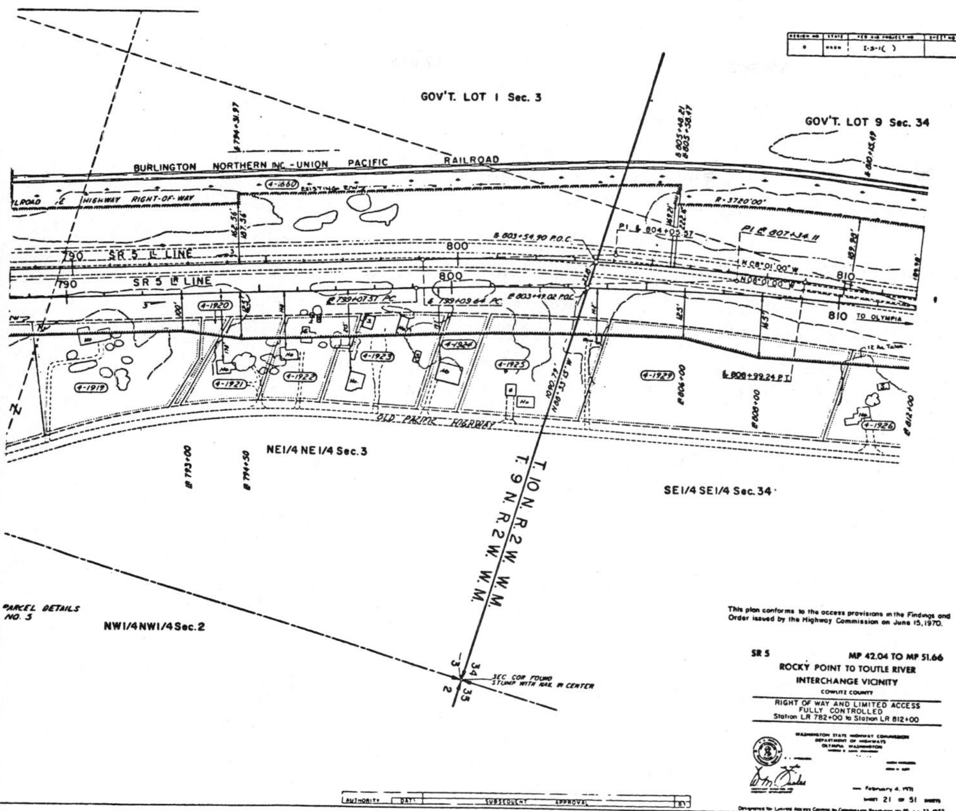

Figure 4.1. Typical Right of Way Map

PARCEL NO.	NAME	TOTAL AREA	TAKE	LT.	REMAINDER	RT.	EASEMENTS
	OWNERSHIPS						
4-1917	J. ALDRICH		SEE	SHEET 20			
4-1918	B. E. TREISCHEL	3.24 AC.	0.32 AC.			2.92 AC.	
4-1919	E. A. SOWERS	2.44 AC.	0.38 AC.			2.06 AC.	
4-1920	K. DECKERT	0.20 AC.	0.07 AC.			0.13 AC	
4-1921	R. P. SCHUMACHER	0.86 AC.	0.20 AC.			0.66 AC.	
4-1922	R. L. SNAZA	0.92 AC.	0.28 AC.			0.64 AC.	
4-1923	S. LOCKWOOD	1.39 AC.	0.32 AC.			1.07 AC.	
4-1924	E. C. MORRIS	0.65 AC.	0.15 AC.			0.50 AC.	
4-1925	A. R. JANISCH	1.96 AC.	0.36 AC.			1.60 AC.	
1926	D. D. WALSTON	1.14 AC.	0.13 AC.			1.01 AC.	
4-1929	A. JANISCH	3.88 AC.	0.60 AC.			3.28 AC.	
4-1660	BURLINGTON NORTHERN INC.						

Figure 4.2. Typical Ownership Information

on such a map. The right-of-way map is then given to the appraiser with instructions to appraise a specific parcel.

The matter of physical contiguity is an engineering question, whereas unity of ownership is usually a legal question. The right-of-way map is prepared and the boundaries of the properties to be appraised are determined prior to any consideration of unity of use. Therefore, most appraisal contracts between an appraiser and a condemning agency specify that the appraiser is to appraise a parcel which may or may not be the larger parcel. The ultimate determination of the larger parcel must be made by the appraiser. If it is found that the parcel defined by the right-of-way map and appraisal contract does not constitute the larger parcel, the appraiser must insist on a revised contract defining the larger parcel as the property to be appraised. If the property appraised is not the larger parcel, the appraisal is invalid.

The importance of the larger parcel comes into play in a partial taking case where, after the taking, compensable damages and/or special benefits accrue to the remainder parcel. Like many other elements in condemnation appraisal, the tests to determine the larger parcel (i.e., unity of ownership, unity of use, and contiguity) cannot be applied universally and blindly. The federal courts and some state courts have ruled that all three elements of this test need not be present in every instance.

An example of a situation where a right-of-way map may not correctly depict the larger parcel is shown in Figure 4.3. In this case, the entire parcel meets the

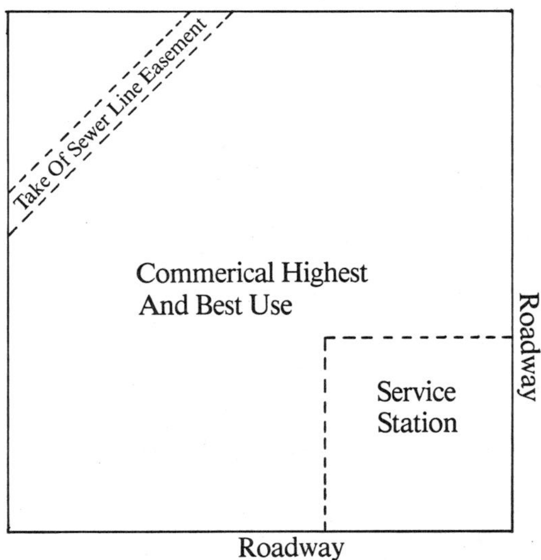

Figure 4.3. Nonunity of Use

tests of unity of title (ownership) and contiguity, but it fails the test of unity of use. Therefore, the service station site is not a part of the larger parcel[2] and cannot suffer compensable damage, nor can it receive a special benefit.

Another situation is shown in Figure 4.4. In this instance, the two sites have unity of ownership, but they are certainly not contiguous or put to the same use.

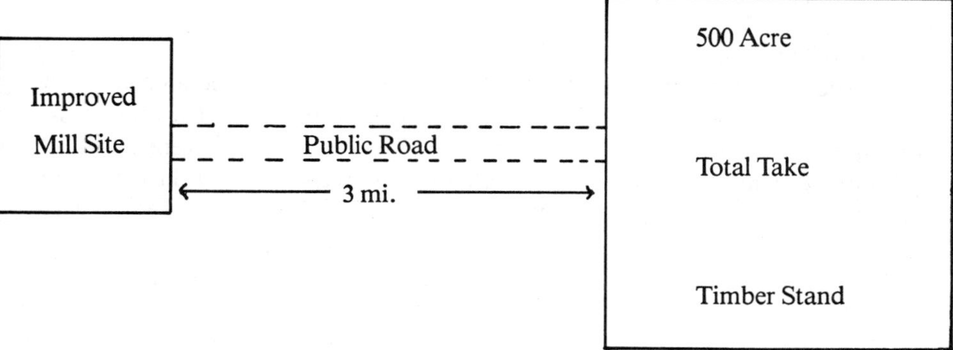

Figure 4.4. Noncontiguous Larger Parcel

However, unity of use has often been defined to include an integrated use.[3] The mill may have been constructed for the sole purpose of processing logs harvested from the 500-acre timber stand; while the two tracts do not have identical uses, they certainly have an integrated use. In some jurisdictions, the larger parcel would be defined as both the mill site and the timber stand. In such a case, damages accruing to the mill site, by reason of the taking of the timber stand, would be compensable.

In an often-cited landmark case in a federal court, it was ruled that two parcels 17 miles apart constituted a single larger parcel. In this ruling the court said:

> The basic question in condemnation cases involving severance damage is what constitutes a "single" tract as distinguished from "separate" ones, and the answer does not depend upon artificial things like boundaries, or upon whether the owner acquired his land in one transaction or even at one time. Whether land condemned is a part of a "single tract" authorizing allowance of severance damage, does not wholly depend upon whether holdings are physically contiguous, since contiguous tracts may be "separate" ones if used separately, and tracts physically separated may constitute a single tract if put to integrated unitary use, or even if possibility of their being so combined in

use in the reasonably near future is reasonably sufficient to affect market value. Integrated use, not physical contiguity, is the test whether land condemned is part of a "single tract" warranting award of severance damage, but physical contiguity is important as bearing on unity of use, and separation remains as evidentiary, not an operative, fact.[4]

It should be noted that, in the above case, the court recognized that separate parcels do not actually have to be utilized for the same use or an integrated use at the date of valuation; rather, if the highest and best use of the properties requires the sites to have the same use or integrated use, they constitute the larger parcel.

Unity of ownership is a very important element in determining the larger parcel. If Parcel *A* in Figure 4.5 is owned by Mrs. Jones, as her sole and separate

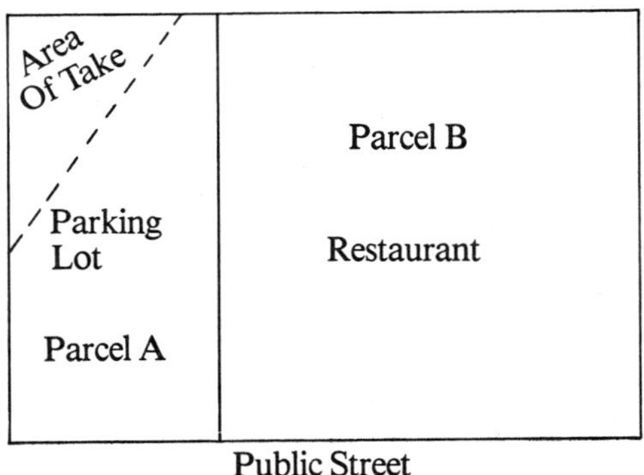

Figure 4.5. Nonunity of Title

property, and Parcel *B* is owned by Mr. and Mrs. Jones jointly, many courts would rule that the larger parcel is Parcel *A* only and no compensable damages can accrue to Parcel *B*, even though the two tracts have contiguity and unity of use.[5]

The appraiser's ability to define the larger parcel allows him to confine his judgments to those parcels or parts of a single parcel that are affected by condemnation. Figure 4.6 depicts a 100-acre farm which is subject to two zoning classifications. A widening of Road *A* requires the acquisition of the southerly 25 feet of the tract. The highest and best use of the property coincides with its existing zoning. The property is owned by a single individual and there is certainly contiguity present, but there is no unity of highest and best use. Thus, the larger parcel is the southerly 500 feet of the ownership and only this part of the tract is subject to compensable damages and/or special benefits.

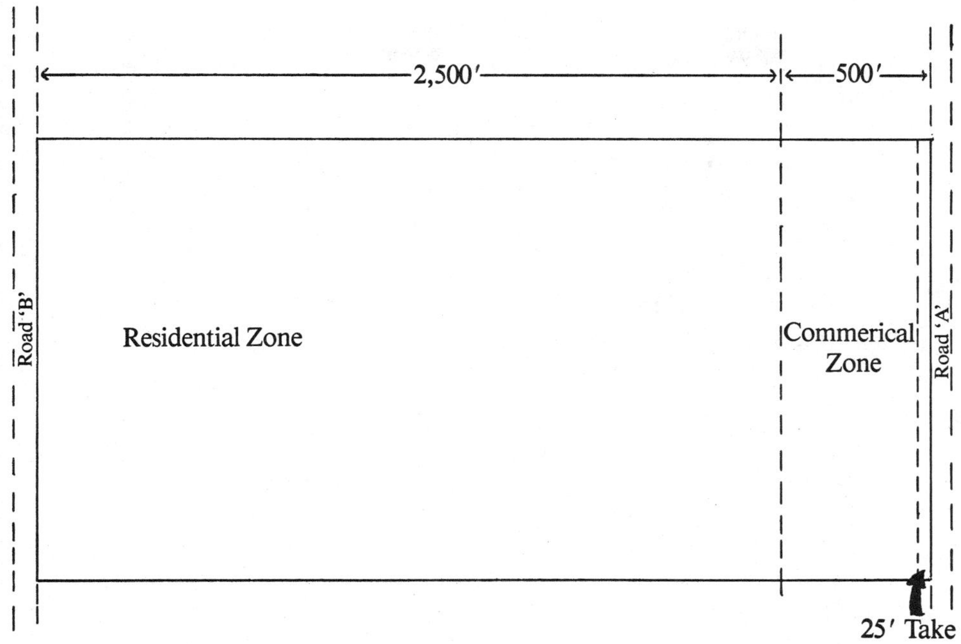

Figure 4.6. Nonunity of Use

This determination eliminates the application of the previously described *back-land theory.*[6] The backland theory would be used much less often if appraisers and others involved in condemnation proceedings had a better understanding of the larger parcel premise. Once the appraiser has made the larger parcel determination, the scope of his study and analysis is narrowed substantially. In the above case, only the southerly 500 feet needs to be appraised; thus, only comparable commercial land sales have to be investigated and analyzed. The need to investigate residential land sales no longer exists.

The preceding example illustrates that more than single ownership and physical parcel size must be studied to define the scope of the appraiser's assignment. Because the rules of determining the larger parcel (i.e., unity of title, unity of use, and contiguity) can be applied in a variety of ways, it is necessary to study each element of this *trinity* in some depth. Although most of the rulings pertaining to the larger parcel involve the question of compensable damages, the rulings are just as applicable to special benefits. It generally has been held that the determination of the larger parcel is a matter of *fact,* not a matter of *law.* Therefore, when a question of the larger parcel arises in a condemnation trial, it is a question to be answered by the jury (or trier of fact), not by the court.[7]

Difficult questions sometimes arise in determining what constitutes a separate or independent parcel or tract of land. The problem has a dual aspect. The first aspect involves the valuation of a parcel taken which is presently or potentially *allied* in use with another parcel. May the parcel taken be valued as in joint and unified use with the other parcel, whether the other parcel is taken or not? May the parcel taken by [sic] considered as a part of the larger parcel which consists of both parcels?

The other side of the same coin involves the question of severance damages to a noncontiguous remainder parcel which is presently or potentially capable of joint and unified use with the parcel taken.

It is apparent that the rule of joinder is simply an outgrowth and development of the fundamental principle in the law of eminent domain that property must be considered on the basis of its highest and best use. Implicit, of course, in the motivation for resort to the rule of joinder is the fact that the consideration of the two parcels as one will be productive of a higher use, resulting in a higher valuation than the aggregate of the valuations of the two parcels as separate parcels.

It follows, equally, that if two parcels are, in fact, separate and devoted to different and inconsistent uses, the taking of one parcel, valuation aside, will do no damage to the other. If, however, there is a unity of use so that both parcels are essentially one, the taking of one parcel may result in serious severance damages to the other.

A few definite rules of law can be laid down. In many cases the court can, as a matter of law, determine that lots are distinct or otherwise, but ordinarily it is a practical question to be decided by the jury or other similar tribunal which passes upon matters of fact (which should consider evidence on the use and appearance of the land, its legal divisions and the intent of its owner and conclude whether on the whole the lots are separate or not).[8] [citations omitted]

Unity Of Title

It is generally held that for one or more parcels to be considered a single larger parcel, it is essential that they be owned by the same individual or group of individuals.[9] There are a few cases, however, which have held otherwise. In a Kansas case, for instance, the court held that three contiguous parcels of land, owned by three different individuals and being used as one farm operation by agreement of the three, were a single larger parcel and, therefore, ". . . injury to each [parcel] resulting from the whole taking may be considered."[10]

Unity of ownership or title does not necessarily mean that the quality of the title is identical. Two parcels, one owned in fee and one owned equitably by a vendee's interest in a real estate contract, could be considered to have a unity of title.[11] One California case held that unity of title existed where an individual owned one parcel in fee and was the equitable owner of an abutting parcel, because he had exercised an option to purchase the second parcel.[12] In another California case, however, it was held that when the interest in the second parcel existed only by an unexpired, but unexercised, option, no unity of title existed.[13]

Unity of title generally requires equal legal control over the ownership and future of the lands in question. Acquisition of the parts of a whole at different times does not destroy unity of title,[14] nor, in some cases, does the fact that one parcel is owned by an individual and the second parcel is owned by a corporation under the control of that individual.[15] Some courts, however, have ruled conversely, as in a Pennsylvania case where the court ruled:

> Here we have separate parcels of land being used by distinct legal entities, i.e., the condemned parcel, the scrap yard was operated by appealees individually as co-partners, and the uncondemned parcel, the foundry, was operated, [and owned] by [the corporation], a Pennsylvania Corporation, the latter of which we now hold cannot, as a matter of law, be considered as a unit for condemnation purposes.
>
> Here the corporate shareholders are requesting that the corporate enterprise, voluntarily formed for certain business advantages, ought to be disregarded for their benefit in order to receive increased damages as a result of the present condemnation proceedings. This we refuse to do.[16]

A fee interest in one parcel and a leasehold interest in an abutting parcel, as depicted in Figure 4.7, can operate as one larger parcel for the remaining term of the lease.[17] Similarly, if three individuals independently own separate parcels of land and lease them to a fourth individual, there could be a unity of title during the term of the lease for all the parcels,[18] the beneficial effects of which would flow to the lessee.

Unity Of Use

The second part of the larger parcel trinity requires that the parcel or parcels of land possess the ability to be devoted to the same use as, or an integrated use with, the land from which the taking is made. It is generally not the existence or nonexistence of actual unity of use which is considered, but rather the unity of *highest and best use* which is the controlling factor.[19] If a property is not being utilized to

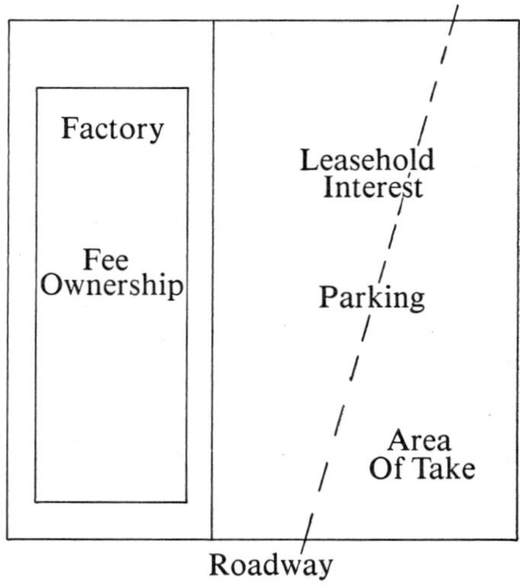

Figure 4.7. Leasehold Larger Parcel

its highest and best use, but has a common highest and best use, the existing utilization of the land does not generally destroy the unity of use.[20] There are, however, some courts which have ruled conversely.[21] These decisions, which seem contrary to the well-established premise that property is appraised for its highest and best use, are generally based on the reasoning that the unity of use has to be present and existing because potential unity of use is too speculative and conjectural to be considered.[22]

It is important that the appraiser recognize that stronger proof of unity of use is required when the parcels are not currently being utilized as a unit, but merely have a highest and best unity of use. "The question of unity of use of two or more tracts is a question of fact to be determined upon the facts and circumstances of the particular case, and is not to be based upon fanciful claims, speculation or conjecture, and in such cases the burden of proof is upon the landowner to prove his claim."[23]

Political boundaries do not interrupt the continuity of use if the government's land-use controls permit a continuous highest and best use.[24] Also, unity of use does not require physical adjacency; there may be physical separation by such things as streets,[25] railroads[26] and creeks,[27] but again this type of separation requires stronger proof of unity of use.

Contiguity

The third element of the larger parcel trinity, contiguity, normally requires physical contiguity to be present for a larger parcel to exist. However, it is not always mandatory. Various jurisdictions have ruled differently on this issue. Most courts hold unity of title and unity of use as the most important test of the larger parcel.[28] The courts' usage of the term *single tract,* as distinguished from *separate* ones, is best reflected by unity of use, but does not preclude a reasonable separation. The existence of such separation does, however, require study by the appraiser. The appraiser must be able to answer in the affirmative to the question: "Is it probable that the separated tracts would sell as an integrated single entity, even with the separation?" before the separated tracts can be considered as a single larger parcel. As a Rhode Island court put it:

> Quite a different situation is presented when, as here, the two parcels in question are unequivocally separated from each other by fixed and definite boundaries, such as a highway. In such a case it is generally held that the two tracts can be considered as one only when they are so inseperably [sic] connected in the use to which they are applied that the taking of one necessarily and permanently injures the other.[29]

Sometimes a larger parcel exists in the before situation but, in the after situation, the parcel is severed by the taking and becomes two separate parcels. Such a situation is illustrated by Figure 4.8. Although the property had unity of ownership, unity of use, and contiguity in the before situation, it certainly lacks contiguity in the after situation. Also, it is quite possible that one or both of the tracts have a different highest and best use after the taking than they did before. It is highly unlikely that a unity of use, or integrity of use, exists between the two parcels in the after situation; thus, it is unlikely they would be sold as a single parcel

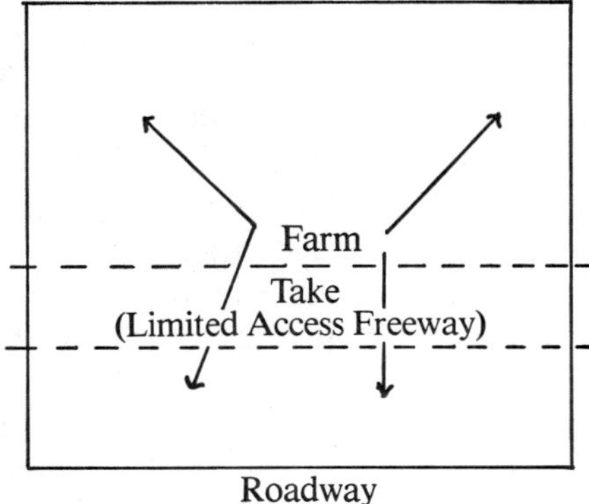

Figure 4.8. Two Larger Parcels—After

and, in all probability, they would properly be considered two separate larger parcels.

Conversely, Figure 4.9 illustrates a situation where two separate tracts, in the before situation , could become a single larger parcel in the after situation. If Parcel *A* could be developed to a greater density in the after situation by using Parcel *B* for required parking, special benefits could accrue; in those jurisdictions that allow the offsetting of special benefits[30] against both damages and the value of the property taken, the property owner may not be entitled to any monetary compensation.

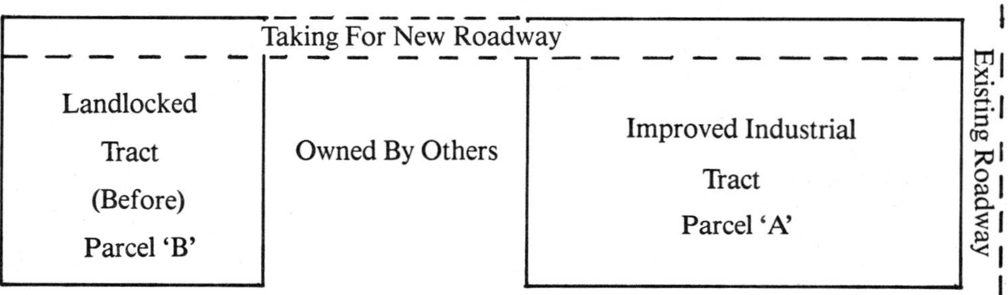

Figure 4.9. One Larger Parcel—After

Another problem which the courts have addressed upon occasion is illustrated in Figure 4.10. This could be described as the problem of the *paper plat*. If a tract exists as depicted by Parcel *A*, the whole parcel is, of course, considered as the larger parcel and the entire remainder parcel is subject to potential compensable damages by reason of the taking. In regard to Parcel *B*, however, the determination as to the larger parcel will often depend upon the specific status of the *paper plat*.

If the property owner has not dedicated the proposed street rights-of-way, or has granted only easements thereto while retaining the underlying fee, and no lots have been sold, the courts have generally ruled that all of Parcel *B* constitutes the larger parcel. The current status of the particular *paper plat* appears to be the key in determining the larger parcel. If the plat processing is beyond its initial stages, there could be two separate larger parcels (Lots 1 and 9) with Lots 2 through 8 falling outside the larger parcel and not subject to any compensable damages and/or special benefits.

An Ohio court expressed this situation well in saying:

> As an allotment develops, as it progresses from open land to individual lots, there comes a point where the lots not only can be but must

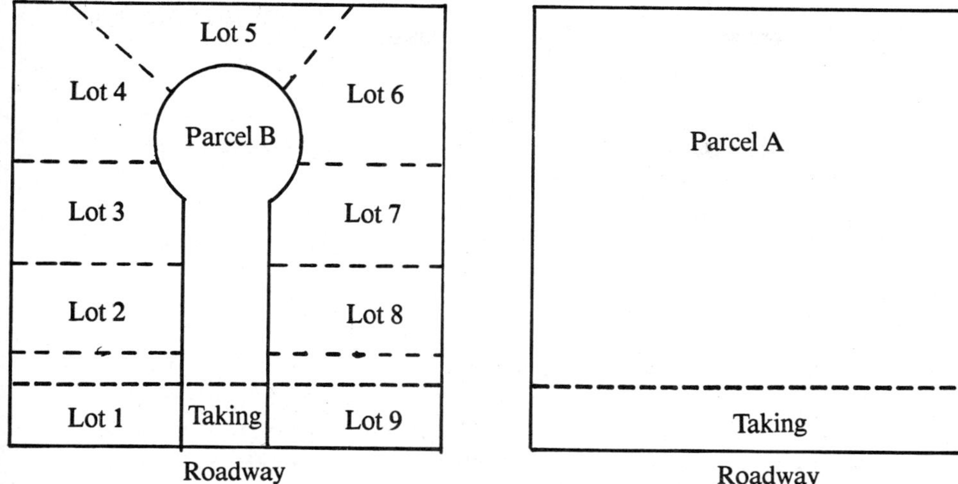

Figure 4.10. Paper Plats

be considered as separate entities. When this point arrives and a part of the allotment only is taken, consisting of a number of lots, the question arises as to what is the remaining land to which damage may occur. Is it the whole remaining subdivision, or is it just the fragment of an individual lot not taken?

Whether certain lots, taken by appropriation proceedings, constitute part of an entire tract so as to entitle the owner of the remaining continuous lots to damages within the rule is principally a question of unity of use and, as such, constitutes a factual matter to be determined by the jury under proper instructions.[31] [citations omitted]

Summary

The *larger parcel* is a premise unique to eminent domain valuation. The premise asserts that it is the larger parcel which is considered in condemnation valuation, and a parcel must generally possess unity of title, unity of use, and contiguity to classify as the larger parcel. Court rulings clearly indicate that all three of these elements need not be present in every instance. The courts have been most lax in requiring physical contiguity, but unity of use and unity of title have been almost universally held to be prerequisites of the larger parcel.

The courts in the various jurisdictions disagree as to whether unity of use must be an existing unity or a highest and best unity of use. The latter would appear to be prevalent in the majority of jurisdictions.

Unity of title is generally a legal question. The quality of the title of the various tracts making up the larger parcel need not be identical, but, as a general rule, if the same individual or group of individuals controls the title and future use of all the tracts, unity of title is considered to be present. Physical contiguity, which is generally an engineering determination, is not always necessary, nor does it follow that a whole parcel constitutes the larger parcel just because it possesses contiguity. Right-of-way maps do not control the determination of the larger parcel and, in fact, they may have no bearing on the question.

Unity of use is an appraisal question and the ultimate determination of the larger parcel is the strict purview of the appraiser. This contention is strongly supported by two court rulings. First:

> The method of valuation of the parcels taken, whether as a separate entity or in a relationship to the whole tract, then becomes a matter of opinion of appraisers to be weighed by the jury. . . . We conclude that in this case the use of either method of valuation by the expert witnesses was proper and their testimony admissible, subject only to the risk of nonpersuasion.[32]

Secondly:

> Where the property taken is less than the entire tract, other considerations arise. The highest and best use of the part taken may be as a separate and distinct piece of property unrelated to the entire property endowing such part with a fair cash market value. On the other hand the highest and best use of the part taken may be so related to the entire property that the value of the part taken for its highest and best use is dependent upon the value of the entire tract. Such a relation or dependence may present an issue of fact and either party is entitled to present his theory of independent or dependent valuation.[33]

The proper application of the larger parcel premise can reduce the scope and complexity of the appraisal assignment. Also, it will often eliminate the misapplication of the backland theory.

The various court applications of the larger parcel premise are quite contradictory. It is therefore important that the appraiser fully understand the court's application of this premise in the jurisdiction where the property being appraised is located. Any question regarding the legal permissibility of the appraiser's larger parcel determination must be addressed by legal counsel.

If a question as to the legal acceptability of the appraiser's determination of the larger parcel does exist, the appraiser must obtain legal instructions from the appropriate attorney, with supporting citations as to the legal acceptability of such a determination. If these instructions are contrary to the appraiser's determination of the larger parcel (assuming the legal instructions are reasonable and supported by applicable citations), the appraiser must alter his determination to conform with applicable jurisdictional law. This is the only way the appraiser can fully comply with his professional obligation. The inclusion of such legal instructions in the appraiser's report has another advantage in that it enables the appraiser to protect his own position.

Notes

1. American Institute of Real Estate Appraisers and the Society of Real Estate Appraisers, *Real Estate Appraisal Terminology,* rev. ed., Byrl N. Boyce, ed. (Cambridge, Mass.: Ballinger Publishing Company, 1981), p. 148.

2. Obrien v. City of New York, 32 A.D.2d 1059, 304 N.Y.S.2d 74.

3. United States v. Mattox, 375 F.2d 461.

4. Baetjer v. United States, 143 F.2d 391.

5. Glendenning v. Stahley, 173 Ind. 674, 91 N.E. 234.

6. See Chapter 2, "Legal Measurements of Just Compensation."

7. Arkansas State H'way Comm. v. Arkansas Real Estate Co., 471 S.W.2d 340.

8. Julius L. Sackman, *Nichols' The Law of Eminent Domain,* rev. 3rd ed. (New York: Matthew Bender, 1979) Vol. 4A § 14.31, and 1980 Supp. p. 218.

9. Commonwealth, Dept. of Highways v. Dennis, 409 S.W.2d 292 (Ky.).

10. Smith County Commissioners v. Labore, 37 Kan. 480, 15 P. 577.

11. State Highway Comm. v. Miller, 83 S.D. 124, 155 N.W.2d 780.

12. County of Santa Clara v. Curtner, 245 Cal. App.2d 730, 54 Cal. Rptr. 257.

13. People v. Hemmerling, 58 Cal. Rptr. 203.

14. Baetjer v. United States, 143 F.2d 391.

15. M.T.M. Realty Corp. v. State, 47 Misc.2d 44, 261 N.Y.S.2d 815.

16. Sams v. Redevelopment Authority, 431 Pa. 240, 244 A.2d 779.

17. Chicago, etc., R. Co. v. Dresel, 110 Ill. 89.

18. Berman v. Urban Redevelopment Authority of Pittsburgh, 324 A.2d 811 (Pa.).

19. Baetjer v. United States, 143 F.2d 391.

20. United States v. Mattox, 375 F.2d 461.

21. Cole Investment Co. v. United States, 258 F.2d 203.

22. City of Washington v. Koch, 456 S.W.2d 628 (Mo.).

23. Ives v. Kansas Tpke. Authority, 184 Kan. 134, 334 P.2d 399.

24. Northeastern, etc., R. Co. v. Frazier, 25 Neb. 42, 40 N.W. 604.

25. Tucker v. Massachusetts C. R. Co., 118 Mass. 546.

26. State v. Hoblitt, 87 Mont. 403, 288 P. 181.

27. Ibid.

28. Barnes v. North Carolina State Highway Comm., 250 N.C. 378, 109 S.E.2d 219.

29. Sasso v. Housing Authority of the City of Providence, 111 A.2d 226 (RI).

30. See Chapter 13, "Benefits—General and Special."

31. In re Appropriation For Highway Purposes, 15 Ohio App.2d 131, 239 N.E.2d 110.

32. Territory of Hawaii v. Adelmeyer, 45 Hawaii 144, 363 P.2d 979.

33. Department of Public Works & Buildings v. Oberlaender, 92 Ill. App.2d 174, 235 N.E.2d 3, aff'd 42 Ill.2d 410, 247 N.E.2d 888.

CHAPTER 5
HIGHEST AND BEST USE

"Fundamental to the concept of value is the theory of highest, best and most profitable use. . . . Highest and best use for land is *the use that, at the time of appraisal, is the most profitable likely use.*"[1] This statement holds true in condemnation appraisal. The courts have universally held that property acquired under the sovereign's power of eminent domain is to be valued in recognition of its highest and best use.[2]

When an appraisal involves a partial acquisition, the appraiser must make two separate and distinct highest and best use estimates. To determine a property's highest and best use in the before situation, any special influences of the proposed project are disregarded. To estimate the highest and best use of a property in its after situation is often more difficult, because it is necessary to study the impact of the proposed project in such areas as pending zone changes by reason of the project, conformance of the remainder property to existing zoning and setback requirements, and general changes in the neighborhood. It must be realized that, in the after situation, a whole new real estate environment is created by reason of the project.

The appraiser must keep in mind that the estimate of the property's highest and best use in the after situation is a totally independent study of the property, not a modification of the study of the property's highest and best use in the before situation. If the appraiser does not estimate the property's highest and best use correctly, in both the before and after situations, it will be impossible to estimate the property's value correctly.

Many definitions of highest and best use have evolved over the years; some are more appropriate than others for purposes of condemnation appraising. Many of the definitions have been expanded to incorporate explanations and restrictions adopted by the courts in their rulings on eminent domain cases. In some instances, the appraiser may find that no single, published definition of highest and

best use is appropriate for the appraisal of a specific property in a specific jurisdiction. Therefore, it becomes necessary, at times, for the appraiser to develop his
or her own definition of highest and best use incorporating applicable clauses
from various published definitions.

Comparison of Definitions

Two widely used definitions of highest and best use are compared below. *Appraisal Terminology and Handbook* defines the term as:

> The most profitable *likely* use to which a property can be put. The
> opinion of such use may be based on the highest and most profitable
> continuous use to which the property is adapted and needed, or likely
> to be in demand in the reasonably near future. However, elements af-
> fecting value which depend upon events or a combination of occur-
> rences which, while within the realm of possibility, are not fairly
> shown to be reasonably probable, should be excluded from consider-
> ation. Also, if the intended use is dependent on an uncertain act of an-
> other person, the intention cannot be considered.

> The use of land which may reasonably be expected to produce the
> greatest net return to the land over a given period of time. That legal
> use which will yield to land the highest present value. Sometimes
> called optimum use.[3]

Real Estate Appraisal Terminology says that highest and best use is:

(A) That reasonable and probable use that supports the highest
present value, as defined, as of the effective date of the appraisal.

(B) Alternatively, that use, from among reasonably probable and
legal alternative uses, found to be physically possible, appropri-
ately supported, financially feasible, and which results in highest
land value.

(C) The definition immediately above applies specifically to the highest and best use of land. It is to be recognized that in cases where
a site has existing improvements on it, the highest and best use
may very well be determined to be different from the existing use.
The existing use will continue, however, unless and until land
value in its highest and best use exceeds the total value of the
property in its existing use. See interim use.

(D) Implied within these definitions is recognition of the contribution of that specific use to community environment or to com-

munity development goals in addition to wealth maximization of individual property owners.

(E) Also implied is that the determination of highest and best use results from the appraiser's judgment and analytical skill, i.e., that use determined from analysis represents an opinion, not a fact to be found. In appraisal practice, the concept of highest and best use represents the premise upon which value is based. In the context of most probable selling price (market value) another appropriate term to reflect highest and best use would be most probable use. In the context of investment value an alternative term would be most profitable use.[4]

For general appraisal practice, the second definition supersedes the first because the second terminology book is an updated revision of the earlier work. However, there are some cogent points in each of these definitions which should be considered by the appraiser engaged in eminent domain valuation and the attorney engaged in condemnation trial work.

The first sentence of the first definition is an excellent, precise description of highest and best use: *"The most profitable likely use to which a property can be put."*[5] The rest of the definition is explanatory in nature. The definition excludes speculative uses from consideration, as the courts have done. In the words of one court "[e]vidence which is remote, speculative or conjectural will not be allowed as proof of land value in condemnation cases."[6]

This is not to say that a highest and best use *"to hold for a speculative rise in market value"* is not a proper determination of highest and best use; the courts have allowed testimony of such use. Such a use, in the words of the court, ". . . is a matter of such common knowledge that argument to the contrary is unrealistic."[7] The appraiser is advised, however, to exclude the word "speculative," or "speculation," from the description of highest and best use to avoid the possibility of the court or the trier of fact misunderstanding its use.

Use of the term *reasonably probable* in the highest and best use definition has been widely accepted by the courts. "[T]he fact that the property is merely adaptable to a different use is not in itself a sufficient showing in law to consider such different use as a basis for compensation. It must be shown that such use of the property is so reasonably probable as to have an effect on the present value of the land."[8]

In the first definition, the statement ". . . if the intended use is dependent on an uncertain act of another person, the intention cannot be considered," may be overly restrictive in some jurisdictions. The courts have generally reverted back to *reasonable probability* in such instances. For example:

> Proof of use of lands in combination with other lands [not owned by the condemnee] is not excluded from [consideration in] a condemnation case, "if the possibility of such connection is reasonably sufficient to affect market value."
>
> This is part of the question of highest and best use. "Value may be determined in light of the special or higher use of the land when combined with other parcels."
>
> It is elemental that the burden of proof of the highest and best use contended by the defendant-landowners, as well as the burden of proof of fair market value, is upon the defendant-landowner. Accordingly, if they contend for a use involving utilization or combination with other lands they have the burden of showing "the reasonable probability" of such use.[9] [citations omitted]

In such an instance, however, the appraiser must be cautious in writing the appraisal report and in testifying, because the question of *reasonable probability* is generally considered a preliminary question for the court, not a question for the appraiser. In the case quoted above, the court went on to say:

> In determining the question of law as to whether a sufficient showing is made of the "reasonable probability" the court will want to hear *facts* and not some experts' ultimate opinion about the very problem the court is to decide. An expert, of course, may be used to present factual matters. Nor are we stating that expert testimony may not be offered on technical problems such as the adequacy of a sewer line. What we are stating is that we will not hear experts give their opinion that there is or is not the required "reasonable probability."[10]

If the court determines, as a matter of law, that a *reasonable probability* for a specific use exists, the appraiser is then generally allowed to testify before the trier of fact in regard to that use.

One concept that is incorporated in the second definition but missing from the first, is the recognition that the vacant land may have a different highest and best use than the property as improved. The recognition of this concept is extremely important in eminent domain valuation; if it is ignored, the appraiser may very well analyze himself into an extremely uncomfortable situation on the witness stand. Such a situation is discussed in detail later in this chapter.

The very first sentence of the second definition of highest and best use says it all, with the balance of the definition being explanatory in nature. Paragraph (D) of this definition would appear to have no basis in eminent domain law. It is a social statement rather than an economic one. By the time an appraisal for condemnation is made, the sovereign has already determined that the project for which the property is taken will further *community development goals*. Because the sovereign is the representative of the community, it could be said that, under this definition, the highest and best use of a condemned parcel is always that use for which it is being condemned.

For example, under provision (D), a wooded urban site may have its highest and best use as a public park,[11] while under the first definition, the highest and best use of the site may be for residential subdivision purposes. Public parks seldom sell on the open market, therefore, it would be rather difficult for the appraiser to estimate the site's market value and for the courts to determine just compensation for the taking. For this reason, the inclusion of such a provision in the definition of highest and best use for purposes of eminent domain valuation is unacceptable.

In general, the second definition, with the exclusion of paragraph D, is well suited for eminent domain valuation. It is especially desirable because it clarifies that the appraiser's determination of highest and best use is an opinion, not a fact, and is therefore no better than the appraiser's judgment and analytical skill.

Highest and Best Use of Property, as Improved

As noted earlier, a tract of land, considered as vacant, may have a highest and best use different than that of the whole property as improved. Classic appraisal theory requires that "[l]and is valued as if vacant and available for its highest and best use."[12] The adoption of this procedure in eminent domain valuation would result in an accurate conclusion, but one that may be totally unbelievable to the court because of the procedure used to develop it. Figure 5.1 illustrates a situation where the appraiser may be well advised to deviate from standard appraisal procedure.

Assume that the appraiser has developed the following conclusions after investigating and analyzing the property depicted in Figure 5.1.

Highest and best use of site, as if vacant	multifamily
Before value of site as if vacant $3.00/sq. ft.	$36,000
After value of site as if vacant $3.00/sq. ft.	$33,000
Highest and best use of property as improved	single-family
Before value of property, as improved	$92,500
After value of property, as improved	$91,500
Before value of site for single-family purposes $1.00/sq. ft.	$12,000
After value of site for single-family purposes $1.00/sq. ft.	$11,000

If the appraiser were allowed to report and testify only on the before and after value conclusions, no problems would arise. The conclusions would be simply:

Before value	$92,500
After value	91,500
Difference between before and after values	$ 1,000

However, the appraiser is seldom allowed to report on or testify to only the conclusions, particularly with an experienced and knowledgeable attorney undertaking the appraiser's cross-examination. As one court said:

> When a witness, having qualified gives his opinion as to the value of the land sought to be condemned, he may properly give his reasons upon direct examination for his conclusion. As the element of highest and best use is an important factor to be considered in reaching a conclusion in respect to value it would seem clear that one who is entitled to give an opinion as to the value of real property should necessarily be in a position to give an opinion also with respect to its highest and best use.[13][citations omitted]

Using classic appraisal methodology, the appraiser's before computations, or abstraction of component values, might look like this:

Land value (12,000 sq. ft. @ $3.00)	$36,000
Value of dwelling	55,000
On-site improvements	1,500
Total before value	$92,500

Using the cost approach, the appraiser's computations in the before situation might take this form:

Reproduction cost of dwelling (2,200 sq. ft. @ $40.00)		$88,000
Less depreciation:		
Physical deterioration	$ 9,000	
Economic obsolescence (misplaced improvement)	24,000	
Total depreciation		(33,000)
Value of dwelling		55,000
Contributory value of on-site improvements		1,500
Total improvement value		$56,500
Land value (12,000 sq. ft. @ $3.00)		36,000
Total property value		$92,500

The appraiser's after value computations would then be:

Land value (11,000 sq. ft. @ $3.00)	$33,000
Value of dwelling	57,000
On-site improvements	1,500
Total	$91,500

The appraiser's after value cost approach computations are then:

Reproduction cost of dwelling (2,200 sq. ft. @ $40.00)		$88,000
Less depreciation:		
Physical deterioration	$ 9,000	
Economic obsolescence (misplaced improvement)	22,000	
Total depreciation		(31,000)
Value of dwelling		$57,000
Contributory value of on-site improvements		1,500
Total improvement value		$58,500
Land value (11,000 sq. ft. @ $3.00)		33,000
Total		$91,500

It can be seen that the economic obsolescence of the dwelling is reduced by $2,000 in the after situation by redistributing the ratio of land to building value. However, it would take an unusually persuasive appraiser to convince a client, or a jury, that the value of the dwelling has increased $2,000 by the taking of a 10-ft. strip from the rear of the site. The appraiser will, of course, protect himself by including in the appraisal report a statement such as:

> Where the value of the land and improvements are shown separately, the value of each is segregated as only an aid to better estimating the value of the whole; and the value shown for either may, or may not, be its fair market value.

Unfortunately, such a statement is usually forgotten or ignored by the reader of the appraisal report and the trier of fact.

Under the circumstance shown in Figure 5.1, the appraiser should consider the advisability of abandoning standard appraisal methodology and appraising the land at the highest and best use of the property as improved rather than vacant. Such a procedure would result in the following before value computations:

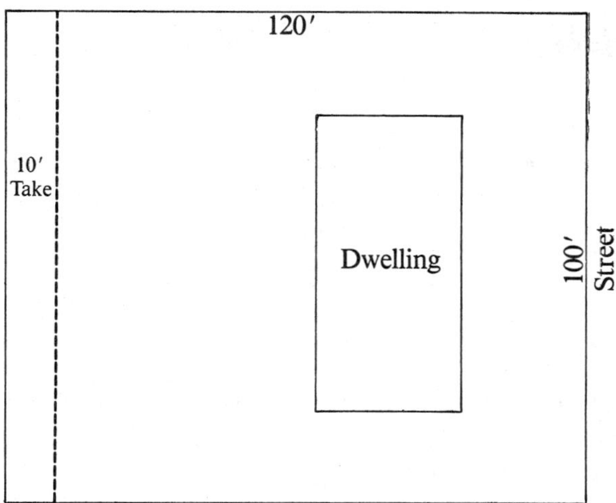

Figure 5.1. Highest and Best Use as if Vacant

Land value (12,000 sq. ft @ $1.00)	$12,000
Value of dwelling	79,000
On-site improvements	1,500
Total	$92,500

With the cost approach, the before value would be calculated:

Reproduction cost of dwelling (2,200 sq. ft. @ $40.00)	$88,000
Depreciation (physical deterioration)	9,000
Value of dwelling	$79,000
Contributory value of on-site improvements	1,500
Total improvement value	$80,500
Land value	12,000
Total	$92,500

The after value computations would then be:

Land value (11,000 sq. ft. @ $1.00)	$11,000
Value of dwelling	79,000
On-site improvements	1,500
Total	$91,500

Computations of the cost approach in this after situation would be:

Reproduction cost of dwelling (2,200 sq. ft @ $40.00)	$88,000
Depreciation (physical deterioration)	9,000
Value of dwelling	$79,000
Contributory value of on-site improvements	1,500
Total improvement value	$80,500
Land	11,000
Total	$91,500

Adopting this procedure does not alter the conclusion of the appraiser. It merely provides a computational process which is more persuasive and believable to those not familiar with real estate valuation techniques. Nevertheless, this procedure will undoubtedly leave the appraiser open to questions regarding multi-family dwelling land sales in the area at $3.00 per square foot. This argument can be derailed by a simple explanation of the consistent use theory, which is described later in this chapter.

It is advisable for the appraiser to include both the classic appraisal computations and the highest and best use, as improved, computations in the report. This procedure will serve a dual purpose. First, if the appraisal report is reviewed by a person knowledgeable in real estate valuation such as a condemnor's review appraiser, it will prevent the reviewer from criticizing the appraiser for abandoning the classic appraisal methodology and, at the same time, it will demonstrate that the results are identical, regardless of the procedure used. Also, the inclusion of both sets of computations will notify legal counsel that the appraiser has deviated from classic appraisal methodology and illustrate why he has done so. This will enable the attorney to better prepare for trial.

All Available Uses

As previously mentioned, the courts have universally acknowledged the concept of highest and best use. The appraiser may take the position that he has appraised the property for a specific use (i.e., the appraiser's estimate of highest and best use), but the courts have rejected this position. The majority of courts that have addressed this question have ruled that a property is not to be valued for a specific use, but rather in light of all available uses to which the property might, in reason, be applied.

A Tennessee court clearly defined its position on this matter:

> In this state we have adopted the view that "value in view of all available uses" is the proper phrase to use in valuation as against the phrase

"value for the best use" as is used by the minority of the states. We are bound by the majority view, that is that we consider the "value in view of all available uses." It is well said that we use this phrase to warn the jury against awarding the "value for a particular use."[14] [citation omitted]

A Massachusetts court used the same reasoning when it ruled:

The sum to be awarded for real estate taken is the fair market value of the property, having reference to all the uses to which it is adapted. Its value for any special purpose is not the test, although it may be considered, with a view of ascertaining what the property is worth in the market for any use for which it would bring the most.[15]

At first glance, these rulings may appear to contradict the appraiser's concept of highest and best use. This is not the case, however, because the courts recognize the concept of highest and best use and its importance in determining market value. The courts have adopted the *all available uses* concept in an attempt to avoid receiving testimony from various witnesses as to the value of the property for different specific uses, "for such evidence opens wide the door to unlimited vagaries and speculations concerning problematical prices which might under possible contingencies be paid for the land, and distracts the mind of the jury from the single question—that of market value—the highest sum which the property is worth to persons generally, purchasing in the open market in consideration of the land's adaptability for any proven use."[16]

It may be that this distinction between highest and best use and all allowable uses is merely a question of semantics and of little concern to appraisers, but the distinction may ultimately determine whether an appraiser's testimony is ruled to be admissible or excluded from consideration by the courts. As stated by a Nebraska court:

The power company also asserts that the trial court erred in permitting, over objection, the testimony of witnesses as to their opinions as to the value of the property for use as a filling station. In this respect one witness was permitted to testify that the corner was worth $14,000 as a filling station site. Sump [the witness] was permitted to state that the corner was worth $15,000 as a filling station site. The evidence was erroneously admitted. The rule is: Witnesses should not be allowed to give their opinion as to the value of property for a particular purpose, but should state its market value in view of any purpose to which it is adapted. The condition of the property and all its surroundings may be shown as well as its availability for any particular use. If it has a peculiar adaptation for certain uses, this may likewise be shown, and if such peculiar adaptation adds to its value the owner is entitled to the benefit of it. Where these facts and circumstances are shown, the only question as to value that is properly in issue is the reasonable market value at the time the property is taken or damaged. We conclude that the trial court erred in admitting the evidence as to the value of the property for use as a filling station.[17] [citations omitted]

It can be seen that there is no conceptual conflict between the appraiser's *highest and best use* and the court's *all available uses*. The appraiser who concludes that the highest and best use of a site is for a service station site, and values the property being condemned based on sales of comparable service station sites, is not in conflict with the *all available uses* concept. Such valuation procedures automatically incorporate the fact that all of the sites, the one being appraised and any comparable sale sites, have potential for uses other than their highest and best use as a service station site. Therefore, the appraiser must simply be cautious in his terminology when testifying in jurisdictions which have adopted the concept of *all available uses*.

All available uses does not generally include the use for which the property is being condemned. In other words, it is the value of the land taken which is to be estimated, not the value of the land to the *taker*. In some instances, however, the highest and best use of the property is, in fact, the use to which the condemnor will put the land. This type of situation often arises in the acquisition of recreational properties such as golf courses. In this circumstance, the property's highest and best use and the use for which the property is being taken could be identical, and the appraiser could properly estimate its value for this use.

This is not inconsistent with court rulings that land should not be valued for the use to which the condemnor will put it. As explained by the court:

If, in the present case, it is solely the state's need which creates the market then, of course, this special need must be excluded in the evaluation of the property. However, only the special value which the property has to the taker cannot be considered by the trier of fact. Where the basis for value to the taker is the same as it is with respect to others, the jury is entitled to consider the fact that the state is a part of the market.[18]

However, it was ruled in a case involving a potential dam site, which had an extremely high cost of construction and maintenance:

Where only the condemnor is financially able to put the property to a specific use, such use is considered too remote and speculative to merit consideration in determining market value.[19]

These cases illustrate that so long as there is a market for a special use other than the condemnor itself, that use may be considered in arriving at estimates of highest and best use and of market value.

Consistent Use Theory

"Consistent use affirms that a property in transition to another use cannot be valued on the basis of one use for land and another for improvements."[20] Two applications of the consistent use theory, as it is applied to mineral deposits and to timberland, have already been discussed in this text.[21]

At first glance, the consistent use theory seems to need little explanation. However, a review of appraisal reports, appraisal testimony, and court rulings indicates otherwise. The consistent use theory is most often misapplied in using the cost approach. For example, consider once again the property shown in Figure 5.1. In this situation, it would be a violation of the consistent use theory for the appraiser to value the land for multifamily purposes, and then value the improvements for single-family purposes, without deducting the economic obsolescence present in the dwelling.

This misapplication can also be carried through to the market data approach by improperly analyzing comparable sales. For instance, assume the appraiser has valued the land for multifamily purposes at $36,000 and then makes the following analysis of the sale of a comparable dwelling on a residential site:

Sale price	$100,000
Land value (12,000 sq. ft @ $1.00)	12,000
Value of improvements	$88,000
Value of on-site improvements	3,500
Value of dwelling	$84,500

The appraiser compares the property shown in Figure 5.1 to the sale property as follows:

Land—subject property is superior	
($36,000—$12,000)	$ 24,000
On-site improvements—subject property is inferior	
($3,500—$1,500)	− 2,000
Dwelling—subject property is inferior.	− 5,500
Net adjustment	$ 16,500
Sale price of comparable	+ 100,000
Indicated value of subject property	$116,500

It can be seen that substantial error results when the consistent use theory is misapplied by valuing land for multifamily purposes and improvements for single-family dwelling purposes. The New York court addressed a similar situation when it said:

> The claimant was awarded $55,500 for the entire taking of her property. It was concluded that the highest and best use for this property was commercial. At the time of the appropriation there was a dwelling house and combination garage and workshop on the property. The trial court awarded $40,850 as the market value of the land and $14,700 for the value of the building. The expert for the claimant as well as the state testified that the buildings would of necessity have to be removed from the property to permit its use for commercial purposes. It was error, therefore, to award anything for the value of the buildings while at the same time fixing the land value for commercial usage since the two bases are entirely inconsistent. Under the facts here the commercial value of the land was in no way enhanced by the value of the building.[22] [citations omitted]

Although it is relatively easy for the appraiser to understand and properly apply the consistent use theory, it is often difficult to explain its application persuasively to a jury. It is difficult for a lay person to accept the fact that a large, well-kept, single-family dwelling has no value. In fact, the courts have, on occasion, refused to accept the consistent use theory and made erroneous rulings.[23]

The appraiser must remember that, although it is a violation of the consistent use theory to value a parcel for two uses that are mutually exclusive, it is permissible to value a parcel for two uses that are not incompatible and can take place simultaneously. A potato farm that attracts a great number of water fowl can have a highest and best use for both farming and recreational hunting, because neither use is necessarily mutually exclusive.

Interim Use

An *interim use*, also referred to as a *transitional use*, is "[t]hat existing and relatively temporary use where the transition to highest and best use is deferred. A building or other improvement may have a number of years of remaining life yet may not enhance the value of the land which has a higher use, except as an interim-use taxpayer while the land is in transition."[24]

One property may, in effect, have two highest and best uses—one for a relatively short period and one as the permanent highest and best use. Developing a property to its ultimate highest and best use may be inadvisable at the time of the appraisal because of market conditions or other factors, such as the unavailability of mortgage money. The property owner can choose to either let the property lie fallow until it is ripe for development to its ultimate highest and best use, or put it to an interim use and at least receive some benefit from the property until its ultimate highest and best use is realized. An example of an interim use would be the utilization of potential subdivision land for agricultural purposes. One court ruled that such an analysis was proper:

> In the case at bar, witness Barnes substantiated his estimates with competent testimony as to the value, nature and use of the property as a dairy farm and also . . . sufficiently demonstrated an increasing demand for the property as a residential development site. Certainly a future purchaser of the Wallace property might well desire to continue the interim use of the dairy operation to offset any costs and interest charges that might exist during the piecemeal process of a housing development. There is nothing incompatible about or inconsistent in these two uses of the property.[25]

The best way to determine whether interim improvements, i.e., those incompatible with the land's ultimate highest and best use, actually contribute any value to the property as a whole is to analyze sales of comparable properties in the same economic position. Because such sales are seldom available, however, various methods of estimating an improvement's interim contributory value have been promulgated.

One of these methods involves valuing the income that can be realized during the interim period as if it were income from a lease, and valuing the land as if it were a leased fee reversion. For example, assume a 50-acre farm, which has an ultimate highest and best use for subdivision purposes, can be leased for $5,000 net per year during an estimated interim period of three years, at which time the land will be ready for development. Further assume that similar land currently ready for development is selling for $6,000 per acre. Therefore, the property under appraisal, if it were ready for development, would have a value of $300,000. The proper discount, or interest, rate applicable to this type of investment is 10%. The value of the property can then be estimated by computing the present value of the income stream and the present value of the reversion as follows:

Value of income stream:	
$5,000 income × 2.486852[26]	$ 12,434
Value of reversion:	
$300,000 × .751315[27]	225,395
Present value of property	$237,829
Rounded	$238,000

Another way to estimate the contributory value of interim improvements is to use the building residual technique of capitalization. Assume a lot improved with a single-family dwelling, which has commercial potential and a current value, recognizing this potential, of $30,000. The property will rent for $300 net per month, or $3,600 per year. In light of the lot's commercial potential, the improvements have a remaining economic life of only five years. An appropriate return rate is 8%. With this information, the contributory value of the improvements can be computed:

Annual net income	$ 3,600
Income imputable to land ($30,000 × .08)	2,400
Income residual to improvements	$ 1,200
Value of improvements ($1,200 ÷ .28*)	$ 4,286
Land value	30,000
Total indicated property value	$34,286
Rounded	$34,300

*8% interest rate plus 20% recapture rate.

Although this methodology is widely used, it contains a flaw. Assume that the current value of the land, recognizing its commercial potential, is $60,000, not $30,000. The computation of the contributory improvement value would then be:

Net annual income	$ 3,600
Less income imputable to land ($60,000 × .08)	4,800
Income residual to improvements	$ 0
Contributory value of improvements	0
Land value	60,000
Total property value	$60,000

It is quite probable that the land, if vacant, could not be rented during the interim period. Although the property is capable of producing $300 per month in net income, this capability is present only because of the existing dwelling; the above computations indicate that the improvements add nothing to the value of the property as a whole.

To correct this error, another method of estimating the contributory value of interim improvements has been developed.[28] This procedure calls for adding the present value of the interim income stream created by the improvements to the current land value. Compare the preceding calculations with the computations used in this method:

Annual net income from property, as is	$ 3,600
Annual net income from property, as if vacant	0
Income imputable to improvements	$ 3,600
Indicated present worth of improvements ($3,600 $\times$ 3.992710)[29]	$14,374
Land value	60,000
Total property value	$74,374
Rounded	$74,500

If the land, if vacant, could be rented to produce a net income, that income would be deducted from the net income produced by the property as improved. In the above example for instance, if the land, if vacant, could be leased as a parking lot during the interim period for a net rental of $1,000 per year, the income imputable to the improvements would then be $2,600, and the indicated contributory value of the interim improvements would be $2,600 $\times$ 3.992710, or $10,381.

The longer the estimated interim time period, the less valid is this procedure; to estimate an interim use period longer than five years can be considered speculation and conjecture. Because the property owner is not receiving any return on the land, this valuation method should be applied only in situations where the interim period is relatively short and, perhaps, where the land is appreciating relatively rapidly. The appraiser should not use this valuation procedure if comparable sales exist; the procedure is not intended to eliminate the need for market research. Also, the results of this procedure should not be adopted blindly, but must be correlated with the realities of the marketplace. Due to the simplicity of this procedure, it is often misused by the uninitiated appraiser and by the advocate.

At times, interim improvements will have a contributory value beyond that created by their income-producing capabilities. Many real estate lenders will not make loans on unimproved properties, but they will lend on improved properties regardless of the ratio of land to building value. This factor can sometimes affect market value, as can the fact that improvements can be depreciated for income tax purposes and give the purchaser an income tax write-off which would not exist otherwise.

In arriving at an estimate of highest and best use, the appraiser must remember the doctrine of reasonable probability. If the amount of time between the effective date of the appraisal and the time when the property is expected to reach its ultimate highest and best use is too great, the appraiser's conclusion of highest and best use becomes remote and speculative and will be rejected by the courts.

Land Use Regulations

Land use regulations play an important role in the appraiser's determination of a property's highest and best use. The appraiser cannot, of course, conclude a highest and best use which is illegal under applicable land use regulations unless there is a reasonable probability that the regulations will be changed to allow this use within the foreseeable future. The effect of land use regulations on highest and best use, and on the value of property, is discussed in detail elsewhere in this work.[30]

Enhancement and Blight

Condemnation blight is the diminution in the market value of a property due to pending condemnation action; *project enhancement* is the increase in a property's market value in anticipation of a public project requiring condemnation action. The appraiser cannot properly consider either of these factors in the before situation when estimating highest and best use or value.[31] The appraiser "shall disregard any decrease or increase in the fair market value of real property, prior to the date of valuation, caused by the project for which the property is to be acquired, or by the likelihood that the property would be acquired for the project other than that due to physical deterioration within the reasonable control of the owner."[32]

Condemnation blight, which decreases property values, most often occurs when public projects are announced long before property acquisition is actually commenced or when the acquisition program is not completed in a timely manner. Urban renewal projects are a classic example of this situation. Once an urban renewal project is announced, tenants tend to vacate buildings, vacancy rates escalate, property maintenance is often ignored, and vandalism tends to occur; these factors have a depressing effect on property values within the project limits. All of these items, except for physical deterioration within the reasonable control of the owner, must be disregarded by the appraiser in estimating the property's highest and best use and its market value.

If a property is located within a designated urban renewal area, it is often advisable for the property owner to retain the services of an appraiser well before the actual appraisal will be required. If this is done, the appraiser can analyze and inspect the property and neighborhood before the deteriorating impact of the urban renewal designation has had a chance to distort the actual *before situation*.

Project enhancement may also have a dramatic effect on property values. Zoning may be changed to accommodate a pending public project which will require all or part of the rezoned property to be acquired. An example of such a situation is shown in Figure 5.2. The property was zoned for single-family dwelling purposes, but a new freeway was announced and the property was subsequently rezoned for multifamily dwellings. The appraiser must decide whether the property in question was rezoned because of the pending project or in spite of it. This determination will have a substantial impact on the appraiser's estimate of highest

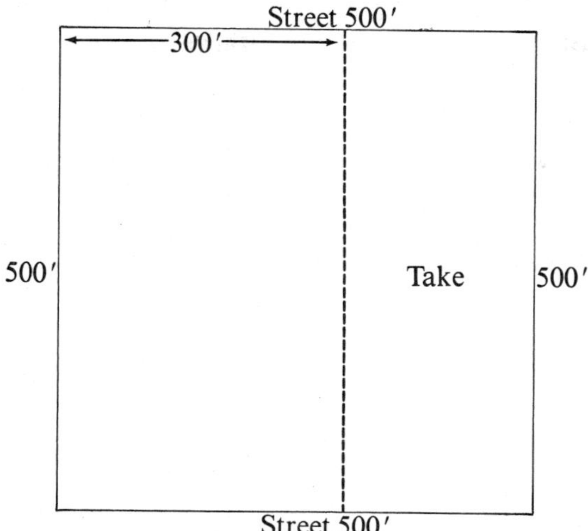

Figure 5.2. Project Enhancement—Change in Zoning

and best use and market value in the before situation.

For instance, assume the appraiser concludes that the property would not have been rezoned except for the pending highway project. If values for single-family dwelling land were 50¢ per square foot, and multifamily land values were $1.25 per square foot, the appraiser's computations, in a jurisdiction following the *federal rule,*[33] would be as follows:

Before value (250,000 sq. ft. @ 50¢)	$125,000
After value (150,000 sq. ft. @ $1.25)	187,500
Difference between before and after values (just compensation)	$ 0

The value of the taking is 100,000 sq. ft. @ 50¢ = $50,000, but this is more than offset by the benefit of 75¢ per square foot to the remainder property, or 150,000 sq. ft. @ 75¢ = $112,500. Under the premise of project enhancement, the appraiser must ignore the rezoning in the before situation, because it would not have occurred if the project were not planned.

On the other hand, if the appraiser concluded that the property would have been rezoned despite the highway project, the conclusion of highest and best use, in both the before and after situations, would be for multifamily dwelling purposes and the value estimates would be computed as follows:

Before value (250,000 sq. ft. @ $1.25)	$312,500
After value (150,000 sq. ft. @ $1.25)	187,500
Difference between before and after values (just compensation)	$125,000

If the highest and best use of a property changes to a more valuable use immediately before the announcement of a public project and the date of valuation, project enhancement may be indicated. In such a case, it is the responsibility of the appraiser to investigate the possibility and determine whether project enhancement has actually occurred.

A classic example of project enhancement is illustrated by a property that has a gravel deposit on it. Before the announcement of a road project requiring acquisition of the property for right-of-way purposes, there was no foreseeable market demand for the gravel. However, the pending project will create a demand for the material. In this case, the appraiser must not consider the demand for the gravel in the before situation because the demand was created by the project itself and is therefore a project enhancement.

Summary

Highest and best use is the most profitable likely use to which a property can be put. The appraiser's estimate of highest and best use is an integral part of the appraisal process because, without an accurate estimate, the appraiser cannot accurately estimate the market value of the property being appraised. In the appraisal of property subject to partial acquisition, two independent highest and best use estimates are made—one in the *before situation* and one in the *after situation.*

Many definitions of highest and best use have been promulgated over the years. The appraiser must take care to use the definition that is applicable to the property being appraised in the specific jurisdiction in which it is located.

The highest and best use of a site as if vacant may be different from the highest and best use of the property as improved. In such instances, the appraiser may wish to include two sets of computations: the classic appraisal computations, which reflect the obsolescence present in the improvements due to their nonconformity to the highest and best use of the land as if vacant, and another set computing the land value for the property's highest and best use as improved.

Most courts have held that a property should be valued for *all available uses,* rather than for a specific use. This concept is not in conflict with the appraiser's interpretation of highest and best use; rather, it is an attempt on the part of the courts to eliminate the possibility that the trier of fact will add together the values of the property for several specific uses to arrive at a conclusion of just compensation.

It is improper to value the land for one use and the improvements for another as this violates the consistent use theory and has been soundly rejected by the courts. There are several methods of estimating the value of improvements for properties which are in transition from one use to another. The appraiser should be familiar with all these procedures and adopt the methodology that best represents the actions of buyers and sellers in the market.

> The fair market value of the property taken, or the entire property if there is a partial taking, does not include an increase or decrease in value before the date of valuation that is caused by (1) the proposed improvement or project for which the property is taken; (2) the reasonable likelihood that the property would be acquired for the improvement or project; or (3) the condemnation action in which the property is taken.[34]

A change in the highest and best use of a property immediately preceding the announcement of a public project and the date of valuation is an indication that condemnation blight and/or project enhancement may have occurred. However, it is sometimes difficult to make a conclusive determination in this regard. Therefore, appraisers may disagree in their conclusions concerning the existence of condemnation blight and/or project enhancement, and this will often have a material impact on their value estimates.

It is implicit in all definitions of highest and best use that the use must be legal. Any estimate of highest and best use must be reasonably probable at the date of the appraisal or in the reasonably near future. An estimate of highest and best use cannot be remote, speculative, or conjectural in nature. The key to determining whether a specific highest and best use can be considered by the appraiser is whether the potential for that use has an effect on market value as of the effective date of the appraisal. If there is a recognized effect due to the potential use of the property in the marketplace, the appraiser not only may, but must, recognize that effect and consider it in the estimate of market value.

Notes

1. *The Appraisal of Real Estate*, 7th ed. (Chicago: American Institute of Real Estate Appraisers, 1978), p. 43.
2. Mississippi and Rum River Boom Co. v. Patterson, 98 U.S. 403, 25 L. Ed. 206.
3. *Appraisal Terminology and Handbook*, 4th ed. (Chicago: American Institute of Real Estate Appraisers, 1962), p. 92.
4. American Institute of Real Estate Appraisers and the Society of Real Estate Appraisers, *Real Estate Appraisal Terminology*, rev. ed., Byrl N. Boyce, ed. (Cambridge, Mass.: Ballinger Publishing Company, 1981), pp. 126-127.
5. *Appraisal Terminology and Handbook*, p. 92.
6. City of Santa Cruz v. Wood, 252 Cal.

App.2d 52, 60 Cal. Rptr. 26.

7. State v. Whitlow, 243 Cal. App.2d 504, 52 Cal. Rptr. 336.

8. Dep't of Transportation v. Great Southern Enterprises, 225 S.E.2d 80 (Ga.).

9. United States v. 70.39 Acres of Land, 164 F.Supp. 451.

10. Ibid.

11. *The Appraisal of Real Estate,* pp. 43-44.

12. Ibid., p. 43.

13. People v. Alexander, 212 Cal. App.2d. 84, 27 Cal. Rptr. 720.

14. Davidson County Bd. of Ed. v. First American Nat. Bank, 301 S.W.2d 905 (Tenn.).

15. Conness v. Commonwealth, 184 Mass. 541, 69 N.E. 341.

16. Sacramento Southern R. Co. v. Heilbron, 156 Cal. 408, 104 P. 979.

17. Petition of Omaha Public Power Dist., 168 Neb. 120, 95 N.W.2d 209.

18. State v. Arnold, 218 Or. 43, 341 P.2d 1089.

19. Julius L. Sackman, *Nichols' The Law of Eminent Domain,* rev. 3rd ed. (New York: Matthew Bender, 1979), Vol. 4, § 12.314, citing Continential Land Co. v. U.S., 88 F.2d 104, 58 S. Ct. 36.

20. *The Appraisal of Real Estate,* p. 46.

21. See Chapter 2, "Legal Measurements of Just Compensation."

22. Spano v. State of New York, 22 App. Div.2d 757, 253 N.Y.S.2d 730.

23. State, Dep't. of Highways v. Luster, 277 So.2d 181 (La.).

24. *Real Estate Appraisal Terminology,* p. 137.

25. Arkansas State Highway Comm. v. Wallace, 459 S.W.2d 812.

26. *The Appraisal of Real Estate,* Appendix B, Compound Interest Tables, 10%, Column 5, p. 576.

27. Ibid., Column 4.

28. Laurence Sando, "Theories of Valuation for Interim Use," *The Appraisal Journal,* January 1964, pp. 29-34.

29. *The Appraisal of Real Estate,* Appendix B, Compound Interest Tables, 8%, Column 5, p. 565.

30. See Chapter 6, "Land Use Regulations."

31. King v. Mayor & Council of Rockville, 249 Md. 243, 238 A.2d 898.

32. Uniform Relocation Assistance and Real Property Acquisition Policy Act of 1970 (P.L. 91-646) § 42.11 (c)(1).

33. See Chapter 2, "Legal Measurements of Just Compensation."

34. "Uniform Eminent Domain Code," 1974. § 1005, p. 10.9.

CHAPTER 6
LAND USE REGULATIONS

The appraiser's estimate of highest and best use must be a *legal use;* therefore, zoning and other land-use regulations are of utmost importance to the appraiser in determining highest and best use and estimating value. Market value is not inherent in the tangible real estate; rather, it flows from the utility the real estate offers. Therefore, it can be said that market value is nothing more than measured utility.

Value is controlled by utility, scarcity, demand, and purchasing power. All of these factors are influenced by zoning and other land-use regulations, so it is imperative that the appraiser be completely familiar with the applicable land-use regulations and their impact on the utility, and therefore the value, of the property under appraisal. Land-use regulations are part of the sovereign's police power and, over the past few years, they have multiplied almost geometrically. A partial list of land-use regulations might include the following:

Building Codes:	Environmental impact statement
structural codes	regulations
fire codes	Shorelines management ordinances
electrical codes	Flood plain management ordinances
plumbing codes	Platting ordinances
health codes	Shortplat ordinances
Comprehensive plans	Rent controls
Zoning ordinances	Timber harvesting controls
Offstreet parking ordinances	Air/water/noise pollution controls

Because some of these land-use ordinances are quite recent, the courts have not yet addressed the question of their impact on properties subject to eminent domain proceedings. However, the likelihood of obtaining an environmental development permit and the impact of this requirement on market value has been addressed by at least one court.[1] Some jurisdictions have ruled that a land use designated in a comprehensive plan takes precedence over the land use designated in a zoning ordinance if there is a conflict between the two, although, historically, comprehensive plans have been considered planning tools rather than enforceable ordinances. Also, some municipalities have denied development permits based on their comprehensive plans, even though they have no ordinance to implement the plan.

It is becoming increasingly complicated and risky to obtain all but the most basic development permits, so most recent land sales have been contingent on the purchaser's ability to obtain necessary permits to proceed with the contemplated development. This trend has added a new dimension to the appraisal of developable land in eminent domain proceedings.

Typically, the sale of a developable tract of land is closed only after the purchaser has procured all necessary permits for development. Therefore, the purchaser incurs no risk as to whether development permits will be available. But the property being appraised for eminent domain purposes is without any development permits and is, therefore, in a different economic position than the sale property. Developable land sales without *subject to procurement of permits clauses* are often unavailable, so the appraiser must adjust the price of the sale property to reflect the superior economic position it had, as of the date of closing, as compared to the property being appraised.

In analyzing such sales, it is important for the appraiser to determine the date when a *meeting of the minds* between the buyer and the seller took place. Sales of this nature often do not close and become a matter of public record until months, and sometimes years, after the buyer and seller have agreed on the price and the other terms of the sale. Therefore, by the time it is recorded, the sale may actually be several months old, and the appraiser must consider an adjustment for its date of sale.

Due to the complexity of the development permit process, some investor/developers who are acquiring raw land, by purchase or option, are processing all necessary development permits to approval and, at that time, reselling the land; in this way, they make a profit, not on the actual development, but on the incremental value realized by the existence of the development permits. An analysis of such sales and resales can help the appraiser determine the proper adjustment, when comparing properties which sold *subject to procurement of permits* with properties sold (or being appraised) without permits or permit clauses.

Each additional permit required to develop a tract of land to its physical and economic highest and best use increases the risk that the site can be legally developed for such use. Potential purchasers in the marketplace will consider this added risk in determining the price they are willing to pay for the land. When the risk increases, the potential purchaser wants a greater return, which often results in a diminution of raw land value. Unlike the land's physical limitations, land-use regulations are written and interpreted by man. They can be revised by man and they can have the human trait of stubbornness against change. These regulations define the legally permitted uses to which a property may be put. No matter how irrational they may seem to the appraiser, they are the law within which the real estate market must function and within which the appraiser must estimate value. They cannot be ignored simply because the appraiser disagrees with them or because they don't serve the client's interest.

Existing Nonconforming Use

Some properties are classified as pre-existing nonconforming uses under existing zoning. This situation generally occurs when the improvement of a property predates the applicable zoning ordinance, or when the ordinance has been changed since construction of the improvements. A nonconforming use is defined as:

> A use which was lawfully established and maintained but which, because of a subsequent change of a zoning ordinance, no longer conforms to the use regulations of the zone in which it is located. A nonconforming building, or nonconforming portion of the building, shall be deemed to constitute a nonconforming use of the land upon which it is located. Such uses preclude additions or changes without municipal approval.[2]

Zoning nonconformity may have a detrimental or a beneficial effect on a property's market value. If a nonconforming use exists, the appraiser must extensively investigate and analyze the specific ordinance provisions governing nonconforming uses and determine how the nonconformity affects the market value of the property.

Some zoning ordinances require that a nonconforming use be terminated upon the sale or transfer of the property, while others preclude the use of the property for a nonconforming activity if it has been vacant for a specific period of time, such as one year. Also, some ordinances preclude the enlargement or repair of a nonconforming use, and many will not allow an improvement to be rebuilt if it is even partially destroyed by a disaster such as a fire or flood. In such a situation, the owner of a property valued at $100,000, which is 50% destroyed by fire, will be unable to restore the improvement. He may receive a fire insurance settlement for the physical loss sustained, but will not be able to recover the additional loss of market value. A provision that forbids repair or structural alteration of nonconforming improvements will often decrease the remaining economic life of the improvements.

The appraiser must analyze these factors to determine whether they have any effect on the market value of the nonconforming property being appraised. In verifying sales of nonconforming properties, it is important for the appraiser to establish whether the buyer was aware of the nonconformity at the time of purchase and, if so, whether he understood the implications of the nonconformity. If a value penalty or benefit due to the nonconformity is reflected in the market, the appraiser must reflect it in his estimate of value. If, on the other hand, market analysis indicates that no change in market value can be attributed to the nonconformity, the appraiser must report this fact. The appraiser cannot report a value differential merely because, in his opinion, there should be one.

In addition to determining whether a nonconforming use exists prior to an acquisition under the power of eminent domain, the appraiser must be aware that a partial acquisition may result in the remainder property becoming a nonconforming use. If this is the case, the appraiser must make the same type of investigation and analysis in the after situation as outlined above for the pre-existing nonconforming use. Some zoning ordinances provide that a property which becomes nonconforming due to a partial acquisition by a governmental agency will continue to be treated as a conforming use. In this instance, the appraiser need not be concerned with the penalty provisions for nonconforming uses within the ordinance, e.g., the inability to renovate or to rebuild if the improvements are destroyed by fire. The appraiser need only concern himself with the physical nonconformity to surrounding properties and its potential effect on value, and not with the property's legal nonconformity.

A property may benefit from its pre-existing nonconformity, particularly in the area of density and occupancy. For instance, assume that a 6,000-sq. ft. site is improved with a 10-unit apartment structure. The property is now subject to a zoning ordinance which requires 1,000 sq. ft. of land area for each dwelling unit. Vacant land under the same zone classification in the neighborhood is selling for $3,000 per allowable unit. However, other land, similar to the site being appraised, but under a zone classification which requires only 600 sq. ft. of land area per unit, is selling for $2,500 per allowable unit. Based on these data, it can be said that the subject site reflects a value enhancement due to its nonconformity.

Value of site as nonconforming (10 units @ $2,500)	$25,000
Value of site as if vacant (6 units @ $3,000)	18,000
Value enhancement due to pre-existing nonconformity	$7,000

Variances

Most zoning ordinances provide for variances, or special-use permits, under certain circumstances. These variances may, for example, reduce setback requirements, allow a preschool facility in a residential area, or modify building density requirements. A zoning variance is:

> A change or variance in the use of property at a particular location which does not conform to the regulated use set forth in the zoning ordinance for the area surrounding that location. It is not an exception or change of the legally applicable zoning.[3]

To consider the variance's effect on property value, the appraiser must confirm that the variance is transferable and runs with the land, rather than running to the owner of the land. It is the market value of the property which is to be valued, not the value of the property for a specific use or to a specific user. The possible impact on value attributable to an existing variance is analyzed and determined in the same way that a nonconformity's effects are investigated.

In the case of a partial acquisition, the appraiser must determine whether a variance will automatically be extinguished or continued. On some occasions, it would be necessary to obtain a variance to develop the remainder land to its highest and best use after the taking. In such a case, the appraiser must determine whether there is a reasonable probability of obtaining the variance and what effect this reasonable probability may have on the market value of the remainder parcel. Care must be taken, however, because many zoning ordinances provide for variances for new construction only; they make no provision to allow a variance for nonconformity occurring after initial construction, which may be the case in a partial acquisition.

Zoning In Anticipation Of A Project

It has generally been held improper for a governmental entity to zone, or refuse to rezone, a property in order to purposely depress the property's value so that it may be acquired more cheaply in an eminent domain proceeding in the future. "Zoning cannot be used as a substitute for eminent domain proceedings to defeat the payment of just compensation by depressing values and so reducing the amount of damages to be paid when private property is to be taken for public use."[4]

In fact, it has been ruled that any governmental action, or inaction, intended solely to depress the value of property to be condemned is an improper action by the government. "An easement which otherwise would have been extinguished upon request of the landowner, may not be used by a government to diminish the value of the fee simple interest in the land in order to allow that government or other public agency to acquire said fee simple interest by eminent domain at a lesser cost for a purpose entirely different from that for which the easement originally existed. Such action would be an abuse of governmental authority, resulting in a denial of due process, no different in principle than using the zoning process for the purpose of depressing values in eminent domain proceedings."[5]

For this reason, it is incumbent upon the appraiser to investigate any governmental action concerning the allowable uses of the property being appraised for a reasonable length of time preceding the condemnation action. The actual length of time will depend on how long the project for which the property is being acquired has been contemplated. Interviews with the property owner are helpful in determining whether there has been any change in the zoning or any refusal to rezone by the government. If any hearing has been held on a rezoning of the property, the appraiser must review the minutes of the hearing and determine the reasons for the legislative action taken.

If the appraiser concludes that a zoning action was taken in anticipation of the acquisition of the property by a government body, this must be considered in the estimates of highest and best use and of market value. The appraiser may conclude that (1) the action taken would have been the same if the acquisition were not pending; (2) there is a reasonable probability that the action taken would have been different if an acquisition were not anticipated; or (3) the action taken would definitely have been different had there been no anticipation of an acquisition.

If it is concluded that the action would have been the same, with or without the anticipated acquisition, the appraiser need only report the zoning activity. If, however, the appraiser concludes that the zoning action was affected, or a reasonable probability exists that it was affected, by the anticipated acquisition of the property in question, the question must be specifically addressed in the appraisal report. If the action has had a depressing effect on the property's value, this must be disregarded. An acceptable approach to this situation from an appraisal standpoint is demonstrated by the following excerpts from an actual appraisal report, prepared for a condemnor:

> PRESENT ZONING: The present zoning is "R-7.5" which allows single family dwelling use with a maximum lot size of 7,500 sq. ft. Therefore, the existing commercial enterprise located on the Subject Property is nonconforming to the zoning ordinance.
>
> HIGHEST AND BEST USE OF THE LAND IF VACANT: In making a "before situation" appraisal for highway purposes, it must be assumed that there is no contemplated taking of the Subject Property nor any highway construction anticipated which would affect the Subject Property. If the proposed taking and/or construction has affected the Subject Property in any way, such effects must be adjusted for in arriving at an estimate of market value in the before situation.
>
> In my investigation, it was learned that Subject Property abuts a

property which is zoned "M-G" (general manufacturing) and is presently being used for a commercial/manufacturing use. It was further learned that both the Subject Property and the property to the north of Subject were being used for commercial/manufacturing uses, thus making them nonconforming to the existing "R-7.5" residential zone. On May 19, 1966 the owner of Subject and the owner of the property north of Subject requested that the Clark County Planning Commission rezone the property "M-G" so the zoning would conform to the property to the south of Subject, as well as to the uses to which the properties were actually being put.

The minutes of the May 19, 1966 Planning Commission show the following:

"1. A letter was submitted by the district highway engineer which read in part:

a. . . . we feel that if this change in zoning was approved, it would increase the value of the property and represent an undue expenditure of public funds.

b. . . . and it is anticipated that the right of way along the route of I-205 will be purchased the first part of 1967. [appraisal report written in 1971]

c. We would like to urge that the planning commission refuse this zone change in light of the forthcoming purchase of right-of-way and the construction of I-205.

"2. The Highway Commission was represented at the Planning Commission meeting."

It is specifically called to the client's attention that Subject has been appraised as if it had been rezoned to general manufacturing on May 19, 1966—not as if a reasonable probability exists for such rezoning as of the effective date of this appraisal.

The appraiser concluded that the property would have been rezoned to the *M-G* designation had it not been for the state's interference with the zoning application and the improper consideration, by the county planning commission, of the anticipated acquisition of the property by the state. Therefore, the appraiser's approach, under these circumstances, was warranted.

An appraiser who encounters a situation similar to the above is well advised to seek appropriate legal counsel before writing his report, because there are some intricacies of the law which need to be addressed in such situations. For instance, the California court ruled:

> The distinction between the governmental entity imposing the improper restrictions in the guise of zoning and the governmental unit taking property for which the constitution demands it pay just compensation creates a critical problem in case at bench. A zoning restriction imposed to depress value with a view of future eminent domain proceedings itself creates a cause of action in inverse condemnation against the governmental unit enacting the zoning ordinance.[6]

However, in establishing this rule, the court limited its applicability to instances where the condemnor and the zoning authority were the same governmental entity.

It is not improper for a zoning authority to base its decisions, in part, on a proposed project which will involve governmental acquisition of real estate; it is improper, however, for the zoning authority to purposefully take action to depress the value of a property so that it may be acquired at a lower price. If the zoning authority takes action, the proximate cause of which is the proposed public project, the appraiser must disregard the zoning action in his appraisal of the property in the before situation. However, if the eminent domain proceedings involve only a partial acquisition, the appraiser must consider the zoning action in estimating the value of the property in the after situation.

For example, assume a partial taking as shown in Figure 6.1. The property consisted of 50 acres of land before the taking and was zoned for its highest and best use of single-family residential development. The condemnor proposed acquisition of 20 acres of the property for the construction of a new limited-access highway. The county planning commission rezoned the property for multiple dwelling purposes, primarily so that the remaining area could act as a buffer zone between the proposed highway and the surrounding single-family dwelling areas. Therefore, after the rezoning, the property being appraised had a highest and best use for multifamily dwelling purposes.

In the appraiser's before valuation, the rezoning to multifamily use cannot be considered because it was predicated upon the proposed highway project. Therefore, the before value must be based on single-family zoning and highest and best use. In the after situation, however, the appraiser must base his value estimate on the multifamily dwelling zoning and highest and best use, because the zoning change was a direct result of the proposed highway project.

If land with a highest and best use for single-family residential development is selling for $10,000 per acre, and land with a highest and best use for multifamily dwelling development is selling for $15,000 per acre, the before and after values in

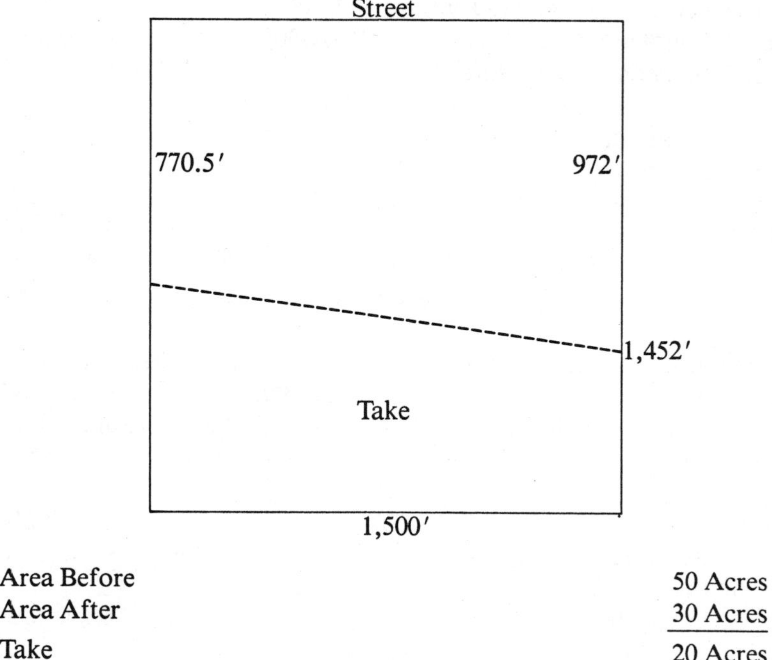

Area Before	50 Acres
Area After	30 Acres
Take	20 Acres

Figure 6.1. Rezone Due to Pending Public Project

jurisdictions that allow the offsetting of special benefits against the taking might be computed:

Before value:	
50 acres @ $10,000	$500,000
After value:	
30 acres @ $15,000	450,000
Difference between before & after	
values (just compensation)	$ 50,000

In jurisdictions that do not allow special benefits to be offset against the taking, the computations would be:

(1)	Value before taking (50 acres @ $10,000)	$500,000
(2)	Value of part taken (20 acres @ $10,000)	− 200,000
(3)	Remainder value before taking	$300,000
(4)	Remainder value after taking	
	(30 acres @ $15,000)	− 450,000
(5)	Damages	$ 0
(6)	Special benefits (30 acres @ $5,000)	− 150,000
(7)	Net damages	$ 0
(8)	Value of part taken	+ 200,000
(9)	Total difference (just compensation)	$200,000

Now, assume that the rezoning would have occurred regardless of the proposed project. In this case, the property would be valued under its multifamily dwelling zoning and multifamily highest and best use in both the before and after situations. Here the benefit offset rule would make no difference in the calculations:

Before value (50 acres @ $15,000)	$750,000
After value (30 acres @ $15,000)	− 450,000
Difference between before and after values (just compensation)	$300,000

Probability Of Rezoning

"[I]t is a well established rule of law that a jury, in determining the fair market value of condemned land, may consider zoning changes which were reasonably probable at the time the land was taken."[7] The question of the probability of re-

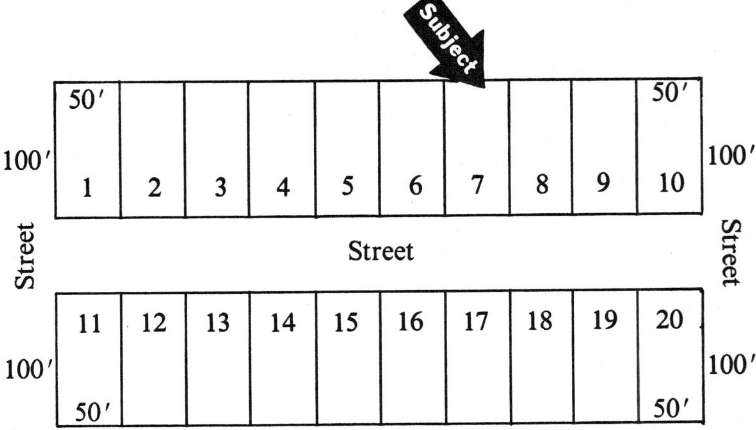

Figure 6.2. Probability of Rezone

zoning is fertile ground for the unscrupulous, the naive, and the dreamer. Therefore, there is a considerable amount of case law on the subject. Problems arise in this area because some appraisers always seem to conclude that a reasonable probability of rezoning exists, while others never conclude that this probability exists. Most court rulings on the subject state that an appraiser *may* consider reasonably probable zone changes but, ethically and professionally, the appraiser *must* consider reasonably probable zoning changes.[8]

The ultimate judge of whether there is reasonable probability for a rezoning is not the appraiser or even the court, but the buyers and sellers in the marketplace. For instance, assume lot 7 in Figure 6.2 is being appraised. The entire neighborhood is currently zoned for single-family dwelling purposes. A search of public records discloses the following sales, all occurring in the past six months.

Lot No.	Price	Price/Sq. Ft.
1	$30,000	$6.00
3	32,000	6.40
4	27,500	5.50
6	34,000	6.80
9	30,000	6.00

The following lot sales, occurring in the last six months, were also found:

Lot No.	Price	Price/Sq. Ft.
11	$7,500	$1.50
16	8,000	1.60
18	8,250	1.65

These last three lots, located on the south side of the street, have been developed with single-family dwellings since their purchase. The five lots on the north side of the street remain undeveloped, and verification of the sales with the purchasers indicates they were purchased for commercial development in anticipation of a rezoning.

Under the circumstances, it makes no difference what the appraiser thinks about the chances of having the area rezoned. Buyers and sellers speak louder than appraisers in such instances, because they are talking with money. Even if the purchasers were overenthusiastic about the potential for a rezoning, the evidence indicates that there are enough overenthusiastic buyers to create a market value of $5.50 to $6.40 per square foot for the property being appraised. It is not the appraiser's function to determine what constitutes a good buy or a bad buy; he only estimates the price at which a property can be sold on the open market.

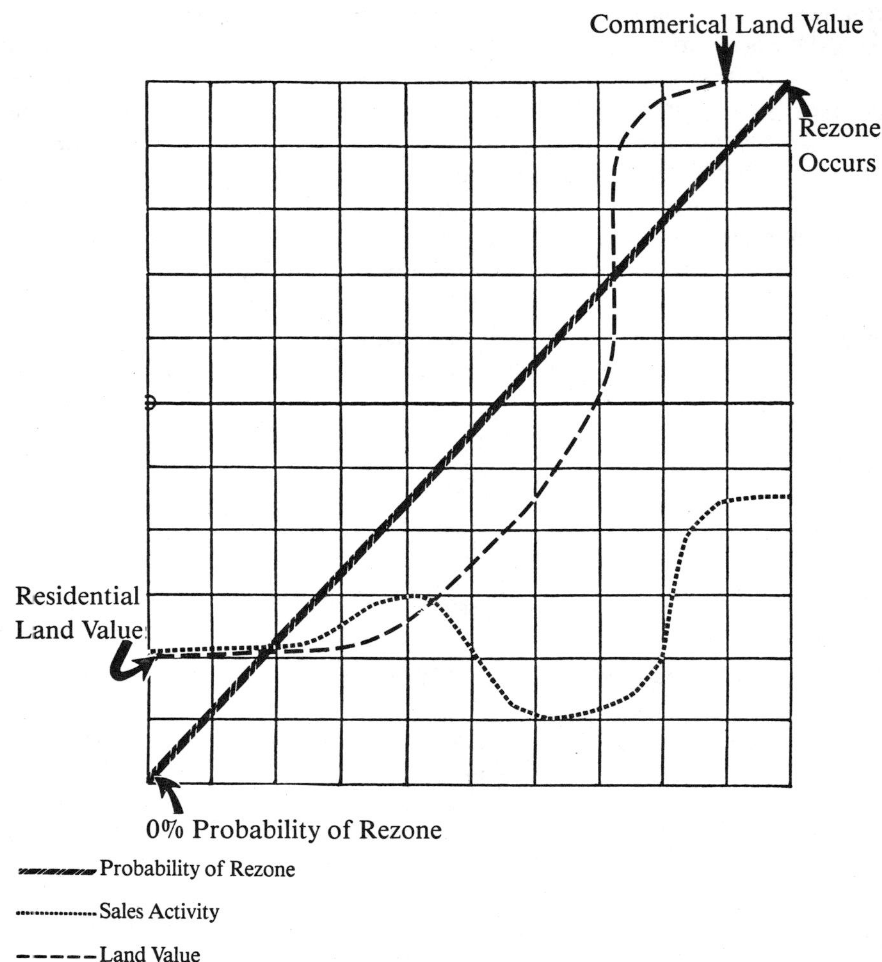

Figure 6.3. Price—Market Activity/Rezone Probability Relationship

Authoritative texts and courts have recognized this factor. As one court put it:

> The test, of course, is not either possibly [sic] or probability of rezoning in absolute terms, but the fair market value of the locus in the light of the chances as they would appear to the hypothetical willing buyer and seller. . . .

> We think that the "market effect" principle . . . is the crux of the test to be applied. The ultimate enquiry in any condemnation case is the

market value of the condemnee's land. Evidence which has a material bearing on market value should be admissible, without regard to whether it relates to an eventuality that might or might not occur in the "near" or more "distant" future, as long as the prospect of the event has substantial present influence on market value. It seems to us that the real purpose of the "near future" and anti-"remote or speculative" qualifications of the rule . . . is to exclude consideration of an asserted prospective rezoning which is nothing much more than a figment of a bullish owner's imagination.[9]

Unfortunately, market evidence is not always so clear. As the possibility of an area being rezoned to a more intensive use begins to develop, prices in the neighborhood begin to rise, and property owners in the area withhold their properties from the market in order to enjoy the benefits of rapidly escalating values as the potential rezoning comes closer to becoming a reality. The relationship between sales activity, values, and the potential for rezoning is graphically displayed in Figure 6.3. Due to this slump in market activity, the appraiser using the Market Data Approach is often forced to use residential sales with no rezoning potential and develop a reliable increment of value for the property's commercial potential, or to use commercial sales and develop a reliable discount to reflect the fact that the property being appraised is not, as an established fact, zoned for commercial purposes.

Under no circumstances can a property, under the doctrine of reasonable probability, be appraised as if it were already rezoned to the higher use. As stated by the New Jersey court:

> The important *caveat* is that the true issue is not the value of the property for the use which would be permitted if the amendment were adopted. Zoning amendments are routinely made or granted. A purchaser in a voluntary transaction would rarely pay the price the property would be worth if the amendment were an accomplished fact. No matter how probable an amendment may seem, an element of uncertainty remains and has its impact upon the selling price. At most a buyer would pay a premium for that probability in addition to what the property is worth under the restrictions of the existing ordinance. In permitting proof of a probable amendment, the law merely seeks to recognize a fact, if it does exist. In short if the parties to a voluntary transaction would as of the date of taking give recognition to the probability of a zoning amendment in agreeing upon the value, the law will recognize the truth.[10]

The courts appear to favor the practice of using comparable sales with zoning the same as the existing zoning on the property being appraised, rather than using higher-zoned sale properties and discounting them, but the ultimate decision is generally left to the judgment of the appraiser. If there is little doubt that the property will be rezoned, and the discount applicable to the higher-zoned sales would be comparatively minimal, it may be advisable to use sales of higher-zoned property. On the other hand, if there is only a marginal increment in value attributable to the probability of a rezoning, it is generally best to utilize sale properties that have the same zoning as the property being appraised and adjust the values upward. In any case, it is often advisable for the appraiser to include and discuss both lower- and higher-zoned sales in his report. This procedure establishes absolute minimum and maximum values for the property being appraised.

If the appraiser concludes that a property has a highest and best use physically and economically contrary to its existing zoning, he must make an exhaustive analysis of the possibility of having the property rezoned. In an often-cited Illinois case, the court set forth some of the factors that must be considered in arriving at a conclusion as to the reasonable probability of obtaining rezoning.

> Without purporting to set forth all of such factors, some of the significant factors may be the rezoning of nearby property, growth patterns, change of use patterns and character of neighborhood, demand within the area for certain types of land use, sales of related or similar properties at prices reflecting anticipated rezoning, physical characteristics of the subject and of nearby properties and, under proper circumstances, the age of the zoning ordinance. . . .

> It should be clear from the foregoing that while permitted in some jurisdictions, a witness in this state may not be offered solely to render an expert opinion as to whether or not a legislative body will in fact grant a rezoning. This applies, as well, to a member of that legislative body. A witness offered, however, as an expert valuation witness, may in the course of explaining the basis for his determination, testify to a reasonable probability of rezoning if such is a factor in arriving at his valuation and if warranted by the matters in evidence suggesting a basis for such rezoning."[11]

The reasoning for this ruling was spelled out in an earlier decision by the same court when opinion testimony was not permitted from an attorney who was a *zoning expert*. "The difficulty of anticipating what any legislative body is going to do is obvious, and the practice of permitting prognostication on legislative policy, we determine, should not be encouraged."[12]

These rulings do not, of course, preclude the appraiser from interviewing zoning officials and members of the legislative body that would make the ultimate decision on the rezoning request. In fact, this should be done if it is at all possible. It is sometimes possible to obtain a commitment from the zoning administrator as to whether he would make a favorable or unfavorable recommendation to the legislative body on a particular rezoning request. If this is possible, the appraiser should determine whether the legislative body routinely follows the administrator's recommendation or often overrides it.

It is becoming increasingly difficult for appraisers to obtain opinions from members of legislative bodies in regard to potential rezoning due to the adoption of the *appearance of fairness* doctrine in many jurisdictions. This doctrine holds that it would be unfair, or at least appear unfair, for a public official to offer an opinion on the advisability of proposed legislative action before all interested parties have had a chance to be heard. It has also been held, under this doctrine, that it is not proper for a public official to meet and discuss proposed legislative action without inviting all interested parties to the discussion, i.e., a public hearing. A member of a legislative body therefore cannot, at least theoretically, arrive at a decision as to the advisability of proposed legislative action until all public hearings have been held and all interested parties have had an opportunity to express their opinion. For this reason, it is often impossible for an appraiser to have a meaningful discussion with a member of a legislative body about the potential of obtaining rezoning.

The burden of proving there is a reasonable probability of rezoning is generally on the property owner, because he is the one who will benefit by a rezoning which allows a higher and better use for his property, and thus a higher value and condemnation award. This is not always the case, however. If the eminent domain proceedings involve a partial acquisition, and the question of reasonable probability relates to the remainder parcel only, the burden of proof then generally falls on the condemnor. In this case, it is the condemnor who will benefit from the rezoning, because a higher and better use after the partial taking will result in a higher after value and a lower condemnation award.

Summary

Market value is measured utility, and the utility of property is directly affected by a variety of land-use ordinances. The number of land-use ordinances has risen sharply over the past few years, and the appraiser must be thoroughly familiar with them and their potential impact on the value of property being appraised.

Because of the promulgation of land-use ordinances, particularly the ordinances requiring development permits, many developable land sales now occur only after the purchaser has procured all necessary development permits. These types of sales place sale properties in a better economic position than the typical property being appraised for eminent domain purposes because development permits seldom exist on the latter property. For this reason, it is often necessary for the appraiser to make downward adjustments in sale properties to reflect the risk inherent in a property without development permits.

Zoning ordinances are the most common type of land-use regulation. Nearly all zoning ordinances have provisions for pre-existing nonconforming uses and for the allowance of variances. In analyzing a property under appraisal, the appraiser must determine if it is nonconforming to the zoning ordinance and whether a variance exists on the property. If either of these factors is found, the appraiser must investigate the impact of this factor on the market value of the property.

The appraiser must also determine whether a zoning action has taken place or been denied, and how this has affected the property being appraised. The appraiser must determine whether the action or nonaction was influenced by the anticipated acquisition of the property in an attempt to depress its value or in light of the proposed public improvement for which the property is being condemned. If the latter circumstance applies, the appraiser must not consider the zoning action, or lack of zoning action, in estimating the market value of the property prior to the taking. However, if the property being appraised is subject to a partial acquisition, the remainder parcel must be appraised giving consideration to the zoning action, or lack of zoning action.

If the appraiser finds that a governmental action was taken in an attempt to depress the value of the property being appraised so that it could be acquired by the condemning agency at a lower price, he is well advised to seek legal counsel in regard to the specific procedure to be utilized in appraising the property. It is well established that governmental action taken to depress property values in anticipation of an eminent domain proceeding is in violation of the provision requiring the payment of *just compensation,* and the appraiser must therefore disregard this governmental action.

When a question concerning the probability of a rezoning arises, it is generally a question of law to be determined by the court. If the court finds that a probability of rezoning exists as a matter of law, the question of the probability of rezoning is then a matter to be determined by the trier of fact or jury. In fact, the question is totally immaterial unless the existence of such probability has an influence on the value of the property being appraised.

It is not the opinion of appraisers as to the probability of rezoning that is important, but rather the actions of buyers and sellers in the marketplace. If it is concluded that rezoning is probable or imminent, the property being appraised is not valued as if the rezoning has occurred, but rather in recognition of the probability that it may occur. Thus, its value will be less than if it were rezoned in order to reflect the risk and cost inherent in actually obtaining the rezoning.

Factors to consider in determining whether a reasonable probability exists for a rezoning include: 1) rezoning of nearby property, 2) growth patterns, 3) any change in use patterns, 4) changes in the character of the neighborhood, 5) demand within the area for certain types of land use, 6) sales of related or similar properties at prices reflecting anticipated rezoning, 7) physical characteristics of the subject property and nearby property, and 8) the age of the zoning ordinance. Also, examination of a municipality's comprehensive plan may reveal the municipality's planning goals and its attitudes toward property in the neighborhood of the one being appraised. However, the above factors are not accepted by all jurisdictions. Kaltenbach's *Just Compensation Resume* summarizes the question of a probable rezone this way:

> In considering this question, courts of different jurisdictions appear to emphasize different factors. In some cases, weight has been given to the fact that an application for rezoning has been made, and weight has also been given to the opinions of the officials on the zoning board. In other cases the emphasis has been upon the physical aspects of the matter, such as the location of the property, the use made of properties nearby, the traffic on the streets, and other physical factors. Some courts state that the physical factors without more are sufficient to indicate the probability of a change, while others require that applications to the zoning board shall have been made, and that there be some showing that there is a reasonable probability that the application will be granted. The probability of a change in some jurisdictions is regarded as a question of law, while in others it is regarded as a question of fact. In one case when a change in zoning was made after the taking it was held that evidence of this change might be proper at the retrial of the case.[13]

Not only *may* an appraiser consider the probability of a rezoning and its effect on market value, but he *must,* from a professional and ethical standpoint, consider such reasonable probability and its impact on market value.

Notes

1. Laurel, Inc. v. State, 362 A.2d 1383 (Conn.).
2. American Institute of Real Estate Appraisers and the Society of Real Estate Appraisers, *Real Estate Appraisal Terminology,* rev. ed., Byrl N. Boyce, ed. (Cambridge, Mass.: Ballinger Publishing Company, 1981), pp. 174-175.
3. Ibid., p. 261.
4. Symonds v. Buckley, 197 F.Supp. 682.
5. Washington Metropolitan Area Tran-

sit Authority v. One Parcel of Land, 413 F.Supp. 102.

6. People, Dep't of Public Works v. Southern Pacific Transp. Co., 109 Cal. Rptr. 525.

7. Martens v. State, 554 P.2d 407 (Ak.).

8. American Institute of Real Estate Appraisers, Regulation No. 10, *Code of Professional Ethics and Standards of Professional Conduct,* Canon 5, Guideline 6, p. 12 (Adopted Nov. 13, 1981).

9. Moschetti v. City of Tucson, 9 Ariz. App. 108, 449 P.2d 945.

10. State v. Gorga, 26 N.J. 113, 138 A.2d 833.

11. Lombard Park Dist. v. Chicago Title & Trust Co., 103 Ill. App.2d 1, 242 N.E.2d 440.

12. Park Dist. of Highland Park v. Becker, 60 Ill. App.2d 463, 208 N.E.2d 621.

13. Henry J. Kaltenbach, *Just Compensation Resume* (Warrenton, Va.: Right of Way Consultants, Inc., 1969), § 1-4-7.1, pp. 9-10.

CHAPTER 7
COST APPROACH TO VALUE

The cost approach to value is:

> "[t]hat approach in appraisal analysis which is based on the proposition that the informed purchaser would pay no more than the cost of producing a substitute property with the same utility as the subject property. It is particularly applicable when the property being appraised involves relatively new improvements which represent the highest and best use of the land or when relatively unique or specialized improvements are located on the site and for which there exist no comparable properties on the market.[1]

The major steps in applying the cost approach are: 1) estimate the reproduction (or replacement) cost of the improvements as of the date of appraisal, 2) estimate the amount of depreciation present in the improvements, 3) deduct total depreciation from the estimated reproduction cost to arrive at an indicated value of the improvements as of the date of appraisal, and 4) add the estimated value of the land to the indicated improvement value to arrive at an indication of total market value.

The appraiser is well advised to explain the appraisal process to the trier of fact in some detail before testifying in regard to a specific property he has appraised. The appraiser should emphasize that the three approaches to value are not independent of one another, and that he does not utilize the single most applicable approach, but rather all three approaches, if possible, because they are all integral parts of the appraisal process. The indicated value of the property by each of the approaches is then correlated into a final estimate of value, giving consideration to the relative strengths and weaknesses of each approach in relation to the specific property under appraisal.

Most courts do not seem to understand that each of the three aproaches to value is an integral part of the valuation process. Many court rulings appear to assume that the three approaches to value are totally independent of one another, and that only the *most applicable* approach is utilized in the appraisal of a specific parcel of land.

The Washington court has recognized the relationship between the three approaches to value. Citing *The Appraisal of Real Estate*[2] as its authority, the court described the three approaches as:

1. The current cost of reproducing a property less depreciation from deterioration and functional and economic obsolescence.
2. The value which the property's net earning power will support, based upon a capitalization of net income.
3. The value indicated by recent sales of comparable properties in the market.[3]

Citing the Washington case, however, the Massachusetts court said:

Whatever the relative importance or usefulness of the three methods to the real estate profession, however, they have not been viewed as equally applicable or as interchangeable under the law of eminent domain as it has developed in our cases. More specifically, the introduction of evidence concerning value based upon DRC [Depreciated Reproduction Cost] computations has been limited to special situations in which data cannot be reliably computed under the other two methods.[4]

The Massachusetts ruling appears typical of the prevailing attitude in a number of jurisdictions, which hold that "[m]arket value of property which is not unique and is not a specialty should not be valued on the basis of reproduction cost less depreciation."[5]

By statutory law, effective March 31, 1979, the State of California specifically allows consideration of reproduction cost as long as the improvements enhance the value of the property for its highest and best use. The California Evidence Code states "[w]hen relevant to the determination of the value of property, a witness may take into account as a basis for his opinion the value of the property or property interest being valued as indicated by the value of the land together with the cost of replacing or reproducing the existing improvements thereon, if the improvements enhance the value of the property or property interest for its highest and best use, less whatever depreciation or obsolescence the improvements have suffered."[6]

The minority rule which excludes consideration of cost data seems to have developed for a number of reasons. The courts may fear that the sum of the independent values of the land and buildings may not represent market value. As one court said:

> In [another case] this court held that, to avoid confusing and misleading the jury, evidence presented at trial may properly be confined to the value directly at issue, that is, the value of the improved land as a whole, and that evidence of separate values of the land and improvements was inadmissible. The problem which may occur from the admissibility of such evidence is that the jury may conclude that the market value of the property is the sum of the different values stated by the witnesses. It may fail to consider the various other factors, such as the real estate market in the area of the property, which a professional appraiser, with his experience and judgement, must weigh in determining the market value. The trial court, therefore, erred in admitting evidence of the underlying figures used by the appraisal witnesses.[7] [citations omitted]

A second fear the courts have stated in reference to the admission of testimony concerning reproduction cost is the violation, on the part of the appraiser, of the *consistent use theory*.[8] "Implicit in the utilization of evidence of reproduction cost is the fact that the structure adds value."[9] Using the cost approach, the unwary (or unscrupulous) appraiser can overlook areas of depreciation and, in doing so, violate the consistent use theory.

Another reason the courts may hesitate to allow reproduction cost testimony is due to a weakness in human nature, not in the approach itself. Federal Judge James Carter described this weakness:

> No matter how carefully a judge attempts to instruct a jury that certain evidence is only background material or not direct evidence of value, there is no assurance that he can, in a complicated case, put that over to a jury; and the impact of direct testimony of dollars and cents of "reproduction cost less depreciation," will tend to mislead a jury in fixing, as they should, what the willing buyer and willing seller would arrive at in the market place, and would divert them from their consideration of comparable sales as to the best evidence of value and from properly considering all the factors that an expert would consider, i.e., whether the comparable sales were sufficiently close in time, size, description, and the various other factors underlying the expert's opinion.[10]

These minority rulings do not, of course, restrict the appraiser from using the cost approach in arriving at a final estimate of value; they merely exclude testimony in regard to his findings. The appraiser has an ethical and professional obligation to develop a cost approach to value in any instance where the results of that approach will assist in better estimating the value of the property.[11] In an attempt to reduce appraisal fees, some condemnors will offer appraisal contracts with the provision that the appraiser need only apply the market data approach to value. An appraiser must reject any such contract unless the cost and income approaches will be of no assistance whatsoever in estimating the value of the property, or he is prepared to apply *all applicable approaches* for the appraisal fee offered despite the contract provisions. Without using all applicable approaches to value, the appraiser has simply not made an analysis that is thorough enough for trial purposes. The cost approach can be of assistance not only in arriving at a final conclusion of value, but also in allocating the elements of value and damages in partial taking cases.

Reproduction Cost

In appraisal terminology, the distinction between reproduction cost and replacement cost is quite clear. Reproduction cost is the current cost to physically reconstruct the improvements using the same or highly similar materials; replacement cost is the cost of constructing improvements equal in utility to those being appraised.

For example, a lumber mill constructed in 1920 may be a 4 in. × 4 in. wood-frame structure with a sawtooth roof and 3-in. thick wood decks over 18 in. × 18 in. floor framing. If reproduction cost is to be estimated, the cost estimate will include the cost of reconstructing these facilities using the same or similar materials. If the appraiser is using replacement cost, however, the general description of the building may be a steel-frame structure with steel skin, concrete floors, and a gable roof, which has better lighting than the existing facility. Replacement cost is differentiated from reproduction cost by the removal of many, if not all, of the items of construction excesses. Although there is a clear distinction between replacement cost and reproduction cost in appraisal terminology, these terms are not clearly distinguished by the courts in most jurisdictions. Most court citations use the term *reproduction cost,* but many others use the terms *reproduction* and *replacement* interchangeably.

The *Uniform Eminent Domain Code* provides for the use of the cost approach as follows:

Section 1111. *(Reproduction Or Replacement Cost.)* A valuation witness . . . may consider, as a basis for an opinion of value, the cost of reproducing or replacing existing improvements on a property sought to be taken which enhances its value for its highest and best use, less any depreciation resulting from physical deterioration or from functional or economic obsolescence.[12]

The authors of the code go on to make this comment:

> Section 1111 authorizes use of reproduction or replacement cost data as one factor supporting opinion evidence as to the value of improved property. . . . The cost of "reproduction" refers to the cost of duplication with the same or similar materials and appearance, and is not necessarily the same as the cost of "replacement" (i.e., providing a substitute facility of equal functional utility).
>
> Under this section, the evidence may be used only for the purpose of proving the market value of the land with the improvements on it, to the extent they enhance its value for its highest and best use, but not to prove the value of the improvements separate from the land. This section is not applicable, of course, if the improvements are detrimental to the use, and thus diminish the value, of the property for its highest and best use.[13]

Because many courts fail to distinguish between reproduction and replacement costs, the appraiser must be cautious in using these terms on the witness stand. If the terms are utilitzed, the appraiser must explain their precise meanings from an appraisal standpoint.

The standard methods of estimating reproduction or replacement cost are: 1) the quantity survey method, 2) the unit-in-place method, 3) the market method, and 4) the cost service method.[14] These methods are listed in what is generally considered their order of accuracy, with the most accurate being the quantity survey method and the least reliable the cost service method. No matter which method is used by the appraiser, it is important that all indirect costs be included in the cost estimate.

In all cases, the appraiser must, of course, make an accurate, detailed property inspection before a cost estimate can be made. Although many of the computations may be made after the appraiser's field inspection, following a detailed field inspection checklist during the physical inspection of the property is highly recommended. This practice avoids multiple trips to the property to obtain data overlooked during the first inspection and, more important, prevents embarrassing situations on the witness stand. The appraiser should not answer inquiries about construction detail by saying "I don't know," "I didn't notice," or worse, "No, that item of cost is not included in my reproduction cost estimate."

When the appraiser cannot testify to the size of the hot water tank in the single-family dwelling under appraisal, the typical juror will often ignore the fact that he doesn't know the size of the hot water tank in his own home. Rather, he will begin to wonder how the appraiser was able to estimate the reproduction cost of the hot water tank without knowing its size. The juror may also speculate that if the appraiser missed that item of reproduction cost, he may have missed other items and made other errors in the appraisal process.

Experienced appraisers often develop their own field inspection checklists; there are also a number of published forms available. Figure 7.1 is a copy of the field inspection form utilized in conjunction with the *Marshall and Swift Computer Cost Service*. For purposes of illustration, this form has been completed for an existing, freestanding, wood-frame restaurant building on a 68,659-sq. ft. site. The building contains 11,104 square feet of first floor area and 1,028 square feet of second floor office area. The results of this cost estimate are shown in Table 7.1.

Whether the appraiser uses a segregated, or unit-in-place method of cost estimating or a square foot method, a detailed field inspection sheet is essential. Even if the appraiser engages independent cost estimators to arrive at an estimated reproduction cost, a detailed field inspection form will help the appraiser describe the improvements in the appraisal report and on the witness stand.

The appraiser must avoid representing himself to the trier of fact as both an *expert appraiser* and an *expert cost estimator*. In a Rhode Island case,[15] a "petitioner contended that the trial court erred in refusing to allow his witness, a realtor and appraiser, to testify as an expert concerning the cost of replacing a portion of fence lost in an eminent domain proceeding. The court held that the exclusion of the appraiser's testimony as to the substantial cost of a needed replacement fence was not error because the qualifications of a witness as an appraiser do not establish him as a qualified fence builder and hence his testimony would be hearsay."[16]

If the cost approach is an important element in the appraiser's value conclusion, he is well advised to obtain at least one contractor's cost estimate. After obtaining the contractor's cost estimate, the appraiser should develop at least one other reproduction cost estimate or use one developed by a cost service, if necessary. If the appraiser adopts the contractor's cost estimate with no other evidence, the estimate is not the opinion of the appraiser, but of the contractor. Under such a circumstance, the appraiser could be excluded from testifying in regard to the reproduction cost of the improvements because it is not his opinion and, therefore, is hearsay evidence. A simple solution to this problem is for the appraiser to obtain two independent reproduction cost estimates, by using two separate contractors or two different methods of cost estimating, then consider both

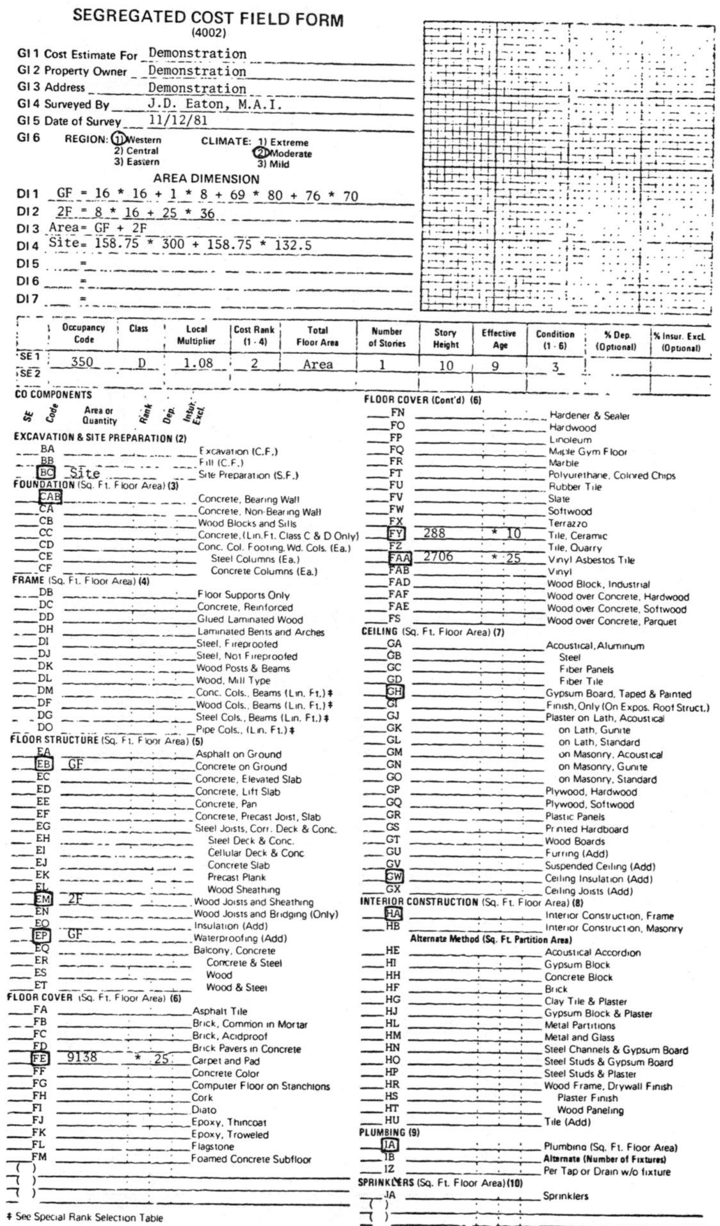

SEGREGATED COST FIELD FORM
(4002)

GI 1 Cost Estimate For Demonstration
GI 2 Property Owner Demonstration
GI 3 Address Demonstration
GI 4 Surveyed By J.D. Eaton, M.A.I.
GI 5 Date of Survey 11/12/81
GI 6 REGION: (1) Western   CLIMATE: 1) Extreme
    2) Central   (2) Moderate
    3) Eastern   3) Mild

AREA DIMENSION

DI 1 GF = 16 * 16 + 1 * 8 + 69 * 80 + 76 * 70
DI 2 2F = 8 * 16 + 25 * 36
DI 3 Area = GF + 2F
DI 4 Site = 158.75 * 300 + 158.75 * 132.5
DI 5 =
DI 6 =
DI 7 =

	Occupancy Code	Class	Local Multiplier	Cost Rank (1 - 4)	Total Floor Area	Number of Stories	Story Height	Effective Age	Condition (1 - 6)	% Dep. (Optional)	% Insur. Excl. (Optional)
SE 1	350	D	1.08	2	Area	1	10	9	3		
SE 2											

CO COMPONENTS

SE / Code / Area or Quantity / Rank / Dep. / Insur. Excl.

EXCAVATION & SITE PREPARATION (2)
BA — Excavation (C.F.)
BB — Fill (C.F.)
BC — Site — Site Preparation (S.F.)

FOUNDATION (Sq. Ft. Floor Area) (3)
CAB —
CA — Concrete, Bearing Wall
CB — Concrete, Non-Bearing Wall
CC — Wood Blocks and Sills
CD — Concrete, (Lin. Ft. Class C & D Only)
CE — Conc. Col. Footing, Wd. Cols. (Ea.)
CF — Steel Columns (Ea.)
— Concrete Columns (Ea.)

FRAME (Sq. Ft. Floor Area) (4)
DB — Floor Supports Only
DC — Concrete, Reinforced
DD — Glued Laminated Wood
DH — Laminated Bents and Arches
DI — Steel, Fireproofed
DJ — Steel, Not Fireproofed
DK — Wood Posts & Beams
DL — Wood, Mill Type
DM — Conc. Cols., Beams (Lin. Ft.) ‡
DF — Wood Cols., Beams (Lin. Ft.) ‡
DG — Steel Cols., Beams (Lin. Ft.) ‡
DO — Pipe Cols., (Lin. Ft.) ‡

FLOOR STRUCTURE (Sq. Ft. Floor Area) (5)
EA — Asphalt on Ground
EB — GF — Concrete on Ground
EC — Concrete, Elevated Slab
ED — Concrete, Lift Slab
EE — Concrete, Pan
EF — Concrete, Precast Joist, Slab
EG — Steel Joists, Corr. Deck & Conc.
EH — Steel Deck & Conc.
EI — Cellular Deck & Conc
EJ — Concrete Slab
EK — Precast Plank
EL — Wood Sheathing
EM — 2F — Wood Joists and Sheathing
EN — Wood Joists and Bridging (Only)
EO — Insulation (Add)
EP — GF — Waterproofing (Add)
EQ — Balcony, Concrete
ER — Concrete & Steel
ES — Wood
ET — Wood & Steel

FLOOR COVER (Sq. Ft. Floor Area) (6)
FA — Asphalt Tile
FB — Brick, Common in Mortar
FC — Brick, Acidproof
FD — Brick Pavers in Concrete
FE — 9138 * 25 — Carpet and Pad
FF — Concrete Color
FG — Computer Floor on Stanchions
FH — Cork
FI — Diato
FJ — Epoxy, Thincoat
FK — Epoxy, Troweled
FL — Flagstone
FM — Foamed Concrete Subfloor
( )
( )
( )

‡ See Special Rank Selection Table

FLOOR COVER (Cont'd) (6)
FN — Hardener & Sealer
FO — Hardwood
FP — Linoleum
FQ — Marble Gym Floor
FR — Marble
FT — Polyurethane, Colored Chips
FU — Rubber Tile
FV — Slate
FW — Softwood
FX — Terrazzo
FY — 288 * 10 — Tile, Ceramic
FZ — Tile, Quarry
FAA — 2706 * 25 — Vinyl Asbestos Tile
FAB — Vinyl
FAD — Wood Block, Industrial
FAF — Wood over Concrete, Hardwood
FAE — Wood over Concrete, Softwood
FS — Wood over Concrete, Parquet

CEILING (Sq. Ft. Floor Area) (7)
GA — Acoustical, Aluminum
GB — Steel
GC — Fiber Panels
GD — Fiber Tile
GH — Gypsum Board, Taped & Painted
GI — Finish, Only (On Expos. Roof Struct.)
GJ — Plaster on Lath, Acoustical
GK — on Lath, Gunite
GL — on Lath, Standard
GM — on Masonry, Acoustical
GN — on Masonry, Gunite
GO — on Masonry, Standard
GP — Plywood, Hardwood
GQ — Plywood, Softwood
GR — Plastic Panels
GS — Printed Hardboard
GT — Wood Boards
GU — Furring (Add)
GV — Suspended Ceiling (Add)
GW — Ceiling Insulation (Add)
GX — Ceiling Joists (Add)

INTERIOR CONSTRUCTION (Sq. Ft. Floor Area) (8)
HA — Interior Construction, Frame
HB — Interior Construction, Masonry
Alternate Method (Sq. Ft. Partition Area)
HE — Acoustical Accordion
HI — Gypsum Block
HH — Concrete Block
HF — Brick
HG — Clay Tile & Plaster
HJ — Gypsum Block & Plaster
HL — Metal Partitions
HM — Metal and Glass
HN — Steel Channels & Gypsum Board
HO — Steel Studs & Gypsum Board
HP — Steel Studs & Plaster
HR — Wood Frame, Drywall Finish
HS — Plaster Finish
HT — Wood Paneling
HU — Tile (Add)

PLUMBING (9)
IA — Plumbing (Sq. Ft. Floor Area)
IB — Alternate (Number of Fixtures)
IZ — Per Tap or Drain w/o fixture

SPRINKLERS (Sq. Ft. Floor Area) (10)
JA — Sprinklers
( )
( )

Figure 7.1. Field Inspection Form

HEATING, COOLING & VENTILATION (Sq. Ft. Floor Area) **(11)**

____ KA — Electric (Cable, Panel or Baseboard)
____ KB — Electric Wall Heaters
____ KC — Forced Air
____ KD — Floor Furnace
____ KE — Gas Steam Radiator
____ KF — Gravity Furnace
____ KG — Heaters, Vented
____ KH — Hot Water
____ KI — Hot Water, Radiant
____ KJ — Space Heat, Gas
____ KK — Space Heat, Steam
____ KL — Steam, with Boiler
____ KM — Steam, without Boiler
____ KN — Air Cond. Hot and Chilled Water
____ KO — Air Cond. Warm and Cooled Air
[KP] * 25 — Package Heating & Cooling
____ KQ — Heat Pump
____ KR — Evaporative Cooling
____ KS — Refrigerated Cooling
____ KT — Ventilation
____ KU — Wall Furnace
____ UAM — Window Air Conditioner (Each)
____ UAN — Window Evaporative Cooler (Each)

ELECTRICAL (Sq. Ft. Floor Area) **(12)**

____ LA — Electrical & Lighting
____ LB — Unfinished Area

EXTERIOR WALL (Sq. Ft. Wall Area) **(13)**

SE	Code	In. Thick	Area or Quantity	Rank	Dep.	Insur. Excl.	
							Masonry Walls
____	[MA]						Adobe Block
____	MB						Brick, Block Back-Up ("Thick)
____	[MC]	8	1612				Common ("Thick)
____	MD						Cavity ("Thick)
____	ME						Face Brick (Add)
____	MF						Concrete Block ("Thick)
____	MR						Concrete, Reinforced ("Thick)
____	MH						Concrete, Tilt-up ("Thick)
____	MI						Stn. Ashlar Veneer, Block ("Thick)
____	MJ						Stone, Rubble ("Thick)
____	MK						Pilaster
____	ML						Bond Beams
____	MM						Insulation (Add)
							Curtain Walls
____	MN						Concrete, Precast
____	MU						Concrete and Glass Panels
____	MV						Metal and Glass Panels
____	MW						Stainless Steel and Glass
____	[MX]		300				Bronze and Glass
____	MY						Stone Panels
____	MAA						Steel Studs and Stucco
____	MZ						Tile, Clay ("Thick)
____	MAB						Facing Tile (Add)
							Wood or Steel Framed Walls
____	MAD						Aluminum Siding
____	MAE						Asbestos Siding
____	MCA						Asbestos Shingles
____	MAF						Shingles
____	[MAG]		900				Shakes
____	MAH						Stucco on Wire and Paper
____	MAI						on Sheathing
____	MAJ						Wood Siding on Paper
____	[MAK]		3190				on Sheathing
____	MAL						Veneer, Common Brick
____	MAM						Face Brick
____	MAN						Stone
____	MAO						Used Brick
____	MAP						Siding, Vinyl Surface
____	MCB						Hardboard
____	MAQ						Textured Plywood
____	MAR						Board and Batten Box Frame
____	MAS						Log, Rustic
____	[MAU]		4320				Insulation (Add)
							Wood or Steel Skeleton Frames
____	MAT						Aluminum Cover
____	MAV						Sandwich Panels
____	MAW						Corrugated Steel on Steel Frame
____	MAX						on Wood Frame
____	MBA						Transite
____	MBB						Siding, Post and Girder Frame
____	MBC						Sheathing (Add)
____	MBD						Steel Hanger Doors, Sml. (Sq. Ft. Door)
____	MBE						Steel Hanger Doors, Lge. (Sq. Ft. Door)

EXTERIOR STAIRS (Number of Flights) **(28)**

____ NA — Steel
____ NB — Wood
____ ND — Concrete
____ NE — Concrete & Steel
____ NC — Fire Escape

STORE FRONT (Sq. Ft. Store Front) **(15)**

____ OB — Store Front

ELEVATORS (Sq. Ft. Floor Area) **(20)**

____ TA — Elevators († Occupancies Only)
__( )__
__( )__
__( )__

‡ See Special Rank Selection Table.

FORM 4002 REV. 5

ELEVATORS (Cont'd) (Number of Shafts & Stops per Shaft) **(20)** ‡

Shfts. Stops/Shaft

____ TB — Multi-story Fully Automatic
____ TC — Multi-story Passenger Operated
____ TE — Small Car - 2 or 3 Stops
____ TI 1 — Freight Elevator (Manual Doors)
____ TI 2 — Freight Elevator (Power Doors)
____ TK — Sidewalk Elevators
____ TL — **Escalator** (Enter Number of Stairways)

WALL ORNAMENTATION (Sq. Ft. Ornamented Area) **(16)**

____ PA — Brick Face, Split
____ PC — Face, Standard Size
____ PD — Select Common
____ PE — Used
____ PF — Cast Stone
____ PG — Concrete Block, Imitation Stone
____ PH — Screen
____ PI — Slumpstone
____ PJ — Granite
____ PK — Limestone
____ PL — Marble
____ PM — Metal Screen
____ PN — Sandstone Veneer
____ PO — Stone Veneer, Local
____ PP — Rubble
____ PQ — Special
____ PR — Slate
____ PS — Stucco on Masonry
____ PT — Terra Cotta
____ PU — Tile, Ceramic
____ PV — Mosaic
____ PW — Vitrolite

ROOF STRUCTURE (Sq. Ft. Ground Floor Area) **(17)**

____ QA — Concrete Joists, Slab
____ QC — Precast Joists and Deck
____ QE — Thin Shell Concrete
____ QF — Lamella
____ QG — Steel Joists, Concrete Slab
____ QH — Gypsum
____ QI — Precast Plank
____ QJ — Steel Deck, Gypsum
____ QK — Steel Deck
____ QL — Composition Deck
____ QM — Wood Deck
[QAA] GF — Wood Joists, Wood Deck
____ QO — Composition Deck
____ QP — Precast Plank Deck
____ QR — Exposed Beams and Sheathing
____ QS — Open Steel System for Corr. Metal
____ QT — Open Wood System for Corr. Metal
____ QN — Monitor (Add)
____ QQ — Sawtooth (Add)
____ QU — **Trusses, Steel**
____ QAB — Longspan Girders, Steel
____ QV — Timber Trusses
____ QW — Glued Laminated Girders
____ QX — Steel Space Frame
____ QY — **Marquee**, Wood Frame (Sq. Ft. Marquee)
____ QZ — Steel Frame

ROOF COVER (Sq. Ft. Ground Floor Area) **(18)**

____ RA — Aluminum
____ RB — Aluminum Shingles
____ RC — Asbestos Shingles
[RD] GF * 40 — Built-Up Composition
____ RE — Composition, Roll
____ RF — Composition, Shingles
____ RG — Concrete Tile
____ RH — Copper
____ RI — Galvanized Steel
____ RJ — Hypalon-Neoprene
____ RK — Lead
____ RL — Porcelain Enamel Shingles
____ RM — Shakes
____ RN — Shakes-Fire Resistant
____ RO — Slate
____ RP — Tar and Gravel
____ RQ — Terne
____ RR — Tile
____ RS — Transite
____ RT — Wood Shingles
[RU] GF — Insulation (Add)

BASEMENTS (31)

Basement Wall (Sq. Ft. Base Wall Area)

____ *A — Brick Masonry ("Thick)
____ *B — Concrete Block ("Thick)
____ *C — Concrete, Reinforced ("Thick)
____ *D — Rubble Masonry ("Thick)
____ *E — Waterproofing (Add)

Interior Construction (Sq. Ft. Floor Area)

____ *NO — Finished
____ *NP — Partially Finished
____ *NQ — Unfinished
____ *NR — Parking

Electrical & Lighting (Sq. Ft. Floor Area)

____ *NX — Finished
____ *NY — Plain Lighting
____ *NZ — Unfinished
__(31)__ — Floor
__(31)__
__( )__
__( )__

Figure 7.1. Field Inspection Form (Continued)

Table 7.1

Cost Estimate For: Demonstration
Property Owner: Demonstration
Address: Demonstration
Surveyed By: J.D. Eaton, M.A.I.
Date Of Survey: 11/12/81

Occupancy: Restaurant

Class: D
Effective Age: 9 Years
Number of Stories: 1.0
Floor Area: 12,132

Cost Rank: 2.0 Average
Condition: 3.0 Average
Average Story Height: 10.0
Cost as of: 11/81

Component	Units	Cost	Replacement Cost New	Depr
Excavation & Site Preparation:				
Site Preparation	68,659	0.10	6,866	5,630
Foundation:				
Concrete, Bearing Walls	12,132	1.13	13,709	11,241
Floor Structure:				
Concrete on Ground	11,104	1.88	20,876	17,118
Wood Joists and Sheathing	1,028	3.66	3,762	3,085
Waterproofing	11,104	0.33	3,664	3,004
Subtotal			28,302	23,207
Floor Cover:				
Carpet and Pad	9,138	2.18	19,921	14,941
Tile, Ceramic	288	5.30	1,526	1,373
Vinyl Asbestos Tile	2,706	0.99	2,679	2,009
Subtotal			24,126	18,323
Ceiling:				
Gypsum Board, Taped & Painted	12,132	0.89	10,797	8,854
Ceiling Insulation	12,132	0.34	4,125	3,383
Subtotal			14,922	12,237
Interior Construction:				
Interior Construction, Frame	12,132	6.21	75,340	61,779
Plumbing:				
Plumbing	12,132	5.50	66,726	54,715
Heating and Ventilating:				
Package Heating & Cooling	12,132	2.94	35,668	26,751
Electrical:				
Electrical	12,132	5.49	66,605	54,616
Exterior Wall:				
Common Brick	1,612	11.73	18,909	15,505
Bronze and Glass	300	24.54	7,362	6,037
Shakes	900	7.38	6,642	5,446
Wood Siding	3,190	8.27	26,381	21,632
Insulation	4,320	0.32	1,382	1,133
Subtotal			60,676	49,753
Roof Structure:				
Wood Joists, Wood Deck	11,104	3.52	39,086	32,051
Roof Cover:				
Built-Up Composition	11,104	0.96	10,660	6,396
Insulation	11,104	0.65	7,218	5,919
Subtotal			17,878	12,315
Total			449,904	362,618
Architect's Fees	6.9%		31,043	25,455
Replacement Cost New	12,132	39.64	480,947	
Depreciation	(19.3%)		(92,874)	
Depreciated Cost				388,073
Additions:				
Concrete Flatwork	984	1.00	984	984
Asphalt Paving	31,200	0.60	18,720	18,720
Landscape			2,500	2,500
Land	68,659	1.75	120,153	120,153
Total Cost			623,304	530,430
Rounded To Nearest $1,000			623,000	530,000

Cost Data by Marshall and Swift

cost estimates, and finally arrive at his own opinion as to the reproduction cost of the improvements. The problem of hearsay can also be encountered when the appraiser utilizes a published cost service as his sole source of data.

Disregarding the hearsay rule, using a cost service to estimate reproduction cost has still been viewed rather skeptically by some courts.

> They [the appraisers] relied largely upon reproduction costs calculated on a rule of thumb, cubic footage basis, less depreciation. . . . [T]he rule of thumb basis for estimating cost of reproduction, used by the Agency appraisers, has been described as being "not even approximately accurate, except for a few highly standardized types of structures." 2 Orgel, Valuation Under Eminent Domain, §193 (1953). There is no showing that this was such a standardized structure. Accordingly, if such testimony is repeated on a new trial the jury should be cautioned . . . that the cubic foot cost method of computing reproduction cost is not entitled to great weight in such a case as this even in arriving at reproduction cost.[17]

Depreciation

Depreciation is a loss in the value of improvements from all causes; it is the difference between the current cost of reproducing or replacing the improvements, new, and the amount, in dollars, they add to the value of the land as of the date of appraisal. Whenever the courts have considered reproduction cost in eminent domain proceedings, they have universally recognized that *depreciated reproduction cost* rather than reproduction cost, new, is the proper measure of value.[18] The courts have also generally recognized the various forms of depreciation, including obsolescence as well as physical deterioration.[19]

In the analytic process, the appraiser will often break down the estimate of depreciation into several categories:[20]

> Physical deterioration: curable or incurable.
> Functional obsolescence: curable or incurable.
> Economic obsolescence: incurable.

Each of these forms of depreciation is measured by different means. Some forms of depreciation are curable and can be measured by the cost to cure, while others may be incurable and are measured by capitalizing the rent loss created by the presence of the depreciation.[21]

This type of analysis is a valuable appraisal tool, but presenting it to a judge or jury will often lead only to confusion and/or disinterest. Terms or phrases such as *curable physical deterioration* or *incurable functional obsolescence caused by a superadequacy* may have precise meanings in the real estate appraisal profession, but they are meaningless to the layman. If the appraiser uses such terms on the witness stand, the jury may be confused or, worse, may feel they are being *talked down to* or given a *snow job*. The appraiser who uses a detailed breakdown method of estimating the depreciation present in the property is well advised to find a method of explaining his methodology in simple layman's terms before taking the witness stand.

Table 7.2

Comparable Sales

	Sale 1	Sale 2	Sale 3	Sale 4
Price	$240,000	$255,000	$216,000	$275,000
No. of units	12	12	10	14
Building size	10,200 sq. ft.	10,400 sq. ft.	8,000 sq. ft.	12,250 sq. ft.
Building age (effective)	7	15	14	12
Contributory value of garages	0	$12,000	$10,000	0
Contributory value of on-site improvements	$3,600	$4,500	$5,000	$4,200
Estimated land value	$24,000	$24,000	$21,000	$25,000

If adequate market data are available, the abstraction method of estimating depreciation is an excellent appraisal tool and is ideal for jury presentation. For example, assume the appraisal of a 12-unit apartment house that has an effective age of 12 years. Further assume that preliminary analysis indicates that 1) the land value is $24,000, 2) the garage facilities have a contributory value of $7,500, 3) the on-site improvements have a contributory value of $4,800, and 4) the estimated reproduction cost of the apartment structure itself is $265,200. Market investigation uncovers four recent comparable sales, which have been analyzed as shown in Table 7.2. The depreciation present in the property being appraised can be estimated by analyzing the comparable sales, utilizing the following six steps:

1) Estimate the reproduction cost of each comparable improvement in the same way that the reproduction cost of the property being appraised was estimated.
2) Compute the price paid for each comparable improvement by deducting the estimated land value and contributory value of the secondary improvements not included in the reproduction cost estimate (garage, on-site improvements, etc.) from the total sale price.
3) Deduct the price paid for the improvement from its reproduction cost, which results in the total depreciation in the comparable improvement.

4) Divide total depreciation by the effective age of each comparable to obtain the average annual depreciation suffered.
5) Divide the annual depreciation in the improvement by its reproduction cost to obtain an annual rate of depreciation.
6) Multiply the annual rate of depreciation by 100 to convert it to an annual percentage of depreciation.

For purposes of illustration, assume Step 1 produced an estimated reproduction cost of the apartment structure in Sale 1 of $24 per square foot, or $244,800. Step 2, applied to Sale 1, would result in an indicated price for the apartment structure of $212,400, computed as follows:

Sale price		$240,000
Less:		
Garage value	$ 0	
On-site improvement value	3,600	
Land value	24,000	
Total deductions		27,600
Sale price of apartment structure		$212,400

Step 3 would indicate the total depreciation present in Sale 1 as follows:

Reproduction cost	$244,800
Indicated price of improvement	212,400
Total depreciation present	$ 32,400

Annual depreciation (Step 4) is therefore $32,400 total depreciation ÷ 7 years effective age, or $4,629. The annual rate of depreciation (Step 5) can be developed by dividing the annual depreciation, $4,629, by the reproduction cost of the improvement, $244,800, which results in an annual depreciation rate of .0189. The figure multiplied by 100 (Step 6) indicates 1.89% depreciation per year.

Table 7.3 shows the results of applying the six steps to each of the comparables. The comparables indicate annual depreciation rates applicable to the property under appraisal from 1.77%–1.89% per year. Applying this rate to the 12-year effective age of the property being appraised indicates a range of depreciation from (1.77% × 12 years) 21.24% to (1.89% × 12 years) 22.68% or, in dollars, from ($265,200 × .2124) $56,328 to ($265,200 × .2268) $60,147.

From this analysis, the appraiser might correlate his conclusions by the cost approach as follows:

Reproduction cost of apartment	$265,200
Less depreciation (22.5%)	− 59,670
Indicated value of apartment	$205,530
Contributory value of garage	7,500
Contributory value of on-site improvements	4,800
Total indicated improvement value	$217,830
Estimated land value	24,000
Total indicated property value by the cost approach	$241,830
Rounded	$242,000

This type of analysis can be clearly and convincingly presented to a jury, particularly when the appraiser uses charts similar to those shown in Tables 7.2 and 7.3.

Table 7.3

Sales Analysis in
Abstraction Method of Depreciation

	Sale 1	Sale 2	Sale 3	Sale 4
Price	$240,000	$255,000	$216,000	$275,000
Less garage value	0	(12,000)	(10,000)	0
Less on-site improvement value	(3,600)	(4,500)	(5,000)	(4,200)
Less land value	(24,000)	(24,000)	(21,000)	(25,000)
Improvement value	$212,400	$214,500	$180,000	$245,800
Reproduction cost	$244,800	$299,000	$241,500	$312,250
Less improvement value	(212,400)	(214,500)	(180,000)	(245,800)
Improvement depreciation	$32,400	$84,500	$61,500	$66,450
Depreciation per year	$4,629	$5,633	$4,393	$5,538
% depreciation per year	1.89%	1.88%	1.82%	1.77%

In applying the abstraction method of estimating depreciation, it is sometimes advisable to estimate the reproduction cost of secondary improvements (such as the garages and on-site improvements in the foregoing example) and include them in the total reproduction cost. In such a situation, the contributory value of the secondary improvements is not extracted from the sale price of the comparable properties, and the indicated rate of depreciation is applicable to the reproduction cost of all improvements. Including the reproduction cost of these secondary improvements is particularly advantageous when the value ratios between primary and secondary improvements are similar in the comparable sale properties and the property under appraisal.

Summary

"Although there is a marked difference of opinion [by the courts] as to the competency of reproduction cost less depreciation, the weight of authority supports the proposition that such evidence is admissible on direct examination provided the adaptability of the improvement to the land is established. . . ."[22] The appraiser must be aware of the court's attitude toward the cost approach and the admissibility of reproduction cost estimates before attempting to testify. A jury will not be impressed with an appraiser who testifies that his conclusion of value had been based primarily on an approach that the court subsequently rules inadmissible. The statement ". . . reproduction cost evidence almost invariably tends to inflate valuation"[23] indicates the court's lack of confidence in reproduction cost evidence. Although the majority of the courts allow evidence on reproduction cost and the cost approach, most have developed safeguards in regard to its admission. As stated in *Nichols'*, "When this inherently inflationary attribute of reproduction cost evidence is considered in light of the misleading exactitude which such evidence almost inevitably imparts to a jury unsophisticated in the niceties of economics, the justification for placing substantial safeguards upon its admission is apparent."[24]

Even in jurisdictions that do not allow testimony in regard to reproduction cost or the cost approach, the appraiser is ethically and professionally obliged to use this approach in the appraisal process if it will assist in developing a more accurate and reliable conclusion of value. Whether the data developed in the cost approach is admissible or not, it can be of invaluable assistance to the appraiser in allocating the elements of value and damages in partial taking cases. In any case, the appraiser must make a detailed inspection of the improvements noting all material construction details. An extensive field inspection checklist is very helpful in documenting all necessary physical and construction data.

No matter how the cost approach was applied in the appraisal process, the appraiser should present the data to the trier of fact as clearly and simply as possible. The market method of reproduction cost estimating and the abstraction method of estimating depreciation can generally be presented most clearly and convincingly.

If the appraiser anticipates testifying as to reproduction cost, he should avoid claiming expertise in cost estimating; he should utilize the market method of cost estimation or obtain cost data from two independent sources to ensure that his testimony will not be considered hearsay.

Notes

1. American Institute of Real Estate Appraisers and the Society of Real Estate Appraisers, *Real Estate Appraisal Terminology*, rev. ed., Byrl N. Boyce, ed. (Cambridge, Mass.: Ballinger Publishing Co., 1981), p. 63.

2. *The Appraisal of Real Estate,* 5th ed. (Chicago: American Institute of Real Estate Appraisers, 1967), p. 60.

3. State v. Wilson, 6 Wash. App. 443, 493 P.2d 1252.

4. Correia v. New Bedford Redevelopment Authority, 377 N.E.2d 909 (Mass.).

5. In re Oakland Street, City of New York, 213 N.Y.S.2d 973.

6. California Evidence Code, § 820.

7. Dep't of Transportation v. Quincy Coach House, Inc., 1 Ill. Dec. 13, 356 N.E.2d 13, Rev'd 29 Ill. App.3d 616, 332 N.E.2d 21.

8. See Chapter 5, "Highest and Best Use."

9. Julius L. Sackman, *Nichols' The Law of Eminent Domain,* rev. 3rd. ed. Vol. 4 (New York: Matthew Bender, 1979), § 12.313.

10. United States v. 70.39 Acres of Land, 164 F.Supp. 451.

11. American Institute of Real Estate Appraisers, Regulation No. 10, *Code of Professional Ethics and Standards of Professional Conduct,* Canon 5, Guideline 1, p. 12 (Adopted Nov. 13, 1981).

12. "Uniform Eminent Domain Code," 1974 § 1111, p. 11.11.

13. Ibid., Author's Comment.

14. *The Appraisal of Real Estate,* 7th ed., 1978, pp. 263-272.

15. Palazzolo v. Rayhill, 394 A.2d 690 (R.I.).

16. *Nichols',* Vol. 5, § 18.4[1].

17. Riley v. District of Columbia Redevelopment Land Agency, 246 F.2d 641.

18. Commonwealth, Dep't of Highways v. Gibson, 523 S.W.2d 885 (Ky.).

19. Harvey School v. State of New York, 14 Misc.2d 924, 180 N.Y.S.2d 724.

20. *The Appraisal of Real Estate,* 7th ed., 1978, pp. 236-262.

21. Ibid.

22. *Nichols',* Vol. 5, § 20.2[1].

23. Ibid.

24. Ibid.

CHAPTER 8
INCOME APPROACH TO VALUE

The income approach to value is "[t]hat procedure in appraisal analysis which converts anticipated benefits (dollar income or amenities) to be derived from the ownership of property into a value estimate. The Income Approach is widely applied in appraising income-producing properties. Anticipated future income and/or reversions are discounted to a present worth figure through the capitalization process."[1] In other words, a factor (or rate) is developed from market data and applied to the net income of a property to indicate the property's market value. The factor (or rate) is simply a ratio between income and value.

In the past 15 years, the income approach has been modified and expanded more dramatically than any other concept in real estate appraisal. The fourth edition of *The Appraisal of Real Estate,* published in 1964, devoted 89 pages to the development and application of the income approach; the seventh edition of the same text has over 30% more material on the development and application of the income approach. Prior to 1971, the basic appraisal course sponsored by the American Institute of Real Estate Appraisers, *Course I,* was taught in 10 days and covered all aspects of the theory of real estate appraisal. In 1971, this course was divided into two segments; the second half, *Course IB,* covering the theory of the income approach, lasted 10 days. In 1980, *Course IB* was expanded to teach capitalization theory and techniques in 15 days. In addition, a special 5-day course was developed in the 1960s to teach the Ellwood method of capitalization. The Ellwood method is now taught as part of the capitalization series and a new real estate investment analysis course has been added to the Institute's curriculum.

The appraisal methodology used to develop a property's anticipated net income has remained virtually unchanged over the years; the only innovation has been the introduction of an income projection term shorter than the remaining economic life of the improvements. The major changes in the income approach

116

have involved capitalization rate concepts and construction. Because these new concepts have been introduced recently, there is little case law on the court's attitude toward or acceptance of them.

The courts differ in their acceptance of the income approach to value in eminent domain cases. All jurisdictions appear to accept evidence developed through the income approach when the property in question is income-producing and there are not enough market data to develop the market data approach to value. Both California[2] and Pennsylvania[3] provide for the admission of income approach information as a matter of statutory law. "The Uniform Eminent Domain Code" states:

> A valuation witness . . . may consider, as a basis for an opinion of value, the actual or reasonable net rental income attributable to the property when used for its highest and best use, capitalized at a fair and reasonable interest rate.[4]

The code allows the expert to *consider* the income approach to value, but it does not necessarily allow for testimony in this regard. By way of explanation, the code states "[a] valuation witness . . . may consider as the basis of his opinion of value any nonconjectural matters ordinarily relied upon by experts in forming opinions as to the fair market value of property, whether or not they are admissible in evidence."[5]

The attitudes of the various courts in regard to the probative value of income approach evidence vary greatly. One court considered the income approach to value "the 'surest index' of value in the ordinary case of income producing properties."[6] Another court stated, "[c]apitalized rental value is not the sole criterion of fair market value, even when lands have been rented for years and there is no evidence of sales to go by. It is only one of the relevant factors to be considered in determining fair market value and we cannot say that inadequate weight must have been given to that factor in the instant case because it was not regarded as controlling."[7] A more skeptical court held that "[t]he only conclusion possible in this particular instance is that . . . the capitalization method is simply too hazardous and too uncertain. It would be completely unfair to the government to compel it to pay on any such formula, and would make a mockery of the concept of just compensation."[8]

Gross Income Estimate

The first step in the income approach is to estimate the gross annual rental income the property being appraised would produce if it were 100% occupied. To accomplish this, the appraiser will usually investigate and analyze the actual rent schedule of the property under appraisal, if there is one, and then compare the rent schedules of similar properties. From this analysis, the appraiser estimates the economic, or market, rent applicable to the property under appraisal.

If the property under appraisal is rented, and the appraiser's conclusion of economic rent deviates from the actual rent schedule, he has a professional and ethical obligation to present strong market support for the deviation.[9] The courts seem reluctant to accept anything other than a property's actual rent schedule. As stated in *Nichols'*, "[e]stimates of earning out of conformity with actual earnings should, in the main, be disregarded."[10]

Some courts have rejected income approach testimony because the property under appraisal was not actually rented. In *City of Chicago* v. *Giedraitis* the court said, "[w]e know of no instance in which speculative or future anticipated rentals were held to be competent valuation factors. . . . Since the Giedraitis property was owner occupied and no actual rental had been made or was even anticipated, it is clear that the trial court did not err in striking testimony based upon such improper elements."[11] However, an Alabama court took an opposite view when it held that evidence of rental value is admissible even where the owner occupied the property himself and did not actually rent it.[12]

"Occasionally, a landowner may seek to introduce evidence of rents which will be received from a projected improvement of the land condemned. Such evidence is generally rejected."[13] The appraiser is well-advised to avoid using the land residual technique of land valuation whenever possible,[14] because it is highly probable that any testimony in regard to a value estimate developed by this procedure will be excluded.[15] It is possible, in fact, that the value estimate itself will be excluded from testimony. This methodology may be used in an appraisal report to support the market data approach to value when market evidence is weak, but it appears to have no place in the courtroom.

In estimating the gross income attributable to a property, the appraiser must exclude any income that would be considered business income, rather than real estate rental income. It is the real estate, not the business, which is being acquired under the sovereign's power of eminent domain.[16] "It is, accordingly, well settled that evidence of the profits of a business conducted upon land taken for the public use is not admissible in proceedings for the determination of compensation which the owner of the land is to receive."[17] Evidence of business volume may properly be admitted, however, when it can be shown that this is the basis of market value and/or economic rent within the industry.[18]

For example, a Missouri court ruled it an error to instruct the jury to consider the amount of fuel being pumped by a service station being condemned only to show the property's highest and best use. Evidence showed that service station properties were sold and rented on a dollar amount per gallon of gasoline pumped; therefore, the higher court ruled that "[i]n view of the evidence offered and received, we think the instruction was erroneous and misleading and particularly prejudicial to respondant [sic]."[19]

Good professional practice requires that the appraiser use rent comparables in estimating the economic rent of the property being appraised, whether or not the conclusion conforms to the property's actual rent schedule. A few courts exclude testimony in regard to comparable rentals, but most follow the same rules they have adopted in regard to the admissibility of comparable sales.

Vacancy and Credit Loss

The second step in the income approach is to estimate a vacancy and credit loss factor applicable to the property under appraisal and deduct this amount from the gross scheduled income of the property to produce an estimated effective gross income of the property. "In considering rent for capitalization purposes it is usually essential to deduct a normal reserve for vacancies. Thus the resultant capitalization figure is based on normal earnings and does not excessively penalize property in bad times nor inflate its value in boom times. It is axiomatic that a reasonably prudent investor will provide such a safety margain in his calculations in weighing the relative attractiveness of a new investment."[20]

The appraiser usually estimates the vacancy rate by analyzing the quality and durability of the projected income and the vacancy level of comparable properties under similar circumstances. At times, however, it has been held that it is not improper to exclude a vacancy factor.[21] This practice may become even more prevalent as the courts begin to rule on cases involving the mortgage-equity method of capitalization, in which the projected income term is the typical ownership period, not the economic life of the property improvements. A vacancy factor may be particularly unnecessary where the projected ownership term is equal to or less than the existing lease term and the tenant is of high quality.

Expenses

"In considering evidence of . . . rents as an element in the determination of market value care must be taken to distinguish between gross rents and net rentals. It is the latter which is ordinarily considered as an evidentiary factor in the valuation process."[22] Therefore, the appraiser must deduct expenses from the effective gross income of the property. Expenses are estimated by the appraiser and deducted from the effective gross income of the property to arrive at an estimated net income. These expenses are often broken down into fixed expenses, operating expenses, and a reserve for the replacement of short-lived items.[23]

With more appraisers utilizing a projected ownership term, rather than the property's economic life, some are not establishing specific reserves for replacements. Instead, they are including some of these items in their estimate of annual repairs and maintenance and/or considering the probable condition of these short-lived items and their effect on the probable resale price of the whole property at the end of the projected ownership term. This procedure tends to project a more accurate cash flow picture, which can be of assistance to the appraiser who wishes to make a cash flow analysis as part of the appaisal process.

In estimating the expenses applicable to a property being appraised, the appraiser should be cognizant of expense trends as well as the historical expenses of the property. The actual expenses incurred by comparable properties can also help the appraiser make accurate expense projections. It will be persuasive evidence if the appraiser can testify that his estimate of expenses is 30% of the property's effective gross income and that the comparable rentals (or the comparable sales utilized in the market data approach) were experiencing expenses ranging from 28% to 32% of their effective gross income.

Net Income

Using the factors just discussed, the appraiser can compute the estimated net income for the property being appraised. The steps are:

> Gross income − vacancy and credit loss = effective gross income
> Effective gross income − expenses = net income

The appraiser should prepare a detailed stabilized income and expense statement for purposes of clarity. This statement can be presented to the trier of fact or, for that matter, it can be included within the appraisal report very effectively, following the format shown in Table 8.1. Further justification of the appraiser's estimate may be presented as shown in Table 8.2 or, even more simply, as shown in Table 8.3. If the specific situation demands it, this analysis may be presented both as a percentage of gross income and in dollars per applicable unit of comparison (e.g., per apartment unit, per room, per square foot) as shown in Table 8.4.

The appraiser must convince the trier of fact and the reader of the appraisal report of the accuracy of the net income estimate or his development of an appropriate capitalization rate, no matter how clearly and convincingly it is presented, will be of little interest or value.

Capitalization Process

The mathematics of the capitalization process are quite simple. The entire process is based on the fact that there is a direct relationship between a property's value and the net income it can produce. Any appraiser, even one with minimal experience in the appraisal of income-producing properties, is aware of this relationship

Table 8.1

**Subject Property
14-Unit Apartment Building
Reconstructed Operating Statement**

	3 Years Ago	2 Years Ago	Last Year	Projected Stabilized
Gross income:				
Scheduled rent	$31,080.	$33,600.	$35,280.	$35,280.
Vacancy and credit loss	(1,243)	(3,380)	(2,470)	(2,822)
Subtotal	$29,837.	$30,220.	$32,810.	$32,458.
Laundry income	1,260.	1,580.	1,848.	1,750.
Other income	0	300.	50.	0
Effective gross income	$31,097.	$32,100.	$34,708.	$34,208.
Less expenses:				
Fixed:				
Real estate taxes	$ 2,100.	$ 2,400.	$ 2,500.	$ 2,600.
Insurance	0	0	520.	175.
Total fixed expenses	$ 2,100.	$ 2,400.	$ 3,020.	$ 2,775.
Operating:				
Utilities	$ 1,848.	$ 1,830.	$ 1,950.	$ 1,900.
Advertising	820.	830.	858.	840.
Office expenses	137.	140.	142.	150.
Professional management	2,089.	2,115.	2,297.	2,272.
Resident manager	840.	840.	840.	840.
Professional fees	300.	50.	320.	300.
Repairs and maintenance	2,675.	1,850.	4,032.	1,850.
Cleaning	324.	375.	309.	350.
Yard and ground care	240.	280.	280.	280.
Miscellaneous expenses	0	40.	100.	50.
Total operating expenses	$ 9,273.	$ 8,350.	$11,128.	$ 8,832.
Reserves:				
Drapes and carpets	$ 0	$ 0	$ 0	$ 560.
Appliances	0	0	0	1,680.
Roof	0	0	0	230.
Total reserves	$ 0	$ 0	$ 0	$ 2,470.
Total expenses	$11,373.	$10,750.	$14,148.	$14,077.
Net income	$19,724.	$21,350.	$20,560.	$20,131.

Table 8.2

**Income and Expense Comparison
Per Unit**

	Rental 1	Rental 2	Rental 3	Subject Stabilized
Gross income:				
Scheduled rent	$2,400.	$3,120.	$2,340.	$2,520.
Vacancy and credit loss	(96)	(250)	(164)	(202)
Subtotal	$2,304.	$2,870.	$2,176.	$2,318.
Laundry income	112.	128.	120.	125.
Other income	8.	0	0	0
Effective gross income	$2,424.	$2,998.	$2,296.	$2,443.
Less expenses:				
Fixed:				
Real estate taxes	$ 175.	$ 190.	$ 172.	$ 186.
Insurance	12.	15.	14.	13.
Total fixed expenses	$ 187.	$ 205.	$ 186.	$ 199.
Operating:				
Utilities	$ 132.	$ 140.	$ 128.	$ 136.
Advertising	62.	60.	56.	60.
Office expenses	8.	10.	12.	11.
Professional management	170.	210.	161.	162.
Resident manager	60.	61.	48.	60.
Professional fees	0	25.	12.	21.
Repairs and maintenance	128.	140.	113.	132.
Cleaning	28.	30.	27.	25.
Yard and ground care	18.	23.	22.	20.
Miscellaneous expenses	0	8.	0	4.
Total operating expenses	$ 606.	$ 707.	$ 579.	$ 631.
Reserves:				
Drapes and carpets	$ 35.	$ 44.	$ 32.	$ 40.
Appliances	115.	130.	117.	120.
Roof	15.	20.	16.	16.
Total reserves	$ 165.	$ 194.	$ 165.	$ 176.
Total expenses	$ 958.	$1,106.	$ 930.	$1,006.
Net income	$1,466.	$1,892.	$1,366.	$1,437.

Table 8.3

**Income and Expenses Comparison
Per Unit**

	Rental 1	Rental 2	Rental 3	Subject Stabilized
Effective gross income	$2,424.	$2,998.	$2,296.	$2,443.
Expenses:				
Fixed	$ 187.	$ 205.	$ 186.	$ 199.
Operating	606.	707.	579.	631.
Reserves	165.	194.	165.	176.
Total expenses	$ 958.	$1,106.	$ 930.	$1,006.
Net income	$1,466.	$1,892.	$1,366.	$1,437

and has been exposed to the formulas $I \div R = V$ and $F \times I = V$, which are graphically shown in Figure 8.1. The factor F is simply the reciprocal of the rate R. Thus, the reciprocal of 5% is $1 \div .05 = 20$ and vice versa; the reciprocal of 20 is $1 \div 20 = .05$, or 5%.

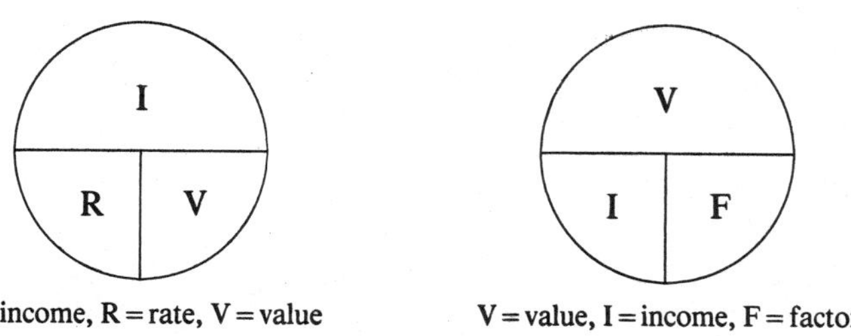

I = income, R = rate, V = value   V = value, I = income, F = factor

Figure 8.1.

By use of the formulas graphically displayed in Figure 8.1, it can be seen that if any two elements of the formula are known, the third can be covered to reveal the formula to compute it. For instance, using the *IRV* formula, if a property sold for $100,000 *(V)* and had a net income of $9,000 *(I)* per year, the unknown element in the formula is the rate, or R, and the formula is $I \div V = R$ or $9,000 \div 100,000 = 9\%$. If this rate was applicable to a property under appraisal, which had a net income of $12,000, the value of the property could be computed as follows:

$$I \div R = V, \text{ or } \$12,000 \div .09 = \$133,333.$$

Table 8.4

Subject Property
14-Unit Apartment House
Reconstructed Operating Statement

	Total	Percent of Scheduled Gross Rent	Per Unit
Gross income:			
Scheduled rent	$35,280.	100.0	$2,520.
Vacancy and credit loss	(2,822.)	8.0	202.
Subtotal	$32,458.	92.0	$2,318.
Laundry income	1,750.	5.0	125.
Other income	0	0	0
Effective gross income	$34,208.	97.0	$2,443.
Less expenses:			
Fixed:			
Real estate taxes	$ 2,600.	7.4	$ 186.
Insurance	175.	.5	13.
Total fixed expenses	$ 2,775.	7.9	$ 199.
Operating:			
Utilities	$ 1,900.	5.4	$ 136.
Advertising	840.	2.4	60.
Office expenses	150.	.4	11.
Professional management	2,272.	6.4	162.
Resident manager	840.	2.4	60.
Professional fees	300.	.9	21.
Repairs and maintenance	1,850.	5.2	132.
Cleaning	350.	1.0	25.
Yard and ground care	280.	.8	20.
Miscellaneous expenses	50.	.1	4.
Total operating expenses	$ 8,832.	25.0	$ 631.
Reserves:			
Drapes and carpets	$ 560.	1.6	$ 40.
Appliances	1,680.	4.7	120.
Roof	230.	.7	16.
Total reserves	$ 2,470.	7.0	$ 176.
Total expenses	$14,077.	39.9	$1,006.
Net income	$20,131.	57.1	$1,437.

Although the relationship between value, income, and rate of return is ingrained in the appraiser's mind, experience has shown that the typical juror has not spent long periods of time sitting around thinking about it. It is therefore necessary for the appraiser to explain this relationship to the jury. If this is not done, a good portion, if not all, of the jury will not follow his testimony regarding the capitalization process. The appraiser must educate the jury in this matter with great care. An almost perfect balance is needed. The appraiser must explain this relationship so clearly and precisely that it cannot be misunderstood; at the same time, he must avoid the appearance of talking down to the jurors. The appraiser must impress upon the jurors that they are not expected to have this knowledge because they are not experts in the field of valuation or finance; however, they must acquire a general understanding of the capitalization process to properly fulfill their duties as jurors in the particular case under consideration. The appraiser's explanation will be most effective if it is presented to a jury in both written and verbal form. It might be wise to equate the relationship between value, income, and rate of return with something familiar to most jurors, such as the operation of a savings account.

If the trier of fact is not a jury, but a judge or commission, the appraiser's task may be simplified or obviated. The degree to which a jury must be educated on the capitalization process will depend largely on the complexity of the appraiser's testimony. If the appraiser will testify on developing an applicable capitalization rate from market sales, the jury need only understand:

Comparable property's income ÷ comparable property's price = rate
Subject property's income ÷ rate = subject property's value.

If, on the other hand, the appraiser's testimony will involve concepts such as the band-of-investment method of rate selection, the Inwood Tables, or the Ellwood Tables, the jury must understand these more complex methods of rate selection. It must be remembered, however, that the appraiser's job is not to conduct a capitalization seminar, but rather to give the jury enough information to ensure that they understand the income approach testimony. The application of a capitalization rate is a simple mathematical process. It is the selection and/or development of a proper rate that can seem complex to the uninitiated. The introduction of residual techniques, equity yield rates, equity dividend rates, and the like can totally confuse the appraiser and the attorney who are not continually involved in income-producing property valuations, to say nothing of a trier of fact. Also, practicing appraisers or attorneys who have not availed themselves of the continuing educational opportunities available will find themselves woefully behind the times. Unfortunately this condition, to the chagrin of the appraiser, is often brought to light under cross-examination.

Each method of capitalization rate selection or development has some built-in assumptions regarding the nature of the income stream, the income projection term, the form of the investment yield rate, the amount of money recaptured over the projection term, the recapture term, and the recapture rate. Table 8.5 lists the assumptions inherent in straight capitalization, Inwood annuity capitalization, Hoskold annuity capitalization, and the mortgage-equity method of capitalization.

Table 8.5

Built-in Assumptions
For Various Capitalization Methods

	Straight	Inwood	Hoskold	Mortgage-Equity
Net income	Declining	Level annuity	Level annuity	Level, or stabilized
Projection term	Estimated economic life	Lease term or estimated economic life	Estimated economic life	Holding period or lease term
Investment yield	Risk rate	Risk rate	Risk rate and "safe" rate	A weighting of mortgage interest rate and equity yield rate
Amount recaptured	Building investment	Capital investment	Building investment	Part or all of mortgage plus equity reversion
Recapture term	Estimated economic life	Lease term or remaining economic life	Estimated economic life	Projected holding term or lease term
Recapture rate	Reciprocal of estimated economic life	Sinking fund at investment yield rate for lease term or remaining economic life	Sinking fund at estimated "safe" rate for estimated remaining economic life	Sinking funds at mortgage and equity yield rates

These rates and methods of capitalization are discussed in depth in *The Appraisal of Real Estate.*[24] A detailed description of the mortgage-equity method of capitalization and the Ellwood premise, which is an extension of the mortgage-equity method, can be found in the *Ellwood Tables.*[25] A reading of *Burritt Mutual Savings Bank* v. *City of New Briton*[26] could prove interesting for comparative purposes. Although this is a tax review case, it contains one of the most detailed descriptions of the income approach laid down by any court.

In selecting a method of capitalization for application to any specific property, it is required that the assumptions built into the method of capitalization represent the actual conditions found in the property being appraised. If the property's income stream is expected to remain level due to a triple net, long-term lease, the straight-line method of capitalization cannot be used; similarly, if it has been concluded that the typical purchaser of the property will probably establish a *safe rate sinking fund* to provide for investment recapture, the Hoskold method of capitalization is called for. "[O]f great importance, is the selection of a proper method of depreciation, amortization, or recapture of investment in the building."[27]

Knowing the basic assumptions that are built into the capitalization method selected by the appraiser is not enough. The appraiser must know the assumptions that are built into all methods of capitalization and why the other methods were not selected and are not applicable to the property under appraisal.

The courts have time and time again recognized the importance of selecting the proper capitalization rate to be applied to the net income of the property being valued. Various courts have stated, "[i]n the whole process the vital factor is the capitalization rate"[28] and "[p]erhaps the most vital factor in the process of capitalization of income is the determination of the capitalization rate."[29] "The capitalization or interest rate selected and applied to the formula used here reflects the degree of risk in the undertaking involved. It is an extremely important figure in the computation because a change of even a fraction of one percent will produce a surprisingly material change in the result."[30]

Because the courts recognize the importance of the capitalization rate, it is imperative that the appraiser support his rate selection with sound factual data and present that data to the trier of fact. "Absent foundation information about the relevant capitalization rate the witness should not be permitted to express an opinion on market value by use of the income approach to value."[31]

The most easily understood method of rate selection is selection by direct comparison. On several occasions, the federal court has approved the admission of comparable sales, even if their sole purpose was to establish the ratio between income and sale price (overall rate).[32] Table 8.6 illustrates the development of overall capitalization rates from comparable sales, which can directly be applied to the net income of the property being appraised. This form of analysis, presented graphically to the trier of fact, is convincing evidence. Although the appraiser may have to analyze such data further in the appraisal report or in later testimony, its preliminary presentation in the format shown in Table 8.6 is generally most persuasive to the trier of fact. When the appraiser needs to break down the overall rate into components of return on investment and recapture, or into debt service and equity dividend rates, the trier of fact can better follow the appraiser's analysis if there is a clear understanding of how the overall rate was established in the first place.

Table 8.6

**Rate Selection
by Direct Comparison**

	Sale 1	Sale 2	Sale 3	Subject
1. Confirmed sale price	$147,500	$237,500	$225,000	N.A.
2. Effective gross income	24,240	35,976	36,736	$ 34,208
3. Expenses	9,850	13,272	14,880	14,077
4. Net income (2 − 3)	$ 14,390	$ 22,704	$ 21,856	$ 20,131
5. Overall rate (4 ÷ 1)	.097559	.095595	.097138	N.A.
Rounded	9.76%	9.56%	9.71%	

If the appraiser chooses an annuity or mortgage-equity method of rate selection, he must fully understand the construction of this rate and be able to demonstrate it in court. Furthermore, the appraiser must be able to distinguish how the adopted rate relates to the real estate market and to competitive investments. As one court said:

> . . . Capitalization of income comprehends the use of a rate of return in comparable investments. . . . There was no testimony whatsoever about comparable investments. [The appraiser] merely used a formula from a handbook of factors for present value of an annuity of $1.00 per year.[33]

The construction of an annuity factor can be demonstrated to a jury, or to another trier of fact, by demonstrating the accumulation of interest in a savings account. For example, assume an appraiser wanted to illustrate how an annuity factor is constructed. The jurors could be asked to assume that they deposited $100 in a savings account today, at 6% interest compounded annually, and wanted to know what the account balance would be at the end of two years. This computation is shown using a deposit of $1.00 for arithmetic convenience.

Deposit	$1.00
Interest for Year 1 ($1.00 × .06)	.06
Balance at end of Year 1	$1.06
Interest for Year 2 ($1.06 × .06)	.0636
Balance at end of Year 2	$1.1236

The balance for a $100 deposit would be $100 × 1.1236 or $112.36.

The appraiser can then ask the jurors to assume that they want to end up with a $100 balance in their savings account at the end of two years. How much do they need to deposit to accumulate this amount? This can be computed by taking the previous factor of 1.1236 and dividing it into one, which results in a factor of .889996. This factor, applied to the $100, results in a required deposit of $100 × .889996, or approximately $89. The accuracy of this factor can be proven as follows:

Deposit	$ .889996
Interest in Year 1 (.889996 × .06)	.053400
Balance at end of Year 1	$ .943396
Interest in Year 2 (.943396 × .06)	.056604
Balance at end of Year 2	$1.000000

Therefore, it can be said that the right to receive $100 two years from now is currently worth $89. But what if $100 would be received each year for two years? What is that right currently worth? That can be determined by adding the factors for Years 1 and 2 together:

Factor for payment deferred 1 year	.943396
Factor for payment deferred 2 years	.889996
Present worth of right to receive $1.00 per year for two years	1.833392

Thus, the current right to receive $100 per year for two years is $100 × 1.833392, or $183.34. The right to receive $100 one year from today is currently worth $100 × .943396, or $94.34, and the right to receive $100 two years from today is currently worth $100 × .889996, or $89. So the total current value from the two payments is $94.34 + $89, or $183.34.

Terminology

Problems with appraisal terminology have continually plagued the appraisal and legal professions and have, at times, hampered effective communication. The problem appears to be particularly prevalent with regard to the income approach to value. The most glaring error caused by a misunderstanding in terminology is found in Section 19.21(1) (Existing Rent of Similar Property) of *Nichols'*, which states:

> Generally, evidence of the rental value of similar neighboring property is not considered competent in proving the fair rental value of the property condemned. [*Nichols'* footnote 17] It has been stated that while rental value of a parcel, the market value of which is an issue, may be received as some indication of the fair market value of that parcel, the rental value of similar premises, as distinguished from actual sales near in time, is not sufficiently relevant to warrant the extension of the field of controvesy and fact finding which is entailed in its admission.[34]

After reading this passage, the appraiser might logically conclude that, as a general rule, evidence as to comparable rentals will not be allowed in support of the appraiser's estimate of the economic rent applicable to the property being valued. However, the cases cited by *Nichols'* in its footnote 17 clearly indicate that the term *rental value,* as used by *Nichols'* (and some courts), does not refer to *economic rent* nor to the rent received by comparable properties.

A typical case cited by *Nichols'* under footnote 17, in support of the position stated above, reads in part:

> Missouri cases support the principle that the particulars of a lease dealing with comparable land, and an expert's opinion with regard to the value of the comparable land based upon computations involving the rental terms, are not admissible on the issue of damages to the condemned land. *State* v. Vorhof-Duenke Co., 366 S.W.2d 329. [further citations omitted] The rule is one of expediency and its application spares the court and jury from a time consuming enquiry into collateral matters of limited relevance. In *Vorhof-Duenke,* supra, the court said at p. 340: "There is no merit to the defendant's contention that the court erred in refusing to allow their witness to testify as to the market value of comparable real property computed from the witness' knowledge of the lease on the property and its terms. The capitalization of rentals may tend to show the value of the particular property under lease, but an expert witness cannot give an opinion of the value of similar land in support of his opinion of the value of the land in question."[35]

As an authority this case cites *Nichols'*, which states, "A witness cannot state his opinion of the value of neighboring land."[36]

Confusion in this matter does, in fact, exist. This is clearly illustrated by the fact that the citations under *Nichols'* footnote 17 are contrary to the position stated above. First is the citation of the California Evidence Code, which states:

> 818. For the purpose of determining the capitalized value of the reasonable net rental value attributable to property or property interest being valued as provided in Section 819 or determining the value of a leasehold interest, a witness may take into account as a basis for his opinion the rent reserved and other terms and circumstances of any lease of comparable property if the lease were really made in good faith within a reasonable time before or after the date of valuation.[37]

Providing even greater evidence that confusion exists in this matter is a case cited by *Nichols'* under footnote 17 as being contrary to the code's statement.

> Ohio has adopted the majority view that evidence of comparable sales is admissible on direct examination as substantive proof of the fair market value of the property to be appropriated where such sales were concluded between purchasers who were willing but not required to buy, and sellers who were willing but not required to sell. *Masheter v. Hoffman* (1973), 34 Ohio St. 2d 213, 298 N.E.2d 142.

> It is noted that *Masheter v. Hoffman, supra,* deals with sales of comparable property and not comparable rents. However, we can perceive no basis for distinguishing between comparable sales and comparable rentals, and the principle of *Masheter v. Hoffman, supra,* must also apply to comparable rentals. Evidence of comparable rental prices may therefore be introduced on direct examination as substantive proof of fair market rent.[38]

The *rental value* referred to by the courts, as it relates to the property being appraised, is simply the market value of the property as indicated by the income approach to value. However, the *rental value* referred to by the courts, as it relates to comparable properties, is not the rental amount reserved by these properties, but the indicated market value of the properties developed by capitalizing the rent of the comparable property by a capitalization rate chosen by the appraiser. The scenario of this procedure goes something like this:

1. The appraiser locates a comparable rental which has a gross annual income of $50,000 per year.
2. The appraiser estimates the vacancy and credit loss for the comparable, say 7% ($3,500), and develops an effective gross income for the comparable of $50,000 − $3,500 = $46,500.

3. The appraiser next estimates the expenses of the comparable at 35% of effective gross income, or $46,500 × .35 = $16,275.
4. Next, the appraiser computes the net income of the comparable at $46,500 − $16,275 = $30,225.
5. Then the appraiser estimates a capitalization rate applicable to the comparable, say, in this instance, 10.5%.
6. The appraiser then computes the indicated value of the comparable at $30,225 ÷ .105 = $288,000 (rounded).
7. The appraiser then treats the $288,000 as if it were a bona fide sale price of the comparable and makes a comparative analysis between the comparable and the property being appraised as would normally be the procedure in applying the market data approach to value.

In all but the most unusual circumstances, the courts have soundly rejected this procedure, and rightfully so. In at least one case, the appraiser concealed from the court and the trier of fact that the *comparables* to which he was testifying were developed by the above procedure and were not, in fact, bona fide sales.[39] This was discovered in the cross-examination. The appraiser deceived the court with phrases such as "My next comparable, after adjustment for time, indicates a value of X dollars." The appraiser then went on to describe the *comparable* as if it were a bona fide sale, and made a comparative analysis between the comparable and the property under appraisal.

It is this type of conduct, on the part of appraisers, which prompts courts, on occasion, to make statements such as "[t]here has been widespread and growing distrust of expert testimony in our courts,"[40] "[i]n any case where expert opinion is admissible the particular kind of opinion desired by any party to the investigation can be readily procured by paying the market price therefore,"[41] and "[i]f I were to give my interpretation of an expert witness, you wouldn't like it, and the lawyers wouldn't like it . . ."[42]

The appraiser must understand this confusion on the part of the courts and the legal profession. It is imperative that the trier of fact understand that the appraiser is using comparable rental properties to assist in estimating the economic, or market, rent applicable to the property being valued in the same manner that a comparable sale property is used to assist in estimating a property's value in the market data approach. The general adoption of uniform names for the approaches to value would go a long way in eliminating the confusion of terminology between the legal and appraisal professions. The three standard approaches to value are: the cost approach, the income approach, and the market data approach.

Each of the approaches to value develops an indication of the *market value* of the property under appraisal. For greater clarity, each of the approaches could include the phrase *"to market value,"* i.e., the *cost approach to market value,* the *income approach to market value,* and the *market data approach to market value.* Much confusion could be avoided by eliminating such terms as *sound value* and *physical value* when referring to the indicated market value of a property as developed by the cost approach to (market) value, and by eliminating terms such as *rental value, economic value,* and *rent approach,* when referring to the indicated market value of a property as developed by the income approach to (market) value.

Summary

The income approach is a procedure in the appraisal process which develops the anticipated net income from a property into an indication of market value by use of a rate, or factor. This process is known as capitalization and, by the application of the income approach, the appraiser acknowledges that a relationship exists between the amount of net income a property can produce and its market value. Over the past few years, capitalization theory has been modified and expanded more than any other element within the appraisal process. The admissibility of much of this new theory has not yet been ruled upon by our highest courts.

The courts' universally recognize the income approach to value, but the various jurisdictions have different rules regarding its admissibility. Some jurisdictions will allow its admission under all circumstances, while others only allow its admission in cases involving income-producing properties when comparable sales are not available. The courts have generally acknowledged that it is a property's net income that is capitalized, and that the selection of a proper capitalization rate is vital to the capitalization process.

The steps taken by the appraiser in developing an indication of market value by the income approach are:

1. Estimate gross income.
2. Estimate vacancy and credit loss.
3. Compute indicated effective gross income (Step 1 minus Step 2).
4. Estimate expenses:
   A. Fixed
   B. Operating
   C. Reserves
5. Deduct expenses from the effective gross income to arrive at an indicated net income.
6. Select the applicable capitalization rate.
7. Apply the capitalization rate to net income to arrive at an indication of the market value of the property being appraised.

A detailed description of these steps is provided in *The Appraisal of Real Estate*.[43]

The appraiser has an obligation to ensure that the trier of fact understands the relationship between income, value, and rate of return demonstrated in the capitalization process in order to adequately comprehend the appraiser's testimony in regard to the property being appraised.

The appraiser must have a thorough understanding of all methods of capitalization rate selection and the residual techniques.[44] He must know what assumptions are built into the method of capitalization rate selected for use in a particular instance, as well as the assumptions of all the available methods of capitalization rate selection. This is the only way the appraiser can be sure to choose the proper capitalization rate selection method and be able to justify that choice. The most easily understood method of rate selection is selection by direct comparison. The appraiser should present his testimony in regard to the application of the income approach graphically as well as verbally. This will increase the probability that the trier of fact will follow and understand the appraiser's testimony.

The appraiser and the attorney must share a clear understanding of the various terms utilized in the income approach to value. The meaning of these terms must then be concisely conveyed to the court and the trier of fact. Without a thorough understanding of the terminology used by all parties, the trier of fact may disregard competent evidence and/or the court may rule competent evidence inadmissible. As a general rule, the court will reject any attempt by an appraiser to testify in regard to the value of any property other than that being appraised, by capitalization of rental income or otherwise. However, many courts recognize the validity of using comparable rental properties to assist in estimating the economic, or market, rent of the property being valued, and they will admit testimony in regard to these comparable rental properties.

Notes

1. American Institute of Real Estate Appraisers and the Society of Real Estate Appraisers, *Real Estate Appraisal Terminology*, rev. ed., Byrl N. Boyce, ed. (Cambridge, Mass: Ballinger Publishing Co., 1981), p. 132.

2. *California Evidence Code*, § 8.19.

3. *Pennsylvania Eminent Domain Code* (P.L. 84), § 705, ¶(2).

4. "Uniform Eminent Domain Code," 1974, § 1110, p. 11.10.

5. Ibid., § 11.06, p. 11.7.

6. In re James Madison Houses, 17 A.D.2d 317, 234 N.Y.S.2d 799.

7. Demetria Sifuentes v. United States, 1 Cir., 168 F.2d 264.

8. United States v. 49,375 Square Feet of Land, 92 F.Supp. 384.

9. American Institute of Real Estate Appraisers, Regulation No. 10, *Code of Professional Ethics and Standards of Professional Conduct*, Canon 5, Guideline 5, p. 12 (Adopted Nov. 13, 1981).

10. Julius L. Sackman, *Nichols' The Law of Eminent Domain,* rev. 3rd ed., Vol 5. (New York: Matthew Bender, 1979), § 19.22[1].

11. City of Chicago v. Giedraitis, 14 Ill.2d 45, 150 N.E.2d 577.

12. Kayo Oil Co. v. State, 340 So.2d 756 (Ala.).

13. *Nichols',* Vol. 5, § 19.22[2].

14. *The Appraisal of Real Estate,* 7th ed. (Chicago: American Institute of Real Estate Appraisers, 1978), p. 149.

15. Port of New York Authority v. Howell, 68 N.J. Super. 559, 173 A.2d 310.

16. In matter of City of Rochester, 234 App. Div. 583, 255 N.Y.S. 801.

17. *Nichols',* Vol. 5, § 19.3[1].

18. Ibid.

19. St. Louis Housing Authority v. Bainter, 297 S.W.2d 529 (Mo.).

20. *Nichols',* Vol. 5, § 19.23.

21. In re Lincoln Square Slum Clearance Project, 15 A.D.2d 153, 222 N.Y.S. 786.

22. *Nichols',* Vol. 5, § 19.21.

23. *The Appraisal of Real Estate,* Chapter 19, pp. 345-363.

24. Ibid., see Chapters 19, 20, 21, and 22, pp. 364-460.

25. L. W. Ellwood, *Ellwood Tables for Real Estate Appraising and Financing,* 3rd ed. (Chicago: American Institute of Real Estate Appraisers, 1974).

26. Burritt Mutual Savings Bank v. City of New Briton, 20 Conn. Sup. 476, 140 A.2d 324.

27. Ibid.

28. Ibid.

29. United States v. Tampa Bay Garden Apartments, Inc., 294 F.2d 598.

30. United States v. Whitehurst, 337 F.2d 765.

31. Eikelberger v. State, Dep't of Highways, 429 P.2d 555 (Nev.).

32. United States v. Certain Interests in Property, 239 F.Supp. 822.

33. United States v. 158.76 Acres of Land, etc., 298 F.2d 559.

34. *Nichols',* Vol. 5, § 19.21[1].

35. State ex rel. State Highway Comm. v. Scott, 544 S.W.2d 340 (Mo.).

36. *Nichols',* Vol. 5, § 18.45[1].

37. *California Evidence Code,* § 818.

38. Pokorny v. Local 310, Int. Hod Carriers, 35 Ohio App.2d 178, 300 N.E.2d 464.

39. Case citation omitted due to pending ethics complaint.

40. *Nichols',* Vol. 5, § 18.4.

41. Roberts v. New York El. R. Co., 128 N.Y. 455, 28 N.E. 486.

42. Brown & Vaughn Dev. Co. v. Commonwealth, 339 Pa. 589, 143 A.2d 815.

43. *The Appraisal of Real Estate,* Chapters 17, 18, 19, 20, 21, and 22.

44. *The Appraisal of Real Estate,* Chapters 17, 18, and 19.

CHAPTER 9
MARKET DATA APPROACH TO VALUE

The market data approach is:

> [T]raditionally, an appraisal procedure in which the market value estimate is predicated upon prices paid in actual market transactions and current listings, the former fixing the lower limit of value in a static or advancing market (price wise), and fixing the higher limit of value in a declining market; and the latter fixing the higher limit in any market. It is a process of analyzing sales of similar recently sold properties in order to derive an indication of the most probable sales price of the property being appraised. The reliability of this technique is dependent upon (a) the availability of comparable sales data, (b) the verification of the sales data, (c) the degree of comparability or extent of adjustment necessary for time differences, and (d) the absence of non-typical conditions affecting the sales price.[1]

The application of this approach produces an estimate of value for a property by comparing it with similar properties that have been sold recently or are currently offered for sale in the same or competing areas. Procedures used to estimate the degree of comparability between two properties involve sound judgment decisions concerning their similarity with respect to many value factors such as location, construction, age and condition, layout, equipment, design, utility, and desirability. The sales prices of properties judged to be most comparable tend to set a range within which the value of the Subject Property will fall. Further consideration of the comparative data should lead to a logical estimate of the probable price for which the property could be sold as of the date of the appraisal. This is the Market Data Value indication.[2]

Over the years, the term *market data approach* has been criticized as misleading because all approaches to value require the use of market data. In fact, the use of this term may on occasion contribute to the courts' inability to acknowledge that, like the market data approach, the income and cost approaches also result in indications of market value.

Some appraisal professionals avoid the use of the term *market data approach* and, instead, use the term *sales comparison approach*. There is, in fact, a trend underway to replace the term *market data approach* with *sales comparison approach*. Upcoming appraisal textbooks will reflect this new terminology. This change will take time, however, and the term *market data approach* will remain in use for some time to come.

The term *sales comparison approach* has not been adopted for use in this text because the legal profession and the courts have a common understanding of the *market,* or *market data,* approach. Condemnation appraisal is not the proper arena in which to introduce new terminology. So many appraisal terms are misunderstood by lawyers and the courts, that it seems imprudent to abandon one that is universally understood. Therefore, appraisers should be cautious about introducing the term *sales comparison approach* in their reports and testimony. In the field of litigation appraising, the use of standard terminology is preferred until the new terminology has gained wide acceptance in other areas of appraisal and is generally understood by nonappraisers involved in real estate litigation.

The courts appear to prefer the market data approach to value overwhelmingly. "Ordinarily, if there are sales of comparable property at or near the time the condemned property is taken, evidence in regard to such sales would be more appropriate than any other method in determining the market value of the property taken."[3] In a few jurisdictions, this preference can cause courts to exclude any other approach to value if comparable sales are available. For instance, "[t]o be consistent with our many decisions holding the omission of evidence as to capitalization of revenue or cost of reproduction to be proper because of the nonavailability of evidence of comparable sales of similar lands, we hold the availability of evidence of comparable sales of similar lands operates to exclude from evidence testimony as to other methods for determining the fair market value."[4]

Admissibility of Comparable Sales Data

Evidence of comparable sales has been admitted in nearly all jurisdictions, but the reasons for admitting such evidence vary. "Evidence of sales of comparable properties may be offered under three conditions: (I) on direct examination of expert or lay witnesses as independent substantive evidence of the value of the property to which the comparison relates, or (II) on direct examination of the value-witness to give an account of the factual basis upon which he founds his opinion on the issue of value of the real estate in controversy, or (III) on cross-examination of the value-witness to test his knowledge, experience and investigation and thus affect the weight to be given to his opinions."[5]

The minority position is that sales may only be admitted on cross-examination. The reasoning for the exclusion of this sales data on direct examination is two-fold. First, it is argued that the admission of such testimony opens up too many collateral issues, and "proves nothing. It is therefore irrelevant, improper, and dangerous."[6] Secondly, it is argued that testimony by an appraiser in reference to the price, terms, and conditions surrounding a sale is hearsay evidence because the witness was not a party to the transaction nor was he present at the time of the closing.[7] The trend, however, is definitely to allow direct evidence of comparable sales on direct examination.[8] "Actual experience in the trial of land damage cases in states in which evidence of this character is admitted does not show the objections mentioned above to be as formidable as supposed. If the admission of such evidence is regulated with reasonable judgment by the presiding justice, it throws light upon the issue before the jury as nothing else can."[9] Some jurisdictions have, in fact, enacted legislative exception to the hearsay rule so as to allow evidence of comparable sales on direct examination.[10]

It is probably of little consequence to the appraiser whether the sale price of a comparable is admitted as direct evidence of the value of the property being appraised or as support for the appraiser's opinion of market value. It may be significant, however, insofar as the sale presented as direct evidence of the market value of the property under appraisal must, as a general rule, have a higher degree of comparability than the sale submitted as support for the appraiser's opinion of market value. In fact, a court will often rule on the comparability of a sale, as a matter of law, before the appraiser is allowed to testify to the price of the comparable.[11]

Most jurisdictions allow the price of comparable land to be admitted as direct, or independent, evidence of the market value of the property in dispute.[12] Under such circumstances, this rule of admissibility is an exception to the hearsay and best evidence rules.[13] The reasoning behind this exclusion from the rules is well stated in a Montana case:

> All expert opinion is based on "hearsay" to a great extent and much of what is presented by such witnesses is "secondary" evidence. We feel we can achieve speedy litigation and still preserve the truth by the rule adopted here. It must be shown that the witness is expert and that the sales are comparable and recent. With these safeguards plus the fact that the witness has his professional reputation riding on his testimony we feel that the repugnancy of this line of testimony is reduced, if not eliminated altogether. The development of a value pattern by

one experienced in the business and knowledgeable as to the area involved will best bring uniformity to the market value determination in the most efficient manner.[14]

When a comparable sale is admitted only in support of the appraiser's opinion, it generally does not have to possess the same high degree of comparability as does the sale submitted as direct evidence of value. In such a case, "there is less reason for being strict in regard to similarity, because the evidence serves the purpose only of supporting the credibility of the estimate of value given by the witness."[15] When such support testimony is given, it is not usually necessary for the court to rule on its comparability before admitting the sale price of the comparable property. The price is not admitted as direct evidence of value but, rather, to assist the jury in measuring the reliability of the expert's ultimate opinion of value.[16]

Sale of Subject

An historical sale of the property in dispute is universally admitted as direct evidence of the value of the property as long as the sale was recent and voluntary, there were no changes in the property's condition, and no material fluctuations have occurred in the property's value since the date of sale.[17] No rule has been set down as to what constitutes *recent;* whether the sale of a property is recent enough to allow it into evidence is generally within the discretion of the court.[18]

For instance, the federal court excluded from evidence a sale occurring two years prior to the date of valuation for being too remote in time,[19] but, in another case, the same court admitted into evidence the purchase price of the property in dispute, which occurred 14 years prior to the date of valuation.[20] The Michigan court recently ruled that "[a] nine year interval between the purchase of the land and its condemnation does not render the purchase price patently inadmissible."[21] Evidence may, of course, be admitted to explain the circumstances of such a sale, and it has been held that consideration must also be given to any appreciation between the date of sale and the date of condemnation.[22] Therefore, an appraiser must make an adjustment for the date of sale if it is warranted.

In one form or another, a number of courts have held that the prior sale price of the property being condemned is the best evidence of value. It is imperative, therefore, that the appraiser investigate and completely analyze any fairly recent sale of the property being appraised. Although an appraiser may conclude that comparable sales more than two years old are too remote in time to be meaningful, such a conclusion would not necessarily apply to an earlier sale of the property being appraised. Some users of appraisal services require that all sales of an appraisal property occurring within a specific period prior to the appraisal date be reported and analyzed. For instance, the Washington State right of way manual states:

ITEM 4-DELINEATION OF TITLE

Here show all sales of the Subject Property occurring within the previous five years. Each sale is tabulated in order of occurrence showing the grantor, grantee, date of sale, Auditor's volume and page, confirmee, and the sale price . . .

Following each sale, state an opinion on whether the sale can be considered as evidence of value. Any physical changes to the property made after each such sale are briefly described, such as additional construction remodeling, etc. Also indicate the probable effect of remodeling, etc., upon market value. If more than one sale has occurred, an explanation is given for any change in price which could not be equated to physical changes, such as: contract sale vs. cash sale, change in neighborhood development, changes in general economics, etc. If the sale can be considered as evidence of value, the sale information and the appraiser's analysis thereof are reported on a Market Data Form (HWY Form 261-020) and included in the report. If the sale cannot be considered as evidence of value, the appraiser inserts a brief narrative instead of a Market Data form giving the details of the sale, any physical changes subsequent thereto and an explanation of why the sale cannot be considered as evidence of value.[23]

The manual on *Uniform Appraisal Standards for Federal Land Acquisitions* recognizes the importance of prior sales of the property being appraised.

Prior sales of identical property: Since compensation is measured by market value, prior sales of the same property, reasonably recent and not forced, are the best evidence of market value. Accordingly, the appraiser has an obligation to determine what the owner paid for the property. Adjustments for changes in market conditions may have to be made, or the prior sale may have been made under circumstances which render it irrelevant to a determination of the fair market value as of the date of taking, but each appraisal report should include a statement with respect to the consideration accorded to the immediate past sale of the property condemned.

Because of its pertinency, the admission of evidence of a sale of the property condemned has been sustained even though a considerable period of time elapsed between the sale and the taking. Too frequently it has been found that the very property being condemned was recently purchased by the condemnee at a price far under that which he is claiming but that no real effort had been made to bring out the fact of such sale. It is essential that such sales be included by the appraiser in his report and that the fact of such a sale be adduced either by way of direct testimony of the Government's witness or by way of cross-examination of the landowner's witness.

In addition to including in his appraisal report the latest sale of the property (regardless of when it was made and with whatever statement is deemed warranted concerning its relevancy to the value as of the date of taking and the adjustments, if any, made to reflect that value), all sales of the Subject Property within 10 years of the date of taking should be included in the reported history of the Subject Property.[24] [citations omitted]

As noted above, it is not adequate for an appraiser to simply report a prior sale of the property in question; he must also analyze the sale to determine its relevancy and report the results of his analysis. If it is found that the sale occurred so much before the date of appraisal as to be meaningless, this should be stated. If it is found that the sale did not represent market value and was not an arms length transaction, that conclusion, and the reasoning behind it, should also be reported. Statements such as "based upon my analysis of the sale of the subject property, which occurred six months ago, I am of the opinion that the sale did not represent market value" *just won't wash*. Why didn't it represent market value? If changes in the property since the date of sale, such as rezoning, improvement, or destruction, render the prior sale meaningless in reference to current value, these factors must be reported and explained.

If it is found that a prior sale of the property is, in fact, relevant to its current value, this sale should then be analyzed like any other comparable sale. Often, but not always, the only adjustment necessary is for the date of sale. Federal review appraisers have approved appraisal reports in which the appraiser adjusted a sale of the subject property, which occurred within one year of the date of valuation, upward for date of sale and topography, and downward for flood potential, lack of landscaping, and soil conditions. The property under appraisal had been directly affected by Mt. St. Helens' volcanic activity between the date of sale and date of valuation. Admittedly, such instances are rare, but because physical changes in a property can occur rapidly, the appraiser must take great care in verifying the sale.

The appraiser may justifiably conclude that the prior sale of subject should be given greater weight in the final estimate of value due to the lack of adjustments required for physical differences. However, this is not necessarily true as a matter of law, because the prior sale price of the property in question is only one of many factors to be considered in arriving at a final estimate of value. As stated by the federal court, "[w]e reject the conception that a prior sale or sales of condemned property must always, as a matter of law, be given more weight in condemnation proceedings than sales of comparable property. Recent sales of the very property condemned are entitled to considerable weight, but sales of similar property are entitled to weight also; and the relative importance of the two is dependent upon the facts in the particular condemnation proceedings."[25]

If the appraiser has made a *time increment* or *appreciation/depreciation* study, it should support the final estimate of the property's value when the results of the study are applied to the prior sale price of the property; if it does not, a clear explanation of the divergence must be included in the appraisal report.

During cross-examination, any question concerning an appreciation/depreciation rate must be answered with great care. Counsel may try to apply an appraiser's *offhand* answer regarding general property appreciation/depreciation rates to a prior sale of the property in dispute, which may degrade the appraiser and his final estimate of value. Leading questions such as, "Do you agree with the article in the local paper last week which stated that property values in this county have increased 15% over the last year?" should never be answered with a simple *yes* or *no*. The appraiser must first determine whether such an article did, in fact, appear in the local paper and, if so, whether it was accurately represented by counsel's question; secondly, the appraiser must let it be known that appreciation (and depreciation) rates fluctuate, depending on a great number of variables, such as property location, property type, property size, price ranges, and available financing. Although 15% might be an average rate of appreciation for a large geographical area, it would not necessarily be correct to apply this rate to any specific property.

Comparable Sales

The appraiser will generally investigate, analyze, and consider many sales before selecting those which are the most pertinent in the valuation of the property under appraisal.[26] Because it is usually market value that the appraiser is attempting to estimate and "[t]the best evidence of such value is like and comparable sales within a reasonable time preceding the condemnation,"[27] it is imperative that the selection process be made only after all implications are considered.

The comparables selected must be the best, from an appraisal standpoint and, whenever possible, there should be no question as to their admissibility. If the appraiser feels that a comparable sale may be inadmissible, but it is absolutely necessary for the proper estimation and support of value, the sale may be included, but its questionable admissibility should be pointed out, either in the appraisal report itself, or separately, depending upon the discovery rules within the jurisdiction.[28]

The best comparable sales, from an appraisal standpoint as well as from a legal standpoint, are those that are most *similar.* To the appraiser, this means those properties requiring the least adjustments to equalize them to the property under appraisal. The courts recognize ". . . that 'similar' does not mean 'identical,' but means having a resemblance, and that property may be similar in the sense in which the word is here used though each possess various points of difference."[29] The degree of similarity will, of course, vary from case to case, so it is not possible for appraisers, or the courts, to arrive at a formula to test for comparability or similarity. In one instance, adjustments totalling more than 15% of the sale price may very well indicate that the property is, in fact, not a *comparable sale,* but in another instance, a sale with total adjustments of 15% of the sale price might turn out to be the most *comparable sale* available.

Before a property can be considered a *comparable,* the appraiser must ascertain whether the sale constituted an *open market transaction.* In other words, did the sale occur under the conditions commensurate with market value?[30]

1. Were both the buyer and seller typically motivated?
2. Were both parties well informed, or well advised, and each acting in what he considered his own best interest?
3. Was the property allowed exposure in the open market for a reasonable length of time?
4. Was payment made in cash or its equivalent?
5. Was financing, if any, on terms generally available in the community at the time of sale and typical for the property type in its locale?
6. Did the price represent a normal consideration for the property sold unaffected by special financing amounts and/or terms, services, fees, costs, or other credits incurred in the transaction?

If these questions can all be answered affirmatively, the sale probably meets the criteria necessary for an arm's-length transaction. An affirmative answer to question 1 eliminates *forced sales* of all description and all sales in which the price paid was affected by a personal relationship between the parties. A positive answer to question 4 will eliminate sales involving trades or exchanges for other real or personal property.

A negative answer to some of the above questions does not necessarily mean the sale was not an open market, arm's-length transaction. For example, a seller may have paid a portion of the purchaser's financing fees. If the amount of fees actually paid by the seller can be determined, this may be used as the basis of an adjustment to the indicated sale price. Or the sale may have been a contract sale, in which case evidence in this regard may or may not be admissible, depending on the jurisdiction and the specific terms and conditions of the sale.

In determining whether a contract sale is admissible within a specific jurisdiction, applicable case law must be carefully analyzed. A distinction must be made between a *contract of sale* (real estate contract) and a *contract to sell* (such as an earnest money contract). A *contract to sell* is sometimes referred to as a *sale contract*[31] and this can create confusion. Case law is somewhat divided on the admissibility of *installment sales;* most jurisdictions appear to allow their admissibility, taking the position that if the offered sale is a contract of sale this fact affects the weight of the evidence, not its admissibility. As *Nichols'* has stated, "[i]f evidence were to be excluded of all sales every cent of which was not cash, the door would practically be closed as to the evidence of other sales."[32] The admission of evidence in regard to *contracts to sell,* such as earnest money contracts, has met with mixed reactions. As a general rule, unexercised options are not admissible.[33] Similarly, "[a]dmissibility may not be accorded to sales which are made either partially or fully in exchange for other property."[34]

As a general rule, sales should be personally verified by the appraiser with either the buyer or the seller. If neither is available, verification of the sale with a broker or the attorney who handled the transaction is generally satisfactory. Verification of a sale with the broker or attorney and with the buyer or seller generally produces the greatest amount of helpful information.

It is common in the real estate appraisal profession for an appraiser to employ research assistants or associate appraisers to do much of the field research required for an appraisal, including, at times, the verification of sales. This practice may be perfectly adequate for an appraisal report, but is unacceptable for trial purposes. As the Colorado Court put it:

> By this statute [¶38-1-118,C.R.S. 1973] a legislative exception to the hearsay rule was created, but it is limited in its aplication. The use in this statute of the terms "personally" and "communicated directly" do not mean by or through someone other than the witness.[35]

The New Jersey courts, by statute,[36] allow testimony as to comparable sale prices so long as the appraiser has verified the sales with the buyer, the seller, or the broker. This provision has been expanded by New Jersey case law to include attorneys as well:

> The cited statute was designed to overcome [existing case law excluding testimony to comparable sales] but it unaccountably does not list attorneys along with brokers as valid sources of information as to sales to be adduced in evidence.

. . . It should hereafter be understood that an expert may properly cite an attorney participating in the transaction as a source of confirmation of a comparable sale used by the expert in arriving at his valuation of the Subject Property.[37]

The weight of authority holds that sales to a purchaser having the power of eminent domain are not admissible.[38] However, there have been exceptions to this rule. It has been stated that ". . . the burden is upon the party who offers such evidence to establish as a preliminary fact that the purchase, concerning which evidence is offered, was made without compulsion, coercion or compromise."[39] If the appraiser is to use such a sale, he must verify it with all parties involved and explain the results of such verification explicitly in his report and testimony.

If the seller made the initial contact and offered the property to the purchaser, this fact can be strong evidence of no unusual compulsion. Also, an historical review of the number of parcels acquired versus the number condemned by the purchaser over a period of time can give some insight into any possible undue compulsion to buy or sell. Sales to purchasers with the power of eminent domain do not necessarily set a pattern as being either above or below the market value of the property. "A company condemning land might be willing to give more than its worth, and the owner of the land might be willing to take less than its worth, that is, less than its market value, rather than have a lawsuit."[40]

The appraisal profession recognizes that accurate adjustments can sometimes be made for *conditions of sale.* "Conditions of sale are a primary consideration in the initial screening process to eliminate sales that do not meet basic criteria for meaningful comparison. Conditions of sale for which adjustment is practical, such as nontypical financing, receive consideration within the adjustment process."[41]

For example, an FHA discount paid by a seller for a purchaser's financing can generally be accurately determined by proper sales verification. The discount may be deducted from the gross sale price of the property to develop the effective price the seller actually received for the property. In the same way, an atypical contract of sale may be accurately converted to a *cash equivalency*[42] price.

Comparisons

The appraisal profession and the courts generally agree that basic adjustments are made for date of sale, location, and physical characteristics. As is the case with sales to an entity with the power of eminent domain, "[t]the party offering the sales claimed to be comparable has the burden of proving, as a preliminary to the introduction of the prices involved in such sales, that they are similar both in character and locality to the land being condemned."[43] "[N]o fixed or general rule has or could be laid down which governs the degree of similarity that must exist between the properties sold and that condemned to make evidence of that sale or sales admissible. . . ."[44]

The date of sale of a comparable property is, of course, most important in a rapidly changing market.[45] In at least one instance, an appraiser was allowed to testify in regard to sales used in a *time increment* or *value increase/decrease* study in support of a time adjustment, even though the sale properties were not *comparable*.[46] Whether or not the specific data utilized in such a study are admissible, a time increment study should be undertaken by the appraiser. This remains true whether the appraiser makes time adjustments or not. Even if the appraiser is unable to testify about the specifics of such a study, he will generally be allowed to testify that his time adjustments, or lack of adjustments, were based on such a study. Sales occurring after the date of taking have met with mixed reception. The use of these sales falls under what is often termed the *hindsight rule*.

It has long been argued that sales subsequent to the date of taking should not be submitted as evidence, or considered by the appraiser, for two reasons. First, the use of such sales gives the appraiser information that would not have been available to the *hypothetical purchaser* on the date of taking; therefore, the appraiser would be considering market factors unknown as of the date of value. The second objection is that subsequent sales may reflect *project enhancement,* which the appraiser must disregard in estimating the value of a property at the time of taking.

As a general rule, "[s]ales occurring after the date of taking can be used to show the value of the Subject Property in the 'before' situation. It is also the general rule that comparable sales which reflect an enhanced value brought about by the making of the improvement are not admissible."[47] [citations omitted] However, sales occurring subsequent to the date of taking have generally met with greater acceptance when used by the appraiser in estimating a property's *after value* in a partial taking case than in evaluating a property in its *before situation.* Such sales will often demonstrate damages or special benefits accruing to a remainder parcel.

Both appraisers and attorneys must be aware of the law in the applicable jurisdiction regarding the admissibility of sales subsequent to the date of taking. This information is necessary even if the appraiser does not anticipate using such sales because the appraisers testifying for the opposing party may. If the admission of such sales is not clear in the specific jurisdiction, the appraiser should have available alternative sales to which he can testify if sales subsequent to the date of taking are ruled inadmissible.

The degree of proximity required of any specific sale property will vary with the type of property being appraised and sales activity in the area. The courts have, on many occasions, recognized this fact. "No general rules can be laid down as to the distance at which other land ceases to be similar enough in location to the land in question so that evidence as to its sale price is inadmissible to prove the value of the latter land. The determination of this question depends upon the character of the land involved and the facts and circumstances of a particular case."[48]

If an appraisal involves a single-family dwelling located within a subdivision, it will probably not be necessary for the appraiser to leave that subdivision to locate comparable sales. If, however, the property under appraisal is an interstate freeway commercial site, properties 100 miles away can be termed *comparable* insofar as comparables are not always found in the immediate vicinity of the property being appraised, and the property being appraised and the *comparable property* would very probably be competing for the same customer—the interstate system user.

The test of whether properties are comparable in terms of location is not the physical distance between them, but whether the properties are within *economic proximity.* As stated by the Texas court:

> The distance between the condemned property and the property involved in an alleged comparable sale is important in determining whether both are in the same economic use area. Our Supreme Court holds that "evidence of recent sales of other property in the City of Austin, meeting the test of similarity, should be admitted," thus indicating that it is now settled in Texas, that evidence of "comparable and similar sales of comparable and similar properties located anywhere within the metropolitan trade areas, if a city property is involved, or within the same type of marketable land area, if rural property is involved" can be admitted.[49]

However, the best rule of thumb for the appraiser is that, all else being equal, the best comparables are those physically closest to the property being appraised. If the appraiser retained by one party in a dispute must go far afield to find truly comparable properties, it is likely that the appraiser retained by the opposing party will have to do likewise. However, the appraiser must be cautious. One assistant U.S. attorney has been known to use an 8 ft. × 10 ft. map of the United States in closing arguments to point out the location of the *comparable sales* used by the opposing party's appraiser.

A comparison of the physical characteristics of two properties can, of course, cover many items. The specific characteristics requiring adjustment, or at least consideration, will vary with the type of property involved. An extensive list of the differing physical characteristics of the two properties can often be developed, but the appraiser need only consider and include in his appraisal report those differences that reflect themselves in the marketplace. However, the appraiser should include all such differences in his notes, whether or not an actual adjustment is called for, so that he will be able to testify competently on cross-examination.

Many appraisers have found that about one-third of the typical adjustments called for in the appraisal of a single-family dwelling will represent 85%–90% of the difference in value between the two properties. The mere existence of specific physical differences between two properties does not mean adjustments are required. An adjustment is necessary only if the difference is reflected in the price at which sellers are willing to sell and buyers are willing to buy.

In comparing properties' physical characteristics, it is often desirable, and sometimes absolutely necessary, to compare properties on the basis of a common unit of measure. The common denominators for comparing vacant land are price per square foot, price per acre, price per front foot, whole site comparison, and, in some instances, price per developable (or typical) unit. This last unit of measure is often used for land having a highest and best use for multifamily dwelling purposes. The appraiser should use the unit of comparison which is common in the area and produces the most reliable range of value for the property being appraised. A proper unit of comparison generally establishes a much clearer pattern, or trend, of values than an improper unit of comparison.

The units of comparison in use for improved properties are as varied as the number of uses to which property can be put. In appraising unique or specialty properties, the appraiser will often spend as much time determining the common denominator as he will in performing the rest of the appraisal. A list of applicable units of comparison for typical property types follows.

Property Type	Unit of Measurement
Single-family dwellings	Sq. ft. or per room
Motels/hotels	Per room, GRM
Apartments	Per sq. ft., per room, per unit, GRM
Retail	Per sq. ft. or per front foot
Warehouse	Per sq. ft.
Freight terminals	Per door
Theaters	Per seat
Dairy or beef farms	Per head per acre
Parking garages	Per stall
Gasoline service stations	Per gallon pumped

The unit of comparison that develops the clearest pattern of value is the one typically used by buyers and sellers in the marketplace and, therefore, this is the one the appraiser should use.

Presentation of Comparative Data

The appraiser can choose from several format options when presenting comparable sales data and analysis in the appraisal report and in appraisal testimony. In some instances, however, a condemning agency will specify the manner in which the adjustments of comparable sales should be presented in the appraisal report. For instance, ". . . a narrative comparative analysis of each comparable sale is made explaining how the sale relates to subject with regard to those features which tend to influence market value. . . . If market investigation shows adjustment to be necessary, the Appraiser sets forth the facts together with the analysis and reasoning which led him to the conclusion drawn. Each adjustment is reported in an individual specific dollar amount indicating whether plus or minus. . . . A comparative analysis in chart form may be an aid to the Appraiser and may be helpful to the reader."[50]

Such a comparative analysis might follow the form shown in Table 9.1. Some condemning agencies do not require specific adjustments to be included within the appraisal report and, in fact, they discourage it. Regardless of the reporting requirements, the appraiser must make detailed and accurate notes of his comparable analysis and adjustments. Also, a determination of the format of comparable sales data and analysis for presentation to the trier of fact must be made, generally in conjunction with legal counsel. In all but the simplest cases, a verbal presentation of sales data and analysis is inadequate. To supplement the verbal testimony, the appraiser should submit sales data and analysis in graphic form.

As noted above, there are several methods of presenting data for trial purposes. Each has its advantages and disadvantages. The format shown in Table 9.1 has the advantage of appearing detailed, well thought out, and mathematically correct. If the trier of fact disagrees with a specific adjustment made by the appraiser, it can replace its judgment for the appraiser's and mathematically recompute the indicated value of the subject property. The danger of using this type of presentation is that it opens the appraiser to severe cross-examination as to the reasons for each and every adjustment made or not made. When using this type of presentation, the appraiser should be prepared to freely admit the possibility that a $500 adjustment could just as easily be estimated at $400 or $600.

Table 9.2 illustrates the presentation of adjustment factors by percentages. The total net percentage adjustment is then applied to the original sale price (whole or per unit) of the comparable. This method of presentation has the same advantages and disadvantages as presenting specific dollar adjustments. In using this method of adjustment, it must be kept in mind that the adjustments were made as of the date of sale. In other words, the appraiser is working with historical dollars, as of the date of sale, rather than current dollars, as of the date of valuation.

Table 9.1

Comparison Chart—Single Family Dwelling

Item	Subject	Sale 1	Sale 2	Sale 3	Sale 4
Sale price	N.A.	$75,000	$85,000	$82,500	$78,500
Sale date	N.A.	Equal 2 Mo.	+ $5,100 1 Year	+ $4,950 1 Year	+ $2,350 6 Mo.
Site value	$12,000	+ $2,000 $10,000	− $500 $12,500	Equal $12,000	+ $1,000 $11,000
Design/appeal	Average	Equal	Equal	− $2,000 Superior	Equal
Quality/condition	Good	Equal	Equal	Equal	Equal
Age	1968	Equal 1970	− $2,000 1975	Equal 1968	Equal 1970
Size	1,450 sq.ft.	+ $1,250 1,400 sq.ft.	− $1,750 1,520 sq.ft.	− $1,250 1,500 sq.ft.	Equal 1,450 sq.ft.
Bedrooms/baths	3/2	Equal 3/2	− $1,000 4/2.5	Equal 4/2	Equal 3/2
Utility	Average	Equal	Equal	Equal	Equal
Auto storage	600 sq.ft. garage	Equal 560 sq.ft. garage	Equal 540 sq.ft. garage	Equal 620 sq.ft. garage	Equal 600 sq.ft. garage
Other	N.A.	Equal	− $750 Superior built-ins	Equal	Equal
Net adjustment	N.A.				
Indicated value of subject		$78,250	$84,100	$84,200	$81,850

For instance, assume a recent land sale for $7.50 per square foot. The property is comparable to the property being appraised, except that it is 10% inferior in location. The adjustment would be calculated:

Sale price	$7.50
Location adjustment (10%)	+ .75
Indicated value of subject	$8.25

However, now assume the sale was not recent, but occurred two years ago for $6.52 per square foot. Assume also that, in addition to the location adjustment, a 15% upward time adjustment is required. The adjustment process might be:

Sale price		$6.52
Adjustments:		
Time	+15%	
Location	+10%	
Net adjustment	+25%	+1.63
Indicated value of subject		$8.15

There should be no difference between the indicated value of the subject property produced by these two processes. The reason there is a difference is that the location adjustment in the latter instance was not 75¢, as it was in the former, but rather $6.52 × .10, or 65¢, because the 10% adjustment was applied to the historical sale price. This can be corrected in one of two ways. A time adjustment can be

Table 9.2

Comparison Chart—Single-Family Dwelling

Item	Subject	Sale 1	Sale 2	Sale 3	Sale 4
Sale price	N.A.	$75,000	$85,000	$82,500	$78,500
Sale date	N.A.	Equal 2 Mo.	+6% 1 Year	+6% 1 Year	+3% 6 Mo.
Site value	$12,000	+3% $10,000	−1% $12,500	Equal $12,000	+1% $11,000
Design/appeal	Average	Equal	Equal	−2%	Equal
Quality/condition	Good	Equal	Equal	Equal	Equal
Age	1968	Equal 1970	−2% 1975	Equal 1968	Equal 1970
Size	1,450 sq.ft.	+2% 1,400 sq.ft.	−2% 1,520 sq.ft.	−2% 1,500 sq.ft.	Equal 1,450 sq.ft.
Bedrooms/baths	3/2	Equal 3/2	−1% 4/2.5	Equal 4/2	Equal 3/2
Utility	Average	Equal	Equal	Equal	Equal
Auto storage	600 sq.ft. garage	Equal 560 sq.ft. garage	Equal 540 sq.ft. garage	Equal 620 sq.ft. garage	Equal 600 sq.ft. garage
Other	N.A.	Equal	−1% Superior built-ins	Equal	Equal
Net adjustment	N.A.	+5%	−1%	+2%	+4%
Indicated value of subject		$78,750	$84,150	$84,150	$81,640

made first, and all subsequent adjustments can be applied to the time-adjusted sale price as follows:

Sale price	$6.52
Time adjustment (+ 15%)	+ .98
Adjusted sale price	$7.50
Location adjustment (+ 10%)	+ .75
Indicated value of subject	$8.25

The other method to correct for this factor is to recognize the time adjustment required in each of the adjustments. In other words, if the subject is 10% superior to the comparable in location, but the comparable price is 15% below the current value of the comparable because of the date of sale, the proper adjustment for location, as applied to the historical sale price, is 10% plus 15% of 10% (for time), or 11.5%. The adjustment process now would be:

Sale price		$6.52
Time adjustment	+ 15.0%	
Location adjustment	+ 11.5%	
Net adjustment	26.5%	1.73
Indicated value of subject		$8.25

For simplicity and clarity in trial presentations, the first method, adjusting the sale price for date of sale prior to other adjustments, appears to be preferable.

It has been said that the use of "[s]ome adjustment techniques [such as the preceding one] tend to exaggerate results, particularly if all are subtractions, and others to minimize, if all [are] additions. For example, a + 20% [adjustment] for location versus a $5 sale would suggest a + $1 [adjustment]. But if the $5 sale were first . . . [adjusted upward] 45% for other elements, reflecting $7.25, a + 20% [adjustment] would be $1.45. . . . To level these variations or to expand them appropriately, each adjustment may be multiplied by the product of previous adjustments."[51]

For example, equality between properties would indicate a factor of 1.00, a 10% superiority of the property being appraised would result in a factor of 1.10, and a 5% inferiority of the property being appraised would develop a factor of .95. Applying this procedure to the preceding example, it can be seen that the process automatically adjusts for the date of sale as applied to the location adjustment. To illustrate:

Sale price		$6.52
Adjustments:		
Time	15%	
Location	10%	
Net adjustments		
(1.15 × 1.10)		× 1.265
Indicated value of subject		$8.25

However, this is not the case in multiple adjustments. To illustrate, assume a comparative analysis between a property under appraisal and a comparable sale indicates the adjustments shown in Table 9.3. It can be seen that the time adjustment, of +15%, was applied before making any of the other adjustments. Adding the adjustments together indicates a total adjustment of +65%, which results in a final value indication for the property under appraisal of $12.38 per square foot.

Table 9.3

Comparative Analysis—Percentage Adjustments

Sale price per square foot		$6.52
Time adjustment (15%)		.98
Time-adjusted sale price per square foot		$7.50
Other adjustments:		
Topography	+20%	
Location	+15%	
Shape	− 5%	
Utilities	+25%	
Access	+10%	
Net adjustment	+65%	4.88
Indicated value per square foot		$12.38

The factoring system of adjustment, given the same circumstances, results in the value indication shown in Table 9.4. It can be seen that there is a substantial difference in the results produced by the two techniques, in this case nearly 10%.

Historically, this factoring technique has been taught[52] to appraisal students and its use has been encouraged because "[t]he comparison process cannot be reduced to an exact mathematical formula [and this factoring method of comparison] . . . is an example of the orderly mental process through which an appraiser might go in weighing the plus and minus items as between two properties."[53] This factoring technique is no longer included in modern appraisal texts.[54] In fact, one recent appraisal text states, "[i]n the past some appraisers felt that it was not proper to add these percentages together; it was more accurate to convert them to decimal form and multiply them by each other to get the net adjustment figure. . . . This figure known as a 'composite adjustment' would then be multiplied by the comparable's sale price to give an indicated value of the appraised property. This composite adjustment derived by multiplication is generally considered no longer valid."[55]

Table 9.4

Comparative Analysis—Factoring Adjustments

1.15 (Time) × 1.20 (Topography) × 1.15 (Location) × .95 (Shape) × 1.25 (Utilities) × 1.10 (Access) = 2.08

Indicated value per square foot ($6.52 × 2.08) = $13.56

The appraiser is particularly discouraged from using this factoring technique when presenting comparable sales data and analysis to a trier of fact. This process complicates an otherwise easily understood method of estimating market value. Also, the appraiser will be hard pressed to testify on cross-examination as to the actual dollar adjustment made for any individual item. Another reason to avoid this process is that the attorney representing the opposing party can take a composite factor developed by the appraiser and convert it to a net adjustment by adding and subtracting the percentage adjustments; using this figure, he can illustrate to the trier of fact that the appraiser's analysis develops a totally different indication of value than the one the appraiser has testified to and is advocating.

For example, assume an appraiser is testifying on behalf of a property owner who owns 35,000 square feet of land area. The appraiser utilizes the composite factor developed in Table 9.4 and produces an indicated value for the subject property of 35,000 sq. ft. @ $13.56, or $475,000, rounded. The attorney representing the condemnor could then ask the appraiser on cross-examination to add and subtract the percentage adjustments as shown in Table 9.3 and reveal the indicated value of the property based upon these computations. The results would be 35,000 sq. ft. @ $12.38, or $433,000, rounded—some $42,000 less than the appraiser's original figure. Because the adding and subtracting of percentage adjustments is easier to understand, the trier of fact may very well accept these later calculations rather than those originally presented. In such an instance, to the delight of the condemnor's counsel, the newly computed value indication of $433,000 may be closer to the condemnor's indication of value than the condemnee's.

Table 9.5

Comparison Chart—Single Family Dwelling

Item	Subject	Sale 1	Sale 2	Sale 3	Sale 4
Sale price	N.A.	$75,000	$85,000	$82,500	$78,500
Sale date	N.A.	Equal 2 Mo.	+ 1 Year	+ 1 Year	+ 6 Mo.
Site value	$12,000	+ $10,000	− $12,500	Equal $12,000	+ $11,000
Design/appeal	Average	Equal	Equal	Negative Superior	Equal
Quality/condition	Good	Equal	Equal	Equal	Equal
Age	1968	Equal 1970	− 1975	Equal 1968	Equal 1970
Size	1,450 sq.ft.	+ 1,400 sq.ft.	− 1,520 sq.ft.	− 1,500 sq.ft.	Equal 1,450 sq.ft.
Bedrooms/baths	3/2	Equal 3/2	− 4/2.5	Equal 4/2	Equal 3/2
Utility	Average	Equal	Equal	Equal	Equal
Auto storage	Equal 600 sq.ft. garage	Equal 560 sq.ft. garage	Equal 540 sq.ft. garage	Equal 620 sq.ft. garage	Equal 600 sq.ft. garage
Other	N.A.	Equal	− Superior built-ins	Equal	Equal
Net adjustment	N.A.				
Indicated value of subject		$78,250	$84,100	$84,200	$81,850

Another method of presenting comparable sales data and comparative analysis is shown in Table 9.5. This method can be altered slightly by excluding the specific indications of value for the property being appraised by each comparable, and simply showing whether the specific comparable analysis indicates a value for the property under appraisal above or below the sale price of the comparable. Applying this technique to the data shown in Table 9.5 would change the last line in the chart to:

	Sale 1	Sale 2	Sale 3	Sale 4
Indicated value of subject	$75,000 +	$85,000 −	$82,500 +	$78,500 +

Both this last method and the method illustrated in Table 9.5 have an advantage in that they avoid showing specific adjustments for each item of dissimilarity between the properties. Properly presented, they can illustrate to the trier of fact that appraising is not an exact science and that adjustments do not merely involve mathematical processes or formulas, but rather a subjective comparison in which the appraiser's experience and judgment are more important than arithmetic computations. On the other hand, these methods of presentation open the appraiser to intense cross-examination in regard to specific itemized adjustments and often, in final argument, it is asserted that the appraiser's work was *sloppy* and his final estimate of value only a *guess*.

Regardless of the method of sales presentation, some appraisers prefer to testify to one sale that is clearly superior to the property under appraisal and one that is clearly inferior to the property under appraisal, without adjustment, to establish a minimum and maximum value for the property in dispute. In certain instances, this procedure can be quite effective, especially when the highest and best use of the property is not being disputed. On occasion, however, it has been ruled that the trial court has the right to limit the number of sales which can be admitted by each appraiser or each party to the lawsuit.[56] In such an instance, the appraiser should carefully examine whether he wants to use part of his allocated number of sales for this purpose.

It is not necessary for the appraiser to testify to comparable sales in all jurisdictions. In fact, one court has said ". . . these witnesses were testifying as expert land appraisers, and that having so qualified, their opinion evidence, within the bounds of their expertise, would be acceptable in evidence even without giving the basis for the opinion."[57] Another court put it this way: "On direct examination [the appraiser] stated in general terms that his estimates of value were based on his experience in dealing with coal properties and on comparable sales. He was not asked to identify any particular sale he relied on. It was not necessary, in order for his testimony to have probative value, that he identify the comparable sales"[58]

When testifying in a jurisdiction in which the appraiser may, but is not required, to justify his opinion of value, it is essential that the appraiser support his opinion on direct examination, by comparable sales as well as by other means. If this is not done, prudent counsel for the opposing party will probably not ask for the appraiser's comparables on cross-examination or may even decline to cross-examine the witness altogether, particularly if the appraiser is well-qualified and has a good reputation as an expert witness. This leaves the appraiser's opinion naked before the trier of fact, a circumstance which opposing counsel will be quick to point out during his final argument. He may say, "Who are you going to believe? My appraiser, who testified to all of these comparable sales in the area, or the other appraiser, who testified to a totally unsupported guess?" Such a final argument is generally very persuasive.

Most jurisdictions require that an expert explain and support his opinion of value before the court will allow the opinion to be considered by the trier of fact. The Oregon court has said "[t]he witness testified that, taking into consideration adjustments, two parcels were comparable; but he failed to state what the adjustments were. It would have been improper for the court to admit the sale price until the adjustments were explained."[59] In Rhode Island, the court said:

> In the L'Etoile case [*L'Etoile* v. *Director of Pub. Works,* 89 R.I. 394, 402,153 A.2d 173] the opinion of an admitted real estate expert as to the fair market value, based solely on his long experience, was held to have been properly excluded for the reason that to have admitted it without supporting data would have denied the opposite party an opportunity to conduct an intelligent cross-examination.[60]

In a later case, the same court said "[a]n expert may not give an opinion without describing the foundation on which his opinion rests."[61]

An extreme example of this requirement for justification and support of opinion evidence is illustrated by a New York case in which the court said:

> The claimant's appraiser did not give a dollar and cents adjustment in any instance between the comparable and the Subject's land; neither did he give a breakdown percentage-wise nor state the factors which entered into his judgment. His failure to do so affords no basis for a review of his testimony and it is insufficient to justify an award.[62]

When testifying in a jurisdiction that has a propensity to favor specific supporting data, analysis, and documentation, the appraiser might be wise to present sales data and analysis by the method demonstrated in Tables 9.1 or the one shown in Table 9.2.

Summary

The market data approach to value is most widely accepted by the courts, at times to the exclusion of any other approach to value. Most courts will allow testimony on direct examination of sales of similar property in technical violation of the hearsay rule. These sale data are admitted as direct evidence of the market value of the property being appraised in some jurisdictions, while in others the evidence is admitted only in support of the expert's opinion. Those jurisdictions that do not admit comparable sales data into evidence on direct examination will generally allow it on cross-examination to test a witness's opinion.

The price at which the property being appraised was sold is admissible if the transaction was proximate in time to the date of valuation or taking, and no major physical changes to the property have taken place between the sale date and the date of valuation. It has been said that the prior sale of the property in dispute is the best evidence of its value. The appraiser has a professional obligation to consider and report any recent sale of the property being appraised, regardless of whether the price paid was market value and whether or not that price supports the appraiser's ultimate opinion of the property's value.

The appraiser's selection of comparable sales is of utmost importance. Forced sales and sales to purchasers having the power of eminent domain generally do not meet the criteria of an arm's-length transaction and will not be admitted as *comparable sales*. Similarly, sales in which the consideration was other than cash or its equivalent are usually not considered *comparable sales*. Real estate contract or contract sales have, however, been admitted. The fact that a sale does not meet all the criteria of an open market transaction does not mean the appraiser cannot consider it, only that he cannot testify in regard to the sale.

Once an appraiser learns the price and terms of a *nonmarket* sale, how can he avoid considering it? The bell cannot be *unrung,* the appraiser cannot totally erase the knowledge of the *nonmarket* sale from his mind. Considering a sale, or any other factor, does not mean that it has had any influence on the appraiser's final value estimate. The appraiser is certainly allowed and, in fact, should consider all sales with which he is familiar. The appraiser should be prepared to testify, "I considered that sale, but gave it no weight because . . ."

A federal court has ruled on whether an expert witness's testimony should be allowed to stand, after it appeared that the witness had based his appraisal, in part, on sales made to the United States under the shadow of condemnation. The judge said:

> Be that as it may, it would be absurd to exclude a qualified expert's appraisal because he had considered such evidence; indeed he ought to consider it; it is part of the data on which his opinion should rest. It is just because he is an expert, and for that reason able to give its proper weight to all data, that he is allowed to appraise the property at all. No court has held, so far as we can find, that his opinion shall not be received because it is so based in part; and we should not follow its ruling, if there were one, unless we had no escape.[63]

When Justice Holmes was serving as Chief Justice of the Supreme Judicial Court of Massachusetts, he also addressed this issue: "An expert may testify to value, although his knowledge of details is chiefly derived from inadmissible sources, because he gives the sanction of his general experience. But the fact that an expert may use hearsay as a ground of opinion does not make the hearsay admissible."[64]

This is not to say that an appraiser's opinion will be admitted if his value estimate is based entirely on sales that do not meet the criteria of market value. "Where a witness testifies as to value and bases his opinion entirely upon improper considerations and incompetent and inadmissible matters, his testimony may be properly stricken from the record."[65]

If verification of a sale indicates that the price was representative of market value, the appraiser should then determine the overall comparability of the sale property. If the property being appraised could have fairly competed for the sale property's buyer, had it then been competitively offered, the sale property can generally be considered a *comparable sale*. If the sale property meets this test of comparability, the appraiser may then make a comparative analysis of the sale property and the property being appraised.

Adjustments are made to the sale property for date of sale, differences in location, and differences in physical characteristics. Also, on occasion, an additional adjustment is required for conditions of sale. The indicated values of the property being appraised, as developed in the comparative analysis of each of the sale properties, is then correlated into a final value estimate by the market data approach to value. This correlated value is *not* an average of the various value indications developed by the comparable sales. It has been ruled, on several occasions, that to average the comparable sales prices is a *faulty procedure*.[66]

The appraiser will often have several options as to how he will present comparable sales data and analysis in the appraisal report. However, appraisal reporting guidelines may limit these options. The appraiser also has several choices in selecting the format for presenting sales data and analysis to the trier of fact. This selection should never be made by the appraiser alone, but only by mutual agreement between the appraiser and legal counsel. Applicable case law concerning the amount of support and reasoning required to validate an opinion of value may also influence the manner in which the appraiser presents sales data and analysis.

Notes

1. American Institute of Real Estate Appraisers and the Society of Real Estate Appraisers, *Real Estate Appraisal Terminology,* rev. ed., Byrl N. Boyce, ed. (Cambridge, Mass.: Ballinger Publishing Company, 1981), p. 160.

2. *The Appraisal of Real Estate,* 7th ed. (Chicago: American Institute of Real Estate Appraisers, 1978), p. 69.

3. United States v. 100 Acres in Marin County, 468 F.2d 1261.

4. Lataille v. Housing Authority of City of Woonsocket, 280 A.2d 98 (R.I.).

5. Hays v. State, 342 S.W.2d 167 (Tex.).

6. East Pennsylvania R. Co. v. Hiester, 40 Pa. 53.

7. National Bank of Commerce v. City of New Bedford, 175 Mass. 257, 56 N.E. 288.

8. Village of Lawrence v. Greenwood, 300 N.Y. 231, 90 N.E.2d 53.

9. Julius L. Sackman, *Nichols' The*

Law of Eminent Domain, rev. 3rd ed. Vol. 5 (New York: Matthew Bender, 1979), § 21.3[1].

10. Colorado, § 38-1-118, C.R.S., 1973; New York, See Lawrence v. Greenwood, 300 N.Y. 231, 90 N.E.2d 53 for statutory citings Pennsylvania, Public Law 84 (1964) (Eminent Domain Code), § 705 (2) (i); California Evidence Code, § 816.

11. People v. Murata, 161 C.A.2d 369, 326 P.2d 947.

12. Jones v. United States, 258 U.S. 40, 66 L. Ed. 453, 42 S.Ct. 218.

13. United States v. 18.46 Acres of Land, 312 F.2d 287.

14. State Highway Comm. v. Greenfield, 145 Mont. 164, 399 P.2d 989.

15. West Kentucky Coal Co. v. Commonwealth, 368 S.W.2d 738 (Ky.).

16. Bowers v. Fulton County, 176 S.E.2d 219 (Ga.).

17. Commonwealth of Kentucky, Dept. Of Highways v. Whitledge, 406 S.W.2d 833.

18. Lembo v. Town of Framingham, 330 Mass. 461, 115 N.E.2d 370.

19. United States v. 765.56 Acres of Land, 174 F.Supp. 1.

20. United States v. Becktold Co., 129 F.2d 473.

21. Petition of Michigan State Highway Comm. v. McGuire, 185 N.W.2d 187 (Mich.).

22. Virgin Islands Housing Authority v. 15.5521 Acres of Land, 230 F.Supp. 845.

23. Washington State Dept. of Transportation, *Right of Way Manual,* Chapter 4, Appendix 4-2, Appraisal Report Guide, Part IIC, Item 4, pp. 8-9 (Revised 11/10/76).

24. *Uniform Appraisal Standards for Federal Land Acquisitions* (Washington, D.C.: U.S. Government Printing Office, 1973) § A-4., p. 8.

25. United States v. Certain Land in City of Fort Worth, Texas, 414 F.2d 1026.

26. *The Appraisal of Real Estate,* 7th ed., pp. 274-275.

27. Onego Corporation v. United States, 295 F.2d 461.

28. See Chapter 17, "Writing the Report."

29. City of Chicago v. Vaccaro, 408 Ill. 587, 97 N.E.2d 766.

30. See Chapter 1, "Origin of Eminent Domain and Just Compensation."

31. State v. Bowling, 414 S.W.2d 551 (Mo.).

32. *Nichols',* Vol. 5, § 21.3[1].

33. Phillips Petroleum Co. v. City of Omaha, 171 Neb. 457, 106 N.W.2d 727.

34. *Nichols',* Vol. 5, § 21.1.

35. Denver Urban Renewal Authority v. Hayutin, 583 P.2d 296 (Colo.).

36. N.J.S.A. 2A:83-1.

37. New Jersey Sports and Exposition Authority v. Cariddi, 164 N.J. Super 127, 395 A.2d 895.

38. T.V.A. v. Bailey, 115 F.2d 433.

39. Hannan v. United States, 76 U.S. App. D.C. 118, 131 F.2d 441.

40. Yonts v. Public Service Co., 179 Ark. 695, 17 S.W.2d 886.

41. *The Appraisal of Real Estate,* 7th ed., p. 296.

42. *Real Estate Appraisal Terminology,* p. 42.

43. Dep't. of Public Works and Buildings v. Exchange Nat. Bank, 356 N.E.2d 376 (Ill.).

44. City of Evanston v. Piotrowiez, 20 Ill.2d 512, 170 N.E.2d 569.

45. City of St. Louis v. Vasquez, 341 S.W.2d 839 (Mo.).

46. City of Los Angeles v. Retlaw Enterprises, Inc., 16 Cal.3d 473, 546 P.2d 1380.

47. City of Tucson v. Ruelas, 508 P.2d 1174 (Ariz.).

48. *Nichols',* Vol. 5, § 21.31[1].

49. Hays v. State, 342, S.W.2d 167 (Tex.).

50. Washington State *Right of Way Manual,* § A-4, p. 13.

51. John Cotton, "Market Data: Adjustment Techniques," *Condemnation Appraisal Practice,* Vol. II (Chicago:

American Institute of Real Estate Appraisers, 1973), p. 107.

52. *The Appraisal of Real Estate,* 4th ed., 1964, p. 355.

53. Ibid., p. 355.

54. *The Appraisal of Real Estate,* 7th ed., p. 69.

55. George F. Bloom and Henry S. Harrison, *Appraising the Single Family Residence* (Chicago: American Institute of Real Estate Appraisers, 1976), p. 262.

56. United States v. 1,053.27 Acres of Land in Osage Co., Kan., 446 F.2d 1234.

57. Arkansas State H'way Comm. v. Hartsfield, 248 Ark. 821, 454 S.W.2d 82.

58. West Kentucky Coal Co. v. Commonwealth, 368 S.W.2d 738 (Ky.).

59. State H'way Comm. v. Callahan, 242 Ore. 551, 410 P.2d 818.

60. Hunt v. Director of Pub. Works, 99 R.I. 111, 206 A.2d 91.

61. Nasco, Inc. v. Director of Public Works, 116 R.I. 712, 360 A.2d 871.

62. Geffen Motors, Inc. v. State, 307 N.Y.S.2d 389, 334.D.2d 980.

63. United States v. Delano Park Homes, 146 F.2d 473.

64. National Bank of Commerce v. City of New Bedford, 175 Mass. 257, 56 N.E. 288.

65. City of Gilroy v. Filice, 221 Cal. App.2d 259, 34 Cal. Rptr. 368.

66. Latham Holding Co. v. State of New York, 16 N.Y.2d 41, 209 N.E.2d 542, 261 N.Y.S.2d 880.

CHAPTER 10
SPECIAL-PURPOSE PROPERTIES

A special-purpose property is "[a] property devoted to or available for utilization for a special purpose, such as a clubhouse, a church property, a public museum, a public school, and so on. It also includes other buildings having value, such as hospitals, theatres, breweries, etc., which cannot be converted to other uses without large capital investment."[1] The identifying features of a special-purpose property are:
1. The property has physical design features peculiar to a specific use.
2. The property has no apparent market other than to an owner-user.
3. The property has no feasible economic alternate use.[2]

Special-purpose properties, referred to as specialties[3] in some jurisdictions, have caused the courts to avoid adopting market value as the exclusive test of just compensation. Special-purpose properties "are unique and are generally not of a type bought and sold on the open market. Hence, there is no market value in the ordinary sense of the term, since market value presupposes a willing buyer and willing seller, which do not ordinarily exist in such a case. In cases of such a character, therefore, market value will not generally be the measure of compensation."[4]

A uniform method of measuring compensation for the taking of special-use properties has never been developed and, therefore, the potential for widely divergent value testimony is great. For this reason, there is a great deal of case law on the proper methodology to be applied in the valuation of special-purpose properties, but few specific guidelines exist for the appraiser to use in the valuing such properties.

The "Uniform Eminent Domain Code" provides that ". . . the fair market value of property for which there is no relevant market is its value as determined by any method of valuation that is just and equitable."[5] The U.S. Supreme Court has said that "[t]he fair market value of property, in the absence of an actual market, is the estimated or imputed fair market value based on sufficient evidence which justifies a conclusion as to the fair market value which would be established when an informed seller disposes of his property to an equally informed buyer."[6]

It can be seen that the courts are reluctant to completely abandon the market value concept. However, to ensure that an owner is fully compensated for his property, the courts have used such terms as *value to the owner, intrinsic value,* and *value in use.* Due to the complexity of the valuation and the legal problems involved in the condemnation of a special-purpose property, this type of case presents a valuation challenge to the appraiser and a legal challenge to the attorney.

Property Classified as Special-Purpose

The specific type of property being appraised will have some bearing on the valuation approach employed by the appraiser. Some properties that have been classified by the courts as special-purpose include:

Churches[7]	Cemeteries[10]
Schools	Golf clubs[11]
Public utilities	Theatres[12]
Clubhouses[8]	Museums
Dam sites and reservoir sites	Private lakes
Mill sites	Duck clubs
Freight terminals[9]	Banks
Camps	Stadiums
Specialized industrial uses	Amusement parks
(i.e., packing plants, laundries,	Car washes[13]
etc.)	Hospitals[14]
	Nursing homes[15]

The appraiser must not automatically assume that a property is special-purpose simply because like properties have been so classified in the past. To be truly special-purpose, a property must have: 1) physical features peculiar to its specific use, 2) no apparent market other than the current owner-user, and 3) no feasible economic alternate use. The most convincing evidence that a property is, in fact, a special-use property is the absence of sales of similar property. Lack of sales data and the classification of a property as a specialty:

> . . . may afford a basis for the application of more liberal rules of evidence or a different measure of value.

> Relaxation of rules may take various forms:
> 1. Modifications of the yardstick of compensation.

    a. The market value measure applied but rules of evidence relaxed.

    b. Use of measures other than market value.

2. Use of appraisal methods other than the market data approach.

    a. Use of the cost approach and evidence of costs allowed.

    b. Use of the income approach and income data, which may include business done and profits earned, allowed.

3. Variations and proof more or less peculiar to special purpose properties.[16]

The classic approaches to value are sometimes applicable to the valuation of special-purpose properties. The reliability of these approaches often suffers, however, because adequate data on which to base an estimate of value are lacking and the criteria for acceptable data in the appraisal process must be relaxed.

Market Data Approach

"One factor that makes a property special purpose is the lack of sales of similar properties. Therefore, little can be said of this approach when discussing special purpose properties."[17] Nevertheless, it should be realized that the degree of comparability required between a property under appraisal and a sale property is often relaxed when appraising a special-purpose property. This is particularly true in terms of geographic comparability. "[I]f land is not of a character commonly bought and sold, [the court] should allow evidence of the sales of similar land located at some distance from the land taken."[18]

When comparable sales are available, the most perplexing issue facing the appraiser is often the determination of the proper unit of comparison. This is particularly true when appraising the more unusual types of special-purpose properties. In valuing these unique properties, the appraiser may wish to investigate units of comparison which have been helpful in the past. The following list may prove instructive:

Property Type	Unit of Measure
Hospital or nursing home	Per bed
Log dumps	Per 1,000 board feet in and out of dump
Chemical waste sites	Per cubic ft. or per drum of storage space
Theaters/churches	Per seat
Freight terminals	Per door
Duck clubs	Per gun
Cemeteries	Per plot
Funeral homes	Per case
Campgrounds	Per campsite

This is not a complete list, of course, but it does illustrate the diverse units of measurement which the appraiser may encounter in applying market data techniques to special-purpose properties.

Income Approach

The income approach is applicable to special-purpose properties that have rental income potential; it is not applicable, of course, to properties such as churches and municipal buildings. Several problems are typically encountered in applying the income approach to special-purpose properties with income-producing potential.

Most special-purpose properties are owner-occupied, and it is therefore difficult, if not impossible, to find adequate comparable rental data to make an accurate and reliable estimate of the property's economic rent. This creates another problem in that the only income data often available is the net income from the property owner's business, including both business profit and a return on the real estate. Therefore, "[t]he appraiser of special-use properties requires a closer familiarity with the particular type of operation or business conducted than in evaluation of properties suitable for a variety of uses."[19]

Often, the appraiser must develop a stabilized net income from the business operation and the return on the real estate. After developing this estimate, the appraiser encounters a third problem. He must either extract the net income attributable to the business from the total net income, so the residual net income attributable to the real estate can be capitalized into an indication of value, or develop a capitalization rate high enough to reflect the value of the real estate only when it is applied to the total stabilized net income from both the business and the real estate.

Whichever method he uses, the appraiser faces the difficulty of developing and supporting a capitalization rate applicable to the special-use property being appraised. Because sales and rental data for such property are not available, it is generally not possible to develop a capitalization rate directly from market data. An appropriate capitalization rate must be developed by indirect methods, analyzing the quality attributes of the property being appraised as a real estate investment and comparing this investment with other real estate and nonreal estate investments available in the marketplace.

Under normal conditions, the profits from a business operated on a site to be acquired by eminent domain are not admissible in court. It is generally held that "[e]vidence derived from a commercial business upon land taken for public use is ordinarily inadmissible as a basis upon which to ascertain market value in a condemnation proceeding because it is too speculative, remote and uncertain."[20] "It is, accordingly, well settled that evidence of the profits of a business conducted upon land taken for the public use is not admissible in proceedings for the determination of the compensation which the owner of the land shall receive."[21] However, this is not necessarily true when the subject of the condemnation action is a special-purpose property. "In some jurisdictions and some situations, the income from the business conducted on the property and values arrived at by using such income may be admissible. This is another area in which the courts have, of necessity, been more liberal in the allowance of proof when dealing with special purpose properties."[22]

The reasons for admitting evidence of business profits seem mixed. "[W]here a property is so unique as to make unavailable any comparable sales data, evidence of income has been accepted *as a measure of value.*"[23] [emphasis added] Other courts have admitted the net profit from a business operated on condemned land, not as evidence of the value of the property, but merely to demonstrate the *productivity* of the property. "Although the profits of a business do not determine the value of the land, it is proper to show, in arriving at the market value, that it is valuable for certain purposes and productive to the owner."[24] As stated by one court:

> Business profits, it is well recognized, are no sure test of land value for they depend not only on location but on other factors; the same location may be fruitful of profit to one and not so to another. This does not mean, however, that in determining the value of the land no consideration is to be given to its productive capacity which, in such circumstances as are present in this case, has an important bearing on value.
>
> As a practical matter, a prospective purchaser would hardly fail to consider whether or not the business conducted on the premises had proved profitable, for this would be a measure of the desirability of the location, if not to him then to other purchasers. The precise weight to be accorded to this factor is a matter of judgment on which experts may differ, and of this the jury is the final judge. . . .[25] [citations omitted]

In light of these various court rulings, it is incumbent upon the appraiser and the lawyer to determine: 1) whether the property being condemned would be classified as a special-purpose property by the court with jurisdiction; 2) if so, is the net profit from the business operated on the property admissible; and 3) if admissible, for what purpose—as a *criterion of value* or as *evidence of productivity.*

Cost Approach

In valuing a special-purpose property, it has been held that the reproduction cost, or replacement cost minus depreciation, may be considered and, in fact, "may even be the only method in some situations."[26] "Usually, reproduction costs or replacement costs are used as the starting point, *with no recognition being made of the distinction in these two terms*. Some courts have required costs to be those of an identical structure, despite increasing criticism against such an approach."[27] [emphasis added] Therefore, it is critical for the appraiser and the attorney first to determine whether the property being appraised is in a jurisdiction requiring the reproduction cost of an identical structure; if this is not required, they then must ascertain whether a reproduction cost estimate or a replacement cost estimate is more applicable under the circumstances. It is, of course, important that the appraiser clearly identify, both in the appraisal report and to the trier of fact, whether reproduction cost or replacement cost has been utilized. The distinction between these terms must be made clear.[28]

In applying the cost approach to value, the appraiser first estimates the value of the land. The land underlying a special-use improvement will often have a different highest and best use as if vacant than it does as improved with the specialty. If the special-use improvement could be located on a different, less valuable, site, the appraiser must choose either to value the site as if vacant and available for its highest and best use or for its existing use. If the former methodology is adopted, the appraiser must compensate for the fact that the improvements could offer equal utility on a less valuable site by deducting from the reproduction or replacement cost of the improvement the difference between the value of the site for its highest and best use as if vacant and the value of the site for its current use, i.e., the cost of acquiring an equally desirable substitute site. This is essentially the economic obsolescence in the improvements.

For example, consider a church located on the 200 ft. × 120 ft. site shown as Block A in Figure 10.1. Assume the improvements have a reproduction cost of $500,000, and the underlying land, zoned for commerical use, has a value for commerical purposes of $5.00 per square foot, or $120,000. The land in Blocks D and F is zoned for residential use, allows church utilization, and has a value of approximately $1.50 per square foot. If the subject improvements could serve the parishioners as well on Block D or F as they do on Block A, economic obsolescence of the improvements is indicated.

Under such circumstances, the appraiser could value the property (assuming no other forms of depreciation) as follows:

Reproduction cost of improvements	$500,000
Value of site for church use	
(24,000 sq. ft. @ $1.50)	36,000
Total indicated value	$536,000

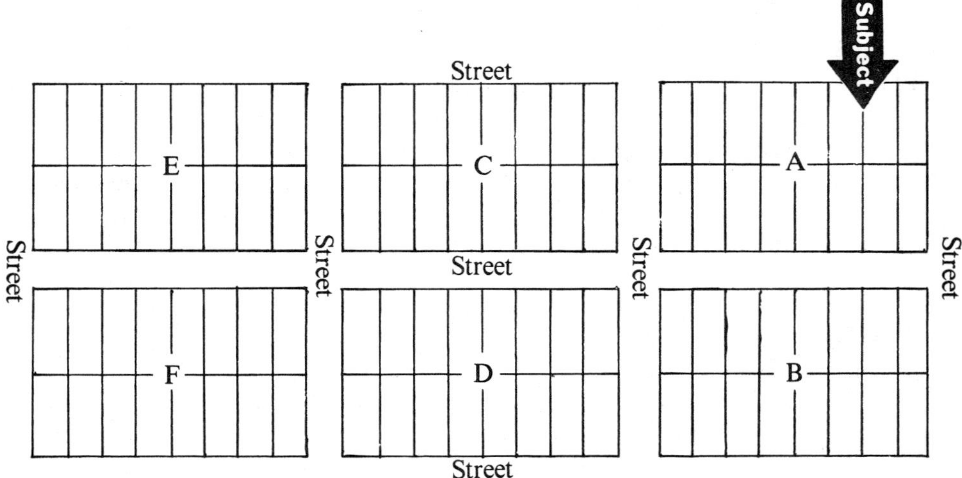

Figure 10.1. Special-Purpose Property—Economic Obsolescence

Or the appraiser may elect to value the site for its highest and best use and reflect the economic obsolescence in the improvements as follows:

Reproduction cost of improvements	$500,000
Less economic obsolescence ($120,000 value of site for highest and best use less $36,000 value of equally desirable substitute site for church purposes)	(84,000)
Indicated improvement value	$416,000
Site value for highest and best use	120,000
Total indicated value	$536,000

Both procedures will result in the same conclusion. The procedure selected by the appraiser will depend on the specific circumstances and the availability of market data. It is often advisable to use both procedures in the appraisal report to ensure the complete understanding of reviewers or other readers of the report. In the same way, a discussion of both procedures on the witness stand will ensure understanding by the trier of fact and severely limit the effectiveness of any cross-examination intended to confuse the trier of fact or diminish the appraiser's credibility.

The most difficult aspect of applying the cost approach to special-purpose properties is the accurate estimation of depreciation. "Although physical depreciation by inspection is not difficult, functional or economic depreciation is much more difficult to determine. . . ."[29] Generally, economic and functional obsolescence is measured using market data. However, it is the lack of market data which identifies a property as a specialty. Therefore, "[i]n assessing the value of a church, for example, the appraiser will have to exercise some effort and ingenuity in determining what elements affecting the utility of the subject church are superior or inferior to similar churches. Each church may have its own needs, however. Ultimate determination of the amount of depreciation will rest on the appraiser's judgment, assuming that the appraiser has made an adequate investigation of the factors that affect the utility and enjoyment of a particular property and that he has attempted to gauge such factors of the subject against what might be considered as the norm in properly improved facilities of the same type."[30]

Due to the lack of factual data from which to estimate depreciation, the cost approach has come under severe criticism, even though it is sometimes the only measure of value available. This was the conclusion reached in an extensive research report regarding the valuation and condemnation of special-purpose properties:

> It [the cost approach] is mechanical from its inception. Reproduction costs of a building may have no correlation whatever to value, market or otherwise. If value is to be reached, it is by appropriate allowances for depreciation. The ultimate basis of depreciation is the appraiser's opinion, which is no better than his experience, knowledge, and judgment. As a practical matter, failure to recognize depreciation is to the owner's advantage. Some indefiniteness of depreciation might be avoided if the starting point were replacement cost; i.e., starting with a building functionally equivalent to the subject. Nevertheless, the Cost Approach is the only method that can be used on some special purpose properties that do not have production of income as their purpose.[31]

Substitute Facilities

The doctrine of substitute facilities is not actually a valuation or appraisal technique, but a concept which has evolved from court decisions. The condemnation appraiser and condemnation attorney should be familiar with this doctrine. The New Jersey court defined the substitute facilities doctrine well when it said:

> We think the rule of substitute facilities is a just and sensible one. Henceforth, therefore, when the State or some other condemnor takes property which is already devoted to some public use by a mu-

nicipality or other agency of government, the requirement of just compensation will be met by the condemnor furnishing an adequate, substantially equivalent substitute facility, which need not, however, be an exact duplicate of what has been taken. This may either be done by the condemnor actually constructing the replacement facility, . . . or it may take the form of a monetary award in an amount deemed sufficient to construct an adequate substitute for what has been taken.[32]

Generally, the substitute facilities doctrine is applied to publicly owned properties such as public schools, municipal buildings, and sewer and water treatment plants. However, ". . . a number of cases have given consideration to the cost of a substitute facility where private property has been taken."[33] The logic of applying the doctrine to privately owned nonprofit facilities was stated in a federal case as follows:

The government also urges that the substitute facilities measure of just compensation is totally inapplicable to any condemnee other than a governmental entity. . . .

For several reasons we think the government's position with respect to private owners of nonprofit community facilities is untenable. In the first place we are dealing with the measure of the duty of indemnification imposed by the "taking clause" in the Fifth Amendment:

"Nor shall *private* property be taken for public use, without just compensation."

In view of the express reference to *private* property and the absence of any reference to public property, it is inconceivable that the framers of the amendment intended to impose greater obligation of indemnification on the national government toward the states and their subdivisions than toward private owners. Accepting the interpretation that it protects the value of community uses, there is no basis for distinguishing between governmental and private community uses. Moreover, acceptance of the appellee's position would inevitably put the government in a position in which, for economic reasons, it would be forced into unfortunate and possibly discriminatory choice-of-location decisions. One can envision, for example, the choice between a highway route traversing land occupied by a private or a public univeristy; the condemnation for emergency office use of a parochial school or a public school; the destruction of a church rather than a City Hall to permit the building of a federal courthouse. It seems to us an impermissible [sic] suggestion that the fifth amendment puts the government in the position of making such choices on the basis that it would be required to pay less by way of fair compensation to the private owners of such community facilities."[34]

The "Uniform Eminent Domain Code" also provides for application of this substitute facilities doctrine. It states:

> The fair market value of property owned by a public entity or other person organized and operated upon a nonprofit basis is deemed to be not less than the reasonable cost of functional replacement if the following conditions exist: (1) the property is devoted to and is needed by the owner in order to continue in good faith its actual use to perform a public function, or to render nonprofit educational, religious, charitable, or eleemosynary services, and (2) the facilities or services are available to the general public.[35]

If applicable case law dictates that the property in question be valued on the basis of the substitute facilities doctrine, the appraiser must obtain an adequately supported legal opinion to this effect. To apply the doctrine, the appraiser estimates the replacement cost and adds to it the value of the land, making no deduction for depreciation. Again, however, the value of the site should be based on the cost of acquiring a substitute site, not on the value of the subject site for a higher and better use.

Summary

A special-purpose property is one with a physical design peculiar to a specific use, no apparent market other than to an owner-user, and no feasible economic alternate use. The lack of comparable sales data is generally the key in distinguishing a special-purpose property.

The courts have been reluctant to totally abandon the market value concept in the valuation of special-purpose properties; instead, they tend to relax the rules of evidence and comparability in evaluating these properties. The three classic approaches to value used in the appraisal of real estate all have severe limitations when applied to special-purpose properties due to the absence of adequate market data. Many appraisers tend to apply the cost approach to value in appraising special-purpose properties because of the mechanical nature of this approach. Without adequate market data, however, the estimate of depreciation, particularly functional and economic obsolescence, generally lacks support.

Because the three standard approaches to value are not reliable, the appraiser is encouraged to use a commonsense approach in estimating the value of special-purpose properties. The valuation of such properties often requires some ingenuity on the part of the appraiser. The abandonment, or at least modification, of the three standard approaches to value by the appraiser has been heartily approved by the courts. Due to the unique nature of special-purpose property, the appraiser must often develop a complete understanding of the business operation conducted on the premises.

Many jurisdictions apply the substitute facilities doctrine to special-purpose properties that have a community use. This is particularly true when these properties are government-owned, but in some jurisdictions the doctrine has been expanded to include privately held property that is put to a community use on a nonprofit basis and is available to the general public. The substitute facility doctrine requires that compensation be the replacement cost of the improvements, without depreciation, plus the value of a substitute site. In some jurisdictions, this can be accomplished by the condemnor actually constructing such a substitute facility.

Because of the unique nature of special-purpose properties and the lack of market data pertaining to them, there is a considerable amount of divergency in value testimony.

> The extent and nature of the taking, as well as the nature of the specific property involved, can affect the appraisal approach and the proof that would establish value. Factors that it is believed will assist in solving special purpose problems include:
> 1. Avoid "market value" or qualify the definition of "market value" in takings from special purpose properties of a public or nonprofit owner.
> 2. Use more extensive consideration of income in valuing income-producing special purpose properties.
> 3. Allow more leeway as to proof admissible to establish the value of special purpose properties.
> 4. Avoid the Cost Approach, if possible, and the confining of proof to this approach. For the approaches used, use reproduction cost rather than replacement cost.
> 5. Consider extension of allowing the cost of a functionally equivalent substitute as compensation when dealing with other than publicly owned special purpose properties.
> 6. Value in use for special purposes, which is a form of value to the owner, must be recognized if the owner is to be indemnified for his loss.

7. Exercise a more extensive investigation and ingenuity by appraisers in determining and considering factors that affect the value of special purpose properties, particularly if an attempt is made to measure depreciation. . . .

The more factors that an appraiser can consider and the more reasons that he can use in arriving at his opinion, the more reasonable is his opinion. Opinions of value should be less extreme in either direction, and constitutional compensation should be more likely.[36]

Notes

1. American Institute of Real Estate Appraisers and the Society of Real Estate Appraisers, *Real Estate Appraisal Terminology,* rev. ed., Byrl N. Boyce, ed. (Cambridge, Mass.: Ballinger Publishing Co., 1981), p. 226.

2. George L. Schmutz, *Condemnation Appraisal Handbook,* revised by Edwin M. Rams (Englewood Cliffs, N.J.: Prentice-Hall, Inc., 1963), p. 163.

3. In re Lincoln Square Slum Clearance Project, 15 A.D.2d 153, 222 N.Y.S.2d 786.

4. Julius L. Sackman, *Nichols' The Law of Eminent Domain,* rev. 3rd ed. (New York: Matthew Bender, 1979) Vol. 4, §12.32[1].

5. "Uniform Eminent Domain Code," (1974) § 1004 (a), p. 10.7.

6. Tlingit and Haida Indians of Alaska v. United States, 389 F.2d 778.

7. *Encyclopedia of Real Estate Appraising,* rev. ed., Edith J. Friedman, ed. (Englewood Cliffs, N.J.: Prentice-Hall, Inc., 1968). See Chapter 36, "Appraisal of Church Property," pp. 782-822.

8. Ibid. See Chapter 38, "Appraisal of a Country Club," pp. 837-842.

9. *Appraisal Reporting Techniques,* Vol. 4 (Chicago: American Institute of Real Estate Appraisers, 1954). See "Appraisal of a Truck Terminal," pp. 1-30.

10. *Encyclopedia of Real Estate Appraising.* See Chapter 35, "Appraisal of Cemeteries," pp. 772-781.

11. Ibid. See Chapter 38, "Appraisal of a Country Club," pp. 837-842.

12. Ibid. See Chapter 43, "Appraisal of Motion Picture Theaters," pp. 908-930.

13. Ibid. See Chapter 34, "Appraising an Automobile Laundry," pp. 763-771.

14. Ibid. See Chapter 41, "Appraisal of Hospitals and Medical Centers," pp. 881-889.

15. Ibid. See Chapter 42, "Appraisal of Nursing Homes," pp. 890-907.

16. Edward E. Level, *Valuation and Condemnation of Special Purpose Properties,* National Cooperative Highway Research Program Rep. No. 92 (Washington, D.C.: Highway Research Board, 1970), p. 5.

17. Ibid., p. 13.

18. United States v. 84.4 Acres of Land, 224 F. Supp. 1017, aff'd 348 F.2d 383.

19. *Encyclopedia of Real Estate Appraising,* p. 761.

20. Shelby County R-IV School District v. Herman, 392 S.W.2d 609, (Mo.).

21. *Nichols',* Vol. 4, § 12.3121[1].

22. *Valuation and Condemnation of Special Purpose Properties,* p. 22.

23. *Nichols',* Vol. 4, § 12.3121[1].

24. Sanitary Dist. of Chicago v. Pittsburgh, Ft. W. and C. Ry. Co., 216 Ill. 575, 75 N.E. 248.

25. State Roads Commission v. Novosel, 117 Me. 552, 102 A.2d 563.

26. *Nichols',* Vol. 4, § 12.32[3][b].

27. Ibid.
28. See Chapter 7, "Cost Approach to Value."
29. *Nichols'*, Vol. 4, § 12.32[3][b].
30. Ibid.
31. *Valuation and Condemnation of Special Purpose Properties,* p. 18.
32. State Commissioner of Transportation v. Township of South Hackensack, 65 N.J. 377, 322 A.2d 818.
33. *Nichols'*, Vol. 4, § 12.32 [3][d].
34. United States v. 564.54 Acres of Land, 506 F.2d 796.
35. "Uniform Eminent Domain Code," (1974), § 1004 (b), p. 10.7.
36. *Valuation and Condemnation of Special Purpose Properties*, p. 47.

CHAPTER 11
DAMAGES IN PARTIAL TAKING CASES

Damages, "[i]n condemnation, [is] the loss in value to the remainder in a partial taking of a property. Generally, the difference between the value of the whole property before the taking and the value of the remainder after the taking is the measure of the value of the part taken and the damages to the remainder. Two types of damages are recognized: consequential and severance."[1] Damages cannot result, of course, when the sovereign acquires the entire ownership because compensation is made for the taking of the total property, and there is no remainder left to damage.

Real Estate Appraisal Terminology defines consequential damages and severance damages as follows:

> CONSEQUENTIAL DAMAGES—A damage to property arising as a consequence of a taking and/or construction on other lands. In many states owners may be compensated for damage as a consequence of a change in grade of a street which adversely affects ingress to and egress from the affected property. In some states property owners are not legally entitled to consequential damages which occur to their real estate. Owners may not be compensated for damage to business, frustration, and loss of goodwill which result as a consequence of a taking or construction by the government.[2]

> SEVERANCE DAMAGES—It is the diminution of the market value of the remainder area, in the case of a partial taking, which arises (a) by reason of the taking (severance), and/or (b) the construction of the improvement in the manner proposed.[3]

It can be concluded, therefore, that all consequential damages arise from the taking of, or construction on, property other than that consequently damaged, and that this type of damage may or may not be compensable or actionable. Severance damages are generally considered compensable.

Terminology in regard to damages creates confusion between the appraisal and legal professions. Although the appraisal definition of consequential damages specifies that the damage always results from the taking of, or construction on, property other than that consequentially damaged, *Nichols'* states, "[a] distinction must be drawn between consequential damages to a remainder area where part of a tract is physically appropriated and consequential damages to a tract no part of which is physically appropriated. In the latter case, the damage must be peculiar to such land and not be such as in [sic] suffered in common with the general public. In the former case, it matters not that the injury is suffered in common with the general public. The sole test in such case is whether the damage complained of is directly attributable to the taking."[4]

This definition conflicts with the appraisal profession's use of the term *consequential damages*. Thus, the terms *consequential damages* and *severance damages* have caused considerable misunderstanding between appraisers, lawyers, and the courts. "The term 'consequential damage' is ambiguous in character, and is not truly relevant to any discussion respecting the different classes of damage. In the proper sense of the term, all damages must of necessity be consequential, since all damage is the consequence of an injurious act. The use of the term introduces an equivocation which is detrimental to any hope of a clear settlement of the question."[5]

To avoid confusion, the terms *consequential damages* and *severance damages* will not be used here; instead, the terms *compensable damages* and *noncompensable damages* will be used. Any further classification of damage is too pedantic for the purposes of this discussion.

Measure of Damage

Damages can only result in the case of a partial taking.[6] The taking need not be a physical taking, but may be the taking of a property right. "In this regard, what constitutes a 'taking' of private property is not susceptible of facile definition, but it is axiomatic that 'it is the character of the invasion [by the sovereign], not the amount of damage which results from it . . .' which determines the question of whether there has been a taking."[7] For instance ". . . a material injury to the easement of view is a taking of property. . ."[8] It is the damage to that part of the tract not taken which is compensable, in addition to the property or property right actually taken. This damage arises from the actual taking and/or from the use of the land taken in the manner proposed.

Damages are often dependent on the construction on, or other utilization of, the land acquired by the condemnor. For example, if the acquisition depicted in Figure 11.1 is for public park purposes, any damages to the remainder would be

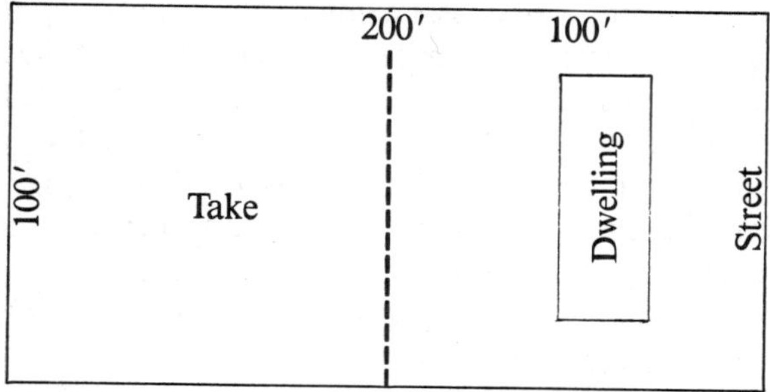

Figure 11.1. Utilization of the Area Taken

considered differently than if the land were being acquired for construction of a limited-access interstate freeway. Before an appraiser begins to estimate damages to a remainder property, he must thoroughly understand the proposed use of the portion of the tract being acquired by the condemning agency.[9]

It is also necessary to fully understand what rights are being acquired by the condemnor. An owner is entitled to consideration for the damage the condemnor has the power to inflict. Nevertheless, it cannot be assumed that the condemnor will put the property taken to that use which is most damaging to the remainder.[10] The appraiser must determine whether the condemnor is required to put the land taken to the specific use proposed on the date of valuation, or whether the condemnor has the right to expand or change the use of the land taken at some future date.

For instance, Figure 11.2 depicts a proposed taking for a new limited-access

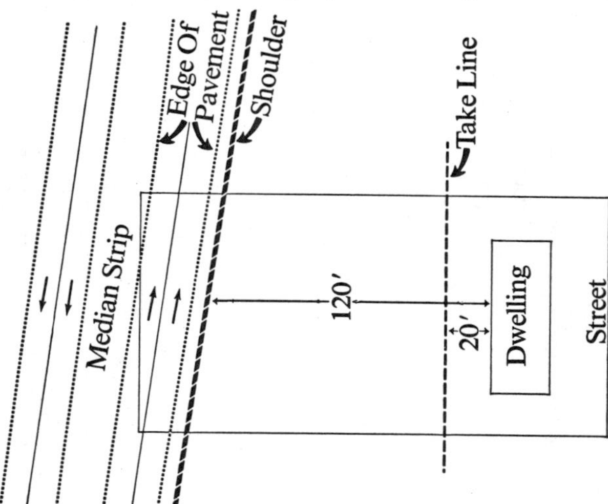

Figure 11.2. Proposed Utilization of the Land Taken

highway and shows the proposed construction of this project. The appraiser must consider whether the condemnor is limited in its utilization of the area taken, or whether the condemnor may, at a later date, expand or realign the highway facility bringing the traveled roadway to within 20 feet of the dwelling located on the remainder. If the latter is the case, as it generally is, the damage is not measured as if such expansion had, or even will, take place, but rather in recognition of the condemnor's right to expand its use without additional compensation. It is not what the condemnor actually does or plans to do with the land acquired that determines the amount of damage suffered by the remainder, but rather what the condemning agency acquires the right to do.[11]

This type of damage is generally measured by analyzing sales of properties similar to the property under appraisal in the after situation. This analysis will often show whether buyers and sellers in the marketplace believe that the likelihood of future highway expansion is so great as to affect the current market value of the property in question.

Another question the appraiser must consider is whether a condemnor can, at a future date, partially or totally change the use for which the property is being acquired. Can the municipality acquiring land for park purposes later convert the land into a garbage dump? Consider the situation shown in Figure 11.3. In this factual situation, the easement for the construction and maintenance of a drainage canal was acquired. A number of years later, the condemnor devised a plan to use the canal maintenance area as a public bicycle and pedestrian path as well as for canal maintenance. The condemnor's right to put the easement area to this

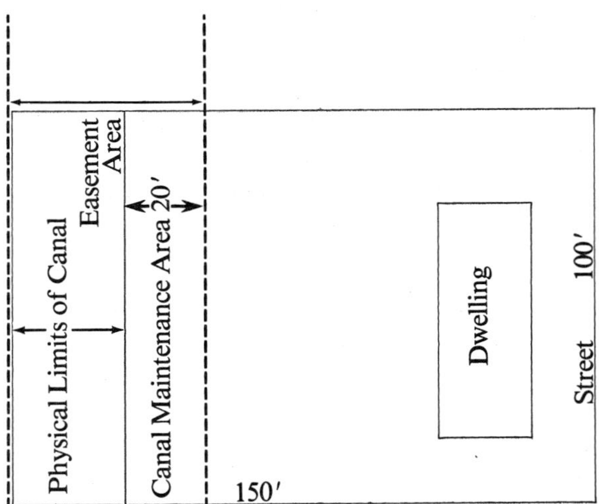

Figure 11.3. Rights Acquired

additional use, without acquiring any additional right or paying additional compensation, hinged, in this instance, on the specific terminology of the original easement.

The example illustrates the importance of determining exactly what rights are being acquired by the condemnor. If satisfactory clarification cannot be provided by the acquiring agency, the appraiser must obtain legal instructions in regard to the rights being acquired. For self-protection, the appraiser must explicitly state what rights are assumed to be acquired in both the appraisal report and in valuation testimony.

In many jurisdictions, the appraiser is not technically required to specifically identify or estimate the dollar amount of damages; he need only estimate the market value of a property before the partial acquisition and the market value of the remainder property immediately after the proposed acquisition and public construction. From a practical standpoint, however, it is imperative that the appraiser attempt to isolate and identify all elements of damage present in the remainder property. This is not to say that the appraiser must, or even should, estimate a specific dollar amount for each of the damage items, only that he acknowledge and consider each.

Whether the appraiser is working under the *federal rule* or *state rule* of measuring just compensation,[12] the procedural steps of valuation are the same. The estimate of damages should include no more conjecture or speculation than is allowed in the appraiser's estimates of market value before and after acquisition. Damage estimates must exclude highly improbable damages, but reflect those damages that would be considered significant by prudent buyers and sellers. In considering damages ". . . the general rule is said to be that where it is possible to separate the element of damage to remaining lands due to the use of the land taken from the owner, from the damage thereto flowing from the use of lands taken from others for the same project, the measure of damage is limited to that caused by the use of the land taken from the owner."[13] However, it is recognized ". . . that it is difficult, if not impossible, to separate one element from the other, and that under the circumstances the owner of the remainder area is entitled to all damage caused by the use of the entire project."[14]

The appraiser measures damages, not as an end in itself, but to assist in better estimating the value of the remainder tract. In other words, the estimate of damage is the basis for arriving at a proper adjustment, which will be applied to various market data in valuing the property in the after situation. One of the most commonly used and reliable methods of estimating damage is by analyzing comparable sales using the matched pairs technique. Damages can also be estimated by capitalizing the net rent loss resulting from the damage item.

A third method of estimating a proper adjustment for damage is known as the *cost to cure*. This method can be used in situations where a property has suffered a damage which can be physically and economically corrected,[15] e.g., correction of drainage, replacement of fencing, reestablishment of physical access, and replacement of sewage or water systems. Under no circumstances, however, can the cost to cure measure of damage be applied if the cost to cure exceeds the diminution in value if such cure were not undertaken.[16]

Again, the cost to cure estimate is only an aid to help the appraiser estimate the value of the remainder tract; it is not to be considered a separate damage item.[17] If the restoration or correction of the damage requires action outside of the remainder tract, this restoration cost, or cost to cure, cannot be considered. "The owner's right to compensation cannot be made to depend upon the question whether adjacent land could easily be bought."[18]

If the appraiser uses the cost to cure method to determine a proper adjustment, he must be careful to include *all the costs* that will be incurred. It must be remembered that the property is being appraised in its *uncured condition*. In other words, a purchaser of the property in the after situation will acquire it recognizing the need to cure the damage and incur the *direct costs* of the correction. Many appraisers make the mistake of not considering an *entrepreneur's profit* in determining a cost to cure adjustment.

To illustrate the fallacy of this methodology, assume two identical (or nearly identical) single-family properties (Parcels A and B), each having a before value of $75,000 as shown in Figure 11.4. An underground utility easement will be acquired across both parcels. After a detailed analysis of comparable properties,

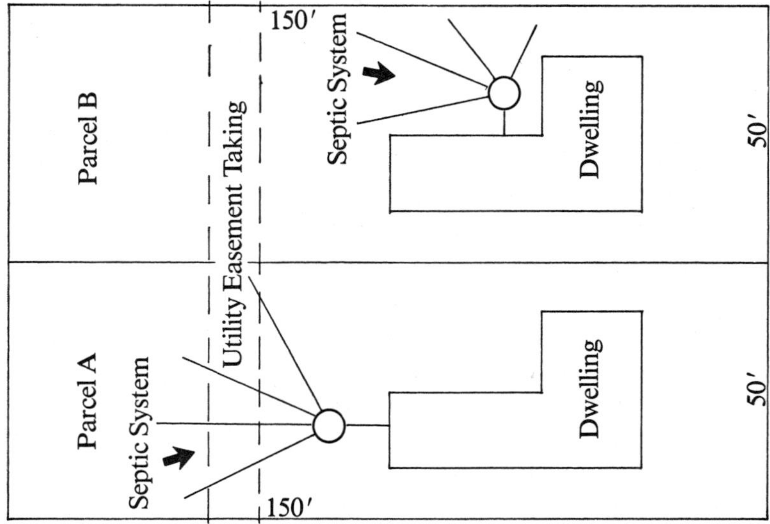

Figure 11.4. Partial Taking

the appraiser concludes that the existence of such an easement, in and of itself, has not resulted in any diminution in the values of properties similar to Parcels A and B. However, the septic tank and drain field systems serving Parcel A are located within the easement area and will, therefore, have to be relocated. No such condition exists on Parcel B.

The appraiser obtains a firm bid from a local contractor who can replace the septic tank on Parcel A for $3,500, including lawn repair, and have the new system installed about 30 days after the authorization to begin work is received. Therefore, the appraiser makes the following conclusions:

Valuation of Parcel A

Before value	$75,000
After value ($75,000—$3,500 cost to cure)	71,500
Difference	$ 3,500

Valuation of Parcel B

Before value	$75,000
After value	75,000
Difference	0

The appraiser must remember that the value of Parcel A in the after situation is in its *as is* condition.

Assume that immediately after the easement taking both Parcel A and Parcel B are placed on the open market for sale; Parcel A is listed at $71,500 and Parcel B at $75,000. Now, a potential purchaser inspects both of the properties and decides to acquire one of them. Which one will the purchaser buy? Will the purchaser buy Parcel B, which has a functioning and operable septic system, for $75,000, or will he acquire parcel A for $71,500, knowing that an additional $3,500 will have to be spent to install a new septic system?

It is obvious that a prudent purchaser would acquire Parcel B, and thereby avoid waiting for the installation of a new septic system and the hassle of obtaining the necessary septic tank installation permits from government agencies and dealing with the contractor or contractors installing the new septic tank system and repairing the landscape. This situation might be compared to a building contractor offering to sell a potential purchaser a newly completed house, or to build an identical house on the lot next door for the same price. Obviously, the purchaser will take the existing house, all else being equal, to avoid the hassle and delay which accompany any construction project.

Returning to the example, it is obvious that Parcel A has been damaged in excess of the *direct cost to cure*. The purchaser who acquires Parcel A, in its *as is* after condition, will need some incentive to undertake the construction project required as a result of the taking. This factor must be recognized by the appraiser in determining a proper *cost to cure* adjustment factor. The appraiser can recognize this factor by adding an *entrepreneurial profit* to the direct cost to cure, either in the form of a percentage of the contract bid or as a flat dollar amount. Both methods are acceptable, but to give no consideration whatsoever to entrepreneurial profit when estimating an appropriate cost to cure adjustment is ludicrous.

In considering the cost of replacement fencing, care must be taken to recognize all forms of depreciation in the remainder fencing. For example, assume the property shown in Figure 11.5 includes, in the before situation, a perimeter chain link fence of 600 L′, which has a replacement cost of $7.50 per L′ and a contributory, or depreciated, value of $5.75 per L′, or $3,450. The difference between the contributory value of the fencing and its replacement cost can be attributed to physical deterioration.

A partial acquisition occurs which will include the taking of 100 L′ of the fence. The value of the fence taken then is 100 L′ @ $5.75, or $575. However, it may be that the remaining fencing will suffer from additional functional obsolescence because it has a 100 L′ gap in it. It will cost $7.50 per L′, or $750 to close the gap. Thus, the proper procedure for estimating the contributory value of the fence before and after the taking would be:

Before value (600 L′ @ $5.75)			$3,450
After value:			
Replacement cost of fencing			
(500 L′ @ $7.50)		$3,750	
Less depreciation:			
Physical (500 L′ @ $1.75)	$875		
Functional (excess cost over			
value to reconnect fencing			
100 L′ @ $1.75)	175		
Total depreciation		1,050	
Total value of fencing—after			2,700
Just compensation for taking and			
damages to fencing			$ 750

The total or partial taking of a private water supply system or sewage disposal system may be analyzed in much the same way. Inspecting the property closely and interviewing the property owner is the only way to determine whether such underground improvements will be affected by the proposed acquisition. If the system must be replaced, it is imperative that the appraiser determine whether the local health authority will allow the replacement and, if so, under what terms and conditions. Assuming physical replacement can be accomplished, the cost of such replacement should then be established.

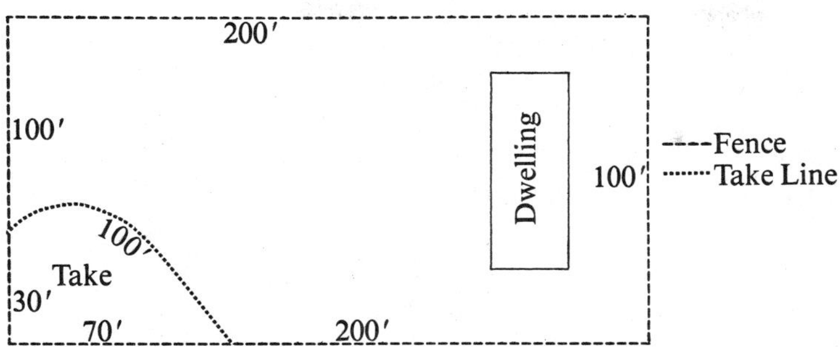

Figure 11.5. Partial Taking of Fence

It is of little consequence how many dollars an appraiser assigns to the value of the portion of the sewage disposal system taken and how much is assigned to damages to the remainder of the system not taken. Normally, the value of that part of the system taken plus damages to the remainder property will inevitably equal the cost of restoring the remainder system. Because it is difficult, in some areas, to estimate the cost to drill a well, a *well agreement* may be made between the condemnor and the condemnee whereby the condemnor agrees to replace the well taken, at its cost, with one of equal quality on the remainder site. In such a situation, the appraiser can usually assume that the remainder property includes a domestic water system equal to the one which existed before the taking.

Regardless of the methodology used, the estimation of compensable damage in the appraisal study must be done thoroughly and in logical steps.

Valuation Procedure

The appraiser's first step is to determine the larger parcel or parcels in the before situation.[19] It is important that the appraiser's determination of the larger parcel reflect the trinity of unity of use, unity of ownership, and physical contiguity. The second step is to estimate the highest and best use of the property in the before situation.[20] In doing so, the appraiser must try to ignore the fact that he will later be considering an after situation. The appraiser should adhere to the principle of *reasonable probability* in estimating both the highest and best use and the larger parcel. As a third step in the valuation process, the market value of the property being appraised must be estimated in the before situation, utilizing all applicable approaches to value. In all but the most unique circumstances, all three of the standard approaches will have some applicability. Again, the appraiser should try to ignore the fact that an after situation will later be considered.

The fourth step starts the procedure all over again, but this time in the after situation. The appraiser begins by determining the larger parcel in the after situation. A property may consist of one larger parcel in the before situation and two in the after situation, or vice versa.[21] As stated by one court:

> It is unfortunate that no witness on either side was asked to express an opinion as to the market value of the two remainder tracts if sold separately. . . . [I]n the absence of evidence to the contrary it may be assumed that the highest and best use of a farm cut in two by a condemnation remains the same after the taking as before, and that its highest value is still as a single unit, [but] this case is different. . . . The case presents a classic instance in which the remainder tracts should have been evaluated separately.[22]

The fifth step is the estimation of the remainder parcel's highest and best use. In making such an estimate in the after situation, the appraiser should give specific consideration to several factors, including the proximity of the new public improvement to the remainder parcel and the possible existence of special or general benefits by reason of the project.[23] The reduction in the land area and the change in the shape of the remainder parcel are also important considerations, as are changes in access to the remainder property and the nature of the public improvement to be constructed. In the after situation, the appraiser should consider all the elements a typical buyer and seller would consider. The final step is to estimate the value of the remainder property, again using all applicable approaches to value.

In estimating the value of the remainder tract, it is important for the appraiser to consider all observations made in estimating the highest and best use of the tract in the after situation and the effect, if any, of the proposed public improvement. It is also important that he look beyond the immediate boundaries of the remainder property for other forces that could affect the property's after value.

For example, Figure 11.6 illustrates the before and after situation of a single-family dwelling affected by the widening of an interstate highway. In the before situation, access to and from the property could be gained via the frontage road and the interstate, or via the frontage road and County Roads 1 and 2. In the after situation, the depth of the remainder parcel was only nominally reduced and the traveled lanes of the frontage road were no closer to the dwelling than before. However, the project called for: 1) the closure of the intersection of the interstate and County Road 1, 2) the closure of the intersection of County Road 2 and the interstate, and 3) the construction of a new roadway extending County Road 2 to connect with a new interchange on the interstate. The remainder parcel would suffer from some circuity of travel due to the closure of the two intersections, but this item of damage was ruled noncompensable before the trial.

Based on these facts alone, it would appear that the property in question suf-

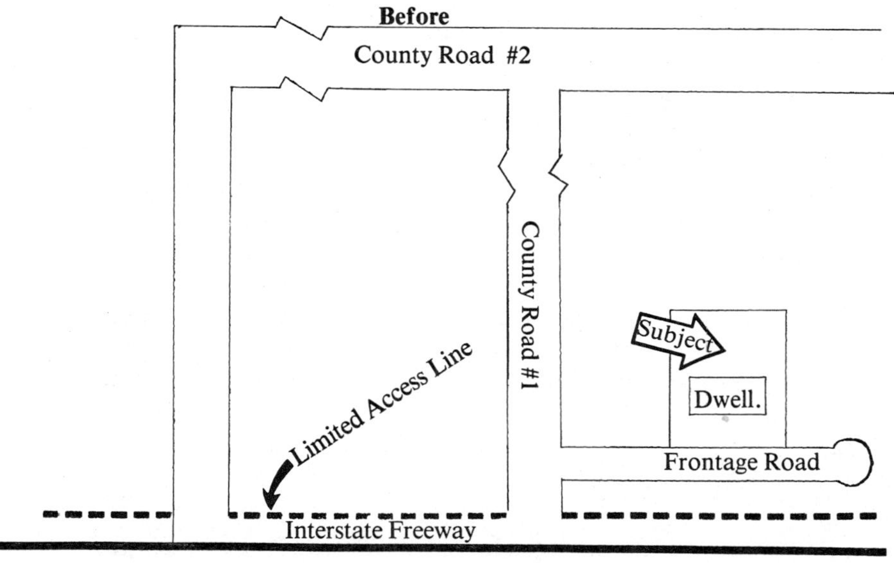

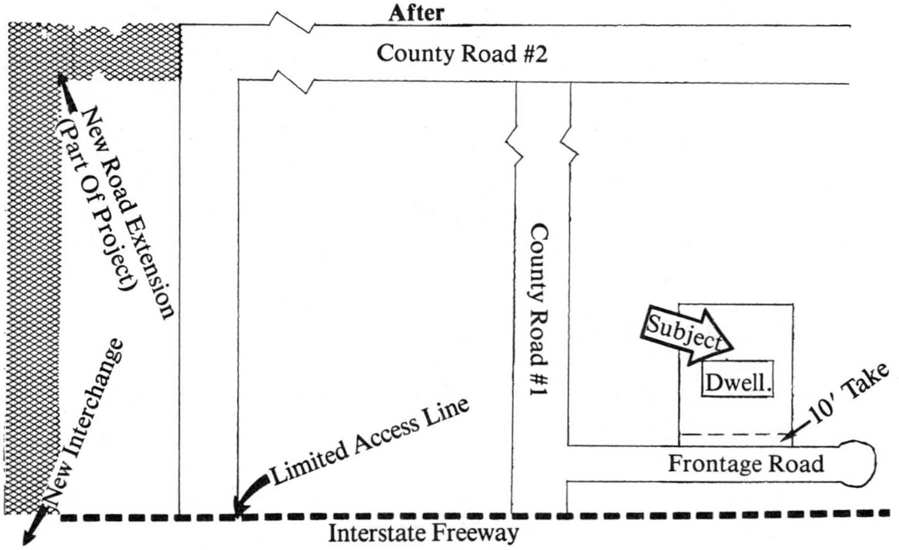

Figure 11.6   Damage—Loss of Adequate Access

fered little, if any, diminution in value by reason of the taking and that no compensable damage had occurred. However, the appraiser for the property owner testified during the trial that, in the preceding 15 years, County Road 1 was flooded an average of 45 days per year at a point two miles from the remainder property, and that during future flooding the only access to the remainder property would be by rowboat. As there were no plans to alleviate this flooding, the appraiser testified to extensive damage to the subject remainder. After an extended recess of the trial, at the request of the condemning agency, the condemnor stipulated in court that it would expand its project to include elevating County Road 1 so as to alleviate future flooding.

The difference between the appraiser's estimate of a property's before value and its after value is the value of that part of the tract taken, as a part of the whole, plus damages to the remainder, if any. Damages reflect the judgment of the appraiser and are based on market analysis, which often requires using different comparable sales in the after situation than in the before situation. A damage estimate is not an arbitrary percentage based on the appraiser's *vast years of experience*. As L.W. (Pete) Ellwood said:

> I believe experience can teach lessons which may lead to sound judgment. I believe sound judgment is vital in selecting the critical factors for appraisal. But, I also believe the bright 17-year-old high school student in elementary astronomy can do a better job estimating the distance to the moon than the old man of the mountains who has looked at the moon for 80 years. So, I find it difficult to accept the notion that dependable valuation of real estate is nothing more than experience and judgment.
>
> I would not give a red cent for an appraisal by the "expert" who beats his breast and shouts; "I don't have to give reasons. I've had 40 years experience in this business. And, this property is worth so much because I say so."
>
> After all, value is expressed as a number. And, no man lives who, through experience, has all numbers so filed in the convolutions of his brain that he can be relied upon to choose the right one without explicable analysis and calculation.[24]

Nevertheless, the appraiser must use common sense. For instance, assume an appraiser is appraising the property depicted in Figure 11.7 in an after situation, with the dwelling located three feet from the fenced right-of-way and its roof overhang on the line. It is not enough for the appraiser to conclude that the dwelling suffers no proximity damage just because no comparable sales of dwellings

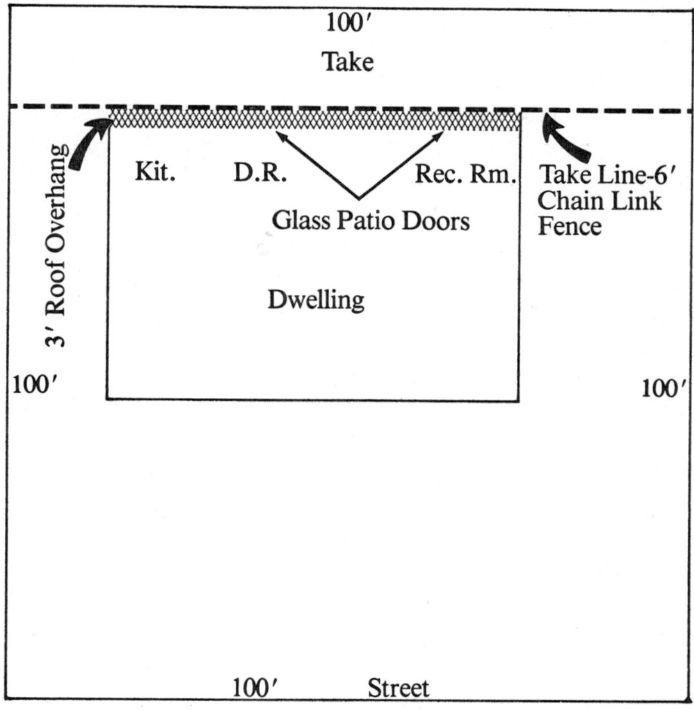

Figure 11.7. Proximity Damage

three feet from an interstate highway right-of-way can be found in the market-place. The appraiser must use some sound judgment in such matters, whether or not strong market evidence exists.

Some condemnors' right-of-way procedures seem to encourage the appraiser to conclude that a remainder property has suffered no damage. A staff appraiser is given a specific amount of time to complete an assignment or a fee appraiser is given a flat fee to complete such an assignment. If damages (and/or special benefits) are not found, the sales, income, and cost data used in appraising the property in the before situation may still be applicable in the after situation; if damages (and/or special benefits) are found, it is often necessary for the appraiser to collect and analyze a new set of cost, income and sales data, which, of course, is much more time-consuming. In this way, the appraiser may be tempted to ignore potential damages. Conversely, the condemnee's appraiser is often faced with a comment such as, "I don't want you to make an appraisal unless you can come up with damages." The appraiser must guard against all such pressure, and be wary of anyone attempting to influence his judgment. Suggestions on handling these situations are discussed later in this work.[25]

Damage Causes

It is simply impossible to develop an all-inclusive list of potential damages that may accrue to property in a partial taking case. "The different elements of damage to remaining land recoverable when part of a tract is taken are as numerous as the possible forms of injury."[26] However, there are some types of damages which occur regularly.

In considering damages, the appraiser must remember that some state constitutions provide for the payment of compensation only when property is taken, while others require payment of compensation when a property is taken *or damaged*. Therefore, in the former case there must be an actual taking of a property right before compensable damages occur. In the latter case, compensable damages may result even where no actual taking has occurred, but the damage must be one peculiar to the property in question, not one suffered in common with the general public.[27]

If the appraiser is unclear as to the compensability of an item, a properly supported legal opinion should be obtained. If the compensability of the damage item is not clearly established by applicable law, the attorney should inform the appraiser of this fact and instruct him to prepare two after appraisals—one including the questionable damage item and one excluding it. In this way, the appraiser will be prepared to testify on this issue regardless of the court's ruling. Sometimes, it is possible for an attorney to submit the questionable item of damage to the court for its determination prior to the condemnation trial.

The appraiser must avoid going on a witch-hunt looking for damages. "[D]amages are never presumed, and they will not be allowed if based on speculation or conjecture."[28] Unless the alleged damage has a demonstrable impact on the market value of the remainder property being appraised, it cannot be considered by the appraiser.[29] Such items of damage are considered too remote and speculative to merit consideration. For this reason a court disregarded an owner's contention that the construction of a railroad across his land would result in tramps using his barn.[30] In another case, a court ruled that a farmer's contention that his laborers would stop work to watch trains go by did not merit consideration.[31]

The existence of damages can most easily be discerned in cases where the highest and best use of the property is diminished in the after situation from that use existing in the before situation.[32] There may be a complete change in the highest and best use of the property, or the highest and best use that existed in the before situation may have to be modified. Generally, the most dramatic change in the highest and best use of a tract occurs when a property is landlocked, or left without legal access, in the after situation. From a technical standpoint, it can be said that such a remainder does not have a highest and best use, but merely helps hold the world together; its only practical use is its sale to an abutter.

The property may actually lack a market value, in the true sense of the word. The number of potential buyers for such property is often so severely limited that the property cannot, for all practical purposes, be placed on the open market. The number of abutting owners to a landlocked parcel will often have a bearing on its value in that these owners are often the only potential buyers for the remainder property. Another factor to be considered is the contribution the remainder property would make if merged with the various abutting ownerships.

The value of landlocked properties is typically measured by analyzing similarly situated properties which have sold recently. Some appraisers question whether such sales can technically be called *comparable sales*. These properties are generally not available on the open market and the sellers are under undue compulsion to sell because of the limited number of potential buyers and the fact that the seller has no legal access to it. It is often difficult, if not impossible, to locate sale properties that are physically similar to the property under appraisal, but these sales are generally the only evidence on which the appraiser can base his after value estimate.

Due to the absence of physically comparable sales, the appraiser must often make a *landlock study* to estimate the property's loss in value due to the lack of access. Such a study is illustrated in Figure 11.8. Based on the information pro-

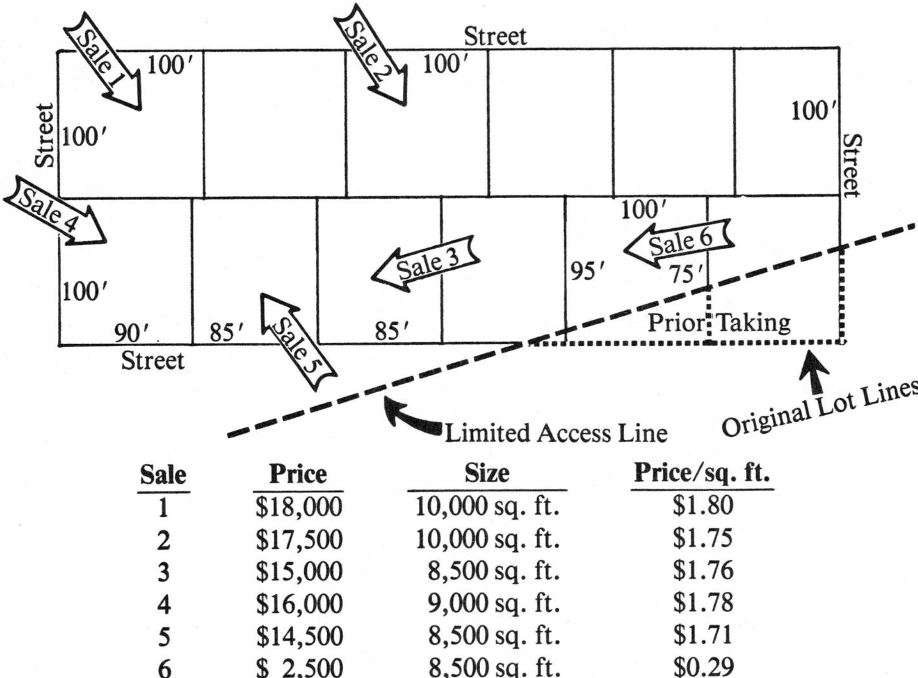

Sale	Price	Size	Price/sq. ft.
1	$18,000	10,000 sq. ft.	$1.80
2	$17,500	10,000 sq. ft.	$1.75
3	$15,000	8,500 sq. ft.	$1.76
4	$16,000	9,000 sq. ft.	$1.78
5	$14,500	8,500 sq. ft.	$1.71
6	$ 2,500	8,500 sq. ft.	$0.29

Figure 11.8. Landlock Study

vided, it might be concluded that the landlocked parcel (Sale 6) would sell for about $1.75 per square foot if it had access. In fact, it sold for 29¢ per square foot, indicating a diminution in value due to its landlocked condition of 29¢ ÷ $1.75, or 83%.

It is necessary to make a number of landlock studies to develop a pattern of value diminution. These studies may show a pattern in price paid per square foot, total price paid, or percent of price paid, as compared to prices paid for surrounding properties which are not landlocked. It is quite possible that the details of these studies will not be admissible, but this does not alter the fact that such studies are often the only basis for an appraiser's estimate of the value of the landlocked remainder. Even if the specifics of landlock studies are not admissible, the appraiser is generally allowed to, and should, testify that he has made the studies and that his conclusion as to the diminution in value of the property appraised (or its after value) is based on these studies.

A change in the shape of a tract due to a partial acquisition may have a damaging effect on the value of the remainder. The change in shape may make it impossible to develop the site with a building having the same degree of efficiency as the one that existed in the before situation. If the property is farmland, some inefficiencies may be created in the areas of cultivation or irrigation. Generally, the effect that an irregular shape has on the market value of the property is measured using comparable sales; however, a capitalized rent loss can be used in some instances.

A reduction in the size of a tract can result in a substantial reduction in the value of the remainder tract, particularly if the reduction transforms the remainder property into a nonconforming use under applicable land-use regulations. A taking could reduce the size of the tract below the minimum area required by applicable regulations, or the remaining amount of frontage, depth, or width could fall below the minimum required. If the property in question is improved, the taking may result in inadequate front, side, or rear yard setbacks. A taking could also create nonconformity in the amount of off-street parking required, or leave a remainder with too high a ratio of building to land area. If any of these conditions are found to exist, the effect of the nonconformity must be determined.

The applicable land-use regulation may have a provision which automatically provides that nonconforming properties are considered conforming if the nonconformity was created by a partial acquisition by a public agency. If not, the appraiser must determine if there is a reasonable probability that a variance could be obtained from the land-use regulation. The effect of the nonconformity on property maintenance, fire insurance rates, and the owner's ability to finance the property must also be ascertained. Depending on the specific effect of the reduction in size, the diminution in value can be measured using comparable sales or the capitalization of rent loss. In some instances, the appraiser can use the cost to cure, as in a case where the improved parking taken is replaced on a portion of the remainder not used for such a purpose in the before situation.

In considering a reduction in the size of a parcel, it is imperative that the appraiser keep in mind the concept of before and after value. Under the state rule (value of the part taken as a part of the whole plus damages to the remainder), it may be necessary to allocate the total difference between the before and after values to the value of the part taken and to damages to the remainder, but it is much safer to do so only after completing the before and after value estimates. If this is not done, the appraiser may be *double damaging* the property and thereby duplicating compensation. A Kentucky case illustrates this potential problem.

> The second basis for damages given by the two witnesses was that, by reason of lack of depth, a portion of the separated parcel had a reduced value for lot purposes. They computed the damages on the basis of percentages of a desirable lot depth. For example, at one end of the separated parcel, where the depth was only 55', one of the witnesses said that the value had been reduced 75%, so he computed that the original potential lot with a value of $1,000 had been damaged to the extent of $750. The trouble with this is that the landowners had already been allowed compensation in the award for the land *taken,* for the land that would have added the necessary depth to the 55' lot. In other words, if the back 75% of the lot is *taken,* and paid for, the landowner should not recover again, in the form of resulting damages, another 75% of the potential lot value. To do so would allow 150% recovery.
>
> It may be that if 75% of a lot were taken so as to render valueless, because of its smallness, the remaining 25%, the owner should be paid the full value of the lot. But he cannot be paid the value of the part taken and be awarded that value again as damages to the remainder.[33]

If the appraisers involved in this case had used a computational format like the one described in Chapter 2 of this text, or the form shown in Tables 2.1 and 2.2, this error would not have been made.

The taking or alteration of access rights, including changes in grade, physical access, light, view, and air, can result in damage to a remainder parcel. The change of a street grade, without a physical taking, is not compensable in all jurisdictions, so compensability must first be determined. A change of street grade can result in increases in the development costs of the remainder property or can eliminate existing driveway or road approaches. Therefore, the physical and economic practicability of replacing such approaches should be considered. In doing so, it may be necessary to investigate the need for a curved driveway, retaining walls and slopes, and the loss of usable site area needed for driveway fills or cuts. A change in grade can also alter the physical setback required for buildings on a site.

For example, Figure 11.9 shows the before and after situation of a single-family dwelling. In the before situation, the site was on grade with the street. After the taking, however, the street will be eight feet above the level of the site. To establish a new road approach at an acceptable slope, say 12%, it will be necessary to extend the drive about 67 feet beyond the right-of-way line, which would require removing the garage from its present location. Also, assuming a 2:1 slope of the driveway fill, more than 1,000 square feet of the site must be devoted to fill for the drive.

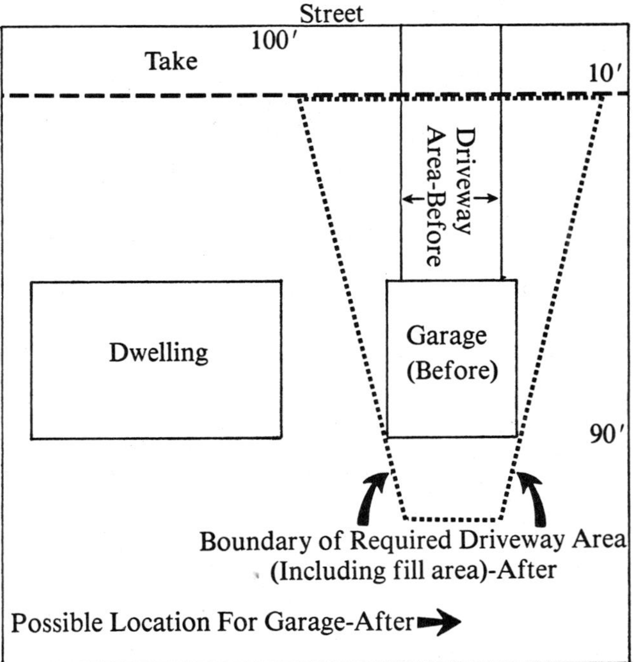

Figure 11.9. Change in Grade

The measure of damage in this instance would be the cost to construct the new approach plus either (a) the cost to demolish the garage and the diminution in the value of the property due to the lack of garage facilities, or (b) the cost of relocating the garage further back on the site to accommodate the new drive, whichever (a or b) is less. Further consideration would, of course, have to be given to the potential diminution value due to the greater amount of site area required for fill and driveway purposes and the fact that the site and improvements are eight feet below street grade. Any loss in value caused by these factors would generally be measured using comparable sales.

The severe loss, or limitation, of access, light, view, or air can alter the highest and best use of a property. Estimating these damages will require the use of different comparable sales in the after situation than in the before situation; thus, it can be said that such diminution in value is measured by the use of comparable sales.

The term *proximity damages* refers to damages "caused by the proximity of the remainder to the improvement being constructed, such as a highway. It may also arise from proximity to an objectionable site or improvement, dirt, dust, noise, or vibration."[34] This type of damage is typically measured using comparable sales. Once again, it is often impossible to find recently sold properties that are similar enough to the subject property in the after situation to use for direct comparison. Therefore, a *proximity study*, similar to the landlock study previously described, should be developed by the appraiser.

The appraiser investigates and analyzes several comparable properties which have sold recently and are located near public facilities similar to the proposed public improvement. The appraiser then compares each of these sale properties with other properties which have sold and are comparable to them, except for their proximity to the public improvements. From such studies, the appraiser can develop a range of potential damage attributable to the proximity of such a public facility.

At times the appraiser may find that there is no price difference between properties in close proximity to a public facility and similar properties located some distance away. However, before the appraiser concludes that no damages are attributable to proximity to the public facility, he must further investigate all of the sales utilized in the various proximity studies. It may be that although the eventual price paid for the properties reflects no proximity damages, a much longer time was required to sell properties near public facilities.

Table 11.1 illustrates such an analysis. If adequate data are available, a meaningful statistical analysis of the typical amount of time required to sell a property can be developed. Assume that the appraiser uses the data in Table 11.1 to conclude that dwellings close to a freeway can be sold in about 270 days, or nine months, while comparable properties away from the freeway are typically selling in about 90 days, or three months. If this is the case, the appraiser should consider the cost of holding the property for an additional six months as a possible measure of proximity damages. It is highly unlikely that a residential property can be rented while it is actively being marketed, so it is unlikely that any income can be generated with which to offset the holding costs. The appraiser should also consider whether the owner of the property is paying higher sales costs (e.g., a greater real estate commission) than the costs paid by owners of property removed from the freeway.

It is not necessary for the appraiser to make any conclusions as to why a property's value is diminished by its proximity to a public facility such as a freeway; in fact, it is probably advisable to avoid this issue. Some elements that one would normally assume are present in proximity damages, such as noise, have on occasion been ruled noncompensable.[35] It is probably best for the appraiser to simply determine, through market evidence, that single-family properties some distance from the freeway sell for X dollars, while comparable properties next to the freeway sell for Z dollars less. This procedure has been approved by the courts.

In making the appraisal, it is not only permissible, but necessary to consider all of the facts and circumstances that a prudent and willing buyer and seller, with knowledge of the facts, would take into account in arriving at its market value. The testimony of the defendant's expert which is here under attack indicates that he conformed to that formula. He properly and candidly included the facts that the new

Table 11.1

Proximity Study

Sale	List Price	Sale Price	Location	Days to Sell
1	$ 80,000	$79,500	On Freeway	265
2	82,500	82,500	No Prox.	64
3	87,750	84,000	No Prox.	108
4	78,000	78,000	No Prox.	92
5	67,500	67,500	On Freeway	272
6	62,000	60,000	No Prox.	87
7	71,000	70,000	No Prox.	70
8	65,000	65,000	No Prox.	91
9	95,000	92,500	On Freeway	294
10	91,000	90,000	No Prox.	36
11	97,500	97,500	No Prox.	102
12	100,000	97,500	No Prox.	76
13	57,000	56,000	On Freeway	198
14	60,000	60,000	No Prox.	94
15	55,500	55,000	No Prox.	87
16	62,500	62,000	No Prox.	38

freeway adjacent to the property, with the attendant increase in traffic and noises, were among the factors considered in making his appraisal. But *there was no attempt to segregate and place a separate money value thereon.* We think the trial court was well advised in admitting his testimony and that no prejudicial error was committed.[36] [added emphasis]

Like permanent takings, temporary takings may result in damages. Temporary damages can result when a condemnor acquires a permanent property right, fee or easement, plus a temporary easement beyond the permanent property right for construction of the proposed public improvement. After the initial construction of the public improvement is completed, the construction easement is extinguished and the unencumbered fee interest in the land reverts back to the owner. The fact that a taking is temporary in nature does not relieve the sovereign from paying just compensation.

Damages that result from temporary construction easements are usually based on the economic rent of the affected area for the term of the temporary easement; in the absence of rental data, the appropriate rate of return on the land for the term of the easement is estimated. For example, consider a partial taking of the farm shown in Figure 11.10. Assume that this 80-acre farm has a before value of $1,000 per acre and comparative analysis indicates that land encumbered by a permanent gas-line easement is diminished in value by 50%. Assume also that the temporary construction easement shown will have a term of 18 months and that

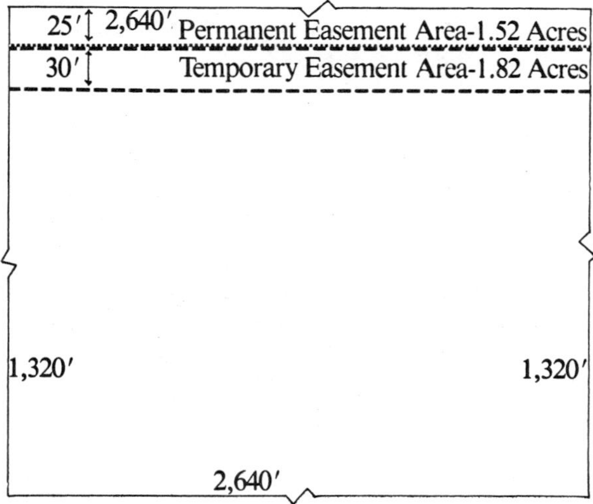

Figure 11.10. Temporary Construction Easement

comparable farmland will rent for $100 per acre per year. The property's after value would be computed:

76.66 acres @ $1,000		$76,660
1.52 acre permanent easement @ $500		760
Fee value of 1.82 acre temporary		
easement area @ $1,000	$1,820	
Less rent loss (1.82 acres @ $100		
× 1.5 years)	− 273	
Value of temporary easement area		1,547
Total after value		$78,967
Rounded		$79,000

If comparable rentals were not available, the appraiser would have to estimate an appropriate rate of return on the temporary easement area and adjust the value of the area to compensate the owner for losing the beneficial interest in the property for 18 months. If the rate of return were 10% per year, the property value in the after situation would be computed as follows:

76.66 acres @ $1,000		$76,660
1.52 acre permanent easement @ $500		760
Fee value of 1.82 acre temporary		
easement area @ $1,000	$1,820	
Less return on temporary easement area		
($1,820 @ 10%/year × 1.5 years)	− 273	
Value of temporary easement area		1,547
Total after value		$78,967
Rounded		$79,000

The rent loss (or appropriate return) is seldom converted to a present value through the application of a discount rate. Usually, the land area affected is so small and the term of the temporary easement so short that such a discounting process would be rather pedantic. Only when the rent loss is substantial and/or the temporary easement is of extended duration does the appraiser need to discount the rent loss, or return on investment, to a present value.

Noncompensable Damages

Some damages, as a matter of law, are noncompensable. However, care must be taken in determining compensability because, in some jurisdictions, an item of damage is compensable only if it is accompanied by a partial acquisition. An example of a noncompensable damage item might be the diversion of traffic which leaves a property with a highest and best use in the after situation inferior to its use in the before situation.[37]

Under no circumstances do damages that are remote or speculative merit consideration.[38] Generally, damages resulting from the sovereign's police power are noncompensable.[39] These actions would include changes in traffic patterns that increase or decrease traffic,[40] temporary blockage of a street or highway,[41] and deprivation of access, light, view, and air caused by a newly constructed limited-access highway.[42] Other items of damage which are generally noncompensable include loss of business,[43] tenant relocation,[44] moving of personal property,[45] and frustration of owners' plans.[46]

An annoyance or inconvenience[47] such as circuity of travel[48] is often ruled noncompensable because the damage is shared with the public in general and is not peculiar to the remainder property. For the same reason, noise, dust, and fumes from highway traffic are generally ruled noncompensable.[49] Since the introduction of successful inverse condemnation avigation easement suits, however, there is a trend toward recognizing noise as a compensable damage item in all types of condemnation so long as the damage has a detrimental effect on the property's market value in the after situation. Also, when noise levels reach an unreasonable level, they have been ruled compensable, even when no physical taking has occurred. For instance:

> The instant case does not involve a physical taking of respondent's property. This fact does not prevent an award for damages under Article 1, Section 16, the Washington constitution (amendment 9). Generally, compensation is not allowed in such circumstance where the injury or damage is one suffered in common with the general public. On the other hand, where the injury or damage is special or peculiar to the particular property involved and not such as is common to all the property in the neighborhood, compensation may be allowed not as a distinct element of damage, but only as it may affect the market value of the property. The measure of damages is the difference between the fair market value before and after the infliction of the damage. . . .

> We believe the [freeway] ramp to be constructed in this case may create an echo chamber for one-way traffic immediately adjacent to the south end of respondent's warehouse and may thereby materially affect the fair market value of respondent's property. This is a special damage differing in kind from the damage sustained by other properties due to the improvement in question. In this situation the jury may consider noise as a factor, if it is a factor, in determining the before and after fair market values of respondent's property. It is not, how-

ever, to be singled out separate and apart from all of the other relevant factors in determination of the market values.[50]

A reasonable fear of danger due to the taking and/or proposed construction and operation of public improvements, if such fear is well-founded, has universally been held to be compensable.[51] However, fear of danger that is unfounded has met with mixed reaction. Those jurisdictions ruling that unfounded fear is a compensable item take the position that any item that has a detrimental effect on the market value of the remainder property is a proper consideration.[52] On the other hand, other jurisdictions have ruled that unfounded fear is not a proper consideration because the damage was not caused by the condemnor's taking, but rather by "the ignorance, prejudice or folly of those who wrongly conceive and believe that it will cause them damage."[53]

Summary

Damage, as used in condemnation, is the loss of value of a remainder property in a partial taking case brought on by the taking and/or the construction and operation of a proposed public improvement. The appraiser is advised to avoid using the terms *consequential damages* and *severance damages* because of the existing confusion in regard to their precise definitions. In conjunction with the sovereign's right of eminent domain and its act of condemnation, the appraiser need only segregate damages into categories of compensable damages and noncompensable damages.

The owner is not compensated for what the sovereign plans to do with the land acquired, but, rather, for all damage the condemnor will have a right to inflict on the remainder property. The appraiser must therefore fully understand not only what the condemnor proposes to do with the land taken, but also all of the things it is acquiring a right to do.

Damages are estimated in order to better estimate the market value of a property being appraised in the after situation. Damages are not individual items of consideration and an owner is not entitled to compensation for each on an individual basis. The three most commonly used measures of damage are: 1) damage indicated by analysis of comparable sales, 2) cost to cure, and 3) capitalized rent loss.

To ensure that all elements affecting value are considered, the appraiser must perform the appraisal assignment in a logical progression. The steps to be followed by the appraiser in valuing property in a partial taking are:

1) Estimate larger parcel before acquisition.
2) Estimate highest and best use before acquisition.
3) Estimate market value before acquisition.

4) Estimate larger parcel after acquisition.
5) Estimate highest and best use after acquisition.
6) Estimate market value after acquisition.

The possible damages to a remainder parcel are so varied that an all-inclusive list cannot be prepared. Damages are definitely indicated when the highest and best use of the property has been diminished in the after situation from that existing in the before situation. Not all damages to remainder property are compensable; remote and speculative damages have universally been held noncompensable. Many damages have been ruled noncompensable when the damage is not accompanied by a taking, but they are considered compensable when accompanied by a taking. Therefore, the appraiser should not make blanket assumptions regarding the compensability or noncompensability of a particular damage item. The appraiser should ask legal counsel to determine the compensability of any damage item in question.

Notes

1. American Institute of Real Estate Appraisers and the Society of Real Estate Appraisers, *Real Estate Appraisal Terminology*, rev. ed., Byrl N. Boyce, ed. (Cambridge, Mass.: Ballinger Publishing Co., 1981), p. 69.

2. Ibid., p. 57.

3. Ibid., p. 218.

4. Julius L. Sackman, *Nichols' The Law of Eminent Domain*, rev. 3rd ed. (New York: Matthew Bender, 1979), Vol. 4A, § 14.1.

5. Ibid.

6. In re Condemnation of 2719,21, 11 E. Berkshire St., 343 A.2d 67 (Penn.).

7. Florida East Coast Properties, Inc. v. Metropolitan Dade County, 572 F.2d 1108.

8. Bramson v. Berea, 293 N.E.2d 577 (Ohio).

9. See Chapter 15, "Construction of the Public Improvement."

10. United States v. River Rouge Impvmt. Co., 269 U.S. 411, 46 S.Ct. 144.

11. Manlius Center Road Corp. v. State, 370 N.Y.S.2d 750.

12. See Chapter 2, "Legal Measurements of Just Compensation."

13. Public Service Elec. & Gas Co. v. Oldwick Farms, Inc., 125 N.J. Super 31, 308 A.2d 362.

14. *Nichols'*, Vol. 4A, § 14.21[1].

15. State Highway Comm. v. Speck, 230 Ark. 712, 324 S.W.2d 796.

16. Arkansas State Hway. Comm. v. Ptak, 263 Ark. 105, 364 S.W.2d 794.

17. Dep't of Transportation v. Gonterman, 354 N.E.2d 76 (Ill.).

18. *Nichols'*, Vol. 4A, § 14.22.

19. See Chapter 4, "The Larger Parcel."

20. See Chapter 5, "Highest and Best Use."

21. *Nichols'*, Vol. 4A, § 14.24.

22. Commonwealth, Dep't of Highways v. Rowland, 420 S.W.2d 657 (Ky.).

23. See Chapter 13, "Benefits—General and Special."

24. L.W. Ellwood, *Ellwood Tables for Real Estate Appraising and Financing* (Ridgewood, N.J.: L.W. Ellwood, 1959), Preface p. IX.

25. See Chapter 21, "Standards of Practice."

26. *Nichols'*, Vol. 4A, § 14.24.
27. Feltz v. Central Nebraska P.P. & I. Dist., 124 F.2d 578.
28. State, Dep't of Highways v. Gordy, 322 So.2d 418 (La.).
29. United States v. Chandler-Dunbar Water Power Co., 229 U.S. 53, 33 S.Ct. 667.
30. Louisville, etc. R. Co. v. Hall, 143 Ky. 497, 136 S.W. 905.
31. Yazoo, etc. R. Co. v. Jennings, 90 Miss. 93, 43 So. 469.
32. State, Dep't of Highways v. Beatty, 288 So.2d 900 (La.).
33. Commonwealth v. Raybourne, 364 S.W.2d 814 (Ky.).
34. *Real Estate Appraisal Terminology*, p. 194.
35. Fairchild v. Oakland etc., R. Co., 176 Cal. 629, 169 P. 388.
36. State Road Comm. v. Rohan, 487 P.2d 857 (Utah).
37. Labriola v. State, 351 N.Y.S.2d 464, rev'd 36 N.Y.2d 328, 368 N.Y.S.2d 147, 328 N.E.2d 781.
38. United States v. Chandler—Dunbar Water Power Co., 229 U.S. 53, 33 S.Ct. 667.
39. Morshead v. California Regional Water Quality Control Board, 119 Cal. Rptr. 586.
40. Commonwealth, Dep't of Highways v. Yates, 383 S.W.2d 340 (Ky.).
41. Commonwealth, Dep't of Highways v. Fister, 373 S.W.2d 720 (Ky.).
42. State v. Calkins, 50 Wash.2d 716, 314 P.2d 449.
43. Stripe v. United States, 337 F.2d 818.
44. Springfield, etc., R. Co. v. Schweitzer, 173 Mo. App. 650, 158 S.W. 1058.
45. Pause v. Atlanta, 98 Ga. 92, 26 S.E. 489.
46. United States v. Easement & Rt. of Way, etc., 447 F.2d 1317.
47. Wyoming State Highway Dep't. v. Napolitano, 578 P.2d 1342 (Wyo.).
48. Houghs v. Mackie, 1 Mich. 554, 137 N.W.2d 289.
49. Commonwealth, Dep't of Highways v. Cleveland, 432 S.W.2d 825 (Ky.).
50. City of Yakima v. Dahlin, 485 P.2d 628 (Wash.).
51. Texas Electric Service Co. v. West, 560 S.W.2d 769 (Tex.).
52. Collins Pipeline Co. v. New Orleans East, Inc., 250 So.2d 29 (La.).
53. City of Meriden v. Zwalniski, 88 Conn. 427, 91 A. 439.

CHAPTER 12
DEVELOPMENT APPROACH

"The most characteristic illustration of the rule that market value is not limited to value for the existing use and the situation in which it is most frequently invoked (and also most frequently abused), is where evidence is offered of what the value of a tract of land that is used for agricultural purposes (or is vacant and unused) would be if cut up into house-lots."[1] This approach to value is commonly known as the *development approach* or *anticipated use method* of valuation. It is "[a] method of estimating the value of vacant land. The usual application is to raw, unsubdivided land by deducting from the estimated gross selling price, the direct expense of development such as cost of streets, utilities, sales, advertising, and overhead (taxes, carrying charges, inspection). Profit and 'time lag' (interest on the money invested for the time needed to complete the project) are also deducted, after which the land value is indicated."[2]

This method of land valuation has also been referred to by various courts as the *lot method*[3] and *the developer's residual approach.*[4] The development approach to value has not been given special treatment in this text merely because it is widely applied in eminent domain valuation. It has been singled out for two other reasons. First, there has been a great deal of controversy and confusion among the various courts as to the applicability of this approach, and, therefore, a considerable amount of case law has developed on the subject. Secondly, in many cases the development method has been applied under the wrong circumstances or in the wrong way.

There is no *single, right way* to apply the development approach to value. Because the approach is continually misapplied, the American Institute of Real Estate Appraisers has developed and published *Subdivision Analysis,* an educational memorandum on subdivision analysis and the development approach to value.[5] There are seven different methods of subdivision analysis demonstrated in this publication; all of them are correct, but some are more applicable under certain circumstances.

Applicability

The development approach becomes the primary, and sometimes the only, method of valuation when:

1. The appraiser concludes through proper market analysis that the property in question does, in fact, have a highest and best use for subdivision purposes;
2. Comparable before and/or after sales are lacking; and
3. Adequate market and/or technical data are available with which to reliably estimate the value of the property being appraised by the development approach.

In analyzing a property's highest and best use for subdivision purposes, the appraiser must consider factors such as supply and demand, zoning, available utilities, the direction of population growth, physical characteristics of the property being appraised, and local legislative attitudes towards development of properties in the area. The property in question may range from raw acreage to a site nearly 100% developed. With a more developed site, of course, there is a stronger case for determining a highest and best use for subdivision purposes and for using the development approach to value. It is also advantageous to have data on some recent sales of developed lots which were originally part of the tract being appraised so that the demand for developed lots is demonstrated by factual market data. "The bald assertion by the condemnee or his witnesses that such a demand exists is not enough. Such a demand must be established by competent proof."[6]

If comparable sales are available, they should be used in evaluating the property under appraisal. If the sale property is truly comparable, it will have the same potential as the property being appraised. As one court put it, ". . . the comparable sales relied upon by both expert witnesses in valuing the subject property involved properties purchased by developers for development purposes and accordingly were sales in which development costs had been considered and were reflected in the sale price. To add an increment to the value established on the basis of these sales [is] to inflate and distort the market value of the Subject Property."[7] A New York case stated, "[t]he court actually valued the property as having a residential development potential by relying upon the state's comparable sales. In the present case there was no need for a separate increment value to be found by the appraisers or the court because the market data inherently included the value in raw acreage sales."[8]

This is not to say that under such circumstances the development approach should be totally disregarded; rather, it should be used to support the indicated value of the property developed using comparable sales. The process used in the development approach can often give the appraiser greater insight into the relative comparability of the sale property. Although many condemning agencies will not allow the development approach to be used as the only measure of value, they recognize it as supportive evidence. For instance:

"Item 4—Valuation of Property

A. Site Analysis and Evaluation

Rules:

. . . .

"The employment of the hypothetical subdivision to develop raw land value may be introduced to support market value and to illustrate the amount of money a prudent purchaser would likely pay for raw subdivision land. However, due to the many variables and speculative elements, *the estimate of value is never based solely upon such hypothesis.*"[9] [emphasis added]

If the appraiser cannot find any raw acreage sales with development potential comparable to the property being appraised, he may want to reexamine his original analysis of supply and demand for developed lots and his estimate of the property's highest and best use. If no actual market data as to retail lot prices, development costs, sellout times, etc., are available in the neighborhood, the appraiser should again review his analysis of supply and demand and his estimate of highest and best use. Technical data can be obtained from engineering firms active in the area of plat design and development cost estimating, or from contractors engaged in the installation of underground utilities and/or construction of other subdivision improvements.

Appraisal Procedure

If the development approach is applicable, the appraiser must apply it in a logical progression. The development approach to value is nothing more than the *land residual technique* applied to land with a highest and best use for subdivision purposes. In fact, if an owner/developer were going to develop lots and lease them on a long-term basis rather than sell them, the two procedures would be identical.

The procedure outlined below is typical in the application of the development approach to value. It is not necessarily the only process which will work, nor is this process best in every instance.

First, the appraiser should determine the number and size of the lots which can be developed. After completing his highest and best use analysis, the appraiser should be totally familiar with the applicable subdivision ordinances as to minimum lot sizes, widths, and depths; minimum street right-of-way width; pavement width; etc. He must bear in mind, however, that land often is not developed to its maximum allowable density or to the minimum improvement requirements. Analyzing existing subdivisions and lot sales in the area will help determine the *typical conditions,* as well as the *minimums and maximums* legally allowed.

It is often advisable, particularly in preparing for trial, to request that an engineering consultant help lay out the most economically and physically practical plan for subdividing the property. Topographic maps of the property in question can be extremely useful in this process. The appraiser and the engineer should work together to construct a subdivision plan which will develop marketable lots and still produce the greatest residual value for the raw acreage in its present state.

The appraiser will work with a *paper plat* showing the number, size, and shape of anticipated lots and the proposed street rights-of-way and open space. He will accurately estimate the *retail value* of each lot by comparing the proposed lots with similar, fully developed lots in the same neighborhood which have sold recently. If no such lot sales exist, it is possible to estimate the value of the lots using the *abstraction method*[10] of site valuation. However, if the abstraction method of value is necessary because there are no comparable lot sales in the area of the property being appraised, the appraiser should again reconsider his estimate of highest and best use.

It is not always necessary to estimate the retail value of each potential lot within the parent tract; often, it will suffice to estimate only the average or typical value of the lots. From this estimate, the cumulative retail market value of all potential lots within the property under appraisal can be computed.

The next step in this process is to estimate the direct cost of physically developing the tract under appraisal into a completed subdivision. Such costs will include items such as engineering, street construction, installation of underground utilities, street light installation, and construction of sidewalks. Also to be considered are indirect development costs such as the increasing development fees charged by local municipalities to generate additional revenues and/or discourage additional development within its boundaries. A further indirect cost to be considered is the cost of advertising and sales. The cost of administration and overhead during the development and sellout period must also be estimated. These costs would include taxes, insurance, interest charges, financing fees, and inspection fees. This information can be obtained from the actual market experience of similar developments, from engineers, from contractors, from real estate agents, or from a combination of these sources.

By deducting the estimated direct and indirect costs of development from the cumulative retail value of all the potential lots, the appraiser can calculate how much of the amount remaining is attributable to entrepreneurial (developer's) profit, raw land value, and any necessary discount for the time required for full absorption of all lots by the market.

It is necessary to deduct a profit factor from the value of the lots to compensate the developer for his time, trouble, and risk. It is also necessary to deduct for time here because, in any subdivision of substantial size, a consideratble period could elapse from the beginning of the development process to the sale of the last lot. Therefore, the developer could be receiving his net income over a period of years, and the income stream must be converted into a current value by discounting it at an appropriate risk rate. Applying the appropriate discount rate will result in the indicated market value of the property being appraised in its present, undeveloped condition.

The preceding steps may be summarized as follows:

1. Prepare subdivision layout to determine number, typical size, and shape of potential lots;
2. Estimate the retail value of lots;
3. Estimate direct development costs;
4. Estimate indirect development costs;
5. Compute income residual to developer's profit and land (Step 2 minus Steps 3 and 4);
6. Deduct developer's profit from Step 5;
7. Estimate amount of time required to develop and sell out subdivision;
8. Discount anticipated income streams into a current indicated raw land value.

The federal court has summarized the procedural steps of the development approach as follows:

> In arriving at their values, the owner's witnesses took into consideration the market data of sales of adjacent subdivided lots and made deductions for selling and advertising expenses, engineering and development costs, overhead costs, taxes, buyer's anticipated profits, and for acreage lost for streets, etc., in order to reflect or indicate the value of the property at the time of taking. In this case, the data relied on was derived from the market and facts as had been generated in the development of adjacent land. This method is referred to as the "developer's residual approach."[11]

Figure 12.1 illustrates how a relatively small tract (19.90 acres) might be subdivided into 60 lots. Table 12.1 shows how the development approach could be applied to this property. All direct unit costs have been applied to a linear footage of streets; this methodology is commonly used in making preliminary estimates of this type and is also used in some cost manuals.[12]

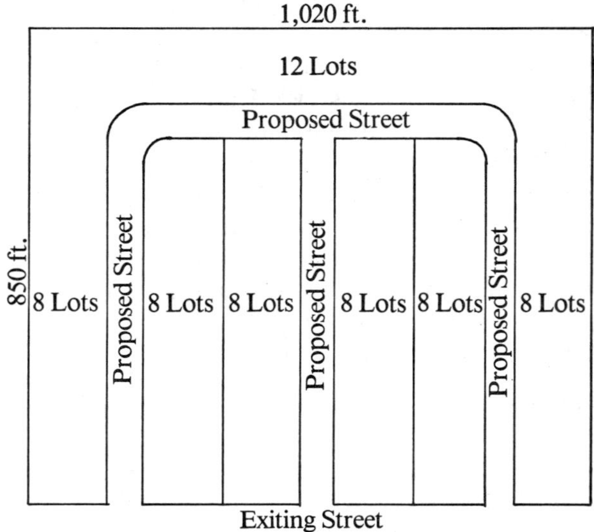

Figure 12.1. Proposed Subdivision Layout

The costs per unit used in Table 12.1 include all engineering, plan, and inspection fees. Direct costs can generally be more accurately estimated with various unit costs than with a cost per linear foot of street. Unit costs might include the cost per actual street light, sewer manhole, or fire hydrant. Per cubic yard of grading or per cubic yard of base rock measurements are also generally accurate. The costs used in Table 12.1 were selected merely to demonstrate the application of the development approach, and they should not be construed as typical or all-inclusive. The sellout time, developer's profit factor, and discount rate utilized were also selected for demonstration only.

Both the appraiser and the attorney should be aware of the basic assumptions built into this methodology. First, it is assumed that the expenses of development will occur steadily over each of the three years of the project, and that sales income will be spread evenly over the life of the project. In this instance, this means that exactly 20 lots will be sold each year.

These assumptions will be true only under the most unusual circumstances. This particular procedure has merit, however, because it is probably the most easily understood application of the development approach. Also, the actual pattern of development expenses and sales income may approximate the assumptions built into this method enough to warrant its use. After all, the development approach is an appraisal tool, not an exact mathematical formula. In using this methodology, the appraiser should be aware of the value differential which will result if the sales income and expenses are treated as they are actually anticipated,

Table 12.1

Development Approach to Value

Step 1. 19.90 acres @ 3.02 lots per acre =		60 lots
Step 2. 60 lots @ $17,500 =		$1,050,000
Step 3. Direct costs:		
Grading (2,740 L' @ $6.72)	$18,413	
Base rock (2,740 L' @ $8.96)	24,550	
Paving (2,740 L' @ $20.14)	55,184	
Curbs & gutters (2,740 L' @ $11.10)	30,414	
Concrete walks (2,740 L' @ $10.40)	28,496	
Sewer main (2,740 L' @ $12.40)	33,976	
Sewer laterals (2,740 L' @ $9.50)	26,030	
Sewer manholes (2,740 L' @ $2.43)	6,658	
Fire hydrants (2,740 L' @ $4.27)	11,700	
Street lighting (2,740 L' @ $6.50)	17,810	
Water main (2,740 L' @ $13.20)	36,168	
Water laterals (2,740 L' @ $3.25)	8,905	
Electric (2,740 L' @ $7.25)	19,865	
Total direct costs		(318,169)
Step 4. Indirect costs:		
Overhead & sales cost		
($1,050,000 @ 10%)	$105,000	
Management & supervision	36,000	
Taxes & insurance	12,500	
Total indirect costs		(153,500)
Step 5. Developer's profit & raw land value		$ 578,331
Step 6. Developer's profit ($1,050,000 @ 20%)		(210,000)
Net before cost of capital		$ 368,331
Step 7. Sellout in 3 years @ 20 lots per year.		
Step 8:		
Annual income stream ($368,331 ÷ 3)		$ 122,777
Discount rate factor (present worth of one per		
period, 3 years, 12%)		× 2.401831
Indicated raw land value		$ 294,890
Indicated value per acre ($294,890 ÷ 19.90)		$ 14,819

rather than as if they are spread evenly over each year. If the differential is significant, the appraiser may have to use one of the more complex methods of applying the development approach, which are demonstrated in the Institute memorandum mentioned earlier.[13]

Problem Areas

Much of the data used in applying the development approach can be supported by documented market evidence. However, there are two areas in which the appraiser must make conclusions which cannot be readily supported by market evidence. First, the appraiser's estimate of the sellout or market absorption period is affected by so many factors that the appraiser could spend hours answering hypothetical questions about how various economic trends could affect the development's estimated absorption time. He might be asked, "What if mortgage interest rates went up three points? What if the largest employer in the area reduced its work force by 50%? What if two competing subdivisions opened up directly across the street?"

In preparing to estimate absorption time, the appraiser should be fully familiar with the economic factors affecting the market in which the property being appraised is located. After ascertaining the general economic trends in the area, the appraiser should determine the geographic boundaries of the areas that will compete with the parcel under appraisal. This may be a neighborhood, a city, or an entire county. After this determination is made, the appraiser should make a physical inventory of the lots in developed subdivisions which could compete with lots developed from the parcel being appraised. Investigation should also be made as to whether any preliminary plats have been submitted for projects which could foreseeably compete with the property being appraised.

Next, the appraiser should ascertain the number of dwellings constructed in the neighborhood on an annual basis over the past several years. The results of this study, under normal circumstances, will indicate how many lots can be absorbed annually within the market area of the subject property. From this local, economic information, the appraiser can logically estimate the absorption time required to sell the subdivision anticipated for the property under appraisal. The appraiser must be careful in this area. If he testifies that a hypothetical subdivision of 400 lots can be sold out within two years, when historically only 150 lots have been absorbed each year in the entire area of competition, the court or trier of fact will be skeptical.

The appraiser's estimate of sellout time can be supported by some historical data, but the second problem area is even more a matter of pure judgment. The appraiser must estimate an appropriate developer's profit to be deducted from the retail price of the developed lots. In Table 12.1 a developer's profit amounting to 20% of the retail value of the lots was adopted for purposes of illustration. Most developers compute potential profit as a percentage of gross retail sales, so the procedure used to compute developer's profit in the table is representative of the typical thinking and actions of buyers in the marketplace.

However, the appraiser should recognize and acknowledge that not all developers make profit projections as a percentage of gross retail sales. Some developers provide for profit at a certain dollar amount per lot, others will project profit as a percentage of raw land costs, and still others will estimate profit as a percentage of raw land costs plus development costs. No matter which method of computing profit is used by the developer, the question for the appraiser remains: How much should be allowed for developer's profit in applying the development approach to value?

One method that can help the appraiser select an appropriate profit factor is to extract the actual profit earned by developers of completed subdivisions similar to the one contemplated for the property being appraised. Table 12.2 illustrates how a developer's profit can be extracted from sales data. In actual practice, of course, several subdivisions would be analyzed in the manner illustrated in Table 12.2 to establish a pattern of the net profit typically obtained by developers.

Table 12.2

Abstraction of Developer's Profit

22-acre parcel purchased for $286,000 and subdivided into 66 lots which sold for an average price of $14,500 each.

1. Gross retail price (66 lots @ $14,500)		$957,000
2. Direct costs	$270,000	
3. Indirect costs	140,000	
4. Total development costs		410,000
5. Profit and land cost		$547,000
6. Land cost		286,000
7. Profit		$261,000
8. Percent of profit ($261,000 ÷ $957,000)		27.3%

All figures above were verified by the developer.

The problem with this procedure, however, is that the computations are based on the amount of money the developer ended up with after the development was completed. In fact, the amount of money the developer received is not of concern to the appraiser; rather, the appraiser wants to know what the developer envisioned when he purchased the raw acreage. Unless the computed 27.3% profit factor is the amount of profit the developer anticipated when he purchased the land, it has little, if any, value to the appraiser in estimating an appropriate profit factor to apply to the property being appraised.

The computations shown in Table 12.2 may support the appraiser's conclusion as to an applicable profit factor, but his decision must be based on the expectations of the developer when he went into the project, not what he eventually got out of it. Therefore, extremely careful and extensive sales verification is required. It may also be helpful for the appraiser to determine whether developers active in the area have any general rules of thumb for anticipated profit which they use when purchasing raw acreage for subdivision purposes.

The Court's View

In an all too infrequent moment of lucidity and comprehension, one court stated:

> It is significant that the method of valuation used by [the appraiser] has been recognized by the American Institute of Real Estate Appraisers. Indeed, income capitalization in general and the anticipated use or development method in particular are standard appraisal practices. It would be unwise for us to require exclusion of such a widely recognized method of valuation through unduly rigid evidentiary rules.[14]

However, when the property in question is raw land and no steps have been taken towards subdivision development, either legally or physically, ". . . the 'lot method' approach to valuation may not be used."[15] Nor can the development approach be used just because a legal plat of the property being appraised has been recorded. "[T]he fallacy of treating land as subdivision land or as farmland depending upon whether or not a plat thereof had been recorded, is the conclusion that there is magic in the recording of a subdivision plat. Obviously the highest and best use of the land is not transformed from one thing into another by this ministerial act."[16]

This is not to say that the subdivision plan of a tract of land is inadmissible. These plans generally are admissible, but only in support of a witness's opinion as to the highest and best use of the land.[17] For this reason, it is often good trial strategy for a condemnor to stipulate that the highest and best use of the land is for subdivision purposes, if the question of highest and best use is not contested. This stipulation will often preclude the submission of any specific development plan, which will severely restrict the effective presentation of the condemnee's case. "Where both parties have conceded or agreed upon adaptability to the highest and best use of the land in question, the introduction of a plat showing the land as subdivided lots is merely cumulative and is subject to misconception by the jury, and should therefore be excluded by the trial court."[18]

As a general rule, it can be said that as a tract of land physically and legally progresses from a state of raw acreage to a completed subdivision, the development approach also progresses from inadmissibility to admissibility. These two extremes were discussed in a federal case.

> It may well be that even though the highest and best use of a property is for a residential subdivision, if no meaningful steps have been taken in that direction, viz., construction expenses and actual lot sales, then a "lot method" appraisal or a "developer's residual" approach, as it is also known, would be inapproporiate. But that is not the situation here. The status of the subdivision and its availability for sale within the reasonably foreseeble future was an actual and real one, certainly not hypothetical, remote or speculative. Someone about to purchase the property on . . . the date of condemnation, would have to regard it as having a highest and best use as a subdivision and, in determining what purchase price he would be willing to pay, would have to consider all factors, including sales price for individual lots and additional expense of development, in arriving at his decision.

> This is not a case where a landowner dreamily contemplates the use to which his property may be put at some undefined future time but rather one where the property is geographically suited for development; is located in a booming developmental area; has been subdivided into lots according to a duly certified map, has been cleared and graded and improved with the creation of a spring-fed lake; the construction of access roads, and the digging of a deep well sufficient to supply water to 150 homes; and where actual sales of lots as identified on the map have taken place, the deeds of which contain building restrictions compatible only with a residential real estate development.[19]

Nichols' addresses the admissibility of the development approach by stating that:

> It is well settled that if land is so situated that it is actually available for building purposes, its value for such purposes may be considered, even if it is used as a farm or is covered with brush and boulders.

> In some cases, however, condemnees have attempted to go so far as to show the number of lots into which a tract is divisible, estimate sales prices per lot and sales prices of comparable sales in the vicinity. In

such cases, however, the courts have uniformly adopted the approach that raw land as such, with little or no improvements or preparation for subdivision, may not be valued as if the land were in fact a subdivision. Thus, the "lot method" approach to valuation may not be used.[20]

But *Nichols'* goes on to say:

> In the case of land that has actually been fully subdivided, or nearly so, the courts are in agreement that the "lot method" or "developer's residual approach" valuation is proper. The problems involved in the partially developed subdivision have evaporated. The costs to the developer are no longer speculative, the value of the individual lots in the market may be ascertained with as much certainty as in any other condemnation proceeding, and the possibility of such a use is no longer remote.[21]

Thus, the *admissibility* of the development approach is not questioned in most jurisdictions when the property being appraised is either raw land or fully subdivided land. In the latter circumstance, the appraiser should carefully analyze his determination of the larger parcel.[22] If the lots affected by the taking are fully developed and salable as separate entities, it is possible that each individual lot represents a separate larger parcel and each should be appraised independently.

A problem arises when the land being appraised is neither raw acreage nor a fully developed subdivision, but falls somewhere in between these two extremes. There is no clear-cut rule applicable to such hybrid properties; for one property, a legal plat may have been filed, and on another, a portion of the property may have been physically and legally subdivided. There is simply no uniform rule as to what point the development process must reach before the development approach is admissible.[23]

The weight of authority, however, appears to favor starting with a raw acreage value and adding *incremental upward adjustments* for subdivision potential, legal steps taken towards actual subdivision, and physical steps taken towards actual subdivision development. Under such circumstances, "[t]he rule is clear. The actual market value of the lots insofar as that value is presently enhanced by the property's availability for subdivision may be shown, but the *possible future value* if subdivision were made may not be shown."[24] "There being no dispute that the most advantageous use of claimants' property at the time of taking was as a potential residential subdivision, the correct rule to be applied 'was to treat the premises not as raw acreage nor as part of the completed development but as a potential subdivision site giving the acreage an increment in value because of that potential use.' "[25] [citations omitted] "Whenever such an increment must be added to the raw acreage value to reflect a property's subdivision potential, then the specific increment which is selected and applied must be based upon sufficient evidence and be satisfactorily explained."[26] [citations omitted]

There is conflicting case law as to the admissibility of the actual costs of subdivisions such as the engineering fees and platting fees incurred by the owner of the property being appraised. Some jurisdictions allow the admission of such evidence, but only to better estimate the incremental value present in the property under appraisal, not as a separate value or damage item.[27] In other words, only the contributory value, not the actual cost, of such items may be considered.

The courts' resistance to admitting the development approach stems from a fear that testimony in regard to such an approach may mislead the trier of fact into determining just compensation on the basis of a fully developed subdivision, rather than on the land as it actually existed on the date of taking. Before attempting to present a case, or testify as to a value, based upon the development approach, extensive review of applicable law in the appropriate jurisdiction is required. This review must be made in light of the specific circumstances surrounding the property under appraisal.

Extensive pretrial conferences between the attorney and the appraiser will be required; the admissibility or nonadmissibility of the development approach may turn on a single question put to the appraiser by the attorney and/or on the appraiser's response to that question. The variability of the courts' view of the development approach was recently illustrated by a federal court decision in which the court said:

> There is some authority for the proposition that valuation evidence based on the lot method of appraisal should never be admitted in condemnation cases involving unimproved raw land. . . . We think the better view, however, is that a lot method appraisal can be admitted in appropriate cases . . ."[28]

The absence of definite rules in this matter was well stated in a lengthy discussion by the Indiana court:

> The line of demarcation between those circumstances in which testimony of specific intended use and lot by lot evaluation is admissible and those circumstances under which it is not, is too finely drawn for us to follow. We remain uninstructed as to the appropriate method for "properly guarding" such evidence so as to allow its admission.[29]

The Hybrid Property

As noted previously, the admissibility of the development approach is less in doubt when the property being appraised is either raw acreage or fully subdivided; divergence in rulings is most prevalent when the property being appraised falls somewhere between these extremes. Factual circumstances, applicable case law, and/or the condemnor's appraisal reporting requirements may necessitate some modification of the *pure* development approach to value. This modification may involve only the written and/or verbal presentation of the approach, or factual situations may require modification to the actual application of the approach.

To illustrate the application of the development approach in a before-and-after situation, assume the following set of circumstances:

1. The tract of land depicted in Figure 12.2 contains 25 ± acres and was acquired 10 years ago by a broker/developer.

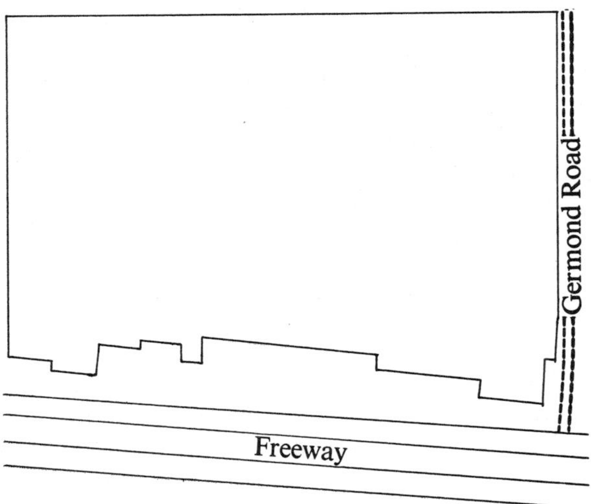

Figure 12.2. Plot Plan—Raw Land

2. *A preliminary plat,* or master development plan, of the land was submitted to the planning commission three years ago. This plan is depicted in Figure 12.3.
3. While the planning commission was considering the master plan, it was learned that the state planned to widen the freeway right-of-way to the east, which would have a direct effect upon the property. For this reason, the property owner requested only preliminary approval of the "master plan"

(Figure 12.3) and final approval on the development of the easterly portion of the property, consisting of the 14 lots depicted in Figure 12.4.

4. The preliminary master plan (Figure 12.3) and the final plat (Figure 12.4) were both approved.

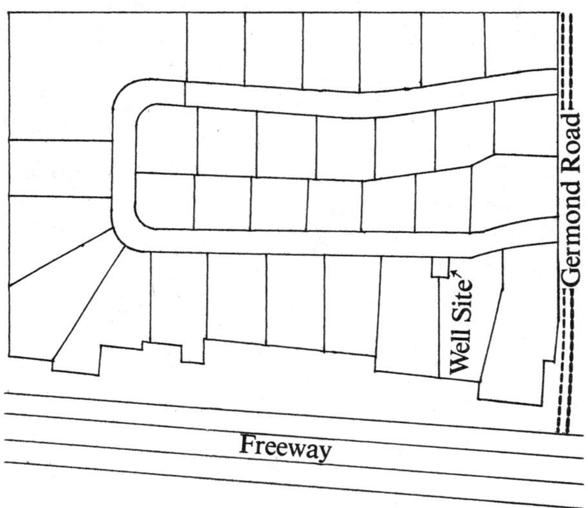

Figure 12.3. Master Development Plan

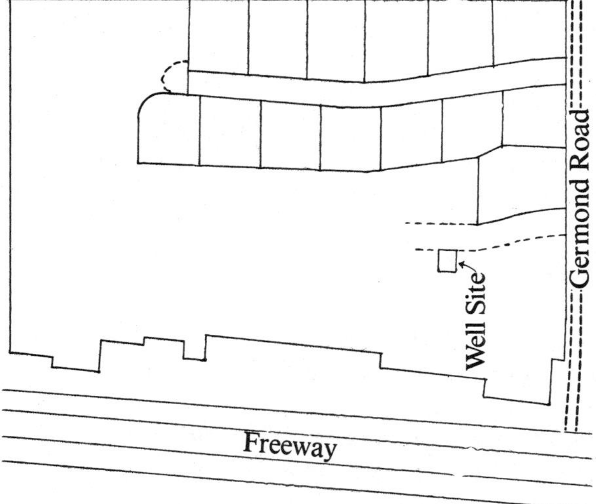

Figure 12.4. Final Plat

5. The property is located in a rural area, about 10 miles from a small city with a population of 40,000. There is no public water or sanitary sewer facility in the area.
6. In developing the easterly 14 lots of the property, the owner drilled a well and constructed a community water system adequate to supply domestic water to all 32 lots proposed in the original master plan.
7. The easterly 14 lots were developed and sold.
8. About one year later, the state's right-of-way plans were made public and the owner made no attempt to develop the tract further.
9. The state's right-of-way plan is superimposed over the original master plan in Figure 12.5. Because the original 14 lots were sold, the "larger parcel" is the unplatted portion of the tract consisting of 15.21 acres.

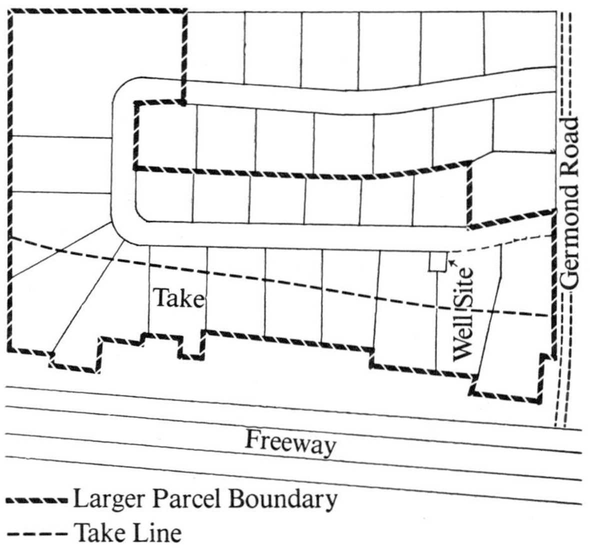

Figure 12.5. Larger Parcel

10. In the before situation, the tract is quite unique in that:
    a. It abuts a successful existing subdivision;
    b. A community water system is available to it;
    c. It is suitable for development with septic tanks;
    d. It has "preliminary master plan" approval;
    e. Preliminary engineering is complete on the tract; and
    f. Proposed streets have been *roughed in*.

Due to the unique nature of the tract, a market search uncovered no comparable sales. Analysis of the site indicates that the highest and best use of the tract, in the before situation, is completion of subdivision improvements in conformity with the original master plan. Based on the foregoing factors, the development approach to value is deemed appropriate.

Research indicates that all lots in the original subdivision sold for $12,500, regardless of their size, and that lot prices at a more recently completed subdivision across the freeway were $12,750, regardless of size. Based upon these data, a developed lot price of $12,750 is considered reasonable. With information from an engineering consultant, cost indexes, analysis of comparable subdivisions, and the appraiser's *data files,* the following development costs can be estimated.

Direct costs:
    (Final plat & construction
    engineering, grading, clearing,
    streets, and water lines) $55,000
Indirect costs:
    Overhead and sales expense   15% of gross sales
    Management and supervision   10% of direct costs
    Taxes during sellout $1,000

A two-year sellout period has been estimated based on the historical experience of the abutting subdivision and the subdivision across the freeway.

From the above data, the estimated before value of the property can be computed. These computations are shown in Table 12.3. Analyzing the remainder in the after situation leads to the conclusion that the highest and best use of the remainder tract is for residential subdivision and that the best method of subdivision follows the plan shown in Figure 12.6. To analyze the property in the after situation, the following factors must be considered:

1. Only nine lots can be developed, so nine lots have been lost.
2. The property contains 9.85 acres in the after situation.
3. The water system becomes an overimprovement.
4. All previous *master plan* approvals are void and all historical engineering data are of little or no value.
5. The average lot size is larger than in the before situation.
6. The tract will have 1,300 L' of frontage on the new frontage road and few interior streets will need to be constructed.
7. The new frontage road will carry a fairly high volume of traffic.

Investigation indicates that lots fronting on arterials or frontage roads are typically larger than interior lots, but this advantage is offset by the disadvantage of fronting on a highly traveled street.

Table 12.3

Before Situation—Value Computations

Gross sales (18 lots @ $12,750)		$229,500
Direct costs:		
Final platting & engineering, grading & clearing, street improvements, water lines		55,000
Subtotal		$174,500
Indirect costs:		
Sales and overhead ($229,500 × .15)	$34,425	
Management & supervision ($55,000 × .10)	5,500	
Taxes	1,000	
Total indirect costs		40,925
Net before return on capital and profit		$133,575
Discount income stream for two years @ 10% ($133,575 ÷ 2) × 1.735537*		$115,912
Less profit ($229,500 × 10%)		22,950
Indicated value of land "as is"		92,962

($92,962 ÷ 15.21 acres) $6,111.90 per acre
(rounded) $6,100 per acre

*Present worth of $1.00 per annum for two years @ 10%.

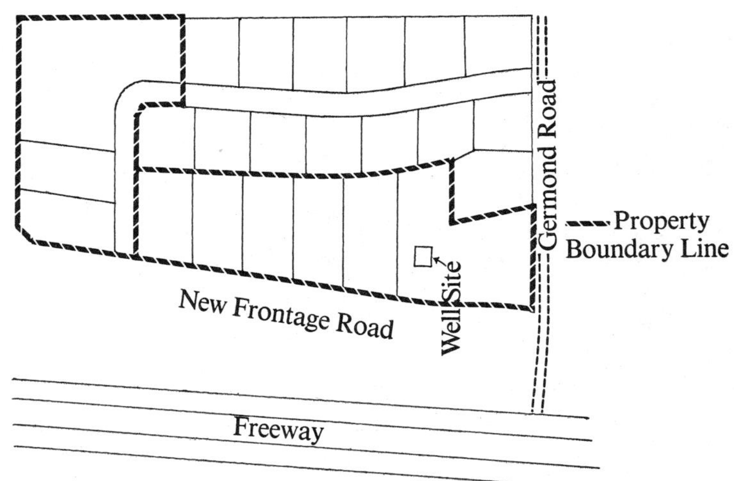

Figure 12.6. Plot Plan—After Situation

Based on these data, discussions with a consulting engineer, reference to cost indexes, and actual costs of comparable subdivisions, an indication of the *after value* of the property could be computed as shown in Table 12.4. In the after situation, street improvements per linear foot increased because part of the new street had not previously been roughed in. Also, water costs per linear foot increased because the water line could not be stubbed across the street. Engineering expenses per lot increased because preliminary engineering had been invalidated by the taking.

Table 12.4

After Situation—Value Computations

Gross sales (9 lots @ $12,750)		$114,750
Less direct costs:		
Engineering, grading, street improvements, water lines		40,900
Subtotal		$ 73,850
Less indirect costs:		
Sales & overhead ($114,750 × .15)	$17,213	
Management & supervision ($40,900 × .10)	4,090	
Taxes	400	
Total indirect costs		21,703
Net before profit,		$ 52,147
Less profit ($114,750 × .10)		11,475
Indicated land value		$ 40,672
or ($40,672 ÷ 9.85 acres) $4,129 per acre		
(rounded) $4,100 per acre		

Under the federal rule,[30] the appraiser's conclusion would be:

Before value (15.21 acres @ $6,100—rounded)	$92,800
After value (9.85 acres @ $4,100—rounded)	40,400
Difference	$52,400

Under the state rule,[31] the appraiser's conclusions would be:

Value before taking (rounded)	$92,800
Less value of part taken (5.36 acres @ $6,100)	32,696
Remainder (before)	$60,104
Less remainder after taking (rounded)	40,400
Damage	$19,704

Less special benefits	0
Net damage	$19,704
Plus value of part taken	32,696
Total difference	$52,400

The foregoing example demonstrates a relatively simple application of the pure development approach to value in a partial taking case. As the complexity of applying the approach increases, the chances of it being approved by either the court or a condemnor's review appraiser decreases. It may be necessary to modify the development approach or its presentation to ensure that it will be accepted. For example, in analyzing the before situation of the tract (Figure 12.3), the appraiser must first investigate and verify sales of vacant land which are comparable to the parcel under appraisal but without development improvements. The costs to develop each comparable are then estimated as the costs to develop the property under appraisal were estimated. For comparative purposes, it is often convenient to convert these cost factors to a cost per lot or cost per acre. This process is demonstrated in Table 12.5, using a hypothetical comparable sale of 20.2 acres which sold for $79,000. In actual practice, the appraiser may want to break this adjustment down for "comparable's lack of a water system, comparable's lack of preliminary engineering, etc."

From an appraisal standpoint, the comparative analysis shown in Table 12.5 is nothing more than a slightly modified application of the development approach to value. However, the development approach has not been used to estimate the value of the property under appraisal; rather, it has been used by the appraiser to assist in estimating and supporting a proper adjustment for the physical and economic differences between the comparable property and the property under appraisal. This adjustment factor is subsequently utilized in the market data approach to value.

Although this methodology may seem a bit devious (and perhaps it is), it is sometimes necessary for appraisers to resort to such procedures to ensure the acceptance of standard appraisal practices, which are widely recognized in the industry as valuable appraisal tools. This process is much like giving your dog his medication rolled up in a piece of hamburger; it's good for him—he just doesn't know it. The use of this methodology can mean the difference between the acceptance or rejection of an appraisal report by a condemnor's review appraiser. It can also mean the difference between the *admissibility* or *inadmissibility* of valuation testimony.

If an adjustment methodology has been used, the appraiser may want to meet with legal counsel to consider how much detail about the specific elements of the adjustment factor they want, or will be allowed, to present under direct examination. The appraiser may choose to testify only about the differences in the comparable and the property under appraisal, and the gross adjustment called for. He may state:

> I considered the fact that the sale property has no water system and the property under appraisal has a water system. I also considered the fact that the preliminary master plan has been approved for the subject, but none exists for the comparable; etc. After considering these differences, the indicated adjustment factor would be + $2,200 per acre, which would indicate a value for the property being appraised in the after situation of $6,100 per acre, or $92,800, rounded.

Table 12.5

Development Land—Comparative Analysis

	Comparable	Subject
Size	20.2 ac.	15.21 ac.
Number of potential lots	26	18
Gross sales @ $12,750	$12,750	$12,750
Direct costs per lot	(5,079)	(3,056)
Indirect costs per lot	(2,731)	(2,274)
Net before capital and profit	$ 4,940	$ 7,420
Discount		
$4,940/2 × 1.735537	$ 4,287	
$7,420/2 × 1.735537		$ 6,439
Less profit 10%	(1,275)	(1,275)
Indicated value per lot "as is"	$ 3,012	$ 5,164
Lots per acre	1.287	1.183
Indicated value per acre "as is"		
$3,012 × 1.287	$ 3,876	
$5,164 1.183		$ 6,109

Indicated per-acre adjustment for subject's well, physical developments, and greater development potential

($6,109 – $3,876)		$ 2,233
(rounded)		$ 2,200

Comparable price	$79,000
Comparable price per acre ($79,000/20.2)	$ 3,911
Adjustment for subject's lesser development cost	2,200
Indicated value of subject per acre	$ 6,111
(rounded)	$ 6,100

Further explanation of this adjustment factor could meet with objection and be ruled inadmissible. If on cross-examination, however, opposing counsel is so bold as to ask "And how, Mr. Appraiser, can you justify this outrageous adjustment of $2,200 per acre?" the appraiser should be prepared to explain this adjustment down to the smallest detail.

Summary

The development approach to value is a method of estimating the market value of a tract of land which has a highest and best use for subdivision purposes. "This procedure involves the comparison of undeveloped land to be appraised with a developed parcel or parcels for which individual lot sale prices are known. If available, data on sales of comparable raw land to developers is the best evidence of value. When such market data is lacking, however, the anticipated use or development procedure may be applicable to raw unsubdivided land, potential residential subdivisions, new neighborhoods, reuse neighborhoods, or industrial centers or parks. In some circumstances this procedure may be the only one available for valuing raw land."[32]

The development approach is simply the land residual technique applied to undeveloped land that has a highest and best use for subdivision purposes. There are many ways to apply the development approach and selecting the correct methodology often depends on the specific facts and circumstances surrounding the property under appraisal. Various applications of the development approach are discussed in detail in other publications.[33]

The best evidence of the value of raw subdivision land is derived from comparable sales. Although the use of comparable sales, when available, is the preferred approach to value, the development approach can, and often should, be used to support the indicated value of the property developed by the market data approach. If an appraiser testifies that the highest and best use of the property is for subdivision purposes and estimates its value using only comparable sales, with no reference whatsoever to the development approach on direct examination, the appraiser may still be subject to cross-examination concerning development cost factors. For instance:

> The appellants' theory was that the highest and best use of the tract was for a subdivision. This being a question and issue, there was no error, based on the record in this case, in allowing cross-examination of their witnesses regarding the cost of improving the property for the sale of lots for dwelling purposes.
>
> The same reasoning applied to the rebuttal testimony offered by the appellee. It being proper to examine the appellants' witnesses as to the

basis of their opinions on costs of subdividing, it was proper for the appellee to introduce evidence on its side as to such costs.[34] [citations omitted]

The procedural steps in applying the development approach to value are as follows:

1. Prepare subdivision layout to determine number, size, and shape of typical lots.
2. Estimate retail value of lots.
3. Estimate direct development costs.
4. Estimate indirect development costs.
5. Compute income residual to developer's profit and land (Step 2 minus Steps 3 and 4).
6. Deduct developer's profits from Step 5.
7. Estimate the amount of time required to develop and sell out the subdivision.
8. Discount anticipated income stream into a current indicated raw land value.

The most difficult items for an appraiser to support with market data are the estimated *sellout,* or *absorption, rate* and appropriate amount of developer's profit to deduct from the retail sale price of the lots. In estimating an appropriate factor for developer's profit, the appraiser must remember that this estimate should reflect what a developer would anticipate as a reasonable profit going into a proposed development project, not the amount of profit which a particular developer actually received at the conclusion of the project. Analyzing the actual profits received by various developers on completed subdivision projects can help the appraiser select an appropriate profit factor to use in the development approach to value, but this is not a conclusive test of the appropriateness of the profit factor.

As a general rule, the courts will not allow the development approach to be admitted into evidence when an attempt is made to apply it to raw subdivision land. On the other hand, when the land under appraisal is fully developed, or nearly so, most jurisdictions will allow the use of the development approach and admit evidence in this regard. Case law regarding the admissibility of the development approach for appraising properties that are neither raw land nor fully developed varies from jurisdiction to jurisdiction, primarily because of the different circumstances of each specific case. Some courts are reluctant to admit development approach testimony because they fear that such testimony will be misconstrued and/or misused by the trier of fact. Due to conflicting case law, it is imperative that an extensive investigation be made as to case law in the applicable jurisdiction prior to any attempts to utilize and/or testify to the development approach to value.

The development approach to value is most often applied to tracts that are between the two extremes of raw acreage and fully subdivided land. Therefore, modification of the procedural steps in applying the development approach is sometimes warranted. As the application of the development approach to value becomes more complex, there is less likelihood that it will be approved by the condemnor's review appraiser or by the court.

The methodology of the development approach to value can be of great assistance to the appraiser in analyzing the differences between a property in the before situation and the after situation. The methodology used in the development approach can be modified and applied to the comparative analysis of sales in the market data approach to value.

Because the development approach to value is complex, and case law concerning its admissibility conflicts, the appraiser should not attempt to use this approach, or testify to it, without the assistance of legal counsel, a consulting engineer, and other technical advisors. It follows, therefore, that the uninitiated appraiser should not attempt to use the development approach to value without associating himself with an appraiser who has had experience in its use. Also, the attorney with little eminent domain trial experience should not attempt to undertake a condemnation case involving the development approach to value without obtaining the assistance of an individual experienced in, and thoroughly familiar with, the legal and appraisal intricacies of this approach.

Applying the development approach to value is generally quite time-consuming and expensive. Similarly, preparation for trial and the trial itself are lengthy procedures for both the appraiser and the attorney, and thus expensive for their client. As a general rule, no other type of condemnation case requires the amount of pretrial conferences and pretrial preparation as a case involving the development approach to value. For these reasons, this type of case should not be undertaken by either the appraiser or the attorney unless the client is fully aware of the potential cost involved and is prepared to pay the price. Under no circumstances can the appraiser or the attorney go to trial without extensive pretrial preparation in a case involving the development approach to value.

Notes

1. Julius L. Sackman, *Nichols' The Law of Eminent Domain,* rev. 3rd ed., Vol. 4 (New York: Matthew Bender, 1979), § 12.3142[1][a].

2. American Institute of Real Estate Appraisers and the Society of Real Estate Appraisers, *Real Estate Appraisal Terminology,* rev. ed., Bryl N. Boyce, ed. (Cambridge, Mass.: Ballinger Publishing Co., 1981), p. 14.

3. United States v. 47.3096 Acres, etc., 583 F.2d 270.

4. United States v. 147.47 Acres of Land, 352 F.Supp. 1055.

5. American Institute of Real Estate

Appraisers, *Subdivision Analysis* (1978).

6. Shillito v. Metropolitan Edison Co., 434 Pa. 131, 252 A.2d 650.

7. Ridgeway Associates, Inc. v. State, 32 App. Div.2d 851, 300 N.Y.S.2d 944.

8. United Artists Theatre Circuit, Inc. v. State, 384 N.Y.S.2d 543.

9. Washington State Dept. of Transportation, *Right of Way Manual,* Chapter 4, Appendix 4-2, Appraisal Report Guide, Part IIC, § 4A, 12, p. 12 (Revised 11/10/76).

10. *The Appraisal of Real Estate,* 7th ed. (Chicago: American Institute of Real Estate Appraisers, 1978), p. 147.

11. United States v. 100 Acres in Marin County, 468 F.2d 1261.

12. *Marshall Valuation Service* (Los Angeles: Marshall and Swift Publishing Company, 1979), § 66, p. 1 (Revised 5/80).

13. *Subdivision Analysis.*

14. Dash v. State, 491 P.2d 1069 (Ak.).

15. *Nichols',* Vol. 4, § 12.3142[1][a].

16. State v. Maplewood Heights Corp., 302 N.E.2d 782 (Ind.).

17. Southern Indiana Gas and Electric Co. v. Riley, 260 Ind. 643, 299 N.E.2d 173.

18. City of Lafayette v. Beeler, 381 N.E.2d 1287 (Ind.).

19. United States v. 147.47 Acres of Land, 352 F.Supp. 1055.

20. *Nichols',* Vol. 4, § 12.3142[1][a].

21. *Nichols',* Vol. 4, § 12.3142[1][d].

22. See Chapter 4, "The Larger Parcel."

23. Dover Housing Authority v. George, 107 N.H. 202, 220 A.2d 156.

24. *Nichols',* Vol. 4, § 12.3142[1], N. 15.

25. County of Suffolk v. Firester, 37 N.Y.2d 649, 376 N.Y.S.2d 458, 339 N.E.2d 154.

26. Ridgeway Associates, Inc. v. State, 32 App. Div.2d 851, 300 N.Y.S.2d 944.

27. State v. Chang, 50 Haw. 195, 436 P.2d 3.

28. United States v. 47.3096 Acres, etc., 583 F.2d 270.

29. City of Lafayette v. Beeler, 381 N.E.2d 1287 (Ind.).

30. See Chapter 2, "Legal Measurements of Just Compensation."

31. Ibid.

32. *The Appraisal of Real Estate,* 7th ed., p. 147.

33. *Subdivision Analysis.*

34. Forest Preserve Dist. of Cook County v. Krol, 12 Ill.2d 139, 145 N.E.2d 599.

CHAPTER 13
BENEFITS—GENERAL AND SPECIAL

General and special benefits, like damages, can only occur in the case of a partial acquisition. When a total parcel is acquired, there is no remainder to which the benefits could accrue. Benefits, as used herein, are defined as "[t]he beneficial factors which arise from a public improvement for which private property has been taken in condemnation. There are two classifications of benefits, General Benefits, Special Benefits."[1] Every treatise on eminent domain includes an attempt to define and differentiate between general benefits and special benefits; none of these attempts has been completely successful. A sampling of these definitions follows:

> SPECIAL BENEFITS—Those benefits which accrue directly and solely to the advantage of the property remaining after a partial taking.[2]

> GENERAL BENEFITS—The benefits which accrue to the community at large, to the area adjacent to the improvement, or to other property similarly situated as that taken but which property is not taken.[3]

> SPECIAL BENEFITS—Benefits deductible in ascertaining the amount of damages to be awarded in eminent domain, as resulting from the improvement for which the land is taken and peculiar to condemnee's property or interest, not being shared by all the property in the vicinity.[4]

> GENERAL BENEFITS—For the purposes of the rule that "general benefits" are not to be deducted from compensation or damages in eminent domain:—Those benefits from the improvement which are

enjoyed, not only by the property of the condemnee concerned in the litigation, but also by other property.[5]

SPECIAL BENEFITS—Value accruing to the remainder of a property by reason of acquisition and use by the State or a portion of such property where such value is special to said remainder and not enjoyed by the general public. Benefits may be special although other owners on the facility receive similar benefits.[6]

GENERAL BENEFITS—Washington law does not clearly define general benefits. Because of this we have only attempted to explain special benefits and will assume that any benefits which are not 'special' may be properly considered to be 'general' benefits.[7]

Nichols' divides benefits into three separate classifications:

(1) Benefits peculiar to a particular estate by reason of its direct relation to the improvement;

(2) Local or neighborhood benefits, or those accruing to a well-defined and limited part of a city or town by reason of its proximity to the improvement;

(3) General benefits, or those which affect the community as a whole and perhaps raise the value of land in an entire city or town.[8]

The text goes on to explain that cases involving eminent domain do not separate benefits into these three, natural classifications; rather, ". . . benefits are arbitrarily divided into two classes, general and special, the special benefits including the peculiar benefits and to some extent the local ones."[9]

The courts do not seem to have fared any better in their quest for differentiating between special and general benefits. As one court said:

There is probably more judicial discord as to what is or is not a special benefit than in any other area of the law of eminent domain. Where there is an actual physical improvement to the property, such as the draining of a swamp, it is easy to see a special benefit. It is equally easy to recognize, at the other end of the spectrum, a general benefit such as an improved system of highways, since everybody in a community benefits from such an improvement. The difficulty lies in the amorphous grey area between these two extremes.[10]

"Upon this subject there is a great diversity of opinion and more rules, different from and inconsistent with each other, have been laid down than upon any other point in the law of eminent domain."[11] "This definition of and distinction between general and special benefits, while fundamentally sound, is too general to admit of ready application to specific situations. The difficulty arises not so much from recognition of the basic principles categorizing special and general benefits as in the application of the same to particular factual situations. The application of the distinction between general and special benefits is influenced by the nature of the eminent domain proceedings and the manner in which special benefits are to be utilized."[12]

The current status of special and general benefits was well summarized by Joseph M. Montano:

> Benefits have been classified into two general categories—general and special. The distinction, if indeed one can truly be made, is necessary because in most states it is only special benefits that can be considered as a proper offset against the damages to the residue or value of the land taken, or both. Courts use different terminology to define and distinguish benefits, and for the most part become hopelessly embroiled in an academic discussion of the difference between the two. The Courts appear to have lost sight of the essential thing (i.e., whether the remainder has in fact been benefited) and rather become preoccupied with a futile attempt to use magic words to distinguish between the two categories.[13]

Existence of Benefits

The appraiser and the attorney must first decide whether any benefits are present and, if so, does it make any difference whether the benefits are considered general or special? Of course, benefits can only accrue to a remainder property in a partial taking case. Therefore, the appraiser must carefully consider what constitutes the *larger parcel*.[14] Although a parcel may be owned by the same condemnee and may, in fact, be benefited by the project, benefits cannot accrue unless the parcel is an integral part of the larger parcel. Benefits are not caused by the taking of a portion of a tract of land, but by the use to which the condemnor will put the land taken.[15] It is important to differentiate between *project enhancement,*[16] which must be disregarded in the valuation of a property, and benefits.

Rules of Setoff

The existence of benefits and whether such benefits are general or special in nature have become important issues because of the different *benefit setoff rules* promulgated by various jurisdictions. It has been noted that five, separate benefit setoff rules are currently used by various jurisdictions in the United States. These five basic rules are:

Rule 1. Benefits, whether special or general, cannot be considered.

Rule 2. Special benefits only can be offset against damages to the residue, but not against the value of the land taken.

Rule 3. Special benefits and general benefits can be offset against damages to the residue, but not against the value of the land taken.

Rule 4. Special benefits can be offset against both the damages to the residue and the value of the land taken.

Rule 5. Special and general benefits can be offset against both damages to the residue and value to the land taken.[17]

Attempts have been made to classify each jurisdiction under one of these five rules. However, there is so much conflicting case law and statute law regarding the offsetting of benefits in some jurisdictions that a precise and totally accurate list which would be applicable in all circumstances cannot be prepared. As the following comments from various treatises dealing with the federal law on the offsetting of benefits illustrate, there is much confusion on this subject.

A controversial setoff question relates to the character of benefits that may be considered. Too frequently it is loosely stated, on the basis of dicta removed from context, that only special benefits may be considered, and general benefits must be excluded. It is the federal view that such position is supportable only if special benefits encompass all real and direct project benefits, and general benefits are equated to nonproject-related value appreciation.[18]

Federal Rule.—The federal rule holds that benefits may be offset against the part taken and the damage to the remainder. "In arriving at just compensation an offset should be made against the value of the thing taken, and the damage to the remainder, whatever enhancement in value may have resulted from the public work requiring the taking." (Dick v. United States, 169F. Sup 491)[19]

The setoff of general benefits, however, has been disapproved by the federal courts.[20]

Under federal law benefits *must* be considered and they are nonetheless to be offset even though the same benefits are enjoyed by other lands having the same relationship to the project. . . . While there are cases in which distinctions are attempted to be drawn between "general" and "special" benefits, the Department of Justice has urged in several briefs filed in federal appellate courts that the attempted dis-

Table 13.1

Benefit Offset Rules

Jurisdiction	Rule 1	Rule 2	Rule 3	Rule 4	Comments
United States				X	
Alabama	X				Offset, against damages allowed on highways, water conservation districts, and water management districts.
Alaska		X			
Arizona		X*			
Arkansas				X*	
California		X*			Counties are not construed as a municipal corporation.
Colorado		X			Court refuses to draw distinction between general and special benefits—each case determined on own particular facts.
Connecticut				X	
Delaware				X	
Dist. of Columbia				X	
Florida		X*			Setoff allowed for road right-of-way, canal, water control facility, and levies.
Georgia		X			Law is not clear as to whether general benefits can be offset.
Hawaii				X	Setoff against damage only when take is for road widening or realignment.
Idaho		X			
Illinois			X		Special benefits have been defined so broadly that they include general benefits as typically defined.
Indiana		X*			
Iowa	X				
Kansas				X*	
Kentucky				X	
Louisiana		X			Courts refuse to draw distinction between general and special benefits—each case determined on own particular facts.
Maine				X	
Maryland				X	
Massachusetts				X	
Michigan		X			
Minnesota				X	
Mississippi	X				

State	1	2	3	4	Comments
Missouri				X	But, special assessment for benefit against property, under state's taxing power, can be simultaneously imposed.
Montana		X			
Nebraska		X			Courts refuse to draw distinction between general and special benefits—each case determined on own particular facts.
Nevada		X			
New Hampshire				X	
New Jersey				X*	
New Mexico			X		No distinction is made between special and general benefits.
New York			X		No distinction is made between special and general benefits.
North Carolina				X	A statute authorizing setoff against general benefits has been held constitutional if allowed under specific statute.
North Dakota		X*			
Ohio		X*			Case law conflicts with state constitution—special assessment may be imposed simultanteously with taking.
Oklahoma	X				
Oregon		X			
Pennsylvania				X	
Rhode Island		X			
South Carolina				X*	Conflict in law exists—most recent cases follow rule 4.
South Dakota		X*			
Tennessee		X			
Texas		X			Courts refuse to draw distinction between general and special benefits—each case determined on own particular facts.
Utah		X			
Vermont				X	
Virginia		X			Both general and special have been offset against damages in condemnation for at least highways, bridges, and ferries.
Washington				X*	Optional deferment of benefits provided—see text.
West Virginia			X		
Wisconsin		X			Highway condemnations allow setoff of both special and general benefits.
Wyoming		X			

*Benefit offset not allowed for other than municipal corporation.

tinction only obscures rather than clarifies the issue and is of little practical significance.[21]

In federal condemnation cases both special and general benefits must be offset against compensation for the part being acquired and/or damages.[22]

In each specific case, legal counsel must decide where the weight of authority lies and advise the appraiser as to whether general benefits can or cannot be offset against the taking and/or damage. If it is concluded that only special benefits can be offset against the taking and damages in a federal case, it would appear that no jurisdiction follows Rule 5. Therefore, it can be said that only the first four rules noted above are currently in use.

Table 13.1 attempts to classify each jurisdiction by the benefit offset rule which is most prevalent therein. There are many exceptions and much conflicting case law in these jurisdictions. Therefore, it would not be prudent to base a conclusion as to this question solely on the information in Table 13.1 without thoroughly researching applicable case law, statutory law, and constitutional law.

An example of a unique statute relating to condemnation and special benefits was adopted by the State of Washington in 1974.[23] It provides that, if the condemnor is asserting special benefits, the owner of the property has two options: 1) he can proceed with the condemnation trial to its conclusion with the trier of fact considering both the value of the taking and damages and offsetting these by the special benefits; or 2) the owner can proceed with the trial under the conditions that neither the condemnor nor the condemnee can present evidence in regard to any special benefits and that the trier of fact cannot consider any special benefits.

If the second option is selected, the owner must agree to allow the condemnor to place a lien on the remainder property in the amount of the just compensation found by the trier of fact. The selection of this option "is subject to the consent by the property owner to the creation and recording of a lien against the remainder in the amount of the fair market value of any property taken plus the amount of damages caused by such acquisition to the remainder of the property without offsetting the amount of any special benefits accruing to a remainder of the property, plus interest as it accrues"[24] at the rate of 5% per annum. This lien can be removed by several different methods: by mutual agreement between the parties, by payment of the lien by the owner, or by holding a new trial within six years of the date of the condemnation to determine the amount of special benefit, if any, which actually accrued to the property due to the construction of the public project.

The stated purpose of this statute was "to provide procedures whereby more just and equitable results are accomplished when real property has been condemned for a highway, road or street and an award made which is subject to a setoff for benefits inuring to the condemnee's remaining land."[25] What is more likely to happen, however, is that a single condemnation will be expanded from one trial to two trials, six years apart.

Undoubtedly, the condemnor will take the position that any increase in the value of the property was caused by the special benefit of the public construction, while the condemnee will hold that any value increase was natural appreciation or caused by other factors. It is apparent that the complexity of this type of litigation is recognized by attorneys for both condemnors and condemnees; since the statute was adopted, only one property owner has taken the second option mentioned, and that decision was reversed by the State Supreme Court remanding the case back for a new trial which, as of this writing, has not taken place.[26] A state-by-state discussion of this question is covered throughly in the *American Law Review*[27] and in *Nichols'*.[28]

Because this issue is controversial, several publications have summarized the applicable law in various jurisdictions. One source states:

State Rules.—The state rules as setoff vary as indicated:

1. About 14 states follow the federal rule that special benefits can be set off against both damages to the remainder and the value of the part taken. [Rule 4]

2. About 20 states follow the rule that special benefits may be set off against damages to the remainder but not against the value of the part taken. [Rule 2]

3. In a few states benefits cannot be considered at all. [Rule 1]

4. Only a few states follow the rule that both general and special benefits may be set off against both the severance [i.e., compensable] damages and the value of the part taken. [Rule 5][29]

An article in *Condemnation Appraisal Practice*[30] reaches the following conclusions:

Rule	No. of Jurisdictions
No offset allowed. [Rule 1]	4
Offset allowed against damages only. [Rule 2]	18
Offset allowed against taking and damages. [Rule 4]	10
Offset allowed, but not definite against what element.	17

Another text concludes that in two jurisdictions ". . . neither general nor special benefits can be considered for setoff purposes"; in eight jurisdictions consideration is given to ". . . both general and special benefits for setoff purposes"; in 16 jurisdictions ". . . special benefits may be setoff against both the value of the part taken and damages to the remainder"; and ". . . special benefits may be setoff only against the damages to the remainder" in 29 jurisdictions.[31] The results shown in Figure 13.1 indicate that four jurisdictions follow Rule 1, 24 follow Rule 2, three follow Rule 3, and 20 follow Rule 4. The applicable benefit setoff rule will often dictate the format that the appraiser must use in reporting his conclusions.[32]

Reasoning For Rules

The various setoff rules in existence today have evolved from constitutional law, statute law, and case law. Detailed discussion of the reasoning behind the various jurisdictions' adoption of one of the five rules is beyond the scope of this work. A general understanding of their reasoning, however, can help the appraiser apply the applicable rule.

Rule 1—*Benefits, whether special or general, cannot be considered.* This rule originates from the fact that many state constitutions provide that private property cannot be taken or damaged without the payment of just compensation. In some of these jurisdictions, the courts have historically ruled that just compensation must be paid in money, so the receipt of a benefit by the landowner cannot be substituted. In other jurisdictions, constitutional provisions exclude from consideration, in arriving at just compensation, "any advantage that may result to the owner on account of the improvement for which it is taken."[33]

Rule 2—*Special benefits only can be offset against damages to the residue, but not against the value of the land taken.* Again, this rule exists because many state constitutions require that the sovereign pay just compensation for the taking of property, and case law supports the position that such payment must be made in cash. In many of these jurisdictions, however, there is no special constitutional provision which requires the payment of just compensation for damages. Therefore, it has been established by case law that, although the property owner must be compensated for damages to the remainder property, the compensation may be in the form of benefits, rather than cash, because the requirement for payment is not a constitutional one.

Rule 2 prohibits the setting off of damages by general benefits. "Viewed as a matter of justice, it seems much fairer to exclude the general benefits. They are very difficult to assess accurately, and, as they usually arise from an increase in population or business prosperity expected to follow the improvement, they will never be received if the results hoped for do not follow. Moreover, the owner whose land is taken is placed in a worse position than his neighbor whose estate lies outside the path of the improvement and who shares in the increased values without any pecuniary loss. The owner may also well argue that the general taxes which he pays are justified only by the general benefit that he receives from the undertakings and improvements made under public authority."[34] "And, even as a constitutional question, it may well be argued that it is not 'just compensation' when a man is singled out arbitrarily and deprived of a share in the increased prosperity of his fellow citizens, merely because the public happens to want his land."[35]

Rule 3—*Special benefits and general benefits can be offset against damages to the residue, but not against the value of the land taken.* This rule is similar to Rule 2, but it provides that general as well as special benefits may be offset against damages. "As a matter of reasoning it was argued with much force that the general benefits derived from the taking actually do reduce the damage which the owner sustains, and he cannot be heard to complain that his fellow citizens receive equal benefits without paying for them. They are not in litigation with the public. He demands compensation for the taking of his land, and can ask only to be placed as well off as he was before it was taken."[36]

Rule 4—*Special benefits can be offset against both the damages to the residue and the value of the land taken.* This rule is often referred to as the *before-and-after rule,* or the *federal rule.*[37] This rule exists simply because it ensures that the property owner is in exactly the same monetary position in the after situation as in the before situation. The constitutions of jurisdictions using this rule generally have been interpreted as not necessarily requiring the actual payment of just compensation in cash, but rather that the property owner be in as good a position monetarily after the taking as he was before. In Missouri it was ruled that compensation paid in anything other than money was unconstitutional; however, the court went on to rule that the condemnor, through its power of taxation, could levy a special assessment against the property for the benefit it received, so the end result was the same.[38]

Rule 5—*Special and general benefits can be offset against both damages to the residue and the value of the land taken.* This rule is similar to Rule 4 except that it holds that both general as well as special benefits may be offset against the taking and damages. As noted previously, this rule does not appear applicable in any jurisdiction unless, of course, the apparent position of the United States Justice Department prevails in a federal condemnation case.

General Benefits

A complete list of general benefits cannot be prepared, because the specific circumstances of each partial taking may differ. Often, a benefit will be ruled as general in one instance and special in another. For example, improved drainage has

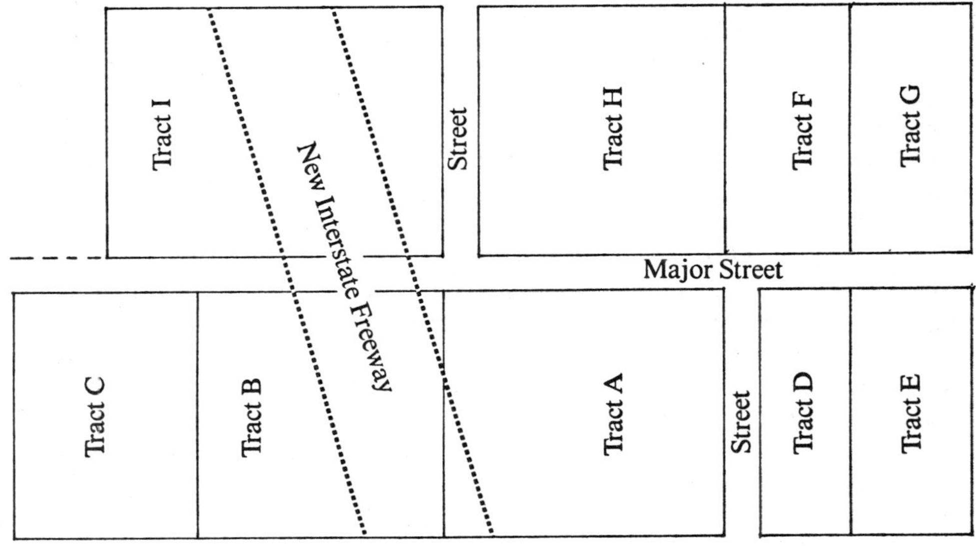

········Limited Access Line

Figure 13.1. General Benefits

been ruled as both a general benefit[39] and a special benefit.[40] Similarly, an Arizona court[41] rules that an increase in traffic was a general benefit, while a New York Court[42] ruled such an increase to be a special benefit. It is interesting to note that, in most cases, if an increase in traffic creates a benefit, it must be considered, but if the increase in traffic has a detrimental effect on a property's value, the damage is generally considered to be noncompensable and cannot be considered.[43]

General benefits are those that accrue to an entire neighborhood or community and have a beneficial effect on the values of properties where no taking or damage has occurred as well as the value of properties which have been taken or damaged. The typical example of a general benefit is the construction of an interstate highway. The construction will generally have a beneficial effect on property values in the neighborhood because it will improve access to shopping and employment centers. This may, in turn, result in land value increases, new housing starts, and new subdivisions in the area.

Usually, most property owners in the area will contribute no land to the project, nor will they be damaged by it; however, they will share in the benefits created by the project. It is often argued that the public improvement is being paid for with tax dollars, and the owner whose land is damaged should not have such damage reduced by the amount of general benefit he will receive because the owner has already paid for the benefit by paying taxes. Figure 13.1 illustrates the situation described above. In most circumstances, the benefits received by any property owner in the area will be classified as general.

Special Benefits

Although the circumstances shown in Figure 13.1 indicate that none of the properties was specially benefited, this is not always the case. Properties which abut the roadway may receive a greater benefit than the community as a whole. This benefit must, of course, accrue from the construction of the roadway, not from the taking. Special benefits are particularly likely to accrue if an interchange is part of the improvement project, as depicted in Figure 13.2. In this instance, it

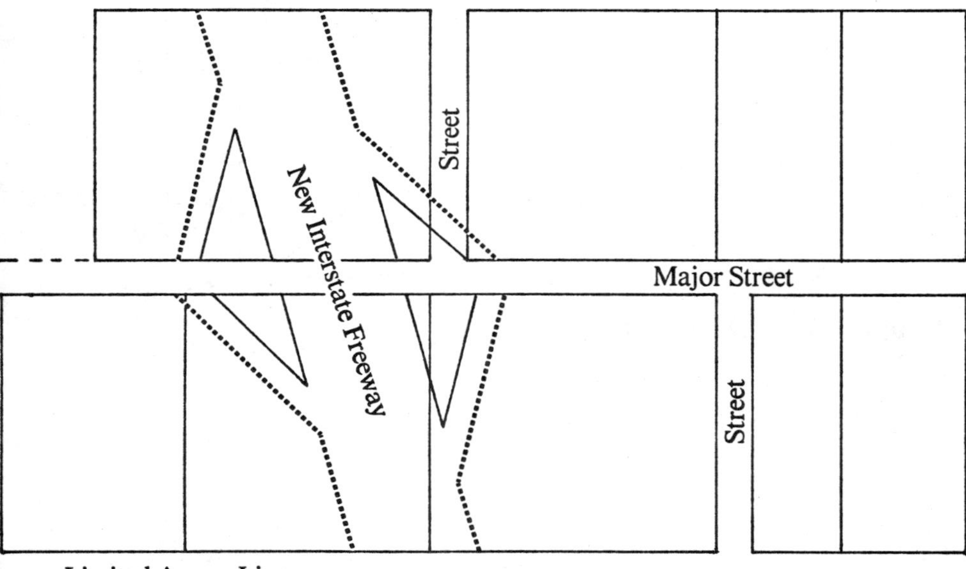

Figure 13.2. General and Special Benefits

could be said that construction of the roadway creates a general benefit, while construction of the interchange ramps results in a special benefit to some properties in the immediate vicinity. Thus, those properties may receive both general and special benefits. Situations of this nature illustrate why the courts are reluctant to distinguish between special and general benefits.

Figure 13.3 and 13.4 show special benefits caused by improved drainage. In the before situation, the property in Figure 13.3 might be inundated on occasion by surface water runoff. The remainder parcel to the right of the proposed road construction, however, could be protected from future inundation because the roadway would have a damming effect on future water runoff.

Figure 13.4 illustrates an actual situation concerning a property owner, who continually removed a beaver dam from his property because it backed up water and caused severe flooding. However, each time the beavers would rebuild the dam and flooding would reoccur. Because of the periodic flooding of the property, its highest and best use was for seasonal pasture; if the property did not flood, its highest and best use would have been for subdivision purposes.

As a part of the state highway construction, the state was required to place a culvert under the roadway adequate in size to accommodate maximum water flow from the creek. To accomplish this it was necessary for the state to remove the beaver dam and to take measures to see that the dam was not reconstructed.

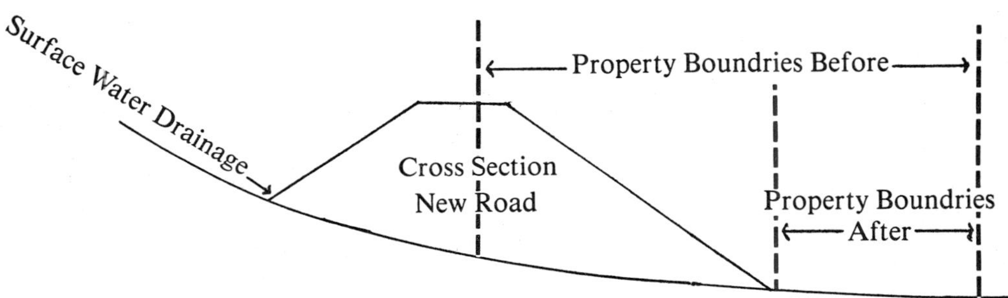

Figure 13.3. Special Benefits

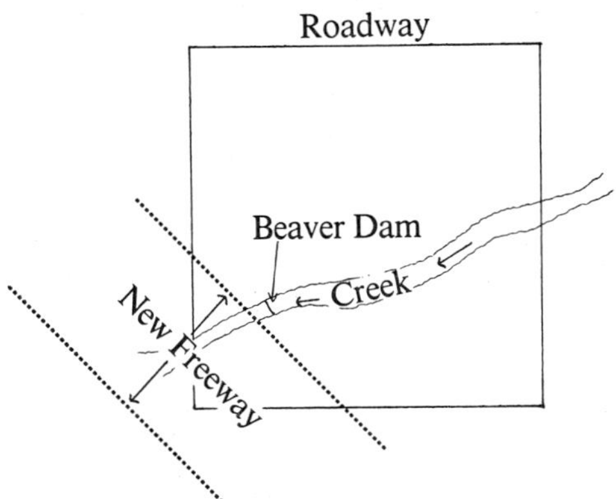

Figure 13.4. Special Benefits

Therefore, the state trapped all of the beavers in the area and relocated them to a different stream some distance from the existing dam. This action, of course, eliminated the flooding of the property in question and changed its highest and

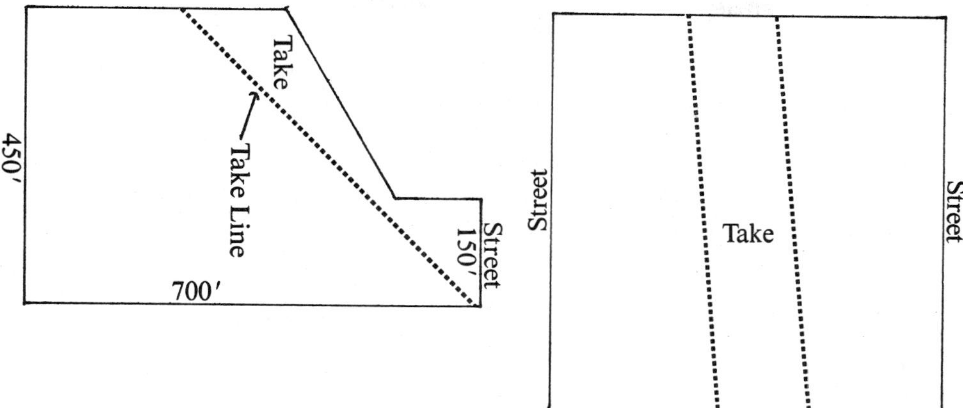

Figure 13.5. Special Benefits   **Figure 13.6. Special Benefits**

best use from seasonal pasture in the before situation to subdivision land in the after situation. The remainder property clearly received a special benefit.

Figure 13.5 depicts another potential special benefit situation. This property will have more than 450 feet of road frontage in the after situation, as compared to 150 feet of road frontage prior to the taking. This increased frontage could increase the utility of the site substantially, depending on its highest and best use.

Figure 13.6 illustrates a situation in which a property might receive special benefits due to an increase in its marketability and a change in its highest and best use. In the before situation, the property was zoned for low-density residential and farm use, while in the after situation it is, or could be, zoned for multifamily purposes. This situation is often quite similar to the problem appraisers face when trying to predict the *reasonable probability* of a rezoning in the before situation.[44]

The probability of a rezoning in an after situation like the one shown here can often be determined with greater certainty than in a before situation. This is true for two reasons. First, the highway (or other public project) has often been in the planning stages for years and the property in question, although still zoned for low-density residential and farm use, may be designated for multifamily use in the local government's comprehensive plan, which also designates the location of the long-planned highway (or other public improvement). Secondly, a review of planning commission actions will sometimes reveal a definite pattern, which indicates that the planning commission tends to zone land abutting an interstate highway or other public facility for multifamily use so the multifamily dwellings can be used as a buffer between the highway and surrounding lower-density uses.

A special benefit may also occur when a taking creates a corner lot from what was originally an inside lot. This before-and-after situation is depicted in Figure 13.7. Under these circumstances, the highest and best use of the site may remain commercial in both the before-and-after situations, but the site may have greater appeal and utility, and therefore value, in the after situation because of its increased visibility (or advertising appeal) and/or increased accessibility.

As has been previously noted, one of the easiest ways to determine whether a property has been damaged is when its highest and best use has diminshed in the after situation from that which existed before the taking.[45] The converse is true in discerning special benefits. Figure 13.8 shows a property in its before-and-after situations. In the before situation, the 20-acre tract was restricted to one road approach and one single-family dwelling because all other rights of access were

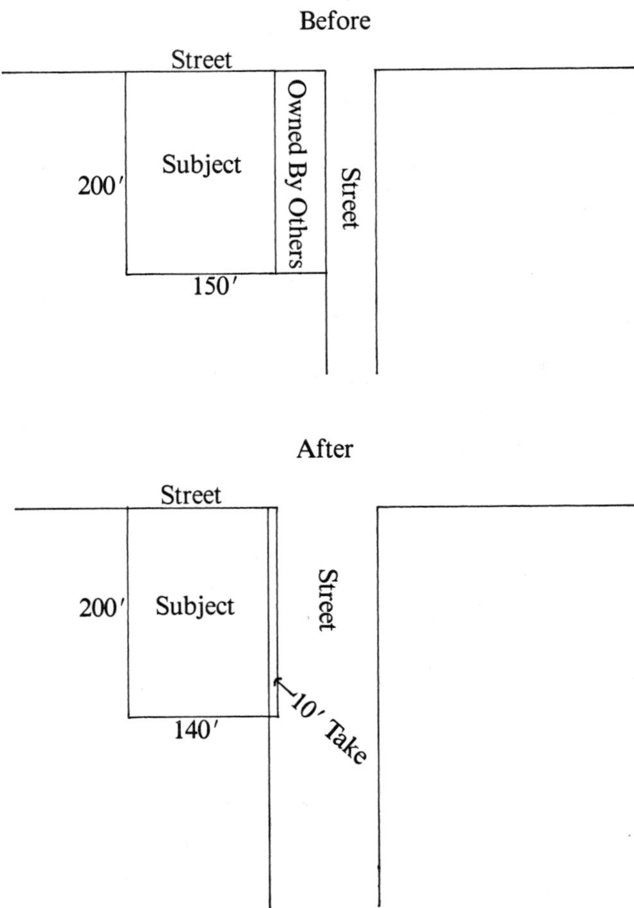

Figure 13.7. Special Benefits

Before

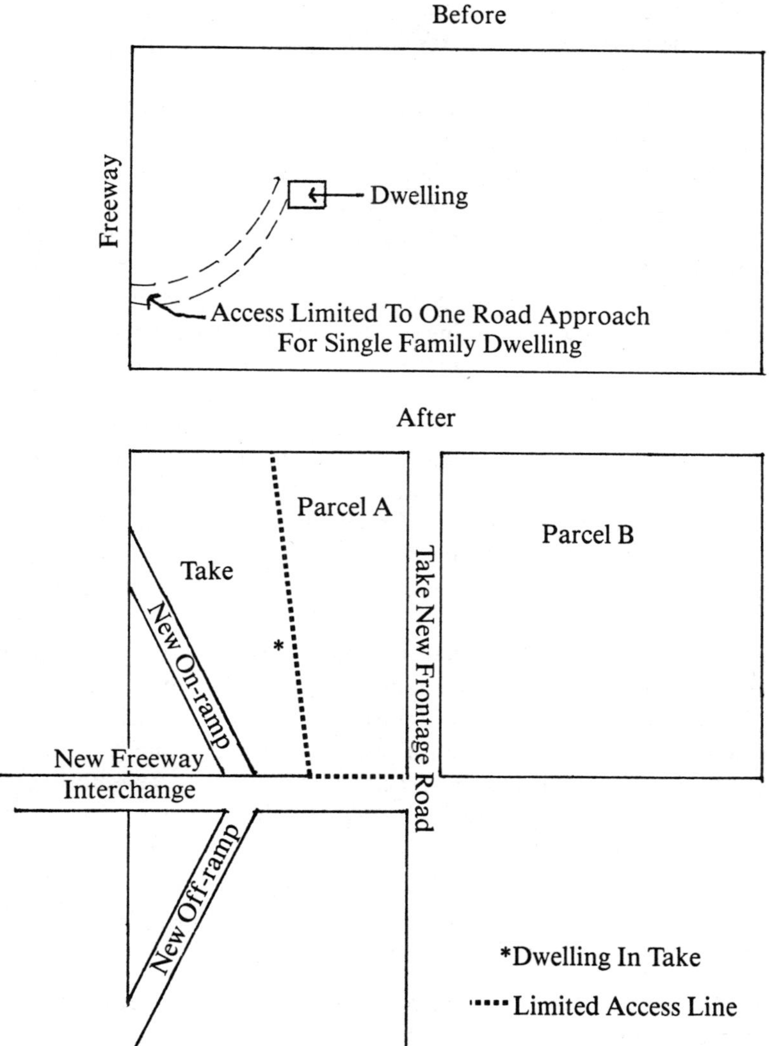

Figure 13.8. Special Benefits

previously acquired by the condemnor. Therefore, from a practical standpoint, any other estimate of the property's highest and best use must be dismissed as speculative.

In the after situation, the tract is located on an interchange and is severed by a newly constructed frontage road. Five acres of the tract and the single-family dwelling located on the site have been acquired. Parcel *A* contains five acres and has a highest and best use for commercial purposes; parcel *B* contains 10 acres and has a highest and best use for residential subdivision purposes. It is obvious that this property has been specially benefited. Even if accompanied by screams of agony from legal counsel, the appraiser should nonetheless consider the real possibility that two larger parcels exist in the after situation—one west of the frontage road and one east of the road.

A word of warning is required if this property is located in a jurisdiction which provides for the offsetting of benefits against both the damages and the value of the taking (Rule 4). Such a situation will often result in the property owner receiving no compensation because the combined values of the commercial land and the subdivision land after the taking will be considerably greater than the property's value before the taking. Market evidence may overwhelmingly support such a conclusion. Difficulties are encountered, however, when the condemnor tries to convince the jury that the little, old widow who owns the property should be paid nothing. The condemnor has just taken her house and five acres of her land, and then claims they owe her nothing. What does she want with a potential restaurant/service station site and a potential 30-lot subdivision? *She has no place to live!* In such a case, the condemnor's road is all uphill, regardless of the strong market evidence or the predominance of statutory and case law supporting his position.

Figure 13.9 illustrates a special benefit which is often overlooked—the transfer of financial obligation. In the before situation, the owner of this farm owns and maintains some 10,560 linear feet of fencing. As part of the construction project, the condemnor will be responsible for installing fencing along its easterly right-of-way line and to maintaining this fencing into perpetuity. Therefore, the landowner has been relieved of the financial reponsibility of maintaining some 2,720 linear feet of fencing, which could well represent a special benefit.

The appraiser must remember that it is not necessary for only one property to receive a special benefit; many properties may be benefited and the benefit can still be classified as special. As stated by the Arizona court:

> We believe that the following benefits are "special benefits" therefore, offsetable:
>
> (1) the unique benefit—a benefit not shared by any other parcel, and
> (2) the special benefit—a benefit which may be shared by other parcels along the roadway similarly situated.
>
> We would classify as non-offsetable or "general" benefits the following:
>
> (1) the local or neighborhood benefit—a benefit shared with other parcels not abutting the road but in the near vicinity and

(2) the general or community benefit—a benefit shared with other parcels in the community arising from the fulfillment of the public object which justified the taking.[46]

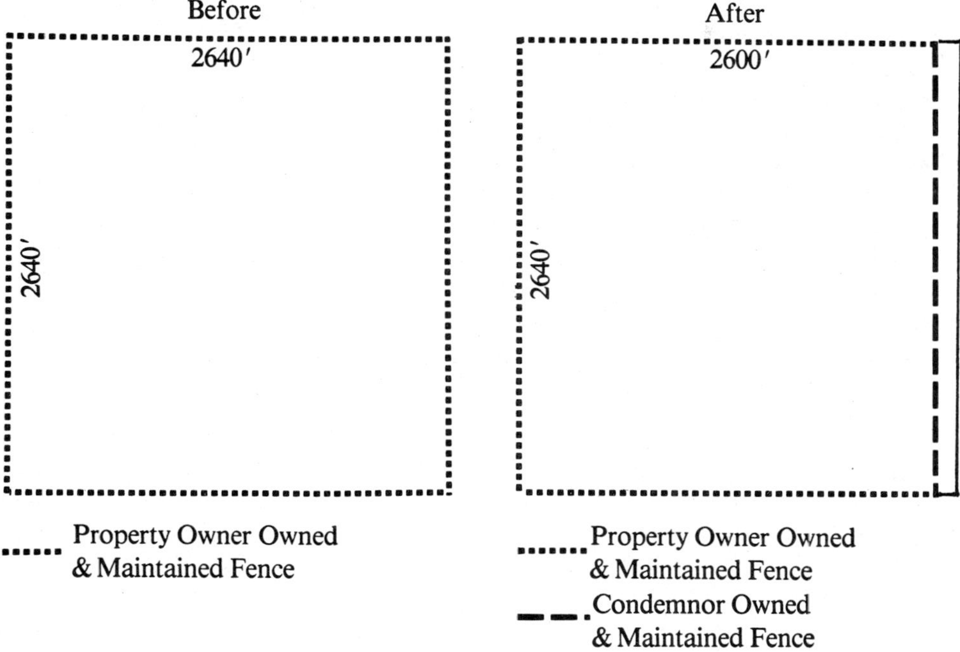

Figure 13.9. Special Benefits

"The test is not whether the improvement affects one or more owners by creating special advantages to their property; but whether the benefits are in fact such as add anything to the convenience, accessibility, and use of the property as contradistinguished from benefits arising incidentally out of the improvement and enjoyed by the public generally."[47] For instance, all four quadrants of a highway interchange could receive special benefits.

Figure 13.10 depicts six contiguous ownerships. In the before situation, the street on which these tracts front had no sidewalks. In many jurisdictions, the construction of a sidewalk in front of these dwellings would represent a special benefit to each of the tracts and, therefore, the sidewalk construction would be offsetable against the taking and/or damages in some jurisdictions. However, Figure 13.10 could also illustrate another common situation in which the applicable jurisdiction would impose a *special assessment* on each of the affected landowners, using the sovereign's power of taxation. If this were the case, the owner would, in effect, pay twice for the same benefit: once by having the amount of the benefit setoff against the value of the taking and/or damages, and again through the owner's payment of this special assessment.

"Unless there is some special statutory provision which leads to a different conclusion, there can be no setoff of the benefits that will result from the improvement for which a piece of land has been taken when it lies within the power of the public authorities to levy a special assessment for the same improvement."[48] "Special benefits are not offset where the condemning authority has the power to require property owners to pay for the improvements through the levy of special assessments. If the rule were otherwise and damages resulting from condemnation proceedings were offset by special benefits and, either before or after the condemnation proceedings, a special assessment was levied against the same land for such benefits, the landowner would be required to pay twice for the same special benefits. That this denies the landowner the just compensation guaranteed to him by the Federal and State Constitutions has been recognized by an overwhelming majority of the courts in the country."[49]

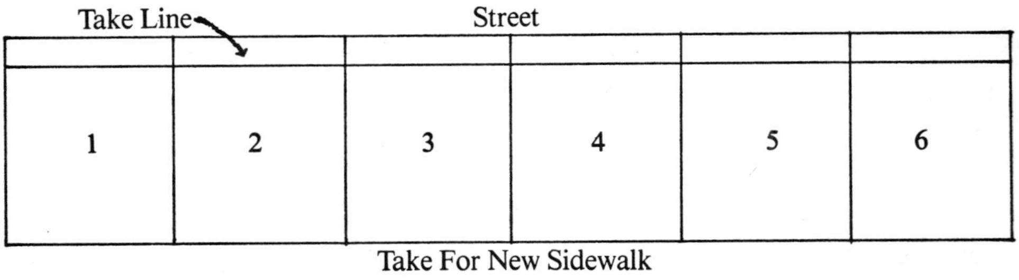

Figure 13.10. Special Benefits

Appraisal Procedures

The procedures used in appraising a property that may be benefited are no different than the procedures used to value properties that have been damaged by a partial acquisition (see Chapter 11). Here, too, the most commonly used, and most reliable, method of estimating benefits is through the analysis of comparable sales, using the matched pairs technique. In many cases, the treatment of damages and benefits is quite similar.

A benefit may reduce the expenses of ownership, and thus increase the net income from the operation of the property, which can be capitalized to indicate the value of the benefit received. Also, a deficiency in a property could be partially or wholly corrected by the construction of a public improvement, thus resulting in a benefit to the remainder. Such a situation may occur when the elevation of a roadway is altered, bringing the new, finished roadway closer to the elevation of the tract of land under appraisal. In the after situation, this could mean that it would cost less to construct a road approach into the property than it would have if the approach was to have been constructed in the before situation.

It can be said that the units of measuring damage can be applied in measuring benefits. Like damages, however, benefits are estimated only to better estimate the market value of the subject property in the after situation.

There are, however, some specific points which should be addressed by the appraiser and/or the attorney when possible benefits are encountered. First, benefits, like damages, cannot be speculative or conjectural. "Only such benefits as are or will be the proximate result of the improvement may be considered, and only such benefits as may be shown to be reasonably probable" and secondly, "the issue of benefits is limited to the particular tract of land of which a portion is taken or damaged."[50] In other words, the trinity of the larger parcel (unity of use, unity of ownership, and contiguity) must be as scrupulously adhered to in a case involving benefits, as it is in a case involving damages. In fact, a review of case law on this issue indicates that the courts tend to apply the tests of the larger parcel somewhat more stringently in cases involving benefits than they do to cases involving damages.

As the burden of proof of damages is on the landowner, the burden of proof of benefits is on the condemnor. Market evidence and appraisal report documentation must be extensive and convincing. It can be expected that the landowner and the landowner's attorney will find the appraiser's conclusion of benefits unacceptable and, in some instances, offensive. However, the appraiser for the condemnor who concludes that benefits exist should also be prepared for resistance from the review appraiser, the negotiator, the condemnor's attorney, and possibly even the head of the condemning agency. In any case, the appraiser should have strong market evidence and report documentation available. If a conclusion of zero compensation is reached, a condemnation trial is sure to follow. When an owner is offered nothing for the taking, he hasn't much to lose by going to trial.

To be considered a benefit, the situation must be permanent.[51] Inconvenience during construction is not a compensable damage; similarly, the rerouting of cars in front of a commercial establishment during construction is not an offsetable benefit.

The appraiser should remember that project enhancement must be disregarded in the before situation[52] and that, in most jurisdictions, general benefits must be disregarded in the after situation.[53] However, this is extremely complicated, particularly when special benefits are present and rapid natural land appreciation is taking place at the same time. The complexity of such a situation is illustrated in Figure 13.11. None of the properties shown are restricted in use by a zoning ordinance or any other land-use regulation. The properties are located in a rapidly growing residential area and the north-south street shown is the major traffic arterial connecting residential development, to the west of the area, with the central business district and employment center of the city.

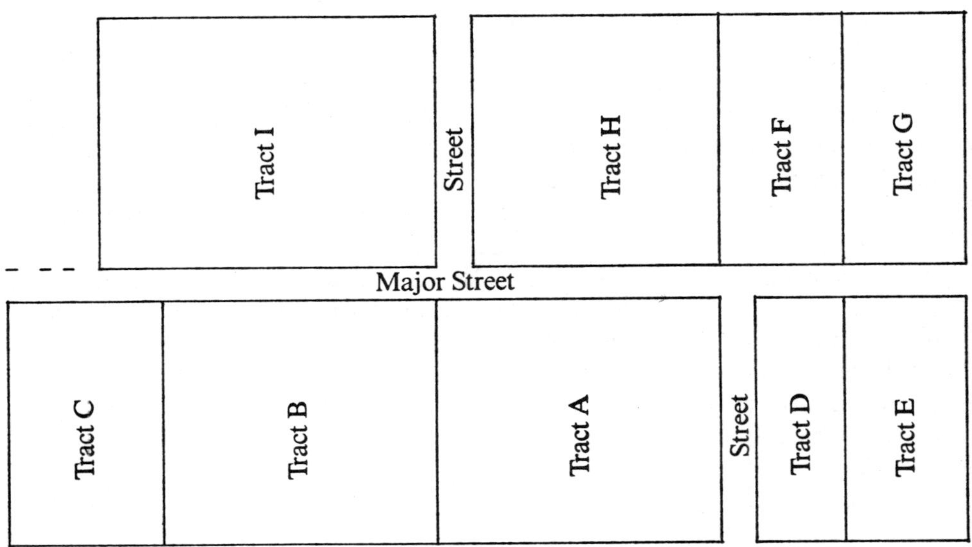

Figure 13.11. Tracts Affected by Proposed Freeway

The history of real estate activity for the parcels shown is as follows:

1960-1964	No sales or construction activity.
1965	Tract *A* sold for $5,000 per acre.
1967	Interstate highway plans (shown in Figure 13.12) were announced.
1968	Tract *A* sold for $10,000 per acre.
1968	Tract *E* sold for $7,000 per acre.
1971	Tract *A* sold for $32,000 per acre.
1972	Tract *B* (after the taking) sold for $27,500 per acre.
1973	Tract *C* sold for $28,000 per acre.
1973	Tract *E* sold for $12,000 per acre.
1973	Tract *G* sold for $15,000 per acre.

In 1974 several appraisals were obtained of Tract H in the before-and-after situations shown in Figure 13.12. The appraisers were asked to estimate the value of the property as of 1974; they were instructed to disregard any project enhancement in the before situation. Because the property is located in a jurisdiction that allows special benefits to be offset against both the taking and damages (Rule 4), the appraisers were also instructed to disregard any general or special benefits the property might reflect in the before situation. In the after situation, the appraisers were instructed to disregard general benefits, but to consider any special benefits. The appraisers were further instructed, as is typical, to assume in the after situation that the proposed public inprovement had been completed in accordance with plans and specifications.[54]

From these historical data and careful verification, and from price increment studies made in similar neighborhoods with no highway construction pending, each appraiser had to estimate the amount of project enhancement, general benefits, and special benefits reflected by each of the various sales to arrive at a legally acceptable before-and-after value estimate. Needless to say, the final determination of these questions, and the question of just compensation, was made by the trier of fact.

This illustration uncovers another fact which is recognized by appraisers and others, but does not appear to have been clearly addressed by the courts or covered in the typical *appraisal guidelines* prepared by various condemning agencies. In appraising property subject to a partial acquisition, the before value of the property is to be estimated as of the date of taking, as if no proposed public tak-

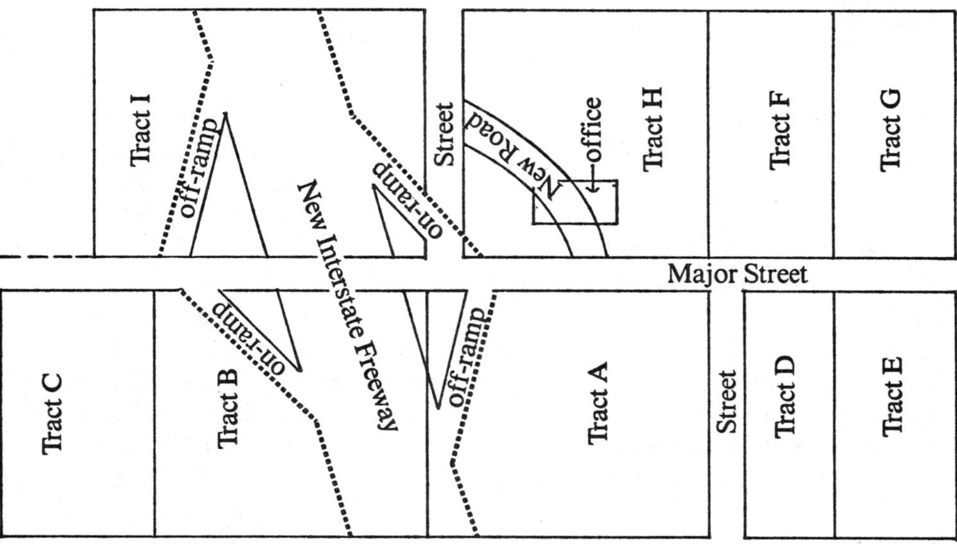

·······Limited Access Line

Figure 13.12. Proposed Taking for Freeway

ing or improvement project were contemplated. The after value of the property, on the other hand, is also to be estimated as of the date of taking, but as if the taking had already occurred and the public improvement project were, in fact, complete.

Returning to the illustration, it can be seen that these assumptions conflict. At the time of trial in 1975, it was anticipated that the entire interstate project, which would convey substantial special benefits to the remainder property, would be completed in 1977. However, the appraisals in the after situation were made, in accordance with legal instructions supported by case law, as if the interstate project were already complete. Factually, it is now anticipated that the interstate project scheduled for completion in 1977 will actually be completed in late 1983 or early 1984. Therefore, the benefits which were assessed against the owner in 1975 will not actually accrue until eight years after the assessment.

Such a situation is not so critical when damages are involved because the condemnor is acquiring the right to inflict said damages anytime it desires. Also, as previously stated, any inconvenience caused by construction of the public improvement is not a compensable damage anyway.[55] However, this factor is important in a benefits case. To illustrate, assume that Tract H, shown in Figure 13.12, contained a total of 12 acres in the before situation and had a before value of $15,000 per acre, or $180,000. In addition, there was an office building located in the taking with a contributory value of $100,000. Further assume that the taking consisted of three acres, and the remaining nine acres had a value, assuming the public project was complete, of $32,500 per acre, or $292,500. Therefore, *theoretical just compensation* could be computed as follows:

Before value:	
Land, 12 acres @ $15,000	$180,000
Office building	100,000
Total before value	$280,000
After value (9 acres @ $32,500)	292,500
Difference *(just compensation)*	$ -0-

Now let it be assumed that the remainder property will not receive its benefit until the construction of the public improvement is complete, some eight years hence. The benefit that the property will receive at that time is $32,500 − $15,000, or $17,500 per acre, totaling $157,500 for the nine acres. Therefore, it can be said that the owner of the remainder property has the right to receive $17,500 per acre, or $157,500, in eight years. Assuming a 12% discount, or interest, rate is applicable in this instance, the present worth of the right to receive $157,500 in eight years can be computed as $157,500 × .403883[56] = $63,612.

Therefore, it can be said that the current value of the estimated benefit is

$63,612 \div 9$ acres, or $7,068 per acre, and the after value of the property considering the present worth of the benefit to be received in eight years is $15,000 + $7,068, or $22,068, rounded to $22,000 per acre. Based on this premise, *theoretical just compensation* could be computed as:

Before value:	
Land (12 acres @ $15,000/acre)	$180,000
Office building	100,000
Total before value	$280,000
After value (9 acres @ $22,000)	198,000
Difference *(just compensation)*	$ 82,000

The authors of the *Uniform Eminent Domain Code* recognize the tremendous effect that a time delay can have on compensation. The *Code* states:

Section 1006. [Compensation to Reflect Project as Planned]

(a) If there is a partial taking of property, the fair market value of the remainder on the valuation date shall include increases or decreases in value caused by the proposed project including any work to be performed under an agreement between the parties.

(b) The fair market value of the remainder, as of the date of valuation, *shall reflect the time when the damage or benefit caused by the proposed improvement or project will be actually realized.*[57] [emphasis added]

The authors' comment in regard to subsection (b) is particularly enlightening:

Under subsection (b), the determination of fair market value of the remainder is not based on the often unrealistic view that the improvement has already been completed on the valuation date, but must be computed in a manner that will take into account any anticipated delay before the benefit or damage to the remainder is actually realized. If a subsequent change in plans causes additional damage, the property owner may obtain relief in a proceeding after judgment.[58]

At least one court has recognized the effects of time lags. In attempting to apply the previously noted statute[59] regarding special benefits, the Washington Supreme Court said:

There is obvious inequity in allowing a present offset of yet-to-be-constructed special benefits. Some benefits may eventually accrue to

> the property while others may not. And the value of the special bene-
> fit is, to a degree, speculative prior to completion of any construction
> project. It is clear our legislature enacted the above statutes and has
> allowed condemnees to postpone the determination of special bene-
> fits, if any, in order to remedy this inequity and achieve more just re-
> sults in condemnation cases. . . . The separate valuation proceeding
> helps insure against speculative special benefit offsets. Both con-
> demnor and condemnee benefit from a precise determination of spe-
> cial benefits.[60]

If a considerable time lag is anticipated between the date of valuation and the date an anticipated damage or benefit will actually occur, the attorney and the appraiser should consider altering the standard practice of evaluating property in the after situation as if the public improvement were complete. If the time interval between the date of valuation and the date of anticipated project completion is some distance in the future, they should also consider whether the estimated benefit is realistic or falls within the realm of speculation and conjecture. If the latter is the case, the benefit should be disregarded. A second alternative, of course, is to apply a discount factor to reflect the time delay, thus considering the current value of a damage or benefit as opposed to its future value.

Summary

Remainder properties often receive benefits due to the construction of a public improvement. The appraiser must be aware of such potential benefits and how these benefits are classified and treated in various jurisdictions. There is a considerable amount of disparity among the various jurisdictions and, at times, within the same jursidiction as to how benefits are treated.

Generally, all jurisdictions will fall under one of the following benefit offset rules:

1 Benefits of any type cannot be considered.
2 Special benefits can be offset against damages to the remainder property, but not against the value of the taking.
3 Both special and general benefits can be offset against damage, but not against the value of the land taken.
4 Special benefits can be utilized to offset both the damages to the remainder and the value of the land taken.
5 Both special and general benefits can be used as an offset against both damages to the remainder property and value of the land taken.

Nevertheless, both appraisers and attorneys are advised that there are many exceptions to these rules in the various jurisdictions. For instance, of the 48 jurisdictions that appear to allow benefit offset in one form or another, 12 specifically exclude such offset when the condemnor is other than a municipal corporation.

The existence of benefits is generally measured by the appraiser through the analysis of market data; this is the same procedure used to determine the existence and amount of damages in the after situation.

General benefits are those that benefit the community at large and have a beneficial effect on the value of properties which have not been taken or damaged, as well as on the value of properties which have been directly affected by the taking. Conversely, special benefits are those that arise because of the particular relationship between the remainder parcel and the public improvement. The fact that more than one property receives the benefit from a public project does not mean that the benefit cannot be classified as special; for example, all four properties on the quadrants of a new interchange may receive special benefits.

The types of benefits that can accrue to a remainder parcel are as numerous as the types of damage that can accrue to a remainder parcel. No clear distinction can be made between a special benefit and a general benefit because such a conclusion will often depend upon the circumstances of the specific case. In fact, in several cases, the same benefit has been classified as general in one instance, and special in another.

Because a great number of forces affect real estate values, it is often difficult to differentiate among natural real estate appreciation or decline, project enhancement, general benefits, and special benefits. However, because the law in some jurisdictions requires such differentiation, the appraiser may be required to make detailed studies of real estate value trends in areas that are comparable to the area in which the property under appraisal is located, but not under the influence of the public project, in order to develop a sound and supportable basis for his determination.

In estimating the after value of a remainder property that will receive an offsetable benefit, it is important that the appraiser determine that the benefit will accrue within the reasonably foreseeable future. If this cannot be done, the appraiser should reanalyze the anticipated benefit in conjunction with legal counsel. It could ultimately be concluded that the anticipated benefit will be realized so far in the future that to consider it would be speculative; or it could be that the future benefit should be discounted to a present worth in light of its distant date of accrual.

Notes

1. American Institute of Real Estate Appraisers and the Society of Real Estate Appraisers, *Real Estate Appraisal Terminology,* rev. ed., Byrl N. Boyce, ed. (Cambridge, Mass.: Ballinger Publishing Co., 1981), p. 28.

2. Ibid., p. 226.

3. Ibid., p. 116.

4. James A. Ballentine, *Ballentine's Law Dictionary*, 3rd ed., William S. Anderson, ed. (Rochester, N.Y.: The Lawyers Co-operative Publishing Co.; San Francisco: Bancroft-Whitney Co., 1969) p. 1197.

5. Ibid., p. 517.

6. Washington State Dept. of Transportation, *Right of Way Manual*, Chapter 4, Appendix 4-2, Appraisal Report Guide, Part 1C, § 2b. p. 1 (Revised 11/10/76).

7. Ibid., 2c.

8. Julius L. Sackman, *Nichols' The Law of Eminent Domain*, rev. 3rd ed. (New York: Matthew Bender, 1979) Vol. 3, § 8.6202.

9. Ibid., § 8.6203.

10. Taylor v. State ex rel. Herman, 467 P.2d 251 (Az.).

11. *Nichols'*, Vol. 3, § 8.62.

12. Territory of Hawaii v. Mendonca, 46 Hawaii 83, 46 Hawaii 126, 375 P.2d 6.

13. Joseph M. Montano, *Recognition of Benefits to Remainder Property in Highway Valuation Cases*, National Cooperative Highway Research Program Report No. 88 (Washington, D.C.: Highway Research Board, 1970), p. 1.

14. See Chapter 4, "The Larger Parcel."

15. Hoyt v. Stamford, 116 Conn. 402, 165 A. 357.

16. See Chapter 5, "Highest and Best Use."

17. *Recognition of Benefits in Highway Valuation Cases*, p. 3.

18. Clyde O. Martz, "The Federal View of Damages and Benefits," *The Appraisal Journal*, April 1969, p. 206.

19. *Divergencies in Right-of-Way Valuations*, National Cooperative Highway Research Program Report No. 126 (Washington, D.C.: Highway Research Board, 1971), p. 9.

20. *Nichols'*, Vol. 3, § 8.6211[1].

21. *Uniform Appraisal Standards for Federal Land Acquisitions* (Washington, D.C.: U.S. Government Printing Office, 1973) § A-10, p. 20.

22. Appraisal Report Guide, *Right of Way Manual*, Part 1C, § 2.

23. Laws of 1974, 1st Ex. Sess., Ch. 79 §§ 1-6; RCW § 8.25.210 (Wash.).

24. Ibid., § 8.25.220(4).

25. Laws of 1974, 1st Ex. Sess., Ch. 79 §§ 1-6; RCW § 8.25.210 (Wash.).

26. State v. Green, 578 P.2d 855 (Wn.).

27. 145 A.L.R. 1, "Deduction of Benefits in Determining Compensation"; 13 A.L.R. 1149, "Eminent Domain Deduction of Benefits in Determining Compensation or Damages in Proceedings Involving Opening, Widening, or Otherwise Altering Highway."

28. *Nichols'*, Vol. 3, § 8.6211, "Rules of Setoff in Each Jurisdiction."

29. *Divergencies in Right-of-Way Valuations*, p. 9.

30. Clifton W. Enfield and William A. Mansfield, "Special Benefits," *Condemnation Appraisal Practice* (Chicago: American Institute of Real Estate Appraisers, 1961), pp. 207-222.

31. George L. Schmutz, *Condemnation Appraisal Handbook*, revised by Edwin M. Rams, (Englewood Cliffs, N.J.: Prentice-Hall, Inc., 1963), pp. 133-134.

32. See Chapter 2, "Legal Measurements of Just Compensation."

33. Iowa Const., Art. I. § 18.

34. *Nichols'*, Vol. 3, § 8.6205.

35. Ibid.

36. Ibid.

37. See Chapter 2, "Legal Measurements of Just Compensation."

38. Newby v. Platte County, 25 Mo. 258.

39. Portland, Oregon City Ry. Co. v. Penny, 158 P. 404 (Ore.).

40. State v. Cady, 400 S.W.2d 481 (Mo.).

41. Phoenix Title and Trust Co. v. State, 425 P.2d 434 (Az.).

42. Vanech v. State, 270 N.Y.S.2d 357.

43. Iowa State Highway Commission v. Smith, 248 Iowa 869, 82 N.W.2d 755.

44. See Chapter 6, "Land Use Regulations."

45. See Chapter 11, "Damages in Partial Takings," fn.32.

46. Taylor v. State ex rel. Herman, 467 P.2d 251 (Az.).

47. Hempstead v. Salt Lake City, 32 Utah 261, 90 P. 397.

48. *Nichols'*, Vol. 3, § 8.6209.

49. City of St. Louis Park v. Engell, 168 N.W.2d 3 (Minn.).

50. *Nichols'*, Vol. 3, § 8.6203.

51. Reading, etc., R. Co. v. Balthaser, 119 Pa. 472, 13 A. 294.

52. See Chapter 5, "Highest and Best Use," fn.32.

53. See Figure 13.1.

54. *Recognition of Benefits in Highway Valuation Cases,* p. 8.

55. Wyoming State Highway Dep't. v. Napolitano, 578 P.2d 1342 (Wyo.).

56. *The Appraisal of Real Estate,* 7th ed. (Chicago: American Institute of Real Estate Appraisers, 1978), Appendix B, Compound Interest Tables, 12%, column 4, p. 587.

57. "Uniform Eminent Domain Code," 1974, § 1006, p. 10.11.

58. Ibid., "Comment," p. 10.12.

59. Laws of 1974, 1st Ex. Sess., Ch. 79 §§ 1-6; RCW § 8.25.210 (Wash.).

60. State v. Green, 578 P.2d 855 (Wn.).

CHAPTER 14
EASEMENT ACQUISITIONS

The ownership of real estate is endowed with a bundle of rights which may be held by one party or spread among a number of parties.[1] A right or interest in property is referred to as an estate, the most basic being a fee simple estate, the unimpaired ownership of the real estate subject only to the governmental limitations of escheat, eminent domain, taxation, and police power. When the bundle of rights is split between two or more parties, lesser estates are created. This is the case when a contractural limitation on a fee simple ownership is created by the establishment of an easement.

An easement is simply the right to perform a specific action on a particular parcel, or a portion of a parcel, without owning the underlying fee. A continuous easement across multiple tracts of land is often referred to as a right-of-way. This term is particularly common when referring to easements for roadway or railroad purposes.[2] Such easements are referred to as *easements in gross,* as opposed to appurtenant easements, which are easements used in conjunction with property owned in fee by the owner of the easement.[3] An easement is an estate which may be severed from the bundle of rights and can be defined in terms of time and space.

Easement Duration

Easements may be temporary in nature, with either a specific or an indefinite termination date. A common temporary easement having a specific termination date is a temporary construction easement. This easement is necessary when more space is needed to construct a facility than will be needed to operate and maintain it after construction is completed. Such easements generally have a specific termination date, but some temporary easements will have an indefinite termination date. For example, an easement for ingress and egress through a tract of timberland for the purpose of harvesting the timber will terminate upon completion of the harvest.

There are some roadway easements which terminate upon abandonment of the roadway. However, the courts generally regard such an abandonment clause as having little, if any, bearing on the amount of compensation due a fee owner for the taking of an easement. "A condemnor cannot demand a perpetual easement with one breath and insist with the next that he be excused from paying full compensation for the perpetual easement on the grounds that there is a bare possibility that he may abandon the perpetual easement on some uncertain day before the last lingering echo of Gabriel's horn trembles into ultimate silence. This is true because the law of eminent domain deems the possibility of the abandonment of a perpetual easement by non-user [sic] so remote and improbable it will not allow the contingency to be taken into consideration in determining the value of the easement."[4]

Permanent, or perpetual, easements are generally acquired for electrical transmission lines; sewer, water, and other utility lines; highways; and other public facilities. Often, an easement will be both temporary and permanent, as is the case with a sewer line easement. If an easement width of 40 feet is required for installation of a sewer line, but only 25 feet is required for its maintenance and operation, a 15-ft. temporary construction easement is acquired in addition to a 25-ft. permanent easement.

Easement Occupancy

In terms of space, an easement may be defined as subsurface, surface, or overhead. Subsurface easements are required to install sewer lines, water lines, communication lines, and tunnels; common surface easements allow for drainage, flowage, railroads, and highways. Avigation, air, noise, and line of sight easements are overhead easements. Some easements may involve the rights to two or even all three types of space, as is the case of a high-power transmission line. The lines and the upper portion of the tower occupy overhead space, the tower rests on surface area, and the foundation footings for the tower occupy subsurface space.

From a strictly technical point of view, an easement cannot be exclusively a surface easement. An easement for roadway purposes must include enough subsurface rights for removal of topsoil and installation of base rock and paving and enough overhead, or above surface, rights for practical use of the roadway. Although a *pure surface easement* cannot exist from a practical standpoint and possess any utility, many easements, such as easements for roadways and railroads, are still commonly referred to as surface easements. Only when the encroachment below and/or above the surface of the ground is extreme or excessive for the intended surface use of the easement area is the easement classified as multiple-space occupancy.

Specialty Easements

Some of the most common easements create no unique problems for the appraiser. Properties encumbered by easements for roadway, railroads, power transmission lines, sewer lines, and slopes (or cuts and fills) are often plentiful in the market; thus, with diligence, the appraiser has enough data to make an accurate market analysis of the effect of such easements on a property's market value. In fact, studies have been published on the impact of some of the more common easements, such as power transmission line easements.[5] However, easements come in many varieties because an easement can be created for almost any purpose as long as the right, or estate, to be acquired can be severed from the underlying fee. Some of these unique, or specialty, easements create difficult valuation problems for the appraiser and, therefore, require individual consideration.

Flowage Easements

A flowage easement grants the easement owner the right to flood the fee owner's land. Such an easement is often taken in conjunction with a hydroelectric or flood control project. The easement will generally define whether the easement owner has the right to flood the land occasionally or permanently. If the right is to flood permanently, the fee owner retains only the land under the water; such an easement acquisition can damage the land to nearly 100% of its fee value. The fee owner may retain the right to fill the encumbered land (above the flood stage) and to build structures on it, but these rights often require the specific approval of the easement owner.

Occasionally, flowage easements give the easement owner the right to inundate the land only periodically. Such easements are often acquired in addition to permanent flowage easements to allow the easement owner to encroach occasionally above the level of the permanent flowage easement; they also protect the easement owner from damage suits that might arise if the land is eroded by wave action.

A flowage easement will generally be described as encumbering all of the fee ownership lying between a low and high elevation mark. Therefore, the appraiser must have access to accurate topographic maps. He should investigate whether the land to be encumbered is subject to flooding in the before situation and, if so, to what degree and how frequently. If the acquisition involves an occasional flowage easement, the same flooding information will be required for the after situation.

Avigation Easements

Avigation easements are divided into two specific classifications: clearance easements and flight easements. A clearance easement is acquired to assure that no structure exceeds a maximum height, if structures are allowed at all. This will give aircraft an unobstructed view and provide a safety margin for flights that may have to descend due to pilot error, poor weather conditions, etc. The flight easement allows the frequent overflight of aircraft over the encumbered land and constitutes a separate and distinct easement from the clearance easement.[6]

In fact, the courts have, on occasion, refused to consider potential damage from overflights when only a clearance easement was being condemned.

> On this record it must be accepted that the claimed right of clearance is merely a provision for insuring that space shall be unoccupied and vision unobstructed above a designated altitude. Unquestionably this is an aid of avigation. But no flight easement is mentioned or to be inferred, much less claimed, in the present pleadings and, therefore, no servitude can be imposed except for the asserted and precisely limited rights of clearance.

> It is well established that, absent bad faith which is not argued here, the government's determination and explicit assertion of the nature and extent of the estate to be taken are not judicially reviewable. If any subsequent low flying of aircraft over appellee's land should occur and should be said to invade property rights, the acquisition of the right to keep that space clear will not have conferred any attendant right to fly through it.[7]

In a similar situation, another court said:

> [S]ince the government has not acquired a right to fly aircraft over the condemnee's land by these proceedings, it follows that, if the government does cause its aircraft to make flights over the lands of these defendants, or has already done so, at such elevation and with such frequency as to result in taking beyond that described in the Declaration of Taking on file in these cases, or in actual physical damages, the landowners would have a right to bring suit against the government for damages or just compensation.[8]

Because the courts have come to consider overflights as easement takings only recently,[9] minimal law exists as to acceptable methods of measuring damage. For this reason, the federal court[10] has held that a percentage factor applied to the property's before value, based on a mathematical formula,[11] can be used when market data on the property's after value are unavailable. The approved formula considers three factors: 1) the height of the overflight, up to an elevation of 500 feet; 2) the distance the property is located from the center line, extended, of the runway up to 2,000 feet; and 3) the distance between the property and the end of the runway, up to 25,000 feet.

Facade Easements

Facade easements prohibit the fee owner of a property from altering the facade, or exterior, of an existing improvement on his land. Such easements are generally imposed on structures of historical significance and are acquired for the purpose of historical preservation. Facade easements usually apply to a single property and may constitute a taking. However, if such a restriction is placed on all structures within a geographical area, it is usually accomplished with zoning regulations, and, therefore, does not constitute a compensable taking.[12]

Often, the appraiser will be asked to make a before-and-after appraisal of a facade easement when the easement has, in fact, formally been donated by the landowner. Such appraisals are often requested for real estate and federal income tax purposes.

One of the most difficult determinations to be made in facade easement cases is whether a taking has actually occurred, or whether the restriction placed on the land falls under the sovereign's police power.[13] Some jurisdictions have ruled that a facade easement may be taken by police power, even if the ordinance creating the easement is directed at only one parcel of land.[14] The appraiser is well advised to obtain legal verification of this point before the appraisal assignment is undertaken.

Scenic Easements

Scenic easements became more prominent with the adoption of the *Highway Beautification Act of 1965*. The act allocated to each state 3% of the funds apportioned to that state for federal-aid highways in any fiscal year to be "used for landscape and roadside development within the highway right-of-way and for acquisition of interests in and improvement of strips of land necessary for the restoration, preservation, and enhancement of scenic beauty adjacent to such highways."[15]

Scenic easements generally restrict the underlying fee owner from using his land in any manner that would diminish its aesthetic appeal. However, easement forms vary substantially from state to state and from project to project. It is very important that the appraiser make an exact determination of the rights to be acquired in each instance. Scenic easements are generally acquired on land which runs parallel to highway rights-of-way. Studies have been made in an attempt to ascertain the effect on market value resulting from the imposition of a scenic easement on a tract of land.[16]

Scenic easements will often include the forced removal of existing advertising signs and a prohibition against any future signs. Compensation for existing signs must be paid to both the landowner and the owner of the sign in accordance with Title 1 of the Highway Beautification Act.[17] However, the prohibition against future advertising is almost universally accomplished by the sovereign's police power.

In regard to scenic easements, as with facade easements, it is often difficult to determine whether a taking has actually occurred, or whether the sovereign has restricted the use of the land by its police power. Some jurisdictions have ruled that the aesthetic factor alone is a valid basis for police power regulations.[18] On the other hand, the courts in all the states have not yet determined that acquisition of scenic easements is for a *public use,* nor that the expenditure of public funds for scenic easement acquisition is for a *public purpose.*[19] Therefore, the appraiser must clearly distinguish between the rights being acquired by eminent domain and the limitation of rights imposed by the sovereign's police power. Often, this can only be accomplished with the guidance of legal counsel who is thoroughly familiar with the applicable law.

Estates Created

The owner of an easement is said to have a *dominant estate,* while the owner of the underlying fee is said to have a *subservient estate.* A dominant estate is sometimes referred to as an *affirmative easement,* and a subservient estate as a *negative easement.* These terms are somewhat self-explanatory in that the interest in the land held by the owner of the easement dominates the rights retained by the fee owner. Although the fee owner may retain the right to use the land encumbered by an easement, he may not utilize it in any manner that interferes with the easement owner's use of the property for the purposes specified in the written easement; thus, a fee owner's interest in the easement area is subservient to the interest of the easement owner.

Value Considerations

The principles and techniques of appraising land for easement acquisition are the same as those applied to other condemnation appraisals. The only difference is that in appraising land for easement acquisitions, only a partial taking may occur. Even if an entire ownership will be encumbered by an easement, the landowner will still retain his underlying fee interest in the form of a subservient estate. In those jurisdictions using the before-and-after, or federal, rule, the appraiser simply values the property before and after the easement acquisition. As a federal court said in remanding a case for retrial, ". . . we suggest that the measure of appellant's detriment should be the difference, if any, between the fair market value of the land immediately before and after the perpetual easements were imposed by the taking."[20]

Jurisdictions using the taking plus damages, or state, rule will require the appraiser to estimate the value of the easement interest acquired plus damages to the remainder, if any.[21] In applying either rule, the measure of damage caused by an easement acquisition is the loss of salable utility both to the area encumbered by the easement and to the unencumbered portion of the larger parcel.

Some courts, as a matter of law, have ruled that the property's loss in market value is not the proper criteria of value in the case of temporary easement acquisitions.[22] It has been held that the proper measure of compensation is the value of the property for the period it is to be held by the condemnor,[23] or the diminution in the value of the property by reason of the owner's loss of its use and occupancy during possession by the condemnor.[24] The most common measure of damages accepted by the courts is the rental value of the easement area for the period of occupancy by the condemnor.[25]

The damages to land due to the imposition of an easement can range from 0%[26] to 100% of the easement area's fee ownership.[27] Some courts have ruled, as a matter of law, that under certain circumstances compensation for an easement taking is equal to 100% of the fee value of the land encumbered by the easement. "Under our law it is firmly settled that when a permanent easement is taken by eminent domain, depriving the owner of the use of the property, the compensation must equal the full value of the land, as if a fee were being acquired."[28] [citations omitted] Conversely, other courts have ruled that, as a matter of law, compensation for an easement taking cannot equal 100% of the fee value of the land encumbered. As one court put it ". . . what the plaintiff took was merely an easement, which being in law less than the title, can in law only entail compensation for less than the fee title."[29]

The degree of damage for the same type of easement can vary greatly depending on the highest and best use of the land. For example, a pipeline running 25 feet beneath grazing land may have little or no effect upon the productivity, or market value, of the land encumbered with the easement. But, if the pipeline traversed a tract of timberland, the loss of salable utility, or market value, could be great because the pipeline easement agreement typically precludes the growth of timber within the easement area.

Another factor that can alter the degree of damage incurred by reason of an easement acquisition is the location of an easement in relation to the boundary lines of the larger parcel. This is illustrated in Figure 14.1, which depicts the taking of a 10-ft. water line easement from two, single-family residential lots.

The rights acquired from parcels A and B are identical, as are the areas to be encumbered. However, because the easement is located close to Parcel A's boundary line, the tract has lost little, if any, of its original utility. The tract's highest and best use is for development of a single-family dwelling, both before and after imposition of the easement. Parcel B, on the other hand, has probably suffered severe loss of utility due to the easement acquisition. Before the imposition of the easement, the tract's highest and best use was for construction of a single-family dwelling; however, the location of the easement, as it relates to the tract's boundaries, makes such a use impractical in the after situation. The only practical use of Parcel B, after the acquisition of the easement, would be its sale to an abutting owner at a nominal price.

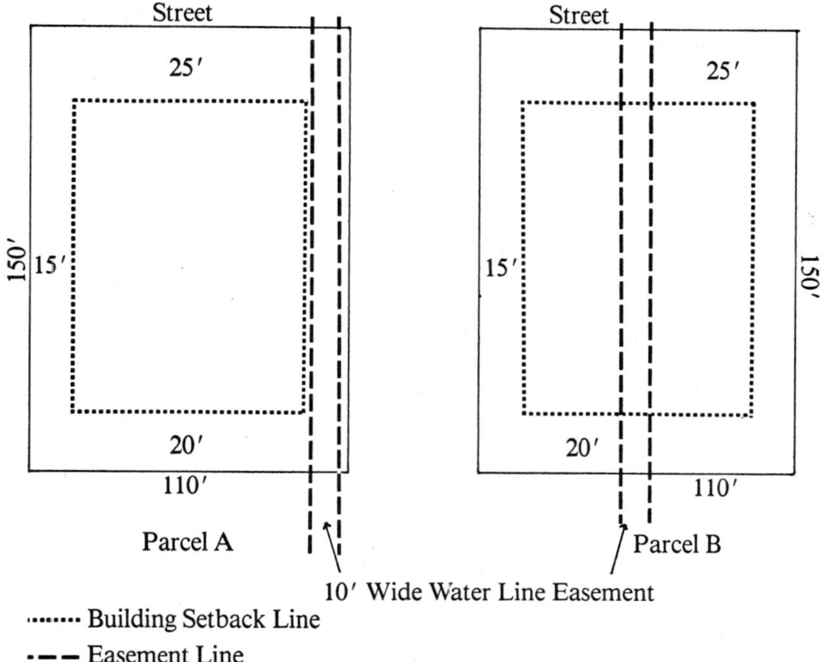

Figure 14.1. Easement Location

The location of an easement as it relates to improvements on the larger parcel is also important. This is illustrated in Figure 14.2. Again, the rights and areas of the parcels encumbered are identical. However, the easement's location on Parcel A could severely restrict the future expansion of the industrial building. In addition, the presence of power lines could obstruct the use of large industrial machinery around the structure, and the towers could hamper the ease and efficiency of freight loading and/or delivery. The only possible loss in Parcel B's utility by reason of the easement acquisition might be minor modification of the employee parking area to accommodate the tower locations. Therefore, it can be seen that the location of an easement, in relation to the larger parcel's boundary lines and to existing improvements can have a substantial effect on the property's market value.

Before the effects of an easement acquisition can be properly evaluated, it is imperative that the appraiser know exactly how the easement area will be used, what rights are to be acquired, and how responsibilities will be divided between the parties. The total impact of an easement acquisition cannot be estimated until

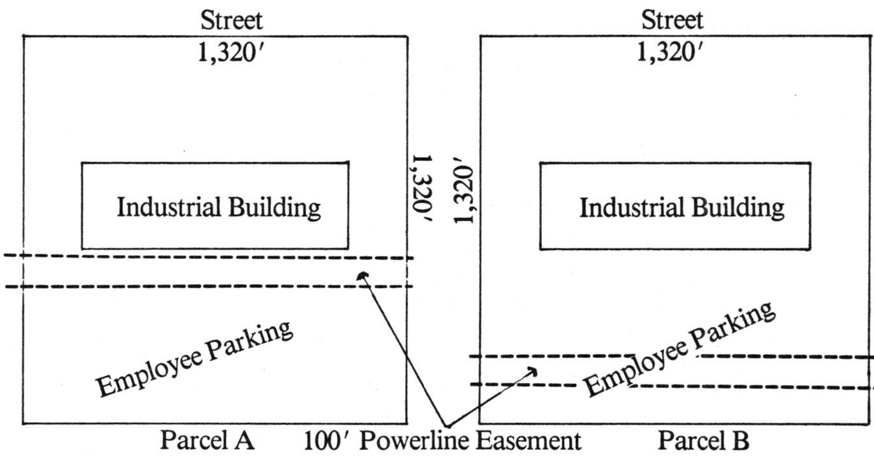

Figure 14.2. Easement Location

the appraiser determines: 1) the loss of present utility, 2) the loss of future utility, 3) the accessory rights to be acquired, and 4) the obligations of the parties. The accessory rights acquired may include the right to maintain the easement area (including the right to spray power or pipeline easement areas); the right to enter onto the property for inspection, repair, and/or replacement; and, on occasion, the right to expand the utilization in the easement area for other purposes, or to expand the area itself without additional compensation, or by a predetermined compensation formula. Power line easements sometimes include a provision that allows the easement owner to perpetually remove *danger trees* from unencumbered areas of the fee owner's larger parcel with little or no compensation, or by a predetermined compensation formula.

In investigating the obligations of the parties, the appraiser should determine 1) whether the easement owner will be responsible for returning the land to its original state after construction, replacement, and/or repairs; 2) who will be responsible for fence repair and maintenance, if any; 3) who is obliged to maintain the easement area, including the control of noxious weeds; and 4) who will be responsible for potential personal injury losses occurring in the easement area.

The following jury instruction lists the potential damage items which an appraiser must consider in estimating the diminution in market value caused by an easement acquisition.

> In arriving at the difference [in market value before and after the easement acquisition], you should take into consideration the actual legal rights taken *and also the following items*: [emphasis added]

(a) depreciation, if any, due to the existence of the pipeline itself;

(b) loss of crops, if any, this year and future years;

(c) loss, if any, of use of pasture due to the use by the corporation of said fifty foot right-of-way and temporary easements this year and in future years;

(d) reasonable expense, if any, to respondents in keeping cattle from said fifty foot right-of-way now and in the future and during periods necessarily required in order to reestablish the crops and pasture on said fifty foot right-of-way;

(e) reasonable expense, if any, to respondents in building and maintaining necessary works to insure proper irrigation of the land during such times as said corporation shall have the right to occupy said fifty foot strip under the terms of the easement;

(f) reasonable expense, if any, to respondents in keeping water from said fifty foot strip during periods of construction, replacement and repair;

(g) reasonable expense, if any, to respondents in leveling and releveling said fifty foot strip and hauling of additional soil to fill settlements;

(h) reasonable extra expense, if any, to respondents caused by said fifty foot right-of-way due to the interference thereof with the operation of said dairy herd farm unit and said cattle feeding farm unit;

(i) reasonable extra expense, if any, to the respondents in puddling the trench in which said pipeline will be laid in preventing water from seeping along said pipeline, and preventing consequent damage;

(j) extra reasonable expense, if any, to the respondents of regrading, replanting and caring for, and seeding said fifty foot right-of-way;

(k) reasonable damages, if any, to crops and land due to the necessity of keeping water off during periods of occupancy of said right-of-way by said corporation under the terms of its easement;

(l) such other reasonable expenses, if any, supported by the evidence, reasonably necessary to restore said premises to normal productivity.[30]

This case was eventually remanded for retrial. In doing so the court said:

> While the listed items may have a bearing on the depreciation in market value which would result from the granting of the easement, they could not be considered as distinct items of damages. It was not proper for the jury to consider them *in addition to the legal rights taken,* the value of which, the jury had previously been told, was the same difference in market value.[31] [emphasis added]

As can be seen, the list of potential damage items which an appraiser must consider is often quite lengthy. The appraisal of a property impacted by an easement imposition may be more complex than if the property were acquired in a fee taking. Full and detailed appraisal reports are required—either a full before-and-after appraisal or an appraisal of the taking plus damages, depending on the rules in the applicable jurisdiction. However, there are occasions when the impact on market value caused by the imposition of an easement will be nominal, or even nonexistent, as could be the case with Parcel A in Figure 14.1.

Nominal Acquisitions

In cases where damages are nominal or nonexistent, it is often unnecessary and impractical, from an economic point of view, to have a fully documented appraisal report prepared. In fact, the fee for a fully documented appraisal report could amount to considerably more than the estimated loss in the property's value. Treatment of nominal acquisitions will vary among condemnors. When such an assignment is encountered, the appraiser should consult with his client to determine the type of appraisal report required. If, however, the appraiser is preparing the appraisal report for trial purposes, a fully documented report should be prepared, regardless of the resulting diminution in value. An unprepared appraiser can look just as incompetent on the witness stand in a case involving $500, as in one involving $500,000.

For large easement acquisition projects such as for a pipeline through a rural area, the condemnor will often analyze land values in the area and make an *administrative determination* as to the amount of compensation each property owner will be offered. This determination is often based on a unit of measure, e.g., X dollars per chain, or linear foot, of easement acquired. Other condemnors use abbreviated appraisal reports when the values involved are minimal. For instance, one condemnor allows "the use of the short form, project type of appraisal report for minimal value acquisitions when the just compensation including cost-to-cure damages is found to be $2,500 or less and no other damages or benefits are found to exist."[32]

It is generally recognized that appraising is not an exact science; some easement takings have such a minimal effect on value that no discernible difference in market value can be ascertained in the marketplace. However, it is also generally recognized "that no property owner (except in a case of special benefits) can be expected to convey land [or an interest therein] to the state without compensation . . ."[33] If no discernible difference in market value before and after an easement acquisition can be demonstrated, some condemnors will make the administrative determination that the property owner be compensated in a nominal amount.

Other condemnors, however, will require that some form of appraisal report be filed to meet applicable acquisition guidelines. In such instances, the appraiser may write an abbreviated report describing the property before and after the easement imposition and concluding that *the difference between the value of the property prior to acquisition of the easement and after the acquisition of the easement is nominal, say $500.* He may not arrive at specific before-and-after values or include any sales data in the appraisal report. This procedure keeps the cost of the appraisal to a minimum and, at the same time, satisfies the condemnor's requirements that an appraisal be made before an offer can be tendered to the property owner. This procedure also avoids a situation, common in minimal taking cases, whereby the appraiser who is unable to justify or support a diminution in the property's value will conclude the same value for the property before and after the easement imposition. Nothing ruins a negotiator's day faster than trying to get a property owner to sign an easement which pays him no compensation whatsoever.

Existing Easements

So far, we have discussed the appraisal of real estate for easement acquisition purposes. The appraiser must also consider the effects of existing easements on a property's utility and value. Easements can be held *in gross* or as an *appurtenance* to other property that is held in fee, usually by the easement owner. An easement held in gross is one that has utility in and of itself or in conjunction with other continuous easements, such as power line easements, utility easements, etc. An easement held as an appurtenance, however, usually has no material utility in and of itself, but is useful only in conjunction with other property. An example of an appurtenant easement is an easement across a tract of land for ingress to and egress from an abutting tract of land which is held in fee by the owner of the easement. The easement would have no material value to its owner if he did not also own the fee to the other tract of land.

Many jurisdictions require that a tract of land encumbered with an easement be appraised considering the easement's negative effect on the property's market value. "Generally, where property burdened with easements is taken by eminent domain, the property must be valued in its existing condition and not as an unencumbered fee."[34] Therefore, the appraiser must be aware of the effects of all easements encumbering a property under appraisal.

The appraiser must also be aware of easements on other lands which may be appurtenant to the parcel under appraisal. Appurtenant easements must be carefully investigated because not all jurisdictions require an appurtenant easement to be legally described in the condemnor's declaration of taking.[35] When an appurtenant easement exists, the fee parcel is appraised considering the beneficial effect of the easement across the other land. In other words, the larger parcel is the fee ownership plus the easement ownership in the abutting land.[36] Similarly, when only the appurtenant easement is acquired, the easement owner's interest is considered in light of his abutting fee ownership. Thus, the larger parcel is the easement ownership plus the abutting fee ownership.[37]

"Ordinarily an easement is appurtenant to a parcel of property known as the dominant tenement. Such dominant tenement will naturally be worth more with the appurtenant easement than without it. When, therefore, there is a destruction of the easement either by a direct taking of the easement itself or by a taking of the servient estate, it has been said that the owner of the easement is damaged to the extent that the value of his dominant tenement has been impaired by such taking."[38] "For purposes of valuation an easement is to be considered as appurtenant to the dominant tenement. *Together they constitute a single entity.*"[39] [emphasis added]

To illustrate this principle, consider the acquisition depicted in Figure 14.3. In appraising Parcel A, the larger parcel is the unencumbered fee of Parcel A plus the dominant estate, or interest, in the access easement across Parcel B. If Parcel A's easement interest across Parcel B were not considered, the tract would be landlocked and could have only a nominal value. But, the existence of the easement gives Parcel A a great deal more utility and value than the tract would have without it. In this instance, Parcel B is not legally affected by the highway acquisition and need not be appraised.

However, if the acquisition were to follow the course shown in Figure 14.4, Parcel B would be directly affected by the highway acquisition and must be appraised. The larger parcel, however, is not the unencumbered fee of the parcel, but the fee as encumbered by the easement. In other words, the easement's detrimental effect on Parcel B's value, if any, must be considered by the appraiser in estimating the tract's before and after values.

Although no portion of Parcel A is being acquired in Figure 14.4, an appraisal of the tract is still necessary. As stated, the fee and the easement interest are a single entity for the purposes of valuation. As in the previous example, the larger parcel is the fee of Parcel A plus the easement interest in Parcel B. In Figure 14.4, it is quite possible that Parcel A will be more severely damaged by the highway acquistion than Parcel B, even though there is no physical invasion of Parcel A.

Situations involving appurtenant easements can become much more complex.

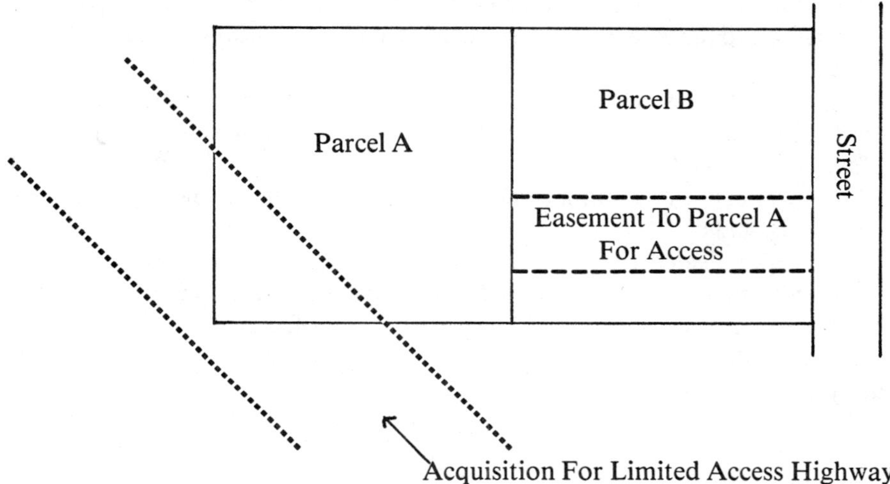

Figure 14.3. Appurtenant Easement

For instance, consider the factual situation illustrated in Figure 14.5. The owner of Parcel B has an easement across Parcel A, and the owner of Parcel A has an easement across Parcel B. The owner of Parcel C has an easement across both Parcels A and B, and the owner of Parcel D has an easement across Parcels A, B, and C. Four appraisals would be required by reason of the taking:

1. An appraisal of Parcel A including the appurtenant easement across Parcel B, but subject to the encumbering easement in favor of the owners of Parcels B, C, and D.

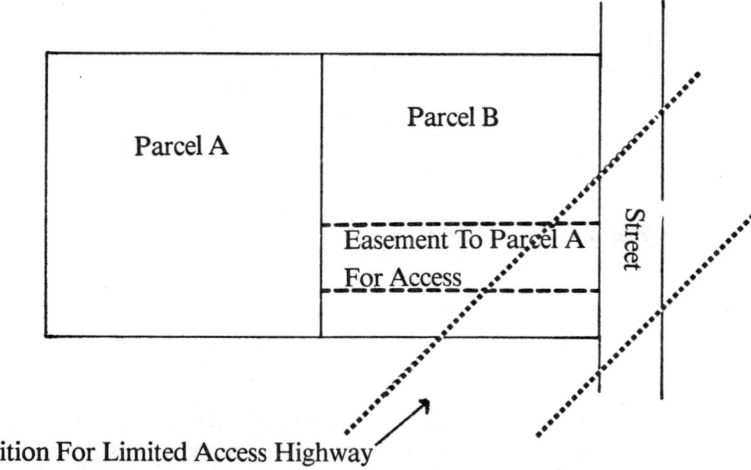

Figure 14.4. Taking of an Appurtenant Easement

2. An appraisal of Parcel B including the appurtenant easement across Parcel A, but subject to the easement across Parcel B in favor of the owners of Parcels C and D.

3. An appraisal of Parcel C including the appurtenant easement across Parcels A and B, but subject to the encumbrance of the easement across Parcel C in favor of the owner of Parcel D.

4. An appraisal of Parcel D together with the appurtenant easements across Parcels A, B, and C.

In such complicated circumstances, it may be advisable for a condemnor to consider constructing a frontage road from Road *B* across Parcel B to connect the existing easement road to Road *B*. Constructing this facility could cost far less than the cumulative compensation due to the owners of Parcels B, C, and D by reason of the elimination of their only legal access.

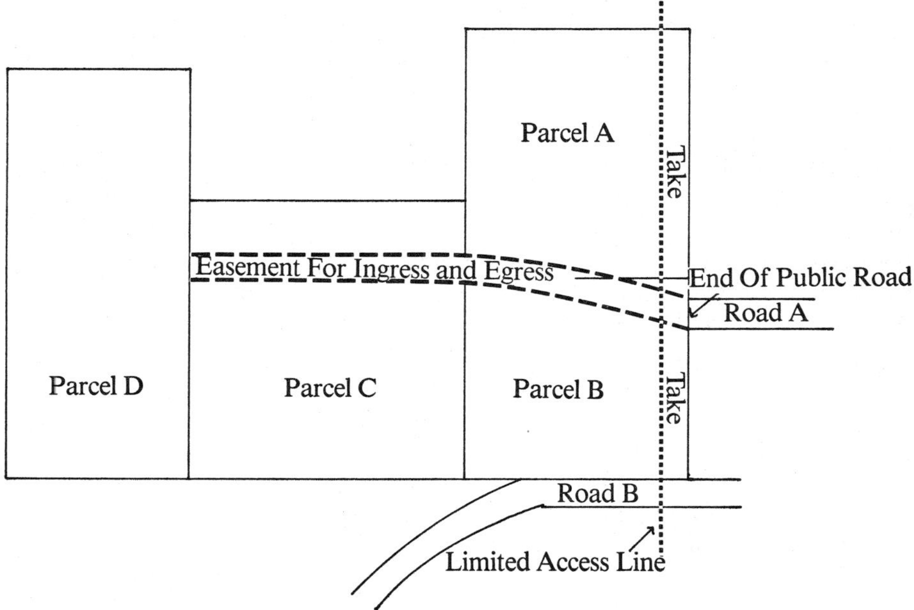

Figure 14.5. Appurtenant Easements

Summary

An easement is the right to do a specific thing to a particular parcel of land without owning the underlying fee. An easement may be temporary or permanent in nature, and it may be classified as subsurface, surface, overhead, or a combination of these types. All easement acquisitions are partial acquisitions because the fee, even though it may be bare land of no utility, will remain with the original owner. Damages due to an easement acquisition are measured by the loss of salable utility in both the area encumbered by the easement and the unencumbered portion of the larger parcel. Damages to the land area encumbered by an easement range from 0% to 100% of the land's fee value.

The appraiser must consider the effects of an easement under three specific circumstances. First, the effect of a proposed easement must be considered in making appraisals for easement acquisition. In this type of assignment, the appraiser must consider the rights to be acquired by the condemnor, the rights remaining with the condemnee, and the obligations and responsibilities of each party. Secondly, consideration must be given to the effect of existing easements encumbering the property under appraisal. Thirdly, consideration must also be given to easements appurtenant to a property under appraisal. It must be remembered that the larger parcel consists of the fee simple ownership plus the appurtenant easement attached to it, viewed as a single entity.

Notes

1. See Chapter 3, "Property Rights."

2. American Institute of Real Estate Appraisers and the Society of Real Estate Appraisers, *Real Estate Appraisal Terminology*, rev. ed., Byrl N. Boyce, ed. (Cambridge, Mass.: Ballinger Publishing Co., 1981) p. 209.

3. James A. Ballentine, *Ballentine's Law Dictionary*, 3rd ed. William S. Anderson, ed. (Rochester, N.Y.: The Lawyers Co-operative Publishing Co.; San Francisco: Bancroft-Whitney Co., 1969), p. 387.

4. North Carolina State Highway Dept. v. Black, 239 N.C. 198, 79 S.E.2d 778.

5. Louis E. Clark, Jr. and F.H. Treadway, Jr., *Impact of Electric Power Transmission Line Easements on Real Estate Values* (Chicago: American Institute of Real Estate Appraisers, 1972).

6. United States v. 48.10 Acres of Land, etc., 144 F.Supp. 258.

7. United States v. 64.88 Acres of Land, etc., 244 F.2d 534.

8. United States v. 4.43 Acres of Land, 137 F.Supp. 567.

9. United States v. Causby, 328 U.S. 256, 66 S.Ct. 1062.

10. Town of East Haven v. Eastern Airlines, Inc., 333 F.Supp. 338.

11. Thomas H. Hall III and William R. Beaton, "A Factor Formula For Valuation of Avigation Easements," *The Appraisal Journal,* January 1965, pp. 29-46.

12. Berman v. Parker, 348 U.S. 26.

13. Julius L. Sackman, *Nichols' The Law of Eminent Domain,* rev. 3rd ed. (New York: Matthew Bender, 1979) Vol. 2A, § 7.519[4].

14. Mayor, etc., of City of Annapolis v. Anne Arundel County, 316 A.2d 807 (Md.).

15. Pub. L. 89-285, 89th Cong. § 301 (a) Amending 23 U.S.C. 319.

16. Donald T. Sutte, Jr., "Scenic Easements," *The Appraisal Journal,* October 1966, pp. 531-548; Howard L. Williams and W.D. Davis, "Effect of Scenic Easements on the Market Value of Real Property," *The Appraisal Journal,* January 1968, pp. 15-32; *Scenic Easements—Legal, Administrative, and Valuation Problems*

and Procedures, National Cooperative Highway Research Program Report No. 56 (Washington, D.C.: Highway Research Board, 1973).

17. 79 Stat. 1028 Amending 23 U.S.C. § 131.

18. Oregon City v. Hartke, 400 P.2d 255 (Ore.).

19. *Scenic Easements—Legal, Administrative and Valuation Problems and Procedures,* National Cooperative Highway Research Program Report No. 56 (Washington, D.C.: Highway Research Board, 1973).

20. Calvo v. United States, 303 F.2d 902.

21. Illinois Telegraph News Co. v. Meine, 242 Ill. 568, 90 N.E. 230.

22. City of Norwood v. Sheen, 126 Ohio St. 482, 186 N.E. 102, A.L.R. 1375.

23. Kimball Laundry Co. v. United States, 338 U.S. 1, 69 S.Ct. 1434.

24. City of Norwood v. Sheen, 126 Ohio St. 482, 186 N.E. 102, A.L.R. 1375.

25. United States v. General Motors Corp., 323 U.S. 373, 65 S.Ct. 357.

26. Fulmer v. State Dep't of Roads, 178 Neb. 664, 134 N.W.2d 798.

27. Central Louisiana Elec. Co. v. Fontenot, 159 So.2d 738 (La.).

28. Chicago Mill and Lumber Co. v. Board of Directors, 236 Ark. 322, 366 S.W.2d 184.

29. Mitchell v. Texas Electric Service Company, 299 S.W.2d 183 (Tex.).

30. Pacific Northwest Pipeline Corp. v. Myers, 50 Wash.2d 288, 311 P.2d 655.

31. Ibid.

32. Washington State Dept. of Transportation, *Right of Way Manual,* Chapter 4, § 4-3.24, ¶A (Revised 11/10/76).

33. Ibid., § 4-3.3, ¶E.

34. *Nichols',* Vol. 4, § 12.411.

35. State ex rel. Lindemann v. Preston, 171 Ohio St. 303, 170 N.E.2d 489.

36. United States v. Welch, 217 U.S. 333, 30 S.Ct. 527.

37. Matter of City of New York (West 10th St.), 267 N.Y. 212, 196 N.E. 30.

38. *Nichols',* Vol. 4, § 12.41[1].

39. Matter of City of New York (West 10th St.), 267 N.Y. 212, 196 N.E. 30.

CHAPTER 15
CONSTRUCTION OF THE PUBLIC IMPROVEMENT

If the acquisition of a parcel of land is a total taking, as opposed to a partial acquisition, the proposed use of the land taken is of no consequence to the appraiser, nor is it of consequence to the attorney once the question of public use and necessity has been adjudicated by the court. At least theoretically, the proposed use of the land taken in a total taking is of no significance to the trier of fact and should have no bearing on its determination of just compensation. Only in the case of a partial acquisition does the proposed use of the land taken need to be considered.

Although some may argue that not all public construction constitutes the construction of a public *improvement,* a discussion of this question is beyond the scope of this work. For the purposes of this discussion, it is assumed that all public construction constitutes public improvements. The value estimate of a remainder property in a partial taking case is generally made assuming the public improvement is complete and operational.[1] Therefore, the appraiser must be able to visualize the remainder property after the proposed public project is complete to estimate its value and reflect the damages and/or special benefits accruing to it.

The appraiser proves that he fully and accurately understands the after situation by his ability to describe it in writing, in an appraisal report, and verbally, from the witness stand. The appraiser must understand not only that portion of the public project which will abut the remainder property, but the entire public improvement.

There is considerable case law indicating that damage to the remainder property is limited to the damage caused by only that portion of the public project which abuts the remainder tract.[2] This theory is based on the fact that ". . . the just compensation assured by the Fifth Amendment [of the U.S. Constitution] to an owner, a part of whose land is taken for public use, does not include the diminution in value of the remainder caused by the acquisition and use of adjoining lands of others for the same undertaking."[3] However, it is generally recognized "that it is difficult, if not impossible to separate one element from the other, and that under the circumstances the owner of the remainder area is entitled to all damage caused by the use of the entire project. A railroad, for instance, is an entire thing. It is impossible for any human intelligence to separate the loss or injury which its operation causes, allocating so much to one portion and so much to another."[4] As one court put it:

> For the purpose of determining severance damage to the part not taken, the part of the defendant's land taken is to be considered as an integral and inseparable part of a single highway project not limited to the segment of the highway on his land but extending so far as the construction and use of the highway has a reasonable tendency to cause detriment to the part not taken and to reduce the market value of his land not taken from the viewpoint of a ready, able and willing buyer.[5]

Engineering Data

The first thing the appraiser must do is familiarize himself with the property being appraised by performing a site inspection, examining the title of the property, and making some preliminary determinations as to zoning, neighborhood trends, and general economic conditions. Once this is accomplished, he should meet with the condemnor's engineer to learn about the proposed construction. If the appraiser has been employed by the condemnee, it is often necessary for the condemnee's attorney to make arrangements for such a meeting. If the condemnor's attorney and/or engineer is uncooperative, the required information may be elicited through interrogatories or by deposition.

The amount and quality of information on construction plans and specifications that is available for review by the appraiser will generally depend on the specific condemnor and the type of public project proposed. If possible, a joint site inspection by the appraiser and the engineer should be made. If the appraiser does not understand the proposed construction perfectly, he must continue to question the engineer until full comprehension of the proposed project is achieved.

Some condemnors designate one engineer to act as the condemnor's *court engineer*. The court engineer testifies in all condemnation cases where engineering testimony is required and is usually available to assist the condemnor's attorney and appraiser to prepare for trial. If the condemnor does, in fact, have a court engineer, it is generally advisable for the appraiser to work with, or at least through, this individual regardless of whether the appraiser has been retained by the condemnor or condemnee. The reasons for this are twofold. First, the court engineer is practiced in explaining complex engineering concepts to lay people because he has had experience in testifying before a trier of fact. Secondly, the court engineer is the individual who will be explaining engineering detail to the trier of fact and it is important that the appraiser obtain all necessary engineering data from the same source.

It is often helpful to the appraiser, and in some instances absolutely necessary, to have the property staked by the condemnor's engineer. Some condemnors resist such requests, but if staking is necessary for the appraiser to fully understand the conditions which will exist in the after situation, the appraiser must insist upon it. In some instances, it may be possible for the appraiser to limit the appraisal report and reserve the right to alter it after staking. However, care must be taken not to limit the report to such a degree that it becomes meaningless or misleading.

It is recommended that the appraiser make arrangements to be notified as soon as staking is in place. Survey stakes have a tendency to disappear or move about, so it is prudent for the appraiser to view and photograph the property as soon as possible after staking is complete. The type and degree of staking required by the appraiser will vary from case to case, depending on the type of proposed public construction and the physical characteristics of the property under appraisal. For instance, in a partial acquisition for construction of a new highway, the appraiser may request that the following items be staked:

1. Pertinent property corners.
2. Take, or right-of-way line.
3. Edge of shoulder of road.
4. Edge of pavement.
5. Centerline of road.
6. Extent of limited-access line, if any.
7. Location of new road approach, if any.

A power line easement acquisition might require staking of the limits of the easement, the tower locations, and the limits of any danger tree areas.

Often, the appraiser is required by law and/or policy to invite the property owner to accompany the appraiser on the property inspection. Whether this is required or not, it is good appraisal practice. If the property is to be staked, the ideal time for a joint inspection is immediately after staking. This is also the ideal time for the attorney to inspect the property with the appraiser and/or owner. If the attorney does not take advantage of this opportunity, he will probably not have another chance to view the property with the staking in place until one or two days before trial, when the property is restaked for inspection by the trier of fact. If the attorney does not understand the circumstances surrounding the remainder property until one or two days before the trial, he may not have enough time to prepare adequately.

Figure 15.1 illustrates one good reason the appraiser and/or the owner's attorney should make a joint inspection of the property with the property owner. In this factual situation, no evidence of a septic tank, drain field, or well was visible from ground level. The applicable health regulations required a totally clear zone 100 feet in diameter around the well, with no drain field, driveway, or other improvement encroaching within this area. When the taking line was determined, the condemnor was not aware of the location of the septic tank drain field. The appraiser and the attorney retained by the condemnee were also unaware of the location of the drain field until the owner pointed it out during a joint inspection of the property. The take line was then staked to verify its location in relationship to the drain field.

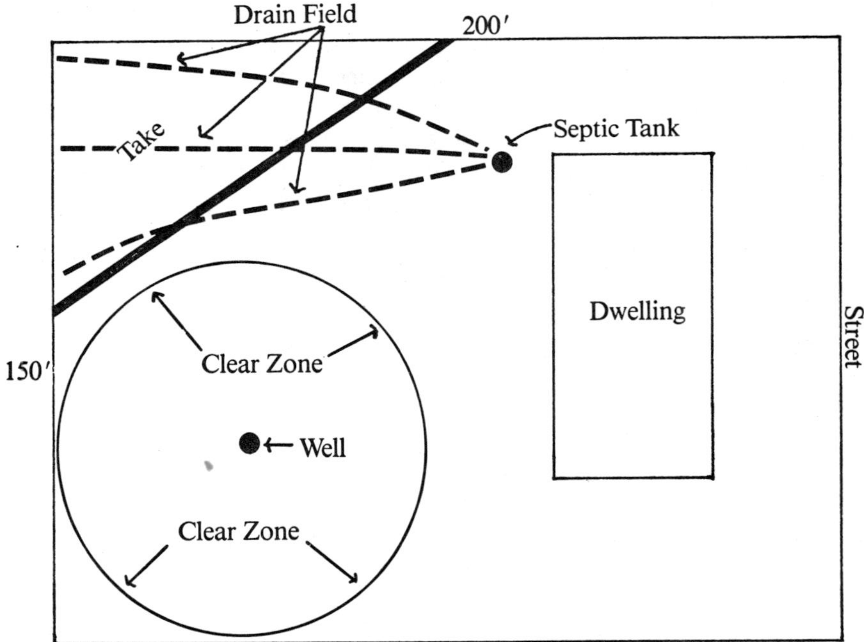

Figure 15.1. Partial Taking

The local health authority was contacted and it was found that the drain field could not be relocated on the remainder and still keep the required 100 feet clear zone around the well. This resulted in the remainder property suffering damage of nearly 100%. When the condemnor was notified of these circumstances, it determined that it would be physically possible and more cost effective to construct a small concrete retaining wall west of the proposed take line and move the take line far enough west to avoid the underground septic tank drain field.

In analyzing the value of the property in the after situation, the appraiser must consider the proposed use to which the condemnor will put the land taken.[6] However, he must keep in mind that the condemnor is generally not limited in the use of the land taken to that proposed at the time of taking unless the condemnor limits or restricts itself to the specific plans and specifications submitted at that time. If such a limitation is made by the condemnor, and the condemnor subsequently expands or changes the use of the land, the condemnee may be entitled to additional compensation.[7] If no such limitation is made, however, the condemnor is not restricted in its use of the land taken and the appraiser should consider what the condemnor is acquiring a right to do, not what he specifically plans to do as of the date of valuation.

On the other hand, the appraiser cannot assume that the condemnor will put the land taken to that use which, in the appraiser's opinion, would be the most damaging to the remainder.[8] Any potential uses must be so reasonably probable as to have a detrimental effect on the current market value of the remainder. As one court stated:

> While it is true that a condemnation award must "once and for all" fix the damages, present and prospective, that accrue reasonably from the construction of the improvements, and in this connection must consider the most injurious use of the property reasonably possible that does mean that the jury may speculate on the possibility of damage from some future abandonment of the improvement. Remote, speculative, or conjectural elements of damage cannot be submitted to or considered by the jury.[9] [citations omitted]

"It has been frequently held that if a portion of a tract is condemned and compensation is paid, the condemnee or his successor in interest cannot recover additional damages because of any subsequent use of the land taken which could reasonably be foreseen at the time of the original condemnation, the theory being that the condemnee was compensated for any use of the condemned property foreseeable at the time of taking."[10] [citations omitted]

The most common partial acquisitions are overhead easements (as for power lines), surface easements or takings (as for roadways), and subsurface easements (as for utility distribution). The specific engineering data typically available and the information needed by the appraiser to value each of these types of takings are discussed in detail below. Of course, if the taking is of a fee rather than an easement, the taking, from a technical standpoint, is of the entire property including the space above the ground and the area below the ground; thus the reference to overhead, surface and subsurface refers to the intended use of the area taken, rather than the form of the taking.

Overhead Use

The most common overhead use is an easement acquired for the construction of electrical transmission lines. Installations involving long-run, high-capacity lines are those which most often require the services of professional appraisers and which can often result in condemnation trials. Topographical maps of the easement area are generally available from the condemnor, along with parcel or ownership strip maps.

Figure 15.2 is an example of a strip map. These maps generally show the location of existing buildings, the limits of the proposed easement acquisition, the ownership of the land, the proposed tower locations, and various physical features of the land such as roads, waterways, fences, etc. Such maps will also delineate danger tree areas, labeled "DTA," which are areas outside of the easement proper where the condemnor will have the right to top or completely remove any trees which it perceives as dangerous to the proposed transmission line. Large- and small-scale aerial photographs are also useful and generally available to the appraiser involved in appraising larger ownerships.

The appraiser will require engineering data on easement widths and areas; danger tree areas, if any; and the types, styles, locations, and heights of towers. The appraiser should also investigate anticipated initial line capacity, anticipated future increases in line capacity, and whether operation of the line is likely to cause any coronas, arcing, TV disturbance, and/or radio interference. Also, any and all safety features of the line should be determined.

If an easement will be acquired, its specific terms and conditions must be analyzed to determine which rights will remain with the underlying fee owner and which will be transferred to the condemnor. A standard easement form used by the U.S. Department of Energy is shown in Figure 15.3. Two specific items on this form should be noted. Paragraph 3(b) gives the government the right to designate additional trees, owned by the fee owner but not specified in the easement, as danger trees for a period of three years and to remove said trees upon payment of their market value to the fee owner. The second item to be noted is that Christmas trees are not construed, for purposes of this easement, as an agricultural crop and the growing of these trees within the easement area is, therefore, prohibited. Formerly, these easements allowed the planting and growing of Christmas trees, but experience showed that the trees were often forgotten by the fee owner and allowed to grow to such heights as to eventually endanger the power line and the government was forced to remove the trees at its own expense.

Surface Use

The most common acquisition for surface use is the fee acquisition for roadway purposes. In appraising partial acquisitions for roadway purposes, the appraiser

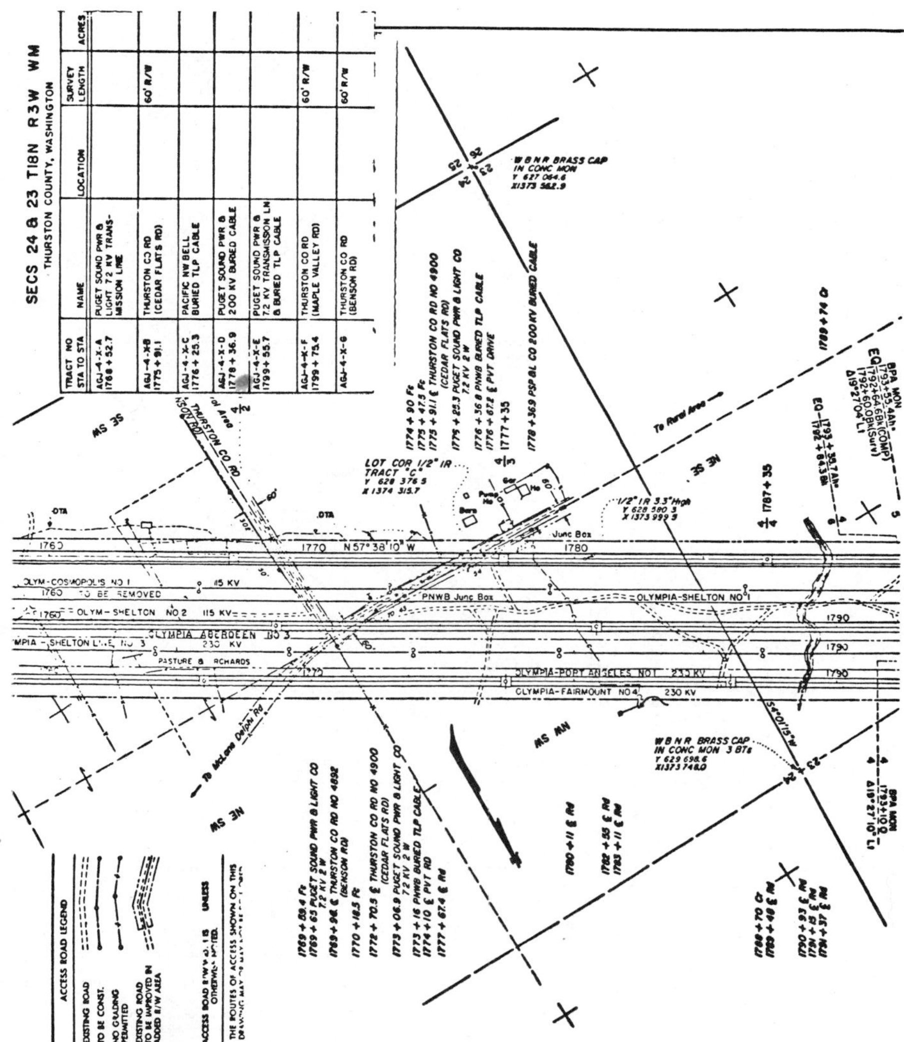

Figure 15.2. Strip Map

generally requires more engineering data than are needed for any other partial taking. Fortunately, most condemnors of road rights-of-way employ competent, full-time engineering staffs and, therefore, engineering data are plentiful. If the appraiser has been employed by the condemnor, much of this data is furnished at the time the appraisal assignment is made; if he has been employed by the condemnee, however, the appraiser may have to ask for each specific document or item of data; often several times.

U.S. DEPARTMENT OF ENERGY — BONNEVILLE POWER ADMINISTRATION

CONTRACT AND GRANT OF EASEMENT
(Transmission Line and Danger Trees)

THIS AGREEMENT made this _______ day of _______ , 19___

between _______

the Grantor, whether one or more, and the UNITED STATES OF AMERICA, Department of Energy, Bonneville Power Administration, pursuant to the Bonneville Project Act, Act of August 20, 1937, Ch. 720, 50 Stat. 731, as amended, 16 U.S.C. 832(1970) and the Federal Columbia River Transmission System Act, Act of October 18, 1974, P.L. 93-454, 88 Stat. 1376, 16 U.S.C. 838 (Supp IV).

WITNESSETH

That the parties hereto covenant and agree as follows:

1. The Grantor, for and in consideration of the sum of _______ ($_______) and the provisions contained in this agreement, does hereby grant and convey to the United States of America and its assigns a perpetual easement and right-of-way for electric power transmission purposes in, upon, over and under the following-described land, to wit:

2. The grant shall include the right to enter and to locate, construct, operate, maintain, repair, rebuild, upgrade, remove and patrol one line of poles or structures and appurtenances thereto, supporting conductors of one or more electric circuits of any voltage, together with the present and future right to clear the right-of-way and to keep the same clear of all structures, trees, brush and any other vegetation, and fire hazards, provided, however, that vegetation and fire hazards shall not include agricultural crops. All such trees, brush, vegetation, structures and fire hazards presently on the right-of-way shall become the property of the United States on the date of acceptance hereof, and may be disposed of by the United States in any manner it deems suitable.

3. The Grantor also hereby grants and conveys to the United States and its assigns:

(a) The right to top, limb, or fell and to remove, set, burn or otherwise dispose of those trees and snags (collectively called "present danger trees") located on land owned by the Grantor adjacent to the transmission line right-of-way that are presently of such height and location that any part thereof could fall within _______ feet of any of the facilities constructed or to be constructed within the transmission line right-of-way; provided, however, it is agreed that the consideration recited herein includes payment for all trees and snags presently and in the future located within the right-of-way, and those trees and snags presently within the area of and located outside said right-of-way as shown on the attached Exhibit.

(b) The United States shall have the right within three years from the date of the initial clearing of the right-of-way to top, limb, or fell and to remove, set, burn or otherwise dispose of danger trees, if any, on the Grantor's land outside of the areas of land described in sub-paragraph (a) above (collectively called "additional danger trees"); and the United States shall pay the owner thereof the prevailing market value.

4. Notice of acceptance of this instrument by the United States shall be given to the Grantor at his last known address within six months from the date hereof or offer shall become void. Upon the issuance of such notice, the United States shall have the right to exercise the rights granted herein.

5. The rights granted herein are subject to easements of record and mineral rights of third parties.

6. In addition to the consideration recited herein, the United States shall repair or compensate the Grantor for damage to agricultural crops, fences, and irrigation and drainage systems within the transmission line right-of-way that occurs during the construction, reconstruction, removal or maintenance of the transmission line(s). Payment for such damage shall be made on the basis of an appraisal approved by the United States.

7. The Grantor agrees to satisfy of record such encumbrances, including taxes and assessments, as may be required by the United States, and obtain such curative evidences of title as may be requested by the United States.

8. The United States shall pay all costs incidental to the preparation and recordation of this instrument, and for the procurement of title evidence.

9. The Grantor covenants to and with the United States that the Grantor is lawfully seized and possessed of the land aforesaid, has a good and lawful right and power to sell and convey the same, that the same is free and clear of encumbrances, except as herein provided, and the Grantor will forever warrant and defend the title to the rights granted herein and the quiet possession thereof against the lawful claims and demands of all persons whomsoever.

10. The provisions hereof shall inure to the benefit of and be binding upon the heirs, executors, administrators, successors and assigns of the Grantor, and the assigns of the United States.

11. Future expenditures to be made by the United States as provided herein are subject to the availability of funds therefor.

12. No Member of or Delegate to Congress or Resident Commissioner shall be admitted to or share any part of this agreement or to any benefits that may arise therefrom, but this provision shall not be construed to extend to this agreement if made with a corporation or company for its general benefit.

_______________________ Witness   Grantor _______________________

Accepted for the
UNITED STATES OF AMERICA _______ (Date)   Grantor _______________________
By _______

                                    Grantor _______________________

Tract No(s) _______   Grantor _______________________

BPA 1410 MARCH 1981

Figure 15.3. Standard Easement Form

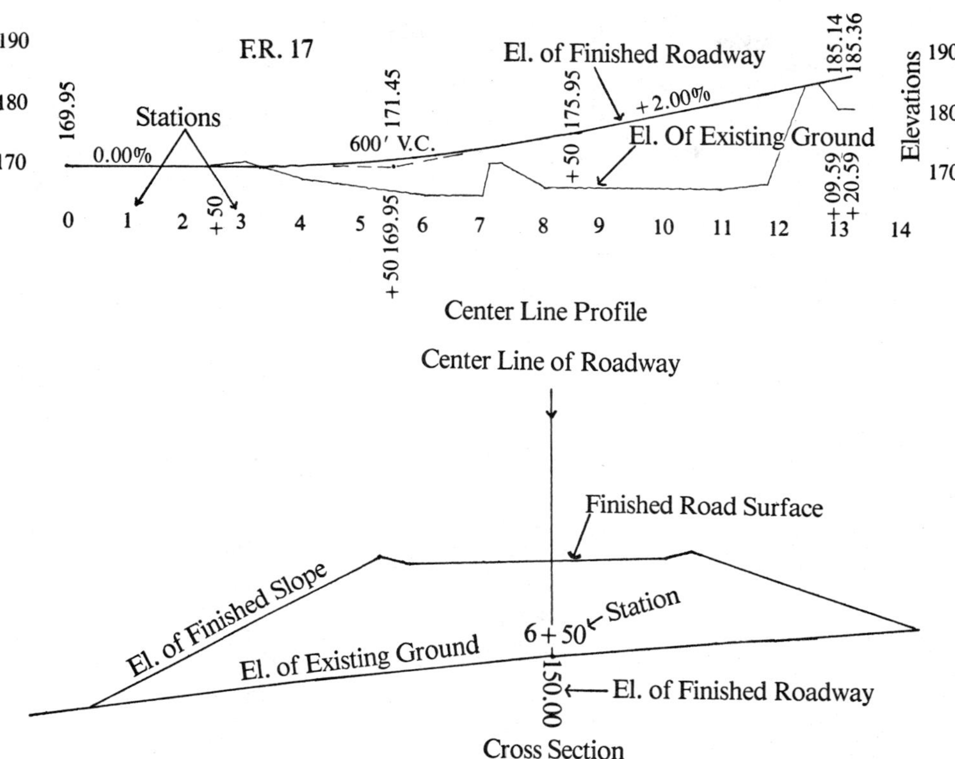

**Figure 15.4. Centerline Profile and Roadway
Cross-Section Maps**

The right-of-way maps prepared by the condemnor are generally informative and of good quality. An example of a typical highway right-of-way map was presented earlier in this work.[11] Centerline profile maps and roadway cross-section maps are also generally available. Examples of these maps are shown in Figure 15.4. It is important to obtain both centerline and cross-section profile maps of proposed highways, as Figure 15.5 illustrates. The centerline elevation map appears to indicate that the taking would cause no loss of view, but the cross-section map clearly shows that the property under appraisal would suffer such a loss. A cross-section map will also help the appraiser determine the feasibility of reconstructing road approaches and driveways.

Figures 15.6 and 15.7 demonstrate why this information is necessary. The right-of-way map in Figure 15.6 would lead one to believe that damages to the remainder, if any, would be nominal. However, Figure 15.7 clearly indicates that the garage will be unusable in its present location after the taking because an acceptable vehicular access to it cannot be constructed. This may also be damaging to the dwelling due to the loss of light, view and air. Some drainage problems may also be present in the after situation.

In addition to showing the areas affected and the location of the improvements, engineering maps will help the appraiser determine whether any ancillary rights are being acquired; these rights might involve slope easements (permanent or temporary), drainage easements, flowage easements (permanent or occasional), construction easements of varying scope, water channel relocations (per-

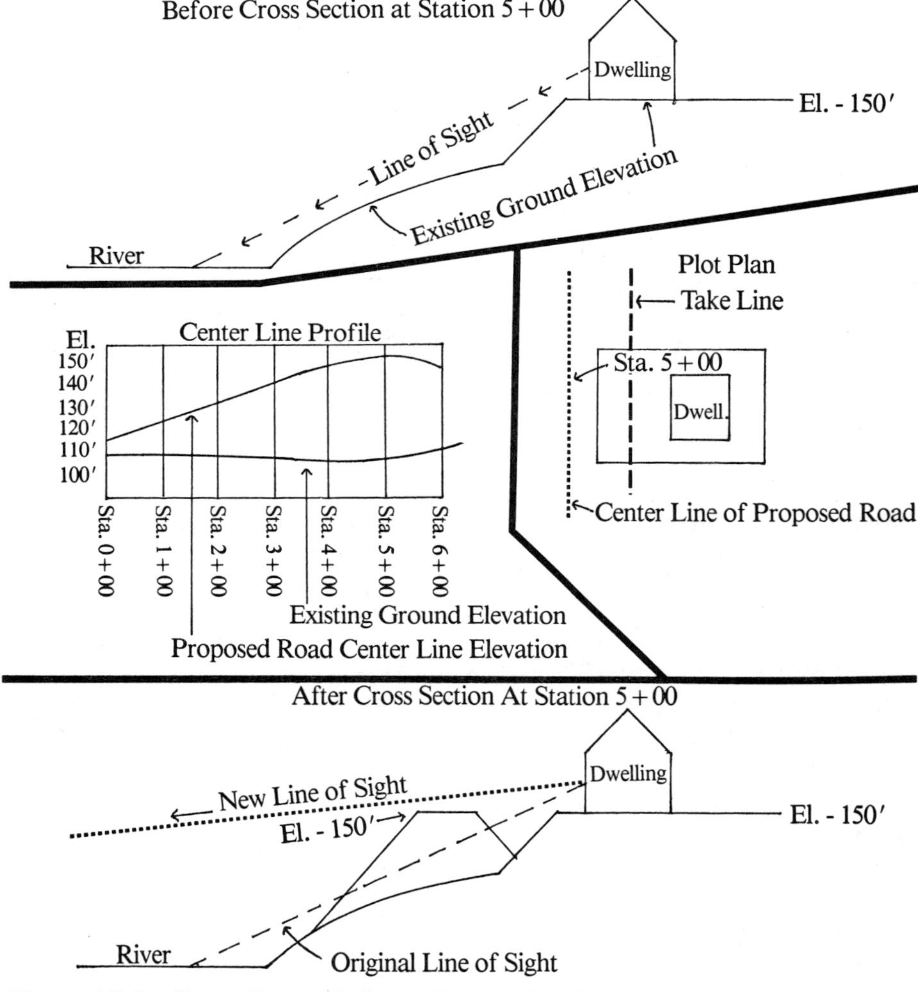

**Figure 15.5. Centerline and Cross-Section Profile Maps
of Proposed Highways**

manent or temporary), limitations on rights of light, view, and air, and any restrictions on road approaches.

The appraiser should obtain detailed plans of drainage, traffic control, and traffic channelization, as well as profiles and cross-sections of any frontage road or interchange on/off ramp that could possibly affect the property being appraised. He must also determine roadway widths, the number of proposed lanes, anticipated traffic volumes, and any plans for the construction of sidewalks and/ or curbs. If fences are to be constructed, he must know the type of fence to be built and determine who will be responsible for its maintenance.

Engineering consultants can help the appraiser estimate the increases or decreases in traffic noise, dust, and headlight glare to be anticipated due to the operation of the proposed improvements. Dust and noise created during construction

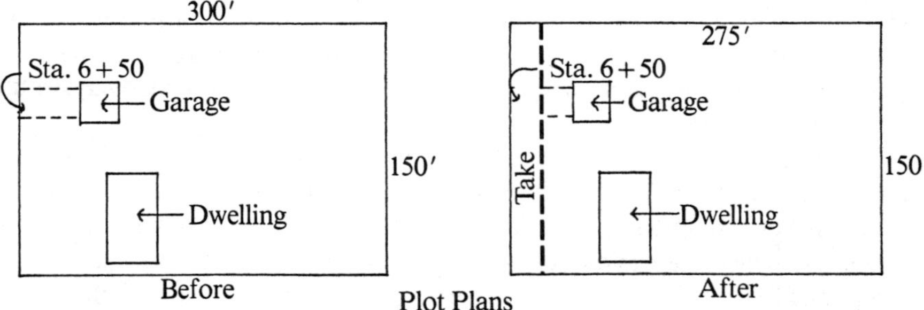

Figure 15.6. Plot Plans

of the improvements are noncompensable damage items. It is dust and noise created by the operation of the completed improvement which may be compensable if they diminish the remainder property's market value and the damage is peculiar to the property being appraised. Large- and small-scale aerial photographs of the property are often available and can be particularly helpful if the engineer has identified the boundary lines of the property and prepared a *clear film* overlay depicting the after situation.

Another common type of surface use is the flowage easement. These may be in

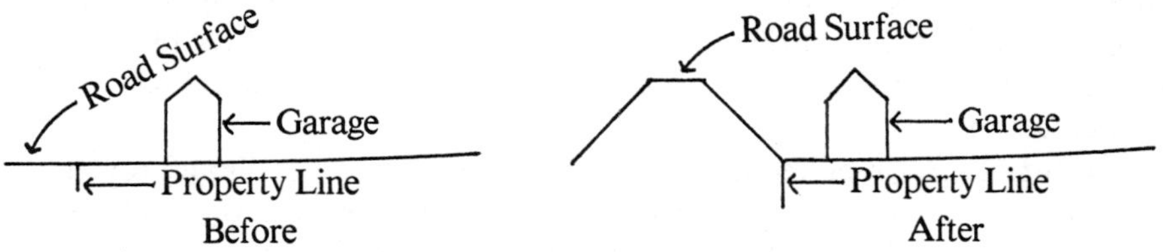

Figure 15.7. Cross Sections at Station 6+50

the form of *occasional flowage easements, permanent flowage easements,* or a combination of these two types. Extremely accurate, small-scale topographic maps are absolutely necessary in appraising flowage easements. It is often left to the appraiser to estimate the amount of land area which will be inundated. Using an accurate topographic map, a steady hand, and a planimeter, this estimate can generally be made with a relatively high degree of accuracy. If the easement specifies occasional inundation, the appraiser must determine how frequently the land will be flooded. This can generally be ascertained by examining available records and questioning the condemnor's engineer. The appraiser should attempt to discover whether the property to be encumbered by the easement has had a history of flooding in the before situation.

Two areas are often overlooked in the appraisal of property for flowage easement purposes. The first item is the potential for damage to the unencumbered portion of the property due to the impairment or elimination of physical access from the fronting roadway to the property and/or from one portion of the property to another. It may be necessary to construct a bridge or a roadway with a culvert to rectify this situation.

The second element is the potential damage or benefit to an unencumbered remainder from a change in the groundwater elevation, caused by the flowage of water to an elevation greater than that which existed before the acquisition of the flowage easement. This can damage an unencumbered remainer by increasing the frequency of flooding, damaging or killing crops and trees, or causing the failure of a septic tank system. On the other hand, an increase in the elevation of the water table could benefit arid land by causing subirrigation to occur and decreasing or eliminating the need to irrigate the unencumbered area by artifical means. If the appraiser is concerned about the probable effect of a flowage easement on surrounding unencumbered land, a hydrology consultant should be employed.

Subsurface Use

The most common subsurface use generally takes the form of an easement for underground utilities such as gas lines, water lines, oil lines, sewer lines, and cables for television, telephone, and electricity. In appraising a property for the acquisition of a subsurface easement, the appraiser must determine the specific use to which the easement area will be put. If a pipeline carrying potentially dangerous material will be installed, the type and safety features of the pipe must be determined. For most subsurface uses, the depth of the pipe or cable should also be ascertained.

It will generally require some research, but the appraiser should investigate how often the condemnor will have to go back onto the property to reopen the ground for inspection and/or repair of the pipe or cable. The easement form to be utilized must be examined to determine: 1) who repairs the surface of the ground; 2) whether any additional temporary construction easements will be acquired and, if so, for how long; 3) whether the underlying fee owner can build on any part of the easement area; and 4) whether the condemnor will construct any surface structures within the easement area such as valves, valve houses, pump stations and manholes. If unsightly surface structures are to be built, the appraiser can often estimate the damage by calculating the cost of planting sight-obscuring shrubbery around the structures. Of course, this method cannot be used if the cost of buying and planting the shrubbery is greater than the diminution in the property's market value brought on by the unsightly structure.

Utility easements can often benefit a property as well as damage it; Figure 15.8 depicts such a situation. Before the easement acquisition and construction of the sewer line, the owner of the property was using a septic tank; all house plumbing

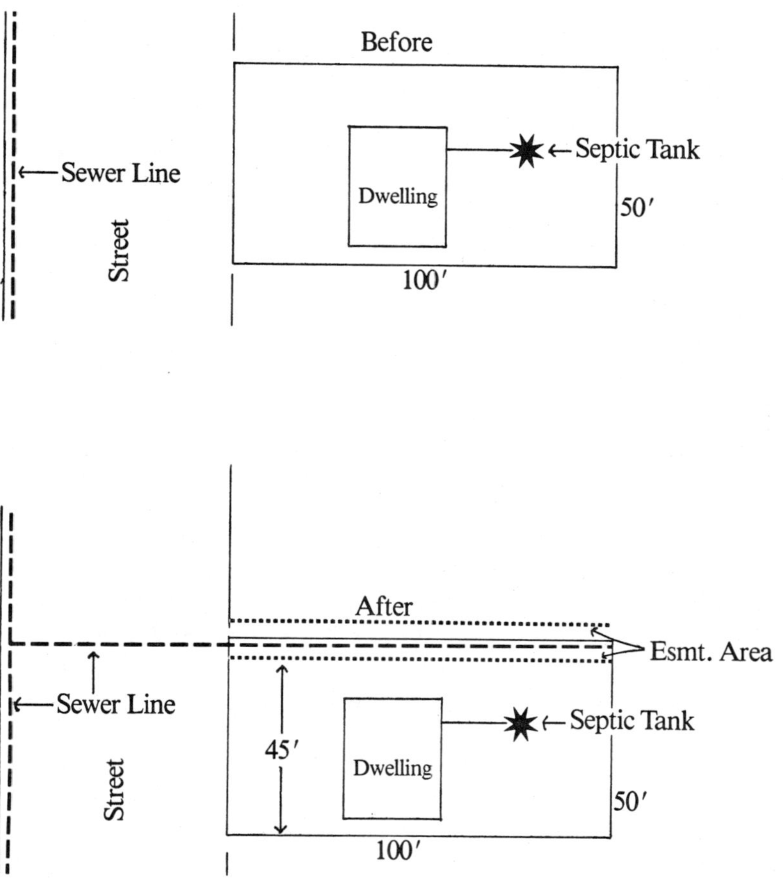

Figure 15.8. Benefits Due to Public Project

was channeled toward the rear of the improvement and connected to the septic tank. In the before situation, to connect the plumbing to the public sewer would have required running a connection line under the public street, reorganizing the pipes within the house to accommodate the sewer connection, constructing an exit through the front wall of the dwelling, and digging a trench through the front yard of the property. The total cost of these improvements was estimated at $1,900. In the after situation, the owner simply connected the public sewer line running along the east side of the property to the existing piping exiting the dwelling. The total cost of this hookup was $235, so a benefit of $1,900 - $235, or $1,665 may have accrued to the property.

Visualizing the After Situation

To ensure complete understanding of the after situation, the appraiser must be able to *paint a picture* of the property after the taking, both verbally and visually. The engineering data used should be verified in writing by the engineer; this document should be retained in the appraiser's file for later reference. The appraiser should always identify the plans and specifications he relied upon in preparing the appraisal report and include the date when these plans were last revised. For instance, the appraiser might include in the assumptions and limiting conditions of the appraisal report a statement such as:

> This appraisal was made under the assumption that the taking and construction of the proposed public improvement will occur as depicted on the Department of Transportation's right-of-way and profile maps for SR 5, MP (mile post) 42.04 to MP 51.66, Rocky Point to Toutle River. Specific reliance has been placed on (1) the right-of-way plans designated as sheet 19 of 51 sheets having an original date of February 14, 1978 and a last revision date of April 16, 1980 and (2) the profile plan designated as sheet 36 of 51 sheets having an original date of February 14, 1978, with no subsequent revision date. If any modification is made to the above referred to plans the appraiser reserves the right to alter her appraisal report to reflect such modifications.

Only with extreme caution should the appraiser rely on an artist's or architect's rendering of an after situation. Those lovely, towering trees which screen the remainder from the public improvement's offending view and noise will only be 18 inches high when planted; the gently sloping, cultivated landward side of the dike or levee may turn out to be quite steep and covered in a riprap of rather large rocks. Depend on the engineering plans and specifications, not the fertile imagination of an artist with a flair for drawing aesthetically pleasing pictures.

To guarantee consistency, and for self-protection, the appraiser should always listen to any engineering testimony given at a condemnation trial. If the engineer's testimony and the information furnished to the appraiser by the engineer are not consistent, this inconsistency must be clarified either before the engineer is excused from the witness stand or before the appraiser takes the stand. Although in most circumstances the appraiser may be ready to admit what he does not know on the witness stand, ignorance about basic engineering data that will affect the property under appraisal in the after situation is totally unacceptable. The appraiser must thoroughly understand the effect the proposed construction may have on the remainder property.

It is imperative that the appraiser and the attorney have an identical understanding of how the engineering plans affect the property being appraised well before the trial. If there is no such understanding, the attorney may not recognize the inconsistency between the engineer's testimony and the engineering data adopted by the appraiser until it is too late and the appraiser's description of the property in the after situation is being torn apart under cross-examination.

If the proposed construction is atypical in any manner, the appraiser should try to locate a similarly constructed public improvement, inspect it, and take aerial and/or ground photos of the similar improvements, as circumstances warrant. It also may be educational for the appraiser to reinspect remainder properties, which he has previously appraised, after the public improvement is complete and operational. At this time, the appraiser can ascertain whether the remainer does, in fact, resemble the verbal and written picture he prepared before the taking. Interviewing the owners of such properties may also be helpful. If the appraiser attempts to inspect a previously appraised property after completion of the public improvements and cannot find the remainder property, it is quite possible that the appraiser's visual and written picture of the remainder was somewhat off target.

Summary

If the government exercises its power of eminent domain and takes the entire property, the purpose of the government's acquisition is of no consequence once the court has ruled that there is a public use and necessity for the acquisition. However, if a property owner is left with a portion of his property, often referred to as the *remainder,* the use to which the condemnor will put the land taken becomes important because it may have a significant effect on the remainder property's value. For this reason, the appraiser and the attorney must be intimately familiar with the proposed public construction.

The appraiser should be prepared to describe fully, both verbally and in writing, the construction and engineering details of the proposed public improvement. He should also determine whether the condemnor must put the land taken to that use proposed at the time of the taking, or whether the condemnor is also acquiring the right to expand or change the use of the land taken at a later date. In any verbal or written presentation made, the appraiser must clearly identify the specific rights which the condemnor is acquiring and describe, in detail, the proposed public construction. A statement such as "The state will build a four-lane freeway" is totally inadequate in describing a proposed government construction.

Several courts have held that damage to a remainder property is limited to the damage caused by only that portion of the public project abutting the remainder property. However, most courts have ruled that it is impossible to separate the damage resulting from that portion of the public project abutting a remainder and the damage caused by that portion of the public project not abutting the remainder. Usually, damage to the remainder caused by the entire public project is considered. To understand the engineering details of the after situation, the appraiser should obtain written data directly from the condemnor's engineer—preferably the same engineer who will testify before the trier of fact if the case goes to trial.

In many instances it is helpful, if not absolutely necessary, to have the property boundaries and significant construction details staked on the ground so that the appraiser and the attorney can better visualize the proposed public construction and the remainder property in the after situation.

The amount of construction or engineering data required will depend on the use to which the property taken will be put and the complexity of the proposed construction. The quantity and quality of engineering data will often depend on the specific condemnor involved and the complexity of the proposed public project. An answer on the witness stand of *"I don't know"* by an appraiser in response to a question regarding the details of the proposed public construction is totally unacceptable. If the appraiser does not know the construction details of the proposed public improvement, he cannot accurately estimate the after value of the remainder property. Responses such as, "I think the property will flood" or "I think the power transmission line will interfere with TV reception" are also clearly unacceptable. The appraiser must demonstrate a clear understanding of the after situation. If he cannot obtain satisfactory answers from the condemnor's engineer, the appraiser should either retain another engineering consultant or limit the appraisal report to those engineering or construction details which are clearly understood.

The appraiser should reinspect the appraised property after the public improvement is complete and operational to determine whether the mental picture of the after situation he developed during the initial appraisal process does, in fact, coincide with the actual, constructed improvement. Such an *after construction* inspection can also help the attorney prepare future land litigation cases.

The appraiser must always refer in his report to the specific plans and specifications which were used in making the appraisal. He should also note when the information was originally prepared and last revised. The appraiser should reserve the right to alter the previous findings if the plans and specifications are changed after the effective date of valuation.

Notes

1. For exceptions, see Chapter 13, "Benefits—General and Special," § Appraisal Procedure.

2. St. Regis Paper Co. v. United States, 313 F.2d 45.

3. Campbell v. United States, 266 U.S. 368, 45 S.Ct. 115.

4. Julius L. Sackman, *Nichols' The Law of Eminent Domain,* rev. 3rd. ed. (New York: Matthew Bender, 1979) Vol. 4A, § 14.21[1].

5. State Highway Comm. v. Bloom, 77 S.D. 452, 93 N.W.2d 572.

6. United States v. 72.35 Acres of Land, etc., 150 F.Supp. 271.

7. McCubbin v. Village of Gretna, 174 Neb. 172, 116 N.W.2d 287.

8. United States v. River Rouge Impvmt. Co., 269 U.S. 411, 46 S.Ct. 144.

9. People ex rel. Dept. of Public Works v. Schultz Co., 123 Cal. App.2d 925, 268 P.2d 117.

10. Texas Electric Service Co. v. Cambell, 328 S.W.2d 208 (Tex.).

11. See Chapter 4, "The Larger Parcel," Figures 4.1 and 4.2.

CHAPTER 16
LEASEHOLD VALUATIONS

Real estate carries with it a bundle of rights to which the owner of the real estate is entitled. One of the most important of these rights, or interests, is often referred to as the *beneficial interest* in the real estate; this is the right of use and occupancy of the realty. Another ownership right is the right to transfer the beneficial interests in property to another person or entity. This act of transference is often accomplished by way of a lease, which is defined as, "[a] written document by which the rights of use and occupancy of land and/or structures are transferred by the owner to another person or entity for a specified period of time in return for a specified rental."[1]

When a tract of land is leased, the fee simple estate is divided in two. The owner of the real estate is said to hold a *leased fee estate,* while the tenant, or lessee, holds a *leasehold estate.* The owner of a leased fee retains the fee to the property, and the rights of use and occupancy are conveyed by lease to others. The owner of the leased fee has two specific rights in the property: 1) the right to receive rent over the period of the lease, and 2) the right to repossess the property upon termination of the lease.[2] The owner of the leasehold estate has the right to use and occupy the realty for the term of the lease, subject to the terms and conditions of the lease, including the payment of rent.[3]

Both the leased fee estate and the leasehold estate can be described as positive or negative. If the rental amount specified in the lease is less than the current economic or market rent, the lessee, or tenant, holds a positive leasehold interest and the landlord holds a negative leased fee estate. Under such circumstances, the lessee, at least theoretically, can sell his beneficial interest in the property for a sum of money; the landlord, on the other hand, will not be able to sell the leased fee estate for as much as he could if the property were not subject to the lease.

If the rent specified in the lease, often referred to as the *contract rent,* is greater than the current economic or market rent, the landlord then has a positive leased

288

fee estate, and the lessee has a negative leasehold estate. Under these circumstances, the owner of the leased fee estate, again theoretically, could sell his interest in the property for more than the property would bring if it were not under the lease; the lessee, however, could not give his leasehold estate away, let alone sell it.

Undivided Fee Rule

It would be unethical for an appraiser to value a property subject to a lease without considering the effect of that lease on the market value of the property unless such consideration "is specifically precluded by the terms of the appraisal assignment."[4] In most condemnation appraisals, the appraiser is instructed to exclude any consideration of existing leases and their effect, if any, on the market value of the property, and to appraise the property as if all interest therein were held by one individual or entity. This concept is often referred to as the *undivided fee rule*.[5] The philosophy behind this rule is that the condemnor is acquiring the fee simple title to the property,[6] not the various, separately held interests in it.

The federal courts,[7] and many of the state courts, have adopted the undivided fee rule.[8] As stated by the Idaho court:

> It was the State's theory of the case at trial and its theory on appeal that the compensation for the value of the land taken and the damages to the remaining property by reason of severance should be assessed in total and only thereafter should that award be apportioned between the lessor Bastian and the lessee Albertson's. The State sought a jury instruction to that effect, but it was denied. The denial of that instruction was error. The mere fact that ownership of land is divided among different persons and of owners of various interest in the title including leasehold does not in and of itself enhance the value of the property.[9] [citations omitted]

"In appraising such property the undivided fee rule is generally adhered to . . .,"[10] and apportionment of the total award is considered only after the total award has been established by the trier of fact. To attempt to do otherwise has been compared to trying to divide a cake before it is ready for slicing.[11] For this reason "[t]he matter of such apportionment is of no concern to the condemnor and is a problem in which only the claimants are involved."[12] "Having participated in the trial to establish the value of the whole, the government should have no concern with or responsibility for the later allocating of the distributive shares, among those owning or claiming subordinant estates or interests in the improved site."[13]

The jurisdictions that have adopted the undivided fee rule have taken the position that the sum of the various estates in a parcel of real estate cannot, as a matter of law, exceed the value of the real estate as a whole.[14] Experienced appraisers know that "[t]he sum of the values, of the fee, subject to the lease, and leasehold interest tends to be the same as the value of the property free and clear."[15] They also acknowledge, however, that ". . . under certain circumstances, the total value of the property as a unit can be more or less than the sum of the fee and leasehold values."[16] Only a limited number of jurisdictions have recognized this second fact.[17]

When the undivided fee rule is abandoned by these few jurisdictions, an alternate rule, referred to as *the aggregate of interests rule,* is generally adopted. In adopting the aggregate of interests rule, the California court reasoned:

> The question to be answered in this case is, of what does the whole really consist, for which payment is to be made by the condemner in one lump sum under § 1246.1, if it so elects? It seems to us that this whole must be the total of what the various involuntary sellers have to sell and not the undivided fee which the condemner is seeking to acquire. The fact that in this situation, by resorting to § 1246.1, the condemner can force the valuation award against it to be a single sum for the entire fee rather than a summation of the various separate sums awarded to the several owners of interests or estates in the total fee, arrived at independently of each other, does not compel the conclusion as a corollary to this requirement that the total fee so valued must of necessity be valued as if it were owned only by one owner, when in fact it is actually owned jointly by more than one owner. In other words, *what § 1246.1 requires in this initial evaluation, in the first phase of this type of condemnation trial, is a valuation of the fee as a whole, but not a valuation of that fee in an undivided state. The two should not be confused and equated as they so often have been.* [emphasis added]

> We base this conclusion on the fundamental nature of the constitutional requirement of just compensation. All of condemnation law, (statutory and decisional) procedure and practice is but a means to this end of just compensation. The power of eminent domain is granted to the executive branch of the state government so that private property may be taken expeditiously for public use whenever it is so needed, but only upon payment of just compensation to the property owner. The right to take private property involuntarily for public use is conditioned and based upon the performance by public authorities of this obligation to pay the owner of private property the just compensation due him. This obligation of the state to make just compensation to the property owner for the property taken has long been

recognized in this state as concomitant with and inseparable from its right of eminent domain.

Just compensation under the Fifth Amendment to the United States Constitution, so far as taking damages are concerned, means the full and perfect equivalent in money of the property taken. The owner is to be put in as good a position pecuniarily as he would have occupied if his property had not been taken from him. We believe that the due process clause of the Fourteenth Amendment of the United States Constitution requires this as well.

In our opinion this is likewise the mandate of Article I, § 14 of our State Constitution. The property owner must be made whole for his loss and be recompensed in an amount of money equal to that loss. In short, just compensation is based on the loss the owner suffers rather than the benefit which the taker receives. What is to be valued for that purpose is what the involuntary sellers have to sell rather than what the public buyer seeks to acquire.[18] [citations omitted]

There is a basic distinction between those jurisdictions that have adopted the undivided fee rule and the California courts' ruling, as stated above. The California court hears a condemnation case, at least for this purpose, as a case *against the owners of the property,* while jurisdictions adhering to the undivided fee rule view a condemnation trial as a case *in rem*—an action against the property itself, not against its owner.

Because there are only about four jurisdictions which have, at one time or another, abandoned the undivided fee rule in favor of the aggregate of interests rule, the appraiser will generally be concerned with the undivided fee rule. Under this rule, the appraiser will value a property encumbered by a lease in the same way he would appraise a property not so encumbered. In other words, the property in question will be appraised as if its fee simple title were held by one individual or entity. This does not mean, however, that the appraiser should not consider the existing rent level specified in the lease in estimating the current economic rent of the property being appraised.

In light of the undivided fee rule, the appraiser retained by the condemnor generally has completed his assignment upon estimating the market value of the property as if it were not encumbered by a lease. This is usually not the case, however, when the appraiser has been retained by the property owner or lessee. Estimating the market value of the unencumberd property is only the first step for this appraiser.

Allocation of Award

The actual procedures of a condemnation trial and the subsequent allocation of the condemnation award vary from jurisdiction to jurisdiction. Some jurisdictions provide that the same trier of fact which determines just compensation also makes the determination of the proper allocation of the total award, but only after first determining total just compensation. As stated by the Illinois court:

> Where it becomes necessary for the jury to assess damages for separate interests in condemnation proceedings, it is the duty of the jury to first fix the fair cash market value of the entire property as between the petitioner and all of the defendants, and then to divide same according to the respective rights of the defendants.[19]

Other jurisdictions hold a separate hearing on the question of award allocation. "The tenant is given his chance to 'fight it out' with his landlord during allocation proceedings where he can point to 'the period of the unexpired term of the lease, the options, if any, therein to renew or of the landlord to terminate, the characteristics of the demised premises and the amount of rent reserved.' "[20] [citations omitted]

The federal courts have continually held that it is improper to present any testimony regarding the allocation of a condemnation award to a jury hearing a condemnation case. "Any contest between persons claiming an interest in the award is heard by the Court and not the jury and only after the award of all interests in the land has been made. Various persons claiming an interest in the land may appear and desire to present proof of fair market value in the first phase of the case, e.g., owners and lessees."[21]

Such two-step condemnation procedures can create strange bedfellows. In the first phase of a trial, the actual condemnation and determination of total compensation, the landlord and tenant are codefendants; they will often work together to develop and present to the trier of fact the strongest case possible for the highest possible award. In the second phase of the trial, the allocation of the award between landlord and lessee, these parties will become adversaries.[22] It is not unknown for the appraiser who testified for the condemnor in the condemnation phase of the trial to subsequently be retained by either the lessor or lessee to estimate and testify in regard to the proper allocation of the total award.

Generally, the appraiser retained by the condemnor will not be involved in the valuation of leased fee estates, leasehold estates, or the allocation of a condemnation award between these two estates. An appraiser retained by a lessor or a lessee in a condemnation action, however, may also be called upon to estimate the proper allocation of the condemnation award. It is also possible that an appraiser totally unconnected with the original condemnation action may be selected by the lessor or the lessee to estimate the apportionment.

The specific methods of calculating the proper allocation of a condemnation award between the lessor and the lessee will vary substantially depending on the jurisdiction in which the property is located and the specific provisions of the lease.

Lease Provisions

The provisions of a lease encumbering a tract which is acquired or damaged are of extreme importance to the appraiser charged with estimating the proper allocation of a condemnation award, or settlement, between the lessor and the lessee of the property. "The value of a leased fee or leasehold interest can be estimated only after ascertaining the duration and terms of the lease. The terms of the lease may cover a wide range of provisions agreed to by the parties. The quantity, quality and durability of the income attributable to the different interests as well as the value of the property at the end of the lease term are affected by the provisions of the lease."[23] A discussion of all the provisions which can be found in various types of leases is beyond the scope of this work, but this information can be found in other texts.[24] The appraiser must, of course, obtain a complete copy of the lease and analyze it in detail. He should address any technical questions regarding the lease provisions to proper legal counsel. The lease provision which will be of utmost importance to the appraiser is the so-called *condemnation clause.*

The condemnation clause will often dictate the formula to be used in determining how much of the condemnation award should be paid to the lessee, if any. In analyzing a lease condemnation clause, the appraiser must answer the following questions:

1 Does the lease contain a condemnation clause?
2 In a total taking, when does the obligation to pay rent cease?
3 Is the lessee to share in the award for a total taking?
4 How is the award for fixtures to be apportioned in a total taking?
5 In a partial taking, how is the award to be split? Is the lessee to share in the award?
6 Is the lessor to share in the award for partial taking of the leased fee with a rent abatement for the lessee? If so, how is the abatement to be determined?
7 If, in a partial taking, the lessor does not share in the award for loss of rental value, is a trust to be established from the award to insure future payment of rent to the lessor?
8 If the lessee remains in possession after a partial taking, who is responsible for repairs? To whose specifications must the repairs be made? Is a trust to be set up from the award to guarantee the repairs? Must the repairs be made within a specific time?
9 Is there an option to terminate on a partial taking? If there is such an option when must it be exercised?

> 10 If there is a partial taking where percentage leases are involved, are the flat rate per rental period and percent of sales in the rent to be revised?[25]

Nichols' contains a number of illustrative condemnation clauses.[26] If the terms of a condemnation clause are to preclude any relief for the lessee, the clause must be drafted very carefully. "This is required because of the attitude of many courts towards condemnation clauses. Courts are reluctant to see lessees deprived of possession without some remedy, and to accomplish this result they construe such clauses strictly against the lessor."[27]

The provisions of the condemnation clause, and the other provisions of the lease, will effectively lead the appraiser to the correct methodology to be used in estimating the allocation of the award between the lessor and lessee. The appraiser should keep in mind that often the individual or entity in possession of the property is not the original lessee, but a sublessee. In such an instance, it is necessary to consider how the total award will be allocated between the lessor, the original lessee, and the sublessee. The original lessee in such a situation is often referred to as the *sandwich man,* and the lease is often referred to as a *sandwich lease.* "In any event, the damages which should be paid to the tenant are not easy to ascertain."[28]

Legal Rules and Methodology of Valuation

A lease will affect the value of the leased fee estate only if it meets two conditions. First, the remaining term of the lease must be of adequate length so that, if the property were placed on the market, a potential purchaser would recognize the lease and be willing to pay more or less for the property because of its existence than if the property were unencumbered by the lease. Secondly, the contract rent[29] must be either higher or lower than existing market, or economic, rent. Again, the difference between the contract rent and the economic rent must be large enough to affect what an able and willing buyer would pay for the property.

Often, but not always, the value of a leased fee estate plus the value of the leasehold estate will tend to equal the market value of the property free and clear of any lease. Experienced appraisers know that this is not always the case but, in a large majority of jurisdictions, the courts have adopted this concept as an absolute truism. It has been said that "[w]hatever advantage is secured by one interest must be taken from another, *and the sum of all the parts cannot exceed the whole.*"[30] [emphasis added] Therefore, appraisers and attorneys generally must work within the confines of this rule.

Proper appraisal practice would require that the leasehold estate and the leased fee estate each be valued separately; the sum of these two estates may or may not equal the market value of the property as if unencumbered.[31] However, to determine the allocation of a condemnation award, a different procedure is required. "The task of determining the value of the unexpired term of a lease is not without its difficulties. Because of restrictions against assignability, the infrequency with which short term leases are sold on the open market; variations in the duration of unexpired terms; and other considerations too numerous to mention, it is virtually impossible to rely exclusively upon the customary test of market value as to leasehold estates and, at the same time, secure to the condemnee the constitutional guarantee of full or just compensation. The actual value, or value to the owner, is usually the best, if not the only adequate test of such compensation."[32]

However, the Indiana court has ruled otherwise:

> The State contends that there was no proper foundation established to support the opinion evidence of appellees' witnesses, particularly complaining that the opinion is based on a capitalization of net profits. State argues that the proper method of valuing a leasehold interest is to take 'the difference between the contract rent and the fair rental value, if any, capitalized for the unexpired term of the lease and discounted by the factor of present worth.' For this proposition the state cites [several New York cases].

> Although decisions from other States, including the New York cases above noted, speak of computing the value of a leasehold by measuring the excess of rental value over the rents to be paid during the remainder of the term, we are unable to find any Indiana authority to this effect.

> Indiana case and statutory law converge upon the concept that fair market value is the proper measure of damages where a leasehold interest is condemned.[33] [citations omitted]

Some courts have, in effect, treated a leasehold interest as they would a special-use property, referring to a leasehold interest as having an *actual value, intrinsic value,* and a *value to the owner.* A Pennsylvania court stated:

> But market value is an unsatisfactory test of the value to a tenant of a leasehold interest. It is really no test at all, because a lease rarely has any market value. Generally it is not assignable at the will of the tenant, and he pays in rent all that the right of occupation is worth. The right of which he is deprived, and for which he is entitled to full compensation, is the right to remain in undisturbed possession to the end of the term. The loss resulting from the deprivation of this right is what he is entitled to recover.[34]

On the other hand, the Massachusetts court has held that, when contract rent and economic rent are equal, the tenant has not been compensably damaged.[35]

Through case law, various courts have established methods and formulas to be used in the valuation of leasehold and leased fee estates so that allocations of condemnation awards can be made. It can be said, without hesitation, that there is no uniformity by the courts in the methods of allocating condemnation awards between lessees and lessors.

A recent Connecticut case held that the leasehold estate is to be valued and apportioned to the lessee, with the balance of the award being allocated to the lessor. The court stated:

> Generally a leasehold has a value if a fair market rental value of the property, sometimes called economic rent, is in excess of the rent reserved in the lease. In the case of the total taking of property, the accepted method of assessing damages to the leasehold is to determine the annual difference between the contract rent and the economic rent, to multiply the annual difference by the number of years left under the lease, and then to discount that sum to determine its present value. In a partial taking such as in the present case, the same rule is generally followed except that the value of the leasehold before and after the taking must be determined. The measure of damages is the difference between the before and after values of the leasehold.[36]

The Tennessee court recently pronounced a similar rule, but this ruling did not make any mention of discounting the rent differential between economic rent and contract rent. It merely stated that the "[a]pportionment between lessor and lessee is accomplished by determining the value of the latter's interest in the taken property, which in turn is calculated by determining the fair rental value of that property for the unexpired term of the lease and subtracting the rent that would actually have been paid for it by the lessee during that term."[37]

The Florida formula conflicts with the Connecticut rule. The Florida court has stated its apportionment formula as follows:

> This method consists of first determining the fair market value of the property being condemned, free of the leasehold estate. The next step in the process consisted of adding to the reversionary value of the fee at the termination of the lease the reserved rent payable during the remainder of the term, and reducing the total to its present worth by application of the appropriate annuity tables. The last figure thus reached represented the witness's opinion as to what constituted the present value of the fee subject to the lease which, when deducted from the present value of the unencumbered fee, left a remainder which represented the value of the leasehold.[38]

There appears to be considerable confusion, on the part of the courts, as to whether it is appropriate to apply a discount factor to the difference between the contract rent and the economic rent to arrive at a proper value of a leasehold estate. This confusion can be illustrated by comparing the findings of two court cases. The Missouri court stated:

> Lessors' next point is that the judgment is excessive for failure to reduce the judgment to present cash value. Lessors' argument is that the leasehold bonus would not have been realized in one lump sum, but in a series of annual installments or accruals of $1250 over the next 7½ (we have concluded 17½) years, but for the condemnation proceedings, and that the court should not commute these future benefits and award them presently in one lump sum at their full value, but should apply a discount factor to arrive at the present worth of the market value as a lump sum payable *in praesenti*.

> We are of the opinion that the discount factor should be applied under the particular facts of this case; that this lessee is entitled only to the capitalized value of the bonus. The principle is that of an annuity. The method is the commutation to a lump sum of the series of periodic benefits which but for the condemnation proceedings would have accrued in the future, the enjoyment of which would have been delayed and withheld until by the passage of time the future dates of accrual arrived. The discounted sum, presently to be awarded in one lump sum, with a given rate of interest compounded, will equal the amounts which would have come due annually by the expiration of time under the operation of the lease.[39]

The Ohio court ruled:

> Discounting is the determination of the present value of future income or benefits. Appellant's theory of discounting leasehold value is that if there is value to the lease, the lessee will receive this value or benefit ratably over eight years and eight months, and if the lessee receives cash for this benefit at one time, the total amount should be discounted because the benefit will come to the lessee all at once and he does not have to wait for it. Some courts have recognized discounting in determining the value of a leasehold.

> However, a majority of courts have ruled that the fair and reasonable market value of a leasehold interest is the full amount of the difference between the fair market rental value of the leased premises for the unexpired term and the rent paid under the terms of the lease.

> Ohio also has not recognized the discount theory in determining fair market value of the leasehold interest in apportionment proceedings between the lessor and lessee in an appropriation case. The value of a leasehold interest is the difference between the lease rent and the fair market rent for the term of the lease and option period. There is no Ohio statute or reported case requiring discounting in determining value of a leasehold in an appropriation case.[40]

The confusion between the two positions by the various courts appears to stem from their comparing cases involving long-term leaseholds with cases involving short-term leaseholds. For example, if a leasehold advantage of $1,000 per year has only three years until expiration, the total value to be received over the remaining term of the lease will be $1,000 × 3 years, or $3,000. If this three-year income stream is discounted at 8%, the present value of the income stream will be $1,000 × 2.577097,[41] or $2,577.10. The difference between the results of these two methods is only 14%. However, if the remaining lease term were 23 years instead of three, the total value received over the remaining term of the lease would be $1,000 × 23 years, or $23,000. Now, if this $1,000 per year income stream were discounted at 8%, the present value of the income stream would be $1,000 × 10.371059[42], or $10,371.06. This results in a 55% differential between the two methods.

In the latter case, the rental advantage was discounted at an appropriate rate to convert it to a present value. This is a standard valuation procedure which is well-recognized in the appraisal profession and must be applied in nearly all instances. However, discounting may not be required in the case of a minimal rental advantage for an extremely short term because the application of a discount factor would have only a nominal effect on the results of the computation.

The absurdity of evaluating a leasehold estate by simply multiplying the lessee's annual rental advantage by the remaining term of the lease becomes more obvious when long-term, positive leasehold estates are considered.

It must be assumed that states, which have retained the majority rule that the leasehold interest is simply the aggregate of the rental advantage over the remaining term of the lease, have not, as yet, considered the consequences if such rulings are applied to a substantial lease advantage over a remaining term of several years. It must be concluded that when such cases are reviewed by the higher state courts in the future, the method of discounting rental advantages described above will become not only the majority rule, but the only acceptable rule.

The Kentucky court recently took the opportunity to review its previously adopted rulings in regard to the valuation of leasehold interests. The court used an example in its ruling, which clearly illustrated the absurdity of its previous formula for computing the value of a leasehold estate. The court said:

While we are reversing the judgment because of failure of the trial court to observe the existing rules of law in this jurisdiction applicable to eminent domain cases, we have decided to reexamine those rules, abolish some of them, and state new rules that will govern in the event of another trial of this case, and will have application in other cases as stated at the end of this opinion.

DETERMINATION AND ALLOCATION OF DAMAGES FOR LEASED PROPERTY

As related to the leased parcel, and the determination of the respective damages of the landowners and the lessees, the evidence in this case was directed in a loose way towards application of the method outlined in *City of Ashland* v. *Price,* Ky., 318 S.W.2d 861. The key to this method is "to ascertain the present fair rental value, compare it with the rent stipulated in the contract and allow the aggregate difference for the period of the unexpired term of the lease."

Aside from the fact that the foregoing method furnishes no criterion or basis for determining the lessee's damages where only *part* and *not all* of the leased property is taken, we have come to the conclusion after thorough reconsideration that the method is completely unsound, unfair and unworkable.

Let us use an illustration that is not far afield from the actual facts of this case: The property as a whole, if sold free and clear of the lease, would have a value of $100,000. The fair rental value would be $12,000 per year (there is testimony in this case that 12% rent is fair for a commerical property). The lessees have contracted to pay only $6,000 per year. Their lease has 20 years to run. The state condemns the entire tract. By applying the method outlined in the Ashland case, the lessees would be damaged $120,000 ($6,000 per year for 20 years) or $20,000 more than the whole property was worth. This is so patently absurd as to establish beyond any question the fallaciousness of the method. The foregoing illustration is not at all inappropriate because in the instant case the lessees were paying $7,200 a year rent; they said the fair rental was $14,400 a year; their lease had 15 years to run; therefore their damage was $108,000. Yet they testified that the leased property as a whole was worth only $120,000 (one said it was worth only $105,000) and the state took less than one-fourth of the area and none of the structures.[43]

The court went on to establish specific rules to be applied in all future leasehold valuation cases tried in the state:

After thorough deliberation we have worked out what we consider to be the most reasonably fair and workable method for determining compensation in cases of condemnation of property that is under lease. Under this method the proof should be directed towards showing, and the instructions should require the jury to find, only the following three values:

A. The fair market value of the leased tract as a whole immediately before the taking, giving consideration to the fact that it has rental value but *evaluating it as if free and clear of the lease.* (This will be factor A.)

B. The fair market value of the leased tract as a whole, immediately before the taking, *if sold subject to the existing lease.* (This will be factor B.)

C. The fair market value of so much of the leased tract as remains immediately after the taking, giving consideration to the fact that it has rental value but evaluating it as if free and clear of the lease. (This will be factor C.) (Of course, if the entire tract is taken by the condemnation, this value will be zero and need not be found by the jury, but for the purpose of the following computations C will be considered to be zero.)

After the jury has fixed the foregoing three values the *judge* will compute and apportion the damages as follows:

(1) Subtract C from A. The result is the total damages payable by the condemnor.

(2) If B is the *same* as or *more* than A, ignore B. In this situation *all* of the damages will go [to] the *landowner,* because the leasehold had no value, by reason of the fact that the existence of the lease has not impaired the market value of the tract.

(3) If B is *less* than A, subtract B from A and then *divide* the difference by A. The result will be the *percentage of ownership interest* the *lessee* is deemed to have had in the leased tract before the condemnation.

(4) *Multiply* the total damages, found under (1) above, by the percentage found under (3) above. The result will be the lessee's share of the total damages. Subtracting his share from the total damages will leave the *landowner's* share.

It is proper for the foregoing computations to be made by the judge because they involve only mathematical computations and not a determination of disputed facts. It would confuse the jury to require them to make the computations.[44]

Julius Sackman summarized the rules applicable in New York State, as developed in the landmark *Great Atlantic and Pacific Tea Company* case[45]:

(1) *As to valuation of leased property.*—The property should be valued as if there were no lease and as if single ownership in unencumbered fee simple absolute prevailed. All appropriate methods of valuation can be utilized—the market data approach, the income approach, and the cost approach. However, if the income approach is used, it must be remembered that "rental value," not the reserved rent, should be capitalized.

(2) *Leasehold value.*—Leasehold value exists only if there is a so-called "bonus value" to the lease—*i.e.,* that the rental value, or economic rental as it is sometimes called, is in excess of the reserved rental. The leasehold value is, of course, computed by applying the appropriate Inwood coefficients to the annual bonus values for each year of the remainder of the lease term and aggregating the results so obtained.

(3) *Complete taking.*—It [sic] there is a complete taking the award is apportioned as follows:

(a) Leasehold value is paid to the lessee.
(b) Unencumbered fee value minus leasehold value equals the amount to be paid to the lessor.

(4) *Partial taking.*—If there is a partial taking the award is apportioned as follows:

(a) Leasehold value prior to the taking minus leasehold value of the remainder after the taking equals the amount to be paid to the lessee. The leasehold value of the remainder is computed by subtracting the reserved rent, as abated, from the rental value of the remainder area.

(b) The damages computed on the basis of the undivided fee rule, minus the amount found under "(a)" immediately above equals the amount due to the lessor.

(5) *Temporary easement or taking of the entire demised premises.*—
If there is a temporary taking of the *entire* premises for a period

shorter than the balance of the leased term, the entire award belongs to the lessee. If, however, the period of the taking is *longer* than the balance of the leased term and if the taking affects the *entire* property, the award is apportioned as follows:

(a) Leasehold value is paid to the lessee.

(b) The award for the temporary taking, computed under the undivided fee rule, minus the leasehold value equals the amount to be paid to the lessor.

(6) *Temporary easement or taking of part of the demised premises.*— If there is a temporary taking of *part* of the premises for a period which is *shorter* than the balance of the leased term, the entire award belongs to the lessee. In such case, of course, the tenant continues to pay the full rent in unabated amount. If, however, as a result of such temporary partial taking, there is an abatement in the rent, the award should be allocated as follows:

(a) If the rent reserved, as abated, is *equal* to or *greater* than the fair rental value of the property either as a temporary remainder area or as the property subject to a temporary easement, then only the landlord is injured by the temporary taking and he should receive the entire award.

(b) If the rent reserved, as abated, is *less* than the fair rental value of the property either as a temporary remainder area or as property subject to a temporary easement, then the award should be apportioned as follows:

1. The present value of the amount of the rental which has been abated should be paid to the lessor.

2. The balance of the award should be paid to the lessee because this represents the decline in the bonus value of the lease.

If the temporary taking of *part* of the demised premises extends *beyond* the balance of the leased term, the award should be broken down into two parts, the first part being allocable to the leased term and the second part being allocable to the reversionary period. The latter part would be paid to the lessor. The first part would be paid to the lessee or the lessor, or apportioned between them, as set forth with respect to takings which expire prior to the end of the leased term.[46]

The foregoing discussion has dealt with the allocation of a condemnation award where a positive leasehold estate exists and the total condemnation award must be allocated between the lessor and the lessee. The other side of the coin, however, is a situation where a positive leased fee estate and a negative leasehold estate exist; i.e., the contract rent is greater than the economic rent. As previously noted, nearly all courts hold that the aggregate value of the various interests in the real estate cannot exceed the value of the real estate as a whole.[47] The only reasoning found to support such a conclusion, other than the fact that a condemnation case is viewed as a case *in rem,* is that any rent received by the lessor in excess of economic rent ". . . must be considered as a *profit* for which he is not entitled to be compensated in condemnation proceedings."[48] This position, however, appears to conflict with the majority rule that ". . . the government may neither confiscate the owner's bargain, nor be required to assume his loss."[49]

Appraisal Rules and Methodology of Valuation

The following discussion relates only to situations involving a positive leasehold estate. If no positive leasehold estate exists, there is no need to allocate a condemnation award because the entire award will go to the owner of the leased fee estate.

Before an appraiser can attempt to value a leasehold or allocate a condemnation award, he must totally understand all the terms and conditions of the lease and be familiar with the condemnation laws in the applicable jurisdiction, specifically those laws relating to a lessee's liability when a leased property is partially or totally acquired. In all instances, the provisions of a condemnation clause within a lease will prevail over statutory and decisional law.[50] Statutory law is generally intended to be applied only when no condemnation clause has been included in the lease. In many jurisdictions, statutory law requires that the tenant continue to pay full contract rent as specified in the lease when a partial taking has occurred.[51] There are, however, some jurisdictions which provide for rent abatement in the case of a partial acquisition.[52]

In analyzing the terms of a lease, the appraiser should take particular note of its expiration date and whether there are any provisions for renewal. If the lease has a renewal clause at the same rent, or another specified rent, and the renewal provision is obligatory on the part of the lessor, the appraiser may assume that the lease will be renewed if the contract rent specified is less than economic rent.[53] This assumption is based upon the premise that, by contract, the lessor must renew the lease, and any prudent lessee would choose to renew a lease if the rent specified is below existing economic rent.

If the lease contains a provision to renew at a new, arbitrated rent, it is generally assumed that the arbitrated rental will equal economic rent at the time of renewal, and the positive leasehold estate will no longer exist.[54] A lessee's unexercised option to purchase the leased property will generally have no additional value and should not be considered by the appraiser.[55] Also, if the lessee is restricted to a specific use by the lease agreement, the property's estimated economic rent for condemnation award allocation must be based on the use of the property specified within the lease, not on the highest and best use of the property.[56]

The appraiser must report his allocation conclusions in accordance with the rules of the applicable jurisdiction where the property is located. However, the appraiser has much more latitude than the legal rules discussed above may imply.

If the appraiser is of the opinion that market value in a total taking case approximates the sum of the values of the various interests that make up the fee simple estate, it is not necessary to evaluate each interest individually. If the appraiser was not involved in the condemnation phase of the action, he must estimate the market value of the property in question as if free and clear. To adopt the value determined by the trier of fact, or a stipulated settlement between the condemnor and the condemnee, is not appropriate for the same reason that an appraiser does not adopt a local taxing authority's assessed value as representing market value. An estimate of the property's market value as if unencumbered by a lease gives the appraiser a basis from which to work. If the property is leased, it must be income-producing; the appraiser, as a part of the appraisal process, will use the income approach to estimate the value of the fee simple estate. In doing so, the appraiser will arrive at conclusions as to the economic rent of the property in question and the capitalization rates that would be applied to the property if it were free and clear of the lease.

By comparing the economic rent arrived at in the valuation of the property unencumbered with the lease, and the contract rent reserved in the lease, with consideration given to the remaining term of the lease, will often give the appraiser an indication as to whether the lessor or lessee will have the major interest in the fee simple value of the property. If it appears that the leased fee estate will represent 75%–85% of the value of the fee simple estate, the value of the leasehold estate should be estimated first and deducted from the value of the whole; the remainder will represent the value of the leased fee estate.

For example, assume the total taking of a property with the economic characteristics shown in Table 16.1. First, the value of the unencumbered fee is estimated and the overall capitalization rate is extracted from market data. Then, the lessee's annual rent advantage is calculated as $4,000, and an 11% discount factor, or risk rate, is selected as applicable to the lease advantage. This rate is seldom available directly from market data, but the risk rate is generally higher than the overall rate applicable to the property as unencumbered for two reasons:

1 The contract rent is less than the economic rent, so the prudent lessor will void the lease at the first opportunity, i.e., because of a direct violation of the lease provisions or on some small technicality.

2 The lessee is in much the same position as an equity owner in a mortgage-equity

situation. Any decline in market value, or market rent in this situation, is suffered by the lessee, not the lessor, so the lessee's position carries with it greater risk than that of the lessor.

The calculations in Table 16.1 show that the indicated rate for the lessor's interest is approximately 9.78%, nearly one-fourth of one percent below the overall rate applicable to the unencumbered fee. In this situation, the owner of the leased fee estate is exposed to less risk than he would be if the property were leased at economic rent. It is rare that a tenant with an annual lease advantage of $4,000 will default on the lease, so the owner of the leased fee estate will generally settle for a lower return than would be required if the property were leased at economic rent and no positive leasehold estate existed. The example also shows that a reversion rate applicable to the leased fee estate was developed. It is necessary to

Table 16.1

Valuation of Leased Fee and Leasehold Estates

Valuation of unencumbered property:		
Net annual economic rent		$ 31,500
Overall capitalization rate (from market)		10%
Indicated fee simple value ($31,500 ÷ .10)		$315,000
Valuation of leasehold interest:		
Net annual contract rent		$ 27,500
Remaining lease term		25 Years
Annual leasehold advantage ($31,500—$27,500)		$ 4,000
Lessee's risk rate		11%
Present worth of one per period factor—25 year—11%		8.421745*
Indicated value of leasehold estate		
($4,000 × 8.421745)		$ 33,687
Valuation of leased fee estate:		
Value of unencumbered fee		$315,000
Value of leasehold estate		33,687
Indicated value of leased fee estate		$281,313
Indicated rate applicable to leased fee estate		
Income stream rate ($27,500 ÷ $281,313)		.097756
Anticipated appreciation:		
Value at end of lease	$315,000	
Current leased fee value	281,313	
Anticipated Appreciation	$ 33,687	
Appreciation per year		
($33,687 ÷ 25)	$1,347.48	
Percent of appreciation per year		
($1,347 ÷ $281,313)		+.004788
Revision rate		.102544

*See *The Appraisal of Real Estate,* 7th ed., (Chicago: American Institute of Real Estate Appraisers, 1978) p. 583.

adjust the rate upward to reflect the fact that the reversion to the lessor is assumed to be $315,000, as opposed to the existing leased fee estate value of $281,313.

To allocate a condemnation award or stipulated judgment, the values developed in Table 16.1 can be converted into percentages of the unencumbered fee value of the property. For example, if a condemnation award of $345,000 were made, the computations for apportionment would be:

Lessee's interest in fee simple estate	
($33,687 ÷ $315,000)	10.69%
Lessor's interest in fee simple estate	
($281,313 ÷ $315,000)	89.31%
Total	100.00%
Allocation of award:	
Lessee ($345,000 award × .1069)	$ 36,881
Lessor ($345,000 award × .8931)	308,119
Total award	$345,000

If the rule in the jurisdiction where the property is located requires that the value of the leased fee estate be deducted from the value of the unencumbered fee, the same methodology may be employed by the appraiser, but simply presented in reverse. The computations developed under this rule are shown in Table 16.2. The slight difference in results is caused by rounding, and the fact that the reversion is assumed to be $315,000, rather than $253,985. The computations for apportionment, again assuming an award of $345,000, would be:

Lessor's interest in fee simple estate	
($283,058 ÷ $315,000)	89.86%
Lessee's interest in fee simple estate	
($31,942 ÷ $315,000)	10.14%
Total	100.00%
Allocation of award:	
Lessor ($345,000 × .8986)	$310,017
Lessee ($345,000 × .1066)	34,983
Total award	$345,000

The lessor's reversion has been computed using a 10% discount rate—the same as the overall rate for the unencumbered fee. The fact that a positive leasehold estate exists neither increases nor decreases the risk of the reversion. However, because the difference between the two rates was only about one-fourth of 1%. The appraiser should try to keep the computations simple to increase the likelihood that the trier of fact will understand them. Applying a 10.25% rate to the rever-

Table 16.2

Allocation of Fee Value of Property

Valuation of unencumbered property:

Net annual economic rent	$ 31,500
Overall capitalization rate (from market)	10%
Indicated fee simple value ($31,500 ÷ .10)	$315,000

Valuation of leased fee estate:

Net annual contract rent	$ 27,500
Remaining lease term	25 Years
Amount of reversion	$315,000
Value of income stream ($27,500 × 9.235809*)	$253,985
Value of reversion ($315,000 × .092296†)	29,073
Indicated value of leased fee estate	$283,058

Valuation of leasehold estate:

Value of unencumbered fee	$315,000
Value of leased fee estate	283,058
Indicated value of leasehold estate	$ 31,942
Indicated rate applicable to leasehold estate	11.74%‡

*Present worth of one per period—25 years @ 9.775787%.

†Present worth of one—25 years @ 10%.

NOTE: The above factors can be determined using a financial calculator or with the compound interest tables and manual interpolation. See *The Appraisal of Real Estate*, 7th ed., (Chicago: American Institute of Real Estate Appraisers, 1978) Appendix B for compound interest tables and p.476 for illustration of interpolation formula.

‡Computed by use of financial calculator or compound interest tables and interpolation.

sion instead of a 10% rate alters the value of the reversion by less than one percent of the property value. It has, in fact, been said that the present value of a lessor's reversion is of no material value when a long-term lease is involved.[57]

There is a very good reason for computing the lesser interest in the fee simple estate and deducting that value from the unencumbered fee value to arrive at an indicated value of the remainder interest. If the appraiser was in error in her conclusion as to the risk rate applicable to the leasehold, valuing the leasehold first minimizes the error. For instance, if the leasehold risk rate should have been 10% instead of 11%, the error in allocating the $345,000 award would be only $2,898, or less than 1%. This computation is shown in Table 16.3.

However, if the lessor's interest were computed first, using a rate of 8.78% instead of 9.78% for the value of the leased fee income stream, the resulting error in allocating the $345,000 award would be $24,910, or about 7% of the total award. These computations are shown in Table 16.4. So, computing the leased fee interest first at 8.78% for the leased fee income stream would reduce the lessee's portion of the total allocation by $24,910; thus, a loss of nearly 70% of the lessee's award would result from this procedure.

The foregoing discussion relates to a total taking; other problems arise when a partial taking occurs. In a partial taking case, the lease condemnation clause becomes critical. For example, consider a partial taking with the following before and after values:

	Land	Building	Total
Before	$60,000	$70,000	$130,000
After	40,000	60,000	100,000
Difference	$20,000	$10,000	$ 30,000

Assume that the property was vacant when the lease was written and that the lessee constructed the improvements. Assume also that the lessee has the right to remove these improvements at the end of the lease term, which is 25 years from the date of taking. The lease required a net land lease payment of $4,500 per year to the lessor and has no lease abatement provisions in the event of a partial condemnation. Applicable return rates on land are currently about 10.5%.

As the figures indicate, the taking and damages equal $30,000. The appraiser should recognize that a leased fee estate is composed of only two components: the right to receive the rental payments during the term of the lease and the right to occupy and use the property at the termination of the lease. It is evident, therefore, that the only lessor right that is affected by the condemnation is the right to

Table 16.3

Analysis of Value Allocation

Indicated fee leasehold simple value of property		$315,000
Value of leased fee estate ($4,000 × 9.077040*)		− 36,308
Indicated value of leased fee estate		$278,692
Apportionment computations		
Lessee ($36,308 ÷ $315,000)		11.53%
Lessor ($278,692 ÷ $315,000)		88.47%
Allocation of award		
Lessee ($345,000 × .1153)		$ 39,779
Lessor ($345,000 × .8847)		305,221
Total award		$345,000

	Lessee	Lessor
Award assuming 11% lessee risk rate	$36,881	$308,119
Award assuming 10% lessee risk rate	39,779	305,221
Difference	−$ 2,898	$ 2,898
Error in allocation of total award ($2,898 ÷ $345,000)		.84%

*Present worth of one per period for 25 years @ 10%. See *The Appraisal of Real Estate,* 7th ed., (Chicago: American Institute of Real Estate Appraisers, 1978) p.576, col. 5.

Table 16.4

Allocation of Award Computations

Indicated fee simple value of property		$315,000
Value of leased fee interest:		
Income stream ($27,500 × 10.0003*)	$275,008	
Reversion ($315,000 × .092296†)	29,073	
Total value of leased fee estate		304,081
Indicated value of leasehold estate		$ 10,919
Apportionment computations:		
Lessor ($304,081 ÷ $315,000)		96.53%
Lessee ($10,919 ÷ $315,000)		3.47%
Total		100.00%
Allocation of award:		
Lessor ($345,000 × .9653)		$333,029
Lessee ($345,000 × .0347)		11,971
Total		$345,000

	Lessor	Lessee
Award assuming 9.78% lessor income stream rate	$308,119	$36,881
Award assuming 8.78% lessor income stream rate	333,029	11,971
Difference	− $ 24,910	$24,910

*Present worth of one per period for 25 years @ 8.78%.

†Present worth of one for 25 years @ 10%.

NOTE: The above factors can be determined by using a financial calculator or with the compound interest tables and manual interpolation. See *The Appraisal of Real Estate,* 7th ed., (Chicago: American Institute of Real Estate Appraisers, 1978) Appendix B for compound interest tables and p.476 for illustration of interpolation formula.

the reversion of the land at the expiration of the lease; the lease payments will remain the same after the taking. Therefore, allocating the taking and damages is simply a matter of estimating the present value of the loss of the lessor's reversionary interest in the property; the balance of the taking and damages will be attributed to the lessee. Therefore:

Total taking and damage		$30,000
Lessor's reversion before		
($60,000 × .082403)[58]	$4,944	
Lessor's reversion after		
($40,000 × .082403)	3,296	
Lessor's interest in award		− 1,648
Lessor's interest in award		$28,352

If, in the previous example, the lessor were to take possession of the building at the end of the lease term, the right of that reversion would also have to be considered. For instance, if it were estimated that the improvements would be valued at 50% of their current value at the end of the lease term, the allocation of the total award would be:

Total award		$30,000
Reversion before:		
Land	$60,000	
Building ($70,000 × .50)	35,000	
Total reversion	$95,000	
Discount factor	× .082403	
Present value of reversion		
before take	$7,828	
Reversion after:		
Land	$40,000	
Building ($60,000 × .50)	30,000	
Total reversion	$70,000	
Discount factor	× .082403	
Present value of reversion		
after take	5,768	
Lessor's interest in award		2,060
Lessee's interest in award		$27,940

This problem would take on another form if, for example, the taking included 25% of the total leased land area and the lease provided for a rent abatement, in the case of a partial acquisition, in direct proportion to the land acquired. The lessor's interest in the award could then be computed as:

Total award		$30,000
Decrease in lessor's reversion		
(per preceding computations)	$2,060	
Current value of lessor's		
rent loss:		
Annual rent loss		
(4,500 × .25)	$1,125	
Discount factor	× 8.739019[59]	
Value of lessor's rent loss	9,831	
Lessor's interest in award		11,891
Lessee's interest in award		$18,109

The allocation procedure can become even more complex. Assume that the lessee who originally constructed the improvements has sublet them to a third party. The economic rent for the property as a whole is $14,950 per year. The net lease payments from the sublessee to the original lessee are $12,000, out of which $4,500 is paid by the original lessee (sandwich man) to the lessor for ground rent. Assume further that the lessor will have the total reversion of the land and reversion of the building, which will have an estimated value of 50% of its current value, upon termination of the lease.

The various interests in the fee simple title can be computed as shown in Table 16.5. The illustration shows that the estimated risk rate applicable to the original lessee's position is 11%. After extraction of the lessor's interest and the sublessee's interest from the value of the fee simple estate, the value of the original lessee's position is $62,439; this results in a rate of return of 11.16%, which approximates the estimated, acceptable range of 11% ± .

However, now assume that a partial taking with damage occurs, as previously described; the after value is $100,000 ($40,000 land value plus $60,000 building value) and the difference between the before and after value of the property is $30,000. The sublease specifies that there will be no rent abatement in the case of a partial taking, but a rent abatement remains in the original ground lease on a pro rata basis of the area acquired, or, in this instance, 25%. The economic rent of the property is $100,000 × .115, or $11,500; thus the sublessee's rent loss is $14,950 − $11,500, or $3,450 per year.

Initial analysis clearly indicates that the sandwich man (original lessee) will not be adversely affected by the taking and/or damage; in fact, the sandwich man's annual net income will actually increase, as shown below.

	Before	After
Contract rent received	$12,000	$12,000
Contract rent paid	4,500	3,375
Net income to sandwich man	$ 7,500	$ 8,625

Because his net income increased after the partial taking, it is clear that the original lessee can hold no claim to any portion of the condemnation award.

The loss suffered by the owner of the leased fee estate can be computed as:

Present value of lost rent ($1,125 × 8.739019)[60]	$ 9,831
Present value of lost reversion ($25,000 × .065785)[61]	1,645
Total loss in present value by lessor	$11,476

The loss suffered by the sublessee can be calculated:

$3,450 rent loss × 7.452678[62] =	25,712
Total losses of lessor and sublessee	$37,188

The total loss borne by both the lessor and the sublessee can be converted to a percentage as follows:

Lessor's loss ($11,476 ÷ $37,188)	30.86%
Sublessee's loss ($25,712 ÷ $37,188)	69.14%
Total loss	100.00%

Table 16.5

Allocation of Value with Sub-Lessee

Assumptions

Property value	$130,000
Annual net economic rent	$ 14,950
Indicated overall capitalization rate ($14,950 ÷ $130,000)	11%
Existing land lease	$4,500 per year for 25 Years
Indicated risk rate applicable to ground lease	10.5%
Existing Sublease	$12,000 per year for 25 Years
Indicated risk rate applicable to sublease	12.75%
Indicated risk rate applicable to original lease	11.5% ±
Reversion to lessor	$60,000 land value + $35,000 building value

Computations

Total property value			$130,000
Value of lessor's interest:			
$4,500 income × 8.739019*		$39,326	
Reversion $95,000 × .065785†		6,250	
Total value of lessor's interest			$45,576
Value of sublessee's interest:			
Economic rent	$14,950		
Contract rent	12,000		
Rent advantage	$ 2,950		
Present value of rent advantage			
($2,950 × 7.4526‡)		21,985	
Subtotal			67,561
Indicated value of sandwich (original lessee) position			$ 62,439
Indicated risk rate to sandwich man			11.16%§

*Present worth of one per period for 25 years @ 10.5%. See *The Appraisal of Real Estate,* 7th ed. (Chicago: American Institute of Real Estate Appraisers, 1978) p.581, col. 5.

†Present worth of one for 25 years @ 11.5%. See *The Appraisal of Real Estate,* 7th ed. (Chicago: American Institute of Real Estate Appraisers, 1978) p.585, col. 4.

‡The present worth of one per period for 25 years @ 12.75%. See *The Appraisal of Real Estate,* 7th ed., (Chicago: American Institute of Real Estate Appraisers, 1978) p.590, col. 5.

§Risk rate computed using a financial calculator or with compound interest tables and manual interpolation. See *The Appraisal of Real Estate,* 7th ed. (Chicago: American Institute of Real Estate Appraisers, 1978) Appendix B for compound interest tables and p.476 for illustration of interpolation formula.

Now, the appraiser can allocate the total award of $30,000 using simple mathematics.

Lessor's allocation ($30,000 award ×	.3086)	$ 9,258
Lessee's allocation ($30,000 award ×	0)	0
Sublessee's allocation ($30,000 award ×	.6914)	20,742
Total award	1.0	$30,000

The number of combinations of property interests is almost endless. There are two important items for the appraiser and the attorney to remember. First, it is important to review each interest in a property to determine whether that interest has been reduced by the taking and damage and, if so, how that loss may be most accurately estimated. Secondly, the appraiser must always work from his own before and after value estimates, and thus his own estimate of the amount of the taking and damages. The appraiser seldom, if ever, knows the circumstances and thought processes which led to the determination of the award or stipulated settlement. It is seldom, if ever, that an appraiser can make an accurate and equitable allocation of an award if he begins with the assumption that someone else's determination, as to the before value, the after value, and/or award, is correct and was determined in a manner identical to that which the appraiser himself would have applied.

The Washington State Appeals Court recently issued an opinion on this very issue:

> Although the state as condemnor and the owners as condemnees agreed that $363,000 was just compensation, the owners did not agree that the fair market value of the respective interests would be determined by reference to that figure, which was not necessarily the fair market value. Rather, it was the best bargain the owners could strike with the State in the condemnation proceedings. The price paid by the State may have been too high or too low. If it was too high, the owners who made the bargain should reap the benefit of it, if it was too low, the owners should share the disappointment. The only way for the court to equitably apportion the proceeds of the condemnation is to ascertain the fair market value of each interest in the property and give each owner his proportionate share.[63]

The above decision was affirmed by the Washington State Supreme Court, which stated:

> We granted a petition for discretionary review in order to consider the

propriety of equitable apportionment of a lump-sum condemnation award; that is, a proportional distribution of a lump-sum award based upon the ratio each separately valued condemned interest bears to the total of all separately valued interests. The trial court refused to apportion the award. The Court of Appeals reversed the trial court and ordered equitable apportionment.[64]

Lease Types

So far, this discussion has only dealt with the type of lease that specifies a rental amount which remains constant throughout the term of the lease. However, this type of lease is becoming less and less common. Continually increasing costs and the general inflation of the past several years, coupled with overall appreciation in most property, have made lessors extremely reluctant to agree to a flat rental amount in leases of any length. Numerous attempts have been made, by the inclusion of various and sundry provisions in many leases, to provide for the above facts in longer term leases, without providing for arbitration of new rental rates, but at the same time being equitable to both the lessor and the lessee.

Leases that call for an automatic, periodic increase or decrease to a predetermined amount, referred to as graduated, or step-up and step-down, leases, present no real difficulty to the appraiser; they simply introduce some additional mathematical calculations into property analysis.[65] Leases that call for unspecified, periodic rent adjustments, however, do cause problems for the appraiser, the attorney, and the trier of fact who are attempting to evaluate leased fee and leasehold estates and to allocate condemnation awards equitably between the lessor and the lessee.

These problematic leases include *percentage leases,* on commercial properties. These leases generally, but not always, specify a minimum rental plus an additional sum, based on a percentage of sales made by the lessee operating a business on the premises. These leases generally apply to retail businesses; they are quite common for restaurants, grocery stores, service stations, and similar enterprises.

Another type of variable rent lease is the *revaluation lease,* which typically provides for the periodic revaluation of the property. This can be an estimate of the market value of the leased property, with a predetermined rate of return to the lessor, or it can be a direct estimate of the economic rent for the property. Under either system, revaluation leases generally provide that the lessee and the lessor each select an appraiser to reevaluate the property. If the two appraisers cannot agree, then the two appraisers select a third appraiser. Then, either the opinion of the third appraiser prevails or the majority rules. It is something like the best two out of three falls.

A third type of variable lease is the *index lease.* These leases usually start at a specified rental, which is adjusted periodically based on the increase or decrease in a specified index. Some of the most commonly used indexes are the *value of the dollar* index and the *Consumer Price* Index. Due to rapid inflation, some index leases now being written require a rent adjustment as frequently as every year.

The problem with variable rent leases, from the viewpoint of the appraiser, is that there is no specific income stream to evaluate; rather, the income stream will fluctuate over the term of the lease, and no one can predict with confidence if the fluctuation will move up or down, when it will occur, and how much fluctuation can be expected.

The appraiser must be very careful in attempting to project future increases in rent levels based on future retail sales, price indexes, and other variable factors. If risk rates can be developed for leasehold estates and leased fee estates from actual sales of these interests, that are subject to the same potential rental fluctuation as the property being appraised, it is generally the best and safest data to utilize. Using these data indicates that fluctuations in rental rates are being anticipated by buyers and sellers in the marketplace and, therefore, are reflected in the prices paid and the risk rates indicated by the sales.

One thing the appraiser must not do is develop a risk rate from the sale of a comparable leased fee or leasehold estate using existing rent levels, and then apply this risk rate to a projected escalating income stream for the property being appraised. The attorney should also be on guard against this practice. For example, assume a leased fee interest in a comparable property sold for $250,000. The sale property's lease provided for a reserved rent of $20,000 per year at the time of the sale, with an annual rental adjustment, based on the cost of living index, over the remaining 10-year life of the lease. A reversion of $250,000 was considered reasonable for this property. The leased fee interest of a property being appraised, on the other hand, is as follows:

> Remaining term, 10 years.
> Rent is $12,500 per year with annual adjustments based upon the cost of living index.
> Current value is reasonably assumed reversion.

The obvious analysis of the data is:

> Sale property:
> $20,000 rent ÷ $250,000 price = 8% rate
> Subject property:
> $12,500 rent ÷ .08% rate = $156,250 value

This is the obvious analysis; however, the following fuzzy thinking is too often applied to such a situation. First, the appraiser concludes, based upon past performance, that the cost of living will increase at the rate of about 10% per year. Therefore, a rent forecast is made as follows:

YEAR		RENT AMOUNT
1		$12,500
2	($12,500 × 1.10)	$13,750
3	($13,750 × 1.10)	$15,125
4	($15,125 × 1.10)	$16,638
5	($16,638 × 1.10)	$18,302
6	($18,302 × 1.10)	$20,132
7	($20,132 × 1.10)	$22,145
8	($22,145 × 1.10)	$24,360
9	($24,360 × 1.10)	$26,796
10	($26,796 × 1.10)	$29,476

The appraiser then converts this projected annual income into a present worth by multiplying each year's income by the appropriate discount factor of 8% for that year. The calculations are:

Year	Rent	Factor	Current Value
1	$12,500	.925926	$11,574
2	$13,750	.857339	$11,788
3	$15,125	.793832	$12,007
4	$16,638	.735030	$12,229
5	$18,302	.680583	$12,456
6	$20,132	.630170	$12,687
7	$22,145	.583490	$12,921
8	$24,360	.540269	$13,161
9	$26,796	.500249	$13,405
10	$29,476	.463193	$13,653

Total current value of income stream $125,881
Value of property at time of reversion (rent level at that time divided by rate, or $29,476 ÷ .08) $368,450.
Present value of reversion ($368,450 × .463193)   170,663
Total present value leased fee estate $296,544
Rounded $297,000

    This type of valuation and analysis procedure, or another equally ludicrous analysis, may be undertaken by appraisers for various reasons, including: 1) improper verification of sale and lease data concerning comparables, causing the index clause in the comparable lease to be overlooked; 2) the inability to recognize that the 8% rate indicated by the sale property reflects the potential increase in rents caused by the index clause in the lease and a potential increase in the reversionary value of the property; 3) general incompetence; and 4) dishonesty, including, at times, advocacy.

It is imperative that the appraiser analyze market data carefully. This type of data is often difficult to obtain in detail; usually, there isn't enough data to allow the appraiser to improperly analyze even a single transaction. In the above example, the potential rent escalation and reversionary value increase or decrease are identical in the sale property and the property under appraisal. It is not necessary for the appraiser to go through extensive mathematical gyrations to apply the market data correctly; nor is it necessary to do so in an attempt to impress the client, the attorney, or the trier of fact.

If the previously described comparable sale had an established rental rate with no rent adjustments, the rate indicated would have undoubtedly been higher than 8%, to reflect the likelihood that the reserved rent would have a lesser value during the latter term of the lease due to the decreasing value of the dollar. In such an instance, comparing these data to the leased fee under appraisal would require more detailed analysis and some adjustment. The appraiser should, however, consider adjusting the risk rate in such an instance, rather than attempting to project what the Consumer Price Index is going to do over the next 10 years.

Summary

Many properties acquired by the sovereign, in whole or in part, by the exercise of its power of eminent domain are under lease; therefore, the interests in the property are not held by a single individual or entity, but by two or more individuals or entities. The individual values of these separate interests are seldom the concern of the condemnor or the appraiser employed by the condemnor. Most condemning agencies have adopted the undivided fee rule, which holds that the value of a property is to be determined as if all of the interests therein are owned by one individual or entity. The majority rule clearly indicates that, as a matter of law, the aggregate value of the various interests held in the real estate cannot exceed the property's value if it were held by one individual.

When a condemned property is subject to a lease, the trial or settlement negotiations are usually separated into two distinct phases. The first phase is the determination of the value of the fee simple estate or, in a partial taking, the determination of *just compensation*. The second phase of the trial, or negotiations, is the allocation of the award determined in the first phase, between the various interests such as the leased fee estate and the leasehold estate. The condemnor has no part in this second phase; rather, it is up to the lessor and lessee to *fight it out*.

The allocation of an award is never undertaken until the amount of the award is determined. The allocation may be determined by the same trier of fact that set the total award, by the court, or by a totally different tribunal at a later date. The procedure will vary from jurisdiction to jurisdiction.

In allocating an award, both the appraiser and the attorney must be thoroughly familiar with all the provisions of the lease, especially those provisions that have a direct bearing on the value of the leased fee and leasehold estates. If there is a condemnation clause in the lease, this clause will materially affect, or totally control, the allocation of the condemnation award. If the lease has no such clause, statutory and decisional law will have a bearing on the award allocation.

Some courts have ruled that the value of a leased fee estate is determined by computing the value of the leasehold estate and deducting this amount from the total award. Other courts have, however, ruled the reverse; the value of the leasehold estate is determined by computing the value of the leased fee estate and deducting that value from the total award, the residual being the value of the leasehold estate. The appraiser must present his valuation and allocation testimony in accordance with the applicable legal rules. However, it is not necessary for the appraiser, in arriving at his conclusions, to compute the various estate values in strict compliance with the legal rules. In general, the appraiser can allocate a condemnation award more accurately if the value of the lesser interest is computed first and deducted from the total award, with the residual representing the greater interest.

Many courts have ruled that the value of the leasehold estate is the annual economic rent of the property, minus the annual contract rent, multiplied by the number of years remaining in the lease. In other words, the income stream is not converted into a present worth. Recently, courts have begun to recognize the absurdity of such a procedure and to adopt new rulings, which provide for the proper discounting of future income streams. It is in everybody's best interests that the courts adopt rules which provide for discounting to avoid inequities to the owners of leased fee estates.

In developing an estimate for the proper allocation of a condemnation award, the appraiser must work from his own before values and, in the case of partial acquisitions, after values. There is no certainty that the total award was made correctly or that it was determined as the appraiser would have in estimating the proper allocation of such an award. The appraiser need only to convert his own opinion of the dollar estimates of the damages to the various estates to percentages of the total damages, so that this percentage can be applied to the previously determined award.

There are, of course, various types of leases. Those that provide for a renewal have given the courts some trouble. But if the lease is favorable to the lessee and the renewal is obligatory on the part of the lessor at the same rent level, it has generally been held that the renewal of such a lease may be assumed for the purpose of valuing the leasehold and leased fee estates. Leases that call for a fluctuating income stream are generally more difficult to analyze and evaluate. The most accurate method of valuing leasehold and leased fee estates in such circumstances, is to attempt to acquire sale and lease data of economically and physically comparable properties and compare these data to the interests held in the property under appraisal. If adjustments for economic differences are required, it is often best to adjust the applicable risk or discount rate, rather than attempt to estimate what the fluctuating income will be for the remaining term of the lease.

Notes

1. American Institute of Real Estate Appraisers and the Society of Real Estate Appraisers, *Real Estate Appraisal Terminology,* rev. ed., Byrl N. Boyce, ed. (Cambridge, Mass.: Ballinger Publishing Co., 1981), p. 149.

2. Ibid.

3. Ibid.

4. American Institute of Real Estate Appraisers Regulation No. 10, *Code of Professional Ethics and Standards of Professional Conduct,* Canon 7, Guideline 9, p. 13 (Adopted Nov. 13, 1981).

5. See also Chapter 3, "Property Rights."

6. Montgomery Ward & Co., Inc. v. City of Sterling, 523 P.2d 465 (Colo.).

7. Garrett v. United States, 407 F.2d 146.

8. Lambert v. Giffin, 257 Ill. 152, 100 N.E. 496.

9. State ex rel. Moore v. Bastian, 546 P.2d 399 (Id.).

10. Julius L. Sackman, *Nichols' The Law of Eminent Domain,* rev. 3rd ed. (New York: Matthew Bender, 1979) Vol. 4, §12.42.

11. Harry T. Dolan, "Unit Rule of Valuation in Federal Condemnation," *The Appraisal Journal,* January 1965, p. 26.

12. *Nichols',* Vol. 4, § 12.42[2].

13. "Unit Rule of Valuation in Federal Condemnation," *The Appraisal Journal,* p. 24.

14. Korfhage v. Commonwealth, 296 S.W.2d 476 (Ky.).

15. *The Appraisal of Real Estate,* 7th ed., (Chicago: American Institute of Real Estate Appraisers, 1978) p. 469.

16. Ibid.

17. *Nichols',* Vol. 4, § 12.42, See f.n. 4.

18. Department of Public Works v. Lynbar, Inc., 62 Cal. Rptr. 320, 253 Cal. App.2d 870.

19. Lambert v. Giffin, 257 Ill. 152, 100 N.E. 496.

20. New Jersey Sports and Exposition Authority v. Borough of East Rutherford, 137 N.J. Super 271, 348 A.2d 825.

21. United States v. 3,276.21 Acres of Land, 194 F.Supp. 297.

22. Clark v. Erich, 217 C.A.2d 627, 31 Cal. Rptr. 628.

23. *The Appraisal of Real Estate,* 7th ed., pp. 461-462.

24. Ibid., pp. 462-469.

25. *Nichols',* Vol. 7A, § 11.08.

26. Ibid., § 11.07.

27. Ibid., § 11.06.

28. *Nichols',* Vol. 4, § 12.42[3].

29. *Real Estate Appraisal Terminology,* p. 59.

30. *Lewis on Eminent Domain,* Vol. 2, 3rd ed., § 7.16.

31. *The Appraisal of Real Estate,* 7th ed., pp. 461-488.

32. Orange State Oil Co. v. Jacksonville Expressway Authority, 110 So.2d 687 (Fl.).

33. State v. Nelson, 296 N.E.2d 908 (Ind.).

34. McMillan Printing Co. v. Pittsburgh, etc., R. Co., 216 Pa. 504, 65 A. 1091.

35. Uhland Club v. Shupbach, 168 Mass. 430, 47 N.E. 113.

36. Gigliotti v. Wood, 397 A.2d 1342 (Conn.).

37. State ex. rel. Dep't of Transportation v. Gee, 565 S.W.2d 498 (Tenn.).

38. Orange State Oil Co. v. Jacksonville Expressway Authority, 110 So.2d 687 (Fl.).

39. Land Clearance for Redevelopment Corp. v. Doernhoefer, 389 S.W.2d 780 (Mo.).

40. Pokorny v. Local 310, Int. Hod Carriers, 35 Ohio App. 2d 178, 300 N.E.2d 464.

41. *The Appraisal of Real Estate,* 7th ed., p. 565, Col. 5 (Present Worth of One Per Period, 3 years @ 8%).

42. Ibid. (Present Worth of One Per Period, 23 years @ 8%).

43. Commonwealth Dept. of Hways. v. Sherrod, 367 S.W.2d 844 (Ky.).

44. Ibid.

45. Great Atlantic & Pacific Tea Co. v. State, 22 N.Y.2d 75, 238 N.E.2d 705.

46. Julius L. Sackman, "Apportionment of Award Between Lessor and Lessee," *The Appraisal Journal,* October 1970, pp. 550-551.

47. Korfhage v. Commonwealth, 296 S.W.2d 476 (Ky.); Lewis on Eminent Domain, Vol. 2, (3rd ed.), § 7.16.

48. Commonwealth Dept. of H'ways. v. Sherrod, 367 S.W.2d 844 (Ky.).

49. James A. Ballentine, *Ballentine's Law Dictionary,* 3rd ed. William S. Anderson, ed. (Rochester, N.Y.: The Lawyers Co-operative Publishing Co.; San Francisco: Bancroft-Whitney Co., 1969), pp. 695-696; Kinter v. United States, 156 F.2d 5.

50. Savin Hill Yacht Club Ass'n v. Savin Hill Yacht Club, 246 Mass. 75, 140 N.E. 299.

51. Gluck v. Baltimore, 81 Md. 315, 32 A. 515.

52. Hinrieks v. New Orleans, 50 La. Ann. 1214, 24 So. 224.

53. Matter of City of New York, 118 App. Div. 865, Aff'd 189 N.Y. 508.

54. Kernochan v. Manhatten R.R. Co., 161 N.Y. 339, 55 N.E. 906.

55. Haney v. Denny, 193 N.E.2d 648 (Ind.).

56. North Coast R. Co. v. Kraft Co., 63 Wash. 250, 115 p. 97.

57. Chicago, etc. R. Co. v. Chicago Mechanics Institute, 239 Ill. 197, 87 N.E. 933.

58. *The Appraisal of Real Estate,* 7th ed., p. 581, Col. 4 (Present Worth of One Per Period, 25 years @ 10.5%).

59. Ibid., Col. 4, (Present Worth of One Per Period, 25 years @ 10.5%).

60. Ibid.

61. *The Appraisal of Real Estate,* 7th ed., p. 585, Col. 4 (Present Worth of One Per Period, 25 years @ 11.5%).

62. *The Appraisal of Real Estate,* 7th ed., p. 590, Col. 5, (Present Worth of One Per Period, 25 years @ 12.75%).

63. State v. Spencer, 16 Wash. App. 841, 559 P.2d 1360.

64. State v. Spencer, 583 P.2d 1201 (Wash.).

65. *The Appraisal of Real Estate,* 7th ed., see page 483 for example.

CHAPTER 17
WRITING THE REPORT

"Condemnation proceedings to acquire private land for public use require a high degree of appraisal skill and considerable judgment by the appraiser. Such problems as estimating the highest and best use for relatively underdeveloped or unimproved property and appraising the value of remaining property in a partial acquisition leave the appraiser open to involvement in court proceedings. The thoroughness with which the appraisal is made and *reported* is the appraiser's greatest protection against professional embarrassment."[1]

From the moment the appraiser accepts an appraisal assignment, his chief thought must be that the culmination of the assignment will be the delivery of a written appraisal report to the client. In appraising for eminent domain, the *purpose* of the appraisal must be clearly understood by the appraiser, the client, and the client's legal counsel. The specific *function* of the appraisal is also important to the appraiser and, while not absolutely necessary, should be understood by the appraiser. The *purpose* of an appraisal defines "[t]he type of value being sought."[2] For eminent domain valuation, the value sought is generally market value. This must be stated in the appraisal report and the term *market value* must be defined. The appraiser should use the definition of market value which has been approved by the courts in the jurisdiction where the property under appraisal is located. The source of this definition should be cited in the appraisal report.

The *purpose* of an appraisal report is "[n]ot the same as function."[3] The *function* of an appraisal is "[t]he reason for which the appraisal is made or is intended to be used. [It r]elates to the character of the decision to be based on the appraisal, *e.g.,* price at which to buy or sell, amount of mortgage to be made. Not the same as purpose."[4] The purpose and function of an appraisal involving a total taking might be worded in the report as follows:

> The purpose of this appraisal is to estimate the market value of the property being appraised. Market value is "[t]he highest price estimated in terms of money which a property will bring if exposed for sale in the open market, allowing a reasonable time to find a purchaser who buys with knowledge of all the uses to which it is adapted and for which it is capable of being used." (Source: *People* v. *Ricciardi*, 23 Cal.2d 390, 144 P.2d 799.)

> The function of this appraisal is to assist the client in its determination of the just compensation due for the taking of the property being appraised.

In the case of a partial acquisition, the definition of market value will remain unchanged, but the purpose and function of the report might be described as follows:

> The purpose of the appraisal is to first estimate the market value of the entire ownership and second to estimate the market value of the remainder. The difference between the two values is then to be analyzed (by the Appraiser) as to the allocation of the value differential to the real property acquired and damages or special benefits to the remaining real property and property rights.[5]

> The function of this appraisal is to assist the client in its determination of the just compensation due for the partial taking of the property being appraised.

Report Format

Much has been written on the proper methodology and format for writing appraisal reports. Most condemning agencies have their own guidelines for writing appraisal reports; these instructions may be similar, but no two sets are identical. Appraisal reporting is discussed in a variety of appraisal publications.[6] Specific report writing guidelines for condemnation appraising may be found in *Uniform Appraisal Standards for Federal Land Acquisitions,*[7] and the guidelines of various condemning agencies.

For example, the Washington State Department of Transportation Appraisal Guideline calls for a "standard narrative form appraisal report . . . using all applicable approaches to value unless the Senior Appraiser provides written authorization for one of the following deviations:

A. Standard Narrative Form Appraisal Report (specifically excluding one or more approaches to value). . . .

B. Short Form, Narrative Type Appraisal Report. . . .

C. Short Form, Form Type Appraisal Report. . . .

D. Short Form Project Type Appraisal Report. . . ."[8]
Deviation *A* is rather meaningless because the standard form appraisal report guidelines allow the appraiser to exclude inapplicable approaches to value. Although a condemning agency may give written approval to exclude an approach to value, the appraiser is ethically obligated to include the approach if it has any applicability. Therefore, it is the applicability of an approach which determines whether it must be included in the report, not the written authorization of a governmental agency.

The above mentioned appraisal guide requires that "[t]he Standard Narrative Form Appraisal Report [must be] organized according to the following format:

SECTION I—IDENTIFICATION AND SUMMARY
Page 1, Certificate of Appraiser (HWY From [sic] 261-015)
Page 2, Summary of Conclusions (HWY Form 261-016)
Page 3, Photographs of all Principal Improvements and/or Feature Affecting Value (HWY Form 261-017)
Page 4, et seq., Narrative Report:
  Item 1—Owner
  Item 2—Address (or location) of Subject Property
  Item 3—Legal Description
  Item 4—Delineation of Title
  Item 5—Purpose of Appraisal
  Item 6—Summary of Appraisal Problems

SECTION II—EVALUATION OF TOTAL OWNERSHIP
Item 1—Assumptions and Limiting Conditions
Item 2—Neighborhood Location and Description
Item 3—Description of Subject Property
  A. Present Use
  B. Accessibility and Road Frontages
  C. Land Contour and Elevations
  D. Land Area
  E. Land Shape
  F. Utilities
  G. Present Zoning
  H. Highest and Best Use of Land if Vacant
  I. Improvements
  J. Specialty Items
  K. Real Estate Taxes
  L. Assessments
  M. Existing Lease or Rental Data
  N. Highest and Best Use of Whole Property as Improved.

D. Land Shape
E. Utilities
   1. Utilities Actually Remaining
   2. Utilities Lost and Possible Corrective Potentials
F. Probable Remainder Zoning
G. Highest and Best Use of Remainder Land if Vacant
H. Improvements
   1. Improvements Remaining in Whole
   2. Improvements Remaining in Part
      a. Descriptions
      b. Rehabilitation Specifications, if rehabilitation feasible
I. Remainder Specialty Item Considerations
J. Estimated Real Estate Taxes
K. Possible Remainder Assessments
L. Lease or Rental Potential
M. Highest and Best Use of Remainder as Improved

Item 4—Valuation of Property Remaining
A. Site Analysis and Evaluation
   1. Comparative Approach, Site Evaluation
      a. General Discussion
         1) Relations
         2) Sales that are Comparable
      b. Comparative Analysis
      c. Correlation and Conclusions by Comparative Approach
   2. Income Approach, Site Evaluation
      a. Data
      b. Analysis
      c. Correlation and Conclusion by Income Approach
   3. Correlation and Final Conclusion, Land Value
B. Approaches to Value, Remainder Whole Property
   1. Comparative [Market Data] Approach
      a. General discussion
         1) Relationships
         2) Sales that are Comparable
      b. Comparative Analysis
         1) Whole Property Comparisons
         2) Comparative Units
      c. Correlation and Conclusion, Comparative [Market Data] Approach

      2. Income Approach
         a. Data
         b. Analysis
         c. Correlation and Conclusion, Income Approach
      3. Cost Approach
         a. Cost New
         b. Accrued Depreciation (Including Analysis and Explanations)
         c. Land Value
         d. Indicated Value by Cost Approach
    C. Correlation of Remainder Value Indications from all Approaches

SECTION IV—ACQUISITION ANALYSIS
    Item 1—Recapitulation
      A. Value of Property before Acquisition
      B. Value of Property after Acquisition
      C. Difference between BEFORE and AFTER values
    Item 2—Explanation of Damages
    Item 3—Explanation of Special Benefits

SECTION V—ADDENDA
    A. Market Data (HWY Forms 261-020 and 261-020A)
    B. Market Data Map
    C. Special Instructions; Charts and Illustrations
    D. Report of Contact with Owner (HWY Form 261-013)
    E. Title Report[9]

Uniform Appraisal Standards for Federal Land Acquisitions requires that the following format be used:

<u>PART I—INTRODUCTION</u>
1. TITLE PAGE. . . .
2. TABLE OF CONTENTS.
3. LETTER OF TRANSMITTAL.
4. PHOTOGRAPHS. . . .
5. STATEMENT OF LIMITING CONDITIONS AND ASSUMPTIONS.
6. REFERENCES. . . .

<u>PART II—FACTUAL DATA</u>
7. PURPOSE OF THE APPRAISAL. . . .
8. LEGAL DESCRIPTION. . . .
9. AREA, CITY AND NEIGHBORHOOD DATA. . . .

10. PROPERTY DATA:
    a. site. . . .
    b. improvements. . . .
    c. equipment. . . .
    d. history. . . .
    e. assessed value and annual tax load. . . .
    f. zoning. . . .

PART III—ANALYSIS AND CONCLUSIONS

11. ANALYSIS OF HIGHEST AND BEST USE. . . .
12. LAND VALUE. . . .
13. VALUE ESTIMATE BY COMPARATIVE (MARKET) APPROACH. . . .
14. VALUE ESTIMATE BY COST APPROACH, IF APPLICABLE. . . .
15. VALUE ESTIMATE BY INCOME APPROACH, IF APPLICABLE. . . .
16. INTERPRETATION AND CORRELATION OF ESTIMATES. . . .
17. CERTIFICATION. . . .
18. LOCATION MAP. . . .
19. COMPARATIVE MAP DATA. . . .
20. DETAIL OF COMPARATIVE DATA.
21. PLOT PLAN.
22. FLOOR PLANS. . . .
23. OTHER PERTINENT EXHIBITS.
24. QUALIFICATIONS. . . .[10]

The appraiser must write the appraisal report in the required format when the condemning agency is the client; however, the appraiser must not allow these regimented reporting requirements to dictate his thinking. When preparing a report for a condemnee, the appraiser will generally have a free hand in determining the format and content of the appraisal report. Regardless of the client, every appraisal report must be tailored somewhat to the specific client.

The inclusion of *boiler plate* is generally unacceptable; preliminary matter should be limited to the appraiser's qualifications, general assumptions and limiting conditions, and the appraiser's certificate. However, even these basic items should be reviewed before being included in an appraisal report. If the appraiser's client is a condemnee, and the appraiser has, in the past, made appraisals for the condemnor, this fact should be included in the appraiser's qualifications. If the appraiser has made other appraisals in the geographic vicinity of the property being appraised, this too should be mentioned.

The assumptions and limiting conditions of the appraisal must be reviewed carefully. If the appraisal is of vacant land, and the assumptions and limiting conditions state that the appraiser has assumed that the improvements on the site are free from termite infestation, the client will see the entire report as sloppy boiler plate. In a partial taking case, the assumptions and limiting conditions must also state that the appraiser has assumed that the proposed public improvement will be completed in a reasonable length of time and that the improvements will be constructed in accordance with the plans and specifications available at the time of valuation. The plans and specifications relied on by the appraiser should be specifically identified by name, page number, original date, and last revision date.

Report Timing

Figure 17.1[11] illustrates the appraisal, or valuation, process in graphic form. It is extremely important to recognize that the very last step in the process is to make a *final estimate* of value and then to prepare a *report of defined value*. When the appraiser sits down to write the appraisal report, he should have all the necessary data at hand; all data should, by this time, be analyzed, applied, and compiled into a final estimate of value.

Some appraisers may ask: *"Why can't I write each section of my report as I come to it? First, I include regional and neighborhood data, then I make my property inspection and write my site and improvement descriptions, and finally I develop each approach to value and write it up. Then, I'm ready to make my final value estimate and write a correlation."* This method is unacceptable, because the appraiser wants to *set the reader up* throughout the report. The appraiser cannot, for instance, establish a basis for land value adjustments, unit costs, and depreciation in the property description section of the report if these factors were not known when this portion of the report was written. The appraiser has written a perfect report when the reader can read to the end of the next to the last page of the appraisal report, which states:

> Based upon the foregoing facts and analysis, I am of the opinion that the market value of the property described herein, as of the___day of _______ 19___ , subject to the assumptions and limiting conditions herein was: [end of page]

and know the answer without turning the page.

At times, the attorney for the client will try to dictate the completion date of the appraisal; sometimes he has just cause for doing so, and sometimes he does not. If the effective date of valuation in the applicable jurisdiction is the date of trial, it may be wise to delay preparing a fully documented appraisal report until just before trial to avoid the costly preparation of two fully documented reports.

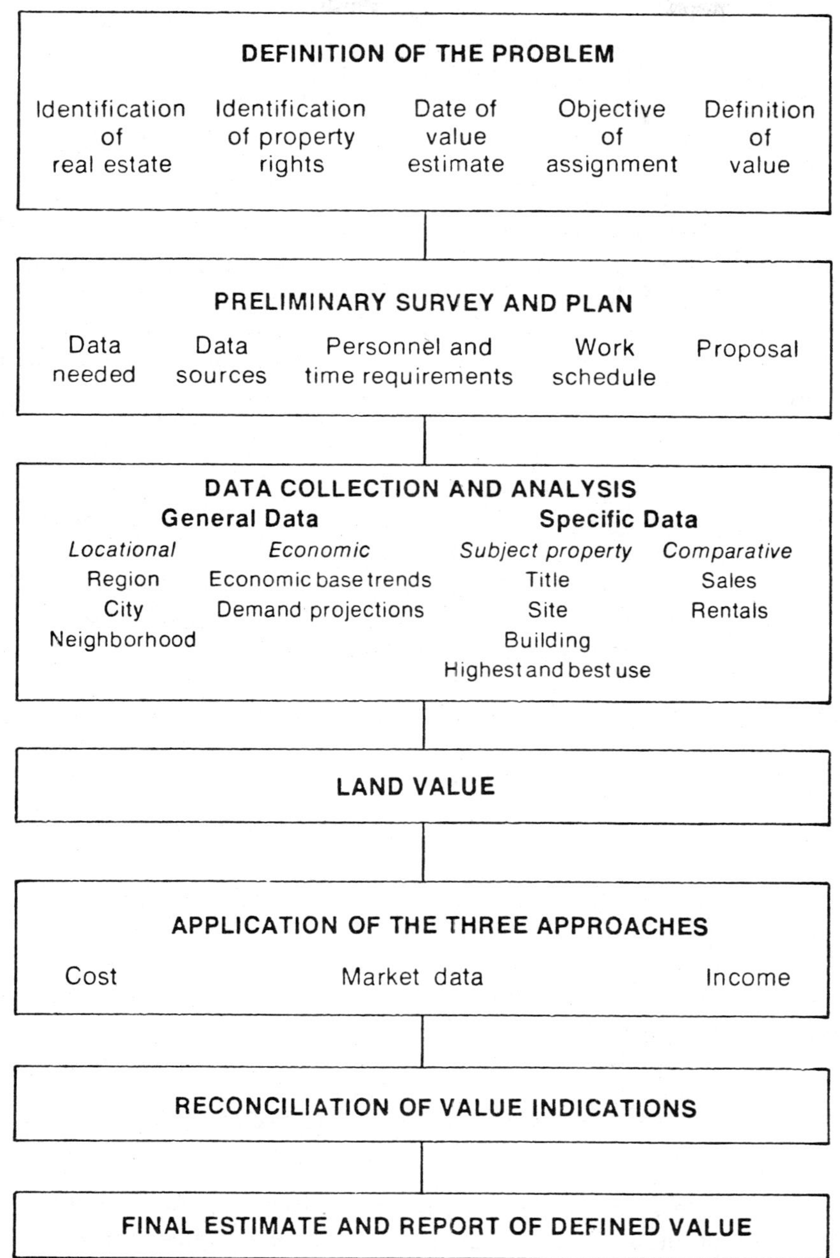

Figure 17.1. Appraisal Process

If, however, the attorney is instructing the appraiser not to finish his appraisal report so the attorney can circumvent applicable discovery rules, the appraiser should not cooperate; he should either finish the report in a timely manner or suggest that the client retain the services of another appraiser. If the discovery rule were always used wisely and fairly, fewer eminent domain proceedings would actually reach the trial stage.

Another possible problem which must be faced by the appraiser arises when the attorney for the client states that no written appraisal report will be needed—ever. This is probably an unwise attempt on the part of the attorney to keep the appraiser's fee down. What the attorney, and the appraiser for that matter, must understand is that the preparation of a documented appraisal report is a form of *trial preparation* for the appraiser. Actually writing down the facts, analysis, and conclusions reached in arriving at a final estimate of value prepares the appraiser to explain his reasoning more clearly to the trier of fact. The attorney's attempt to avoid the cost of a written appraisal report is, without question, a false and foolish economy.

The appraiser must also consider this matter for another reason. Some professional appraisal organizations require that an appraisal report or complete memorandum be prepared and placed in the appraiser's file whenever an appraiser testifies in regard to property valuation.[12] If, by chance, a member or candidate of the same appraisal organization testifies for the opposing party to the dispute, the written reports of both appraisers automatically become subject to review by a committee of the organization.[13] If the appraiser agrees to testify without a written report or memorandum, he may very well find himself writing the report or memorandum, after giving such testimony, on his own time and at his own expense.

Report Content

The content of an appraisal report will depend on the property type, the nature of the taking, and the requirements of the client or the client's legal counsel. The condemnor-client may be very specific as to report content and the methodology to be used in writing the report. For instance, one condemnor describes the application of the market data approach as follows:

> B. APPROACHES TO VALUE, WHOLE PROPERTY
>   RULES:
>
> If the site is improved, the value of the improvement is based upon its contribution to the value of the whole property. All three commonly accepted approaches to the estimate of value, including supporting units of comparison, are employed as applicable. If one or more ap-

proaches to the estimate of value are omitted, the Appraiser states the reason for each omission.

The comparative [market data] method [approach] of presenting market value evidence is the method most acceptable to the Department and to the courts and juries; consequently, the greatest reliance is usually placed upon market comparison. Sufficient highly comparable data is analyzed to provide a sound basis for the conclusion drawn from this approach. The authenticity of the entire approach is directly proportional to the sufficiency and comparability of the data obtained and the accuracy with which it is analyzed.

When studying conditions of sale, any sale based on terms other than cash is studied in order to determine the equivalent cash "market value." Terms of all sales are investigated and reported.

PROCEDURES:
1. Comparative [Market Data] Approach
   a. General Discussion
      1)   Here the Appraiser lays the groundwork for the comparative analysis by a statement as to the extent of his search, the sufficiency and comparability of existing data and the general value bracket within which subject will fall.
      2)   Sales that are comparable are listed identifying each by the sale number on the pertinent Market Data (HWY Form 261-020) [see Figure 17.2 for sample of form] in the Addenda. A format similar to the following is used at the present point in the report:

SALE NUMBER	GRANTOR/GRANTEE	LAND AREA	SALE DATE	SALE PRICE

   b. Comparative Analysis

      Sales of such close comparability as to make adjustments unnecessary when equating them to the property being appraised seldom exist; therefore, a narrative comparative analysis of each comparable sale is made explaining how the sale relates to subject with regard to those features which tend to influence market value. Adjustments found necessary through market analysis are reported in individual specific dollar amounts indicating whether plus or minus, together with the market facts, analysis and reasoning from which they were drawn. Adjustments are not attempted for items of dissimilarity to which the

> market does not react to a measurable degree. The greater the number of adjustments or the larger the amount of any single adjustment, the less valid is the sale as a "comparable."
>
> A comparative analysis in chart form may be of aid to the Appraiser and may be helpful to the reader.
>
> c. Correlation and Conclusion, Comparative [Market Data] Approach
>
> Here the Appraiser explains how he has weighed the various indications of value, what conclusion of value has been reached and why the evidence supports such conclusion.[14]

The above is an excerpt from a 22-page appraisal guide. The appraiser who attempts to apply such a guide for the first time should anticipate some difficulty. A staff appraiser should expect to spend considerably more time on the report than his superior originally anticipated or allocated; a fee appraiser applying such a guide for the first time will consume more time than he anticipated and probably suffer an economic loss on the assignment. The fee appraiser should view this experience pragmatically and be prepared to write off the loss as an *education expense*—no different from the cost of attending a seminar.

Once the appraiser has written a report using this type of guideline, and has received review approval for his effort, future reports become easier. He may want to use the approved report as a guide for writing further reports, rather than referring to the original guide for each report. However, the appraiser should be aware that some review appraisers will overlook minor deficiencies in an appraisal report and permit some deviation from the written guidelines if the report is generally sound and well presented. The written review will often mention these deficiencies, but conclude that they are unimportant and have no bearing on the factual data reported or on the opinion or conclusions presented by the appraiser. Unfortunately, the appraiser rarely sees the written review; thus, if the first report is used as a model for a second report, and the second report is used to write a third, the guideline deficiencies in reports tend to increase geometrically until a report is rejected and returned with a six-page request (demand) for revision. It is therefore advisable for the appraiser to refer to the original guidelines periodically and write a report that strictly follows the original guidelines. Another option is to have the report read by an experienced individual who simultaneously compares the report and the guidelines to ensure compliance.

The stated purpose of appraisal report writing guidelines and procedures is:

a. To insure that the appraiser has considered all the required elements of value in arriving at conclusions of value.

b. To maintain a uniform method of narrative appraisal report writing that will facilitate the appraisal review function.[15]

In other words, a review appraiser can look up Section II, Item 4, Subsection B, ¶1.b in any report reviewed and be confident that he will find the section on the analysis of the market data approach to value in the before situation. This procedure has another benefit for the review appraiser. Because the appraiser is required to specify exact dollar adjustments in the comparative analysis of the property being appraised and the comparable sale, and to specifically analyze the comparable sale in the manner shown in Figure 17.2, the review appraiser can *plug in* the appraiser's specified dollar adjustments and dollar allocations into the form and determine, with mathematical precision, the consistency of the appraiser's analysis. This procedure is sometimes referred to as the *pluginski syndrome* and in this instance negates, to a large degree, the necessity of *thinking* on the part of some review appraisers.

To illustrate, assume that the appraiser has completed Section (6) of the form shown in Figure 17.2 for Comparable 1 as follows:

	Total Value	Unit Value
(6) ANALYSIS:		
a. Extraction Data		
Land: *(give area or front foot for each type)*		
8000 sq. ft.	$ 14,000	$ 1.75
	$	$
Improvements: *(give type and area of each)*		
Dwelling 1530 sq. ft.	$ 39,200	$ 25.62
Garage 540 sq. ft.	$ 2,000	$ 3.70
Land Improvements: *(itemize)*		
Drive, Lawn, & Plantings	$ 1,800	$ Contributory
Total Sale Price	$ 57,000	

The appraiser then makes the following comparative analysis:

The comparable property's site is 1,000 sq. ft. larger than subject's, thus a downward adjustment is required for this factor. The subject is somewhat larger than the comparable, containing 1,620 sq. ft. Subject's 500 sq. ft. garage is slightly smaller than the comparable's, thus a downward adjustment is required for this factor. All other fac-

MARKET DATA

(1) ADDRESS or LOCATION:
(2) PHOTOGRAPH & PLOT PLAN SKETCH

(3) a. Access:
b. Present Use:
c. H. & B. Use:
d. Zoning:
e. Dimensions:
f. Area:
g. Sale Date:
h. Price: $
i. Instrument:
j. Terms:
k. E. Tax No.:
l. Grantor:
m. Grantee:
n. Confirmed with (names / dates)
.... / ....
.... / ....

Taken By: ....Date 	o. Date Inspected ....

(4) LEGAL DESCRIPTION:

(5) PROPERTY DESCRIPTION:

(6) ANALYSIS: TOTAL VALUE   UNIT VALUE
a. Extraction Data
Land: *(give area or front feet for each type)*
$ .... $ ....
$ .... $ ....
Improvements: *(give type and area of each)*
$ .... $ ....
$ .... $ ....
Land Improvements: *(itemize)*
$ .... $ ....

Total Sale Price $ ....

(7) COMPARATIVE ANALYSIS:

.... *Appraiser* Parcel No. .... COMPARABLE SALE NO.: ....

HWY FORM 261-020 REVISED 9/70   PAGE ....

Figure 17.2. Comparative Sale Analysis Form

MARKET DATA   COMPARABLE SALE NO.: .... *(Continued)*

PROJECT: ....

(9)   b.   Cost and Depreciation Data

    A.   Estimated Reproduction Cost New of Main Structure .... sf @ $ ..../sf .... $ ....

    B.   Confirmed Sale Price .... $ ....
        Estimated Land Value .... $ ....
        Estimated Value of Miscellaneous Improvements .... $ ____________
        Total Deductions .... $ ____________
        Contributory Value of Main Structure .... $ ____________

    C.   Accrued Depreciation Reflected by Sale .... $ ....

    D.   Average Annual Depreciation Amount
                    ($ .... , Accrued Depreciation ÷ Age of Structure, ... yrs.) $ ....

    E.   Annual Accrued Depreciation Percentage
                    ($ .... , Average Annual Depreciation ÷ $ .... , Reproduction Cost) .... %

(9)   c.   Income Data

    A.   GROSS INCOME ANALYSIS FROM MARKET

        Confirmed Sale Price $ .... ÷ Annual Gross Income $ .... =
                                   Gross Rent Multiple ....

        Confirmed Sale Price $ .... ÷ Monthly Gross Income $ .... =
                                   Monthly Multiplier ....

    B.   INCOME DATA FROM MARKET

        Annual Economic Gross Income .... $ ....
        Vacancy and Collection Loss .... % .... $ ____________
        Effective Gross Income .... $ ....
        Expenses *(Itemized)*
            Management .... $ ....   Maintenance .... $ ....
            Insurance .... $ ....   Reserves for Replacements .... $ ....
            Taxes .... $ ....   Other .... $ ....
        Total Expenses .... $ ____________
        Net Before Recapture .... $ ____________
        Interest Rate from Market .... %
        Interest Requirement on Investment *(Sale Price x Interest Rate)* .... $ ....
        Residual to Recapture .... $ ....

        MARKET INDICATIONS

        Rate of Recapture *(Residual to Recapture ÷ Contributory Value of Improvement)* .... %

        Operating Ratio ....*(Total Expenses ÷ Annual Economic Gross Income)* .... %

    (The appraiser should develop either or both the above income analyses as appropriate)

Comments:

                                                Grantor: ....

...., *Appraiser* Parcel No. ....   Grantee: ....

tors, including on-site improvements, would appear to be equal between subject and comparable.

For the review appraiser, the amount of adjustment becomes a matter of mathematics:

Price		$57,000
Adjustments:		
Land (1,000 sq. ft. @ $1.75)	$ – 1,750	
Size (90 sq. ft. @ $25.62)	+ 2,306	
Garage (40 sq. ft. @ $3.70)	– 148	
Net adjustment		+ 408
Indicated value of subject		$57,408
Rounded		$57,400

Woe is the poor appraiser whose mathematics don't work out with such precision. If the size adjustment was not made at the rate of $25.62 per square foot, the reviewer who suffers from the *Pluginski Syndrome* will probably have a seizure. However, as noted previously, the appraiser must not let this regimented appraisal procedure and review process constrain his thinking and limit his professional judgment.

One method which may appease the review appraiser is for the appraiser to include an extensive analysis as to why the mathematics of a specific adjustment do not work out precisely. At times, just using the proper words will appease the reviewer. "Probably one of the greatest weaknesses of Appraisers is the inability to communicate their findings without any question of doubt. Report writing is truly an art, and with semantics the problem in our language what it is, this is understandable; however, [the reviewer] must accept this and the Appraiser should make every attempt to project or clarify what is in his 'mind' into the written word, which is also clearly understandable to his client, [and the reviewer] even if it takes more work."[16]

For example, assume that in the appraiser's judgment the size differential between the two properties discussed above should be $1,000 rather than 90 sq. ft. @ $25.62, or $2,306. The appraiser might write, *"Market evidence would indicate that the size differential between these two properties would require an upward adjustment of about $1,000,"* but such a statement might send the review appraiser scurrying for a rejection form. The appraiser might try this statement instead, *"Considering the subject's larger size, and its utility in relationship to its size as compared to the size and relative utility of the sale property, an upward adjustment of $1,000 is indicated."*

This statement may be approved by the review appraiser for one of three reasons. The reviewer may feel that the appraiser has taken away the reviewer's mathematical crutch, but can't quite find anything specific to object to. Or the reviewer may determine that, *mathematically,* the proper size adjustment should have been 90 sq. ft. @ $25.62, or $2,306, but the appraiser used an adjustment of only $1,000 because the property under appraisal was inferior in utility to the sale property in the amount of $2,306 − $1,000, or $1,306. The third possibility is that the review appraiser will accept the adjustment because he is a *good reviewer,* rather than a *poor reviewer,* and recognizes from the appraiser's explanation that he has applied professional judgment. "Reviewers must make every attempt to read or review 'between the lines' to understand what the Appraiser is attempting to convey—this is not easy."[17]

The foregoing discussion may give the reader the impression that the appraiser and the review appraiser are adversaries; nothing could be (or, at least, should be) further from the truth. There are good appraisers and poor appraisers. "Let's also admit that there are good Review Appraisers and poor Review Appraisers. The fact that poor ones do exist does not obviate the necessity for, nor the importance of, the Review Appraiser."[18]

In fact, the review appraiser can be the appraiser's best friend. The reviewer can point out gross errors or foggy thinking before they are exposed to the light of day. The review appraiser can be most helpful in counseling the appraiser before the appraisal report is completed and while the appraiser is applying the appraisal process. The appraiser should use the review appraiser as a sounding board.[19] This is particularly beneficial when the appraiser cannot discuss specific appraisal problems with other knowledgeable appraisers on the same staff or in the same office.

When an appraiser questions a reviewer about applying *a proposed appraisal method* to a specific appraisal problem, and the reviewer responds by tearing the methodology to shreds, the reviewer has shown his greatest worth to the appraiser. It is much better to hear criticism early on, than to have it revealed after the appraisal report is complete or, worse yet, during cross-examination on the witness stand. Because a good review appraiser can be invaluable to the client and the appraiser, it seems incredible that some condemning agencies have adopted rules which prohibit any communication between the apprasier and the reviewer.

One condemning agency, for instance, allows no communication between the appraiser and the reviewer. When the reviewer finds a report which needs to be corrected by the appraiser, he does not contact the appraiser directly, but sends an *intra-departmental communication* (IDC) to the senior appraiser.

> Upon receipt of notice from the Review Appraiser that corrective action is needed . . . the Senior Appraiser:
>
> A.   Confers with the Appraisal Review Section Supervisor and/or

the Review Appraiser as needed.

B. *Does not reveal the Review Appraiser's IDC . . . to the Fee Appraiser under any circumstances.*

C. Takes action to obtain the necessary corrections, including recommending that payment for contracted services be withheld pending contract fulfillment.[20] [emphasis added]

This type of regulation just leads to misunderstanding and wheel spinning and may promote adversary and stubborn postures in all parties involved. Eliminating such rules would greatly diminish the animosity that has developed between some appraisers and review appraisers. Better relations also might result if appraisers would try to develop a true understanding of the reviewer's duties and function. To date, information regarding the duties and function of reviewers has been fragmented and difficult to obtain; recently, however, the National Association of Review Appraisers has compiled a text entitled *Principles and Techniques of Appraisal Review.*[21] Even if the appraiser has no inclination to review an appraisal report, the text is invaluable. It not only defines the duties and functions of the reviewer, but also explains review procedures. With this knowledge, the appraiser is better prepared to write an appraisal report that will *sail through review.*

Both the appraiser and the reviewer must remember that it is not the function of the reviewer to reappraise the property. "This is sometimes difficult for some Reviewers to do. He must be cognizant that he is not assigned to do the appraisal; this has already been accomplished. He must place himself in the position of 'interpreter' rather than 'performer.' He must not attempt to 'second guess' the Appraiser. His function is to make a determination as to whether or not the Appraiser has adequately substantiated and justified the valuation conclusion reached."[22]

Some reviewers for condemning agencies also must decide whether the appraisal report has been written in accordance with the applicable appraisal guidelines and/or the appraisal contract. These reviewers must also make a *DV* (determination of value) based on their review of one or more appraisals. One of the greatest compliments a reviewer can give an appraiser is to approve the appraisal report, but reject the appraiser's final estimate of value. Although the reviewer substitutes his own judgment for the appraiser's in writing a *DV,* the fact that the reviewer approves the report is evidence that the appraiser has written it in accordance with the applicable guidelines, has met all conditions of the appraisal contract, and has adequately substantiated and justified the value conclusion reached. It is only natural for the reviewer to try to find fault with the procedure and analysis used when he disagrees with the final conclusion. Thus, it is a good sign when the reviewer cannot fault the appraiser's work or conclusions, although he maintains a different opinion of value.

As previously illustrated, using the detailed adjustment process in the appraisal report poses a problem in jurisdictions that require full discovery or exchange of appraisal reports. The condemnor's legal counsel may turn prematurely grey when such an exchange is ordered. The appraiser should be prepared to justify why each dollar adjustment was made in precisely the amount reported.

Although the appraiser may have made specific dollar adjustments when comparing properties, using these precise adjustments in an appraisal report can mislead the reader. Using finite adjustments suggests that the appraisal of real estate is an exact science, rather than an art. In analyzing comparable sales, some appraisers conclude that "after analysis, this sale property indicates a value for subject of about X dollars, or in the neighborhood of X dollars." This phrasing can, in fact, be used in stating the indicated value of the property under appraisal by the various approaches to value; then, the final estimate of value can be stated as a precise figure if a single, specific amount is required by law and/or the client.

The minimum content of an appraisal report is often dictated by the professional appraisal organization of which the appraiser is a member or a candidate for membership. For instance, the minimum reporting rules specified by the American Institute of Real Estate Appraisers is stated as follows:

Reporting Rule 1.
Each written appraisal report signed by a Member or Candidate must contain a clear and reasonably complete description of the real estate (or interest in real estate) that is the subject of the appraisal. Each oral appraisal report made by a Member or Candidate must clearly identify the real estate (or interest in real estate) that is the subject of the appraisal.

Reporting Rule 2.
Each written or oral appraisal report signed or made by a Member or Candidate must clearly set forth all of the assumptions and limiting conditions upon which the appraisal is based.

Reporting Rule 3.
Each written or oral appraisal report signed or made by a Member or Candidate must clearly set forth (either specifically or by reference) all of the significant facts upon which the appraisal is based.

Reporting Rule 4.
Each written or oral appraisal report signed or made by a Member or Candidate must set forth a reasonably complete summary of the work done in arriving at each analysis, opinion or conclusion concerning real estate contained in such report as well as the reasoning of the appraiser supporting each such analysis, opinion or conclusion.

Reporting Rule 5.
Each written or oral appraisal report signed or made by a Member or Candidate that contains a valuation of a particular parcal or tract or [sic] real estate must set forth the date of such valuation as well as the date of such appraisal report.

Reporting Rule 6.
Each written or oral appraisal report signed or made by a Member or Candidate that contains a valuation of an estate in land that is less that [sic] the entire fee simple estate must contain a clear statement that (i) the value reported for such estate relates to a fractional interest only in the real estate involved; and (ii) the value of this fractional interest plus the value of all other fractional interests may or may not equal the value of the entire fee simple estate considered as a whole.

Reporting Rule 7.
Each written or oral appraisal report signed or made by a Member or Candidate that contains a valuation of a geographical portion of a larger parcel [sic] or tract of real estate must contain a clear statement that (i) the value reported for such geographical portion relates to such portion only and should not be construed as applying with equal validity to other portions of the larger parcel or tract, and (ii) the value reported for such geographical portion plus the value of all other geographical portions may or may not equal the value of the entire parcel or tract considered as a whole.

Reporting Rule 8.
Each written or oral appraisal report signed or made by a Member or Candidate must contain a statement that the appraiser has no direct or indirect, current or prospective personal interest in the subject matter of the appraisal report and that the appraiser has no personal bias with respect to the parties involved in the appraisal; *provided, however,* that if a statement of this nature cannot be made, then such appraisal report must contain a statement fully and accurately disclosing all such personal interest or bias.

Reporting Rule 9.
Each written appraisal report signed by a Member or Candidate must contain *either* (i) a statement in compliance with Canon 3 of this Regulation acknowledging all significant professional appraisal assistance received from others in arriving at the analyses, opinions or conclusions concerning real estate contained in such appraisal report, *or* (ii) a statement that no one other than the person or persons signing

the report rendered significant professional appraisal assistance in arriving at the analyses, opinions and conclusions concerning real estate set forth in such report.

Reporting Rule 10.
Each written appraisal report signed by a Member or Candidate must contain a certification substantially in the following form:

> "The American Institute of Real Estate Appraisers conducts a voluntary program of continuing education for its designated members. MAIs and RMs who meet the minimum standards of this program are awarded periodic educational certification."

> "I am certified under this program through *(date);* or I was last certified under this program through *(date);* or I have not been certified under this program.

This statement may be expanded by Members who wish to explain non-participation; however, such explanation must be stated in a forthright manner. The statement of certification is also required for form appraisals, either on the form itself or on an attached sheet.

In addition, each written appraisal report signed by a Member or Candidate must contain a certification substantially in the following form:

> "I (we), the undersigned, do hereby certify that I (we) have (or have not) inspected the subject property; that to the best of my (our) knowledge and belief, the statements of fact contained in this report, upon which the analyses, opinions and conclusions expressed herein are based, are true and correct; that this report sets forth all of the assumptions and limiting conditions affecting the analyses, opinions and conclusions contained in this report; and that this report has been made in conformity with and is subject to the requirements of the Code of Ethics and Standards of Professional Practice of the American Institute of Real Estate Appraisers of the National Assocation of Realtors."

If there is more than one signatory of a written appraisal report, each signatory must state whether he or she has or has not personally inspected the subject property.

Reporting Rule 11.
Each written appraisal report signed by a Member or Candidate which relates to residential real estate and states that a neighborhood is declining or is about to decline must contain (either specifically or

by reference) the significant facts and the reasoning of the Member or Candidate supporting such conclusion. Each oral appraisal report made by a Member or Candidate which relates to residential real estate and states that a neighborhood is declining or is about to decline must be supported by specific facts and the reasoning of the appraiser and all supporting data must be contained in the appraiser's file.

Reporting Rule 12.
Each written appraisal report signed by a Member or Candidate must contain a statement substantially in the following form:

> One (or more) of the signatories of this appraisal report is a Member (or Candidate) of the American Institute of Real Estate Appraisers of the National Association of Realtors. The Bylaws and Regulations of the Institute require each Member and Candidate to control the use and distribution of each appraisal report signed by such Member or Candidate. Therefore, except as hereinafter provided, the party for whom this appraisal report was prepared may distribute copies of this appraisal report, in its entirety, to such third parties as may be selected by the party for whom this appraisal report was prepared; however, selected portions of this appraisal report shall not be given to third parties without the prior written consent of the signatories of this appraisal report. Further, neither all nor any part of this appraisal report shall be disseminated to the general public by the use of advertising media, public relations media, news media, sales media or other media for public communication without the prior written consent of the signatories of this appraisal report.[23]

In addition, the American Institute of Real Estate Appraisers' Code of Professional Ethics and Standards of Professional Conduct states that:

> In performing a real estate appraisal assignment, it is improper to arrive at an analysis, conclusion or opinion concerning real estate without utilizing all of the recognized appraisal methods and techniques that will materially and significantly contribute to a proper valuation or evaluation of such real estate or to a solution of the real estate problem under consideration.[24]

The Society of Real Estate Appraisers requires that the following items be included in each appraisal report, as a minimum:

(1) An adequate and definite description of the property being appraised.
(2) The purpose of the appraisal and a definition of the value estimated.
(3) The effective date of the appraisal.
(4) The data and reasoning supporting the value conclusion which may include the comparable sales [market data] approach, the income approach and the cost approach. The exclusion of any of the usual three approaches must be explained and supported.
(5) The final estimate of value.
(6) Special and limiting conditions, if any.
(7) The appraiser's certification and signature.[25]

The appraiser retained by a condemnee is generally given a freer hand in determining the content of the appraisal report. However, it is always advisable to include a thorough explanation of the premises behind the various approaches to value and how they work. It is also advisable to state briefly the legal premise of just compensation and to explain that the appraiser is generally bound by the applicable jurisdiction's concept of just compensation, *i.e.,* market value. The appraiser should indicate that the owner's unwillingness to sell, or the fact that the owner was born and raised on the property has no bearing on market value and, therefore, cannot be considered in the appraisal process.

The appraiser should consult with the client's legal counsel as to the content of the appraisal report. This discussion will give the appraiser an indication of the attorney's understanding of the appraisal process, which, in itself, may help the appraiser determine the appropriate report content. This consultation will also give the appraiser and the attorney the opportunity to review the applicable rules of discovery in the jurisdiction and how these rules may or may not affect the desired report content.

Discovery rules are becoming more and more liberal. Some federal courts require the exchange of appraisal reports, in total, prior to trial. In 1967, a New York court established the following rules in regard to the discovery of valuation evidence:

Special Rule

Exchange of Appraisal Reports in Proceedings for Condemnation, Appropriation and Review of Tax Assessments

(a) In all proceedings for the determination of the value of property taken pursuant to eminent domain, and in all proceedings for the review of tax assessments on real property where value is in issue, the attorneys for the respective parties shall file with the administrative judge of the judicial district in which the proceedings are pending, not later than 30 days before the date set for trial, one copy (or, in the event that there are two or more adversaries, a copy for each of such adversaries) of a report of each appraiser or expert witness whose testimony is intended to be relied upon at the trial, with proof of service upon each adversary of a notice of the filing of such reports.

(b) When the administrative judge shall have received the appraisal reports of all parties, or twenty-eight days before the date set for trial, whichever is earlier, he shall distribute copies of the appraisal reports filed with him to each of the attorneys of record of all other parties to the claim. In proceedings where more than one parcel is involved, the appraisal reports shall only be distributed to the taking or taxing authority and to the claimant or claimants who are owners of parcels which are the subject of the appraisal report.

(c) Each appraisal report shall contain a statement of the method of appraisal to be relied on and the conclusions as to value reached by the expert, together with a complete and detailed statement as to the facts, figures and calculations by which the conclusions were reached. If sales, leases or other transactions of comparable properties are to be relied on, they shall be set forth with such particularity as to permit the transactions to be readily identified. Appraisal reports shall be in compliance with the Standard Form For Appraisal Reports which is obtainable from the Director of Administration for the Third Judicial Department, Courthouse, Albany.

(d) Upon the trial of the proceedings, all parties shall be limited in their proof as to value based on appraisal to matters set forth in their respective appraisal reports. Any party who fails to file an appraisal report as herein required shall be precluded from offering any expert testimony on value.

(e) Upon the application of any party on such notice as the court in which the proceeding is pending shall direct, the court may, upon good cause shown, relieve a party of a default in the filing of a report, extend the time for filing reports or allow an amended or supplemental report to be filed upon such conditions as the court may direct. No such application shall be entertained after the trial of the issue has begun except in extraordinary circumstances.

(f) Motions hereunder shall not be made to the administrative judge.

Standard Form for Appraisal Reports

Note: This report is required by rule of the Appellate Division Third Department, a copy of which appears on the reverse side of this form. Information requested shall be furnished under each category, unless clearly inapplicable to a particular proceeding. Notwithstanding the specification of information on the form, parties shall furnish complete information as to the elements of the appraisal.

I. Introduction
    (a) Title and number of action; Attorney; Reference to the Appropriation Project or Tax Assessment Proceeding.
    (b) Purpose of Appraisal.
    (c) Qualifications of Appraiser.
II. Description of Property
    (a) Ownership, location of subject property and description of neighboring lands.
    (b) Description of land and improvements and facilities available.
    (c) Present use; economic trends; highest and best use; zoning.
III. Description of Acquisition or Explanation of Assessment
    (a) Description of all interests affected with full particulars concerning extent and nature of the appropriation, if such, or the assessment, if such.
IV. Value of Property Before Appropriation or at Time of Assessment
    (a) Describe in detail the valuation and all methods by which it was arrived at. Include data on comparable sales.
V. Value of Property After Appropriation (Not Applicable to Assessments)
    (a) Giving highest and best use of remainder, detail the direct damages and consequential damages, if any, to the land and improvements.
    (b) Allocate damages to the land and the various improvements.
VI. Miscellaneous
    (a) Attach any maps, drawings or photos which are pertinent.[26]

The *Uniform Eminent Domain Code* illustrates this trend toward liberal discovery rules. The *Code* states:

A party to a condemnation action may:

(1)   [By request for production] require any other party to produce for inspection and copying or to furnish a copy, of any written appraisals, reports, maps, diagrams, charts, tables, or other documents in his possession or under his control that contain engineering, economic, valuation, comparable sales, or other data pertaining to the issue of compensation.[27]

An important part of an appraisal report are the graphics, photos, and other exhibits included in the report and the addenda of the report. Appraisers do not always agree as to which items should be included in the body of a report, and which should be left for the addenda. Each appraiser must make his own decision in this regard, keeping in mind the client's reporting requirements and using his own good judgment.

For instance, the body of an appraisal report on a proposed medical office complex might include:

1. Aerial photo of subject (following letter of transmittal).
2. Graph depicting the ratio of doctors to trade area population for the past 20 years.
3. List of nursing homes in the city, including the class of each home and the number of beds it contains.
4. Neighborhood occupancy map (on the page facing the neighborhood data section of report).
5. List of comparable land sales, showing sale number, grantor/grantee, sale date, land size, price, and price per square foot.
6. Detailed reproduction cost estimate.
7. List of rental comparables, showing rental number, lessor/lessee, location, size, rent, and rent per square foot.
8. Reconstructed operating statement.
9. List of properties, including pertinent data used to develop capitalization rate.
10. Graphic analysis of selected overall capitalization rate.
11. List of comparable improved sales, showing the sale number, grantor/grantee, sale date, building size, and price.

The addenda of this report might include the following items:

1. City or regional map.
2. Neighborhood map.
3. Neighborhood aerial photo.
4. Legal description of property (if legal description is short, this would typically be included in the body of the report).
5. Plot plan.

6. Subject photographs.
7. Comparable land sales map.
8. Comparable land sales data and photos.
9. Executed leases on subject property.
10. Comparable rental map.
11. Comparable rental data and photographs.
12. Comparable improved sales map.
13. Comparable improved sales data and photographs.
14. After tax cash flow analysis for various tax brackets.

When an economic or geographic peculiarity has, or may have, affected property values over a large area, a detailed general discussion of this factor can more properly be included in the addenda than in the body of the report.

Written appraisal reports should state the appraiser's findings in the same way a verbal report would. Appraisers seem to have a phobia about using dictating equipment, but this equipment can help the appraiser write a report in a conversational manner; once the appraiser becomes accustomed to it, the actual report writing time will be substantially reduced. When first attempting to dictate a report, the appraiser may be discouraged and want to go back to writing the report out in longhand. Don't do it! Most people will be pleasantly surprised at how well their verbal communciation reads.

Report Appearance

The quality of an appraisal report will be judged on its appearance as often, if not more often than on its content. Many times the appraiser will never meet his client face to face; the only way the client can judge the appraiser is through the written appraisal report. Most appraisers consider themselves professionals, so their product—the appraisal report—must look professional. One way to emphasize the importance of the report's appearance is for the appraiser to divide the appraisal fee by the number of pages in the finished report. The report may cost the client more than $100 per page, and for that much money, the client deserves more than smeared typing, typographical errors, and free hand sketches stuffed into a 25¢ binder.

Some clients will dictate the format and content of the appraisal report. Some government agencies will even specify such oddities as "[a]ll reports are typewritten on legal size *(8½" × 13")* bond paper."[28] (Because legal size paper is generally 8½" × 14", the appraiser will generally have to procure special paper.) Some clients may specify, "The completed report is stapled in the upper left-hand corner only. The report is not to be placed in a folder."[29] Nobody seems to remember when, why, or how these report specifications were first determined, but if that's what the client wants, the appraiser must comply.

A word of warning to both the appraiser and the attorney is in order. The appraiser must not, under any circumstances, take a report in such a format on the witness stand for reference; the attorney should not allow the witness to do so. When opposing counsel sees the report they will start asking very specific factual questions; undoubtedly, the appraiser will have to refer to the appraisal report to answer these questions. After about the fourth question, the appraiser is going to look like a windmill, with papers flying every which way. If the report is typed on erasable paper, the appraiser will begin having problems turning the pages because perspiration from his forehead has dripped on the pages and made them stick together. The type of reference material the appraiser should or should not take on the witness stand is described in detail later in this work.[30]

Often, graphics can make a report more easily understood; therefore, professional sketches and photographs should be included in appraisal reports. Aerial photographs with clear film overlays can be particularly useful in partial taking cases. They can illustrate the relative proximity of the property under appraisal to other geographically identifiable objects, e.g., the proximity of a drug store to various medical offices. Well drawn sketches, such as the one shown in Figure 17.3, can also add to an appraisal report. Letter transfers, sometimes called press type, can be used to give dimensions and label areas and structures. Because most government agencies will require multiple copies of an appraisal report, the appraiser should have access to good photocopying equipment.

Summary

"The thoroughness with which the appraisal is made and *reported* is the appraiser's greatest protection against professional embarrassment."[31] The appraiser must know the purpose of the appraisal and clearly define the value sought, e.g., market value, in terms that are legally acceptable in the applicable jurisdiction. It is not absolutely necessary for the appraiser to know the function of the appraisal, but this knowledge can help the appraiser determine the specific content and format of the appraisal report.

Some clients will specify the format required for an appraisal report, while others will leave the formating totally in the hands of the appraiser. Whatever the client's instructions, an appraisal report must be presented in a logical, sequential manner which leads the reader to the same conclusion reached by the appraiser. The appraiser must avoid the tendency to regiment his thinking along the lines outlined by the client's required format and content.

The writing of an appraisal report should not be begun until the appraiser has completed all necessary investigation, analysis, and computations and has arrived at all the conclusions necessary to complete the report. It is also helpful if the appraiser prepares all graphic materials and photographs which will appear in the report before he starts the actual writing. By doing this, the appraiser will

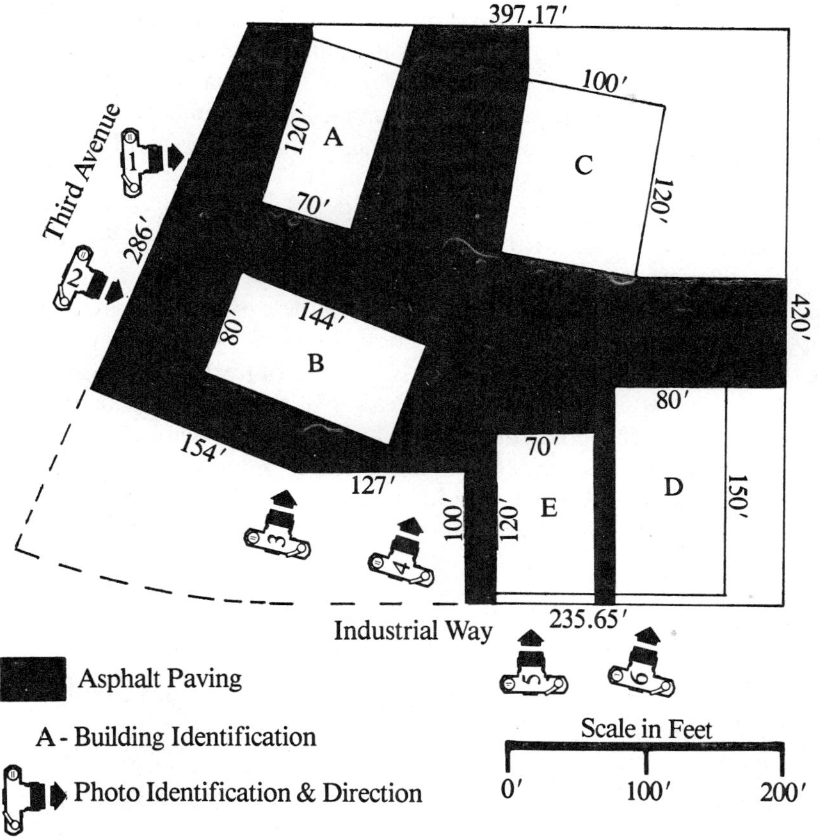

Figure 17.3. Sketch of Subject Property

have all material data in front of him and avoid conflicts between the narrative and graphic portions of the report.

The content of an appraisal report will depend on the nature of the property, the nature of the taking, and the requirements of the client and/or the client's legal counsel. Many condemnors are very specific as to the format and content of appraisal reports. Regardless of the client's requirements, the appraiser should use a report outline or checklist to ensure that no important factors have been overlooked. In writing an appraisal report for a condemnee, it is often advisable to use the condemnor's appraisal report guidelines as a checklist; if the condemnor wants a specific factor covered by its own appraiser, the condemnor's attorney will probably want to know whether this factor has also been considered by the condemnee's appraiser.

There is no single outline for an appraisal report's format and content which can be applied universally because different types of properties are involved. Many publications contain demonstration or illustrative appraisals of different types of properties. *Nichols'* contains more than 30 illustrative condemnation appraisals, including appraisals for condemnors, for condemnees, in total taking cases, in partial taking cases, and appraisals involving leasehold and lease fee cases.[32]

Regardless of the property type or the client's instructions, the appraiser should be certain that any report written meets the minimum reporting requirements set down by the professional appraisal organizations. These requirements should be met whether the appraiser is a member of one of these organizations or not; this is simply good professional appraisal practice. Also, the Realtor® should be aware that the Code of Ethics of the National Association of Realtors also contains minimum reporting requirements when the Realtor® is acting in the capacity of an appraiser.[33] Appraisal report content should be discussed with the client's legal counsel, particuarly when the content may relate to applicable rules of discovery.

The typical appraisal client may judge the quality of an appraisal report as much by its appearance as by its content. Therefore, appraisers should produce only professional quality reports.

Notes

1. William C. Himstreet, *Writing Appraisal Reports* (Chicago: American Institute of Real Estate Appraisers, 1971), p. 28.

2. American Institute of Real Estate Appraisers and the Society of Real Estate Appraisers, *Real Estate Appraisal Terminology,* rev. ed., Byrl N. Boyce, ed. (Cambridge, Mass.: Ballinger Publishing Co., 1981), p. 195.

3. Ibid.

4. *Real Estate Appraisal Terminology,* p. 115.

5. Washington State Dept. of Transportation, *Right of Way Manual,* Chapter 4, Appendix 4-2, Appraisal Report Guide, Part IIC, tab C, p. 9, Item 5 (Revised 11/10/76).

6. See *Communicating the Appraisal: A Guide to Report Writing* (Chicago: American Institute of Real Estate Appraisers, 1982); George L. Schmutz, *Condemnation Appraisal Handbook,* Revised by Edwin M. Rams (Englewood Cliffs, N.J.: Prentice-Hall, Inc., 1963); and *The Appraisal of Real Estate,* 7th ed. (Chicago: American Institute of Real Estate Appraisers, 1978).

7. *Uniform Appraisal Standards for Federal Land Acquisitions* (Washington, D.C.: U.S. Government Printing Office, 1973) § B, pp. 35-38.

8. *Right of Way Manual,* Part IIC, § 4-3.2.

9. Ibid., pp. 1-5.

10. *Uniform Appraisal Standards for Federal Guidelines,* § B, pp. 35-38.

11. *The Appraisal of Real Estate,* 7th ed., p. 52.

12. American Institute of Real Estate Appraisers, Regulation No. 10, *Code of Professional Ethics and Standards of Professional Conduct,* Canon 8, pp. 15-18 (Adopted Nov. 13, 1981). 13, 1981).

13. American Institute of Real Estate Appraisers, Regulation No. 12, Art. III, § 2, pp. 1-2 (Revised May 8, 1978).

14. *Right of Way Manual,* Part II, Item 4 Bl, pp. 14-15.

15. Ibid., Part II, § A3.

16. The National Association of Review Appraisers, ed., *Principles and Techniques of Appraisal Review* (St. Paul, Minn.: Todd Publishing, 1980) p. 20.

17. Ibid.

18. Ibid., p. 7.

19. Ibid., p. 19.

20. *Right of Way Manual,* Part IIC, Chapter 4, § 4-5.09.

21. *Principles and Techniques of Appraisal Review,* pp. 1-385.

22. Ibid., p. 16.

23. Regulation No. 10, *Code of Professional Ethics and Standards of Professional Conduct,* Canon 8, pp. 16-17.

24. Ibid., Canon No. 7, Guideline 1, p. 12.

25. Society of Real Estate Appraisers, *Standards of Professional Practice,* § II.

26. Special Rule, New York Supreme Court, Appellate Division, Third Dept., Albany.

27. "Uniform Eminent Domain Code," 1974, § 702, p. 7.1.

28. *Right of Way Manual,* Part II, § B2.

29. *Right of Way Manual,* Part II B, § B7.

30. See Chapter 19, "The Expert Witness."

31. *Writing Appraisal Reports,* p. 28.

32. Patrick J. Rohan and Melvin A. Reskin, *Nichols' The Law of Eminent Domain,* rev. 3rd ed. (New York: Matthew Bender, 1980) Vol. 8A and 9, Appendix B-2, pp. App-47—App-102.974 (298) (Vol. 8A is also published as Vol. 3A, Part 2 of the treatise entitled *Real Estate Transactions*). (Vol. 9 is also published as Vol. 3B of the treatise entitled *Real Estate Transactions*).

33. National Association of Realtors®, *Code of Ethics,* Article 11 and Standard of Practice 11-1.

CHAPTER 18
PREPARATION FOR TRIAL

The appraiser should begin preparing for trial the moment the appraisal assignment is received. The attorney, of course, should obtain a general understanding of the case and the basis of the dispute when he is retained by the client. The procedure will vary somewhat depending on whether the client is a condemnor or condemnee. If the client is an active condemnor, it generally has one or more staff attorneys or has an attorney on retainer. An active condemnor will also have an *approved appraiser list* and/or a staff of appraisers.

When an appraiser is given an assignment by a condemnor, the attorney who will handle the case is generally known by the appraiser. On the other hand, the attorney does not usually have any input into the selection of the appraiser; in fact, he is often not even aware of the case until the staff or fee negotiators have failed to settle the dispute. When the case is turned over to the attorney, he will generally have the choice of keeping the original appraiser or choosing a new appraiser to replace or assist the first one. Many condemnor's attorneys, as a matter of policy, refuse to go to trial with a staff appraiser, particularly when the compensation at stake is substantial. The reason behind this practice is that many attorneys do not feel that they can convince a trier of fact that the staff appraiser is not an advocate in favor of the condemnor, which also happens to be the appraiser's employer.

When the client is the condemnee, a different situation exists. The client may approach either the attorney or the appraiser first. If the appraiser is contacted first, he should encourage the client to retain legal counsel immediately. If the attorney is contacted before an appraiser has been retained, one of his primary functions is to counsel the client to retain the services of an appraiser. The sooner the appraiser/attorney team is determined the better.

Some attorneys wait until the last possible moment to retain the services of an appraiser. This may be because the attorney is too busy to worry about it until the date of trial is very near, or the attorney may falsely believe that hiring the appraiser late in the game can save the client appraisal fees because the appraiser will not be able to spend as much time on the appraisal and the preparation for trial. Whatever his reason for procrastination, the attorney should retain the services of an appraiser at the outset; the appraiser should decline to accept any assignment if there isn't adequate time to properly complete the appraisal and prepare for trial. "Many good appraisers are in too much of a hurry to try to turn out their appraisal reports for clients who waited too long to hire them. Many mistakes in arithmetic are made. Many items are overlooked in the physical inspection. If the cross-examining attorney can find one mistake, his favorite questions are: And what else did you overlook? And what else did you do wrong? Small details which are missed are blown way out of proportion because you are an expert."[1]

"Successful resolution of a condemnation proceeding, whether from the viewpoint of the condemnor or condemnee, depends upon teamwork between attorney and appraiser and other experts. The value of any parcel being condemned is an elusive thing, difficult of determination. But it is this determination that is the object of the condemnation proceeding. A smoothly functioning appraiser-attorney team represents the client's best, indeed only, chance of obtaining just compensation."[2] This teamwork sometimes breaks down, however, because ". . . the appraiser probably thinks that the lawyer is an unadulterated idiot, because the attorney is unable to tell the appraiser what the law is which will probably control in the case. In turn, the lawyer thinks the appraiser is an unadulterated idiot because the appraiser—as is true of all nonlawyers—always knows what the law is."[3] This attitude can be overcome only by recognizing that ". . . as important as having an expertise in their respective fields of endeavor is the need for the lawyer to be familiar with appraisal methods and problems, and correlatively, the need for the appraiser to have an understanding of court procedure and rules of evidence governing admissibility of appraisal information. Attorneys and experts should aid each other in understanding those matters within their own sphere of expertise which their counterparts should know for purposes of the condemnation proceedings."[4]

Reference to the "appraiser/attorney team" should not be misconstrued to imply that the objectives of the appraiser and attorney are synonymous. The appraiser and the attorney act as a team because, although their goals are not the same, they are compatible. The attorney is an advocate for his client's interest. He strives to obtain the most favorable award for his client—as high as possible for the condemnee-client, and as low as possible for the condemnor-client. The appraiser, on the other hand, is an advocate only for his opinion of value.

Only when the appraiser's opinion of value supports the client and his attorney's concept of the proper amount of compensation can an appraiser/attorney team exist and function effectively. Therefore, it cannot be determined for certain that a "team" relationship actually exists until the appraiser has reached his opinion of value. If the appraiser's opinion of value does not support the client's position, there is no team; if the appraiser's opinion of value does support the client's position, the appraiser and the attorney can function as a team because their ultimate goals are compatible.

Experience has shown that triers of fact have an uncanny knack for distinguishing between the expert witness who is an advocate for his client and is testifying to a false value, and the one who is testifying to his unbiased opinion of value. Experienced condemnation lawyers know this and will dump, without hesitation, the appraiser who taints his value estimate to satisfy the interest of his client. The appraiser who cannot ignore the interests of the client and develop an unbiased, supportable opinion of value will have a short professional career.

Selection of Appraiser

The selection of an appraiser by the attorney, generally in consort with the client, may be one of the most important steps in preparing for trial. Many states have no licensing requirements, and those that do generally have only minimal qualification and testing requirements. In fact, some federal agencies have disregarded state licensing laws and have retained unlicensed appraisers. This decision is based on the theory that the government has the right to select anyone it chooses to appraise government property. It is the government's money that pays the fee and the government's property being appraised, so it is the government's right to determine whom it will retain as an appraiser.

If the attorney is not personally familiar with an appraiser, referrals can generally be obtained from other attorneys, real estate agents, bankers, and various condemnors. When relying on a referral, the attorney should be careful to avoid enlisting the services of a *prostitute* appraiser. There are those appraisers who work only *one side of the street—i.e.,* only for condemnors or for condemnees. This fact, in and of itself, is not an adequate reason to reject a referral. However, if the referred appraiser only works for condemnees, it is advisable to ask some attorneys who represent condemnors about the appraiser; similarly, if the appraiser works only for condemnors, it is advisable to obtain the opinions of attorneys who specialize in representing condemnees. Experience has shown that attorneys have respect for well-qualified, honest appraisers, even if they only work the other side of the street. If, however, the appraiser in question never sees anything but potential shopping center sites or, at the other end of the spectrum, only sees pasture land, attorneys are not generally known for their silence on such matters.

Hiring the prostitute appraiser (or, as some prefer to label him, *the continually over-optimistic* or *over-pessimistic appraiser*), may initially appear to be in the best interest of the client. However, this practice can have serious, negative results. First, opposing counsel may take the tack that "If the other side is going to use that prostitute, then we are going to hire our own prostitute"; this is the fight-fire-with-fire approach. Secondly, hiring a disreputable appraiser will all but eliminate the possibility of a negotiated settlement. Third, the client may draw false hope from the appraiser's often-outlandish conclusions; when the condemnation award does not even approach the appraiser's testimony, the attorney, at least in the eyes of the client, will be partially to blame. Finally, if the appraiser testifies to a value that the trier of fact finds totally unbelievable, the trier of fact's only alternative is to base its award solely on the evidence presented by the opposing party to the dispute.

For instance, if the condemnor's appraiser testifies to a value of $300,000, and the condemnee's appraiser testifies to a value of $400,000, the odds are much greater that the trier of fact will split the difference at $350,000. This would be highly improbable if the condemnee's appraiser had testified to a value of $800,000. When the valuation testimony varies greatly, the trier of fact will generally adopt the premise presented by one party to the suit, to the exclusion of the other; therefore, the award will be based on a single premise and value estimate.

If the appraiser selected has a reputation for competency, objectivity, and a professional demeanor on the witness stand, just the retention of such an appraiser may assist in reaching a negotiated settlement. This is particularly true if the appraiser selected has, in the past, worked with opposing counsel. Opposing counsel will know that the case presented will be creditable, well prepared, and believable.

There is controversy within both the legal and appraisal professions as to whether appraisers should accept assignments from both condemnors and condemnees, particularly in cases involving the same public improvement project. Some condemnors have gone so far as to include a clause in their appraisal contracts prohibiting the appraiser from making appraisals for any condemnee involved with the same project. Of course, the individual appraiser engaged in such work and the individual attorney who retains appraisers on behalf of his clients must determine whether or not to agree to this clause. There are, however, a couple of factors that should be considered in making this decision.

First, the appraiser might not want to restrict himself because an appraiser who has worked for both condemnors and condemnees can so testify as a part of his qualifications. This is particularly effective when an appraiser, testifying on behalf of a condemnee, can state that he has appraised for the condemnor on the same public project; this infers the condemnor's tacit acknowledgment that the appraiser is competent, unbiased, and honest. In this situation, the condemnor can only suggest to the trier of fact that, although the appraiser is well-qualified, this time he has simply made a mistake. Therefore, it has been said that "[u]se of an appraiser whose experience has been primarily on one or the other side of a condemnation should be avoided."[5]

Another factor to be considered is that the appraiser who works for both condemnors and condemnees is, of necessity if not inclination, kept honest. The appraiser's analysis of a sale property simply cannot change from assignment to assignment; once the analysis is made and reported, the appraiser is stuck with it. For instance, in analyzing the *Coulter case,*[6] George C. Hadley explained:

> It happened that in the present proceeding the condemnee's two expert witnesses had been previously employed by the state in a similar capacity. Moreover, each of the witnesses had made studies, appraisal reports, and in one or more instances had testified in court as a state witness in relation to the value of properties in the immediate area. It was developed on cross-examination that one of their appraisals concerned the property adjoining the [property under appraisal], and that another appraisal was in relation to an entire block of property directly across [the street from the property in dispute]. Further cross-examination with respect to sales data (upon which the state's experts were to rely in large measure) disclosed that while these two witnesses had each previously considered the same data helpful in their appraisals of property in this vicinity when appearing for the state, they now chose to disavow the comparability of such transactions.[7]

In selecting an appraiser, the attorney must determine the appraiser's competency and review his general qualifications. Engaging an appraiser who holds a designation from a professional appraisal organization, such as the MAI (Member, Appraiser Institute) designation granted by the American Institute of Real Estate Appraisers or the SREA (Senior Real Estate Analyst) designation awarded by the Society of Real Estate Appraisers, ensures that the appraiser has specific minimum qualifications and is subject to a strict code of ethics. The reputation of the appraiser should also be investigated; this is especially important in smaller communities.

The attorney should determine whether the appraiser will need any special qualifications for the assignment. For instance, an appraiser who is qualified to cruise timber may be helpful in a case involving timberland. Any appraiser selected should be able to assist the attorney in preparation for negotiations, preparation for trial, preparation of exhibits, and, of course, during the trial. It is, perhaps, unfortunate that the attorney must put so much emphasis on the appraiser's demeanor on the witness stand. But if the appraiser falls apart under cross-examination, or direct examination for that matter, he becomes a liability rather than an asset to the attorney.

Once the appraiser has been selected, a contract for appraisal services should be prepared and signed. A condemnor-client will generally have a standard form appraisal contract. These form contracts probably would never be signed if appraisers carefully read them and fully understood their terms. Condemnor contracts generally provide that payment for work does not have to be made until the appraisals are reviewed and approved, but there are no time restraints on how long the condemnor has to complete such a review. Another typical provision of such a contract is that "[i]t is mutually understood and agreed that any dispute relating to the quality or acceptability of work furnished, to the acceptable fulfillment and performance of the contract on the part of the Appraiser, and/or to compensation *shall be decided by the Chief Right of Way Agent, Department of Highways*."[8] [emphasis added] Most contracts also provide for hourly or daily compensation for pretrial and trial work.

A contract between the condemnee and the appraiser is generally much more informal. Some of these contracts specify a flat fee for appraisal services, while others specify a daily fee (and sometimes an agreed maximum). Provisions for pretrial and trial work are generally made. A typical contract form of this type is shown in Figure 18.1. Such contracts are generally made directly between the appraiser and the client. Many condemnees cannot pay the appraisal fee until the condemnation award has been received, so provisions must be made for such payment. Often, the attorney will agree to pay the appraisal fee directly out of the condemnation award. In this way, the appraiser is guaranteed his fee, and payment of a retainer or prepayment of the appraisal fee is obviated.

Selection of Attorney

Sometimes, the tables are turned, and it is the appraiser who counsels the client in selecting an attorney, rather than the attorney assisting in the selection of an appraiser. If the appraiser is active in condemnation work, he may be familiar with local attorneys who specialize in condemnation work or, at least, have some experience in the field. The first thing the appraiser should determine is whether the client has an attorney who handles most of his legal matters; if so, the client should get advice from his regular attorney, if the appraiser can make such a recommendation in good conscience.

The type of property and potential values involved will have some bearing on the selection of the correct attorney. Of course, the ability of the appraiser to work with the selected attorney is also important. Some attorneys are trial lawyers and some are not. If the client's regular attorney is not a trial lawyer, the appraiser should analyze the attorney's law firm and try to determine who, in the particular firm, would probably try the case if it went to trial. The client's regular attorney may not have enough trial experience, but another attorney in the same firm may be well-qualified. If asked to recommend an attorney, the appraiser

CLIENT _______________ ORDERED BY ________ AUTHORITY _______
ADDRESS ____________________________________ PHONE ___________
Date Assignment is Due ____
Agreed Fee (1) $__________ When Due and Payable (2)_______________
Purpose and Function of Assignment ______________________________
Date of Valuation _________ Type of Report _________ No. of Copies ________
Expert Testimony (1) Fee __ Date Services Required____________________
Provision for Pretrial Conference ________________________________
SUBJECT PROPERTY: Address and Location ________________________

LEGAL DESCRIPTION____

PROPERTY DESCRIPTION____

SPECIAL ASSUMPTIONS AND LIMITING CONDITIONS:____________

MISCELLANEOUS DETAILS:_______________________________________

The undersigned agrees that the above sets forth fairly the agreement herein entered into between them this ______ day of ___________________ , 198____ and the work is hereby authorized to proceed.

Client ____________________   Appraisal Firm Name
By _______________________   By _______________________
Title ____________________

(1) Plus travel expense, job costs and reasonable subsistence cost when out of ________________ County. Client also agrees to reimburse Appraisal Firm Name, at regular professional rates for any time required of it, by due process of law to be expended upon the client's affairs.

(2) If the account is past due, or any portion thereof remaining is past due, it is delinquent and the payer agrees to bear simple interest from the due date at one percent per month. Payer also agrees to pay reasonable collection expenses including courts costs and actual attorney's fees.

This appraisal report will be made in conformity with and will be subject to the requirements of the Code of Professional Ethics and Standards of Professional Conduct of the American Institute of Real Estate Appraisers of the National Association of Realtors.

If this contract is not returned fully executed by client by   , it shall become void.

Figure 18.1. Contract for Professional Services

should consider giving the client the names of several attorneys and discuss the strengths and weaknesses of each.

In the end, of course, the client will actually select the appraiser and the attorney. If the individuals chosen do not feel they can work together effectively, it is best that they refuse the assignment. Nothing is worse than a three-party condemnation trial: 1) condemnor vs. condemnee's attorney and condemnee's appraiser, 2) condemnee's attorney vs. condemnor and condemnee's appraiser, and 3) condemnee's appraiser vs. everybody.

The Appraisal Report

There is considerable disagreement in legal circles as to the degree of legal instruction the attorney should initially give the appraiser. If the appraiser is experienced in condemnation appraising, the only instruction needed, at least initially, will be *"appraise the property."* The experienced appraiser knows the rules of determining just compensation, which damage items are compensable and which are not, and the rules regarding the offsetting of benefits in the applicable jurisdiction. More importantly, the experienced appraiser will know when a questionable point of law is encountered and will ask for assistance from legal counsel. The appraiser can usually do a much better job if the attorney is not continually looking over his shoulder.

If the appraiser is employed by the condemnee, he should be apprised of the initial offer made by the condemnor. Some appraisers may say they don't want to know the amount of the offer, but this knowledge may save the client thousands of dollars in appraisal fees. If the appraiser is familiar with the area where the property is located, he will generally be able to arrive at a range of values within which the appraiser's final value estimate will fall. Whether or not the appraiser has knowledge of the condemnor's offer, he should cease work after developing a range of values. At this point, the appraiser should advise the client and the client's legal counsel of the following factors:

1. Appraisal fees due to date.
2. Anticipated appraisal fees to complete appraisal report (if not previously determined).
3. Range of values anticipated on completion of appraisal report.
4. Estimate of time and charges that may be required for court preparation, pretrial conferences, and trial time.

With this information the client and legal counsel can determine their best strategy. The appraiser who completes a fully documented appraisal report, knowing it will be of no financial benefit to the client, may (and probably should) have difficulty collecting his appraisal fee. It is certain that future referrals from the attorney involved in the case will be few and far between.

If the appraiser's preliminary estimate of value is unsatisfactory to the con-demnee-client and the attorney, the attorney will usually try to reemphasize the advantageous aspects of the property and/or the potential damages which may accrue to the property due to the taking and the construction of the public im-provement. It is only natural, of course, that the attorney should want to confirm that the appraiser has considered the important factors affecting the property. However, under no circumstances should the attorney attempt to coerce the ap-praiser into altering a valid estimate of value. Even if the attorney is successful in his persuasion, the appraiser will be unable to testify to the value estimate with conviction and total honesty.

If the value estimate is unfavorable, the attorney must counsel his client as to the alternative steps that can be taken. The condemnee can accept the con-demnor's offer, or attempt to negotiate a higher settlement figure without an ap-praisal. Another option is to hire another appraiser. If this alternative is chosen the costs of hiring an additional appraiser should be discussed. At this point, the attorney has the opportunity to stay in the good graces of the client and, at the same time, lead the client to the conclusion that is in his best interest. The attor-ney need not, and should not, express to the client his own opinion of value or just compensation.

The most advantageous posture for the attorney to take with the client is that serious negotiations cannot begin until the client obtains an appraisal, and that the attorney certainly cannot go to trial without an appraiser. If the results of the appraisal are unfavorable to the client, the next move is the client's. The attorney should maintain the position that, without a valid appraisal, he cannot take the case to trial. Does the client want to take on the cost of another appraisal, and another, and another? By taking this position, the attorney remains friend and counselor to the client, and the appraiser is the bad guy. Clients have a tendency to become more realistic in their ideas of just compensation when they have to shell out money, time after time, to be told that their expectations are unrealistic.

When the range of values reported by the appraiser is favorable, and the client wishes to proceed, the appraiser should begin to develop a well-documented ap-praisal report including applicable photographs, sketches, and charts. The ap-praiser should determine the actual content of the report in conjunction with the attorney and in light of governing court rules, rules of discovery, and the mini-mum requirements for any professionally prepared appraisal report.

At this point, the appraiser should consider the legal date of taking and the legal date of valuation. In many federal condemnations, the declaration of taking is the date of valuation, but the date of taking actually precedes the preparation of the appraisal report. Therefore, the appraiser must bear in mind that whatever is included in the appraisal report must be supported during the trial. There are no second chances in such a situation. On the other hand, many jurisdictions require that the date of valuation be the date of trial. In this case, the appraiser may be required to update the appraisal report just before the trial. This gives the appraiser a second chance to verify all factual data in the report and to strengthen and augment the conclusions reached.

Appraisal Review

The attorney should be given ample time to review the appraisal report carefully. In this review, the attorney should look for data, methods, or approaches that may be inadmissible. He should keep in mind that because a piece of data is inadmissible, does not necessarily mean that the appraiser should not have considered or even relied on such data. For instance, an offer to sell usually is inadmissible. Therefore, it would be improper for the appraiser to testify that he considered the fact that a property abutting the property under appraisal was listed at $5.00 per square foot. It would not, however, be improper for the appraiser to testify that he considered the present listing price of a property abutting the property being appraised. It is the actual *asking price* which is inadmissible, not the fact that it was considered.

In reviewing an appraisal report, the attorney should use a *checklist* to ensure that the appraiser has included all pertinent data. The condemnor's published *appraisal guidelines* are useful for this purpose. *Nichols'* also contains an excellent "pretrial checklist" for use by attorneys.[9]

If the appraiser has been retained by the condemnor, the attorney's review of the report is at least the second, and more likely the third or fourth, review of the appraisal report. Neither the appraiser nor the attorney should assume the report is error-free just because it has withstood a number of reviews. For instance, the following is a quotation from an actual appraisal report, which was reviewed and approved by three governmental agencies, including one on the federal level.

> Even in the before situation water and sewer connections are some distance from this site, something in the nature of 200' to 300' and bringing these facilities onto the site would be rather more expensive than is typical. In the after situation, the circumstance is greatly compounded by the fact that, having brought the utility lines to the toe of the dike at the southwest aspect of the [state highway/county road] intersection, a tunnel would have to be dug under the dike in a northeasterly direction in order to bring those utility connections onto the Subject remainder. The distance involved in that tunneling project would be a minimum of 180'. In an effort to grasp the magnitude of this tunneling project, I have interviewed several convicts who have tunneled out of [the state prison]. They uniformly report that it takes several days for two men to plan such a tunnel and it takes two men

> several days to dig one. . . . For the reasons discussed just above, I
> am of the opinion that the highest and best use of the Subject Prop-
> erty in the after situation is for recreational river access.

After reviewing an appraisal report, the attorney should consider two alternatives. First, he must determine if the employment of a second appraiser is advisable. The answer to this question generally depends on the number of appraisers retained by opposing counsel and, more important, the amount of money at stake. The condemnee's attorney should consider whether there are any provisions for the condemnor to pay the condemnee's expert witness fees in the jurisdiction where the case will be heard. The attorney should also acknowledge that it is unlikely that two appraisers will approach a valuation problem the same way or arrive at exactly the same value. Therefore, the use of two or more appraisers will generally result in the presentation of two or more different approaches and conclusions to the trier of fact. If the trier of fact is a jury, the submission of two or more approaches and conclusions by the same party may adversely affect the outcome of the trial. "The outcome of the trial of a case involving the value of real estate depends upon the presence of well-qualified and thoroughly competent expert witnesses. The trial pattern and the success or failure of the case is in direct ratio to the *quality*, not quantity of the witnesses testifying in the proceedings."[10]

The second alternative the attorney may want to consider is whether to employ a consulting appraiser. The appraiser who values the property and will testify in court must not be an advocate for anything other than his own value estimate. The consulting appraiser is retained strictly as a consultant—he never appraises the property. The consultant can, and should, be an advocate to his client's interest. He is available to the attorney throughout the trial preparation and, if necessary, during the trial itself. The consultant can often find technical flaws in the appraisal which may go unnoticed by the attorney. Also, the consultant can usually look more objectively at the weaknesses of the appraisal approach used than can the appraiser who applied the approaches.

Retaining a consultant should be considered under three circumstances. First, if the attorney has very little condemnation experience, the consultant can be of invaluable assistance to him. Second, in a complex case, the appraiser who is preparing for his own portion of the trial may not have enough time to assist the attorney, to the degree necessary to prepare other portions or elements of the trial. Third, if the case involves highly technical appraisal methodology, even the seasoned condemnation lawyer may need assistance in preparing for and conducting the trial. It is understandable that the attorney may become confused when the appraisal problem involves the use of statistics or the application of some of the newer, more technical aspects of the income approach to value. The consulting appraiser can be of considerable worth in such circumstances.

Attorney/Appraiser Conference

Once the attorney has completed the appraisal review, he should confer with the appraiser. Again, a "pretrial conference checklist" is available for use for such a conference.[11] The first matter to be covered in this conference is any deficiencies in the appraisal report found by the attorney, which may require corrective action. The strengths and weaknesses of the appraiser's approach to the valuation problem should also be discussed in detail. All appraisal methodology has strengths and weaknesses; the appraiser should readily admit to them and explain them in detail to the attorney.

For instance, if the appraiser has relied heavily on the income approach to value, and the market data used to justify the capitalization rate are weak, this fact should be pointed out to the attorney. Then, both parties should decide how best to present the available capitalization data to the trier of fact. Probable cross-examination and redirect examination on this matter should also be discussed. The appraiser should be prepared to discuss with the attorney all elements of market data that were considered, but eventually rejected, because these items may be addressed on cross-examination. If the full exchange of appraisals is not required, the appraiser may want to include these data in the appraisal report itself.

"In preparing to prepare the report and related exhibits, even details not important to arriving at an estimation of value should be noted, since failure to know these facts could, at trial, be used to impeach the appraiser's credibility on cross-examination. For example, properties that at first blush appear to be comparable, but the appraiser subsequently decides are not, should be noted, along with the reasons for their exclusion from consideration. Then, when being questioned about such properties, the appraiser will be able to state his reasons for excluding them, instead of having to answer that he cannot recall the sales in question, or why he decided that they were not comparable, thereby leading the trier to believe that perhaps there were other properties that were comparable, that the appraiser failed to consider them in coming to his conclusion of value, and that perhaps these properties that the appraiser did consider in arriving at his opinion do not represent a true picture of the value of the property being condemned."[12]

Including these rejected data in the report has another advantage in that it informs the attorney of the specifics of these data and why they were not comparable. This information can be invaluable to the attorney in cross-examining the appraiser, testifying on behalf of the opposing party to the dispute, if this appraiser uses these sales as comparables. However, if discovery calls for the exchange of fully documented appraisal reports, the appraiser should exclude data regarding noncomparable sales from the appraisal report and convey this information to the attorney by other means. The appraiser will have enough trouble handling cross-examination without helping the opposing counsel load his gun.

During this initial attorney/appraiser conference, a determination should be made as to what exhibits will be required for trial and who will be responsible for preparing these exhibits. If an exhibit is directly connected with the appraiser's testimony, the appraiser should have the responsibility of preparing, or having prepared, this exhibit. The appraiser can quickly become confused, disoriented, and easy prey for opposing counsel if the exhibit presented does not conform to his report or testimony.

Demonstrative Evidence

The complexity of the case and the amount of money involved will directly affect the number and quality of exhibits required. The attorney and the appraiser must determine which exhibits will be required early on because preparation of exhibits can be time-consuming and a hastily prepared exhibit is much more likely to contain errors than one prepared well in advance of trial. If a witness has to correct an erroneous exhibit during testimony, the correction will be obvious and, every time the trier of fact views the exhibit, the fact that the witness has made an error will be reinforced. It makes no difference to the trier of fact whether the exhibit was prepared by the witness or by another person; the trier of fact views it as the witness's error.

The first place that should be explored for possible exhibits is the appraiser's report and the addenda to the report. Cost approach computations,[13] income approach data and computations,[14] and market data charts[15] should always be viewed as potential exhibits. Photographs should almost always be considered required exhibits: photographs of the property being appraised, photographs of comparable land sales, photographs of comparable rentals, photographs of comparable improved sales, etc. All photographs submitted as exhibits should be in color and at least 8 in. × 10 in. They should be clearly identified with the appraiser's name, the date the photograph was taken, and the property depicted in the photograph (e.g., comparable rental No. 5). Comparable sales or rental maps sometimes make good illustrations, as do detailed before and after plot plans, sketches, and small-scale aerial photographs of the property being appraised, the neighborhood, etc.

The discovery process, or the opposing party's responses to interrogatories, will often help determine which exhibits will most effectively assist in the presentation of testimony. For instance, in one case the condemnor learned through interrogatories that the condemnee's appraiser would testify that a motel being acquired for highway-widening purposes had a minimum economic rent per unit of $16.00 per day, although the actual minimum rent was $9.00 per day. Therefore, the condemnor's attorney and appraiser concluded that a detailed presentation of the income approach data relied upon by the condemnor's appraiser, and exhibits presented in conjunction therewith, was essential. The condemnor's appraiser had made a survey of all motels in the area and had graded each for amenities such as room size, condition, location, and furnishings, and had also determined the minimum rental rate for each property.

These data and analysis were presented to the trier of fact, in this case a 12-person jury, in chart form as shown in Figure 18.2. After explaining this chart, the witness developed the mean of each group of motels. Then, the appraiser graphed the results of the calculations and applied a linear regression, or trend line, formula to the data.[16] This resulted in the following:

Group	Mean Rating	Mean Rent	Projected Rent
1	9.33	$ 8.83	$ 8.20
2	14.00	$ 9.98	$10.46
3	19.00	$12.00	$12.92
4	22.00	$15.00	$14.39
5	28.67	$17.83	$17.55

Motel Quality Rating*

Group #	Motel #	Average Room Size	Pool	Restaurant	Condition	Furnishings	TV	Location	Lounge	Entertainment	Public Rooms	A/C	Overall Quality	Minimum Rate	Total Quality Rating
1	1	271 sq. ft. 1	0	0	1	1	B & W 1	2	0	0	0	0	1	$ 9.00	7
1	2	195 sq. ft. 1	0	1	1	1	3	2	0	0	0	0	1	$ 9.00	10
1	3	320 sq. ft. 2	0	2	1	1	Part. 1	3	0	0	0	0	1	$ 8.50	11
2	4	353 sq. ft. 2	0	1	2	1	3	2	0	0	0	0	2	$11.00	13
2	5	264 sq. ft. 1	2	2	2	1	B & W 1	2	1	0	0	2	1	$ 8.95	15
3	6	396 sq. ft. 3	0	1	2	3	3	3	1	0	0	1	2	$12.00	19
3	7	356 sq. ft. 2	0	3	2	2	3	3	1	0	0	1	2	$12.00	19
3	8	271 sq. ft. 1	0	3	2	3	3	3	0	0	0	2	2	$12.00	19
4	9	400 sq. ft. 3	2	2	2	2	3	3	2	0	0	0	2	$15.00	21
4	10	475 sq. ft. 3	3	1	2	3	3	3	0	0	1	2	2	$15.00	23
5	11	404 sq. ft. 3	2	3	3	3	3	3	0	0	1	2	2	$18.00	25
5	12	406 sq. ft. 3	0	3	2	3	3	2	3	3	3	0	2	$17.00	27
5	13	425 sq. ft. 3	3	3	3	3	3	2	3	3	3	2	3	$18.50	34
SUBJECT		285 sq. ft. 1	2	2	1	1	1	2	0	0	0	0	1		11

*Maximum Quality Rate = 35

Figure 18.2. Motel Amenities/Rental Comparison

The condemnor then presented a second exhibit, Figure 18.3, and explained to the jury that the curved line represented the actual ratio between the mean rating and the mean rent of the various groups of motels, and that the straight line reflected the projected relationship between the various group ratings and an estimate of projected rents based on available data. It was then pointed out that the projected minimum rent for the motel being appraised, based upon its quality rating of 11, was $9.02 per day, as compared to its actual rent of $9.00 per day. The submission of this graph gave the condemnor's attorney the opportunity to present, during closing arguments, a modified version of the graph as shown in Figure 18.4, while at the same time informing the jury that "This is what [the owner's appraiser] is asking you to believe."

The condemnor also submitted exhibits supporting its appraiser's estimate of the motel's occupancy rate (Figure 18.5), gross income (Figure 18.6), and net income (Figure 18.7). With the aid of these exhibits, it was possible for the jury to follow the thought processes of the appraiser and to gain a clear understanding of

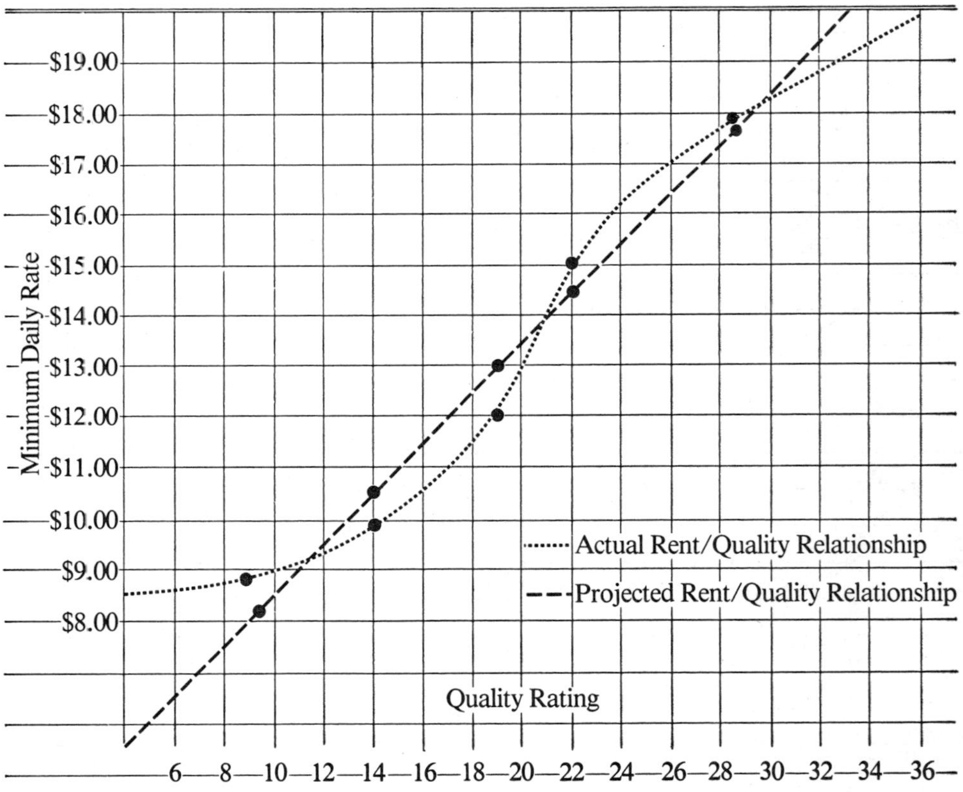

Figure 18.3. Quality/Rate Analysis

the sometimes-confusing income approach to value.

Besides indicating areas that must be emphasized for the trier of fact, the discovery rules or responses to interrogatories will indicate areas of agreement between the parties in dispute. For instance, interrogatories in the above case indicated that the condemnor's appraiser and the condemnee's appraiser were only one-quarter of one percent apart in their estimated overall capitalization rate for the property; therefore, only a brief explanation of the derivation of this rate was required.

The appraiser who becomes responsible for all or some of the exhibits should

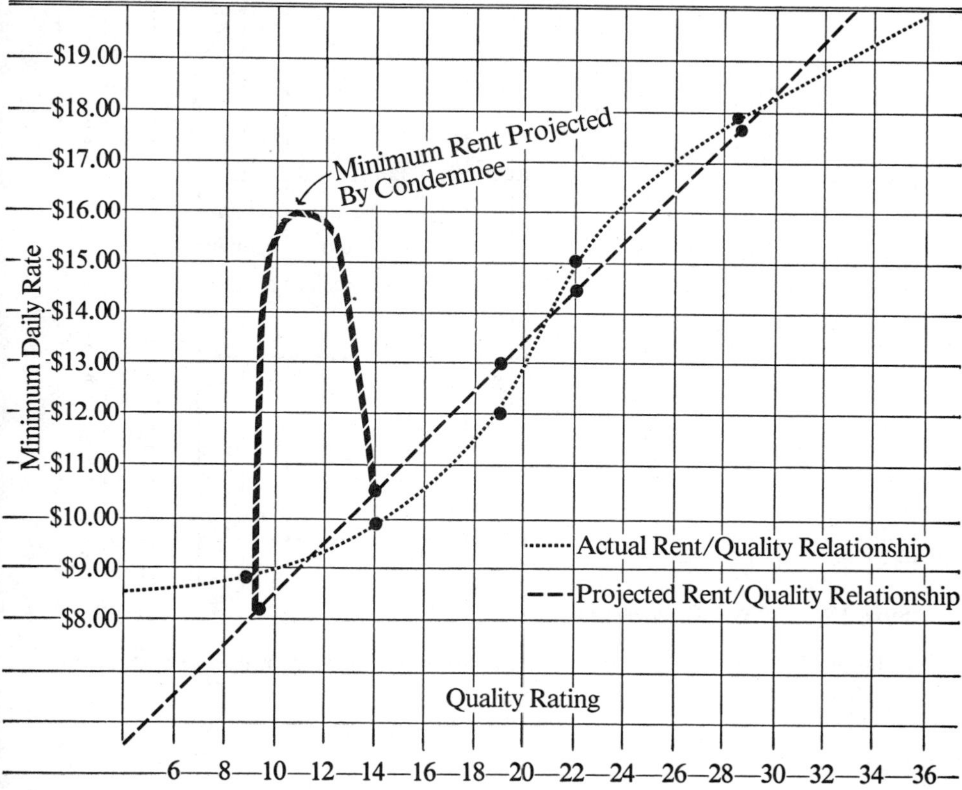

Figure 18.4. Quality/Rate Analysis

be familiar with the layout of the courtroom where the trial will be held. If the appraiser is not familiar with the courtroom, he should visit it before the trial. Then, and only then, can the appraiser determine the proper size and type of exhibits to prepare. Exhibits that are too small for the trier of fact to read clearly are more of a hindrance than a help. The trier of fact will be leaning forward, squinting at the exhibit, and paying no attention whatsoever to the witness's testimony.

The appraiser should also note what equipment is available in the courtroom for displaying exhibits so he can determine whether the exhibits will be set on an easel, pinned to a cork board, etc. All exhibits should be neat, clean, and under-

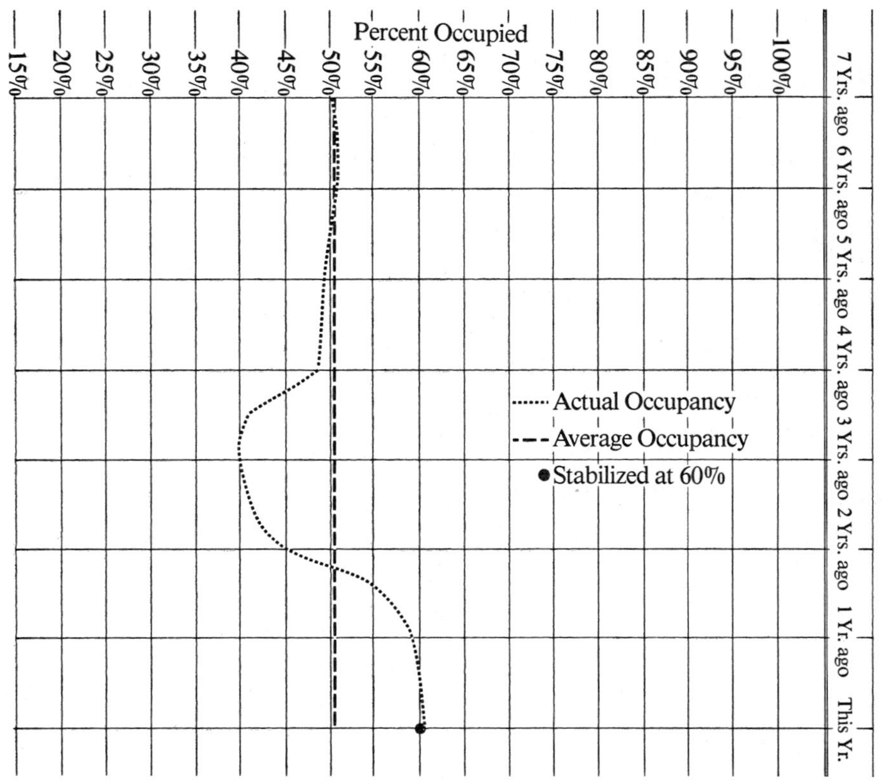

Figure 18.5. Motel Occupancy

standable. The exhibit should look professionally prepared, but not gaudy or too expensive.

Discovery

One important step in preparing for trial is the application of the discovery rules of the jurisdiction where the trial will be held. These rules may require full exchange of documented appraisal reports or no discovery at all. In some jurisdictions, discovery is by deposition of witnesses and/or interrogatories. A standard set of interrogatories, out of a law book, should not be used carte blanche because each condemnation case will have its own peculiarities. Under no circumstances should an attorney send out a set of interrogatories without asking his appraiser, "Is there anything you need to know to make your job easier or to better prepare you for trial?" While the answer to some seemingly trivial question may mean nothing to the attorney, it may reveal to the appraiser the entire valuation approach that the opposing party's appraiser is going to use.

One crucial item of information is, of course, the list of sales which the opposing party's appraiser has used, and will probably testify to, in arriving at his conclusion of value. If a request, by interrogatory, in regard to sales utilized is made, the interrogatory must be worded carefully. Do not ask about all the sales *considered* by the opposing party's appraiser. Appraisers *consider* a great number of sales; they may unconsciously consider all sales known to them, but most are immediately rejected as noncomparable. *"I considered* the sale of the single-family dwelling 45 miles north of town, but rejected it because I am appraising a shopping center 15 miles south of town." The interrogatory should request a list of all sales that were *relied upon* and to which the appraiser will testify. Once this list has been obtained by counsel, a copy should be sent immediately to the appraiser.

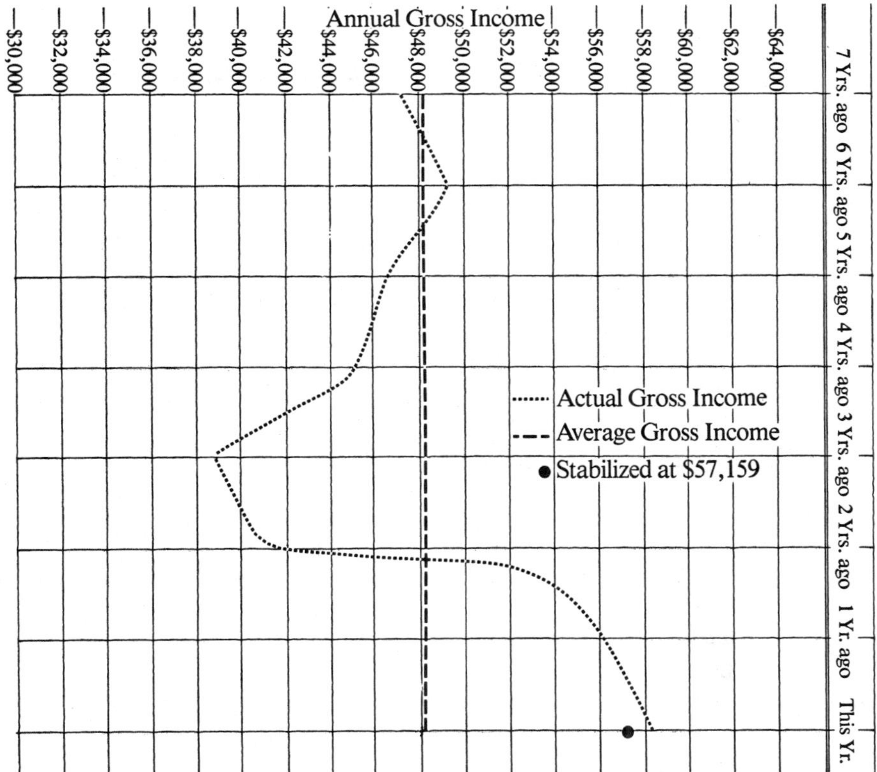

Figure 18.6. Motel Gross Income

Verification of Data

The appraiser and attorney work as a team, and it is the appraiser's responsibility to verify and analyze the sales submitted as comparable by the opposing party to

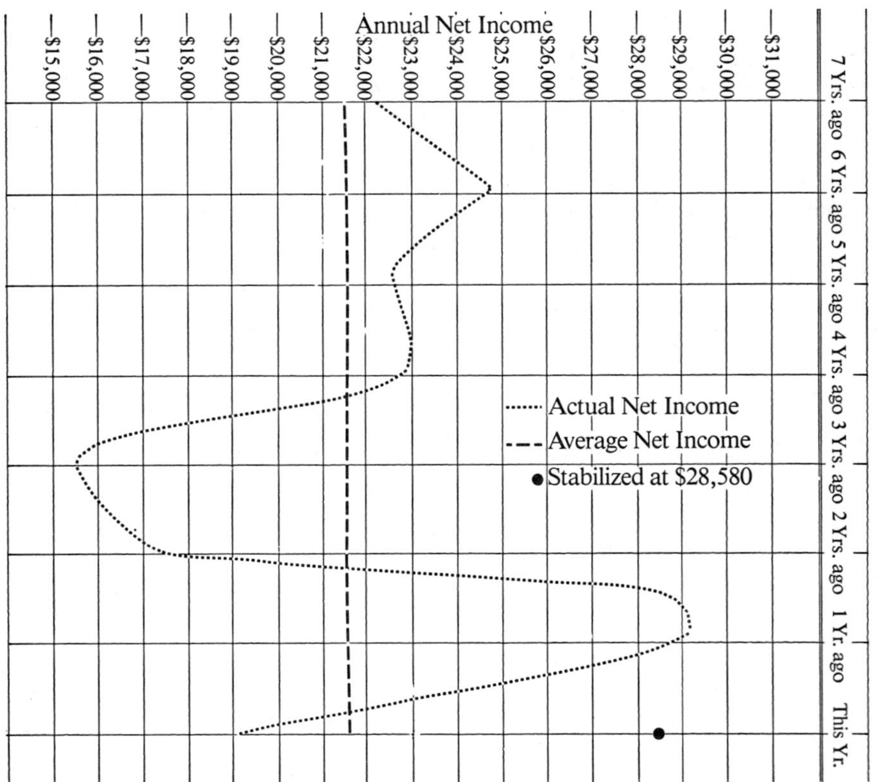

Figure 18.7. Motel Net Income

the litigation. The appraiser should furnish all pertinent data regarding these sales to the attorney. The appraiser should supply the attorney with the following information:

(1) Did the sale, in fact, occur?

(2) Date of sale.

(3) Price.

(4) Terms.

(5) Detailed property description.

(6) Photo of property.

(7) Is the property comparable?

    a. If no, why not?

    b. If yes, why didn't we use it?

   To factually illustrate the importance of this verification, consider the following situation. A hearing in regard to the value of a property was held before a federal judge. The court required the full exchange of appraisals. The claimant's appraiser testified to his opinion of value and the sales he relied on. The attorney for the claimant then asked the appraiser if he was aware of the three sales recited in the defendant's appraiser's report. The exchange continued as follows:

> *Appraiser:* Yes.
> *Attorney:* In reference to Sale 1 in Mr. X's report—are the circumstances surrounding that sale as they were reported?
> *Appraiser:* No, they are not.
> *Attorney:* And why not?
> *Appraiser:* The sale was described in the report as the sale of 600 acres of dry wheat land and the total price paid was divided by the 600 acres to arrive at a price per acre. The fact that the sale included 600 acres of dry wheat land is true, but it also included an additional 600 acres of irrigated wheat land.
> *Attorney:* What about Mr. X's Sale 2?
> *Appraiser:* I found nothing of record in regard to such a sale. The reported seller of the property, who in fact is the owner of the property, was also unaware of the sale, nor did he know the supposed purchaser.
> *Attorney:* And Mr. X's Sale 3?
> *Appraiser:* That sale was reported as the sale of dry wheat land; however, on my inspection of the property I found it to be timberland and as of last Friday, the purchaser has, so far, taken some two million board feet of timber off the property.

After the claimant's appraiser was excused, the court addressed the defendant's attorney as follows:

> *Court:* You may now call your appraiser to the stand—if you dare.
> *Defense Attorney:* Your Honor, may we have a short recess?
> *Court:* You may, but I'll tell you right now; if you put your appraiser on, I'm not going to listen to him.

In addition to verifying the sales supplied by opposing counsel, the appraiser should also reverify his own sales. Although the initial verification may have been done very carefully, it should be repeated, preferably with a different party to the transaction. In one instance, the condemnor's appraiser testified that he did not use a particular sale as a comparable because the purchaser told him that the property was purchased sight unseen. The condemnee's appraiser did use the sale as a comparable and, when cross-examined in regard to the purchaser's knowledge of the sale property, stated that the purchaser had seen the property before purchase. In fact, the appraiser had shown the purchaser the property prior to the sale. The appraiser then produced a photograph of the property with the purchaser in the foreground and, in the background, construction activity that was completed before the date of purchase.

Arithmetic

Computations used in the appraisal report that will be included in the testimony should be checked, double-checked, and triple-checked. Should the attorney ask, "Would you step down to the board, Mr. Appraiser, and show us just how you calculated that?" it doesn't matter how many times the appraiser has rechecked his mathematics. His reaction will be the same. All computations in an appraisal report should be checked prior to trial at least three times, by three different people. If a computational error is made, and the appraiser is asked to prove it, he will invariably copy the erroneous figures directly from his notes. Since the advent of calculators, many people have difficulty doing mathematics in their heads. With 12 jurors and a judge waiting for the appraiser to complete his mental calculations, the difficult becomes impossible.

Mock Examination

When all information has been gathered and all exhibits are prepared, the attorney and appraiser should stage a mock examination. The attorney should ask the appraiser every question he expects to ask him on the witness stand, and the appraiser should answer the questions as if he were in court. This rehearsal should be repeated as many times as necessary until the attorney thinks it is right. Then the attorney, or preferably an associate attorney, should take the position of the opposing counsel and cross-examine the appraiser. This will uncover any weak points in the appraiser's position and give the appraiser and the attorney enough time to strengthen the testimony. "There is no law against rehearsal of your direct examination and, for that matter, of the anticipated cross-examination."[17]

After a few trial runs between the appraiser and the attorney, the process can be abbreviated. In fact, the entire process of preparing for trial can be shortened when each member of the team is aware of what is expected of him and both are confident enough in each other to know that they will perform as required.

Summary

The foregoing discussion presumes that the appraiser's opinion of value supports the client's contention of just compensation. If this is not the case, the appraiser won't be preparing for trial at all, and much of the information in this chapter will not be applicable. In most cases, the appraiser's trial preparation will be curtailed; this may happen early on, as soon as the appraiser has reached a preliminary value range for the property being condemned, or later, just before trial when the condemnor and the condemnee reach a negotiated settlement.

The attorney and the appraiser must function as a team so the attorney may properly represent the client's interest. The composition of this team should be determined as soon as practical. If the client is an active condemnor, the initial appraiser and the attorney are often *thrown together* only after the appraiser has completed his appraisal report. However, the condemnor's attorney will generally have the option of retaining the services of another appraiser. The only totally safe assumption to make is that every parcel of land which is being subjected to the sovereign's power of eminent domain, will result in a trial to determine the compensation due for the taking and/or damage to the property. Therefore, the appraiser should begin preparing for trial as soon as he receives the appraisal assignment, and the attorney should start his preparations immediately after he is retained by the client.

Preparing a condemnation case involves the following steps:

(1)   Appraiser/attorney team is determined.
(2)   Appraiser develops value (or compensation) range.
(3)   Preliminary conference is held between attorney and appraiser.
(4)   Conference is held between attorney and client to develop future strategy.
(5)   Appraiser completes research.
(6)   Conference between attorney and appraiser is held to determine appraisal report content.
(7)   Appraiser completes appraisal report.
(8)   Attorney reviews appraisal report.
(9)   Appraiser/attorney conference is held to determine trial strategy, necessary exhibits, additional information required, and data to be requested from opposing parties through discovery or interrogatories.
(10) Exhibits are prepared.
(11) Appraiser investigates and verifies market data used by opposing party's appraiser as revealed through discovery or interrogatories.
(12) Attorney and appraiser determine line of direct testimony.
(13) Attorney develops specific list of questions to ask appraiser.
(14) Attorney and appraiser hold mock direct examination session.
(15) Attorney and appraiser hold mock cross-examination session.

Notes

1. Patrick J. Rohan and Melvin A. Reskin, *Nichols' The Law of Eminent Domain,* rev. 3rd ed. (New York: Matthew Bender, 1980) Vol. 9, App. C-2(b) (Also Published as Vol. 3, Part 1 of Real Estate Transactions).

2. Ibid., Vol. 7, § 4.05.

3. Fred M. Winner, "The Expert Witness from a Lawyer's Viewpoint," *Condemnation Appraisal Practice* (Chicago: American Institute of Real Estate Appraisers, 1961) pp. 445-452.

4. *Nichols'*, Vol. 7, § 4.05.

5. *Nichols'*, Vol. 7, § 4.04.

6. *B.F. Coulter Co., et al.,* Superior Court, Los Angeles, Case No. 574469.

7. George C. Hadley, "Presentation of the Case," *Condemnation Appraisal Practice* (Chicago: American Institute of Real Estate Appraisers, 1961), pp. 492-512.

8. Washington State Department of Transportation form #261-009, ¶1.

9. *Nichols'*, Vol. 7, § 4.09.

10. Theodore J. Labrecque, "The Court and the Expert Witness," *The Appraisal Journal,* January 1961, pp. 87-93.

11. William H. Crouch, "Pretrial Conference Checklist of Factors Affecting Valuation," *The Appraisal Journal,* October 1964, pp. 523-530.

12. *Nichols'*, Vol. 7, § 4.08[1].

13. See Chapter 7, "Cost Approach to Value," Figure 7.1 and Tables 7.2 and 7.3.

14. See Chapter 8, "Income Approach to Value," Figure 8.1 and Tables 8.1, 8.2, 8.3, 8.4, and 8.6.

15. See Chapter 9, "Market Data Approach to Value," Tables 9.1, 9.2, and 9.5.

16. Linear Regression is a statistical method of finding a straight line that best fits a set of data points. See for explanation and formula, American Institute of Real Estate Appraisers and The Society of Real Estate Appraisers, *Real Estate Appraisal Terminology,* rev. ed., "Simple Linear Regression," Byrl N. Boyce, ed. (Cambridge, Mass.: Ballinger Publishing Company, 1981), pp. 323-332.

17. *Nichols'*, Vol. 7, § 8.05[1].

CHAPTER 19
THE EXPERT WITNESS

An *expert* is "[o]ne who is so qualified, either by actual experience or by careful study, as to enable him to form a definite opinion of his own respecting a division of science, branch of art, or department of trade about which persons having no particular training or special study are incapable of forming accurate opinions or deducing correct conclusions."[1] The *expert witness* is "[a] witness qualified by scientific or specialized knowledge or experience so as to be permitted to testify not only to the facts, but to his opinion respecting the facts, so far as necessary to inform the jury and enable them to understand the issues of fact and arrive at a proper conclusion."[2]

Appraisers, as expert witnesses, are not always regarded favorably by the courts.[3] Some members of the legal profession have also been critical of real estate appraisers and the appraisal profession. As was stated more than 20 years ago:

> Is there any hope that the jury system and the expert witness can live in honest and peaceful co-existence? The chance is slim, but it is still there. Hope here will rest upon an immediate and drastic house and soul cleaning job by reputable appraisal organizations and societies and, what is even more vital, a complete and objective self-analysis by every individual who henceforth will take the stand and qualify as an expert.[4]

Rebuttal to such remarks is, of course, to be expected. For instance, it has been pointed out that the attorney is an advocate for his client and ". . . instructions by an attorney/client to make an improper appraisal, although a reflection of his personal ethics, in no way violate formal pledges of conduct. Accepting and acting on such instructions, however, do constitute a breach of ethics for the appraiser."[5] However, when an appraiser testifies, "I must state that I was legally instructed to appraise the property as though it had potential for industrial use, and that assumption was made in making the appraisal. . . ,"[6] it makes one wonder about the appraiser's and the attorney's intelligence, let alone their ethics.

This *finger pointing* continues today and will probably go on well into the future. Any appraiser or attorney who doesn't have his head in the sand knows that there are unethical individuals in both professions, and that these individuals seem to have an uncanny knack for finding each other.

> [G]roups of self-styled "appraisers" make their living by giving "made to order" appraisal testimony. They are primarily professional witnesses and should be distinguished from professional appraisers. These witnesses are supported by some legal firms who handle condemnation cases in the same manner as personal injury litigation in which distorted claims for damages commonly occur.
>
> Such situations are the probable cause of many major divergencies in court testimony between appraisers. They are and will remain the most difficult to cure.
>
> Some courts contribute to "legalizing" divergency by permitting the uninformed political appointee and the known "actor" to function as an expert witness when a more strict enforcement of qualifying standards would do much to discourage erroneous valuations and unjust awards.
>
> Under present circumstances virtually anyone can qualify as an expert witness. The resultant testimony is often afforded as much credence by the judge, jury, or commission as is the testimony of a competent and qualified appraiser.[7]

There is, however, some hope of eradicating this type of behavior. In a fairly recent ruling, the Tennessee appellate court said:

> [T]he facts in this case at bar point up the need for a change in the rules of evidence pertaining to the qualification of a witness who is permitted to give an opinion as to the value of real estate involved in litigation. Until recent years there were only a limited few people trained in the science of real estate appraising, but it has now reached a professional status that should be recognized by the courts. The American Institute of Real Estate Appraisers has developed real estate appraising to almost an exact science.
>
> Something is wrong with our rules of evidence when a verdict can be

predicated on the opinion of a person completely ignorant of real estate values and the opinions of skilled, knowledgeable, professional experts ignored. It is likened to taking the opinion of a midwife over that of an obstetrician. . . .

[W]e are not satisfied that justice has been done. We have seen a number of cases in this court where we think the ends of justice would have been more nearly met had only qualified expert witnesses been permitted to express an opinion as to real estate values. . . .But until such time as our ancient rules of opinion evidence relating to the real estate values have been modernized these injustices will continue.[8]

Burden of Proof

U.S. courts have employed all three possible rules with respect to the burden of proof in condemnation cases:

(1)   The taking agency has the burden of proving just compensation. It is the moving party and seeks to change the status quo. The condemnor therefore must prove all parts of its case. (Followed in Georgia, Mississippi, and Washington. Illinois and Kentucky also may be placed in this group for want of a further subdivision to fit their unusual procedural practices.)

(2)   Neither party has the burden of proof. The measurement of just compensation involves the question of fact to be determined *in rem* and without adversary pleadings. This rule is based on the theory that the parties are not adversaries, therefore neither should have a greater burden of proof than the others. (Ohio)

(3)   When the taking agency is a governmental subdivision, it is presumed to have made a fair offer, and, accordingly, the landowner has the burden of proof that just compensation requires a sum greater than the amount conceded by the government. (So-called majority rule, followed in at least 24 states.)[9] [citations omitted]

The party which has the burden of proof is generally given the right to *open* and *close* the trial proceedings. In other words, the party with the burden of proof makes its opening remarks first and has the last closing argument. The party with the burden of proof usually will present its case in chief first. The appraiser called by the party with the burden of proof can generally expect to spend more time on the witness stand than other appraisers, because it generally falls upon the first appraisal witness to educate the trier of fact as to the property involved, the appraisal process, appraisal terminology, and other technical matters. In many instances, however, some engineering testimony has been presented and, perhaps, the trier of fact has viewed the property before the first appraiser takes the witness stand. These preliminaries will assist the appraiser in describing the property and/or the public improvement project which necessitates the taking.

The View

The trier of fact is generally given the opportunity to view the property in question. However, some jurisdictions do not provide for a view of the premises by statute, so the question of whether a view of the property will be made is left to the discretion of the court.[10] About the only time a view is denied is when the property in question has been altered so much between the date of valuation and the date of trial that a view might mislead the trier of fact. A view could also be denied if the property in question is a good distance from the location of the trial and a view would, therefore, be extremely time-consuming.

A view of the property in question by the trier of fact can be considered in two different ways. Some jurisdictions allow the trier of fact to consider what was seen in viewing the property as *evidence;* other jurisdictions instruct the trier of fact that what it saw on the view was not evidence, but only background information to better understand the testimony. Realistically, however, the trier of fact is going to consider what it saw on the view in the same light, regardless of the court's instructions.[11] In any case, a view of the property in question by a jury definitely makes presentation of the case easier for both parties to the suit.

Appraiser's Attendance in Court

The appraiser witness should dress in a conservative manner out of respect for the court. The appraiser's appearance is important when he is on the witness stand and when he is simply an observer in the courtroom. The appraiser should be present throughout the trial, except, perhaps, during the closing arguments. The attorney/appraiser team falls apart if half the team is missing or doesn't know what is going on. The appraiser should take notes on the testimony of others, so he can discuss this testimony with legal counsel. The appraiser can be especially helpful to the attorney if explanation is needed concerning the technical elements of the other appraiser's testimony.

The attorney who wants the appraiser in the courtroom only when he is to testify is foolish, unless the attorney has also retained a consultant to assist during the trial. The attorney who dismisses an appraiser because he feels he doesn't need any assistance probably has an ego problem. If the appraiser is dismissed to save money, this is probably a false economy; if two or three extra days of appraisal fees are that critical, the case probably never should have gone to trial in the first place. *Sidney Z. Searles* advises fellow lawyers that "[b]efore undertaking a cross-examination you should consult your own experts; I have found such consultation of considerable assistance, and I would recommend that your expert be present in court to listen, not only to the direct examination of the expert of the adverse party, but the cross-examination as well."[12]

Rather than require the appraiser's continual presence in the courtroom or retain a consulting appraiser, many condemnors assign a staff appraiser to assist legal counsel. This appraiser should be aware of the contents of the condemnor's appraisal report and be fully familiar with the circumstances surrounding the case. Assigning a staff appraiser can release the fee appraiser and, at the same time, provide the appraiser half of the appraiser/attorney team. Any such assignment, however, should not be undertaken by the condemnor without approval of the concept and the staff appraiser by condemnor's legal counsel. Although it is permissible, and sometimes advisable, for a staff appraiser-consultant or an independent consultant to sit at the counsel table with the attorney, it is not advisable, nor is it even considered ethical by some appraisal organizations, for a fee appraiser witness to be seated at the counsel table.[13]

Preparing for the Witness Stand

When the appraiser takes the witness stand, he should take along any notes or materials to which he may need to refer under direct examination and cross-examination. The appraiser should always take a calculator to the stand because he invariably will be asked to make some calculations. All calculators work a little differently, and the witness stand is not the place to try out a new one. A jury is not particularly impressed with an appraiser who doesn't know how to operate a calculator.

To illustrate, consider the following excerpt from an actual trial transcript. The opposing counsel has asked an appraiser to make a mathematical computation and provided the appraiser with a calculator.

> *Opposing Counsel:* I would like you to make a mathematical calculation for me, if you will, please. I would like you to take $47,500 and divide it by 203,000 sq. ft.
>
> *Appraiser:* Since you have a machine . . .
> (attorney hands appraiser calculator)
>
> *Opposing Counsel:* You have entered it backwards.
>
> *Appraiser:* Divided by 203,000.
>
> *Opposing Counsel:* You've got it backwards again.
>
> *Appraiser:* (pause)
>
> *Opposing Counsel:* Perhaps I could assist you to speed the matter up, Mr. [Appraiser]. If you will watch me push

> the buttons on the calculator, which I have in the
> courtroom here, I will push 4-7-5-0-0. . . .

The jury was not particularly impressed, especially when it discovered that the appraiser, in his report, divided 203,000 sq. ft. by the sale price of $47,500 and arrived at a calculated price per square foot of 42.7¢. The actual result of this calculation is $4.27, but the appraiser apparently reasoned that $4.27 was not correct and therefore moved the decimal point one place to the right. The actual sale price of the property was $47,500 ÷ 203,000, or 23.4¢ per sq. ft.

The appraiser should take his entire file, including a copy of the appraisal report, on the witness stand. This material should be carried in a briefcase and, if at all possible, left in the briefcase. Counsel has the absolute right to inspect any paper referred to by the appraiser on the witness stand. Therefore, while on the witness stand, the appraiser must never refer to any document that could embarrass the appraiser or be detrimental to the client's case if examined by opposing counsel.

The appraiser should prepare a set of notes, for use on the stand, which will not be detrimental to him or his client if they fall into the hands of opposing counsel. Notes written in the appraiser's personal form of shorthand are often useful for this purpose. Some attorneys like to take the appraiser's notes and continue to ask the appraiser questions, which to answer the appraiser needs to refer to his notes. He can, of course, ask for his notes back so he may refer to them, but it is more effective for the appraiser to have prepared a second (and sometimes a third) copy of the notes prior to trial. This demonstrates to the cross-examiner that the appraiser is well-prepared for most cross-examination tricks.

Direct Examination

The appraiser's direct examination can be logically broken down into specific sections in order of probable occurrence: 1) qualification as an expert, 2) description of the appraisal process, 3) appraiser's description of work undertaken in appraising the property which is the subject of the trial, 4) description of the property, 5) application of the cost approach, 6) application of the income approach, 7) application of the market data approach, and 8) final correlation of value. If the trial concerns the partial taking of a property, Items 4 through 8 would apply only to the before situation. Upon conclusion of Item 8, Items 4 through 8 would be repeated for the property in the after situation.

As has been stated previously, the attorney and the appraiser should rehearse the appraiser's testimony in preparation for trial.[14] "However, elicitation of testimony from a witness should always have an air of spontaneity about it, and should not, merely because it is well rehearsed, appear to be conducted in a mechanical manner. Only very thorough work by all involved can give the assurance which breeds naturalness."[15] "The trial is the proving ground of the teamwork of the expert and his attorney."[16]

In responding to questions, the appraiser must speak loudly enough to be heard by the trier of fact, the attorneys, and the court reporter. The appraiser should address the jury, not the inquisitor; if the attorney didn't already know the answer to the question, he would not have asked it. However, the appraiser must be careful not to talk down to the jury or to answer questions in a monotone. He should act as naturally as possible on the witness stand and not try to project a false personality.

Qualifying as an Expert

"Qualification is a rather awkward phase to pass through successfully. If the witness is well qualified, recital by him of his experience may be thought of as immodest by the jury; thus he may not be able to establish a rapport with them."[17] The specific methodology for eliciting such testimony should be determined well before trial. Qualification testimony can best be presented to the jury through the attorney's leading questions. For instance, the question, "Who have you made appraisals for?" puts the appraiser in an awkward position. He can reply, "Governmental agencies, lending institutions, industrial clients, and a number of individuals" or he may recite specific clients; this second answer can be quite time-consuming and may make the appraiser look like a braggart in the eyes of the jury. This type of question is asked only by the attorney who is unprepared, lazy, or incompetent.

To most effectively place the appraiser's credentials before the jury, the question should be broken down into several segments. The exchange might proceed as follows:

> *Attorney:* Mr. Appraiser, have you ever made any appraisal for the federal government?
>
> *Appraiser:* Yes.
>
> *Attorney:* And could you tell the jury for which agencies of the federal government you have made appraisals?
>
> *Appraiser:* The United States Army Corps of Engineers, the Bonneville Power Administration, etc.

The attorney can continue with the same form of questions relating to state governmental agencies, local governmental agencies, industrial clients, commercial clients, etc. The appraiser should always mention if he has made appraisals for the condemnor when testifying for the condemnee; in testifying for the condemnor, he should note any appraisals he has made for condemnees where the opposing party was the same condemnor involved in the instant case. The appraiser should also reveal if he has made any appraisals for the county or city in which most of the jurors reside, or if he has made appraisals for one or more of the jurors' employers or their spouses' employers. The specific clientele cited will depend on the type of property being appraised, the location of the property, the location of the trial, the makeup of the jury, etc.

The appraiser's qualifications will generally cover historical employment experience, current employment, general educational background, specialized training in appraising, any teaching experience, professional affiliations and designations and any offices held, any manuscripts or papers published, typical clientele, types of property appraised, expert testimony and experience, and the geographical area of his experience.

"In a condemnation case, the more impressive the qualifications of the expert, the more likely his testimony will convince the jury that his valuation approach is the correct one."[18] Therefore, opposing counsel may willingly stipulate that the appraiser is qualified to testify as an expert. This should not, however, be allowed to happen; it excludes from the jury any specific knowledge of the appraiser's experience and qualifications. Such a stipulation by opposing counsel may be handled in one of two ways. Counsel may state:

> We thank opposing counsel for recognizing the excellent qualifications of our appraiser. In light of counsel's stipulation, I would move for admission of our appraiser's written qualifications so the jury may study and consider them during its deliberations.

Having made this statement, legal counsel should still insist that the jury hear at least the appraiser's important qualifications.

The second method of handling such a stipulation is for counsel to state:

> We thank opposing counsel for recognizing the excellent qualifications of our appraiser. However, we feel the jury would benefit from learning the specific qualifications of our expert so as to give our appraiser's opinion proper weight.

In such a situation, the court is required to allow counsel to present the expert's qualifications to the jury.[19] As put by one court:

> It was error not to permit appellants' expert to state his qualifications. The fact that the commonwealth "accepted" his qualifications went only to whether the court should permit him to testify. It did not meet the further question of what weight the jury might wish to give

his opinion, which might well be governed by its appraisal of his background and experience.[20]

The Appraisal Process

Now the appraiser will describe the appraisal process applicable to all appraisals with emphasis on those portions of the process which were most applicable in appraising the property being acquired. In other words, the appraiser may very well *skim over* the cost and income approaches if a non-income-producing tract of land with no improvements is being appraised. The description of the appraisal process in this instance will focus on the market data approach. At this point, only a brief description of the approaches to value is needed; a detailed description of the applicable approach can best be left until the appraiser actually begins to testify on how he applied each approach to the property being appraised. Because it generally falls on the first appraiser to educate the jury as to the appraisal process, subsequent witnesses need not explain the process in detail.

A description of the appraisal process provides an opportunity to define some appraisal terms which will be used throughout the trial. These terms might include market value, highest and best use, the subject property, and capitalization rate. The appraiser and the attorney should decide which terms will be used and at what points in the description of the appraisal process the attorney will interrupt the appraiser to ask for the definition of a term. The attorney may say, "A moment ago you mentioned the term highest and best use—could you explain to us what appraisers mean when they use this term?" In this way, the terminology is explained to the jury without the appraiser lecturing or talking down to them. Also, counsel's use of the term "us" in his question infers to the jury that they are not expected to be able to answer the question and helps to establish a rapport between the attorney and the jury. The attorney should only interrupt the appraiser's description of the appraisal process at a *natural* breaking point, so as not to destroy the continuity of the description. It is sometimes helpful to draw a diagram of the appraisal process for the jury.

Work Process

The appraiser explains the work process to show the jury that he has made a thorough investigation and that an appraisal consists of more than looking at a property and estimating its value. The work process should be described thoroughly, following the appraisal process step by step. In fact, it is often helpful to refer back to the appraisal process. For instance, in describing the growth, or lack of growth in a neighborhood, the appraiser may state that growth factors are developed as part of the general neighborhood data, which will influence demand projections in the foreseeable future.

Property Description

In verbally describing the property to the jury, the appraiser should, as should be done in the appraiser's written report, attempt to set the jury up to buy the appraiser's final conclusion. If the property suffers from functional obsolescence, this fact should be stated in describing the property. The appraiser should never allow the jury to be surprised when the appraiser makes a deduction for functional obsolescence in applying the cost approach. The appraiser is well advised to include a detailed property description among the reference notes he brings to the witness stand. These notes are most useful when prepared in outline form.

Here again, the attorney can help the appraiser present a full description of the property to the jury by asking several, specific leading questions. Questions such as "Would you describe the land?", "Would you describe the dwelling?", "Would you describe the on-site improvements?", and "Are there any other improvements on the land?" usually lead to a more detailed property description than a question such as, "Would you describe the property?" Again, the first appraiser will generally be expected to give the most detailed description of the property.

Photographs are, of course, helpful in describing the property and their use can shorten the appraiser's testimony. In describing the property, the appraiser should consider whether the jury has viewed the property. If so, the obvious elements of the property can be referred to without in-depth description. In describing specific property elements, it is often advisable for the appraiser to preface his remarks by saying, "As I am sure the jury saw when they viewed the property. . ."

Cost Approach

If the cost approach was not used by the appraiser, he should tell the jury why it was inapplicable. If the cost approach was used, the appraiser should explain in detail the steps taken to develop an estimate of value by this approach. The appraiser should keep in mind that the jury was briefly exposed to the cost approach during the description of the appraisal process. It is important to emphasize that the value estimate developed by the cost approach is an estimate of *market value;* not some obscure *sound value* or *physical value,* etc., but *market value.* The advantages and disadvantages of the various methods of estimating cost and depreciation and the likelihood of these methods being understood by the trier of fact has already been discussed.[21]

The first step is to present to the trier of fact the data used by the appraiser in developing the estimate of land value. The verbal presentation should be augmented by photographs of the comparable site sales and some form of sales comparison chart.[22] Because the cost approach is rather mechanical, it lends itself to graphic display. Therefore, each step of the cost approach should be presented to the jury in chart form, as well as verbally. Even if the appraiser has not separately estimated physical deterioration, functional obsolescence, and economic obsolescence, he should define these terms and emphasize that each form of depreciation was considered in arriving at a total depreciation estimate, irrespective of whether they were independently estimated or estimated as a lump sum, as in the abstraction method of estimating depreciation.

Income Approach

The mechanics of the income approach can be the single most difficult concept for a jury to understand. If the income approach is an integral part of the appraiser's value estimate, it is worthwhile to present the mathematical workings of the approach in extensive detail. The appraiser should first explain the basic steps of the income approach, and then go back and carefully explain and illustrate the capitalization process and the derivation of a capitalization rate. Presentation of these data is extensively covered elsewhere in this work.[23] The methodology utilized by an appraiser in selecting an applicable capitalization rate will have a major bearing on the difficulty of obtaining understanding by the jury. For example, if the capitalization rate was developed by direct comparison, this process can be explained rather simply; on the other hand, if the mortgage-equity method of rate selection was used, extensive explanation may be required.

When a complex method of rate selection must be explained, some appraiser/attorney teams prefer to have the appraiser testify on rate development in a rather general manner on direct examination. For instance, the appraiser might explain that he used the mortgage-equity method of rate selection, which necessitates the consideration of available financing, equity yields required by investors, potential appreciation or depreciation, and the typical ownership term. If opposing counsel wants to delve further into the construction of the capitalization rate, the appraiser should be prepared to explain it. One advantage of waiting until cross-examination to describe the mortgage-equity rate is that, if the jurors get confused and cannot follow the testimony, they will often blame the attorney rather than the witness. If asked to explain a complex capitalization rate, the appraiser should attempt to do so in writing, as well as verbally. When, on cross-examination, an appraiser starts to explain the derivation of a capitalization rate by writing out the Ellwood formula: $R = Y - M(Y + [(1/(1+i)^n)(f/I - 1)(Sp - 1)] - f \mp_{D}^{A}(1/(1 + i)^n))$, the attorney will generally wish he never asked the question.

Only after both the attorney and appraiser are absolutely certain that the jury understands the concept and mathematics of the income approach, should there be any attempt to present the income approach as it relates to the property being condemned. The development of the property's economic rent and stabilized annual net income should be presented to the jury both verbally and in chart form. Mathematical computations should either be presented in a chart, or the appraiser should actually write the calculations while testifying. If the appraiser states, "Based on subject's net income and the cap rate, the value of the property is $150,000," the jury will wonder where the $150,000 came from. The jurors cannot take notes, nor do they have calculators, so a better way to present a final estimate of value by the income approach is to write the computations while explaining them. As the appraiser writes the computations on the blackboard, he might say: "Now that the net income from the property has been estimated and a proper capitalization rate has been selected, a simple mathematical calculation is used to develop the indicated market value of the property. The basic *IRV* formula, which I explained earlier, is used. The income is known and the rate is known, thus the unknown factor is value. Applying the *IRV* formula the computation would be Income ÷ Rate = Value. The net income previously developed was $18,000, and the proper capitalization rate is 12%. Dividing the $18,000 income by the 12% capitalization rate results in a value indication of $150,000."

Explaining such an easy calculation in detail may seem somewhat unnecessary. However, it must be kept in mind that the mere concept of valuing property by the income approach is completely new to the jury. Although the appraiser and the attorney are constantly exposed to the concepts and mechanics of the income approach, the jury is not. And while the appraiser and attorney spent hours and hours (or should have) preparing for trial (analyzing the concepts and mathematics of the income approach as it relates to the specific property in question) the jury is not afforded the opportunity to prepare for trial.

It is extremely depressing to see an appraiser spend several hours on the witness stand carefully explaining the concept and mathematics of the income approach, developing in minute detail the estimate of economic rent, convincingly leading the jury from gross income to net income, and carefully explaining the derivation of the capitalization rate only to ruin the presentation at the last minute by neglecting to show the jury the final computation. Once again, it is extremely important to stress that the value indication developed by the income approach is *market value.*

Market Data Approach

The market data approach to value is most often relied on by the trier of fact. Therefore, it is important that the appraiser/attorney team present this approach to value in a detailed, believable, and accurate manner. Photographs of comparable sales are all but essential. These photographs should be admitted into evidence so that the jury can look at them while the appraiser is describing the comparable sale. This procedure is very effective and, of course, the photographs will also be available to the jury during their deliberations. It is therefore important that the appraiser note the specifics of the comparable sale on the back of each photograph; this information might include the sale number, its location, the date the photo was taken and the appraiser's name.

Graphic presentation of comparable sales data and analysis to the trier of fact has already been discussed.[24] It is generally advisable to prepare such graphic material before the trial so that the sales chart can be professionally drawn and easily read by the trier of fact. It is important for both the appraiser and the attorney to remember that the sale price of a property is generally not admissible until the property's comparability has been established. The establishment of such comparability may be handled in one of two ways.

First, the chart may be prepared without the comparable sale prices and indicated value of the property being appraised by each of the sales. As the appraiser testifies as to the comparability of each sale property, and the analysis thereof, he may testify as to the price of the comparable and, at that point, write the price of the comparable on the sales chart. As the comparative analysis is further developed, the appraiser can write the value of the property being appraised as indicated by each comparable onto the sales chart.

A second, and perhaps cleaner, method of securing admission of a comparable sales chart, which includes the price of each comparable and the value of the property being appraised as indicated by the analysis of the sales, is to verbally submit an adequate amount of testimony on each sale property to establish its comparability to the satisfaction of the court. This testimony will generally include the date of the sale, the location of the sale property, and a general description of its physical characteristics. Once the attorney feels that the appraiser has given enough testimony in regard to the sale for the court to rule on the admissibility of the sale price of the property, the attorney should ask the appraiser the sale price of the property and then move on to the next comparable sale. If opposing counsel objects to the admissibility of the sale price of the property on the grounds that its comparability has not been demonstrated, and the court sustains this objection, the attorney must then elicit more information on the sale property and its comparability from the appraiser until the court is satisfied that the sale is comparable and allows testimony as to the price of the property.

After the appraiser has testified to all comparable sales on the sales chart, in the manner indicated, the attorney can have the sales chart identified by the court. The appraiser can then use the chart in giving detailed testimony to the trier of fact as to items of similarity and dissimilarity for each sale property. Thus, the trier of fact is led through the comparative analysis and adjustment process employed by the appraiser for each comparable sale. Once the appraiser has testified to all sales on the chart in the manner described, the attorney may confidently move for the admission of the chart as evidence. After the chart is admitted, the trier of fact will have the opportunity to study the chart during deliberations. If the chart were not so admitted, the trier would have to try to remember its contents.

This second method of obtaining the admission of a comparable sales chart has an advantage in that it reduces the possibility of numerous objections as to comparability by opposing counsel. The court has ruled that each sale property has an adequate degree of similarity for admission as a comparable, before the appraiser ever begins testifying in regard to the details of the comparative analysis made between the sale property and the property being appraised. Numerous and continued objections during the appraiser's presentation of the comparative analysis can destroy the continuity and effectiveness of the testimony. It can also confuse and break the train of thought of the trier of fact or, worse yet, the appraiser.

Final Correlation of Value

At this point, the appraiser has the opportunity to review with the trier of fact the indicated market value of the property as developed by the various approaches to value. In this portion of the trial, the appraiser should first testify to his final estimate of market value. This allows a chart similar to that shown in Table 19.1 to be placed before the jury or other trier of fact early in this phase of the appraiser's testimony. This chart will assist the appraiser in reviewing and summarizing the testimony with the trier of fact and, at the same time, provide the greatest visual exposure of the appraiser's conclusion. When direct examination is over, opposing counsel will usually remove from view all charts and diagrams presented as a part of the appraiser's direct testimony. The attorney does not want the trier of fact *contaminated* with the appraiser's conclusions any longer than necessary. He will usually remove any visual evidence, under the pretext that the exhibit space will soon be needed for other purposes.

Once a chart such as Table 19.1 is placed before the trier of fact, the appraiser should briefly review how each indication of market value was developed. It should be noted that Figure 19.1 refers to *indicated market value,* not *indicated value* or simply *value.* The fact that all three approaches to value result in an indication of *market value* should be continually emphasized. The appraiser should describe in detail the reasoning he applied to arrive at the final opinion of value and how the results of each approach to value were weighed in that opinion.

The reliability of each approach to value in solving the particular appraisal problem should be explained. If one approach to value has been given primary emphasis, the reasons therefore should be given. The appraiser's testimony should emphasize the strong points of the approach that was given primary weight in the final conclusion. It is also important to explain the weaknesses, under the particular circumstances of the case, of the approaches that were given lesser weight. The earlier testimony of other appraisers, or their anticipated future testimony, will have a bearing on the appraiser's testimony in this regard. If all appraisers agree as to the most reliable approach to value in the instant case, there is no need for detailed testimony on the weaknesses of the other approaches to value. Instead, the importance of properly analyzing the integral elements of the most applicable approach to value should be emphasized.

After Value

If the case involves a partial taking, the appraiser, under direct examination, again reviews Steps 4 through 8 as described earlier, but in the after situation. The procedure followed in the before situation should be repeated with equal clarity and detail in the after situation. It is useless to convince the trier of fact of the accuracy of the before value, if the trier doesn't accept the after value estimate. Awards, in partial taking cases, are not based on before value alone.

If jurisdictional rules require application of the *state* or *taking plus damages* rule, the after value testimony must be framed to comply with the applicable rules. If benefits are not present in the after situation, little alteration will be required and the result will, or at least should, be identical to the results using the *federal,* or *before and after,* rule.

Under the federal rule, the indicated market value of the property in the after situation should be visually presented to the trier of fact in the manner shown in Table 19.1; the *remainder value after take* under the state rule should be presented in the same way. However, the final mathematical calculation under the federal rule might be presented as shown in Table 19.2, while the mathematical computations under the state rule, assuming no benefits, might be presented as shown in Table 19.3. If special benefits are present, the appraiser's conclusions, under the state rule, should be presented as shown in Table 19.4, assuming special benefits were offset against damages.

Table 19.1

Correlation of Appraiser's Estimate of Market Value

Approach To Market Value	Indicated Market Value
Cost Approach	$123,500
Income Approach	$117,000
Market Data Approach	$120,000
Final Estimate of Market Value	$120,000

Cross-Examination

How does the attorney/appraiser team prepare the appraiser for cross-examination? First, they try to determine on what points the appraiser will be most heavily cross-examined. In other words, what are the weakest points of the appraiser's approach to value and, thus, the weakest probable points of his testimony? How can the appraiser best defend himself against cross-examination on these points? The appraiser/attorney team should not assume that the appraisal approach applied is without weak points, or hope that opposing counsel will overlook any weaknesses. They must view their case objectively, pick out the weaknesses, and prepare to defend them against attack.

With proper preparation, opposing counsel should never be able to bring out a weakness of the appraiser's direct testimony that has not been recognized as a

Table 19.2

**Appraiser's Final Conclusions
Federal Rule**

Before Value	$120,000
After Value	− 86,000
Difference	$ 34,000

Table 19.3

**Appraiser's Final Conclusions
State Rule**

Value Before Take	$120,000
Value of Part Taken	− 22,000
Remainder Value Before Take	$ 98,000
Remainder Value After Take	86,000
Damages	$ 12,000
Value of Part Taken	22,000
Total Difference	$ 34,000

weakness by the appraiser/attorney team prior to trial. For instance, in one case, the value estimate of the condemnor's appraiser was 30% below the price actually paid for the property two months prior to the date of taking. The appraiser defended his value estimate on cross-examination so successfully that the trier of fact completely disregarded the prior sale of the property and found the property's market value to be as testified by the condemnor's appraiser.

It has been said that "cross-examination takes the place in our legal system that torture occupied in the medieval systems of civilization."[25] "The purpose of cross-examination is to dilute, neutralize or completely destroy the effect of the witness's direct testimony"[26] and appraisers have sagely been advised that "[c]ross-examination is the anvil of the truth and you must be prepared for a thorough hammering."[27] It is with these thoughts in mind that the appraiser should prepare for cross-examination.

Table 19.4

Appraiser's Final Conclusions
State Rule With Special Benefits

Value Before Take	$120,000
Value of Part Taken	− 22,000
Remainder Value Before Take	$ 98,000
Remainder Value After Take	− 90,000
Damages	$ 8,000
Special Benefits	− 6,000
Net Damages	$ 2,000
Value of Part Taken	22,000
Total Difference	$ 24,000

It can be either a great insult or a great compliment for a cross-examiner to stand after the appraiser's direct testimony and say, "No questions." If the appraiser has presented a strong and detailed case for his opinion of value during direct examination, cross-examination may be declined because the cross-examiner feels the appraiser is so well-prepared and has such presence on the witness stand that any cross-examination would only strengthen the appraiser's direct testimony. Under such circumstances, it is best for the opposing counsel to try to give the trier of fact the impression that the appraiser's approach to the appraisal problem is so ill-conceived that cross-examination would be a waste of time. Cross-examination of a very strong witness can do more harm than good, and the cross-examiner's best course is to get the appraiser out of sight, and hopefully out of mind, of the trier of fact as quickly as possible.

On the other hand, cross-examination may be foregone if the appraiser's direct testimony is not particularly strong or does not materially damage the cross-examiner's case in chief. For example, if the appraiser testifies to a value estimate under direct examination without providing the facts on which he based his opinion, it is often well to forego cross-examination. A cross-examiner might ask, "Do you have any sales to back up your totally unsupported opinion?" to point out to the trier of fact that the opinion is unsupported. However, if the witness answers the question well, the opinion might be much better supported than the cross-examiner ever wanted it to be, and worse yet, the question allows opposing counsel to delve into the question of comparable sales on redirect examination. Often, it is best for the cross-examiner to forego cross-examination and emphasize to the trier of fact during closing arguments that the appraiser's opinion is without basis.

If not covered in the direct examination, it is most important for the cross-examiner to ask the appraiser the assumptions, limiting conditions, and legal instructions under which the appraisal was made. Too often this question is left unasked. Regardless of the answer, this question should not be injurious to the cross-examiner's case. The trier of fact is seldom aware of the *standard* assumptions and limiting conditions under which a typical appraisal is made. For instance, a typical list of the assumptions and limiting conditions of an appraisal involving a partial acquisition can be seen in Table 19.5. While a recitation of the appraisal's assumptions and limiting conditions is not particularly harmful to the appraiser, the cross-examiner might try to convince the trier of fact in final argument that the appraiser seems to have assumed everything and known nothing.

The real advantage of asking for a recitation of the appraisal's assumptions, limiting conditions, and legal instructions is the possibility that one of these assumptions, limiting conditions, or legal instructions is contrary to eminent domain and valuation law in the applicable jurisdiction. For instance, one appraisal report made for a condemnee was prepared under the following limiting condition and instruction:

> Zoning has been completely disregarded. The appraiser has been instructed to value the property based upon the Highest and Best Use of the site, irrespective of present zoning or use.

Another report prepared for a condemnee, covering a warehouse constructed in 1903, was made under the following assumptions:

ASSUMPTIONS

That the owners have a legal right of ingress and egress by deed or prescription. [The property was legally landlocked]

That, *as limited investigation has revealed,* there are no valid, comparable sales of property and buildings. [emphasis added]

That there are no land and buildings in the area currently being rented to provide valid income data. [This might be a proper conclusion to reach after market investigation, but it should certainly not be an assumption.]

Table 19.5

Typical—Partial Acquisition

ASSUMPTIONS AND LIMITING CONDITIONS:

In making this appraisal it was assumed that:

1. No legal questions are considered, such as title, encumbrances, etc. The property is appraised as though free and clear, except as specifically noted within this report.
2. All dimensions and legal descriptions are assumed to be correct as found through available records or on-the-ground inspection.
3. The Subject Property will be under management that is competent and ownership that is responsible.
4. All information as found in data furnished is deemed to be reliable. If any errors are found, the right is reserved to modify the conclusions reached.
5. The sketch and aerial photos, if any, in this report are included to assist the reader in visualizing the property. I have made no survey of the property and assume no responsibility in connection with such matters.
6. While various approaches to value and various mathematical calculations are used in estimating value, these are but aids to the formulation of the opinion of value expressed by the appraiser in this report. In these calculations, certain arithmetical figures are rounded off to the nearest significant amount.
7. The data and conclusions embodied in this appraisal are a part of the whole valuation. No part of this appraisal is to be used out of context, and, by itself alone—no part of this appraisal is necessarily correct as being only part of the evidence upon which the final judgment as to value is based.
8. Employment to make this appraisal does not require testimony in court unless mutually satisfactory arrangements are made in advance.
9. Fair Market Value is defined as: . . . "the amount in cash which a well-informed buyer willing, but not obliged to buy the property, would pay, and which a well-formed seller willing, but not obligated to sell it, would accept, taking into consideration all uses to which the property is adapted and might in reason be applied."
10. Where the value of the land and the improvements are shown separately, the value of each is segregated as only an aid to better estimating the value of the whole; and the value shown for either may, or may not, be its correct Fair Market Value.
11. The signatory of this appraisal report is a Member of the American Institute of Real Estate Appraisers of the National Association of Realtors. The Bylaws and Regulations of the Institute require each Member to control the use and distribution of each appraisal report signed by such Member. Therefore, except as hereinafter provided, the party for whom this appraisal report was prepared may distribute copies of this appraisal report, in its entirety, to such third parties as may be selected by the party for whom this appraisal report was prepared; however, selected portions of this appraisal report shall not be given to third parties without the prior written consent of the signatory of this appraisal report. Further, neither all nor any part of this appraisal report shall be disseminated to the general public by the use of advertising media, public relations media, news media, sales media or other media for public communication without the prior written consent of the signatory of this appraisal report.
12. No study has been made to determine whether structures may have an infestation such as termites or dry rot. In the absence of such study, it is assumed that the property is free from such problems.
13. The proposed public improvement will be constructed in a timely manner in accordance with the plans and specifications thereof as described in the body of this report. Said plans and specifications are shown on map sheet 4 of 7 sheets; Project SR500, M.P. 0.23 to M.P. 2.95, Jct. S.R. 5 at 39th St. to N.E. 66th Ave. Said map sheet 4 bears an approval date of June 2, 1978 and a date of last map revision of March 23, 1979.

> That the replacement [of the property] is necessary to the business and the loss of the subject facility would cause economic harm far in excess of the cost of replacement. [Appraiser estimated value of business, not value of the realty.]

It may surprise the attorney who does not specialize in eminent domain litigation to know that very often real estate appraisals are made under assumptions, limiting conditions, and/or attorney instructions that are unacceptable to the court. When exposed, this flaw can substantially weaken the effectiveness of the witness and, at times, the court may rule that all testimony given by the appraiser/witness should be disregarded by the trier of fact.

It is essential that, before ever acting as an expert witness, the appraiser read "One Hundred Questions on Cross-examination" by Walstein Smith, Jr.[28] Other articles of interest by the same author include "One Hundred Questions on Direct Examination"[29] and "One Hundred Questions Which Will Worry Weak Witnesses."[30] In regard to this latter list of questions, Smith states:

> It does not take 100 questions to upset an expert witness. Sometimes it takes only one question asked at the right moment with the proper voice inflection. However, sometimes it takes a selection of two or three hundred questions to get the right one.[31]

The one hundred questions to worry weak witnesses are divided into ten categories designed to show:

    I. Bias: Factual or Inferred
    II. Collusion and Advocacy
    III. Lack of Real Estate Experience on Special Property Types
    IV. Lack of Appraisal Education, Training, Professional Recognition
    V. Personal Incompetence: Factual or Inferred
    VI. Dishonesty
    VII. Lack of Local Experience
    VIII. Lack of Preparation and Carelessness
    IX. Imperfections of Appraisal Techniques
    X. Trick Questions[32]

Smith summarizes these questions by stating: "[N]ow, after reading these 100 questions, you know why many appraisers refuse to do condemnation appraisals!"[33]

Although the appraiser is an advocate of his opinion, there must be nothing in his testimony or demeanor which suggests advocacy for his client's interest. This is particularly difficult under cross-examination, because the cross-examiner is trying to convince the trier of fact of the appraiser's advocacy, whether it exists or not. The appraiser must remain calm on the witness stand and think before answering each question. He should respond to each question as briefly as possible, but a long series of "yes" and "no" answers should be avoided. Many appraisers begin answering too quickly, and may answer without considering the full ramifications of the question and/or the answer.

The appraiser should never be lulled into a feeling of false security on the witness stand. Be on the lookout, at all times, for trick and hypothetical questions. The question, "Did you consider the sale of 1234 X Street for $50,000" is improper if no proof of such a sale has been submitted. Opposing counsel should object to this question. Hypothetical questions, such as "If a sale of 1234 X street occurred two months ago for $50,000, would that affect your opinion?" are acceptable and should be answered. It is opposing counsel's job to point out to the trier of fact, one way or another, that there was never any proof of such a sale presented.

The appraiser should always be prepared to testify regarding the sales used by the opposing party's appraiser. During cross-examination, a question in regard to such a sale may be answered by stating "Yes, I considered that sale, but felt it was not comparable," or "Yes, I considered that sale, but disregarded it in my final analysis because it sold over two years ago, it was twice the size of the subject property, did not have sewer like the subject, has flooded three out of the last five years, and is subject to a different zone classification than the property being appraised." The first response will generally cause counsel to ask the same question about each and every sale used by other appraisers; the second response will generally lead into an entirely new field of questioning and shorten the cross-examination process.

The following short excerpt contains a couple of important lessons for the appraiser:

CROSS EXAMINATION

Attorney A: So, Mr. [Appraiser] you feel that the volume of traffic past this property is an important factor because it gives it greater exposure?

Appraiser: Yes; and I might add . . . (interrupted)

Attorney A: Your honor, I would ask that the witness be restricted to answering my question—I don't care what he might or might not add.

Court:	Your point is well-taken Mr. [Attorney A]. The witness has answered the question—he need not elaborate on it.
Attorney B:	Your honor, the witness should be allowed to explain his answer.
Court:	I don't think any explanation is necessary at this point. You may ask him about it on redirect.
Attorney B:	I don't know what he was going to say.
Court:	My ruling stands.
Attorney A:	No more questions, your honor.

REDIRECT

Attorney B:	Mr. [Appraiser], in reference to your response to [Attorney A's] last question, *what is it you might add?*

The first lesson to be learned here is that, in responding to a question, the appraiser must choose his words carefully. If the appraiser had responded "Yes, because. . . ," the explanation would probably have gone unchallenged; however, the words "I might add" raised a red flag to the cross-examiner. This brief exchange also shows that a small amount of light humor is not necessarily out of place in the courtroom, particularly near the end of a four-day jury trial, but the appraiser should leave the humor to the court and the attorney. Although appraisers must keep a sense of humor when on the witness stand, they are not hired as comedians and should never, under any imaginable circumstances, attempt humor from the witness stand.

Redirect

Redirect examination of an appraisal witness could more descriptively be called *reconstruction.* Redirect examination gives the attorney/appraiser team a chance to repair any damage done during cross-examination and to clarify any points made confusing, intentionally or not, by opposing counsel. It also allows the appraiser to explain fully his simple "yes" and "no" responses to questions posed on cross-examination, if further explanation is, in fact, desirable.

Final Argument

The final arguments are totally within the purview of the attorneys. The final argument is not the time to explain the techniques of appraisal methodology to a jury; if the jury doesn't understand the case by this time, the attorney may as well save his breath—the case is lost.

There is some debate as to whether the appraiser should stay in the courtroom during the final arguments. The appraiser must abide by the wishes of legal counsel, but should generally encourage counsel to allow him to be excused. If the appraiser is going to stay in the courtroom, how should he react during final arguments? Each time the appraiser's name is mentioned, every member of the jury will turn and watch the appraiser's reaction. The appraiser's attorney will extol the appraiser's virtues; should he blush or shuffle his feet? Does he watch the attorney or stare the jury square in the eye? During final arguments, opposing counsel will often imply that the appraiser is an advocate, a nonprofessional, an incompetent and usually wears a black hat. Again, how does the appraiser, sitting there in the spectator's gallery in full view of the jury, react—with a noncommittal look on the face, staring straight ahead? with a threatening glare at the cross-examiner? or with a smile on his lips? Does he look at the jury or thumb his nose at opposing counsel? If the appraiser is a masochist, he should, by all means, stay. If not, the appraiser should request, and plead with legal counsel if necessary, to be excused from the courtroom.

Summary

Appraisers are allowed to testify as to their opinion of value only because they are classified as experts in the field of real estate valuation. Although appraisers are not always looked on favorably by courts and attorneys, it is generally recognized that their testimony is necessary in a condemnation trial. There always have been, and there probably always will be, individuals who classify themselves as professional appraisers, but arrive at *made-to-order* opinions of value. By the same token, there have been, and probably always will be, an ample number of attorneys to *place the order.*

The specific procedure of a condemnation trial will vary from jurisdiction to jurisdiction. Some jurisdictions provide that the condemnor has the burden of proof, while others place that burden on the condemnee; still other jurisdictions hold that neither the condemnor nor the condemnee has the burden of proof.

It is advisable for appraisers to be present throughout the condemnation trial, except during final arguments. In this way, the appraisers can better assist legal counsel in preparing appropriate questions for both direct examination and cross-examination.

The appraiser should make detailed, but abbreviated, notes for use on the witness stand; he should always keep in mind that any notes used on the stand are subject to inspection by opposing counsel. During testimony, the appraiser should speak clearly and loudly enough to be heard by everyone in the courtroom. He should not speak so fast as to confuse the trier of fact and/or the court reporter. The appraiser should avoid using a monotone and direct his remarks to the jury when answering questions. If the appraiser will be on the witness stand for any length of time, a glass of water should be within easy reach; staring at the pitcher of ice water on the counsel's table can cause the appraiser to lose his train of thought.

The appraiser's direct examination can be broken down into eight logical steps:

1 Qualification as an expert.
2 Description of the appraisal process.
3 Specific work description.
4 Property description.
5 Cost approach.
6 Income approach.
7 Market data approach.
8 Final value estimate.

In a partial taking case, Steps 4 through 8 will be repeated in the after situation. These steps must be modified in the after situation if the jurisdiction requires use of the *state* or *taking plus damages* rule. The appraiser should use as many visual aids (charts, graphs, photos, etc.) as possible to assist the trier of fact in understanding the appraiser's testimony.

An objective analysis of the appraiser's data and methodology will reveal the weakest points of the appraiser's presentation. Recognition of these weaknesses will afford the appraiser/attorney team the opportunity to determine how best to defend or rebut the weaknesses which will undoubtedly be brought out through cross-examination. The purpose of cross-examination is to weaken the appraiser's direct testimony. The attorney who undertakes cross-examination and does not weaken the appraiser's direct testimony is an attorney who should have never cross-examined the witness or who went into the cross-examination unprepared.

Any appraisal methodology or approach has its weaknesses. If the attorney cannot bring them out on cross-examination, he is unprepared. It is not a question of whether an appraiser's direct testimony can be weakened by cross-examination, but rather how much it can be weakened. Redirect examination is an attempt to restrengthen the weak points brought out in the cross-examination; it gives the appraiser an opportunity to explain answers to questions which, under cross-examination, could only be answered with a "yes" or "no." The degree to which the appraiser's direct testimony was weakened by cross-examination will dictate the amount of redirect examination required.

The appraiser should not remain in the courtroom during final argument, unless he is specifically instructed to do so by counsel. Some attorneys will so instruct their appraisers, but most recognize the disadvantage of having the jury's attention drawn to the appraiser, rather than the attorney's argument. The content of the attorney's argument will depend on the circumstances of the particular case. In almost every case, the attorney will point out to the trier of fact, to one degree or another, 1) the superb qualifications of his expert witness, 2) the lack of qualifications of the opposing party's expert witness, 3) the objectivity of his expert, 4) the bias or advocacy of the opposing party's expert, 5) the thoroughness of his expert's work and the reasonableness of the expert's opinion, and 6) the slipshod work of opposing counsel's expert and the absurdity of that expert's opinion. The attorney will also highlight those little items that make each case unique, such as the fact that the property owner was born and raised on the property, or the allegation that the condemnor's appraiser cannot possibly know the value of the property because he doesn't live in the community.

Notes

1. James A. Ballentine, *Ballentine's Law Dictionary,* 3rd ed. William S. Anderson, ed. (Rochester, N.Y.: The Lawyers Co-operative Publishing Co.; San Francisco: Bancroft-Whitney Co., 1969), p. 445.

2. Ibid.

3. See Chapter 8, "Income Approach to Value," footnotes 40, 41, and 42.

4. John P. Hogan, "Ten Court Room Commandments for Appraisers," *Right-of-Way,* October 1969, pp. 21-25.

5. Seymour Simon, "Responsibilities of the Appraiser Accepting Legal Instructions," *The Appraisal Journal,* April 1974, p. 181.

6. Case citation omitted due to pending ethics complaint.

7. *Divergencies in Right-of-Way Valuations,* National Cooperative Highway Research Program Rep. No. 126 (Washington, D.C.: Highway Research Board, 1971), p. 2.

8. Newport Housing Authority, Inc. v. Hartsell, 533 S.W.2d 317 (Tenn.).

9. State v. Nelson, 222 Or. 458, 353 P.2d 616.

10. Jutice v. United States, 145 F.2d 110.

11. Julius L. Sackman, *Nichols' The Law of Eminent Domain,* rev. 3rd ed. (New York: Matthew Bender, 1979) Vol. 5, § 18.31[1].

12. Sidney Z. Searles, "Examination and Cross-Examination of Appraiser in Eminent Domain," *Institute on Planning, Zoning and Eminent Domain,* Southwestern Legal Foundation, 1973, (New York: Matthew Bender & Co., Inc., 1973).

13. American Institute of Real Estate Appraisers Regulation No. 10, *Code of Professional Ethics and Standards of Professional Conduct,* Canon 1, p. 3 (Adopted Nov. 13, 1981).

14. See Chapter 18, "Preparation for Court."

15. Patrick J. Rohan and Melvin A. Reskin, *Nichols' The Law of Eminent Domain,* rev. 3rd ed. (New York: Matthew Bender, 1980) Vol. 7, § 8.04 (also published as Vol. 3, Part 2 of Real Estate Transactions).

16. Ibid., § 8.05[1].

17. Ibid., § 8.04[2].

18. *Nichols',* Vol. 7, § 8.04.

19. Trowbridge v. Abrasive Co. of Philadelphia, 190 F.2d 825.

20. Wolf v. Commonwealth of Puerto Rico, 341 F.2d 945.

21. See Chapter 7, "Cost Approach to Value."

22. See Chapter 9, "Market Data Approach to Value."

23. See Chapter 8, "Income Approach to Value."

24. See Chapter 9, "Market Data Approach to Value."

25. 5 *Wigmore on Evidence* 29 (1940).

26. *Nichols',* Vol. 7, § 8.04.

27. *Right-of-Way,* pp. 21-25.
28. Walstein Smith, Jr., "One Hundred Questions on Cross-Examination," *Real Estate Appraiser,* May 1963, pp. 8-13.
29. Walstein Smith, Jr., "One Hundred Questions on Direct Examination," *Residential Appraiser,* June 1962, pp. 3-6.
30. Walstein Smith, Jr., "One Hundred Questions Which Will Worry Weak Witnesses," *Real Estate Appraiser,* Feb. 1967, pp. 11-16.
31. Ibid.
32. Ibid.
33. Ibid.

CHAPTER 20
APPRAISALS FOR TAX
HEARINGS AND OTHER
LITIGATION

It is not possible to develop a list of all the different types of litigation which could require real estate valuations and testimony by real estate valuation experts. The possibilities are endless; they are limited only by the fertile imaginations of buyers, sellers, and users of real estate and their legal counsels. There are, however, several types of real estate litigation which frequently appear on civil court dockets. A review of these cases reveals that the rules of evidence and appraisal procedures applied are surprisingly similar, if not identical, to the rules and procedures used in condemnation trials. The appraiser who is knowledgeable and experienced in the area of condemnation appraising will find his experience applicable to the appraisal of real estate for most civil litigations.

Some of the most common forms of civil litigation requiring real estate valuations, which are not related to the sovereign's power of eminent domain, are discussed in this chapter. Some forms of civil litigation create no unique valuation problems, while others may create technical problems which the appraiser can solve only with outside assistance.

In many civil litigation cases, there is an irreconcilable conflict between the attorney and the appraiser. If the attorney and the appraiser recognize the conflict, and know why it is incurable, they will generally have a better understanding of each other's needs. A civil litigation action such as a divorce case need not lead to a divorce between the attorney and the appraiser. In many litigation cases, the difference of opinion as to the value of real estate is comparatively minimal. However, the attorney has an obligation to attempt to procure the services of the best (and generally the most expensive) appraiser available, while, at the same time, considering the small amount of money at issue.

The appraiser, on the other hand, must assume that he will be required to testify to his opinion of the value of the real estate. To do otherwise will almost ensure that the appraiser will find himself on the witness stand. Therefore, the appraiser will generally quote his appraisal fee assuming that he must be prepared to testify as to his conclusion of value. This will often draw a comment from the attorney such as, "This is a divorce case, not a million-dollar condemnation," or "I didn't ask you to buy the property—just appraise it."

The appraiser must realize that the attorney can economically justify only a limited appraisal fee because the amount of money involved in some civil litigation cases is not large. But, the attorney must also understand the appraiser's circumstances. The unprepared appraiser can be made to look just as incompetent when cross-examined on the witness stand in a suit involving $10,000 as in one involving $10,000,000. The appraiser's integrity and reputation are at stake every time he takes the witness stand. If an appraiser is unprepared on the witness stand, the members of the legal community will not be so forgiving as to say, "It doesn't matter because he was only testifying in a divorce case."

If the appraiser and the attorney cannot reach a compromise, and the conflict between their positions is incurable, they should part company on good terms. The appraiser may be able to recommend an associate appraiser who is competent to do the work, or he may refer the attorney to an appraiser in another firm. The appraiser's assistance will not be forgotten by the attorney.

Divorce

When the attorney tells the appraiser, "This is only a divorce case, so you won't be called to testify," the appraiser generally can double the odds of winding up on the witness stand. The appraiser may also be able to tell whether the attorney represents the husband or the wife, and who is likely to keep what property. In describing the real estate, the attorney may say, "The only real estate involved is a run-down house and a high-quality office building from which the husband is operating a highly successful professional business." The attorney is probably representing the wife, who will be keeping the house, while the husband retains the office building. The valuation problems resulting from a divorce, or the dissolution of a marriage, might include estimating the market value of a single-family dwelling, valuing complex, special-purpose properties, valuing a leased fee and/or leasehold interest, valuing a part interest in real property, or estimating an equitable partitionment of real property.

The purpose of an appraisal in a divorce action is to estimate the market value of any real estate or interest in real estate involved. The appraisal methodology used to estimate the market value of this property is no different than that employed to estimate the *before* market value of a parcel in condemnation, except, of course, that there is no need to disregard *condemnation blight* or *project enhancement* if the property being appraised happens to be affected by either of these factors.

In addition to valuing real estate in divorce cases, the appraiser is sometimes asked to value, or at least testify as to the correct procedure for valuing, a deferred annuity. In some jurisdictions, the current value of a spouse's retirement plan has been ruled to belong to the community, i.e., the husband and the wife each have an undivided half interest in the current value of the retirement plan. Some attorneys do not fully understand the mathematics involved in valuing a deferred annuity, and they prefer to have a witness present the procedure to the court rather than try to present it themselves through argument.

For example, assume the husband in a divorce action is 55 years of age and will be eligible for retirement at age 62. At that time, his retirement benefits will be $500 per month until his death. Assume also that a proper discount rate is 8% and that mortality tables show that a 55-year-old male has a remaining life expectancy of approximately 20 years. Therefore, the current value of the deferred annuity is the present value of the 20-year annuity deferred seven years (until the husband reaches retirement age). The computation would be:

Factor for 240-month (20 years) annuity	119.554292[1]
Factor for 84-month (7 years) deferment	− 64.159261[2]
Factor for 156-month (13 years) annuity	
Deferred 84 months (7 years)	55.395031
Monthly annuity payment	× $500
Present value of annuity (or interest in	
retirement fund)	$27,698

If asked to prepare a written report or to testify, the appraiser is well-advised to make his computations at various interest, or discount, rates using 1% increments and let the attorneys argue as to the applicable rates.

Inverse Condemnation

Inverse condemnation is a civil suit brought by a property owner against a public, or quasi-public, body that has the power of eminent domain. This type of suit is brought when the property owner believes the public agency has appropriated all or part of his property or property rights without condemnation action and the payment of just compensation. Such a situation may occur when a public agency restricts the use of land and claims that the restriction is an exercise of its police power; the owner, on the other hand, may assert that the restriction goes beyond the agency's police power and is, in fact, a taking of property rights for which compensation is due.

An example of such a case comes from Maine, where the state's conservation statute prohibits owners from filling in marshlands. When an owner of marshland was denied a fill permit, he claimed that the statute went beyond the state's constitutional police power and that the denial of a fill permit constituted a taking of a valuable property right for which he should be compensated. The court ruled:

> The application of the wetlands restriction in the terms of the denial of appellants' proposal to fill, and enjoining them from so doing deprives them of the reasonable use of their property and within section 4704 is both an unreasonable exercise of police power and equivalent to taking within constitutional considerations.[3]

As has been previously indicated, police power rights are continually being broadened by legal interpretation and by new legislation; what has historically been considered a *taking,* is now often viewed as an exercise of the sovereign's police power.[4]

However, the pendulum may be beginning to swing the other way. In 1978 Florida adopted a statute providing that "any person substantially affected by final action of any [state] agency, with respect to a permit, may seek review . . . and request monetary damages and other relief in a circuit court . . ."[5] Similar legislation has been submitted, or is being considered, in California, Illinois, North Carolina, Oregon, and Washington. Also, ". . . attorneys have begun to consider using section 1983 of the 1871 Civil Rights Act in land use litigation. In other types of cases (e.g., 'over-enthusiastic' police), municipalities and/or their officials have been held financially liable for depriving persons of their constitutional rights. This approach might be successful in cases involving taking of property. Section 1988 of the Act also allows awarding of attorney's fees to the prevailing party."[6]

An inverse condemnation suit can also be filed when a public agency and a property owner disagree in their interpretations of previously acquired property rights. For instance, such a situation resulted when a local municipality constructed a retaining wall to prevent road slippage. In 1932 the agency acquired an easement for a roadway, which provided an easement width of 20 feet from the proposed centerline of the road *plus necessary cuts and fills.* In 1934 the roadway was constructed in the configuration shown in Figure 20.1; the roadway was maintained in the configuration until 1975, when there was some slippage of the roadway because the development of the nearby hillside increased the velocity and quantity of water runoff.

To alleviate this slippage problem, the municipality extended the slope of the road fill and constructed a retaining wall to hold the fill in place. The configuration of the roadway after this modification is depicted in Figure 20.2. The municipality claimed that, under its 1932 easement, it had the right to expand the area of

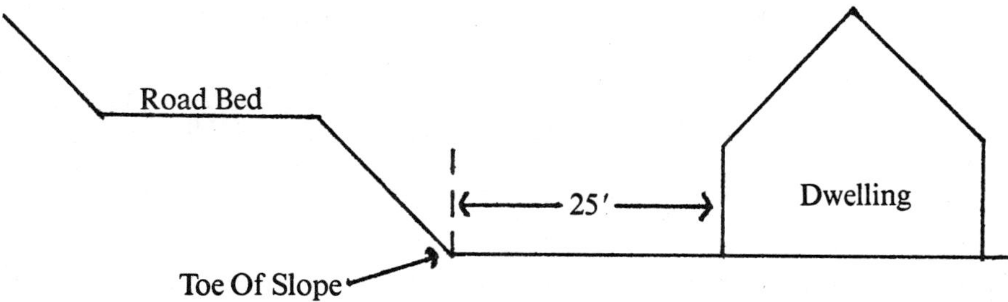

Figure 20.1. Roadway Limits—Before

the slope. The property owner disagreed and brought an inverse condemnation action against the municipality. The jury agreed with the property owner that there was, in fact, an additional *taking* and awarded the property owner *just compensation* for his loss.

When an inverse condemnation suit is filed, the property owner has the burden of proving that the public agency's action constituted a *taking*. If the trier of fact determines that a taking, in a constitutional sense, has not occurred, the trial is over. If, on the other hand, the trier of fact concludes that a taking has occurred, it must then determine *just compensation* for the taking. The appraiser's function in an inverse condemnation case is the same as in a regular condemnation. The appraiser estimates the market value of the property under the valuation rules applicable in the jurisdiction. It is up to the property owner and his legal counsel to prove a taking has occurred, and it is the responsibility of the attorney for the public agency to defend against that claim. The appraiser generally has no participation in, and no responsibility for, this portion of the case. The appraiser must avoid letting his opinion as to whether or not a taking has occurred affect his market value estimate.

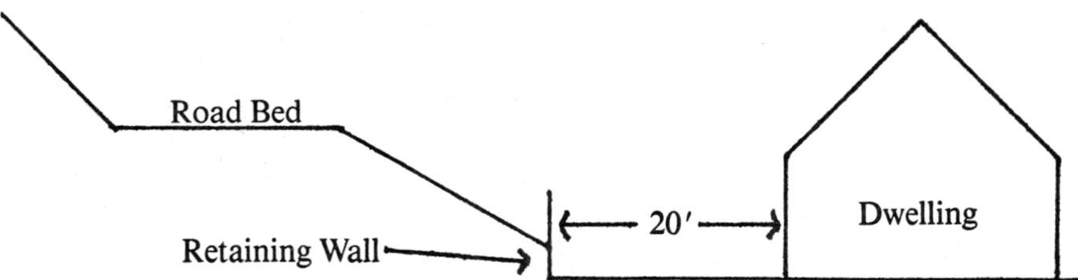

Figure 20.2. Roadway Limits—After

Insurance Claims

Appraisals are made for insurance claim purposes when the insurance company and the insured cannot agree on the amount of property damage sustained. Most losses occur from natural causes such as fire, wind damage, flooding and other water damage, and soil slippage. However, damage can also result from unique occurrences such as tidal waves and volcanic eruptions. Appraisals for insurance claim litigations generally take the same form as appraisals for federal condemnation. That is, the appraiser estimates the market value of the property before the damage and then the market value of the property after the damage has occurred. Often the appraiser must use public records and available photographs of the property to establish the *before* condition of the property. If this is the case, it is important that the appraiser limit his appraisal report and testimony in this regard by clearly specifying the assumptions made about the property prior to the damage.

It is important for the appraiser to understand which items of damage are recoverable, and which are not. A property may suffer diminution in value in excess of the cost to restore it to its original condition. For instance, assume a property is damaged by a landslide in the area. The cost to restore the property to its original physical condition may be $5,000, but the difference between the market value of the property before and after the slide may be $25,000; the extra $20,000 reflects the market's reaction to the potential for landslides in the future. If the appraisal assignment is performed in conjunction with a claim by a property owner against his insurance company, the recoverable loss is only $5,000. However, if the claim is against an abutting property owner (and, thus, his insurance company) who caused the slide by removing a lateral support, the recoverable loss is $25,000, assuming it can be proven that the actions of the abutting owner were the proximate cause of the slide.

Another form of insurance claim is the title insurance loss. This type of loss occurs when the purchaser (or sometimes the mortgagee) of property purchases title insurance and the title insurance company insures the fee title of the property, subject only to the specific exceptions in the policy. If a defect, or encumbrance, in the title to the property that is not specified in the insurance policy exceptions is later found, the title insurance company may be liable for the loss. Three typical types of title loss in which the appraiser may be involved are the existence of a nondisclosed easement, the encroachment onto or enroachment by the subject property, and an incorrect legal description. The loss from any such occurrence is generally measured using a *before and after* methodology identical to that of federal condemnation valuations.

For example, if a property is encumbered by a water-line easement, but was insured as free and clear of easements, the proper valuation procedure would be to estimate the market value of the property as if no easement existed, and then to estimate the market value of the property as encumbered by the easement; the difference between these values, from a legal standpoint, represents the insurable loss up to the maximum coverage of the policy. Often, the title insurance company will bring the original seller of the property into the suit, as a third-party defendant, if this individual transferred the property to the purchaser by way of a warranty deed, without expressly excepting the easement on the face of the deed.

Guardianship/Trustee Matters

An individual who is under legal age or has been ruled incompetent is a ward, and a guardian is responsible for the handling of the ward's affairs. If the ward is under legal age, his parents are his legal guardians. If the individual is an incompetent adult, the court will appoint a guardian for the ward. The powers of a guardian and a trustee will vary from jurisdiction to jurisdiction. However, the actions taken by such a guardian are subject to review by the court and, in many instances, the guardian must get court approval before taking any material action.

When a guardian acts on behalf of a ward in a real estate transaction, an appraiser is often retained to value the property involved so that the guardian has documentation that the transaction contemplated is in the best interest of the ward. In this case, the appraiser may be called to the witness stand to testify to the value of the property so that the court can make a prudent decision on the guardian's motion to take action. Because of the legal and financial responsibilities of a guardian, decisions regarding real estate are generally more carefully investigated, analyzed, and documented than they would be if the guardian were acting on his own behalf.

Appraisal assignments performed in conjunction with guardianship matters can range over the entire spectrum of real estate appraisal and consulting services. Most assignments, however, will involve estimating market value or economic rent and are handled with the same procedures used in estimating the *before value* of a property in a condemnation action.

Fraud and Misrepresentation

Fraud and misrepresentation actions are generally brought by a disgruntled buyer (or lessee) of real estate against the seller (or lessor) and/or the seller's agent. In some cases, the buyer requests that the sale of the property be rescinded and that the seller return all the buyer's money. An appraiser may or may not be involved in such a case. For instance, one case involved a general contractor who had just been awarded a substantial contract to construct a portion of an interstate highway. The contractor was in immediate need of a large quantity of gravel for fill material in conjunction with the highway contract. A nearby property owner offered his property to the contractor, who confirmed the seller's representation as to the quantity and quality of gravel on the site by drilling test holes. The contractor purchased the property, but only after the seller allegedly advised him that a shorelines management permit would not be required to remove the rock. The seller allegedly told the buyer that this fact had been confirmed by the local planning agency.

After closing of the sale, however, the purchaser was advised by the local planning agency that a shorelines management permit would be required before any material could be taken from the site and that it could take several months to obtain such a permit. Due to construction deadlines, the contractor had to acquire another site to obtain the gravel and complete the construction project in a timely manner. The buyer brought suit against the seller and asked for rescission of the sale. The market value of the property was not in question. The issue was whether the seller misrepresented the property to the buyer, and whether the buyer relied on this misinformation. The buyer wasn't interested in the market value of the property; he was unable to use it for his intended purpose in a timely manner and, therefore, did not want the property at any price. The court found that the seller did, in fact, misrepresent the property to the buyer and, therefore, ordered that the sale be rescinded.

Another case in which an appraiser's services were required is described below. In anticipation of selling his property, an owner obtained a survey and had a legal description drawn by an engineering firm. The topography of the site was quite irregular and the land was covered with trees and brush. The engineering firm described the property as "containing 42.6 acres, more or less." The property was placed on the market and sold for $100,000 to a purchaser who intended to develop the property into a mobile home park. The buyer immediately began developing plans for a mobile home park to be submitted to the local planning agency. The applicable land-use ordinance allowed a maximum of eight mobile homes per acre. In preparing the mobile home park plans, the buyer found that he had only 35.4 acres of land, and, thus, could develop the site with only 283 (35.4 × 8) mobile home pads, not 340 (42.6 × 8) pads as he anticipated at the time of purchase.

The purchaser brought suit against the seller asking that the sale price of the property be reduced. The seller brought the engineering firm into the suit as a third-party defendant. The seller alleged that he never represented the property as being any specific size, and that the price paid was a lump sum and was in no way based on the number of acres in the tract or the number of mobile home pads that could be developed on the tract. The buyer testified that he purchased the property with the understanding that it contained approximately 42.6 acres and purchased it because he felt a price of $2,350 per acre was fair.

The buyer retained an appraiser who was legally instructed to appraise the property first as if it contained 42.6 acres and, then, to appraise it again assuming the tract had the same boundary lines but contained only 35.4 acres. The appraiser testified that similar tracts are typically offered, sold, and bought on a price-per-acre basis. Under the first premise, the appraiser's estimate of the tract's market value was $100,000 (42.6 acres × $2,350, rounded); under the second premise, his estimate of market value of the tract was $83,000 (35.4 acres × $2,350, rounded).

The court found no intentional fraud or misrepresentation, but ordered the seller to refund $17,000 to the purchaser, because similar tracts generally sold on a per-acre basis. The court further ordered the engineering firm to pay both the purchaser's and the seller's attorneys' fees because, had it not been for the engineer's error in calculating the size of the tract, there would have been no trial and no fees.

Appraisal assignments involving fraud and misrepresentation are usually similar to assignments to appraise a partial taking in a condemnation case using the before and after rule. The market value of a property in the before situation is based on how it was allegedly misrepresented, and the after value is based on the actual circumstances. The difference, if any, is the amount that the alleged misrepresentation affected the value of the property. It is of no concern to the appraiser whether any actual fraud or misrepresentation occurred. The appraiser must, however, obtain clear, written instructions from legal counsel as to what special elements are to be assumed in both the before and after situations. These instructions must be included within the appraisal report and should be noted in any testimony the appraiser may give in reference to the property.

Bankruptcy

Involuntary bankruptcy may require the services of an appraiser both to value the real estate and to testify to its market value in court. These appraisal assignments are identical in nature to the *before value estimate* made in a condemnation assignment. An appraisal assignment, in conjunction with bankruptcy, often comes about when a creditor attempts to force a debtor into bankruptcy, claiming that the debtor is insolvent, i.e., the debtor owes more than the total value of all of his assets. If the debtor contests the bankruptcy, the value of the real estate owned by the debtor becomes quite important because it may determine the debtor's solvency.

Removal of Lateral Support

A situation requiring the services of an appraiser may occur when an abutting, downhill property owner removes the lateral support necessary to stabilize the abutting, uphill owner's property, thereby causing the uphill property to slide and damage the uphill land and/or improvements. Figure 20.3 depicts the *before* and *after* situation in such an instance. An excavation on the downhill ownership caused a portion of the uphill ownership to become unstable and begin to slide, causing damage to the uphill land and buildings. In such a situation the appraiser's function is to appraise the uphill ownership before the excavation and after the excavation and subsequent slide; the difference between the two values is the amount of damage suffered by the uphill owner.

Often, the appraiser will need to retain a consulting engineer to determine whether the area of the slide can be stabilized and, if so, at what cost. From the illustration shown in Figure 20.3, a soils engineer and a structural engineer concluded that constructing a properly designed, concrete retaining wall at the toe of the excavation would restabilize the area. Cost estimates on constructing the retaining wall and repairing the damage to the uphill land and dwelling were obtained by the appraiser. It was concluded that these costs were less than the diminution in the value of the uphill property which would be suffered if the corrective work were not undertaken. Therefore, the appraiser was correct in using a *cost to cure* adjustment to estimate the property's after value. The computations might be presented as follows:

Before value		$50,000
After value:		
Before value	$50,000	
Cost of retaining wall	− 10,000	
Cost to repair landscaping	− 500	
Cost to repair dwelling	− 2,500	
After value		− 37,000
Difference between before & after values		$13,000

There are two factors to be considered when appraising a property that has become subject to movement. First, the appraiser must be sure that the *cost to cure* adjustment factor, as illustrated above, includes *all* cost to cure items, including an *entrepreneurial profit factor.* This factor was described earlier in this work.[7]

The other factor to be considered by the appraiser is whether the fact that the property once had a sliding problem will affect the property's value, even after the slide condition is physically corrected. Also, there will be considerable divergency, at times, between the opinions of different soils engineers. One might say that a slide can be stabilized for $1,000, and another may say that the cost to stabilize the area is greater than the appraiser's estimate of the property's before value. The appraiser should accept neither opinion blindly. Often, a diligent search of sale records will reveal the sale of a property similar to the one under

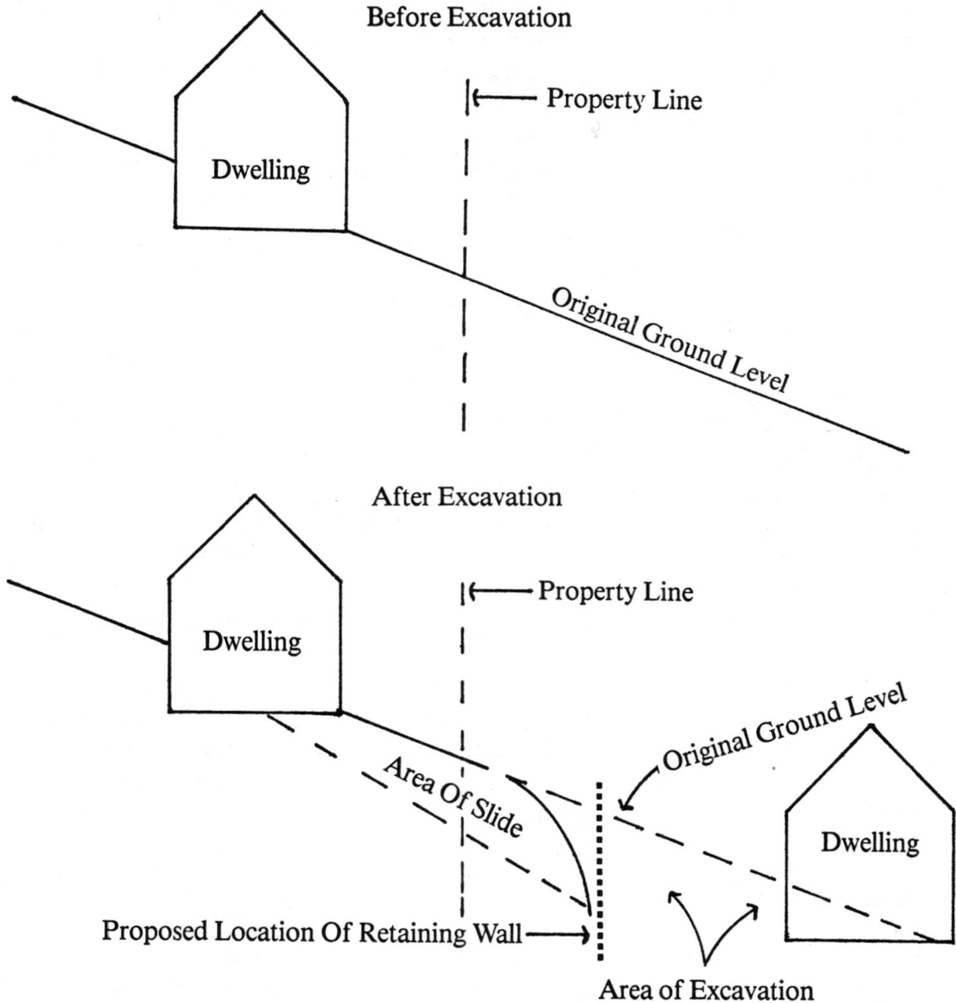

**Figure 20.3. Cross Section—Before Excavation and
After Excavation**

appraisal, which also has a propensity for sliding. This sale property can then be compared with comparable properties not subject to slides, using the matched pairs technique of analysis, to arrive at the diminution in value due to the possibility of future sliding. Even if the properties studied are not highly similar to the one under appraisal or in the same geographical area, their analysis can still be of assistance to the appraiser in making a proper adjustment for the potential sliding on the property being appraised.

The situation shown in Figure 20.3 illustrates that the corrective retaining wall is actually to be constructed on the *downhill owner's property*. In this particular case, the downhill owner was the defendant in the case because his excavating action caused the slide; therefore, the downhill owner offered the uphill owner an easement to construct and maintain the wall as a means of mitigating the total damages to the uphill owner's property. However, this is a unique situation. Generally, the appraiser cannot assume a stabilization project which would involve construction work on any property other than the parcel being appraised. If the slide condition cannot physically be corrected by measures wholly within the boundaries of the subject property, it must be assumed that the property cannot be stabilized.

A slide condition can be caused by factors other than the removal of lateral support. For instance, the construction activity of an uphill owner, such as the paving of previously open ground for a parking lot, can increase the amount or velocity of groundwater running onto the downhill owner's property, thereby oversaturating the soil and causing a slide. The unintentional diversion of a natural water course can have the same result. Similarly, the intentional diversion of a water course can cause damage to the land of a downhill owner and, although such intentional diversion is construed as intentional trespass and is therefore a criminal act, the uphill owner remains liable to the downhill owner for any damages caused.

Whatever the reason for a slide, the damage caused by a slide or by an increase or diversion of a water course is generally measured by the difference between the market value of the property before and after the damage. Therefore, the appraisal methodology applied in federal, partial taking, condemnation actions would also apply in these instances.

Foreclosures

Under normal circumstances, an appraiser will not be involved in a foreclosure action in a manner that will require testimony. In general, the appraiser will only be asked to appraise a property for a lien holder so that the holder can determine the advisability of starting a foreclosure action. However, some jurisdictions provide for the establishment of an *upset bid prices* in a judicial foreclosure. An upset bid price is the minimum amount for which a property can be sold in a foreclosure sale. This price is established to protect any junior lien holders and/or the underlying fee owner.

For instance, assume a property has a market value of $50,000 and is encumbered by a first mortgage of $10,000 and a second mortgage of $2,000; this leaves the underlying fee owner with an equity of $38,000. Without an upset bid price, the first-position lien holder could foreclose its lien and bid in the property at

$10,000, leaving the junior lien holder and the underlying fee owner *out in the cold*.

When a junior lien holder or the underlying fee owner asks the court to set an *upset bid price,* the appraiser may be required to testify. The appraiser will estimate the market value of the property and testify to his estimate. This testimony gives the court a foundation on which to base an upset bid price; in the foregoing example, this price might be in the neighborhood of $35,000.

Private Way of Necessity

A *private way of necessity* is a situation recognized in many jurisdictions. This type of lawsuit may arise in a situation like the one illustrated in Figure 20.4. Parcel B is legally landlocked, and the only practical access to Parcel B is through Parcel A. If the owner of Parcel A refuses to give or sell, at a reasonable price, an easement for ingress and egress to the owner of Parcel B, the owner of Parcel B may bring a suit against the owner of Parcel A to force an access easement across Parcel A to Parcel B. In effect, the owner of Parcel B is given the limited right of eminent domain in this particular situation. Along with this right, the owner of Parcel B acquires the obligation of paying the owner of Parcel A for the taking of the easement area and for any damages to the remainder of Parcel A caused by the taking and the proposed use of the easement.

In appraising a property for a private way of necessity, the appraiser proceeds as he would in a typical condemnation action. In the foregoing example, the owner of Parcel B is the condemnor and the owner of Parcel A is the condemnee. The appraiser must remember that the important factors are the estimate of the market value of Parcel A before the taking, the estimate of the market value of Parcel A after the taking, and the difference between the two estimates. The amount by which the new easement enhances the value of Parcel B is of no consequence.

Usually, a private way of necessity is limited in use. For instance, it may be limited to use for ingress and egress to one single-family dwelling on Parcel B, or it may be limited to use for ingress and egress of logging equipment to harvest the timber on Parcel B. In the second case, the easement for the private way may be extinguished once the harvesting is complete.

The key difference between an appraisal for a private way of necessity and an appraisal in a regular condemnation action is that the party obtaining the private way of necessity will not have all the facts when he first contacts the appraiser. He will not know exactly where the easement will go across the neighboring tract, the width, surface, or finished grade of the proposed private way, or whether any drainage problems will be caused by the proposed construction; if there is a drainage problem, he will not know how it will be corrected. The amount of detail

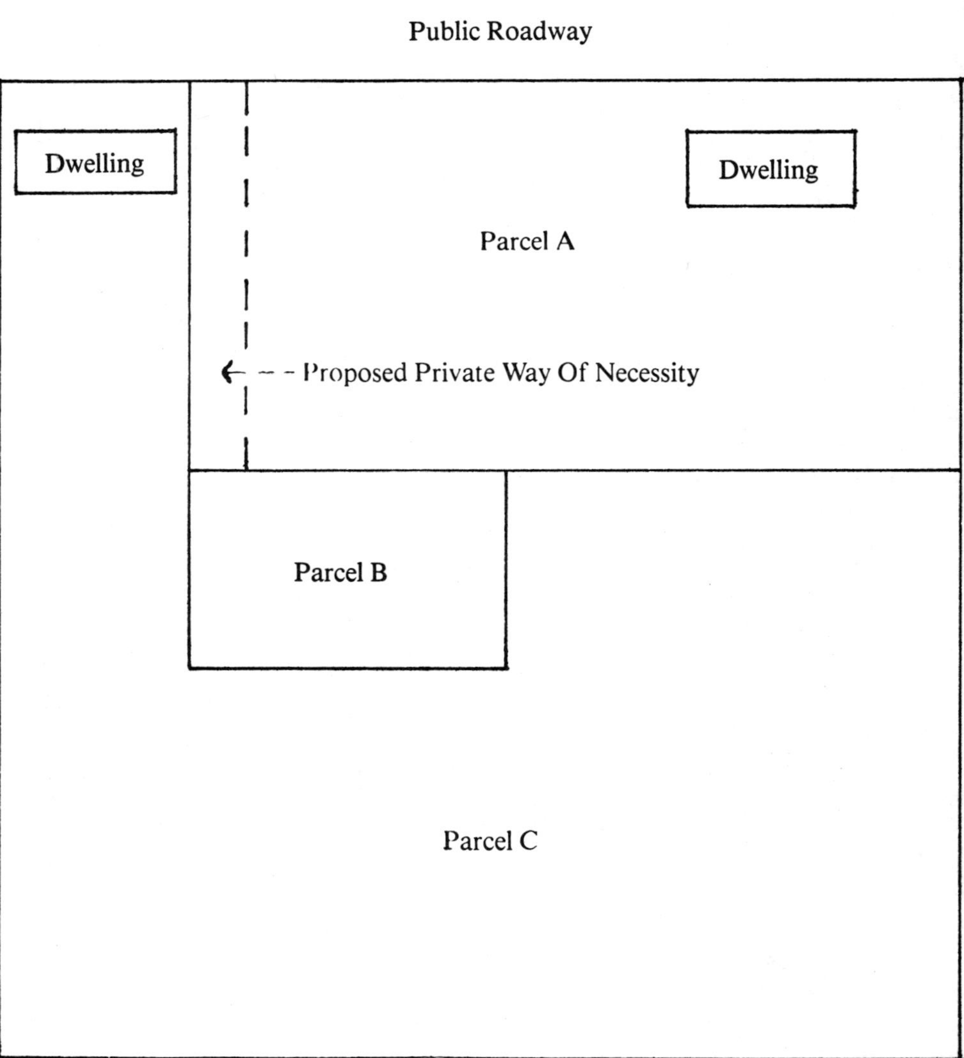

Figure 20.4. Private Way of Necessity

needed by the appraiser will vary from case to case. Nevertheless, the appraiser should develop a complete list of the data needed to complete the appraisal so that these data can be developed by or through the individual obtaining the private way.

Partitionment

A litigation to partition a parcel of property is generally caused by the termination of a partnership, a divorce, or the division of property in an estate. In a partitionment case, the appraiser's assignment is often twofold in nature. First, the appraiser must estimate the value of the whole property as a single entity, as he would for the before valuation in a condemnation case. Then, the appraiser should make a hypothetical division of the property into two parcels of equal value, or into several parcels representing specified percentages of the aggregate value of the total property.

In other words, if the title to the property being appraised is held by a two-person partnership, and each partner has a 50% interest in the partnership, the appraiser would determine how the property could be physically split into two independent parcels of equal value. If a number of persons hold interests in the property to be partitioned, and/or their interests are unequal, the appraiser's job of economically partitioning the property becomes more complex. An example of such an assignment might be the appraisal of a property owned by a four-person partnership or estate, with the partners, or heirs, holding interests of 36%, 26%, 26%, and 12%. Once the appraiser has completed the hypothetical partitionment, he must estimate the market value of each of the partitioned segments of the whole property as separate and distinct entities.

Each step of the appraiser's partitionment assignment will furnish the court with information needed to make a logical and equitable ruling. Sometimes it is physically and/or legally impossible to partition a property in direct proportion to the various interests held. If the interests in a property are 36%, 26%, 26%, and 12%, as previously stipulated, and the property is a large tract of timberland, a partitionment that is both physically and legally equitable can probably be made. However, if the property is a single commercial building, partitionment will not be possible. In such an instance, the court will generally use the appraiser's estimate of the market value of the whole property and order the property to be sold, with the proceeds of the sale divided according to the various interests in the property.

At first glance, it may seem unnecessary to estimate the actual market value of each partitioned portion of the total parcel so long as the proportionment can physically and legally be made, and the market values of the various partitioned parcels coincide with their percentage of interest in the whole parcel. However, in some instances an economic hardship can arise due to the partitionment, even though the partitionment can legally and physically be made. For instance, assume the previous example of a large tract of timberland with ownership interests of 36%, 26%, 26%, and 12%. Further assume that the tract contains 200 acres and has a value of $600,000 before partitionment. It is quite possible, under such circumstances, that the aggregate value of the partitioned parcels would be considerably less than the value of a whole property before partitionment.

Assuming there is a direct relationship between the value of each acre of the tract and the total value of the tract (e.g., each and every acre is worth $3,000), the partitionment will result in four independent ownerships of 72 acres, 52 acres, 52 acres, and 24 acres. It is quite possible that the value of these four parcels will not equal the value of the whole property before partitionment. The cost of moving logging equipment into the area and setting up a logging operation will be the same, whether 24 acres, 72 acres, or 200 acres are to be logged. Therefore, the setup cost will have to be spread over the smaller acreages created by the partitionment, rather than the original 200-acre tract. In fact, it is quite possible that it would not be economically feasible to log the 24-acre parcel as a separate entity at all.

For the abovementioned reasons, the court must know the aggregate market value of all the partitioned tracts so it can compare the value of the whole property with the aggregate value of the partitioned parcels and determine whether the partitionment creates an unreasonable economic hardship for one or more of the individuals holding interests in the property. If an economic hardship is created, the court will often reject the partitionment and will order that the property be sold as a single entity, with the proceeds of sale split among the various owners of the property in proportion to their ownership interests.

Determining exactly how to partition a property is probably the most difficult part of the appraiser's assignment. The appraiser often uses trial and error, drawing different lines of partitionment and appraising the partitioned parcels as if they were remainder parcels in a condemnation proceeding. The appraiser must adjust the line, or lines, of partitionment until the proper interest-to-property-value ratio is achieved. The specific location of the dividing line or lines finally selected by the appraiser is often the subject of severe cross-examination. The appraiser should be prepared for such cross-examination and readily admit that, as a general rule, the property in question could be partitioned in a number of different ways and still maintain the proper ratio of interest to value.

Construction Faults

On occasion, an appraiser is asked to appraise a property recently improved with a building, which was not constructed in accordance with the building specifications and/or applicable building codes. Often, this type of assignment will require the assistance of a structural engineer, a mechanical engineer, or an electrical engineer, depending on the specific deficiency of construction.

Such an appraisal assignment is identical in nature to a partial taking in a condemnation case. The before value of the property is estimated, assuming that the improvement was constructed in strict adherence to the building specifications and all applicable building codes. The after value of the property is then estimated with the improvements in their *as is* condition. The difference between the before and after values is the damage suffered by the property owner. In many instances, the loss of value caused by a construction deficiency can be measured by the cost to cure the deficiency. If this is so, the appraiser's assignment is comparatively easy. When a construction deficiency cannot economically be cured, the appraisal assignment becomes more complex.

Consider an appraisal assignment in which the *cost to cure* a deficiency plays a major role. Figure 20.5 is a plot plan of a single-family dwelling constructed under contract. In locating the dwelling and the attached garage on the site, the contractor measured the minimum required front yard setback incorrectly and situated the 20 ft. × 24 ft. garage only 18 feet from the front lot line, instead of the required 25 feet. The building inspector did not notice the error until construction was complete and an occupancy permit was requested. The permit was

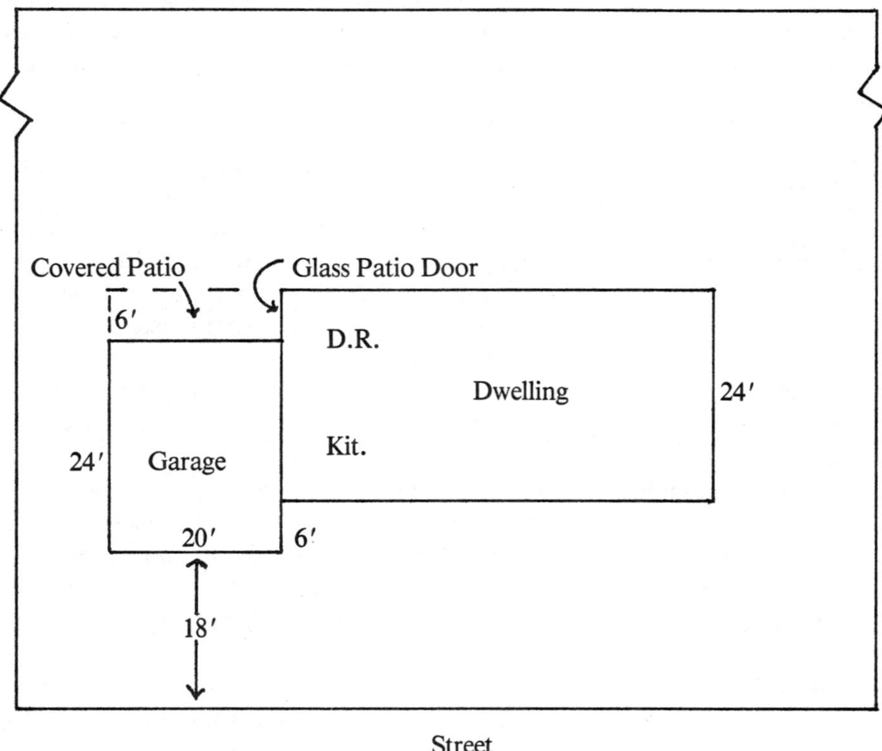

Figure 20.5. Non-Conforming Setback

denied and the contractor applied to the local board of adjustment for a variance to the front yard setback. The variance was also denied and the owner was ordered to remove the 6-ft. encroachment of the garage from the minimum 25-ft. front yard setback.

The options available in this case involved cost to cure versus diminution in value decisions. The options included:

1. Remove six feet of garage and leave an 18-ft. deep garage. (18-ft. deep garages don't hold much market appeal.)
2. Remove six feet off the front of the garage and extend the garage six feet to the rear, eliminating the patio and relocating or removing the sliding glass doors.
3. Remove the garage entirely.
4. Convert the remaining 18-ft. garage into a recreation room.

Each of these options was analyzed by the appraiser in terms of its cost and its impact on the market value of the property. Figure 20.6 illustrates the option selected. The garage was extended to the rear, the patio was uncovered, and the sliding glass doors were relocated. This option could be completed at the least dollar amount of the aggregate of the cost to make the construction alteration, plus the diminution of value between the property's before value and its value after alteration.

Now, consider another example which creates a more complex problem for the appraiser. A two-story, single-family dwelling was constructed on contract for about $200,000. As is too often the case, the plans and specifications of this single-family dwelling were quite sketchy, but the dwelling was constructed in an area with standard building codes. After the construction was completed, an occupancy permit was granted and the owners began to move into the dwelling. While attempting to move a large dresser into the second-floor master bedroom, the new owners learned that the stairway from the first to the second floor was exceptionally narrow. Upon further investigation, it was learned that the stairway was six inches narrower than the minimum width specified by the applicable building code.

After the appraiser inspected the property and discussed the problem with several contractors, it became obvious that the stairway could not economically be widened to the minimum acceptable width. Therefore, the appraiser concluded that any diminution in the property's market value caused by the narrow stairway would have to be measured by market data. The before value of the property was estimated as if the stairway was of minimum code width, and the after value estimate of the property was made in its *as is* condition. The appraiser was able to find a number of sales of comparable properties which had stairways, from the first to the second floor, of adequate width to meet the building code, so the *before value* of the property was easily estimated.

However, being quite familiar with the market area, the appraiser knew that

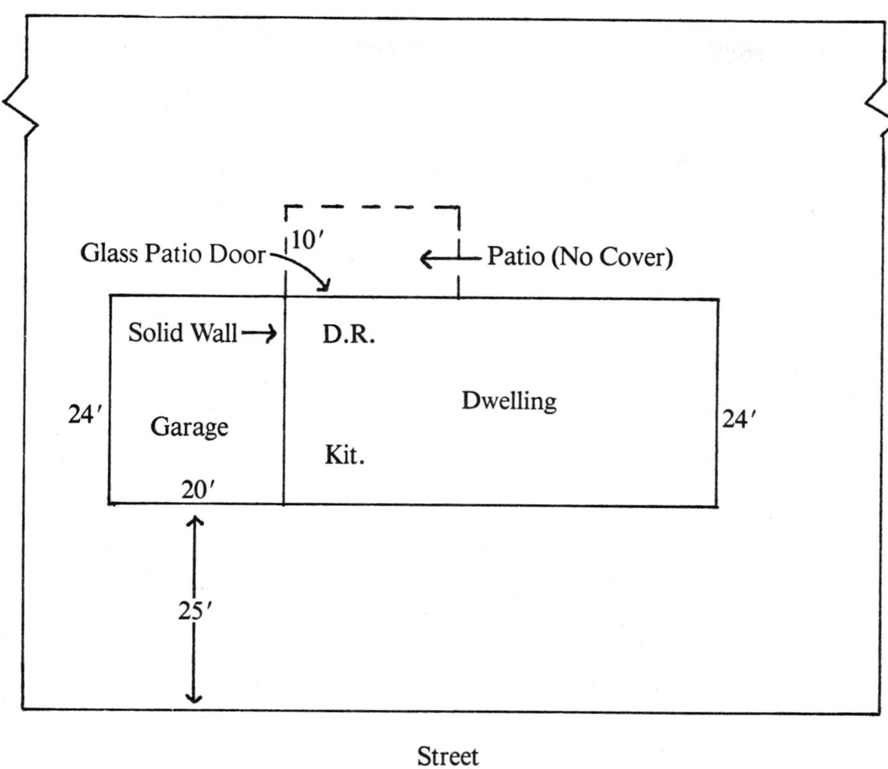

Figure 20.6. Conforming Setback

there would not be many recent sales of comparable, newer two-story houses in the $200,000 price range with stairways six inches narrower than required by the building code. Although the appraiser found the contractor's opinion that no damage was caused by the narrow stairway a bit unrealistic, he also found the owner's contention that the property was damaged in the amount of $50,000 just a wee bit on the high side. Therefore, the appraiser resorted to the classic *matched pairs technique* to arrive at a proper and supportable adjustment for the narrow stairway.

Sales of older, two-story dwellings were investigated. Many of these homes were built before the adoption of the building code, and some had stairways that were narrower than the minimum width required by the current building code. Recent sales of older dwellings with narrow stairways were compared to sales of similar, older homes with wider stairways. From this matched pairs analysis, the appraiser was able to develop a percentage of the diminution in the value of second-floor space caused by narrow stairways. For example, second-floor space might sell for the same price per square foot as first-floor space if the second-floor space is served by a stairway of adequate width; second-floor space served by a narrow stairway, however, might sell for only 85% of the square foot price of the first-floor space.

Using the matched pairs technique often enables an appraiser to develop a measurable and supportable adjustment for the unusual or unique features of a property. It would, of course, be preferable to make a direct comparison between a sale property and the property under appraisal, but, in litigation appraising, the appraiser will often encounter situations which are simply one of a kind. These cases require the appraiser to use some ingenuity in developing a measurable and supportable method of arriving at proper adjustment factors.

Appraiser's Negligence

"As happens in any profession, the conduct or performance of an appraiser occasionally falls short of the standards established by the profession or the expectations of society at large. When such a situation is discovered, it normally is policed satisfactorily within the 'fraternity.' Now and then, however, an appraiser will find himself/herself unhappily defending a lawsuit brought by an equally unhappy employer, client, or other seemingly aggrieved person."[8] This type of litigation is becoming more and more prevalent. If an appraiser steps through the bathroom floor while inspecting a dwelling being appraised, including a limiting condition in the written report which says "It has been assumed that the subject property is free from structural defects and rot," is not going to relieve the appraiser from liability.

A discussion of appraisers' liability for errors in their work product is beyond the scope of this work.[9] It is how such liability is measured that is important here. In some liability cases, appraisers are not required as expert witnesses because the measure of liability is not based on a diminution or difference in value. For instance, in one case an appraiser was retained to furnish the client with an appraisal for mortgage loan purposes. The appraiser made a computational error, which was found several months later, before the loan was closed. The court ruled that the appraiser was liable for the cost incurred by the client, in reference to the appraised property, between the date of the first report and the date of the corrected report; these costs amounted to $256,250.01.[10]

Many appraiser liability cases do require appraisal services because the measure of damage is the difference between the market value of the property as described (and/or certified) by the appraiser and the market value of the property in its *as is* condition.[11] It has been ruled that *cost to cure* is admissible as some evidence of diminished value, but this cost is not necessarily the controlling factor.[12]

In liability cases, as in condemnation trials, the *cost to cure* is a proper measure of damage when it does not exceed the diminution in market value.

Like many appraisals made in conjunction with pending litigation, appraisals made for appraiser negligence cases are identical to appraisals made for condemnation trials using the federal, or before and after, rule. The appraiser assumes the property existed in the before situation as described by the defendant-appraiser in his appraisal report. The after appraisal estimates the property's value in its actual, *as is* condition.

Ad Valorem Taxation

It has been stated previously that the ownership of real estate carries with it inherent rights, commonly referred to as the bundle of rights.[13] The bundle of rights is limited because certain rights are retained by the sovereign, including the sovereign's right of taxation.

Over the years, ownership of real estate has, at least in the eyes of the public, become synonymous with wealth, and, of course, there is no more fertile area to collect taxes than from the wealthy. Ad valorem (meaning according to value) real estate taxation is a natural extension of this philosophy. An appraiser is often asked by the assessing authority, or by a property owner, to appraise a property and to testify to its value for ad valorem tax purposes. All ad valorem taxing authorities work from a base figure of *market value*. In some jurisdictions, the assessed value is 100% of market value, while in others the assessed value is ". . . a statutorily determined percentage of market value."[14]

The procedure to be followed in appealing an assessor's determination of value will vary from jurisdiction to jurisdiction. Generally, however, the appraiser who has completed an appraisal for the property owner should ask for a conference with the assessor and the appraiser who estimated the value of the property for the assessor. If such an informal conference can be held before the assessment roll is closed, the appraiser may be able to convince the assessor that his value estimate is correct and that the prior assessed value of the property should be abandoned in favor of this new value estimate.

One reason such a conference can be effective is that the assessed value of a property is usually arrived at by mass appraisal procedures, giving considerable weight to the cost approach, sometimes to the complete exclusion of the market data and income approaches. The appraiser's estimate of value, on the other hand, has been tailored to the individual property using all approaches to value, and the conclusion is probably much better documented than the original assessed value. Another reason such a conference can be effective is that the assessor is much more likely to admit and correct an error in the privacy of his own office than he would be if he must defend the original assessed value before a hearing board.

Even if the assessment roll is closed, and the assessor cannot change the roll unless ordered to do so by a hearing board or board of equalization, a prehearing conference can still be effective. If the assessor is convinced that the appraiser's value estimate is correct, the assessor can join in the owner's request to the board of equalization, and the assessed value can be altered to coincide with the appraiser's estimate of value.

For an appraiser/assessor conference to be effective, the appraiser must, of course, have a good working relationship with the local assessor. To develop and maintain such a relationship, the appraiser must never be an advocate of anything other than his opinion of value. Also, the appraiser must treat the assessor with professional courtesy and realize that the assessor, like himself, only wants to find the right answer. If someone is going to allege incompetence on the part of the assessor, let the attorney do it during the hearing process. In fact, it is generally best that the attorney not discuss the matter with the assessor until the hearing, or at least not until shortly before the hearing. It is generally more effective to keep the discussions on a nonadvocate, appraiser-to-appraiser basis, at least until all hope of convincing the assessor is extinguished.

The appraisal of real estate for ad valorem tax purposes is a straightforward estimate of market value. The only change in procedure required of the appraiser is in the application of the income approach. It is not possible to arrive at a *stabilized net income* from the operation of the property in question because one of the major expenses of owning the property is its real estate taxes, and these taxes remain unknown so long as the assessed value of the property is in contention. Therefore, the appraiser must estimate the net income of the property before payment of real estate taxes and then add the real estate tax factor to the overall capitalization rate to arrive at an indicated value of the property by the income approach.

For example, assume that analysis indicates that an overall rate of return for properties similar to the one being appraised is 11%. Further assume that real estate taxes on these properties are about $18.50 per $1,000 of market value. If the property being appraised is producing a net income, before payment of real estate taxes, of $15,000 per year, the indicated value of the property will be approximately $116,700, computed as follows:

Overall capitalization rate	.1100
Tax rate ($18.50 ÷ $1,000)	.0185
Total rate to be applied to net income before real estate taxes	.1285
Indicated property value ($15,000 net income before payment of real estate taxes ÷ .1285)	$116,000

These calculations can be proven by deducting the real estate tax expense from the net income, before payment of real estate taxes, to arrive at a true net income; this net income is then capitalized at the 11% overall rate indicated by market data. The computations would be:

Net income before real estate taxes	$15,000
Real estate taxes ($116.732 thousand	
× $18.50)	2,160
Net income	$12,840
Indicated property value ($12,840 ÷ .11)	$116,727
Rounded	$116,700

Hearing and appeal procedures will vary, but usually an initial hearing is held before a local hearing board or board of equalization. The decision of this board can generally be appealed by either party to a state hearing examiner or a state tax appeals board; the final appeal is made to the court.

Estate Taxes

The estate or wealth of a deceased person is also taxed according to value; these taxes are commonly referred to as *death taxes*. Real estate is, of course, included in the assets of many estates.

Estate, or death, taxes are a percentage of the market value of the assets of an estate. Therefore, the appraiser's assignment is generally a straightforward estimate of market value. It is critical that the appraiser determine the desired *effective date* of the appraisal. The heirs have the option of having the assets of the estate valued as of the date of death, or as of six months after the date of death. Although the value of most real property will not change materially over a six-month period, there are some exceptions. For instance, in one case the value of 600 acres of harvestable timberland declined more than 20% between the owner's death and six months thereafter, due to a rapid decline in the stumpage value of the timber on the tract.

Local Improvement Districts

Local government agencies have also found the taxation of real estate to be an effective method of financing local improvement projects. This type of real estate taxation is often referred to as a *special assessment* and is limited to property within a specifically created taxing district, known as a *local improvement district*, or LID.

The local improvement district is a public agency's means of financing an improvement project by assessing the property owners directly affected by the project. This type of assessment is made within the government's power of taxation, not under its power of eminent domain.[15] In some states, the amount of the assessment cannot exceed the benefit accruing to the property,[16] while in other states the only criterion appears to be that the cost of the project be assessed on all of the parcels in the local improvement district in proportion to some equitable ratio, such as per square foot, per acre, per front foot, zone and termini, or assessed value. Some jurisdictions specify by statute the methods of cost proportionment that are equitable and/or defensible.

For instance, in specifying the zone and termini method of assessment, a Washington statute states, "the cost and expenses shall be assessed upon all the property in accordance with the special benefits conferred thereon in proportion to area and distance back from the marginal line of the public way or area improved."[17] The area within the district is divided into zones radiating from the improvements, and each zone is assessed at a different rate. For example, consider three parcels in an LID as shown in Figure 20.7. If the boundary of the LID is 200 feet from the street, and four zones are designated by the municipality, the assessment might be computed at $1.00 per square foot in Zone 1, 75¢ per square foot in Zone 2, 50¢ per square foot in Zone 3, and 25¢ per square foot in Zone 4. The results of this assessment would be calculated as follows:

Zone	Parcel 1	Parcel 2	Parcel 3
1	$2,500	$2,500	$2,500
2	1,875	1,875	1,875
3	1,250	0	1,250
4	125	0	625
Total assessments	$5,750	$4,375	$6,250

This formula is similar to the outdated 4-3-2-1 rule historically used by tax assessors.

The appraiser is most likely to be involved in this type of situation in jurisdictions that require that the special benefit to a property equal or exceed the special assessment placed on the property. The measure of benefit is, again, identical to the before and after valuation procedures for federal condemnation.

Income Tax

In addition to the ad valorem taxes assessed directly against real estate, any in-

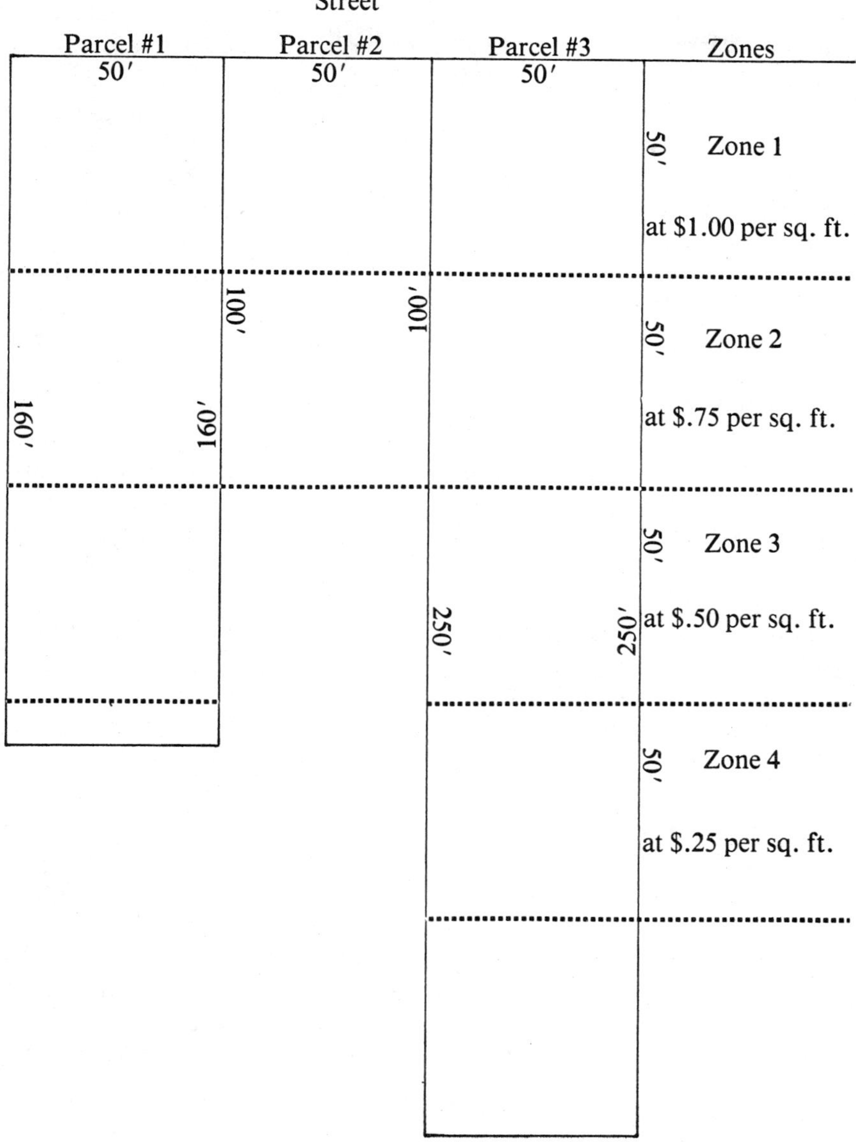

Figure 20.7. Local Improvement District Assessment—Zone and Termini Method

come generated by real estate is subject to taxation through the real estate owner's income tax. Therefore, real estate valuation decisions are also necessary in conjunction with applicable income tax regulations.

The appraiser's function, in regard to income tax, is generally in the area of cost allocation, or the estimate of economic life, rather than in estimating market value. Economic life estimates are made to establish a term for depreciation. Appraisers may also become involved in allocating the cost of the real estate between land and improvements for depreciation purposes, or an appraiser may be asked to allocate a property's value between various parts of the larger parcel. This becomes necessary when an owner purchases a parcel of real estate and then resells a portion of it. The allocation is then used in determining the owner's *cost basis* in that portion of the tract sold.

An appraiser might also be retained to estimate a casualty loss suffered by a property owner. Casualty losses generally result from fire, flood damage, wind damage, and other natural phenomena. If the property owner is not reimbursed by an insurance company for such a loss, the loss can be taken as a deduction for income tax purposes. The appraiser's assignment is to estimate the market value of the property before and after the loss. This procedure is identical to the before and after appraisal made in federal condemnation proceedings.

An appraiser may also be retained in a dispute between a taxpayer and the Internal Revenue Service. For instance, assume a taxpayer purchased a tract of swampland for speculation. After two years of land-use hearings, the taxpayer was given a permit to use the site for dumping solid waste. The land was about 25 feet below grade and had a considerable capacity for such material. The taxpayer then entered into a contract with a local logging firm to pick up and dispose of its solid wood waste on the land.

The taxpayer deducted the depreciation and maintenance of equipment, the wages paid to truck drivers and equipment operators, etc., as business expenses for federal income tax purposes. During a routine audit, the Internal Revenue Service ruled that not all these expenses could be deducted; they considered half of the expenses as *capital improvements* to the land being filled with wood waste. The taxpayer was unable to sway the Internal Revenue Service, so he retained an appraiser and asked that two appraisals of the property be made: 1) an estimate of the market value of the site as if no wood waste had been placed on it; and 2) an estimate of the market value of the site and its *as is* condition, which was with about 12 feet of wood waste fill.

The procedure followed by the appraiser was identical to that used in a before and after appraisal for a federal condemnation case. The appraiser found that local land-use authorities would not allow any construction on the site once it was filled because of the nature of the fill material, which had a tendency to throw off dangerous gases as it decayed. Analysis of market sales of similar disposal sites indicated that the site being appraised did not increase in value as it was filled, as the Internal Revenue Service contended, but rather declined in value as it was filled. Based on these findings, the Internal Revenue Service reversed its ruling; in fact, the taxpayer was able to amend past tax returns to reflect the declining value of the waste site as it was being filled.

Often, only a written appraisal report is required in conjunction with income tax matters. However, on occasion the appraiser may be asked to discuss the appraisal with a tax auditor, or to appear in tax court as an expert witness.

Land-Use Hearings

Included in the bundle of rights inherent in the ownership of real estate is the owner's right of use and occupancy. However, the sovereign has reserved, through the use of its police power, the right to control how the owner of a parcel of real estate uses it.[18] The government's control of land use is generally effected by the adoption of land-use regulations intended to protect the public's health, safety, and general welfare. In other words, land-use regulations effectively place the owner's right to use his land in a subservient position to the interests of the general public. Therefore, public land-use regulations can have an immediate and dramatic impact on real estate values.

Land-use regulations are intended, at least in theory, to maintain and protect real estate values. This is in the public interest because the higher the real estate values, the more taxes can be collected. However, land-use regulations are written by *people* and do not always produce the desired effect. Therefore, appraisers are sometimes called upon to appraise individual properties which have been affected by a land-use regulation or may be affected by a proposed land-use regulation in the future. The appraiser also may be asked to analyze and estimate the probable impact of a proposed land-use regulation on a specific property and to testify as to his conclusions before the initial decision-making body, an appeal board, or even a court.

Appraisers are increasingly being requested to become involved in land-use matters and to testify at land-use hearings. These requests can come from proponents of a proposed land-use matter, opponents of a proposed land-use matter, or from the individuals or agencies empowered to act on such matters.

The appraiser is more often asked to make a general analysis of a proposed land-use regulation's impact on real estate values, than to make an estimate of the market value of a specific parcel of real estate before and after the adoption of a specific land-use regulation. A decision-making body might typically request an analysis of how the value of abutting or nearby single-family dwellings may be affected by a funeral home in a residential neighborhood. The results of such an analysis may assist a planning commission in determining whether it should allow funeral homes to locate in residential areas without any special permit, by special-use permit only, or not at all. Generalized appraisal studies may relate to zoning decisions, shorelines management decisions, board of adjustment decisions, comprehensive land-use planning decisions, forest practices decisions, etc.

Many govermental subdivisions are now requiring that *economic impact statements* as well as *environmental impact statements* be prepared for major real estate projects. In preparing an economic impact statement, the appraiser might be requested to estimate the market value of the real estate project as if complete. This will help determine increases in the area's real estate tax base and, thus, the increase in the area's ad valorem tax income. The appraiser might also be asked to analyze similar projects to determine their impact on surrounding land values. In addition, the appraiser may be requested to assist in estimating the potential gross sales of a proposed commercial project so that an assessment can be made of the possible increase in sales, business and occupation, income, or other applicable taxes.

Most land-use actions require a public hearing. Whether or not the appraiser has submitted a written report to the client, the appraiser will generally be asked to make an oral presentation of his findings at the public hearing. This is assuming, of course, that the appraiser's findings and conclusions support the client's position.

Summary

It would be impossible to list all the different types of civil litigation in which real estate appraisal services might be required. Those discussed here are a mere sampling of the types of situations in which an appraiser might be asked to make an appraisal and to testify at a hearing or civil proceeding. Even when a court is hearing a case of appraiser negligence and liability, real estate appraisers are still needed to make appraisals and to testify in court.

It can be seen by the foregoing sampling that a pattern emerges as to how the measure of damage in litigation cases is determined. Nearly all such cases rely upon the market value of the property before the damage, less the market value of the property after the damage, to represent the award equitably due complainants in such cases.

Due to the unique nature of some civil litigation cases involving real estate, the appraiser cannot expect to find all the answers in this, or any other, text. Occasionally, the appraiser will be faced with an appraisal problem for which there are no written rules of procedure. It is then that the appraiser must use his imagination, ingenuity, and common sense; this is the appraiser's real challenge, this is where he really earns his fee. Before applying any new and imaginative methodology, however, the appraiser should discuss his plans with another qualified appraiser. In this way, he can test its validity before it sees the light of day, or the dark corridors of the courthouse.

Notes

1. *The Appraisal of Real Estate,* 7th ed. (Chicago: American Institute of Real Estate Appraisers, 1978), Appendix B, Compound Interest Tables, 8% Monthly, Column 4, p. 566.
2. Ibid.
3. State v. Johnson, 265 A.2d. 711 (Me.).
4. See Chapter 3, "Property Rights."
5. Chapter 78-85, Laws of Florida.
6. "Statutory Attempts to Protect Private Property Rights," National Association of Realtors, 1981, p. 1.
7. See Chapter 7, "Cost Approach."
8. Stanley J. Fineman, "Law and the Appraiser," *The Appraisal Journal,* October 1981, p. 603.
9. See Ibid., pp. 603-611 for a discussion of appraiser liability.
10. Breckenridge Hotels Corp. v. Real Estate Research Corp., 452 F.Supp. 529.
11. Larsen v. United Federal Savings and Loan Association of Des Moines, No. 238/64765 (S.Ct. Iowa, 1/14/81). Footnote 3, p. 611, 10/81 *Appraisal Journal.*
12. Alva v. Cloninger, 277 S.E.2d 535 (N.C.).
13. See Chapter 3, "Property Rights."
14. American Institute of Real Estate Appraisers and the Society of Real Estate Appraisers, *Real Estate Appraisal Terminology,* rev. ed., Byrl N. Boyce, ed. (Cambridge, Mass.: Ballinger Publishing Co., 1981), p. 19.
15. Fallbrook Irr. Dist. v. Bradley, 164 U.S. 112, 17 S.Ct. 46.
16. Waitaker & Co. v. Sewer Improvement District No. 1, 221 F.2d 649.
17. R.C.W. 35.44.010 (Wash.).
18. See Chapter 3, "Property Rights."

CHAPTER 21
STANDARDS OF PRACTICE

Real estate is one of the basic sources of wealth and its proper use is essential to the economic well-being of any society. If real estate is to be properly used, however, it is essential that business organizations, governmental bodies, individuals and others who own, manage, sell, purchase, invest in and lend money on the security of real estate have ready access to the services of men and women of integrity and independent judgment who are capable of properly valuing and evaluating real estate and making sound determinations as to the manner in which it can or should be used.

The proper valuation and evaluation of real estate and the making of sound determinations concerning its utilization are essential to the orderly growth and development of cities, suburbs and rural areas. In addition, the proper valuation, evaluation and utilization of real estate gives stability to real estate loans and investments and this in turn helps to promote public confidence in the economy that sustains a free society.

. . . .

In a complex, modern society, the professional real estate appraiser often performs a variety of functions and services. In addition to making valuations of individual parcels or tracts of real estate (or interests in real estate) and preparing valuation appraisal reports, the professional real estate appraiser often makes evaluations of real estate (or interests in real estate), renders advice in the form of real estate counseling and prepares evaluation appraisal reports relating to such problems as the highest and best use of a particular parcel or tract of real estate or the marketability or feasibility of a proposed real estate development. These various functions and services require a professional real estate appraiser to make his or her determinations and exercise his or her judgment in a wide variety of complex conceptual and factual situations. . . . Without guidelines to assist the appraiser in resolving the complex ethical questions involved in a modern appraisal practice, the complexity of the ethical problems involved would place an intolerable burden upon a conscientious professional real estate appraiser.[1]

The American Institute of Real Estate Appraisers' Code of Professional Ethics defines the minimum level of conduct below which no member or candidate may fall without being subject to disciplinary proceedings. Ethics can be related to rules governing personal actions, actions within the Institute, and actions with the public. "Ethics, by definition, are standards imposed on persons presumed from the outset to be honest."[2] A code of ethics "cannot make an honest appraiser out of a dishonest one. But codes of ethics . . . never were intended for that purpose."[3] The Institute's Standards of Professional Practice define the minimum level of appraisal performance required of members and candidates; they are in a continual state of change due to the development of new theory and technique.

A code of ethics and written standards of practice are not established to restrict a professional's activities, but rather to help professionals understand the minimum standards expected of them by society as a whole and by other members of the profession. But, "in the final analysis, it is a personal desire for individual excellence coupled with a personal desire for the respect of your peers and the respect and confidence of the society which you serve that provides the most effective incentive to a true professional."[4]   While the major appraisal institutes and societies have established written codes of ethics and standards of professional conduct, and the National Association of Realtors® has adopted standards of practice for its members when acting in the capacity of appraisers,[5] detailed discussion and explanation of these regulations here would be of little value. The Code of Ethics of the American Institute of Real Estate Appraisers is shown as Table 21.1, and the Code of Ethics of the Society of Real Estate Appraisers is shown as Table 21.2. These codes are brief, but their application is explained in detail in the organizations' standards of professional conduct. To fully understand these codes of ethics, the appraiser must examine the detailed explanation which accompany them. The codes of ethics and standards of professional conduct established by the two appraisal organizations do not conflict; in fact, the two codes are virtually parallel.

To include a detailed explanation of codes of professional ethics and standards of professional practice in this text would not alter the conduct of certain individuals, those who some courts and members of the legal profession have referred to

Table 21.1

**American Institute of Real Estate Appraisers
Code of Ethics**

CANON 1
A Member or Candidate of the Institute must refrain from misconduct that is detrimental to the real estate appraisal profession

CANON 2
A Member or Candidate of the Institute must assist the Institute in carrying out its responsibilities to the users of appraisal services and to the public

CANON 3
When performing a real estate appraisal assignment, a Member or Candidate of the Institute must perform such appraisal assignment without advocacy for the client's interests or the accomondation of his or her own interests

CANON 4
A Member or Candidate of the Institute must not violate the confidential nature of the appraiser-client relationship by improperly disclosing the confidential portions of a real estate appraisal report

CANON 5
In securing real estate appraisal assignments and in promoting a real estate appraisal practice, a Member or Candidate of the Institute must refrain from conduct which is deceptive, misleading or otherwise contrary to the public interest

CANON 6
A Member or Candidate of the Institute who has specific knowledge of the requirements of the Institute's standards of professional practice must not deliberately or recklessly fail to observe such requirements

CANON 7
In arriving at an analysis, opinion or conclusion concerning real estate, a Member or Candidate of the Institute must use his or her best efforts to act competently and comply with the Institute's standards of professional practice relating to competency

CANON 8
In communicating an analysis, opinion or conclusion concerning real estate, a Member or Candidate of the Institute must comply with the Institute's standards of professional practice relating to written and oral appraisal reports

as "professional actors" and "expert swearers." Therefore, this chapter will pertain to personal standards of practice, which go beyond the written standards set down by the various professional organizations. The appraiser's implementation of these standards in litigation appraising will be the topic of this discussion.

Advocacy

It has been said that, as appraisers, "we don't win or lose."[6] Some suggest that appraisers should not use the words "win" and "lose" in discussing a court proceeding because to do so indicates advocacy to the client's interest. However, the mere use of these words does not mean an appraiser is the client's advocate. Appraisers must take particular care to ensure that their analyses, opinions, or conclusions concerning real estate are arrived at without bias in favor of the client or the accommodation of their personal interests. However, after arriving at an unbiased analysis, opinion, or conclusion, the appraiser may defend or advocate the correctness of his or her own value estimate.

Like it or not, the statement "No, Mr. Appraiser, in court you don't win, nor do you lose"[7] is not necessarily correct. Every appraiser who testifies in court has a job to do, in which he is assisted by legal counsel. That job is to convince the trier of fact that his estimate of value is correct; in so doing, the incorrectness, or error, of the other appraiser's estimate becomes apparent. If the appraiser does not believe his estimate of value is correct and the other appraiser's estimate is incorrect, he should not be on the witness stand. When an appraiser says, "We won our case," he is not admitting to advocacy; rather, this statement says, "I prevailed in proving the correctness of my appraisal analyses, opinions, and conclusions and thereby convinced the trier of fact that the other appraiser's estimate of value was wrong; I, with my attorney teammate, won."

Admittedly, the terms "win" and "lose" should be used with great care when discussing the outcome of a trial with the uninitiated, but no explanation of the terms should be necessary for the condemnation appraiser or the attorney who specializes in condemnation. In discussions with the uninitiated, the terms either should not be used or they should be explained as they relate to the appriaser. Appraisers "should use their best efforts to avoid the appearance of impropriety even though, in fact, no impropriety exists or is intended. *For example,* if [an appraiser] appears as an expert witness in a legal proceeding before a jury and testifies as to value, [the appraiser] should not join the attorney at the counsel table, either before or after giving such testimony, since such action could be interpreted by the jury as an indication that the appraiser was not impartial in his or her testimony and had a special interest in the outcome of the litigation."[8] Carried to an extreme, this thesis might seem to indicate that the appraiser should have no interest whatsoever in the outcome of a trial. An appraiser's request that legal counsel

Table 21.2

**Society of Real Estate Appraisers
Code of Ethics**

This Code of Ethics is a set of dynamic principles guiding the appraiser's conduct and way of life. It is the appraiser's duty to practice his profession according to this Code of Ethics:

Each member agrees that he shall:

I. Conduct his activities in a manner that will reflect credit upon himself, other real estate appraisers, and the Society of Real Estate Appraisers.

II. Cooperate with the Society of Real Estate Appraisers and its officers in all matters, including, but not limited to the investigation, censure, discipline, or dismissal of members, who by their conduct prejudice their professional status or the reputation of the Society of Real Estate Appraisers.

III. Obtain appraisal assignments, prepare appraisals and accept compensation in a professional manner in accordance with the provisions of the Standards of Professional Practice and Conduct of the Society of Real Estate Appraisers.

IV. Accept only those appraisal assignments for which he has adequate time, facilities, and technical ability to complete in a competent professional manner, and in which he has no current or unrevealed interest.

V. Render properly developed, unbiased and objective value opinions.

VI. Prepare an adequate written appraisal for each real estate appraisal assignment accepted.

VII. Reveal his value conclusions and opinions to no one other than his client, except with the permission of the client or by due process of law, and except when required to do so to comply with the rules of the Society of Real Estate Appraisers.

VIII. Conform in all respects to this Code of Ethics, the Standards of Professional Practice and Conduct, and the By-Laws of the Society of Real Estate Appraisers as the same may be amended from time to time.

advise him of the trier of fact's verdict, however, certainly cannot be construed as advocacy for his client's interest.

Appraisers must understand that they may be under considerable pressure to become advocates of their clients' interests. After all, the appraiser is working for two very strong advocates for the client's interest—the client and the client's legal counsel. "Advocacy on the part of the appraiser is a common cause of divergency [in valuation testimony]. It is understandable when one considers the economic and social atmosphere in which the appraiser functions."[9] The appraiser must make it clear when he accepts the assignment that his employment and/or the appraisal fee are in no way contingent on his conclusions or on any settlement or award. For this reason, among many others, the appraiser should insist on a written contract with the client.

Cross-Examination of Opposing Party's Appraiser

As has been mentioned,[10] the appraiser should be prepared to assist counsel in preparing to cross-examine the opposing party's appraiser. Some appraisers refuse to do this because they believe their involvement could enable counsel to cross-examine the opposing party's appraiser so effectively as to cast discredit on the real estate profession as a whole. If the appraiser holds this belief, this fact must be conveyed to the prospective client and to the client's legal counsel before the appraiser accepts the assignment. The client and his counsel must decide whether to retain the appraiser under these circumstances.

Appraisers who do assist counsel in preparing to cross-examine the opposing party's appraiser generally feel that, if this appraiser is honest and well-prepared, an effective cross-examination will only demonstrate that two qualified experts can have an honest difference of opinon. This fact, in and of itself, will not discredit the profession as a whole. Also, appraisers generally take the position that the analyses, opinions, and conclusions they have developed are well-supported and correct and, in view of the available data and use of proper techniques, the other appraiser must be wrong. If there were no difference of opinion, there would be no trial. These appraisers feel obligated to assist counsel in showing the trier of fact that it is the other appraiser who is in error.

Appraisal Fee

Most appraisal contracts will provide for a flat appraisal fee, or a per diem charge, for the actual appraisal and the written appraisal report. They will also provide for an additional per diem charge for appraisal updating, if necessary, pretrial conferences, preparation for trial, and trial time. Some appraisers specify a greater per diem rate for court testimony than they do for other forms of appraisal services. Admittedly, court testimony is a nerve-wracking experience, but many believe that there is little, if any, justification for charging more for this appraisal service than for other appraisal services.

Appraisers who charge a higher per diem rate for court work attempt to justify it by pointing out that trial work interrupts the appraiser's schedule and last-minute continuances in trial appearances are often encountered; therefore, a higher rate may seem reasonable. They may also argue that, in accepting an appraisal assignment, the appraiser usually has some control over the timing of the work, while in a trial he is at the mercy of the attorney and the court. However, it must be recognized that such a practice may be viewed by some as paying the appraiser more than his regular rate to ensure that his opinion is a favorable one. Therefore, this practice could have the appearance of impropriety and be questionable from an ethical standpoint.[11]

In any case, charging higher fees for court testimony can lead to some embarrassing questions under cross-examination. The opposing attorney may ask, "Isn't it a fact, Mr. Appraiser, that if you were in your office or out in the field doing appraisal work, you would be earning $50 per hour, but here on the witness stand you are charging $100 per hour?" From such a question, the trier of fact can infer that the appraiser had a personal, monetary interest in creating a disparity in value between the parties to ensure that a trial would ensue.

If an appraiser is retained by a condemnee after the condemnor has made an offer of settlement to the condemnee, the appraiser should be made aware of the offer. The appraiser should be certain that the terms of the appraisal contract permit him to perform only the work actually necessary to determine if the result of the appraisal will be of value to the client. Although it is not actually a violation of professional standards to develop a complete appraisal report knowing it will be of no value to the client, this practice certainly should be a violation of the appraiser's personal ethics. Once the appraiser has completed enough work to develop a range of value, he should confer with the client and the client's attorney before proceeding with the assignment. Even if the appraisal will result in a value estimate higher than the condemnor's offer, it will not always be economically practical for the client to spend the funds necessary to have the appraisal completed. Total anticipated attorney and appraiser fees, and other costs of the trial, as well as the impact of relocation allowances, if any, may make it impractical to proceed with the appraisal.

In light of the above factors, it is sometimes advisable for the appraiser and the condemnee-client initially to enter into a contract for an evaluation of the offer tendered by the condemnor, rather than a full appraisal. The appraiser must first evaluate the reasonableness of the offer; if the offer is unreasonable, he should indicate how unreasonable it is, estimate how much it will cost to complete a documented appraisal report of the property in question and, perhaps, recommend further steps which can be taken by the client. He may suggest that the client retain legal counsel, continue negotiations without a written appraisal report, or ask that the condemnor reconsider its original appraisal.

The appraiser seldom knows what the total appraisal fees will be until all testimony is complete and the attorneys begin final argument. However, it is strongly advised that the appraiser compute the total fees due as soon as he is excused by the court and make sure that a statement is hand-delivered to the attorney's office (or postmarked) as promptly as possible. If this is done, the appraiser's bill will be received in the attorney's office, or at least will be postmarked, before the verdict is announced in court. This prevents anyone from claiming that the appraisal fees were, in any way, contingent on the outcome of the trial. It also lessens the possibility that the client or his attorney will approach the appraiser and request a moderation of fees due to an unfavorable verdict.

In accepting an appraisal assignment for a property owner in a condemnation trial, the appraiser should recognize that the condemnee may not be able to pay the entire appraisal fee until the case is settled, either by negotiation or by trial. In such a case, a schedule for the payment of appraisal fees should be determined before any appraisal work is begun and this schedule should be included in the appraisal contract. Some appraisers feel it is their personal, ethical obligation to make arrangements for appraisal fee payments that do not burden the condemnee, so that the condemnee will have the same access to professional appraisal services as the condemnor.

Qualifications and Experience

It is, of course, unethical for appraisers to accept appraisal assignments for which they are not qualified by experience and/or training or to misrepresent their professional qualifications to imply nonexistent experience. If an appraiser is not qualified to accept an appraisal assignment, he may associate himself with a more qualified individual, assuming that the client approves of this plan before entering into an appraisal contract. In doing so, the appraiser must disclose such professional assistance in the appraisal report, so as not to mislead the public. However, it is better, in litigation appraising, for the appraiser to refuse the assignment and acquire his experience and/or training in an assignment that will not involve litigation. It is often possible for an unqualified appraiser to associate himself with another appraiser with expertise in the specific area required, but the unqualified appraiser will have difficulty conferring with the associated appraiser while under cross-examination on the witness stand.

In litigation appraising, the appraiser should analyze his qualifications to accept an appraisal assignment from two points of view. First, is the appraiser qualified by experience and/or training to make an appraisal of the property in dispute? Second, is the appraiser qualified to testify in court? Often, appraisers will accept assignments involving partial takings without knowing the jurisdictional rules of valuation to be applied. In other words, the appraiser might appraise only the portion of the property to be taken, without considering the larger parcel, remainder damages or benefits, or, for that matter, the impact of the specific public improvement for which the property is being acquired.

Although an appraiser may be qualified to appraise a specific property, it does not necessarily follow that he is qualified to accept such assignment if it may include testifying as an expert witness. Of course, the appraiser cannot gain experience as an expert witness without actually testifying. However, the appraiser can get valuable training by attending several civil litigation cases, in which appraisers testify as expert witnesses, before approaching the witness stand himself. In this way, the appraiser can learn court procedures, what to expect on direct examination and cross-examination, and the different methodology employed by various expert valuation witnesses and attorneys. Knowledge acquired in this way is as valuable as any that could be gained in a seminar, and there isn't any tuition.

After the appraiser has attended a number of trials, and feels confident that he has enough training to take the witness stand and testify effectively, it is best to start off slowly. Testifying as to the market value of a single-family dwelling in a divorce proceeding is a good beginning. It is not advisable for the appraiser to start off by testifying in a partial taking condemnation involving complex legal and valuation matters and a great deal of money. The appraiser may be technically competent to take the stand but, without actual trial experience, he can be made to look (and feel) totally incompetent by the skilled, and often ruthless, cross-examiner.

In a noncondemnation case involving real estate values, such as a divorce proceeding, the cross-examiner may be as inexperienced in cross-examining a real estate valuation expert as the novice real estate expert witness is in testifying. This situation provides a mutual learning experience for both the appraiser and the attorney, without the experience being particularly painful for either.

Legal Instructions

"Instructions by the attorney to the appraiser on a matter of law are certainly a proper element to be expressed in the attorney-appraiser relationship, but instructions to the appraiser on valuation are another matter. The appraiser has the choice of accepting or rejecting the attorney's premise. *Once accepted without reservation, the premise becomes the appraiser's responsibility.*"[12] [emphasis added] Sometimes, attorneys try to instruct an appraiser in regard to a valuation determination "under the guise of legal instructions as to a point of law."[13] For instance, an attorney may go beyond *legally instructing* an appraiser by telling him to assume the boundaries of the larger parcel are as specified in the instruction.

As has been previously stated, the determination of the larger parcel depends on three factors: unity of title, unity of use, and contiguity.[14] Unity of title is a legal matter and may properly be addressed by legal instructions. The attorney may also address the question of legal contiguity. However, the question of unity of use (or, more properly, unity of highest and best use) is not a legal question for the attorney; rather, it is a question of highest and best use to be analyzed and determined by the appraiser.

"Some attorneys want appraisers they can influence. This is perhaps understandable [due to the attorney's position as an advocate], but the instructed appraisal is the antithesis of ethical requirements of the profession."[15] Acceptance of a misleading legal instruction from counsel, without reservation by the appraiser, is no different than an appraiser adopting a legal instruction that the property abutting the one under appraisal sold 30 days ago for $1,000,000. The appraiser who states, "I did it that way because the attorney told me to—it was a legal instruction" is often being evasive to avoid fulfilling the requirements of the professional standards of practice. The personal ethics of such an individual need no discussion. If it is presumed that the person who adheres to professional standards is honest, it must also be presumed that the appraiser who does not adhere to professional standards of practice lacks the personal ethics required of an appraiser.

Throughout this work, the appraiser has been advised to obtain legal instruction from appropriate legal counsel. In each case, this has been referred to as legal instruction *"with supporting case law,"* or *"with supporting citations."* Legal "instructions must be valid and well-founded. *Opinions expressed by an attorney that are not valid and are without foundation should be disregarded by an appraiser."*[16] [emphasis added]

The foregoing discussion is not intended to preclude the appraiser from accepting a legal instruction from counsel which is contrary to existing law, if legal counsel is attempting to create *new law.* (It certainly cannot be denied that we need some innovation in certain areas of condemnation law.) However, if this is the case, the circumstances must be fully discussed by the attorney and the appraiser; the legal instructions from the attorney to the appraiser should be very specific, including a thorough dissertation of existing law, with supporting citations, and a detailed explanation of what specific point of law the attorney wishes to challenge and how the legal instruction to the appraiser specifically relates to this challenge. "An appraiser accepting such an assignment, under conditions specifically outlined in writing by counsel, must also be prepared to give an estimate of market value under existing law should the court rule against the 'new' legal premise."[17]

The adoption of any legal instruction must, of course, be conspicuously noted in the appraiser's written appraisal report. Similarly, the instruction must be revealed, on direct examination, by the appraiser testifying in regard to such an appraisal. The appraiser should make it clear to the attorney that the court will be informed of the instruction; this fact may be solicited by the attorney or opposing counsel, or the appraiser may inform the court of this instruction on his own initiative.

Advertising and Bidding

The real estate appraisal profession, like other professional organizations, has been plagued with governmental censure for restricting its members from advertising and fee bidding. For instance, Canon 7 of the American Institute of Real Estate Appraisers' Code of Ethics historically read:

> A member of the Institute must refrain from unprofessional conduct in securing real estate appraisal assignments and in using advertising media in connection with real estate appraisal practice.[18]

However, due to government pressure, the Institute's Canon 7 has been transformed into Canon 5, which reads:

> In securing real estate appraisal assignments and in promoting a real estate appraisal practice, a Member or Candidate of the Institute must refrain from conduct which is deceptive, misleading or otherwise contrary to the public interest.[19]

In explaining this Canon, the Institute states, in part:

> The Institute recognizes the right of its Members and Candidates to utilize advertising media not only to inform prospective clients, users of appraisal services and the public that their professional services are available but also to advise such parties as to the range, nature and cost of such professional services. At the same time, however, it is essential that such advertising not be deceptive, misleading, exaggerated, malicious or calculated to create unrealistic expectations in the minds of the parties to whom the advertising is directed.
>
> The Institute also recognizes the right of its Members and Candidates to engage in the personal solicitation of clients and business in any manner which does not offend the legitimate interests of the public and the profession. Hence, such personal solicitation is prohibited only when it violates the standards set for advertising in general, or when such solicitation implies that the impartiality and objectivity of

the Member or Candidate in performing appraisal services will be adjusted to accommodate the desires of the client.[20]

As with other professions, it is now permissible for appraisers to advertise and solicit appraisal assignments and to enter into competitive bidding. Therefore, each individual appraiser must determine whether he considers advertising for appraisal assignments, other forms of appraisal assignment solicitation, and/or competitive bidding to be a breach of his personal ethics. It is encouraging to note that relatively few attorneys and appraisers solicit business by any means other than referral and reputation.

Members of the legal community have enjoyed public recognition as professionals for a number of years. This is not always the case with members of the real estate appraisal community. Therefore, real estate appraisal professionals must continually strive to strengthen the public's recognition of real estate appraisal as a profession. Unfortunately, legislative and court limitations aimed at policing professions and their members make it increasingly difficult to establish the appraisal industry as a profession in the minds of the public. This effort is also undermined by the fact that inexperienced and nonprofessional appraisers are often encouraged to dabble in the technical area of condemnation appraising.

For instance, one publication on condemnation valuation recommends that the real estate agent supplement his income by doing part-time condemnation appraisal.[21] The publication goes on to suggest to this "part-time condemnation appraiser" that the most effective method of obtaining clientele is to obtain a list of all property owners affected by a proposed public project which will require acquisition of private property and to contact each of these individuals personally to solicit his appraisal business. About the only thing that this publication left out was the suggestion that the part-time condemnation appraiser print up business cards bearing the slogan, "We can get you more."

Summary

Professional standards can be divided into two general categories: professional ethics and personal ethics. The dishonest person who will not abide by the standards of professional practice and the indivdual who does not competently meet the standards of professional practice must have questionable personal ethics. The appraiser with high personal ethics will generally insist on performing well above the minimum rules set forth in the written ethical and practical rules of the major appraisal institutes and societies.

The appraiser must not only avoid becoming an advocate for his client's interest, he must also avoid the appearance of being an advocate for his own interest. The appraiser should make no reference to "winning" or "losing" a condemnation trial, or should use these words with great care; however, the appraiser's use of these terms should not automatically brand him as an advocate for his client's interest. Having an intense interest in the outcome of a legal proceeding does not necessarily indicate advocacy for the client's interest; the appraiser may be motivated by an intense desire to know how effectively he has accomplished his assigned task. A verdict by the trier of fact in a civil litigation dealing with real estate values may be an indication of the appraiser's effectiveness as an expert witness, but it does not necessarily prove or disprove the competence with which the appraiser has performed his assignment.

Legal counsel will expect the appraiser to assist in preparing the cross-examination of the opposing party's appraiser or appraisers. If this violates the appraiser's personal ethics, this fact must be revealed to the client and the client's legal counsel before the appraisal assignment is begun.

If an appraiser concludes that the results of his preliminary analysis will not be of assistance or value to the client, a conference should be held between the client, the client's attorney, and the appraiser before additional appraisal work is undertaken and additional expense is incurred. To complete an appraisal assignment knowing that the results of the appraisal will be of no benefit to the client is, without doubt, not in the client's interest and, therefore, should be contrary to the appraiser's personal ethics.

In appraising for a condemnee, the appraiser must recognize that the client may not be able to pay the appraisal fee until a settlement is reached or the trial is concluded. Therefore, it is important that an understanding in regard to the payment of the appraisal fee be reached before any appraisal work begins. Often, a condemnee's appraiser must wait for payment until the award is received by the condemnee. Some appraisers feel that it is their personal, ethical responsibility to accept such assignments to ensure that the condemnee has the same access to professional appraisal services as the condemnor.

It is, of course, unethical for an appraiser to undertake an assignment for which he is not qualified by experience and/or training. This is doubly important in litigation appraising; in fact, there are two areas of expertise and/or training which the appraiser should possess before accepting such an assignment. First, the appraiser must have the technical experience and/or training to make the actual appraisal and, second, he must have the experience and/or training to act as an expert witness in regard to valuation. If the appraiser has not had trial experience, it can be gained by attending several civil litigation cases involving expert witnesses and real estate valuations. Once the appraiser has gotten some exposure by this procedure, he should feel confident enough to testify in simple civil litigation cases involving real estate valuation.

At times, the appraiser needs legal instructions on matters of law to guide him in arriving at value conclusions with methodologies acceptable to the courts. However, the appraiser should never blindly accept an attorney's instruction in regard to valuation, even if this instruction is in the guise of a legal instruction. Any legal instruction accepted must be received in writing, included within the appraisal report, and recited from the witness stand by the appraiser.

Advertising, which is done in a professional manner, is not misleading, and does not violate the professional organizations' rules relative to the use of their respective logos and designations, and fee bidding are no longer violations of the appraiser's professional ethics. Appraisers are allowed to advertise, enter into competitive bidding for assignments, and to solicit business in other ways. However, members of both the legal and appraisal professions have, by and large, refrained from advertising and/or fee bidding, which displays a high degree of personal ethics on the part of these individuals. Such restraint is an indication that the legal community and the appraisal community will continue to be viewed as professional organizations in the future.

Notes

1. American Institute of Real Estate Appraisers Regulation No. 10, *Code of Professional Ethics and Standards of Professional Conduct,* Preamble, p. 1 (Adopted Nov. 13, 1981).

2. J.B. Featherston, "Ethics: A Matter of Trust," *The Appraisal Journal,* July 1975, p. 328.

3. Ibid., p. 330.

4. *Code of Professional Ethics and Standards of Professional Conduct,* p. 2.

5. National Association of Realtors® *Code of Ethics,* Art. 11, Standards of Practice #11-1 and 11-2.

6. C. Robert Boucher, "We Don't Win or Lose," *The Appraisal Journal,* October 1963, p. 501.

7. Ibid.

8. *Code of Professional Ethics and Standards of Professional Conduct,* Canon 1, p. 3.

9. *Divergencies in Right-of-Way Valuations,* National Cooperative Highway Research Program Report No. 126 (Washington, D.C.: Highway Research Board, 1971), p. 12.

10. See Chapter 18, "Preparation for Trial" and Chapter 19, "The Expert Witness."

11. *Code of Professional Ethics and Standards of Professional Conduct,* Canon 1, p. 3.

12. *Divergencies in Right-of-Way Valuations,* p. 10.

13. Ibid.

14. See Chapter 4, "The Larger Parcel."

15. *Divergencies in Right-of-Way Valuations,* p. 10.

16. *Divergencies in Right-of-Way Valuations,* p. 16.

17. Ibid.

18. *The Appraisal of Real Estate,* 7th ed. (Chicago: American Institute of Real Estate Appraisers, 1978) p. 532.

19. *Code of Professional Ethics and Standards of Professional Conduct,* Canon 5, p. 8.

20. Ibid., Canon 5, p. 8.

21. Henry J. Kaltenbach, *Guide to the Successful Handling of Condemnation Valuation* (Englewood Cliffs, N.J.: Executive Reports Corporation, 1978), pp. 305-308.

TABLE OF CASES ALPHABETICALLY

Case	Chapter	Page	Footnote
People v. Hemmerling, 58 Cal. Rptr. 203.	4	55	13
People v. Murata, 161 C.A.2d 369, 326 P.2d 947.	9	138	11
People v. Sayig, 101 Cal. App.2d 890, 226 P.2d 702.	3	33	34
People, Dep't of Public Works v. Southern Pacific Transp. Co., 109 Cal. Rptr. 525.	6	90	6
People ex rel. Dept. of Public Works v. Schultz Co., 123 Cal. App.2d 925, 268 P.2d 117.	15	275	9
Petition of Michigan State Highway Comm. v. McGuire, 185 N.W.2d 187 (Mich.).	9	139	21
Petition of Omaha Public Power Dist., 168 Neb. 120, 95 N.W.2d 209.	5	71	17
Phillips Petroleum Co. v. City of Omaha, 171 Neb. 457, 106 N.W.2d 727.	9	144	33
Phoenix Title and Trust Co. v. State, 425 P.2d 434 (Az.).	13	236	41
Pokorny v. Local 310, Int. Hod Carriers, 35 Ohio App.2d 178, 300 N.E.2d 464.	8 16	131 297-298	38 40
Port of New York Authority v. Howell, 68 N.J. Super. 559, 173 A.2d 310.	8	118	15
Portland, Oregon City Ry. Co. v. Penny, 158 P. 404 (Ore.).	13	236	39
Priestly v. State, 23 N.Y.2d 152, 295 N.Y.S.2d 659, 242 N.E.2d 827.	3 3	30 33	24 36
Public Service Elec. & Gas Co. v. Oldwick Farms, Inc., 125 N.J. Super 31, 308 A.2d 362.	11	179	13
Reading, etc., R. Co. v. Balthaser, 119 Pa. 472, 13 A. 294.	13	245	51
Redevelopment Comm. of Greenville v. Capehart, 268 N.C. 114, 150 S.E.2d 62.	3	37	55
Ridgeway Associates, Inc. v. State, 32 App. Div.2d 851, 300 N.Y.S.2d 944.	12 12	202 213	7 26
Riley v. District of Columbia Redevelopment Land Agency, 246 F.2d 641.	7	110	17
Roberts v. New York El. R. Co., 128 N.Y. 455, 28 N.E. 486.	8	132	41
Sacramento Southern R. Co. v. Heilbron, 156 Cal. 408, 104 P. 979.	5	71	16
Sams v. Redevelopment Authority, 431 Pa. 240, 244 A.2d 779.	4	55	16
Sanitary Dist. of Chicago v. Pittsburgh, Ft. W. and C. Ry. Co., 216 Ill. 575, 75 N.E 248.	10	166	24
Sasso v. Housing Authority of the City of Providence, 111 A.2d 226 (RI).	4	57	29
Savin Hill Yacht Club Ass'n v. Savin Hill Yacht Club, 246 Mass. 75, 140 N.E. 299.	16	303	50

Case	Chapter	Page	Footnote
Shelby County R-IV School District v. Herman, 392 S.W.2d 609 (Mo.).	10	165	20
Shillito v. Metropolitan Edison Co., 434 Pa. 131, 252 A.2d 650.	12	202	6
Shrader v. Horton, 471 F.Supp. 1236.	3	28	14
Sibson v. State, N.H., 336 A.2d 239.	3	29	15
	3	29	16
Smith County Commissioners v. Labore, 37 Kan. 480, 15 P. 577.	4	54	10
Southern Indiana Gas and Electric Co. v. Riley, 260 Ind. 643, 299 N.E.2d 173.	12	210	17
Southwestern Bell Telephone Co. v. Ramsey, 542 S.W.2d 466 (Tex.).	2	20	8
Spano v. State of New York, 22 App. Div.2d 757, 253 N.Y.S.2d 730.	5	74	22
Springfield, etc., R. Co. v. Schweitzer, 173 Mo. App. 650, 158 S.W. 1058.	11	197	44
St. Louis Housing Authority v. Bainter, 297 S.W.2d 529 (Mo.).	8	118-119	19
St. Regis Paper Co. v. United States, 313 F.2d 45.	15	271	2
State v. Arnold, 218 Or. 43, 341 P.2d 1089.	5	72	18
State v. Bowling, 414 S.W.2d 551 (Mo.).	9	144	31
State v. Cady, 400 S.W.2d 481 (Mo.).	13	236	40
State v. Calkins, 50 Wash.2d 716, 314 P.2d 449.	11	197	42
State v. Chang, 50 Haw. 195, 436 P.2d 3.	12	213	27
State v. Dillon, 175 Neb. 350, 121 N.W.2d 798.	3	39	58
State v. Fonburg, 80 Idaho 269, 328 P.2d 60.	3	31	28
State v. Gorga, 26 N.J. 113, 138 A.2d 833.	6	95	10
State v. Green, 578 P.2d 855 (Wn.).	13	233	26
	13	249-250	60
State v. Hoblitt, 87 Mont. 403, 288 P. 181.	4	56	26
	4	56	27
State v. Independent School Dist. No. 31, 266 Minn. 85, 123 N.W.2d 121.	3	44	71
State v. Johnson, 265 A.2d 711 (Me.).	20	404	3
State v. Lavasek, N.M., 385 P.2d 361.	3	30	21
State v. Maplewood Heights Corp., 302 N.E.2d 782 (Ind.).	12	210	16
State v. Nelson, 222 Or. 458, 353 P.2d 616.	19	377	9
State v. Nelson, 296 N.E.2d 908 (Ind.).	16	295	33
State v. Spencer, 16 Wash. App. 841, 559 P.2d 1360.	16	313	63
State v. Spencer, 583 P.2d 1201 (Wash.).	16	314	64
State v. Whitlow, 243 Cal. App.2d 504, 52 Cal. Rptr. 336.	5	64	7
State v. Widen, 268 Minn. 209, 128 N.W.2d 755.	3	34	42
State v. Wilson, 6 Wash. App. 443, 493 P.2d 1252.	7	102	3

TABLE OF CASES BY JURISDICTION

Case	Chapter	Page	Footnote
United States			
Baetjer v. United States, 143 F.2d 391.	4	51-52	4
	4	55	14
	4	55	19
Bauman v. Ross, 167 U.S. 548, 17 S.Ct. 966.	1	4	13
Berman v. Parker, 348 U.S. 26.	14	258	12
Breckenridge Hotels Corp. v. Real Estate Research Corp., 452 F.Supp. 529.	20	420	10
Calvo v. United States, 303 F.2d 902.	14	259	20
Campbell v. United States, 266 U.S. 368, 45 S.Ct. 115.	15	271-272	3
Carmichall v. United States, 273 F.2d 392.	3	42	64
Chicago v. Taylor, 125 U.S. 161, 8 S.Ct. 820.	3	30	19
Cole Investment Co. v. United States, 258 F.2d 203.	4	56	21
Demetria Sifuentes v. United States, 1 Cir., 168 F.2d 264.	8	117	7
Fallbrook Irr. Dist. v. Bradley, 164 U.S. 112, 17 S.Ct. 46.	20	424	15
Feltz v. Central Nebraska P.P. & I. Dist., 124 F.2d 578.	11	188	27
Florida East Coast Properties, Inc. v. Metropolitan Dade County, 572 F.2d 1108.	11	176	7
Garrett v. United States, 407 F.2d 146.	16	289	7
Hannan v. United States, 76 U.S. App. D.C. 118, 131 F.2d 441.	9	145	39
Harwell v. United States, 316 F.2d 791.	1	4	18
Joiner v. City of Dallas, 380 F.Supp. 754.	1	2	4
	1	2	7
Jones v. United States, 258 U.S. 40, 66 L.Ed. 453, 42 S.Ct. 218.	9	138	12

Case	Chapter	Page	Footnote
United States v. 64.88 Acres of Land, etc., 244 F.2d 534.	14	257	7
United States v. 70.39 Acres of Land, 164 F.Supp. 451.	3	35	44
	5	65	9
	5	65	10
	7	103	10
United States v. 72.35 Acres of Land, etc., 150 F.Supp. 271.	15	275	6
United States v. 765.56 Acres of Land, 174 F.Supp. 1.	9	139	19
United States v. 84.4 Acres of Land, 224 F.Supp. 1017, aff'd 348 F.2d 383.	10	164	18
United States v. Becktold Co., 129 F.2d 473.	9	139	20
United States v. Causby, 328 U.S. 256, 66 S.Ct. 1062.	14	257	9
United States v. Certain Interests in Property, 239 F.Supp. 822.	8	127	32
United States v. Certain Land in City of Fort Worth, Texas, 414 F.2d 1026.	9	142	25
United States v. Certain Lands, 69 F.Supp. 815.	3	42	63
United States v. Certain Property, 306 F.2d 439.	1	6	23
United States v. Chandler-Dunbar Water Power Co., 229 U.S. 53, 33 S.Ct. 667.	11	188	29
	11	197	38
United States v. Cors, 337 U.S. 325, 69 S.Ct. 1086.	1	6	25
United States v. Delano Park Homes, 146 F.2d 473.	9	158	63
United States v. Easement & Rt. of Way, etc., 447 F.2d 1317.	11	197	46
United States v. General Motors Corp., 323 U.S. 373, 65 S.Ct. 357.	14	260	25
United States v. Land in Dry Bed of Rosamond Lake, 143 F.Supp. 314.	3	37-38	56
United States v. Mattox, 375 F.2d 461.	4	51	3
	4	56	20
United States v. River Rouge Impvmt. Co., 269 U.S. 411, 46 S.Ct. 144.	11	177	10
	15	275	8
United States v. Tampa Bay Garden Apartments, Inc., 294 F.2d 598.	8	127	29
United States v. Welch, 217 U.S. 333, 30 S.Ct. 527.	14	266	36
United States v. Whitehurst, 337 F.2d 765.	8	127	30
Virgin Islands Housing Authority v. 15.5521 Acres of Land, 230 F.Supp. 845.	9	139	22
Waitaker & Co. v. Sewer Improvement District No. 1, 221 F.2d 649.	20	424	16

Case	Chapter	Page	Footnote
Florida:			
Orange State Oil Co. v. Jacksonville Expressway Authority, 110 So.2d 687 (Fl.).	16	295	32
	16	296	38
Georgia:			
Bowers v. Fulton County, 176 S.E.2d 219 (Ga.).	9	139	16
Dep't of Transportation v. Great Southern Enterprises, 225 S.E.2d 80 (Ga.).	5	64	8
Pause v. Atlanta, 98 Ga. 92, 26 S.E. 489.	11	197	45
Hawaii:			
State v. Chang, 50 Haw. 195, 436 P.2d 3.	12	213	27
Territory of Hawaii v. Adelmeyer, 45 Hawaii 144, 363 P.2d 979.	4	60	32
Territory of Hawaii v. Mendonca, 46 Hawaii 83, 46 Hawaii 126, 375 P.2d 6.	13	228	12
Idaho:			
Mabe v. State, 83 Idaho 222, 360 P.2d 799.	3	33	33
State v. Fonburg, 80 Idaho 269, 328 P.2d 60.	3	31	28
State ex rel. Moore v. Bastian, 546 P.2d 399 (Id.).	16	289	9
Illinois:			
Chicago, etc. R. Co. v. Chicago Mechanics Institute, 239 Ill. 197, 87 N.E. 933.	16	307	57
Chicago, etc., R. Co. v. Dresel, 110 Ill. 89.	4	55	17
City of Chicago v. Budd, 12 Ill. App.2d 51, 257 N.E.2d 161.	1	6	24
City of Chicago v. Giedraitis, 14 Ill.2d 45, 150 N.E.2d 577.	8	118	11
City of Chicago v. Vaccaro, 408 Ill. 587, 97 N.E.2d 766.	9	143	29
City of Evanston v. Piotrowiez, 20 Ill.2d 512, 170 N.E.2d 569.	9	145-146	44
Dep't of Public Works and Buildings v. Exchange Nat. Bank, 356 N.E.2d 376 (Ill.).	9	145	43
Department of Public Works & Buildings v. Hubbard, 363 Ill. 99, 1 N.E.2d 383.	3	34	40
Department of Public Works & Buildings v. Oberlaender, 92 Ill. App.2d 174, 235 N.E.2d 3, aff'd 42 Ill.2d 410, 247 N.E.2d 888.	2	20	7
	4	60	33
Dep't of Transportation v. Gonterman, 354 N.E.2d 75 (Ill.).	11	180	17
Dep't of Transportation v. Quincy Coach House, Inc., 1 Ill. Dec. 13, 356 N.E.2d 13, Rev'd 29 Ill. App.3d 616, 332 N.E.2d 21.	7	103	7
Forest Preserve Dist. of Cook County v. Krol, 12 Ill.2d 139, 145 N.E.2d 599.	12	222-223	34

Case	Chapter	Page	Footnote
Commonwealth, Dep't of Highways v. Fister, 373 S.W.2d 720 (Ky.).	11	197	41
Commonwealth, Dep't of Highways v. Gibson, 523 S.W.2d 855 (Ky.).	7	110	18
Commonwealth, Dep't of Highways v. Rowland, 420 S.W.2d 657 (Ky.).	11	184	22
Commonwealth, Dept. of H'ways v. Sherrod, 367 S.W.2d 844 (Ky.).	3	34	41
	16	299	43
	16	300-301	44
	16	303	48
Commonwealth, Dep't of Highways v. Yates, 383 S.W.2d 340 (Ky.).	11	197	40
Commonwealth of Kentucky, Dept. of Highways v. Whitledge, 406 S.W.2d 833.	9	139	17
Korfhage v. Commonwealth, 296 S.W.2d 476 (Ky.).	16	290	14
	16	303	47
Louisville, etc. R. Co. v. Hall, 143 Ky. 497, 136 S.W. 905.	11	188	30
West Kentucky Coal Co. v. Commonwealth, 368 S.W.2d 738 (Ky.).	9	139	15
	9	156	58
Louisiana:			
Central Louisiana Elec. Co. v. Fontenot, 159 So.2d 738 (La.).	14	260	27
Collins Pipeline Co. v. New Orleans East, Inc., 250 So.2d 29 (La.).	11	198	52
Hinrieks v. New Orleans, 50 La. Ann. 1214, 24 So. 224.	16	303	52
State, Dep't of Highways v. Beatty, 288 So.2d 900 (La.).	11	188	32
State, Dep't of Highways v. Gordy, 322 So.2d 418 (La.).	11	188	28
State, Dept. of H'ways v. LeDoux, La., 184 So.2d 604.	2	23	16
State, Dep't. of Highways v. Luster, 277 So.2d 181 (La.).	5	74	23
State, Dept. of H'wys. v. Stegemann, La., 269 So.2d 480.	2	21	11
State, through Department of Highways v. Hoyt, La., 284 So.2d 763.	2	21	13
Maine:			
State v. Johnson, 256 A.2d 711 (Me.).	20	404	3
State Roads Commission v. Novosel, 117 Me. 552, 102 A.2d 563.	10	166	25
Maryland:			
Gluck v. Baltimore, 81 Md. 315, 32 A. 515.	16	303	51

Abandonment
Of easement, 87-88, 254-255; Of street, 34
Absorption of lots in development approach,
204-205, 206-209
Abstraction method
Estimating depreciation, 111-113;
Estimating land value, 204
Abutters rights. See access
Access, 29-34. See also light, view, and air
Change in, 184-186, 191-193; Convenient,
30; Deprivation of, to new highway, 197;
Elastic right, 30; Loss of, 188-190;
Reasonable, 30; Suitable, 30
Ad valorem taxation, appraising for, 421-423
Adjustment process
Comparable sales, 142-157
Composite adjustment, 153-154; Dollar
adjustments, 149-150; Percentage
adjustments, 149-155; Time adjustment,
149-155
Detailed, 339
Prior sales of subject, 141
Admissible valuation testimony
Business profits from special purpose
property, 165-166; Comparable sales,
137-139, 142-143; Contract sales, 143-144;
Cost approach data, 114; Development
approach, 210-214; Development costs,
212-213; Exchanges, 144; Income approach
data, 117; Lease of comparable property,
130-133; Market data approach, 137;
Options, 144; Sales after date of take, 146;
Sales to condemnors, 145
Advertising by appraisers, 440-441
Advertising signs, 258
Advocacy
Cause of divergent testimony, 433-435; In

rent forecasting, 315-317; Retained
appraiser showing, 354-355; Staff appraiser
showing, 352; Witness fees indicating,
435-436
Aerial photographs, 276, 281
Affirmative easement, 259
After construction inspection, 285
After situation
Architectural renderings of, 284; As if
public construction complete, 246-250;
Nonconforming use, 85-86; Physical
inspection of property, 285; Presentation to
trier of fact, 389-390; Reasonable
probability of rezone, 92-97; Use of sales
occurring after date of take, 146; Variance,
86-87; Visualization of, 284-285; Zoning in
anticipation of project, 87-92
Aggregate of interests rule, 289-291. See also
unit rule
Air Commerce Act of 1926, 28
Air rights, 28
All available uses, 70-72
Amenities, 116
Amusement parks, 163
Annoyance, 197
Annuity, 128
Life estate, 36-37;
Table construction, 37, 128-129; Value of,
128-129
Annuity factor, 128-129
Anticipated use method. See Development
approach
Apartments
Application of cost approach, 111-113;
Units of comparison, 148; Valuation of land
for, 148
Appearance of fairness doctrine, 97